Applied Probability and Statistics (*Continued*)

CHAKRAVARTI, LAHA and ROY · Handbook of Methods of Applied Statistics, Vol. I
CHAKRAVARTI, LAHA and ROY · Handbook of Methods of Applied Statistics, Vol. II
CHERNOFF and MOSES · Elementary Decision Theory
CHIANG · Introduction to Stochastic Processes in Biostatistics
CLELLAND, deCANI, BROWN, BURSK, and MURRAY · Basic Statistics with Business Applications
COCHRAN · Sampling Techniques, *Second Edition*
COCHRAN and COX · Experimental Designs, *Second Edition*
COX · Planning of Experiments
COX and MILLER · The Theory of Stochastic Processes
DANIEL and WOOD · Fitting Equations to Data
DAVID · Order Statistics
DEMING · Sample Design in Business Research
DODGE and ROMIG · Sampling Inspection Tables, *Second Edition*
DRAPER and SMITH · Applied Regression Analysis
ELANDT-JOHNSON · Probability Models and Statistical Methods in Genetics
GOLDBERGER · Econometric Theory
GUTTMAN, WILKS and HUNTER · Introductory Engineering Statistics, *Second Edition*
HAHN and SHAPIRO · Statistical Models in Engineering
HALD · Statistical Tables and Formulas
HALD · Statistical Theory with Engineering Applications
HOEL · Elementary Statistics, *Third Edition*
HUANG · Regression and Econometric Methods
JOHNSON and KOTZ · Distributions in Statistics
Discrete Distributions
Continuous Univariate Distributions-1
Continuous Univariate Distributions-2
Continuous Multivariate Distributions
JOHNSON and LEONE · Statistics and Experimental Design: In Engineering and the Physical Sciences, Volumes I and II
LANCASTER · The Chi Squared Distribution
MILTON · Rank Order Probabilities: Two-Sample Normal Shift Alternatives
RAO and MITRA · Generalized Inverse of Matrices and Its Applications
SARD and WEINTRAUB · A Book of Splines
SARHAN and GREENBERG · Contributions to Order Statistics
SEAL · Stochastic Theory of a Risk Business
SEARLE · Linear Models
THOMAS · An Introduction to Applied Probability and Random Processes
WHITTLE · Optimization under Constraints
WILLIAMS · Regression Analysis
WOLD and JUREEN · Demand Analysis
WONNACOTT and WONNACOTT · Introduction to Econometric Methods

continued on back

ECONOMETRICS

Ronald J. Wonnacott

Department of Economics
University of Western Ontario

Thomas H. Wonnacott

Department of Mathematics
University of Western Ontario

JOHN WILEY & SONS, INC.

New York · London · Sydney · Toronto

10 9 8 7 6 5

Library of Congress Catalogue Card Number: 77-93485

SBN 471 95960 X

Printed in the United States of America

To Cathy, Doug, Robbie; Cecilia, Rebecca, and Daniel

Preface

This book is written in two parts—elementary and more advanced. Thus, it is designed for an introductory course, followed by a more advanced treatment for the student with better mathematical preparation.

Part I can be used as a one-semester course covering many of the same topics as Johnston's *Econometric Methods* at a more elementary level. It is designed for either undergraduate or graduate students following a semester of elementary statistics (e.g. our *Introductory Statistics*). The objective here is to provide a very simple presentation of the important statistical concepts used in econometrics—without involving the student in heavy mathematics at this early stage. Thus, matrix algebra is never used; in fact, Part I may be taken even without a knowledge of calculus, although students with calculus will be at a clear advantage. While students who cover this material will not become qualified in econometric theory, they should get a good appreciation of the main problems that econometricians face.

The text is kept simple, with the more difficult interpretations and developments reserved for footnotes, starred sections, and the corresponding chapters of Part II. In all instances, these are optional; a special effort has been made to allow the more elementary student to skip these completely without losing continuity. Moreover, some of the finer points are deferred to the instructor's manual. Thus, the instructor is allowed, at least to some degree, to tailor the course to his student's background.

Problems are also starred (*) if they are more difficult, or set with an arrow (⇒) if they introduce important ideas taken up later in the text, or bracketed ( ) if they duplicate previous problems, and thus provide optional exercise only.

Part II is a generalization of Part I, with the chapters in Part II roughly corresponding to the ten chapters in Part I; thus, Chapter 16 is a generalization of Chapter 6, and so on. In designing this book, our objective has been to provide maximum flexibility. Therefore, those who wish to teach the whole book can cover Part I, followed by Part II; or they can teach the corresponding chapters (e.g., 6 and 16) together.

The prerequisites for Part II are courses in calculus and matrix algebra.

Vector geometry is also used extensively, and our experience has been that this is an invaluable aid to understanding; however, it is developed in this text from first principles, and no previous training is necessary. In Chapter 14, there is a self-contained discussion of statistical distributions—the relation of the normal, t, chi-square and F; this provides the necessary background for students who may not have taken a previous course in mathematical statistics.

Part II, using both matrix algebra and vector geometry, leads into the use of more complete advanced texts, such as the one by Malinvaud. Thus, Part II can be used in a first course in econometrics for graduate students with the necessary background in mathematics and statistics; however, we have been surprised to discover that even students with a reasonably sophisticated mathematical background find the very simple treatment in Part I a useful reference. Our experience has been that graduate students in econometrics have a tendency to miss the forest for the trees; they often miss the statistical issues in mastering the matrix manipulations. Hence, many find it very useful, before disappearing into the matrix underbrush, to fully master the basic ideas of Part I.

So many have contributed to this book that it is impossible to thank them all individually. However, a special vote of thanks should go, without implication, to the following for their thoughtful reviews: D. A. Belsley, R. G. Bodkin, T. M. Brown, A. S. Goldberger, L. Hexter, K. R. Kadiyala, T. A. Yancey, and especially F. M. Fisher and G. S. Watson. We are also indebted to our students at the University of Western Ontario who suggested many improvements during a three-year classroom test.

Ronald J. Wonnacott
Thomas H. Wonnacott

London, Ontario, Canada
May, 1969

Contents

ECONOMETRICS

Part I

Elementary Econometrics

Introduction to Regression

1-1 INTRODUCTION

Before undertaking this study of econometrics, the student should have taken a course in introductory statistics, in which a great deal of attention is devoted to making inferences about one variable. In this second course, the emphasis changes to estimating how two or more variables are related. Thus, the economist is typically less interested in describing one variable (consumption) in isolation, than in describing the relationship between variables (i.e., how consumption is related to income). The most useful statistical technique for this purpose is regression.

To illustrate, consider a simple example drawn from agricultural economics; suppose the objective is to discover whether crop yield depends on fertilizer application. If yield (Y) that follows from various fertilizer applications (X) is plotted, a scatter similar to Figure 1-1 might be observed. From this scatter, it is clear that fertilizer does affect yield. Moreover, it should be possible to describe *how*, by an equation relating Y to X. Estimating

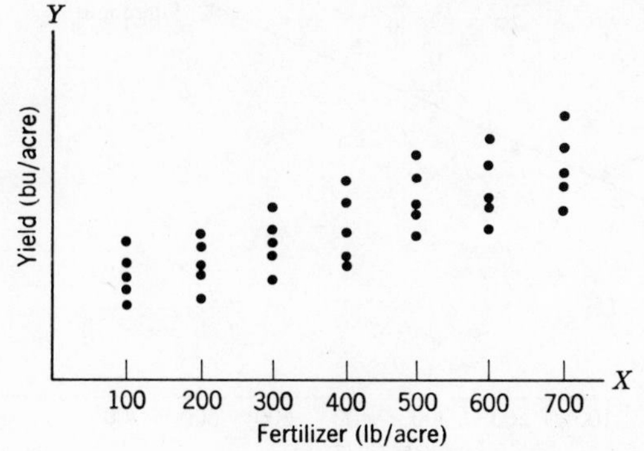

FIG. 1-1 Observed relation of wheat yield to fertilizer application.

an equation is of course equivalent geometrically to fitting a curve through this scatter. This is called the regression of Y on X; as a simple mathematical model, it will be useful as a brief and precise description, or as a means of predicting the yield Y for a given amount of fertilizer X.

This chapter is devoted exclusively to how a straight line may best be fitted. The characteristics of this line (e.g., its slope) may be subjected to statistical tests of significance; but these issues are deferred to Chapter 2. Furthermore, it is possible that Y is related to X in a more complicated nonlinear way; but these issues are deferred to Chapter 4. For now, we assume that the appropriate description is a straight line.

1-2 AN EXAMPLE

Since yield depends on fertilizer, it is referred to as the "dependent" variable Y; since fertilizer application is not dependent on yield, but instead is determined by the experimenter, it is referred to as the "independent" variable X. Suppose funds are available for only seven experimental observations, so that the experimenter sets X at seven different values, taking only one observation Y in each case, shown in Figure 1-2 and Table 1-1.

First, note that if all the points were exactly in a line, as in Figure 1-3*a*, then the fitted line could be drawn in with a ruler "by eye" perfectly accurately. Even if the points were *nearly* in a line, as in Figure 1-3*b*, fitting by eye would be reasonably satisfactory. But in the highly scattered case, as in Figure 1-3*c*, fitting by eye is too subjective and too inaccurate. Furthermore,

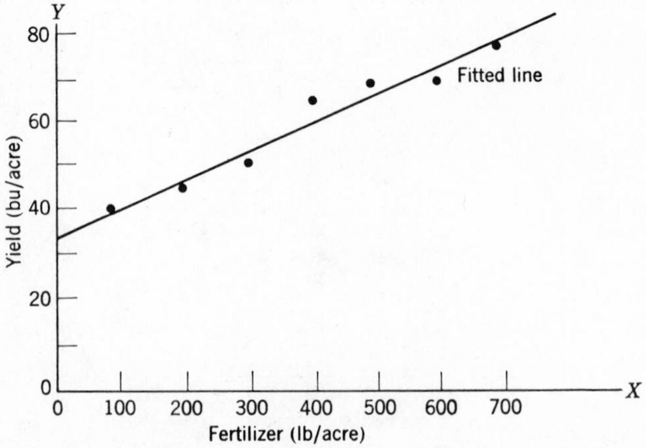

FIG. 1-2 Yields at various levels of fertilizer application.

TABLE 1-1 Experimental Data Relating Yield to the Amount of Applied Fertilizer, as in Figure 1-2

X Fertilizer (Pound/Acre)	Y Yield (Bushel/Acre)
100	40
200	45
300	50
400	65
500	70
600	70
700	80

fitting by eye requires plotting all the points first. If there were 100 experimental observations, this would be very tedious, and an algebraic technique that an electronic computer could solve would be preferable.

The following sections set forth various algebraic methods for fitting a line, successively more sophisticated and satisfactory.

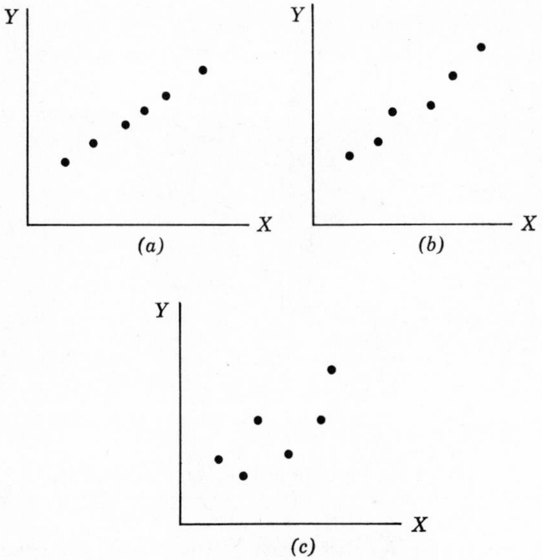

FIG. 1-3 Various degrees of scatter.

1-3 POSSIBLE CRITERIA FOR FITTING A LINE

It is time to ask more precisely, "What is a good fit?" The answer surely is "a fit that makes the total error small." One typical error is shown in Figure 1-4. It is defined as the vertical distance from the observed Y to the fitted line—that is $(Y_i - \hat{Y}_i)$, where $\hat{Y}_i$ is the "fitted value of Y" or the ordinate of the line. We note that the error is positive when the observed Y_i is above the line and negative when the observed Y_i is below the line.

1. As our first tentative criterion, consider a fitted line that minimizes the sum of all these errors,

$$\sum_{i=1}^{n}(Y_i - \hat{Y}_i) \tag{1-1}$$

But this criterion works badly. Using this criterion, the two lines shown in Figure 1-5 fit the observations equally well, even though the fit in (*a*) is intuitively a good one, and the fit in (*b*) a very bad one. The problem is one of sign; in both cases, positive errors just offset negative errors, leaving their sum equal to zero. This criterion must be rejected, since it provides no distinction between bad fits and good ones.

2. There are two ways of overcoming the sign problem. The first is to minimize the sum[1] of the *absolute* values of the errors,

$$\sum |Y_i - \hat{Y}_i| \tag{1-2}$$

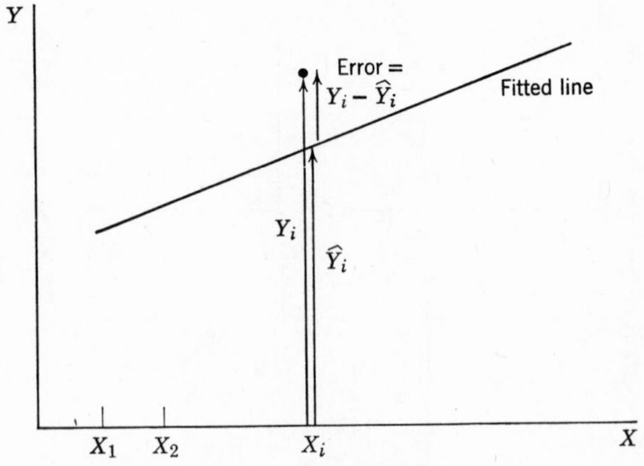

FIG. 1-4 Error in fitting points with a line.

[1] Unless otherwise stated, the summation sign $\sum$ from now on will represent $\sum_{i=1}^{n}$, the sum of all values from $1 \cdots n$.

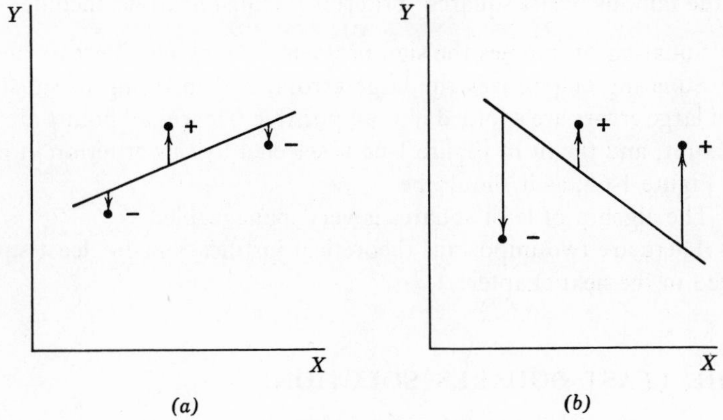

FIG. 1-5

Since large positive errors are not allowed to offset large negative ones, this criterion would rule out bad fits like Figure 1-5*b*. However, it still has a drawback. It is evident in Figure 1-6, that the fit in (*b*) satisfies this criterion better than the fit in (*a*); ($\sum |Y_i - \hat{Y}_i|$ is 3, rather than 4). In fact, the reader can satisfy himself that the line in (*b*) joining the two end points satisfies this criterion better than *any* other line. But it is not a good common-sense solution to the problem, because it pays no attention whatever to the middle point. The fit in (*a*) is preferable because it takes account of all points.

3. As a second way to overcome the sign problem, we finally propose to minimize the sum of the squares of the errors,

$$\sum (Y_i - \hat{Y}_i)^2 \tag{1-3}$$

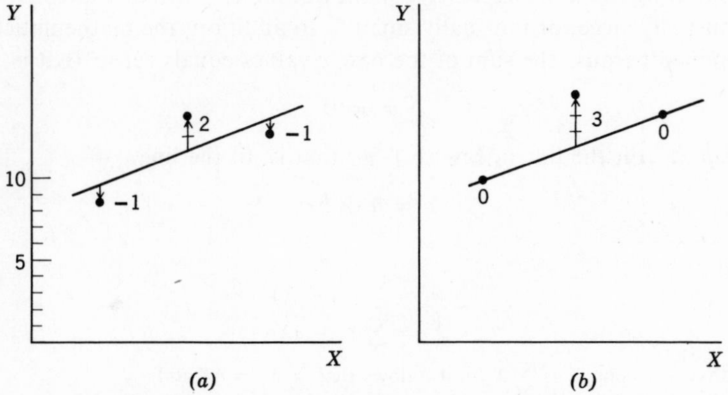

FIG. 1-6

This is the famous "least squares" criterion; its justifications include:

(a) Squaring overcomes the sign problem by making all errors positive.

(b) Squaring emphasizes the large errors, and in trying to satisfy this criterion large errors are avoided if at all possible. Hence, all points are taken into account, and the fit in Figure 1-6*a* is selected by this criterion in preference to Figure 1-6*b*, as it should be.

(c) The algebra of least squares is very manageable.

(d) There are two important theoretical justifications for least squares, developed in the next chapter.

1-4 THE LEAST SQUARES SOLUTION

Our scatter of observed X and Y values from Table 1-1 is graphed again in Figure 1-7*a*. Our objective is to fit a line

$$Y = a_0 + bX \tag{1-4}$$

This involves three steps:

Step 1. Translate X into deviations from its mean; that is, define a new variable x, so that:

$$x = X - \bar{X} \tag{1-5}$$

This is equivalent to a geometric translation of axis, as shown in Figure 1-7*b*; the Y axis has been shifted from 0 to $\bar{X}$. The new x value becomes positive or negative, depending on whether X was above or below $\bar{X}$. There is no change in the Y values. The intercept a differs from the original a_0, but the slope b remains the same.

One of the advantages of measuring X_i as deviations from their central value is that we can more explicitly ask the question: "How is Y affected when X is unusually large, or unusually small?" In addition, the mathematics will be simplified because the sum of the new x values equals zero,[2] that is,

$$\sum x_i = 0 \tag{1-6}$$

Step 2. Fit the line in Figure 1-7*b*; that is, fit the line

$$Y = a + bx \tag{1-7}$$

[2] *Proof.*

$$\sum x_i = \sum (X_i - \bar{X})$$
$$= \sum X_i - n\bar{X}$$

Noting that $\bar{X}$ is defined as $\sum X_i/n$, it follows that $\sum X_i = n\bar{X}$ and

$$\sum x_i = n\bar{X} - n\bar{X} = 0 \qquad \text{(1-6) proved}$$

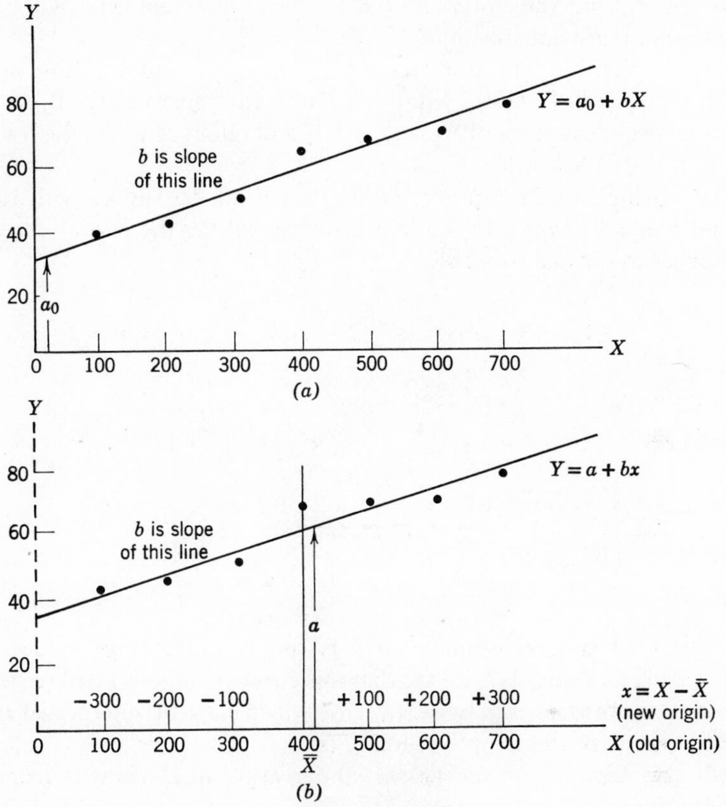

FIG. 1-7 Translation of axis. (*a*) Regression using original variables. (*b*) Regression, translating *X*.

to this scatter by selecting the values for a and b that satisfy the least squares criterion: select those values of a and b that minimize

$$\sum (Y_i - \hat{Y}_i)^2 \tag{1-8}$$

Since each fitted value $\hat{Y}_i$ is on our estimated line (1-7),

$$\hat{Y}_i = a + bx_i \tag{1-9}$$

When this is substituted into (1-8), the problem becomes one of selecting a and b to minimize the sum of squares,

$$S(a, b) = \sum (Y_i - a - bx_i)^2 \tag{1-10}$$

The notation $S(a, b)$ is used to emphasize that this expression depends on a and b. As a and b vary (i.e., as various lines are tried), $S(a, b)$ will vary too, and we ask at what value of a and b it will be a minimum. This will give us our optimum (least squares) line.

The simplest minimization technique is calculus, and it will be used in the next paragraph. [Readers without calculus can minimize (1-10) with the more cumbersome algebra of Appendix 1-1, and rejoin us where the resulting theorem is stated below.]

Minimizing $S(a, b)$ requires setting its partial derivatives with respect to a and b equal to zero. In the first instance, setting the partial derivative with respect to a equal to zero:

$$\frac{\partial}{\partial a}\sum (Y_i - a - bx_i)^2 = \sum 2(-1)(Y_i - a - bx_i)^1 = 0 \tag{1-11}$$

Dividing through by -2 and rearranging:

$$\sum Y_i - na - b\sum x_i = 0 \tag{1-12}$$

Noting that $\sum x_i = 0$ by (1-6), we can solve for a:

$$a = \frac{\sum Y_i}{n}, \qquad \text{or} \qquad a = \bar{Y} \tag{1-13}$$

Thus, our least squares estimate of a is simply the average value of Y; referring back to Figure 1-7, we see that this ensures that our fitted regression line must pass through the point $(\bar{X}, \bar{Y})$, which may be interpreted as the center of gravity of the sample of n points.

It is also necessary to set the partial derivative of (1-10) with respect to b equal to zero,

$$\frac{\partial}{\partial b}\sum (Y_i - a - bx_i)^2 = \sum 2(-x_i)(Y_i - a - bx_i)^1 = 0 \tag{1-14}$$

or

$$\sum x_i(Y_i - a - bx_i) = 0 \tag{1-15}$$

Rearranging

$$\sum Y_i x_i - a\sum x_i - b\sum x_i^2 = 0$$

Noting that $\sum x_i = 0$, we can solve for b:

$$b = \frac{\sum Y_i x_i}{\sum x_i^2} \tag{1-16}$$

Our results[3] in (1-13) and (1-16) are important enough to restate:

[3] To be rigorous, it can be proved with second partial derivation or other techniques, that we actually do have a minimum sum of squares—rather than a maximum or saddle point.

Theorem.

> With x values measured as deviations from their mean, the least squares values of a and b are
>
> $$a = \bar{Y} \tag{1-13}$$
>
> $$b = \frac{\sum Y_i x_i}{\sum x_i^2} \tag{1-16}$$

For the example in Table 1-1, a and b are calculated in the first five columns in Table 1-2; (the last three columns may be ignored until the next chapter). It follows that the least squares equation is:

$$Y = 60 + .068x \tag{1-17}$$

This fitted line is graphed in Figure 1-7b.

Step 3. If desired, this regression can now be retranslated back into our original frame of reference in Figure 1-7a. Express (1-17) in terms of the original X values:

$$\begin{aligned} Y &= 60 + .068(X - \bar{X}) \\ &= 60 + .068(X - 400) \\ &= 60 + .068X - 27.2 \end{aligned}$$

$$Y = 32.8 + .068X \tag{1-18}$$

This fitted line is graphed in Figure 1-7a.

A comparison of (1-17) and (1-18) confirms that the slope of our fitted regression ($b = .068$) remains the same; the only difference is in the intercept. Moreover, we note how easily the original intercept ($a_0 = 32.8$) may be recovered.

An estimate of yield for any given fertilizer application is now easily derived from our least squares equation (1-18). For example, if 350 lb of fertilizer is to be applied, our estimate of yield is:

$$Y = 32.8 + .068(350) = 56.6 \text{ bushels/acre}$$

The alternative least squares equation (1-17) yields exactly the same result. When $X = 350$, then $x = -50$, and

$$Y = 60 + .068(-50) = 56.6$$

TABLE 1-2 Least Squares Calculations (Data from Table 1-1)

(1) X_i	(2) Y_i	(3) $x_i = X_i - X$ $= X_i - 400$	(4) $Y_i x_i$	(5) x_i^2	(6) $\hat{Y}_i = a + bx_i$ $= 60 + .068x_i$	(7) $Y_i - \hat{Y}_i$	(8) $(Y_i - \hat{Y}_i)^2$
100	40	−300	−12,000	90,000	39.60	.40	.16
200	45	−200	−9,000	40,000	46.40	−1.40	1.96
300	50	−100	−5,000	10,000	53.20	−3.20	10.24
400	65	0	0	0	60.00	5.00	25.00
500	70	100	7,000	10,000	66.80	3.20	10.24
600	70	200	14,000	40,000	73.60	−3.60	12.96
700	80	300	24,000	90,000	80.40	−.40	.16
$\Sigma X_i = 2{,}800$	$\Sigma Y_i = 420$	$\Sigma x_i = 0\surd$	$\Sigma Y_i x_i = 19{,}000$	$\Sigma x_i^2 = 280{,}000$			$\Sigma (Y_i - \hat{Y}_i)^2 = 60.72$
$\bar{X} = \frac{\Sigma X_i}{n}$	$\bar{Y} = \frac{\Sigma Y_i}{n}$			$b = \frac{\Sigma Y_i x_i}{\Sigma x_i^2}$			$s^2 = \frac{1}{n-2} \Sigma (Y_i - \hat{Y}_i)^2$
$= \frac{2{,}800}{7}$	$= \frac{420}{7}$			$= \frac{19{,}000}{280{,}000}$			$= 12.144$
$= 400$	$= 60$						and $\boxed{s = 3.48}$
	$\boxed{a = 60}$			$\boxed{b = .068}$			

PROBLEMS

(Save your work in the next three chapters, for future reference.)

1-1 Suppose a random sample of five families had the following income and saving:

Family	Income Y	Saving S
A	$ 8,000	$ 600
B	11,000	1200
C	9,000	1000
D	6,000	700
E	6,000	300

(a) Estimate and graph the regression line of saving S on income Y.
(b) Interpret the intercepts a and a_0.

1-2 Use the data of Problem 1-1 to regress consumption C on income Y.

1-3 To interpret the regression slope b, use equation (1-18) to answer the following questions:
(a) About how much is the yield increased for every pound of fertilizer applied—that is, what is the marginal physical product of fertilizer?
(b) If the value of the crop is $2 per bushel, what is the marginal revenue product of fertilizer? If fertilizer costs $0.25 per pound, would it be economic to apply?
(c) To what price approximately would fertilizer have to fall to make it economic?

⇒1-4 (This question has an arrow because it is an important introduction to material taken up later in the text.) Translate both X and Y into deviations x and y (just as X was translated in Figure 1-7b).
(a) What is the new y-intercept? Does the slope remain the same? Does this not imply that the fitted regression equation is simply

$$y = bx?$$

Draw a diagram similar to Figure 1-7b to illustrate this procedure.
(b) Prove that $\sum x_i y_i = \sum x_i Y_i$; hence we may alternatively calculate b in terms of deviations as

$$b = \frac{\sum x_i y_i}{\sum x_i^2}$$

(c) Using this procedure show how the original intercept ($a_0 = 32.8$) may be recovered.

*1-5 (This question is starred because it is more difficult, and hence is optional. It requires calculus.) Suppose X is left in its original form, rather than being translated into x (deviations from the mean).
(a) Write out the sum of squared deviations as in (1-10), in terms of a_0 and b.
(b) Set equal to zero the partial derivatives with respect to a_0 and b, thus obtaining two so-called "normal" equations.
(c) Evaluate these two normal equations using the data in Problem 1-1 and solve for a_0 and b. Do you get the same answer?
(d) Compare this method of solution with the one used in the text.

*1-6 Suppose that four firms had the following profits and research expenditures.

Firm	Profit, P (Thousands of Dollars)	Research Expenditure, R (Thousands of Dollars)
1	50	40
2	60	40
3	40	30
4	50	50

(a) Fit a regression line of P on R.
(b) Does this regression line "show how research generates profits"? Criticize.

APPENDIX 1-1 AN ALTERNATIVE DERIVATION OF LEAST SQUARES ESTIMATES OF a AND b, WITHOUT CALCULUS

Before estimating a and b, it is necessary to solve the theoretical problem of minimizing an ordinary quadratic function of one variable b, of the form

$$f(b) = k_2 b^2 + k_1 b + k_0 \tag{1-19}$$

where k_2, k_1, k_0 are constants, with $k_2 > 0$.
With a little algebraic manipulation, (1-19) may be written as

$$f(b) = k_2\left(b + \frac{k_1}{2k_2}\right)^2 + \left(k_0 - \frac{k_1^2}{4k_2}\right) \tag{1-20}$$

Note that b appears in the first term, but not in the second. Therefore, our hope of minimizing the expression lies in selecting a value of b to minimize the first term. Being a square and hence never negative, the first term will be

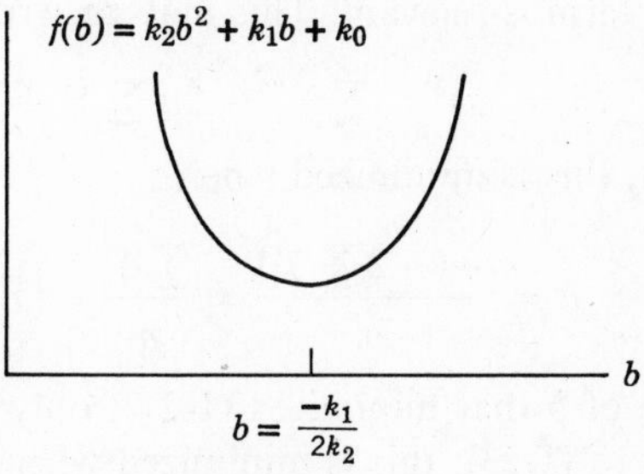

FIG. 1-8 The minimization of a quadratic function.

minimized when it is zero, that is, when

$$b + \frac{k_1}{2k_2} = 0 \tag{1-21}$$

then

$$b = \frac{-k_1}{2k_2} \tag{1-22}$$

This result is shown graphically in Figure 1-8. To restate: *a quadratic function of the form* (1-19) *is minimized by setting*

$$b = -\frac{\text{(coefficient of first power)}}{2\text{(coefficient of second power)}} \tag{1-23}$$

With this theorem in hand, let us return to the problem of selecting values for a and b to minimize

$$S(a, b) = \sum [(Y_i - a) - bx_i]^2 \tag{1-24}$$

It will be useful to manipulate this, as follows:

$$S(a, b) = \sum [(Y_i - a)^2 - 2b(Y_i - a)x_i + b^2x_i^2] \tag{1-25}$$

$$= \sum (Y_i - a)^2 - 2b \sum (Y_i - a)x_i + b^2 \sum x_i^2 \tag{1-26}$$

In the middle term, consider

$$\sum (Y_i - a)x_i = \sum Y_ix_i - a \sum x_i$$
$$= \sum Y_ix_i + 0$$

Using this to rewrite the middle term of (1-26) we have:

$$S(a, b) = \sum (Y_i - a)^2 - 2b \sum Y_ix_i + b^2 \sum x_i^2 \tag{1-27}$$

This is a useful recasting of (1-24), because the first term contains a alone, while the last two terms contain b alone. To find the value of a that minimizes

(1-27) only the first term is relevant. This may be written

$$\sum (Y_i - a)^2 = \sum Y_i^2 - 2a \sum Y_i + na^2$$

According to (1-23), this is minimized when

$$a = \frac{-(-2 \sum Y_i)}{2n} = \frac{\sum Y_i}{n} = \bar{Y} \qquad \text{(1-13) proved}$$

To find the value of b that minimizes (1-27), only the last two terms are relevant. According to (1-23), this is minimized when

$$b = \frac{-(-2 \sum Y_i x_i)}{2 \sum x_i^2} = \frac{\sum Y_i x_i}{\sum x_i^2} \qquad \text{(1-16) proved}$$

chapter 2

Regression Theory

2-1 THE MATHEMATICAL MODEL

So far we have only mechanically fitted a line. This is just a description of the sample observations; now we wish to make inferences about the parent population from which this sample was drawn. Specifically, we must consider the mathematical model that allows us to run tests of significance on a and b.

Turning back to the example in the previous chapter, suppose that the experiment could be repeated many times at a fixed value of x. Even though fertilizer application is fixed from experiment to experiment, we would not observe exactly the same yield each time. Instead, there would be some statistical fluctuation of the Y's, clustered about a central value. We can think of the many possible values of Y forming a population; the probability function of Y for a given x we shall call $p(Y/x)$. Moreover, there will be a similar probability function for Y at any other experimental level of x. One possible sequence of Y populations is shown in Figure 2-1*a*. There would obviously be mathematical problems involved in analysing such populations. To keep the problem manageable, we make a reasonable set of assumptions about the regularity of these populations, as shown in Figure 2-1*b*. We assume the probability functions $p(Y_i/x_i)$:

1. Have the same variance σ^2 for all x_i.
2. Have the means $E(Y_i)$ lying on a straight line, known as the true regression line:

$$E(Y_i) = \mu_i = \alpha + \beta x_i \tag{2-1}$$

The population parameters α and β specify the line; they are to be estimated from sample information. We also assume that

3. The random variables Y_i are statistically independent. For example, a

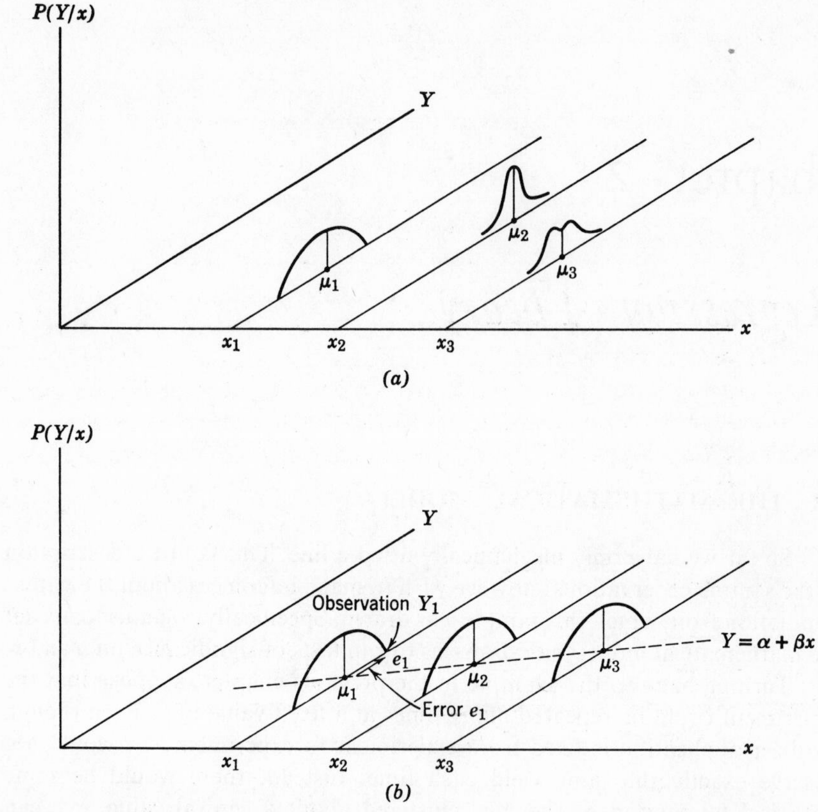

FIG. 2-1 (*a*) General populations of Y, given x. (*b*) The special form of the populations of Y assumed in simple linear regression.

large value of Y_1 does not tend to make Y_2 large; that is, Y_2 is "unaffected" by Y_1.

These assumptions may be written more concisely as:

The random variables Y_i are statistically independent, with

$$\text{mean} = \alpha + \beta x_i \tag{2-2}$$

and

$$\text{variance} = \sigma^2$$

On occasion, it is useful to describe the deviation of Y_i from its expected value as the error or disturbance term e_i, so that the model may alternatively

e is deviation of Y_i from its expected term

be written

$$Y_i = \alpha + \beta x_i + e_i \tag{2-3}$$

where the e_i are independent random variables, with

$$\text{mean} = 0$$

and

$$\text{variance} = \sigma^2 \tag{2-4}$$

We note that the distributions of Y and e are identical, except that their means differ. In fact, the distribution of e is just the distribution of Y translated onto a zero mean.

No assumption is made about the *shape* of the distribution of e (normal or otherwise) provided it has a finite variance. We therefore refer to assumptions (2-4) as the "weak set"; we shall derive as many results as possible from these, before adding a more restrictive normality assumption later.

2-2 THE NATURE OF THE ERROR TERM

Now let us consider in more detail the "purely random" part of Y_i, the error or disturbance term e_i. Why does it exist? Or, why doesn't a precise and exact value of Y_i follow, once the value of x_i is given?

The error may be regarded as the sum of two components:

1. *Measurement error.* There are various reasons why Y may be measured incorrectly. In measuring crop yield, there may be an error resulting from sloppy harvesting or inaccurate weighing. If the example is a study of the consumption of families at various income levels, the measurement error in consumption might consist of budget and reporting inaccuracies.

2. *Stochastic error* occurs because of the inherent irreproducibility of biological and social phenomena. Even if there were no measurement error, continuous repetition of an experiment using exactly the same amount of fertilizer would result in different yields; these differences are unpredictable and are called stochastic differences. They may be reduced by tighter experimental control—for example, by holding constant soil conditions, amount of water, etc. But *complete* control is impossible—for example, seeds cannot be duplicated. Stochastic error may be regarded as the influence on Y of many omitted variables, each with an individually small effect.

In the social sciences, controlled experiments are usually not possible. For example, an economist cannot hold U.S. national income constant for several years while he examines the effect of interest rate on investment.

Since he cannot neutralize extraneous influences by holding them constant, his best alternative is to take them explicitly into account, by regressing Y on x *and* the extraneous factors. This is a useful technique for reducing stochastic error; it is called "multiple regression" and is discussed fully in the next chapter.

2-3 ESTIMATING α AND β

Suppose that our true regression $Y = \alpha + \beta x$ is the dotted line shown in Figure 2-2. This will remain unknown to the statistician, whose job it is to estimate it as best he can by observing x and Y. Suppose at the first level x_1, the stochastic error e_1 takes on a negative value, as shown in the diagram; he will observe the Y and x combination at P_1. Similarly, suppose his only other two observations are P_2 and P_3, resulting from positive values of e. Furthermore, suppose the statistician estimates the true line by fitting a least squares line, applying the method of Chapter 1 to the only information he has—points P_1, P_2, and P_3. He would come up with the solid estimating line in this figure. In Chapter 1 we called this fitted least squares line $Y = a + bx$; now we rename it $Y = \hat{\alpha} + \hat{\beta}x$, to emphasize that $\hat{\alpha}$ is our estimator of α, and $\hat{\beta}$ our estimator of β.

Figure 2-2 is a critical diagram. Before proceeding, the reader should be sure he can clearly distinguish between the true regression and its surrounding e distribution on the one hand, and the estimated regression line on the other.

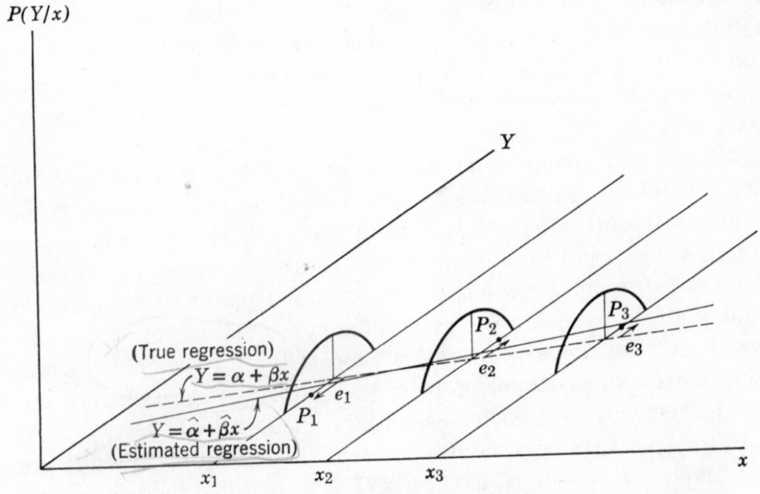

FIG. 2-2 True (population) regression and estimated (sample) regression.

Unless the statistician is very lucky indeed, it is obvious that his estimated line will not be exactly on the true population line. The best he can hope for is that the least squares method of estimation will be close to the target. Specifically, we now ask: "how is the estimator $\hat{\alpha}$ distributed around its target α, and $\hat{\beta}$ around its target β?"

2-4 THE MEAN AND VARIANCE OF $\hat{\alpha}$ AND $\hat{\beta}$

We shall show that the random estimators $\hat{\alpha}$ and $\hat{\beta}$ have the following moments:

$$E(\hat{\alpha}) = \alpha \tag{2-5}$$

$$\text{var}\,(\hat{\alpha}) = \frac{\sigma^2}{n} \tag{2-6}$$

$$E(\hat{\beta}) = \beta \tag{2-7}$$

$$\text{var}\,(\hat{\beta}) = \frac{\sigma^2}{\sum x_i^2} \tag{2-8}$$

where σ^2 is the variance of the error e (the variance of Y).

Because of its greater importance, we shall concentrate on the slope estimator $\hat{\beta}$, rather than $\hat{\alpha}$, for the rest of the chapter.

***Proof of* (2-7) *and* (2-8).** The formula for $\hat{\beta}$ in (1-16) may be rewritten as

$$\hat{\beta} = \sum \left\{\frac{x_i}{k}\right\} Y_i \tag{2-9}$$

where

$$k = \sum x_i^2 \tag{2-10}$$

Thus,

$$\hat{\beta} = \sum w_i Y_i = w_1 Y_1 + w_2 Y_2 \cdots + w_n Y_n \tag{2-11}$$

where

$$w_i = \frac{x_i}{k} \tag{2-12}$$

Since each x_i is a fixed constant, so is each w_i. Thus from (2-11) we establish the important conclusion:

$\hat{\beta}$ is a weighted sum (i.e., a linear combination) of the random variables Y_i (2-13)

From the theory of linear transformations, reviewed[1] in Appendix 2-1b, it follows that

$$E(\hat{\beta}) = w_1E(Y_1) + w_2E(Y_2) \cdots + w_nE(Y_n) = \sum w_iE(Y_i) \tag{2-14}$$

Moreover, noting that the variables Y_i are assumed independent, it follows[2] that

$$\text{var}\,(\hat{\beta}) = w_1^2 \text{ var } Y_1 + \cdots + w_n^2 \text{ var } Y_n = \sum w_i^2 \text{ var } Y_i \tag{2-15}$$

For the mean, from (2-14) and (2-1),

$$E(\hat{\beta}) = \sum w_i[\alpha + \beta x_i] \tag{2-16}$$

$$= \alpha \sum w_i + \beta \sum w_i x_i \tag{2-17}$$

and noting (2-12)

$$E(\hat{\beta}) = \frac{\alpha}{k} \sum x_i + \frac{\beta}{k} \sum (x_i)x_i \tag{2-18}$$

but $\sum x_i$ is zero, according to (1-6).Thus

$$E(\hat{\beta}) = 0 + \frac{\beta}{k} \sum x_i^2$$

From (2-10)

$$E(\hat{\beta}) = \beta \qquad \text{(2-7) proved}$$

Thus $\hat{\beta}$ is an unbiased estimator of β. (Unbiasedness and other desirable characteristics of an estimator—efficiency and consistency—are reviewed in Appendix 2-2.)

For the variance, from (2-15) and (2-2),

$$\text{var}\,(\hat{\beta}) = \sum w_i^2 \sigma^2 \tag{2-19}$$

$$= \sum \frac{x_i^2}{k^2} \sigma^2 \tag{2-20}$$

$$= \frac{\sigma^2}{k^2} \sum x_i^2 \tag{2-21}$$

Again, noting (2-10),

$$\text{var}\,(\hat{\beta}) = \frac{\sigma^2}{\sum x_i^2} \qquad \text{(2-8) proved}$$

A similar derivation of the mean and variance of $\hat{\alpha}$ is left as an exercise.

---

[1] For an introduction to this theory, see for example, Thomas H. Wonnacott and Ronald J. Wonnacott, "Introductory Statistics," New York: John Wiley, 1969.

[2] Since the Y_i are independent, the covariances are zero:

$$\text{cov}\,(Y_i, Y_j) = 0 \qquad \text{for any } i \neq f$$

We observe from (2-12) that in calculating $\hat{\beta}$, the weight w_i attached to the Y_i observation is proportional to the deviation x_i. Hence, outlying observations exert a relatively heavy influence in the calculation of $\hat{\beta}$.

2-5 THE GAUSS-MARKOV THEOREM

This is the major justification for using the least squares method in the linear regression model.

Gauss-Markov Theorem.

Within the class of linear unbiased estimators of β (or α), the least squares estimator has minimum variance.

(2-22)

This theorem is important because it follows even from the weak set of assumptions (2-4), and hence requires no assumption about the shape of the distribution of the error term. A proof is given in Appendix 2-3.

To interpret this important theorem, consider $\hat{\beta}$, the least squares estimator of β. We have already seen in (2-13) that it is a linear estimator, and we restrict ourselves to linear estimators because they are easy to analyse and understand. We restrict ourselves even further, as shown in Figure 2-3; within this set of linear estimators we consider only the limited class that is unbiased. The least squares estimator not only is in this class, according to (2-7); of all the estimators in this class, it has the minimum variance. Therefore, it is often referred to as BLUE, the "best linear unbiased estimator."

The Gauss-Markov theorem has an interesting corollary. As a special case of regression, we might ask what happens if we are explaining Y, but

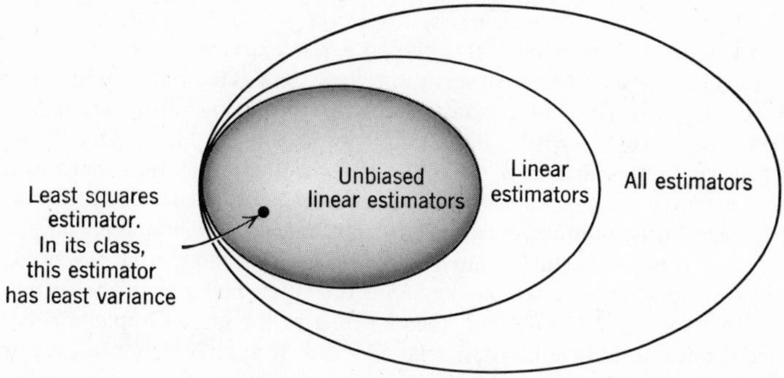

FIG. 2-3 Diagram of the restricted class of estimators considered in the Gauss-Markov theorem.

$\beta = 0$ in (2-2) so that no independent variable x comes into play. From (2-2), α is the mean of the Y population (μ). Moreover, from (1-13) its least squares estimator is $\bar{Y}$. Thus, the least squares estimator of a population mean (μ) is the sample mean ($\bar{Y}$), and the Gauss-Markov theorem fully applies: the sample mean is the "best linear unbiased estimator" of a population mean.

It must be emphasized that the Gauss-Markov theorem is restricted, applying only to estimators that are both linear and unbiased. It follows that there may be a biased or nonlinear estimator that is better (i.e., has smaller variance) than the least squares estimator. For example, to estimate a population mean, the sample median is a nonlinear estimator. It is better than the sample mean, for certain kinds of nonnormal populations.[3] The sample median is just one example of a whole collection of nonlinear estimators known as "distribution-free" or "nonparametric" statistics. These are expressly designed for inference when the population cannot be assumed to be normally distributed.

2-6 THE DISTRIBUTION OF $\hat{\beta}$

With the mean and variance of $\hat{\beta}$ derived in (2-7) and (2-8), we now ask: "What is the shape of the distribution of $\hat{\beta}$?" If we now add (for the first time) the strong assumption that the Y_i are normal, and recall that $\hat{\beta}$ is a linear combination of the Y_i, it follows (Appendix 2-1b) that $\hat{\beta}$ will also be normal. But even without assuming the Y_i are normal, as sample size increases the distribution of $\hat{\beta}$ will usually approach normality; this can be justified by a generalized form[4] of the Central Limit theorem.

We are now in a position to graph the distribution of $\hat{\beta}$ in Figure 2-4; (for the time being, the bottom line in this diagram may be disregarded). Our

---

[3] Populations with thick tails may give rise to a few extreme observations. The sample median "weights" these extreme observations less than does the sample mean, and is therefore more reliable. The classic example of such a thick-tailed distribution is the Cauchy distribution, $p(x) = [\pi(1 + x^2)]^{-1}$. Although it looks roughly "bell-shaped" (in fact it is student's t distribution with 1 d.f.), nevertheless it has such thick tails that the variance is infinite, and even the mean does not exist in a mathematical sense. The mean of a sample from the Cauchy distribution does not obey the Central Limit theorem, and is very unstable. In fact, it is no more stable than a single observation, no matter how large a sample is taken. In this situation, the sample median is obviously better than the sample mean.

[4] As usually stated, the Central Limit theorem proves the large-sample normality of the sample mean; but it applies equally to a sample sum. It applies also to a *weighted* sum of random variables such as $\hat{\beta}$ in (2-13), under most conditions. See for example, D. A. S. Fraser, *Nonparametric Statistics*, New York: John Wiley, 1957. Similarly the normality of $\hat{\alpha}$ is justified.

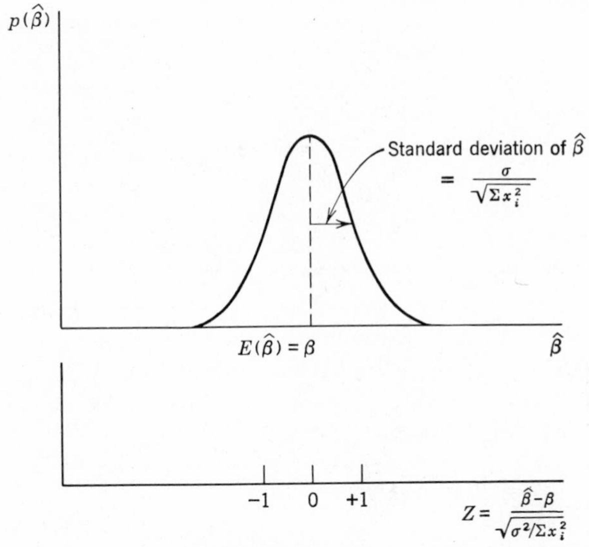

FIG. 2-4 The probability distribution of the estimator $\hat{\beta}$.

objective is to develop a clear intuitive idea of how this estimator varies from sample to sample. First, of course, we note that (2-7) established that $\hat{\beta}$ is an unbiased estimator, so that its distribution is centered on its target β.

The interpretation of its variance (2-8) is more difficult. Suppose that the experiment has been badly designed with the X_i's close together. This makes the deviations x_i small; hence $\sum x_i^2$ small. Therefore, $\sigma^2/\sum x_i^2$, the variance of $\hat{\beta}$ from (2-8) is large and $\hat{\beta}$ is a comparatively unreliable estimator. To check the intuitive validity of this, consider the scatter diagram in Figure 2-5(a). The bunching of the X's means that the small part of the line being investigated is obscured by the error e, making the slope estimate $\hat{\beta}$ very unreliable. In this specific instance, our estimate has been pulled badly out of line by the errors—in particular the one indicated by the arrow.

By contrast, in Figure 2-5(b) we show the case where the X's are reasonably spread out. Even though the errors e remain the same, the estimate $\hat{\beta}$ is much more reliable, because errors no longer exert the same leverage.

As a concrete example, suppose we wish to examine how sensitive Canadian imports (Y) are to the international value of the Canadian dollar (x). A much more reliable estimate should be possible using the period 1948–1962 when the Canadian dollar was flexible (and took on a range of values) than in the period before or since when this dollar was fixed (and only allowed to fluctuate within a very narrow range).

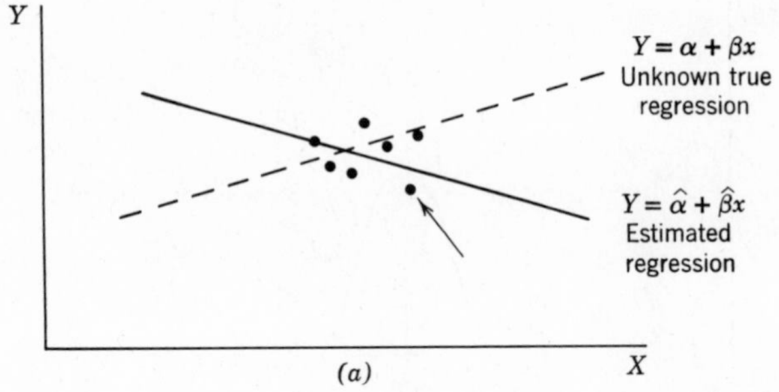

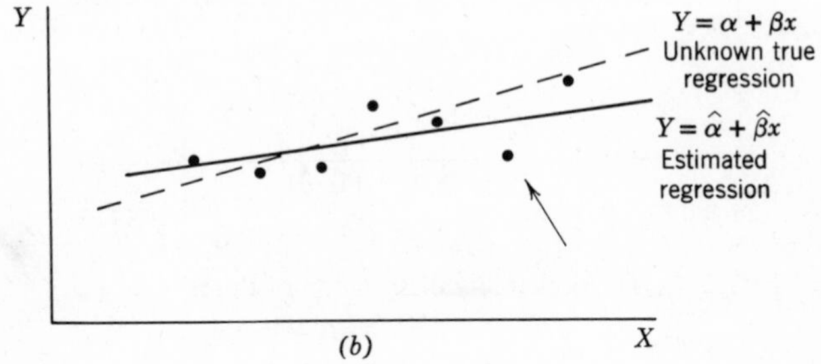

FIG. 2-5 (*a*) Unreliable estimate when X_i are very close. (*b*) More reliable fit because X_i are spread out.

2-7 CONFIDENCE INTERVALS AND TESTING HYPOTHESES ABOUT β

With the mean, variance, and normality of the estimator $\hat{\beta}$ established, statistical inferences about β are now in order. First standardize $\hat{\beta}$, obtaining

$$Z = \frac{\hat{\beta} - \beta}{\sqrt{\sigma^2/\sum x_i^2}} \tag{2-23}$$

where $Z \sim N(0, 1)$, that is, Z is normally distributed, with mean 0 and variance 1, as shown in Figure 2-4.

Since σ^2, the variance of Y is generally unknown, it is estimated with

$$s^2 = \frac{1}{n-2}\sum (Y_i - \hat{Y}_i)^2 \tag{2-24}$$

where $\hat{Y}_i$ is the fitted value of Y on the estimated regression line: that is,

$$\hat{Y}_i = \hat{\alpha} + \hat{\beta}x_i \tag{2-25}$$

s^2 is often referred to as "residual variance," a term similarly used in analysis of variance. The divisor $(n - 2)$ is used in (2-24) rather than n in order to make s^2 an unbiased estimator of σ^2 (see Appendix 2-4). When this substitution of s^2 for σ^2 is made, the standardized $\hat{\beta}$ is no longer normal, but instead has the slightly more spread-out t distribution:

$$t = \frac{\hat{\beta} - \beta}{\sqrt{s^2/\sum x_i^2}} \tag{2-26}$$

where t has $(n - 2)$ degrees of freedom, like s^2. For the t distribution to be strictly valid, we require the strong assumption that the distribution of Y_i is normal. From (2-26) we may now proceed to construct a confidence interval or test an hypothesis.

(a) Confidence Intervals

Let $t_{.025}$ denote the t value that leaves $2\frac{1}{2}\%$ of the distribution in the upper tail: that is,

$$\Pr(-t_{.025} < t < t_{.025}) = .95 \tag{2-27}$$

Substituting t from (2-26)

$$\Pr\left(-t_{.025} < \frac{\hat{\beta} - \beta}{\sqrt{s^2/\sum x_i^2}} < t_{.025}\right) = .95 \tag{2-28}$$

The inequalities within the bracket may be reexpressed:

$$\Pr\left(\hat{\beta} - t_{.025}\frac{s}{\sqrt{\sum x_i^2}} < \beta < \hat{\beta} + t_{.025}\frac{s}{\sqrt{\sum x_i^2}}\right) = .95 \tag{2-29}$$

which yields,

the 95% confidence interval[6] for β:

$$\beta = \hat{\beta} \pm t_{.025}\frac{s}{\sqrt{\sum x_i^2}} \tag{2-30}$$

where $t_{.025}$ has $(n - 2)$ degrees of freedom.

For our example of crop yield in the previous chapter, the confidence interval for β (the effect of fertilizer on yield) is computed as follows: s as

[6] Using a similar argument, and noting (2-6), the 95% confidence interval for α is:

$$\alpha = \hat{\alpha} \pm t_{.025}\frac{s}{\sqrt{n}} \tag{2-31}$$

given by (2-24) is evaluated in the last three columns of Table 1-2. Also noting the values for $\hat{\beta}$ and $\sum x_i^2$ calculated in that table, our 95% confidence interval (2-30) becomes

$$\beta = .068 \pm 2.571 \frac{3.48}{\sqrt{280{,}000}}$$

$$= .068 \pm .017$$

$$.051 < \beta < .085 \tag{2-32}$$

(b) Testing Hypotheses

A two-sided test of any hypothesis may be carried out simply by noting whether or not the confidence interval (2-30) contains that hypothesis. For example, the hypothesis typically tested is the null hypothesis:

$$H_0: \beta = 0 \tag{2-33}$$

that is, fertilizer has no effect on yield. In testing this against the two-sided alternative,

$$H_1: \beta \neq 0 \tag{2-34}$$

H_0 must be rejected at a 5% significance level, since the null value of zero is not contained in (2-32).

Since fertilizer is expected to favorably affect yield, it seems more appropriate to test (2-33) against the one-sided alternative:

$$H_1: \beta > 0 \tag{2-35}$$

First, consider the distribution of the t statistic (2-26), shown in Figure 2-6; (compare this with the slightly less spread distribution of Z shown in Figure 2-4). The rejection region appropriate for the one-sided alternative (2-35) is

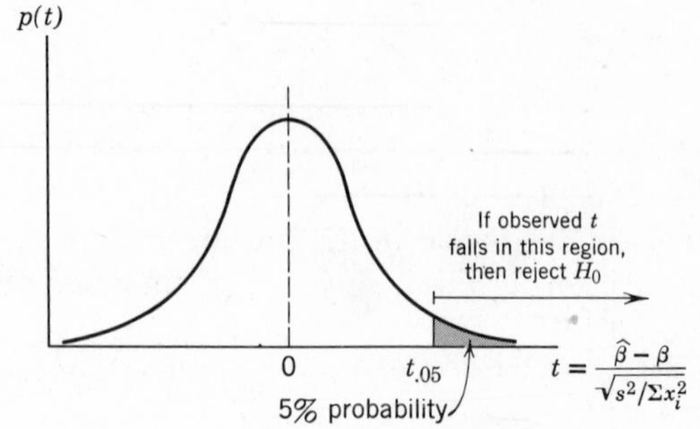

FIG. 2-6 A one-tailed hypothesis test.

defined by the single value $t_{.05}$ leaving 5% of the distribution in the upper tail. Next the observed t value is calculated. Assuming the null hypothesis ($\beta = 0$) is true, this reduces to

$$t = \frac{\hat{\beta}}{\sqrt{s^2/\sum x_i^2}} \tag{2-36}$$

Now an observed t value that falls in the rejection range above $t_{.05}$ may be explained in one of two ways; either H_0 is true and we have been extremely unlucky in observing a sample that is atypical; or the world is not like this after all—that is, H_0 is not true. The implausibility of the first explanation allows us to choose the second, and we reject the hypothesis. But we cannot be certain that the first explanation is not the true one; all we know is that if H_0 is true, there is only a 5% probability that we will make the mistake of rejecting it.

In our example,

$$t = \frac{.068}{3.48/\sqrt{280{,}000}} = 10.3$$

Since this observed value exceeds the critical $t_{.05}$ value of 2.015, H_0 is rejected in favor of H_1 (fertilizer favorably affects yield).

2-8 INTERPOLATION (CONFIDENCE INTERVALS AND PREDICTION INTERVALS)

In the previous section we considered the broad aspects of the model, namely, the position of the whole line (determined by α and β). In this section, we shall consider two narrower problems:

(a) For a given, perhaps new, value of x, say x_0, what is the interval that will predict the *mean* value of Y_0, [i.e., the confidence interval for $E(Y_0)$ or μ_0]? In our fertilizer problem, we may wish, for example, an interval estimate of the mean of the distribution of all possible yields resulting from the application of 550 lb of fertilizer. (Note that we are not deriving an interval estimate of average yield by observing repeated applications of 550 lb of fertilizer; in that case, we could apply the simpler technique of estimating a population mean with the sample mean. Instead we are estimating mean yield for 550 lb of fertilizer from our seven sample values, each of which involved a *different* application of fertilizer. This is clearly a more difficult problem.)

(b) What is the interval that will predict a *single observed* value of Y_0 (referred to as the prediction interval for an individual Y_0). Again using our example, what would we predict a single yield to be from an application of

550 lb of fertilizer? (b) is clearly less predictable than (a). We now consider both in detail.

(a) The Confidence Interval for the Mean μ_0

First we find its point estimator, $\hat{\mu}_0$, then construct an interval estimate around it. The appropriate estimator of μ_0 is just the point on our estimated regression line above x_0. That is,

$$\hat{\mu}_0 = \hat{\alpha} + \hat{\beta}x_0 \tag{2-37}$$

But as a point estimate, this will almost certainly involve some error, because of errors made in the estimates $\hat{\alpha}$ and $\hat{\beta}$. Figure 2-7 illustrates the effect of these errors; the true regression is shown, along with an estimated regression. Note how $\hat{\mu}_0$ underestimates in this case. In Figure 2-8, the true regression is again shown, along with several estimated regressions fitted from several possible sets of sample data. The fitted value is sometimes too low, sometimes too high, but on average, just right.

Specifically we now ask: "What is the distribution of this random estimator $\hat{\mu}_0$?" From Appendix 2-1b, it can be shown that its distribution is normal, with mean and variance derived as follows. By definition,

$$E(\hat{\mu}_0) = E[\hat{\alpha} + \hat{\beta}x_0]$$

But, since x_0 is fixed,

$$E(\hat{\mu}_0) = E(\hat{\alpha}) + x_0E(\hat{\beta})$$

$$= \alpha + x_0\beta$$

$$\boxed{E(\hat{\mu}_0) = \mu_0} \tag{2-38}$$

Hence, $\hat{\mu}_0$ is an unbiased estimator.

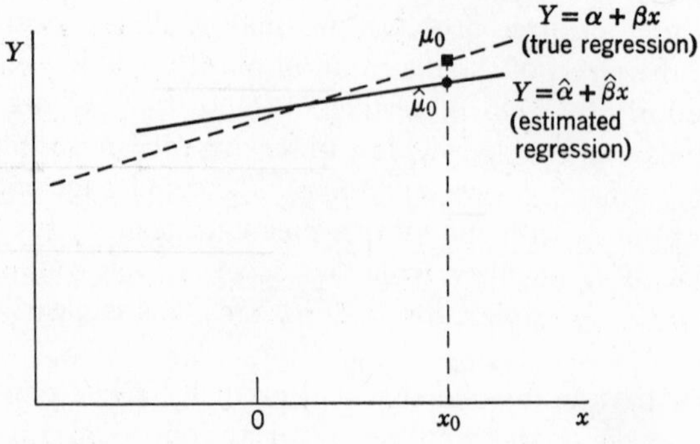

FIG. 2-7 How the estimator $\hat{\mu}_0$ is related to the target μ_0.

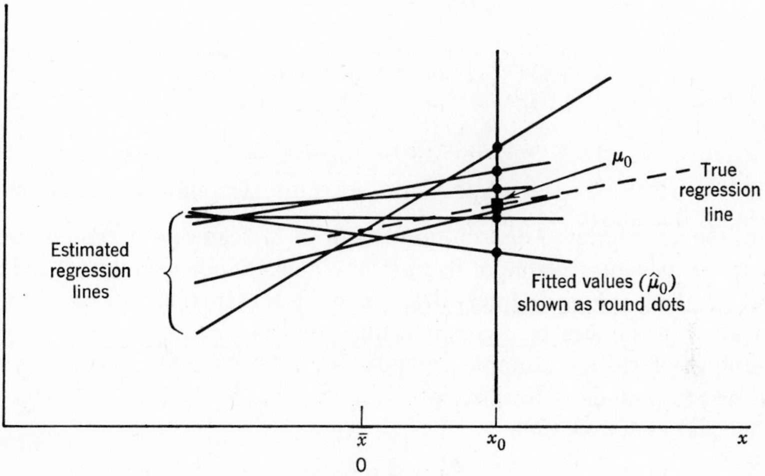

FIG. 2-8 $\hat{\mu}_0$ as an unbiased estimator of μ_0.

Turning to its variance, because $\hat{\alpha}$ and $\hat{\beta}$ are uncorrelated,[7]

$$\text{var}(\hat{\mu}_0) = \text{var}\,\hat{\alpha} + x_0^2\,\text{var}\,\hat{\beta}$$

$$= \frac{\sigma^2}{n} + x_0^2 \frac{\sigma^2}{\sum x_i^2}$$

$$\boxed{\text{var}(\hat{\mu}_0) = \sigma^2\left[\frac{1}{n} + \frac{x_0^2}{\sum x_i^2}\right]} \tag{2-39}$$

To interpret (2-39), we note that this variance (or uncertainty) of $\hat{\mu}_0$ has two components, resulting from the variance (uncertainty) of $\hat{\alpha}$ and of $\hat{\beta}$ respectively. The uncertainty term resulting from $\hat{\beta}$ increases as x_0^2 increases, that is, as x_0 takes on values distant from its central value 0. This also can be seen from Figure 2-8: if x_0 were further to the right, then our estimates $\hat{\mu}_0$ would be spread out over an even wider range. On the other hand, if x_0 were further to the left and closer to its central value then our estimates $\hat{\mu}_0$ would be less spread.

Using standard procedures for constructing an interval estimate from

---

[7] One reason for redefining the X variable as a deviation from the mean was to make the covariance of $\hat{\alpha}$ and $\hat{\beta}$ zero. The proof is straightforward but tedious, so we omit it.

the mean and variance of $\hat{\mu}_0$, it follows that:

The 95% confidence interval for μ_0 is:

$$\mu_0 = \hat{\mu}_0 \pm t_{.025}\, s \sqrt{\frac{1}{n} + \frac{x_0^2}{\sum x_i^2}} \tag{2-40}$$

Again, the appropriate t distribution has $(n - 2)$ degrees of freedom. When x_0 is set at its central value of 0, note how this confidence interval reduces simply to the confidence interval for α in (2-31). In this case there is no uncertainty introduced by errors in estimating β.

For the fertilizer example, suppose we wish to calculate the average yield for 550 pounds of fertilizer application—that is, average yield when x_0 is set at $550 - 400 = 150$:

$$\hat{\mu}_0 = \hat{\alpha} + \hat{\beta} x_0$$

From Table 1-2,

$$\begin{aligned}\hat{\mu}_0 &= 60 + .068(150)\\ &= 70.2 \text{ bushels/acre}\end{aligned}$$

This is the point estimate of average yield. The interval estimate using (2-40) and Table 1-2 is

$$\mu_0 = 70.2 \pm 2.571(3.48)\sqrt{\frac{1}{7} + \frac{150^2}{280{,}000}} \tag{2-41}$$

$$66.0 \le \mu_0 \le 74.4$$

That is, at a 95% confidence level, the true mean will be bracketed within the interval 66.0 to 74.4 bushels/acre.

(b) The Prediction Interval for an Individual Y_0

In predicting a single (future) observed value of Y_0, it may be proved once again, that in a certain sense the best estimate is the point on our estimated regression line above x_0. In other words, the predicted value for Y is

$$\hat{Y}_0 = \hat{\alpha} + \hat{\beta} x_0 = \hat{\mu}_0 \tag{2-42}$$

When we try to find the *interval* estimate for the single Y_0, we will face all the problems involved in the interval for the mean, μ_0. Now, in addition, we face a problem because we are trying to estimate only one observed Y, rather than a more stable average of all the possible Y's. Hence, to our previous variance (2-39), we must now add the inherent variance σ^2 of an individual Y observation, obtaining

$$\sigma^2\left(\frac{1}{n} + \frac{x_0^2}{\sum x_i^2}\right) + \sigma^2 = \sigma^2\left(\frac{1}{n} + \frac{x_0^2}{\sum x_i^2} + 1\right) \tag{2-43}$$

Except for this larger variance, the prediction interval for Y_0 can be proved to be the same as the confidence interval for μ_0, namely:

The 95% prediction interval for an individual Y observation is:

$$Y_0 = \hat{\mu}_0 \pm t_{.025}\, s\sqrt{\frac{1}{n} + \frac{x_0^2}{\sum x_i^2} + 1} \tag{2-44}$$

with the t distribution again having $(n - 2)$ degrees of freedom.

Again using the fertilizer example, suppose we wish to predict a single crop yield if 550 lb/acre of fertilizer are applied. With a 95% chance of being right, we would predict:

$$Y_0 = 70.2 \pm 2.571(3.48)\sqrt{1 + \frac{1}{7} + \frac{150^2}{280{,}000}} \tag{2-45}$$

or

$$60.3 \leq Y_0 \leq 80.1 \tag{2-46}$$

We confirm, as expected, that this is a wider interval than (2-41).

The relationship of prediction and confidence intervals is shown in Figure 2-9. The two potential sources of error in a confidence interval for the mean are shown in Figures 2-9*a* and *b*; these are combined to form the solid band in Figure 2-9*c*. The wider, dotted band in (*c*) gives the prediction intervals for individual Y observations. Note how both bands expand as x moves farther away from its central value of zero; this reflects the fact that x_0^2 appears in both variances.

We emphasize that in formulas (2-40) and (2-44), x_0 may be *any* value of x. If x_0 lies *among* the values $x_1 \cdots x_n$, the process is called interpolation. (If x_0 *is* one of the values $x_1 \cdots x_n$, the process might be called, "using also the other values of x to sharpen our knowledge of this one population at x_0".) If x_0 is out beyond x_1 or x_n, then the process is called extrapolation. The techniques developed in this section may be used for extrapolation, but only with great caution as we shall see in the next section.

See Diagram on Next Page

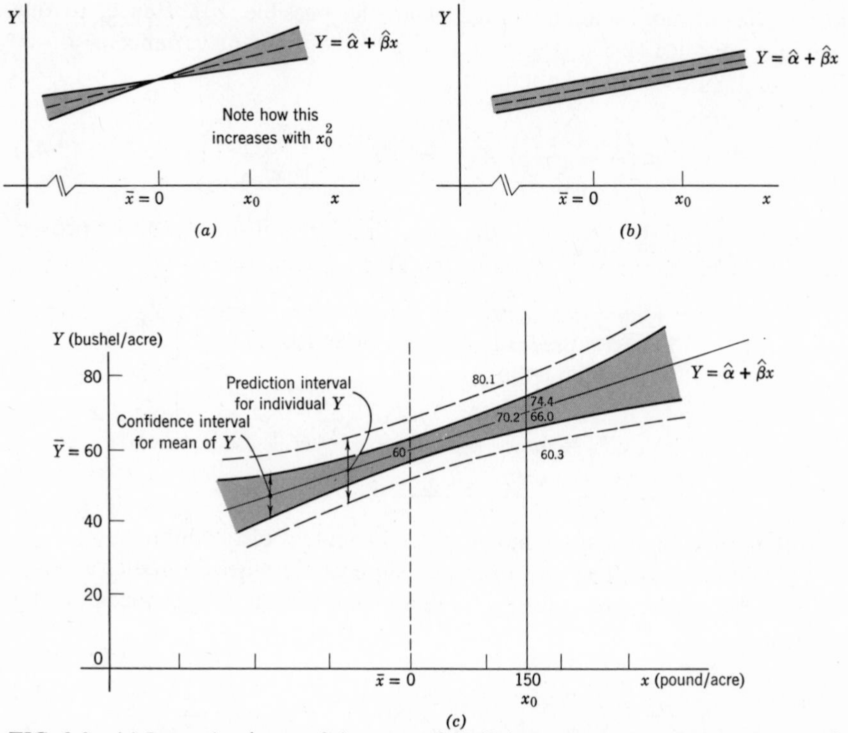

FIG. 2-9 (*a*) Interval estimate of the mean of Y, if there were error only in estimating β. (*b*) Interval estimate of the mean of Y, if there were error only in estimating α. (*c*) Interval estimate for mean of Y and prediction interval for individual Y.

PROBLEMS

2-1 Construct a 95% confidence interval for the regression coefficient β in
   (a) Problem 1-1
   (b) Problem 1-2

2-2 Which of the following hypotheses does the data of Problem 1-1 prove to be unacceptable at the 5% level of significance?
   (a) $\beta = 0$
   (b) $\beta = 1/2$
   (c) $\beta = .1$
   (d) $\beta = -.1$

2-3 At the 1% level of significance, use the data of Problem 1-1 to test the hypothesis that saving does not depend on income, against the alternative hypothesis that saving increases with income.

2-4 Using the data of Problem 1-1, what is your 95% prediction interval for the saving of a family with an income of

(a) \$6000

(b) \$8000

(c) \$10,000

(d) \$12,000

(e) Which of these four intervals is least precise? Most precise? Why?

(f) How is the answer to (b) related to the confidence interval found from (2-31)?

(g) Repeat (a) to (d), calculating a confidence interval for the average saving of all families at each income level. Compare.

2-5 (a) Suppose you are trying to explain how the interest rate (i) affects investment (I) in the U.S. Would you prefer to take observations of i and I over a period in which the authorities were trying to hold interest constant, or a period in which it is allowed to vary widely?

(b) Suppose you have estimated the regression of consumption (C) on income (Y) using data from families in the \$8000 to \$16,000 income range. Would you prefer to predict the future consumption of a family with an \$8000 income, or a family with a \$10,000 income? Why?

2-9 DANGERS OF EXTRAPOLATION

There are two dangers in extrapolation, which we might call "mathematical" and "practical." In both cases, there is no sharp division between safe interpolation and dangerous extrapolation. Rather, there is *continually* increasing danger of misinterpretation as x_0 gets further and further from its central value.

(a) Mathematical Danger

It was emphasized in the previous section that prediction intervals get larger as x_0 moves away from $\bar{x}$. This is true, even if all the assumptions underlying our mathematical model hold exactly.

(b) Practical Danger

In practice it must be recognized that a mathematical model is never absolutely correct. Rather, it is a useful approximation. In particular, one cannot take seriously the assumption that the population means are strung

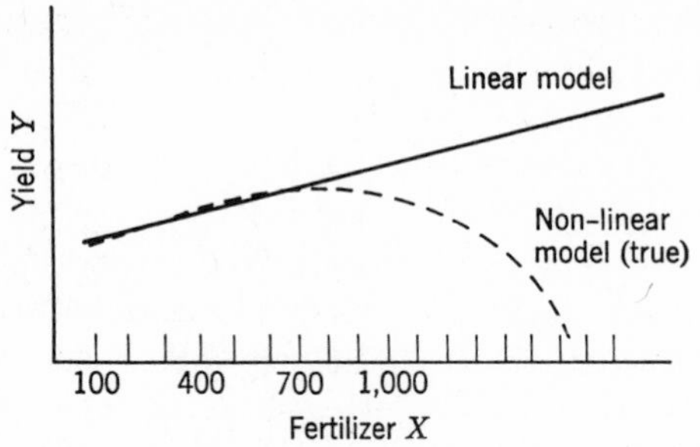

FIG. 2-10 Comparison of linear and nonlinear models.

out in an *exactly* straight line. If we consider the fertilizer example, it is likely that the true relation increases initially, but then bends down eventually as a "burning point" is approached, and the crop is overdosed. This is illustrated in Figure 2-10, which is an extension of Figure 1-2 with the scale appropriately reduced. In the region of interest, from 0 to 700 lb, the relation is *practically* a straight line, and no great harm is done in assuming the linear model. However, if the linear model is extrapolated far beyond this region of experimentation, the result becomes meaningless.

There are "nonlinear" models available, if they seem more appropriate. Moreover statistical tests are available to help determine whether or not they are appropriate. These topics are covered in Chapter 4.

The next section is starred because it is a bit more difficult and theoretical, but it may be detoured without loss of continuity.

*2-10 MAXIMUM LIKELIHOOD ESTIMATION

Sections 2-1 to 2-5, including the Gauss-Markov justification of least squares, required no assumption of the normality of the error term (i.e., normality of Y). In Sections 2-6 to 2-9, the normality assumption was required only for small sample estimation—and this because of a quite general principle that small sample estimation requires a normally distributed parent population to validate the t-distribution. In these last two sections, we make the strong assumption of a normally distributed error throughout. On this premise, we derive the maximum likelihood estimates (MLE) of α and β, that is, those hypothetical population values of α and β that generate the greatest probability for the sample values we observed. These MLE of α and β turn out to be the least squares estimates; thus, maximum likelihood provides another justification for using least squares.

Before addressing the algebraic derivation, it is best to clarify what is going on with a bit of geometry. Specifically, why should the maximum likelihood line fit the data well? To simplify, assume a sample of only three observations (P_1, P_2, P_3).

First, let us try out the line shown in Figure 2-11*a*. (Before examining it carefully, we note that it seems to be a pretty bad fit for our three observed points). Temporarily, suppose this were the true regression line; then the distribution of errors would be centered around it as shown. The likelihood that such a population would give rise to the sample we observed is the joint probability density of the particular set of three *e* values shown in this diagram. The individual probability densities of the three *e* values are shown

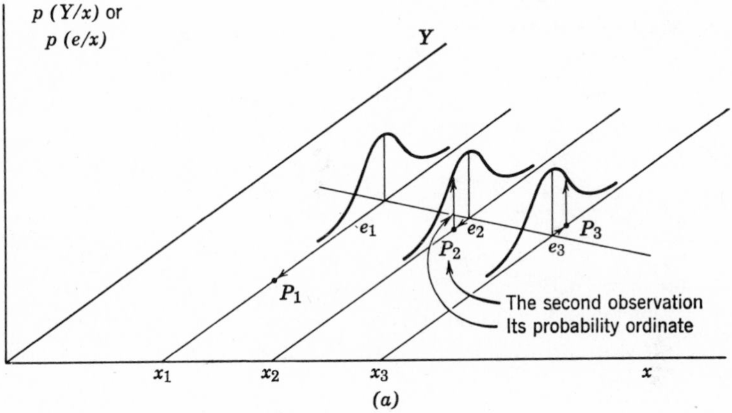

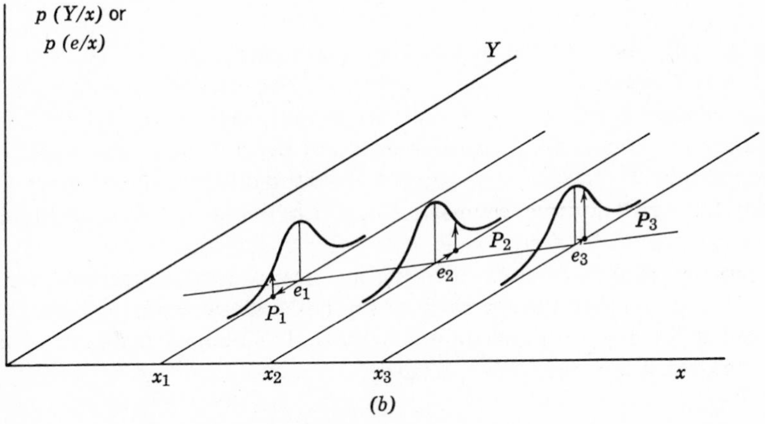

FIG. 2-11 Maximum likelihood estimation. (*a*) *Note*. This is *not* the true population; it is only a hypothetical population that the statistician is considering. But it is not very likely to generate the observed P_1, P_2, P_3. (*b*) Another hypothetical population; this is more likely to generate P_1, P_2, P_3.

as the ordinates above the points P_1, P_2, and P_3. Because the three observations are by assumption statistically independent, the joint probability density (i.e., of getting the sample we observe), is the product of these three ordinates. This likelihood seems relatively small, mostly because the very small ordinate of P_1 reduces the product value. Our intuition that this is a bad estimate is confirmed; such a hypothetical population is not very likely to generate our sample values. We should be able to do better.

In Figure 2-11*b* it is evident that we can do much better. This hypothetical population is more likely to give rise to the sample we observed. The disturbance terms are collectively smaller, with their probability density being greater as a consequence.

The MLE technique is seen to involve speculating on various possible populations. How likely is each to give rise to the sample we observed? Geometrically, our problem would be to try them all out, by moving the population through all its possible values—that is, *by moving the regression line and its surrounding e distribution through all possible positions in space.* Each position involves a different set of trial values for α and β. In each case the likelihood of observing P_1, P_2, P_3 would be evaluated. For our MLE, we choose that hypothetical population that maximizes this likelihood. It is evident that little further adjustment is required in Figure 2-11*b* to arrive at the MLE. This procedure seems to result, intuitively, in a good fit; moreover, since it seems similar to the least squares fit, it is no surprise that we shall be able to show that the two coincide.

There are two other points worth noting. The MLE is derived from our three sample observations; another set of sample observations would almost certainly give rise to another MLE of α and β. The second point is more subtle. The likelihood of any population yielding our sample depends on not only the size of the e terms involved, but also on the shape of the e distribution—in particular σ^2, the variance of e. However, it can be shown that the maximum likelihood *line* does not depend on σ^2. In other words, if we assume σ^2 is larger, the geometry will look different, because e will have a flatter distribution; but the end result will be the same maximum likelihood line.

While geometry has clarified the method, it has not provided a precise means of arriving at the specific maximum likelihood estimate. This must be done algebraically. For generality, suppose that we have a sample of size n, rather than just 3. We wish to know

$$p(Y_1, Y_2 \cdots Y_n) \tag{2-47}$$

the likelihood or probability density of the sample we observed—expressed as a function of the possible population values of α, β, and σ^2. First, consider the probability density of the first value of Y, which is

$$p(Y_1) = \frac{1}{\sqrt{2\pi\sigma^2}} e^{-(1/2\sigma^2)[Y_1-(\alpha+\beta x_1)]^2} \tag{2-48}$$

This is simply the normal distribution of Y_1, with its mean $(\alpha + \beta x_1)$ and variance (σ^2) substituted into the appropriate positions. [In terms of the geometry of Figure 2-11, $p(Y_1)$ is the ordinate above P_1.] The probability density of the second Y value is similar to (2-48), except that the subscript 2 replaces 1 throughout; and so on, for all the other observed Y values.

The independence of the Y values justifies multiplying all these probability densities together to find the joint probability density:

$$p(Y_1, Y_2, \ldots, Y_n)$$

$$= \left[\frac{1}{\sqrt{2\pi\sigma^2}} e^{-(1/2\sigma^2)[Y_1-(\alpha+\beta x_1)]^2}\right]\left[\frac{1}{\sqrt{2\pi\sigma^2}} e^{-(1/2\sigma^2)[Y_2-(\alpha+\beta x_2)]^2}\right] \cdots$$

$$= \prod_{i=1}^{n} \left[\frac{1}{\sqrt{2\pi\sigma^2}} e^{-(1/2\sigma^2)[Y_i-(\alpha+\beta x_i)]^2}\right] \tag{2-49}$$

where $\prod_{i=1}^{n}$ represents the product of n factors. Using the familiar rule for exponentials,[8] the product in (2-49) can be reexpressed by summing exponents

$$p(Y_1, Y_2, \ldots, Y_n) = \left(\frac{1}{\sqrt{2\pi\sigma^2}}\right)^n e^{\Sigma(-1/2\sigma^2)[Y_i-(\alpha+\beta x_i)]^2} \tag{2-50}$$

Recall that the observed Y's are given. We are speculating on various values of α, β, and σ^2. To emphasize this, we rename (2-50) the likelihood function

$$L(\alpha, \beta, \sigma^2) = \frac{1}{(2\pi\sigma^2)^{n/2}} e^{-(1/2\sigma^2)\Sigma[Y_i-\alpha-\beta x_i]^2} \tag{2-51}$$

We now ask, which values of α and β make L largest? The only place α and β appear is in the exponent; moreover, maximizing a function with a negative exponent involves minimizing the magnitude of the exponent. Designating our estimators as $\hat{\alpha}$ and $\hat{\beta}$, the problem is to select values for them that

$$\text{minimize} \sum [Y_i - \hat{\alpha} - \hat{\beta} x_i]^2 \tag{2-52}$$

---

[8] $e^a \cdot e^b = e^{a+b}$ for any a and b.

Moreover, this provides the maximum likelihood solution for α and β, regardless of the value of σ. This is the proposition suggested in the geometrical analysis in Figure 2-11; no matter what is assumed about the spread of the distribution, the maximum likelihood line is not affected by it.

But an even more important conclusion follows from comparing equation (2-52) with equation (1-10). *Maximum likelihood estimates are identical to least squares estimates.* The selection of least squares estimates a and b to minimize (1-10) is identical to the selection of maximum likelihood estimates $\hat{\alpha}$ and $\hat{\beta}$ to minimize (2-52). This establishes our other important theoretical justification of the least squares method: it is the estimate that follows from applying maximum-likelihood techniques to a model with normally distributed error.

The MLE is more difficult to derive for σ^2 than for α and β; moreover, the MLE of σ^2 is biased. This development is left to Appendix 2-4.

2-11 WHEN X IS RANDOM

So far it has been assumed that the independent variable x takes on a given set of fixed values (for example, fertilizer application was set at certain specified levels). But in many cases x cannot be controlled in this way. Thus, if we are examining the effect of rainful on yield, it must be recognized that x (rainfall) is a random variable, completely outside our control. The surprising thing is that with some reinterpretation, most of this chapter is still valid whether x is fixed *or* a random variable, provided we assume, as well as (2-4), that:

The distribution of x does not depend on α, β, or σ^2, (2-53)
and the errors e are normally distributed and (2-54)
independent of the x's.

Of these assumptions, we emphasize the independence of x and e as the most critical. (As we shall see later in Chapter 7, if x and e are correlated, the least squares estimator $\hat{\beta}$ is biased and inconsistent.) When these assumptions are valid, we shall prove among other things, that:

1. $\hat{\beta}$ is still an unbiased estimator of β.
2. The confidence interval for β is still valid.
3. $\hat{\beta}$ is still the MLE of β.

1. If we consider the conditional expectation of $\hat{\beta}$ for a given x (strictly speaking, for a given set of x), this means that we may regard x as fixed, and consider the conditional probability of e. Then, since we make the usual assumptions (2-4), the previous derivation of $E(\hat{\beta})$ in Section 2-4 is still valid;

to emphasize that this is a conditional expectation, we rewrite it with appropriate notation:

$$E(\hat{\beta}/x) = \beta \qquad \text{(2-7) repeated}$$

Since this is true for every given x, it remains true when we average over all x, obtaining

$$E(\hat{\beta}) = \beta$$

2. In the same way, if we considered a given x, the confidence interval for β has a 95% probability of being right (i.e., including the true β). Then if we average over all x, the final probability of being right remains at 95%.

3. The proof that $\hat{\beta}$ is the MLE of β is much the same as in Section 2-10, and is given in Section 2-12 below.

*2-12 MLE OF β WHEN X IS RANDOM

The likelihood of our sample now involves the probability of observing both x and Y. If the x_i are independent, the likelihood function is

$$L = p(x_1)p(Y_1/x_1)\ p(x_2)p(Y_2/x_2) \cdots \tag{2-55}$$

Because of the normality assumption (2-54),

$$L = p(x_1)\frac{1}{\sqrt{2\pi\sigma^2}}\, e^{-(1/2\sigma^2)(Y_1-\alpha-\beta x_1)^2} p(x_2)\frac{1}{\sqrt{2\pi\sigma^2}}\, e^{-(1/2\sigma^2)(Y_2-\alpha-\beta x_2)^2} \cdots \tag{2-56}$$

Collecting the exponents

$$L = p(x_1)p(x_2)\cdots\frac{1}{(2\pi\sigma^2)^{n/2}}\, e^{-(1/2\sigma^2)\Sigma(Y_i-\alpha-\beta x_i)^2} \tag{2-57}$$

Since, according to (2-53), $p(x)$ does not depend on the parameters α, β, and σ^2, the problem of maximizing this likelihood function reduces to the minimization of the same exponent as before. This holds true regardless of how the x_i may be determined. For example, if they are determined by a joint probability distribution, then (2-57) becomes

$$L(\alpha, \beta, \sigma^2) = p(x_1, x_2, \ldots, x_n)\frac{1}{(2\pi\sigma^2)^{n/2}}\, e^{-(1/2\sigma^2)\Sigma(Y_i-\alpha-\beta x_i)^2} \tag{2-58}$$

again requiring the same (least squares) minimization of the exponent.

We conclude that MLE and least squares coincide and may be applied regardless of whether the independent variable x is fixed, or a random variable—provided x is independent of the error and parameters in the equation being estimated. This greatly generalizes the application of the regression model.

APPENDIX 2-1

TABLE 2-1 Linear Transformations and Their Distributions

	Variable	Mean	Variance	Distribution
(a) *Univariate case*				
Original variable	y	μ	σ^2	normal
				↓
Its transformation	$z = my$	$m\mu$	$m^2\sigma^2$	normal
(b) *Bivariate case*				
Original variables	y_1	μ_1	σ_1^2	normal
	y_2	μ_2	σ_2^2	normal
			and covariance σ_{12}	↓
Transformation	$z = m_1y_1 + m_2y_2$	$m_1\mu_1 + m_2\mu_2$	$m_1^2\sigma_1^2 + m_2^2\sigma_2^2 + 2m_1m_2\sigma_{12}$	normal

APPENDIX 2-2 DESIRABLE PROPERTIES OF ESTIMATORS

To be perfectly general, we consider any population parameter θ, and denote an estimator for it by $\hat{\theta}$. We would like the random variable $\hat{\theta}$ to vary within only a narrow range around its fixed target θ. For example, we should like the distribution of $\hat{\beta}$ to be concentrated around β, as close to β as possible. We develop this notion of closeness in several ways.

(a) No Bias

An unbiased estimator is one that is, *on the average*, right on target, as shown in Figure 2-12(*a*). $\hat{\beta}$ is an unbiased estimator of β, because its expected value is β, as in (2-7). In general, we may state:

Definition.

$$\hat{\theta} \text{ is an unbiased estimator of } \theta \text{ if } \quad E(\hat{\theta}) = \theta \tag{2-59}$$

Of course, an estimator $\hat{\theta}$ is called biased if $E(\hat{\theta})$ is different from θ; in fact, bias is defined as this difference:

Definition.

$$\text{Bias } B \triangleq E(\hat{\theta}) - \theta \tag{2-60}$$

where $\triangleq$ means "equal, by definition."

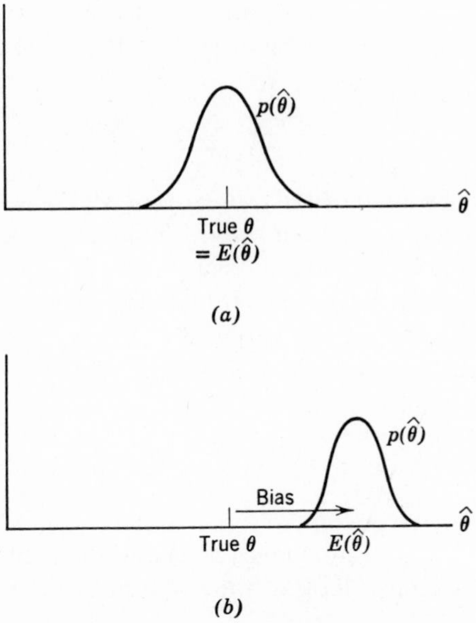

FIG. 2-12 Probability distribution of an unbiased and a biased estimator. (*a*) Unbiased (*b*) Biased.

Bias is illustrated in Figure 2-12(*b*). The distribution of $\hat{\theta}$ is "off target"; since $E(\hat{\theta})$ exceeds θ, there will be a tendency for $\hat{\theta}$ to overestimate.

Some other examples of unbiased estimators are:

1. Given two sample observations Y_1 and Y_2 from a population, then the sample mean

$$\bar{Y} = \tfrac{1}{2}Y_1 + \tfrac{1}{2}Y_2 \tag{2-61}$$

is easily proved[9] to be an unbiased estimator of the population mean μ. It can similarly be shown that

$$\tfrac{1}{3}Y_1 + \tfrac{2}{3}Y_2 \tag{2-62}$$

or, in general,

$$cY_1 + (1 - c)Y_2$$

is an unbiased estimator of μ.

2. The natural intuitive concept of sample variance

$$s_*^2 = \frac{1}{n}\sum_{i=1}^{n}(Y_i - \bar{Y})^2 \tag{2-64}$$

[9] *Proof*. From Appendix 2-1b

$$\begin{aligned} E(\bar{Y}) &= \tfrac{1}{2}E(Y_1) + \tfrac{1}{2}E(Y_2) \\ &= \tfrac{1}{2}\mu + \tfrac{1}{2}\mu = \mu \end{aligned} \tag{2-63}$$

will on average underestimate σ^2, the population variance.[10] But if we inflate it just a little—by dividing by $(n - 1)$ instead of n, we obtain the estimator

$$s^2 = \frac{1}{(n-1)} \sum_{i=1}^{n} (Y_i - \bar{Y})^2 \tag{2-70}$$

which has been proved an unbiased estimator of σ^2. (When we say "has been proved," we mean that it has been proved in advanced texts. If it has been proved in this text, we shall usually say "we have proved".) The student who may have been puzzled in an introductory course by this division by $(n - 1)$ can now see why sample variance is defined this way: we want an unbiased estimator of the population variance.

(b) Efficiency

In estimating μ, both (2-61) and (2-62) are unbiased. In judging which is to be preferred, we must look to their other characteristics. Specifically,

---

[10] In fact, the estimator

$$\frac{1}{n} \sum (Y_i - \mu)^2 \tag{2-65}$$

would have just the right expectation σ^2. This follows because

$$E\left[\frac{1}{n}\sum(Y_i - \mu)^2\right] = \frac{1}{n}\sum E(Y_i - \mu)^2 \tag{2-66}$$

$$= \frac{1}{n}\sum \sigma^2 \tag{2-67}$$

$$= \sigma^2 \tag{2-68}$$

(A simpler but more abstract proof, would be to recognize (2-65) as simply a peculiar example of a sample mean, from the population of $(Y - \mu)^2$. Then according to general sampling theory, the expectation of (2-65) is just the population expectation σ^2.)

Although we have proved that (2-65) is an unbiased estimator of σ^2, it cannot be calculated because μ is unknown. The best the statistician can do is to substitute the observed $\bar{Y}$ for μ, obtaining

$$s_*^2 = \frac{1}{n}\sum (Y_i - \bar{Y})^2 < \frac{1}{n}\sum (Y_i - \mu)^2 \tag{2-69}$$

This inequality follows because the sum of squares $\sum (Y_i - a)^2$ is a minimum when $a = \bar{Y}$, [recall from Section 2-5 that the sample mean $(\bar{Y})$ is the least squares estimator]. Since $\bar{Y}$ and μ typically do not precisely coincide, $\sum (Y_i - a)^2$ will be smaller when $a = \bar{Y}$, than when $a = \mu$.

We conclude that since s_*^2 is less than the unbiased estimator (2-65) it tends to underestimate the population variance σ^2, and hence has a negative bias.

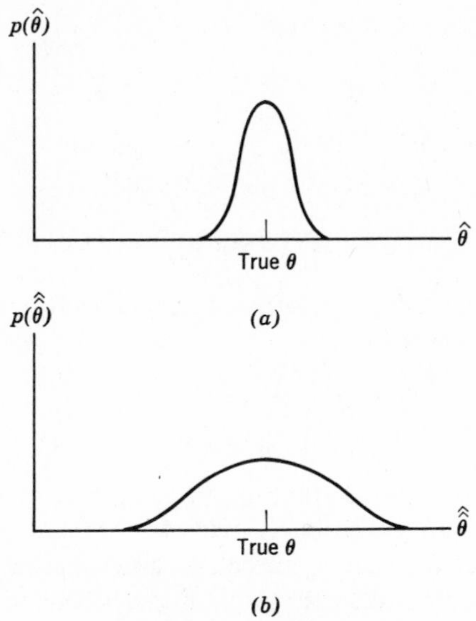

FIG. 2-13 A comparison of an efficient ($\hat{\theta}$) and inefficient ($\hat{\hat{\theta}}$) estimator. Both are unbiased. (a) Efficient. (b) Inefficient.

we should also like the distribution of an estimator $\hat{\theta}$ to be highly concentrated, that is, to have a small variance. This is the notion of efficiency, shown in Figure 2-13. We describe $\hat{\theta}$ as more efficient because it has a smaller variance. A useful relative measure of the efficiency of two unbiased estimators[11] is:

Definition.

$$\text{Relative efficiency of } \hat{\theta} \text{ compared to } \hat{\hat{\theta}} \triangleq \frac{\text{var } \hat{\hat{\theta}}}{\text{var } \hat{\theta}} \tag{2-71}$$

An estimator that is more efficient than any other is called absolutely efficient, or simply "efficient."

Now we are in a position to pass judgement on how the sample mean (2-61) and another weighted average (2-62) compare as estimators of μ. The

[11] For biased estimators, the definition of efficiency is

$$\frac{E(\hat{\hat{\theta}} - \theta)^2}{E(\hat{\theta} - \theta)^2} \tag{2-72}$$

which, of course, is (2-71) if both estimators have 0 bias.

variance of the sample mean is equal[12] to

$$(\tfrac{1}{2})^2 \operatorname{var}(Y_1) + (\tfrac{1}{2})^2 \operatorname{var}(Y_2) = \tfrac{1}{2} \operatorname{var}(Y) \tag{2-74}$$

where var (Y) is the variance of the parent population. On the other hand, the variance of the other estimator (2-62) is equal to

$$(\tfrac{1}{3})^2 \operatorname{var}(Y_1) + (\tfrac{2}{3})^2 \operatorname{var}(Y_2) = \tfrac{5}{9} \operatorname{var}(Y) \tag{2-75}$$

Thus, the sample mean is more efficient. Specifically, applying (2-71), its relative efficiency in this case is

$$\frac{(5/9) \operatorname{var}(Y)}{(1/2) \operatorname{var}(Y)} = \frac{10}{9} \tag{2-76}$$

In fact, it has been proved that in sampling from a *normal* population, the sample mean $\bar{Y}$ is *the* absolutely efficient estimator[13] of μ. For a final comparison, consider the sample median as an estimator of the center of a normal population. It is, like the sample mean, unbiased. But it has larger variance, which approaches, for large sample size n,

$$\frac{\pi}{2n} \operatorname{var}(Y) \tag{2-77}$$

At the same time, the variance of the sample mean is well known to be

$$\frac{1}{n} \operatorname{var}(Y) \tag{2-78}$$

Thus, again using (2-71), the relative efficiency of the sample mean compared to the median is $\pi/2$, or about 1.5. Because it is half again more efficient, $\bar{Y}$ is preferred. It will give us a point estimate that will tend to be closer to the target μ. Or it will give us a more precise (i.e., smaller range) interval estimate. Of course, by increasing sample size (n) we can reduce the variance of either estimator.

Therefore, an alternative way of looking at the greater efficiency of the

---

[12] According to Appendix 2-1. Since Y_1 and Y_2 are independent sample observations,

$$\operatorname{cov}(Y_1, Y_2) = 0 \tag{2-73}$$

Furthermore, the distribution of each sample observation Y_i is the distribution of the parent population Y.

[13] The Gauss-Markov theorem stated that $\bar{Y}$ was the most efficient of the *linear unbiased* estimators. But this is a stronger statement: $\bar{Y}$ is the most efficient of *all* the estimators of μ (whether linear, nonlinear, biased or unbiased), in sampling from a normal population.

sample mean is to recognize that the sample median will yield as accurate a point or interval estimate only if we take a larger sample. Hence, using the sample mean is more efficient because it costs less to sample; note how the economic and statistical definitions of efficiency coincide.

(c) Consistency

Roughly speaking, a consistent estimator is one that concentrates completely on its target as sample size increases indefinitely, as sketched in Figure 2-14. In the limiting case, as the sample size becomes infinite, a consistent estimator $\hat{\theta}$ will provide a perfect point estimate of the target θ.

We now state consistency more precisely. Just as the variance was a good measure of the spread of a distribution about its mean, so

$$\text{mean square error} \triangleq E(\hat{\theta} - \theta)^2 \tag{2-79}$$

is a good measure of how the distribution of $\hat{\theta}$ is spread about its target value θ. Consistency requires this to be zero in the limit:

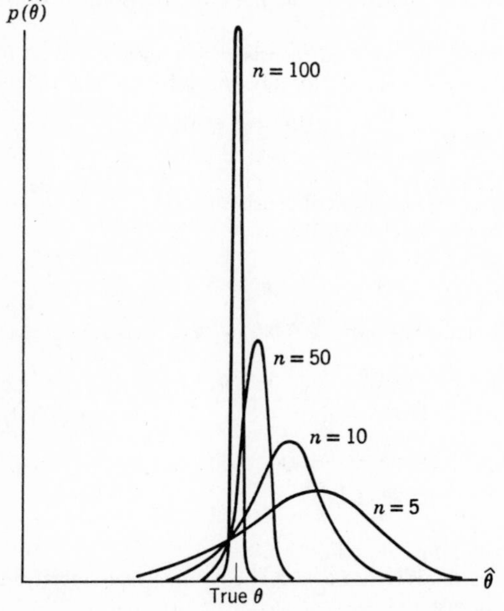

FIG. 2-14 Consistent estimator, showing how the distribution of $\hat{\theta}$ concentrates on its target θ as n increases.

Definition.

$$\boxed{\hat{\theta} \text{ is consistent}^{14} \text{ if } E(\hat{\theta} - \theta)^2 \to 0 \text{ as } n \to \infty} \tag{2-80}$$

Mean squared error is related to bias and variance by the following theorem.[15]

Theorem.

$$\boxed{E(\hat{\theta} - \theta)^2 = B_{\hat{\theta}}^2 + \sigma_{\hat{\theta}}^2} \tag{2-82}$$

Corollary.

$$\boxed{\hat{\theta} \text{ is a consistent estimator iff}^{16} \text{ its bias and variance } \textit{both} \text{ approach zero, as } n \to \infty.} \tag{2-83}$$

If only the bias approaches zero, the estimator is called "asymptotically unbiased"—a condition that is clearly weaker than[17] consistency.

Consistency does not guarantee that an estimator is a good one. For example, as an estimator of μ in a normal population, the sample median is consistent.[18] But it is not a good estimator; the sample mean is preferred because it is both consistent *and* efficient.

As a final example, the sample s_*^2 in (2-64) is a consistent estimator of σ^2. It is true that it is biased; but as $n \to \infty$, this bias disappears; that is, it is

---

[14] This definition is sometimes called "consistency in mean-square." It implies a condition called "consistency in probability": for any positive δ (no matter how small),

$$\Pr(|\hat{\theta} - \theta| < \delta) \to 1 \quad \text{as } n \to \infty \tag{2-81a}$$

This is often taken as the definition of consistency.

(2-81a) may be alternatively written as

$$\hat{\theta} \xrightarrow{p} \theta \tag{2-81b}$$

and read as "the probability limit of $\hat{\theta}$ is θ", or "$\hat{\theta}$ converges in probability to θ."

[15] *Proof.*

$$\begin{aligned} E(\hat{\theta} - \theta)^2 &= E[(\hat{\theta} - \mu_{\hat{\theta}}) + (\mu_{\hat{\theta}} - \theta)]^2 \\ &= E(\hat{\theta} - \mu_{\hat{\theta}})^2 + 2(\mu_{\hat{\theta}} - \theta)E(\hat{\theta} - \mu_{\hat{\theta}}) + (\mu_{\hat{\theta}} - \theta)^2 \\ &= \sigma_{\hat{\theta}}^2 + 0 + (\mu_{\hat{\theta}} - \theta)^2 \\ &= \sigma_{\hat{\theta}}^2 + B_{\hat{\theta}}^2 \end{aligned} \tag{2-84}$$

[16] Iff is an abbreviation for "if and only if."

[17] Asymptotic unbiasedness is also a weaker condition than unbiasedness—since the latter applies for all n, not just $n \to \infty$.

[18] To prove its consistency, we use corollary (2-83), noting that the sample median has zero bias, and a variance given by (2-77) which approaches zero.

asymptotically unbiased.[19] Since it can also be proved that its variance tends to zero, the conditions of corollary (2-83) are satisfied. This concept of a biased, yet consistent estimator is a very important one in econometrics.

PROBLEMS

2-6 A farmer has a square field, whose area he wants to estimate. When he measures the length of the field, he makes a random error, so that his *observed length* 0_1 is a normal variate centered at 200 (the true but unknown value) with $\sigma = 20$. Worried about his possible error, he decides to take a second observation 0_2 and average. But he is in a dilemma as to how to proceed:
(1) Should he average 0_1 and 0_2, and then square?
(2) Should he square first, and then average?
Mathematically, it's a question whether

$$\left(\frac{0_1 + 0_2}{2}\right)^2 \quad \text{or} \quad \left(\frac{0_1^2 + 0_2^2}{2}\right) \text{ is best}$$

(a) Are methods (1) and (2) really different, or are they just two different ways of saying the same thing? [*Hint:* Try a couple of actual values, like $0_1 = 230$ and $0_2 = 200$, and work out (1) and (2).]
(b) If they are different, which has less bias? [*Hints:* This problem will actually be easier if you avoid arithmetic by generalizing from a length of 200 ft to a length of μ, and also use general σ. Furthermore, the *normality* is irrelevant to questions of expectation. Finally, try using $E(0^2) = \mu^2 + \sigma^2$]
(c) Generalize answer (b) to a sample of n measurements.

2-7 A bowl full of many chips has one third marked 2, one third marked 4, and one-third marked 6. If a sample of 2 chips is drawn,
(a) Show that $\bar{X}$ is an unbiased estimator of μ.
(b) Is $(2\bar{X} + 1)$ an unbiased estimator of $(2\mu + 1)$?
(c) Is $(\bar{X})^2$ an unbiased estimator of μ^2?

2-8 To illustrate bias very concretely, consider a sample of $n = 2$ tosses from the population of all tosses of a fair die. The population moments

---

[19] To establish this, we note that

$$s_*^2 = \left(\frac{n-1}{n}\right) s^2 \qquad (2\text{-}85)$$

Thus $s_*^2 \to s^2$ as $n \to \infty$. Since s^2 is unbiased (for any n), it follows that s_*^2 is unbiased as $n \to \infty$.

are easily computed:

$$\mu = 3.5 \qquad \sigma^2 = \frac{35}{12}$$

We shall study sample estimators in two ways:

(a) *Empirical approach* (Monte-Carlo technique)

Repeat the experiment many times. (You can simulate the roll of two dice with the random digits of Appendix Table II.) The result will be a table like:

Result of 2 Tosses	$\bar{X}$	s_*^2	s^2
(3, 1)	2	1	2
(2, 5)	$3\frac{1}{2}$	$2\frac{1}{4}$	$4\frac{1}{2}$
(1, 2)	.	.	.
.	.	.	.
.	.	.	.
Averages	?	?	?

Set up a relative-frequency distribution for $\bar{X}$, s_*^2, and s^2. Calculate the mean of each of these distributions.

1. Does $\bar{X}$ average close to μ?
2. Does s^2 average close to σ^2?
3. Does s_*^2 average close to σ^2?

(*b*) *Theoretical approach*

In (a), if the experiment were repeated endlessly, the relative frequencies would settle down to probabilities. But these probabilities can be calculated very easily, by exploiting the symmetry of the dice. After calculating the relevant probability table, find:

1. $E(\bar{X}) \stackrel{?}{=} \mu$
2. $E(s^2) \stackrel{?}{=} \sigma^2$
3. $E(s_*^2) \stackrel{?}{=} \sigma^2$

⇒2-9 Is the sample mean a consistent estimator of the population mean? Prove your answer.

APPENDIX 2-3 PROOF OF THE GAUSS-MARKOV THEOREM

We shall prove this theorem in the case of simple linear regression for the estimator $\hat{\beta}$. The proof for $\hat{\alpha}$ is left to the reader. This theorem is also generalized for multiple regression in Chapter 16.

First, we insist that our estimator be linear, that is,

$$\hat{\beta} = \sum_{i=1}^{n} c_i Y_i \tag{2-86}$$

where the c_i are constants. In addition we insist that our estimator be unbiased, that is,

$$E(\hat{\beta}) = \beta \tag{2-87}$$

From (2-86)

$$\begin{aligned} E(\hat{\beta}) &= E(\sum c_i Y_i) \\ &= \sum c_i E(Y_i) \\ &= \sum c_i(\alpha + \beta x_i) \\ &= \alpha \sum c_i + \beta \sum c_i x_i \\ &= \beta \text{ iff} \end{aligned}$$

$$\sum c_i = 0 \tag{2-88}$$

and

$$\sum c_i x_i = 1 \tag{2-89}$$

In other words, the c_i must satisfy conditions (2-88) and (2-89) for $\sum c_i Y_i$ to be an unbiased estimator of β.

Now we turn to the condition that our estimator have minimum variance. The variance of $\hat{\beta}$ is given as

$$\text{var}\,(\hat{\beta}) = \text{var}\,(\sum c_i Y_i)$$

and because the Y_i are independent,

$$\begin{aligned} &= \sum c_i^2 \,\text{var}\, Y_i \\ &= (\sum c_i^2)\sigma^2 \end{aligned} \tag{2-90}$$

Since σ^2 is fixed, it is only necessary to minimize

$$\sum c_i^2 \tag{2-91}$$

The problem of minimizing $\sum c_i^2$ subject to the two side conditions (2-88) and (2-89) is best handled by Lagrangian multipliers. This involves setting up the Lagrangian function:

$$g(c_1 \cdots c_n, \lambda_1, \lambda_2) = \sum c_i^2 - \lambda_1(\sum c_i) - \lambda_2(\sum c_i x_i - 1)$$

and setting its partial derivatives with respect to all the c_i, λ_1, and λ_2 equal to zero.

First, setting $\partial g/\partial c_i = 0$, we obtain

$$2c_i - \lambda_1 - \lambda_2 x_i = 0 \qquad (i = 1, 2, \ldots, n) \tag{2-92}$$

That is,

$$c_i = \frac{\lambda_1}{2} + \frac{\lambda_2}{2} x_i \tag{2-93}$$

Then, setting $\partial g/\partial \lambda_i = 0$, we obtain

$$\sum c_i = 0 \qquad \text{(2-88) repeated}$$

$$\sum c_i x_i = 1 \qquad \text{(2-89) repeated}$$

which are a restatement of our two side conditions.

Conditions (2-93), (2-88), and (2-89) must be satisfied for a minimization of the variance subject to the two constraints. Substituting (2-93) into (2-88),

$$\sum \left(\frac{\lambda_1}{2} + \frac{\lambda_2}{2} x_i \right) = 0 \tag{2-94}$$

Similarly, from (2-93) and (2-89),

$$\sum \left(\frac{\lambda_1}{2} + \frac{\lambda_2}{2} x_i \right) x_i = 1 \tag{2-95}$$

$$\frac{\lambda_1}{2} \sum x_i + \frac{\lambda_2}{2} \sum x_i^2 = 1$$

$$0 + \frac{\lambda_2}{2} \sum x_i^2 = 1$$

$$\lambda_2 = \frac{2}{\sum x_i^2} \tag{2-96}$$

To solve for λ_1, we note again that $\sum x_i = 0$; hence, (2-94) can be rewritten,

$$\sum_{i=1}^{n} \frac{\lambda_1}{2} = 0$$

$$n \frac{\lambda_1}{2} = 0 \tag{2-97}$$

$$\lambda_1 = 0$$

Substitution of (2-96) and (2-97) into (2-93) finally yields a solution for c_i

$$c_i = \frac{1}{2} \cdot \frac{2}{\sum x_i^2} \cdot x_i = \frac{x_i}{\sum x_i^2} \tag{2-98}$$

hence $\hat{\beta} = (\sum x_i Y_i / \sum x_i^2)$ is the minimum variance estimator. But this is precisely the least squares estimator, as promised.

APPENDIX 2-4 THE MAXIMUM LIKELIHOOD ESTIMATE OF σ^2

To avoid confusion, we shall rename the variance v instead of σ^2. Since L and $\log L$ will be maximized at the same value of v, we select the value of v to maximize

$$Q = \log L = -\frac{n}{2}\log 2\pi - \frac{n}{2}\log v - \frac{1}{2v}\sum [Y_i - (\alpha + \beta x_i)]^2 \quad (2\text{-}99)$$

where L is the likelihood function (2-51). To find the maximum we set $\partial Q/\partial v = 0$

$$\frac{\partial Q}{\partial v} = -\frac{n}{2}\cdot\frac{1}{v} + \frac{1}{2v^2}\sum [Y_i - (\alpha + \beta x_i)]^2 = 0 \quad (2\text{-}100)$$

Recall that estimating v is part of the larger problem of simultaneously estimating α, β, and v. Hence, we should also set

$$\frac{\partial Q}{\partial \alpha} = 0 \quad (2\text{-}101)$$

$$\frac{\partial Q}{\partial \beta} = 0 \quad (2\text{-}102)$$

Now (2-100), (2-101), and (2-102) may be solved simultaneously for the MLE, of v, α, and β. But in Section (2-10) it was shown that $\hat{\alpha}$ and $\hat{\beta}$ are independent of $\hat{v}$; in other words (2-101) and (2-102) alone may be solved for $\hat{\alpha}$ and $\hat{\beta}$. (The student of calculus is invited to confirm this; his solution of (2-101) and (2-102) for $\hat{\alpha}$ and $\hat{\beta}$ should be the least squares solution.) The only remaining step is to plug $\hat{\alpha}$ and $\hat{\beta}$ into (2-100), and solve for $\hat{v}$:

$$\boxed{\hat{v} = \frac{1}{n}\sum [Y_i - (\hat{\alpha} + \hat{\beta} x_i)]^2} \quad (2\text{-}103)$$

In the special case in which $\beta = 0$ (i.e., in the population Y is not dependent on x), $\hat{\alpha}$ becomes $\bar{Y}$, the last term disappears, and $\hat{v}$ becomes s_*^2. As a special case of (2-103), s_*^2 is, of course, the MLE; but it has been shown (in Appendix 2-2a) to be biased. Using a similar argument, the MLE $\hat{v}$ in (2-103) can be shown to be biased; for this reason it is adjusted by division by

$(n-2)$ rather than n to provide the unbiased estimator:

$$s^2 = \frac{1}{n-2} \sum [Y_i - (\hat{\alpha} - \hat{\beta} x_i)]^2 \tag{2-104}$$

with $(n-2)$ degrees of freedom.[20]

This also illustrates a major limitation of maximum likelihood estimation. It is true that MLE provides an estimate with the very attractive large sample property of consistency; see, for example, how the consistency of the MLE s_*^2 was shown in Appendix 2-2c. However, in small sample estimation it must be used with great caution, since it may be biased; again s_*^2 provides an example.

Further reservations about MLE are dealt with in Chapter 10.

---

[20] Two degrees of freedom are lost in this case because s^2 requires previous calculation of *two* estimates $\hat{\alpha}$ and $\hat{\beta}$.

The concept of "loss of degrees of freedom" is best reviewed by again considering the simplest possible case in which $\beta = 0$, and the variance of the parent population is estimated by the unbiased estimator:

$$s^2 = \frac{1}{n-1} \sum (Y_i - \bar{Y})^2 \tag{2-105}$$

Although there are originally n degrees of freedom in a sample of n observations, one degree of freedom is used up in calculating $\bar{Y}$, leaving only $(n-1)$ degrees of freedom for the residuals $(Y_i - \bar{Y})$ to calculate s^2.

For example, consider a sample of two Y observations, say 21 and 15. Since $\bar{Y} = 18$, the residuals are $+3$ and -3, the second residual necessarily being just the negative of the first. While the first residual is "free," the second is strictly determined; hence, there is only one degree of freedom in the residuals. In general, for a sample size n, it may be shown that if the first $(n-1)$ residuals are specified, then the last residual is automatically determined.

Just as the calculation of $\bar{Y}$ results in the loss of one degree of freedom, the calculation of $\hat{\alpha}$ and $\hat{\beta}$ used to evaluate (2-104) results in the loss of two degrees of freedom.

chapter 3

Multiple Regression

3-1 INTRODUCTORY EXAMPLE

Suppose that the fertilizer and yield observations in Chapter 1 were taken at seven different agricultural experiment stations across the country. Even if soil conditions and temperature were essentially the same in all these areas, we still might ask, "Can't part of the fluctuation in Y (i.e., the disturbance term e) be explained by varying levels of rainfall in different areas?" A better prediction of yield may be possible if *both* fertilizer and rainfall are examined. The observed levels of rainfall are shown in Table 3-1, along with the original observations of yield and fertilizer from Table 1-1.

TABLE 3-1 Observed Yield, Fertilizer Application, and Rainfall

Y Wheat Yield (Bushels/Acre)	X Fertilizer (Pounds/Acre)	Z Rainfall (Inches)
40	100	36
45	200	33
50	300	37
65	400	37
70	500	34
70	600	32
80	700	36

3-2 THE MATHEMATICAL MODEL

The multiple regression technique used to describe how a dependent variable is related to two or more independent variables is, in fact, only an extension of the simple regression analysis of the previous two chapters. Yield Y is now to be regressed on the two independent variables, or "regressors," fertilizer X and rainfall Z. Let us suppose it is reasonable to argue that this relationship is of the form

$$E(Y_i) = \alpha + \beta x_i + \gamma z_i \tag{3-1}$$

like (2-1)

with both regressors x and z measured as deviations from their means. Geometrically this equation is a plane[1] in the three dimensional space shown in Figure 3-1. For any given combination of rainfall and fertilizer (x_i, z_i), the expected yield $E(Y_i)$ is the point on this plane directly above, shown as a hollow dot. Of course, the observed value of Y, shown as a solid dot, is very unlikely to fall precisely on this plane. For example, our particular observed

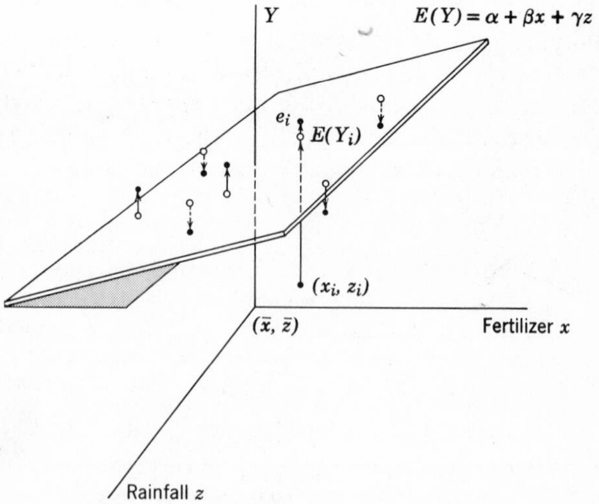

FIG. 3-1 Scatter of observed points about the true regression plane.

[1] It is a plane because it is linear in x and z. Looked at from another point of view, we could say that (3-1) is linear in α, β, and γ. In fact, this latter linearity assumption is the more important of the two, since we are involved in estimating α, β, and γ; it is this assumption that keeps our estimating equations (3-4) linear.

Y_i at this fertilizer/rainfall combination is somewhat greater than its expected value, and is shown as the solid dot lying directly above this plane.

The difference between any observed and expected value of Y_i is the stochastic or error term e_i. Thus, any observed value Y_i may be expressed as its expected value plus this disturbance term

$$Y_i = \alpha + \beta x_i + \gamma z_i + e_i \tag{3-2}$$

like (2-3)

with our assumptions about e the same as in Chapter 2.

β is geometrically interpreted as the slope of the plane as we move in a direction parallel to the (x, Y) plane, keeping z constant; thus β is the marginal effect of fertilizer x on yield Y. Similarly γ is the slope of the plane as we move in a direction parallel to the (z, Y) plane, that is, keeping x constant; hence γ is the marginal effect of z on Y.

3-3 LEAST SQUARES ESTIMATION

Least squares estimates[2] are derived by selecting the estimates of α, β, and γ that minimize the sum of the squared deviations between the observed

---

[2] Maximum likelihood estimates of α, β, and γ are derived in the same way as in the simple regression case; again this coincides with least squares. Geometrically, this involves trying out all possible hypothetical regression planes in Figure 3-1, and selecting that one which is most likely to generate the solid-dot sample values we actually observed.

But first, note that Figure 3-1 involves three parameters (α, β, and γ), and three variables (Y, x, and z). However, there is one additional variable in our system—$p(Y/x, z)$—which has not yet been plotted. It may appear that there is no way of forcing four variables into a three-dimensional space, but this is not so. For example, economists often plot three variables (labor, capital, and output) in a two-dimensional labor-capital space by introducing the third output variable as a system of isoquants. Those for whom this is a familiar exercise should have little trouble in graphing four variables [Y, x, z, and $p(Y/x, z)$] in a three-dimension (Y, x, and z) space by introducing the fourth variable [$p(Y/x, z)$] as a system of isoplanes. Each of these isoplanes represents (Y, x, z) combinations that are equiprobable (i.e., for which the probability density of Y is constant). Thus, the complete geometric model is the regression plane shown in Figure 3-1, with isoprobability planes stacked above and below it. Our assumptions about the error term (2-4) guarantee that the isoprobability planes will be parallel to the true regression plane.

For MLE, we introduce the additional assumption that the error configuration is normal. Then we shift around a hypothetical regression plane along with its associated set of parallel isoprobability planes. In each position the probability density of the observed sample of points is evaluated by examining the isoprobability plane on which each point lies, and multiplying these together. That hypothetical regression which maximizes this likelihood is chosen. The algebra resembles the simple case in Section 2-10; it is easy to show that this results in minimizing the sum of squares (3-3).

TABLE 3-2 Least Squares Estimates for Multiple Regression of Y on X and Z

Y_i	X_i	Z_i	$x_i = X_i - \bar{X}$	$z_i = Z_i - \bar{Z}$	$Y_i x_i$	$Y_i z_i$	x_i	z^2	$x_i z_i$	$\hat{Y}_i = 60 + .06893x + .6028z$
40	100	36	−300	1	−12,000	40	90,000	1	−300	39.9
45	200	33	−200	−2	−9,000	−90	40,000	4	400	45.0
50	300	37	−100	2	−5,000	100	10,000	4	−200	54.3
65	400	37	0	2	0	130	0	4	0	61.2
70	500	34	100	−1	7,000	−70	10,000	1	−100	66.3
70	600	32	200	−3	14,000	−210	40,000	9	−600	72.0
80	700	36	300	1	24,000	80	90,000	1	300	81.3
$\sum Y_i = 420$	$\sum X_i = 2800$	$\sum Z_i = 245$	$\sum x_i = 0$	$\sum z_i = 0$	$\sum Y_i x_i = 19{,}000$	$\sum Y_i z_i = -20$	$\sum x_i^2 = 280{,}000$	$\sum z_i^2 = 24$	$\sum x_i z_i = -500$	
$\hat{\alpha} = \bar{Y} = 60$	$\bar{X} = 400$	$\bar{Z} = 35$								

Estimating equations (3–4) $\begin{cases} 19{,}000 = 280{,}000\hat{\beta} - 500\hat{\gamma} \\ -20 = -500\hat{\beta} + 24\hat{\gamma} \end{cases}$

Solution $\begin{cases} \hat{\beta} = .06893 \\ \hat{\gamma} = .6028 \end{cases}$

Thus our regression is
$$Y = \hat{\alpha} + \hat{\beta}x + \hat{\gamma}z = 60 + .06893x + .6028z$$

Or, in terms of the original X and Z,

$$Y = 60 + .06893(X - \bar{X}) + .6028(Z - \bar{Z}) = 60 + .06893(X - 400) + .6028(Z - 35)$$

$$\boxed{Y = 11.3307 + .06893X + .6028Z}$$

Y's and the fitted Y's; that is, minimize

$$\sum (Y_i - \hat{\alpha} - \hat{\beta}x_i - \hat{\gamma}z_i)^2 \tag{3-3}$$

where $\hat{\alpha}$, $\hat{\beta}$, and $\hat{\gamma}$ are, of course, our estimators of α, β, and γ. This is done with calculus by setting the partial derivatives of this function with respect to $\hat{\alpha}$, $\hat{\beta}$, and $\hat{\gamma}$ equal to zero (or algebraically by a technique similar to that used in Appendix 1-1). The result is the following three estimating equations:

$$\left.\begin{aligned} \hat{\alpha} &= \bar{Y} \\ \sum Y_i x_i &= \hat{\beta} \sum x_i^2 + \hat{\gamma} \sum x_i z_i \\ \sum Y_i z_i &= \hat{\beta} \sum x_i z_i + \hat{\gamma} \sum z_i^2 \end{aligned}\right\} \tag{3-4}$$

Again, note that the intercept estimate $\hat{\alpha}$ is the mean of Y. The second and third equations may be solved for $\hat{\beta}$ and $\hat{\gamma}$. These calculations are shown in Table 3-2, and yield the fitted multiple regression equation.

PROBLEMS

3-1 Suppose a random sample of five families yielded the following data (an extension of Problem 1-1):

Family	Saving S	Income Y	Assets W
A	\$ 600	\$ 8,000	\$12,000
B	1,200	11,000	6,000
C	1,000	9,000	6,000
D	700	6,000	3,000
E	300	6,000	18,000

(a) Estimate the multiple regression equation of S on Y and W.
(b) Does the coefficient of Y differ from the answer to Problem 1-1? Which coefficient better illustrates the relation of S to Y?
(c) For a family with assets of \$5000 and income of \$8000, what would you predict saving to be?
(d) If a family had a \$2,000 increase in income, while assets remained constant, estimate by how much their saving would increase.
(e) If a family had a \$1,000 increase in income, and a \$3,000 increase in assets, estimate by how much their saving would increase.

(f) Calculate the residual sum of squares, and residual variance s^2.
(g) Are you satisfied with the degrees of freedom you have for s^2 in this problem? Explain.

(3-2) Suppose a random sample of five families yielded the following data (another extension of Problem 1-1):

Family	Saving S	Income Y	Number of Children N
A	\$ 600	\$ 8,000	5
B	1,200	11,000	2
C	1,000	9,000	1
D	700	6,000	3
E	300	6,000	4

(a) Estimate the multiple regression of S on Y and N.
(b) For a family with five children and income of \$6000, what would you predict saving to be?

*3-3 Combining the data of Problems 3-1 and 3-2, we obtain the following table:

Family	Saving S	Income Y	Assets W	Number of Children N
A	\$ 600	\$ 8,000	\$12,000	5
B	1,200	11,000	6,000	2
C	1,000	9,000	6,000	1
D	700	6,000	3,000	3
E	300	6,000	18,000	4

Measuring the independent variables as deviations from the mean, we wish to estimate the regression equation

$$S = \alpha + \beta y + \gamma w + \psi n$$

(a) Generalizing (3-4), use the least squares criterion to derive the system of four equations needed to estimate the four parameters.
(b) Using a table such as Table 3-2, calculate the estimates of the four parameters.

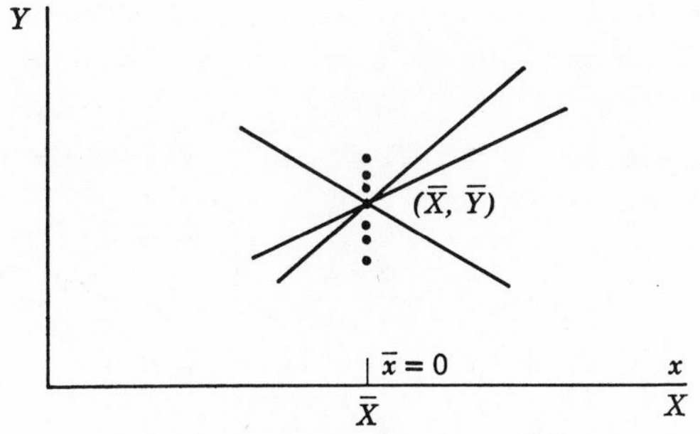

FIG. 3-2 Degenerate regression, because of no spread (variation) in X.

3-4 MULTICOLLINEARITY

(a) In Simple Regression

In Figure 2-5*a* it was shown how our estimate $\hat{\beta}$ became unreliable if the X_i's were closely bunched, that is, if the regressor X had little variation. It will be instructive to consider the limiting case, where the X_i's are concentrated on one single value $\bar{X}$, as in Figure 3-2. Then $\hat{\beta}$ is not determined at all. There are any number of differently sloped lines passing through $(\bar{X}, \bar{Y})$ which fit equally well: for each line in Figure 3-2, the sum of squared deviations is the same, since the deviations are measured vertically from $(\bar{X}, \bar{Y})$. This geometric fact has an algebraic counterpart. If all $X_i = \bar{X}$, then all $x_i = 0$, and the term involving $\hat{\beta}$ in (1-10) is zero; hence, the sum of squares does not depend on $\hat{\beta}$ at all. It follows that any $\hat{\beta}$ will do equally well in minimizing the sum of squares. An alternative way of looking at the same problem is that since all x_i are zero, $\sum x_i^2$ in the denominator of (1-16) is zero, and $\hat{\beta}$ is not defined.

In conclusion, when the values of X show little or no variation, then the effect of X on Y can no longer be sensibly investigated. But if the problem is *predicting* Y—rather than investigating Y's dependence on X—this bunching of the X values does not matter *provided* we limit our prediction to this same value of X. All the lines in Figure 3-2 predict Y equally well. The best prediction is $\bar{Y}$, and all these lines give us that result.

(b) In Multiple Regression

Again consider the limiting case where the values of the independent variables X and Z are completely bunched up on a line L, as in Figure 3-3.

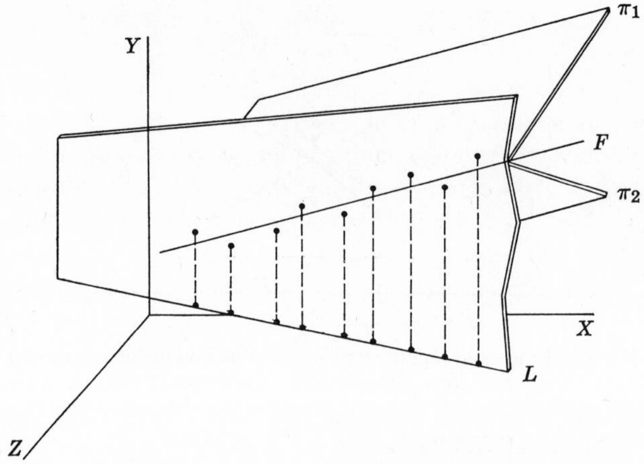

FIG. 3-3 Multicollinearity.

This means that all the observed points in our scatter lie in the vertical plane running up through L. You can think of the three-dimensional space as a room in a house; our observations are not scattered throughout this room, but instead lie embedded in an extremely thin pane of glass standing vertically on the floor.

In explaining Y, multicollinearity makes us lose one dimension. In the earlier case of simple regression, our best fit for Y was not a line, but rather a point $(\bar{x}, \bar{Y})$; in this multiple regression case our best fit for Y is not a plane, but rather the line F. To get F, we just fit the least squares line through the points on the vertical pane of glass. The problem is identical to the one shown in Figure 1-2; in one case a line is fitted on a flat pane of glass, in the other case, on a flat piece of paper. This regression line F is, therefore, our best fit for Y. As long as we stick to the same *combination* of X and Z—that is, so long as we confine ourselves to predicting Y values on that pane of glass—no special problems[3] arise. We can use the regression F on the glass to predict Y in exactly the same way as we did in the simple regression analysis of Chapter 1. But there is no way to examine how X affects Y. Any attempt to define β, the marginal effect of X on Y (holding Z constant), involves moving off that pane of glass, and we have no sample information whatsoever on what the world out there looks like. Or, to put it differently, if we try to explain Y with a plane—rather than a line F—we find there are any number of planes running through F (e.g. π_1 and π_2) which do an equally good job.

[3] In practice, there would be a problem in getting the regression line F, since computer routines typically break down in the face of perfect multicollinearity.

Since each passes through F, each yields an identical sum of squared deviations; thus each provides an equally good fit. This is confirmed in the algebra in the estimating Equations (3-4). When X is a linear function of Z, (i.e., when x is a linear function of z) it may be shown that the last two equations are not independent, and cannot be solved uniquely for $\hat{\beta}$ and $\hat{\gamma}$.[4]

Now let's be less extreme in our assumptions and consider the near-limiting case, where z and x are almost on a line (i.e., where all our observations in the room lie very close to a vertical pane of glass). In this case, a plane may be fitted to our observations, but the estimating procedure is very unstable; it becomes very sensitive to random errors, reflected in large variances of the estimators $\hat{\beta}$ and $\hat{\gamma}$. Thus, even though X may really affect Y, its statistical significance may not be established because the standard deviation of $\hat{\beta}$ is so large. This is analogous to the argument in the simple regression case in Section 2-6.

When the independent variables X and Z are collinear, or nearly so, it is called the problem of multicollinearity. For prediction purposes, it does not hurt provided there is no attempt to predict for values of X and Z removed from their line of collinearity. But structural questions cannot be answered—the *relation* of Y to either X or Z cannot be sensibly investigated.

Example 1

In our wheat yield example, suppose that X is (as before) the amount of fertilizer measured in pounds per acre, and that the statistician makes the incredibly foolish error of defining another independent variable Z as the amount of fertilizer measured in ounces per acre. Since any weight measured in ounces must be sixteen times its measurement in pounds:

$$Z = 16X \tag{3-6}$$

exactly. Thus, all combinations of X and Z must fall on this straight line, and we have an example of perfect multicollinearity. Now if we try to fit[5] a

---

[4] Two linear equations can usually be solved for two unknowns, but not always. For example, suppose that John's age (X) is twice Harry's (Y). Then we can write

$$\begin{aligned} X &= 2Y \\ 5X &= 10Y \end{aligned} \tag{3-5}$$

Note that these two equations tell us the same thing. We have two equations in two unknowns, but they don't generate a unique solution, because they don't provide independent information.

[5] Since the computer program would probably "hang up," suppose the calculations are handcrafted.

regression plane to the observations of yield and fertilizer given in Table 1-1, one possible answer would be our original regression given in (1-18):

$$Y = 32.8 + .068X + 0Z \tag{3-7}$$

But an equally satisfactory solution would follow from substituting (3-6) into (3-7):

$$Y = 32.8 + 0X + .00425Z$$

Another equivalent answer would be to make a partial substitution for X in (3-7) as follows:

$$\begin{aligned} Y &= 32.8 + .068[\lambda X + (1 - \lambda)X] \\ &= 32.8 + .068[\lambda X + (1 - \lambda)(\tfrac{1}{16})Z] \\ Y &= 32.8 + .068\lambda X + .00425(1 - \lambda)Z \end{aligned} \tag{3-8}$$

(3-8) is a whole family of planes depending on the arbitrary value assigned to λ. In fact, all these three dimensional planes are equivalent expressions for our simple two dimensional relationship between fertilizer and yield. While all give the same correct prediction of Y, no meaning can be attached to whatever coefficients of X and Z we may come up with.

Example 2

While the previous extreme example may have clarified some of the theoretical issues, no statistician would make that sort of error in model specification. Instead, more subtle difficulties arise. For example, suppose demand for a group of goods is being related to prices and income, with the overall price index being the first independent variable. Suppose aggregate income measured in money terms is the second independent variable. If this is real income multiplied by the same price index, the problem of multicollinearity may become a serious one. The solution is to use real income, rather than money income, as the second independent variable. This is a special case of a more general warning: in any multiple regression in which price is one independent variable, beware of other independent variables measured in prices.

The problem of multicollinearity may be solved if there happens to be prior information about the relation of β and γ. For example, if it is known a priori that

$$\gamma = 5\beta \tag{3-9}$$

then this information will allow us to uniquely determine the regression plane, even in the case of perfect collinearity. This is evident from the geometry of Figure 3-3. Given a fixed relation between our two slopes (β and γ), there is only one regression plane π that can be fitted to pass through F. This is confirmed algebraically. Using (3-9), our model (3-2) can be written

$$Y_i = \alpha + \beta x_i + 5\beta z_i + e_i \tag{3-10}$$

$$= \alpha + \beta(x_i + 5z_i) + e_i \tag{3-11}$$

It is natural to define a new variable

$$w_i = x_i + 5z_i \tag{3-12}$$

Thus, (3-11) becomes

$$Y_i = \alpha + \beta w_i + e_i \tag{3-13}$$

and a regression of Y on w will yield estimates $\hat{\alpha}$ and $\hat{\beta}$. Finally, if we wish an estimate of γ, it is easily computed using (3-9):

$$\hat{\gamma} = 5\hat{\beta} \tag{3-14}$$

3-5 INTERPRETING AN ESTIMATED REGRESSION

Suppose the multiple regression

$$Y = \hat{\alpha}_0 + \hat{\beta}_1 X_1 + \hat{\beta}_2 X_2 + \hat{\beta}_3 X_3 + \hat{\beta}_4 X_4$$

is fitted to 25 observations of Y and the X's. The least squares estimates often appear in the form:

$$\begin{array}{lccccc} Y = & 10.6 & + \ 28.4X_1 & + \ 4.0X_2 & + \ 12.7X_3 & + \ .84X_4 \\ & (s_0 = 2.6) & (s_1 = 11.4) & (s_2 = 1.5) & (s_3 = 14.1) & (s_4 = .76) \\ & (t_0 = 4.1) & (t_1 = 2.5) & (t_2 = 2.6) & (t_3 = .9) & (t_4 = 1.1) \end{array} \tag{3-15}$$

Here we have 20df (25-5).
For 95% confidence in t ⇒ 2.086

where, for example, s_1 is the estimated standard deviation of $\hat{\beta}_1$, not to be confused with s (the estimated standard deviation of the error term); and t_1 is the[6] t-value that directly corresponds. The bracketed information is used in assessing the reliability of the least squares fit, either in a confidence interval or hypothesis test.

[6] The derivation of this is given in the discussion following equation (5-46) and in Problem 5-9, and more extensively, of course, in Chapters 13 and 15. Thus, t_1 is an extension of the t test (2-36), while s_1 is analogous to the divisor $\sqrt{s^2/\sum x^2}$ in (2-36).

– t refers to number of steps from zero.

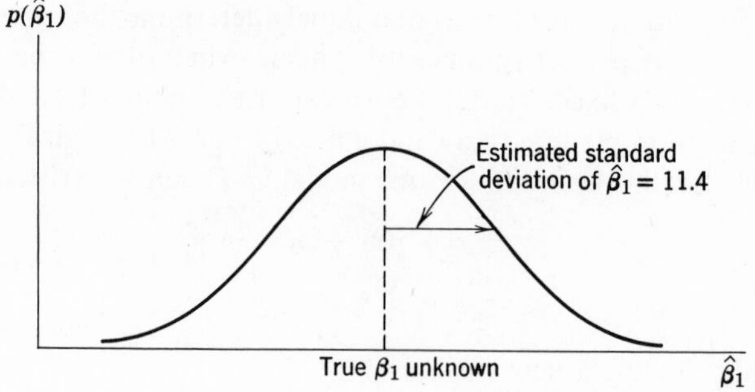

FIG. 3-4 Distribution of the estimator $\hat{\beta}_1$.

The true effect of X_1 on Y is the unknown population parameter β_1; we estimate it with the sample estimator $\hat{\beta}_1$. While the unknown β_1 is fixed, our estimator is a random variable, differing from sample to sample. The properties of $\hat{\beta}_1$ may be established, just as the properties of $\hat{\beta}$ were established in the previous chapter. Thus $\hat{\beta}_1$ may be shown to be normal—again provided the sample size is large, or the error term is normal. $\hat{\beta}_1$ can also be shown to be unbiased, with its mean β_1. The magnitude of error involved in estimation is reflected in the standard deviation of $\hat{\beta}_1$ which, let us suppose, is estimated to be $s_1 = 11.4$ as given in the first bracket below equation (3-15), and shown in Figure 3-4. When $\hat{\beta}_1$ is standardized with this estimated standard deviation, it will have a t distribution.

To recapitulate: we don't know β_1; all we know is that whatever it may be, our estimator $\hat{\beta}_1$ is distributed around it, as shown in Figure 3-4. This knowledge of how closely $\hat{\beta}_1$ estimates β_1 can, of course, be "turned around" to infer a 95% confidence interval for β_1 from our observed sample $\hat{\beta}_1$ as follows:

$$\begin{aligned}\beta_1 &= \hat{\beta}_1 \pm t_{.025}\, s_1 \\ &= 28.4 \pm 2.09\,(11.4) \\ &= 28.4 \pm 23.8 \qquad (3\text{-}16)\end{aligned}$$

($n = 25$ is the sample size, $k = 5$ is the number of parameters already estimated in (3-15), and $t_{.025}$ is the critical t value with $n - k$ degrees of freedom). Similar confidence intervals can be constructed for the other β's.

If we turn to testing hypotheses, extreme care is necessary to avoid very strange conclusions. Suppose it has been concluded on theoretical grounds that X_1 should positively influence Y, and we wish to see if we can statistically confirm this relation. This involves a one-tailed test of the null hypothesis

$$H_0\colon \beta_1 = 0 \qquad (3\text{-}17)$$

against the alternative

$$H_1\colon \beta_1 > 0 \qquad (3\text{-}18)$$

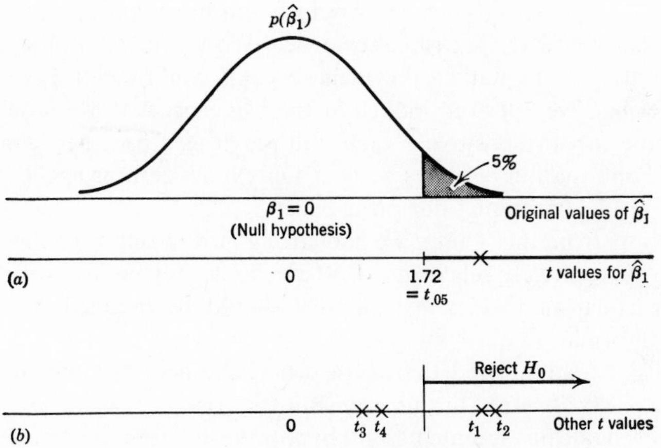

FIG. 3-5 (*a*) Test of β_1. (*b*) Test of other β's.

If H_0 is true, $\hat{\beta}_1$ will be centered on $\beta_1 = 0$, and there will be only a 5% probability of observing a t value exceeding 1.72; this defines our rejection region in Figure 3-5*a*. Our observed t value [2.5 as shown below equation (3-15)] falls in this region; hence we reject H_0, thus confirming (at a 5% significance level) that Y is positively related to X_1.

The similar t values [also shown for the other estimators below (3-15)] can be used for testing the null hypothesis on the other β parameters. As we see in Figure 3-5*b*, the null hypothesis $\beta_2 = 0$ can also be rejected, but a similar conclusion is not warranted for β_3 and β_4. We conclude, therefore, that the results are "statistically significant" for X_1 and X_2; the evidence is that Y is related to each. But the results are not statistically significant for X_3 and X_4.

As long as we confine ourselves to rejecting hypotheses—as with β_1 and β_2—we won't encounter too much difficulty. But if we *accept* the null hypothesis about β_3 and β_4, we may run into trouble.

While it is true, for example, that our t coefficient for X_3 (.9) is not "statistically significant," this does *not* prove there is no relationship between X_3 and Y. It is easy to see why. Suppose that we have strong theoretical grounds for believing that Y is positively related to X_3. In (3-15) this belief is confirmed: Y is related to X_3 by a positive coefficient. Thus our statistical evidence is consistent with our prior belief (even though it is not as strong a confirmation as we might like).[7] To accept the null hypothesis $\beta_3 = 0$ and

[7] Perhaps because of too small a sample. Thus, 12.7 may be a very accurate description of how Y is related to X_3; but our t value is not statistically significant because our sample is small, and the standard deviation of our estimator ($s_3 = 14.1$) is large as a consequence.

conclude that X_3 doesn't affect Y, would be in direct contradiction to both our prior belief and the statistical evidence. We would be reversing a prior belief even though the statistical evidence weakly confirmed it. It would have been better had we not even looked at the evidence. And we note that this remains true for any positive t value, although as t becomes smaller, our statistical confirmation becomes weaker. Only if t is zero or negative, do the statistical results contradict our prior belief.

It follows from this, that if we had strong prior grounds for believing X_3 and X_4 to be positively related to Y, they should not be dropped from the estimating equation (3-15); instead they should be retained, with all the pertinent information on their t values.

It must be emphasized that those who have accepted null hypotheses have not *necessarily* erred in this way. But that risk has been run by anyone who has mechanically accepted a null hypothesis because the t value was not statistically significant. The difficulty is especially acute—as in the case we've cited—when the null hypothesis was introduced strictly for convenience (because it was specific), and not because there is any reason to believe it in the first place. It becomes less acute if there is some expectation that H_0 is true—that is, if there are theoretical grounds for concluding that Y and X are unrelated. Suppose for illustration that we expect a priori that H_0 is true; in such a case, a weak observed relationship (e.g., $t = .6$) would be in some conflict with our prior expectation of no relationship. But it is not a serious conflict, and easily explained by chance. Hence resolving it in favor of our prior expectation and continuing to use H_0 as a working hypothesis might be a reasonable judgment.

We conclude once again, that classical statistical theory provides incomplete grounds for accepting H_0; acceptance must be based also on extra-statistical judgment, with prior belief playing a key role.

* * *

Prior belief plays a less critical role in the rejection of an hypothesis; but it is by no means irrelevant. Suppose, for example that although you believed Y to be related to X_1, X_3, and X_4, you didn't really expect it to be related to X_2; someone had just suggested that you "try on" X_2 at a 5% level of significance. This means that if H_0 (no relation) is true, there is a 5% chance of ringing a false alarm. If this is the *only* variable "tried on," then this is a risk you can live with. However, if many such variables are "tried on" in a multiple regression the chance of a false alarm increases dramatically.[8] Of

[8] Suppose, for simplicity, that the t tests for the significance of the several variables (say k of them) were independent. Then the probability of no error at all is $(.95)^k$. For $k = 10$, for example, this is .60, making the probability of some error (some false alarm) as high as .40.

course, this risk can be kept small by reducing the level of error for each t test from 5% to 1% or less. This has led some authors to suggest a 1% level of significance with the variables just being "tried on," and a 5% level of significance with the other variables expected to affect Y. Using this criterion we would conclude that the relation of Y to X_1 is statistically significant; but the relation of Y to X_2 is *not*—despite its higher t value—because there are no prior grounds for believing it.[9]

To sum up: hypothesis testing should not be done mechanically. It requires:

1. Good judgment, and good prior theoretical understanding of the model being tested.

2. An understanding of the assumptions and limitations of the statistical techniques.

PROBLEMS

3-4 Suppose a multiple regression of Y on three independent variables yields the following estimates, based on a sample of $n = 30$:

	$Y = 25.1$	$+ \; 1.2X_1$	$+ \; 1.0X_2$	$- \; .50X_3$
Standard deviations	(2.1)	(1.5)	(1.3)	(.060)
t-values	(11.9)	( )	( )	( )
95% Confidence limits	(±4.3)	( )	( )	( )

(a) Fill in the blanks.

(b) True or False? If false, correct it.

(1) The coefficient of X_1 is estimated to be 1.2. Other scientists might collect other samples and calculate other estimates. The distribution of these estimates would be centered around the true value of 1.2. Therefore, the estimator is called unbiased.

(2) If there were strong prior reasons for believing that X_1 does not influence Y, it is reasonable to reject the null hypothesis $\beta_1 = 0$ at the 5% level of significance.

(3) If there were strong prior reasons for believing that X_2 does influence Y, it is reasonable to use the estimated coefficient 1.0 rather than accept the null hypothesis $\beta_2 = 0$.

---

[9] Anyone who thinks he would never wish to use such a double standard might suppose that Y is the U.S. price level, X_1 is U.S. wages, and X_2 the number of rabbits in South Australia. With the t values shown in equation (3-15), what would he do?

3-6 DUMMY VARIABLES

There are two major categories of statistical information available to economists: cross section and time series. For example, econometricians estimating the consumption function sometimes use a detailed breakdown of the consumption of individuals at various income levels at one point in time (cross section); sometimes they examine how total consumption is related to national income over a number of time periods (time series); and sometimes they use a combination of the two. In this section we develop a method that is especially useful in analyzing time series data;[10] as we shall see, it also has important applications in cross section studies as well.

(a) Introductory example

Suppose we wish to investigate how the public purchase of government bonds (B) is related to national income (Y). A hypothetical scatter of annual observations of these two variables is shown for Canada in Figure 3-6 and in Table 3-3. It is immediately evident that the relationship of bonds to income

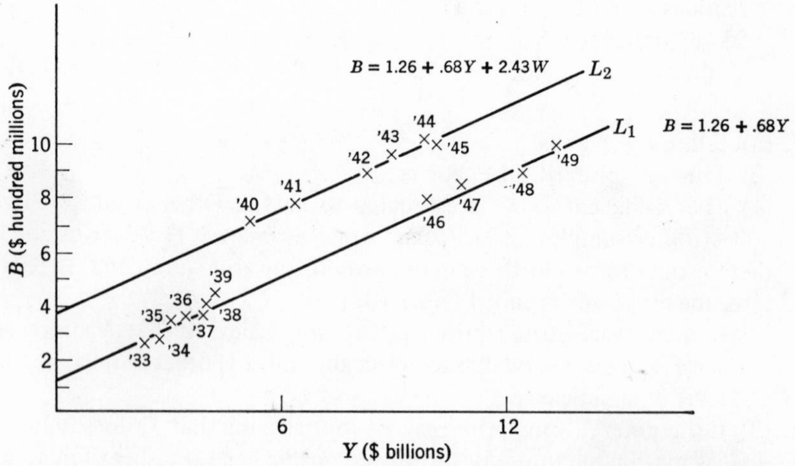

FIG. 3-6 Hypothetical scatter of public purchases of bonds (B) and national income (Y).

[10] There are a number of problems involved in analyzing time series, but most of these are deferred to Chapters 6 and 16.

TABLE 3-3 Calculations for Regression of B on Y and W, where W is a Dummy Variable.

Year	B	Y	W	$y = Y - \bar{Y}$	$w = W - \bar{W}$	yw	By	Bw	y^2	w^2
1933	2.6	2.4	0	−4.44	−.35	1.55	−11.54	−.91	19.71	.12
1934	3.0	2.8	0	−4.04	−.35	1.41	−12.12	−1.05	16.32	.12
1935	3.6	3.1	0	−3.74	−.35	1.31	−13.46	−1.26	13.99	.12
1936	3.7	3.4	0	−3.44	−.35	1.20	−12.73	−1.29	11.83	.12
1937	3.8	3.9	0	−2.94	−.35	1.03	−11.17	−1.33	8.64	.12
1938	4.1	4.0	0	−2.84	−.35	0.99	−11.64	−1.43	8.07	.12
1939	4.4	4.2	0	−2.64	−.35	0.92	−11.62	−1.54	6.97	.12
1940 (War years)	7.1	5.1	1	−1.74	.65	−1.13	−12.35	4.62	3.03	.42
1941 (War years)	8.0	6.3	1	−.54	.65	−.35	−4.32	5.20	.29	.42
1942 (War years)	8.9	8.1	1	1.26	.65	.82	11.21	5.78	1.59	.42
1943 (War years)	9.7	8.8	1	1.96	.65	1.27	19.01	6.30	3.84	.42
1944 (War years)	10.2	9.6	1	2.76	.65	1.79	28.15	6.63	7.62	.42
1945 (War years)	10.1	9.7	1	2.86	.65	1.86	28.89	6.56	8.18	.42
1946	7.9	9.6	0	2.76	−.35	−.97	21.80	−2.77	7.62	.12
1947	8.7	10.4	0	3.56	−.35	−1.25	30.97	−3.05	12.67	.12
1948	9.1	12.0	0	5.16	−.35	−1.81	46.96	−3.19	26.63	.12
1949	10.1	12.9	0	6.06	−.35	−2.12	61.21	−3.53	36.72	.12
	$\sum B = 115$	$\sum Y = 116.3$	$\sum W = 6$			$\sum yw = 6.52$	$\sum By = 147.25$	$\sum Bw = 13.74$	$\sum y^2 = 193.72$	$\sum w^2 = 3.84$
	$\bar{B} = \frac{\sum B}{17} = 6.76$	$\bar{Y} = \frac{\sum Y}{17} = 6.84$	$\bar{W} = \frac{6}{17} = .35$							

Estimating equations (3-4)
$$\begin{cases} \sum By = \hat{\beta} \sum y^2 + \hat{\gamma} \sum yw \\ \sum Bw = \hat{\beta} \sum yw + \hat{\gamma} \sum w^2 \end{cases}$$

or
$$\begin{cases} 147.25 = \hat{\beta}193.72 + \hat{\gamma}6.52 \\ 13.74 = \hat{\beta}6.52 + \hat{\gamma}3.84 \end{cases}$$

Solution:
$$\begin{cases} \hat{\beta} = .68 \\ \hat{\gamma} = 2.43 \end{cases}$$

Thus our estimated regression is: $B = 6.76 + .68y + 2.43w$

Or, expressed in terms of the original variables: $B = 6.76 + .68(Y - \bar{Y}) + 2.43(W - \bar{W})$

$$= 6.76 + .68(Y - 6.84) + 2.43(W - .35)$$

$$\boxed{B = 1.26 + .68Y + 2.43W}$$

follows two distinct patterns—one applying in wartime (1940–1945), the other in peacetime.

The normal relation of B to Y (say L_1) is subject to an upward shift (to L_2) during wartime; heavy bond purchases in those years is explained not by Y alone, but also by the patriotic wartime campaign to induce public bond purchases. B, therefore, should be related to Y *and* another variable—war (W). But this is only a categorical, or indicator variable. It does not have a whole range of values, but only two: we arbitrarily set its value at 1 for all wartime years and at 0 for all peacetime years. Since W is either "on" or "off," it is referred to as a "counter" or "dummy" variable. Our model is

$$B = \alpha + \beta Y + \gamma W + e \tag{3-19}$$

where $W = 1$ for wartime years, and
$ = 0$ for peacetime years.

This single equation is seen to be equivalent to the following two equations:

$$B = \alpha + \beta Y + \gamma + e \quad \text{for wartime} \tag{3-20}$$

$$B = \alpha + \beta Y + e \quad \text{for peacetime} \tag{3-21}$$

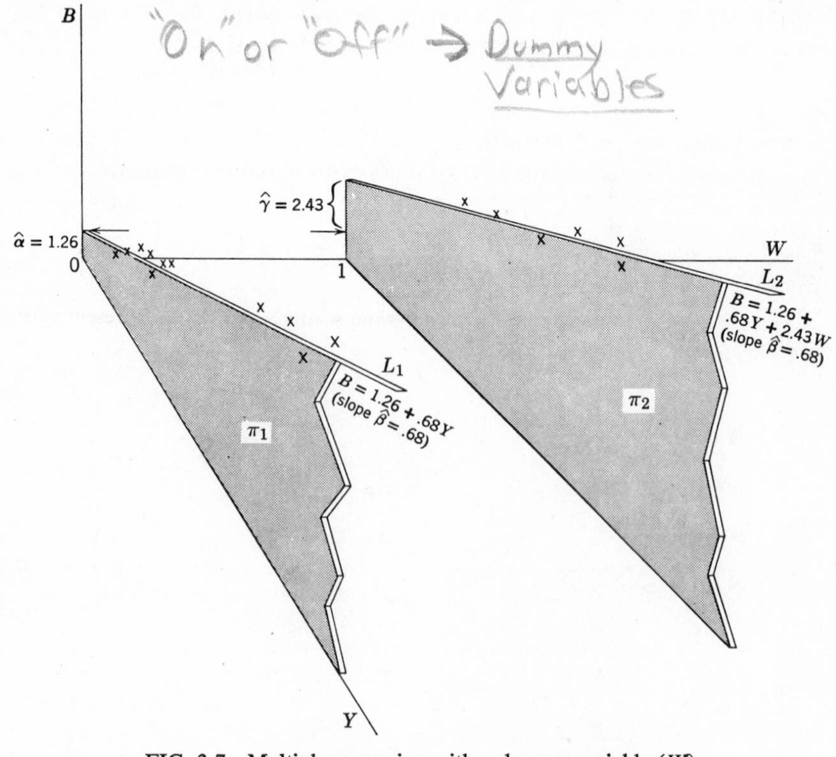

FIG. 3-7 Multiple regression with a dummy variable (W).

W may also be called a "switching" variable. With war and peace, we switch back and forth between (3-20) and (3-21).

We note that γ represents the effect of wartime on bond sales; and β represents the effect of income changes. (The latter is assumed to remain the same in war or peace.) The important point to note is that one multiple regression of B on Y and W as in (3-19) will yield the *two* estimated lines shown in Figure 3-6; L_1 is the estimate of the peacetime function (3-21), and L_2 is the estimate of the wartime function (3-20).

Complete calculations for our example are set out in Table 3-3, and the procedure is interpreted in Figure 3-7. Since all observations are at $W = 0$ or $W = 1$, the scatter is spread only in the two vertical planes π_1 and π_2. Estimation involves a multiple (least squares) regression fit of (3-19) to this scatter. The resulting fitted plane

$$B = \hat{\alpha} + \hat{\beta}Y + \hat{\gamma}W \qquad (3\text{-}22)$$

can be visualized as a plane resting on two supporting buttresses π_1 and π_2. The slopes of L_1 and L_2 are (by assumption) equal[11] to the common value $\hat{\beta}$, and $\hat{\gamma}$ is the estimated wartime shift.

In a dummy variable model—as in any regression problem—it is important to understand why *both* variables Y and W must be included. Even if our only interest is in B and Y, their relationship cannot be properly estimated unless W is taken into account. In other words, since experimental control over the "nuisance" variable W is not possible, its effects must explicitly be removed in the regression analysis. To ignore this variable is to invite a bias in our estimators, as well as an increased variance. To see how bias occurs,

---

[11] This restriction means that L_1 and L_2 are *not* independently fitted. In other words, our least squares plane (3-22) is fitted first; L_1 and L_2 are simply "read off" this plane. Thus L_1 does *not* represent a least squares fit to the left-hand scatter, nor does L_2 represent a least squares fit to the right-hand scatter.

This dummy variable method of fitting a single multiple regression plane and then reading off L_1 and L_2, can be compared to the alternative method of independently fitting two simple regression lines to the two scatters in Figure 3-7. Our model would be:

$$B = \alpha_1 + \beta_1 Y + e_1 \qquad \text{for wartime}$$
$$B = \alpha_2 + \beta_2 Y + e_2 \qquad \text{for peacetime}$$

and the estimated slopes (β_1 and β_2) would generally not be the same.

Estimates of four parameters are required for this model, rather than the three in the dummy variable model (3-19); thus one advantage of the dummy model is that it conserves one extra degree of freedom. Its disadvantage is that it requires an additional prior restriction—that the two slopes are equal. But this is not always a disadvantage. For instance, in our example it may be better to assume the two slopes equal than to independently fit a wartime function to only five observations. The very small wartime sample may yield a very unreliable estimate of slope, and it may make better sense to pool all the data to estimate one slope coefficient.

consider what happens if W is ignored, so that our scatter involves only the two dimensions B and Y. Geometrically, this involves projecting the three-dimensional scatter in Figure 3-7 onto the two-dimensional B-Y plane, as in Figure 3-8a. This is immediately recognized as the same scatter plotted in Figure 3-6; we also reproduce from that diagram L_1 and L_2, our estimated multiple regression using W as a dummy variable. If we calculate L_3, the simple regression of B on Y, it clearly has too great a slope. This upward bias results from the fact that war years tended to be high income years: thus, on the right-hand side of this scatter, higher bond sales that should be attributed in part to wartime would be (erroneously) attributed to income alone.

Bias if ignore W

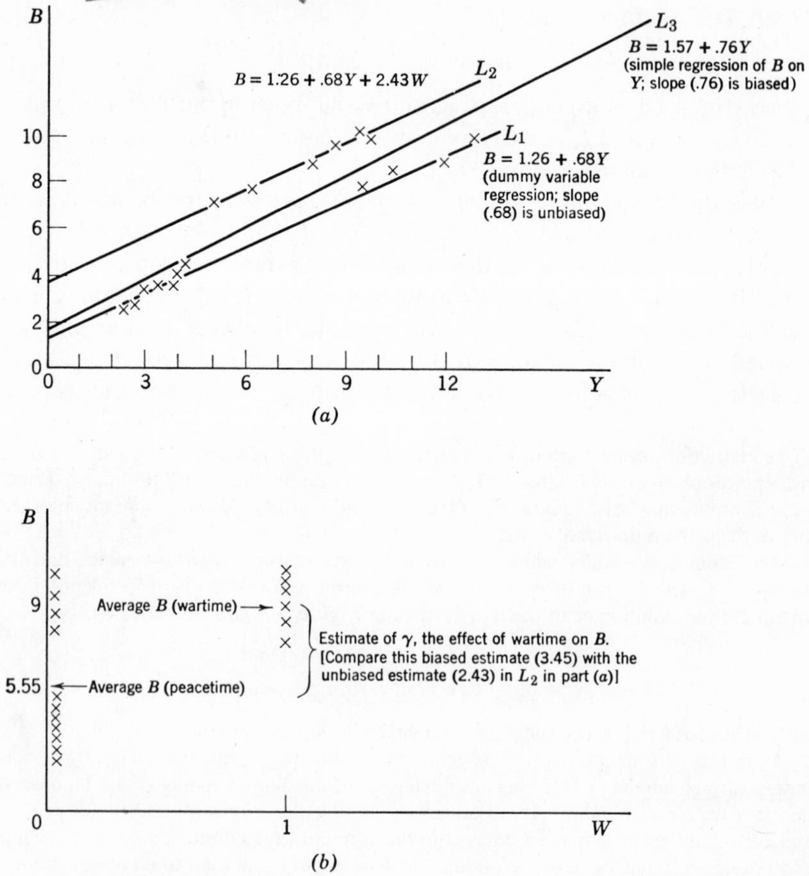

FIG. 3-8 Error when one explanatory variable is ignored. (a) Biased estimate of slope (the effect of Y) because the categorical variable W is ignored. (b) Biased estimate of the effect of W because the numerical variable Y is ignored.

A similar error is to be expected in any investigation of B and W that ignores Y. With no Y dimension, our scatter in Figure 3-7 would be projected onto the B-W plane, as in Figure 3-8b. In this diagram the only way to estimate the wartime effect is to look at the difference in sample means,[12] which is too large. This upward bias would result from the same cause: higher bond sales that should be attributed in part to higher income would be (erroneously) attributed to wartime alone.

This example has illustrated the general nature of dummy variables. This can be applied to a wide variety of problems, but one of the most useful applications is in removing seasonal shifts in time series data, as explained next.

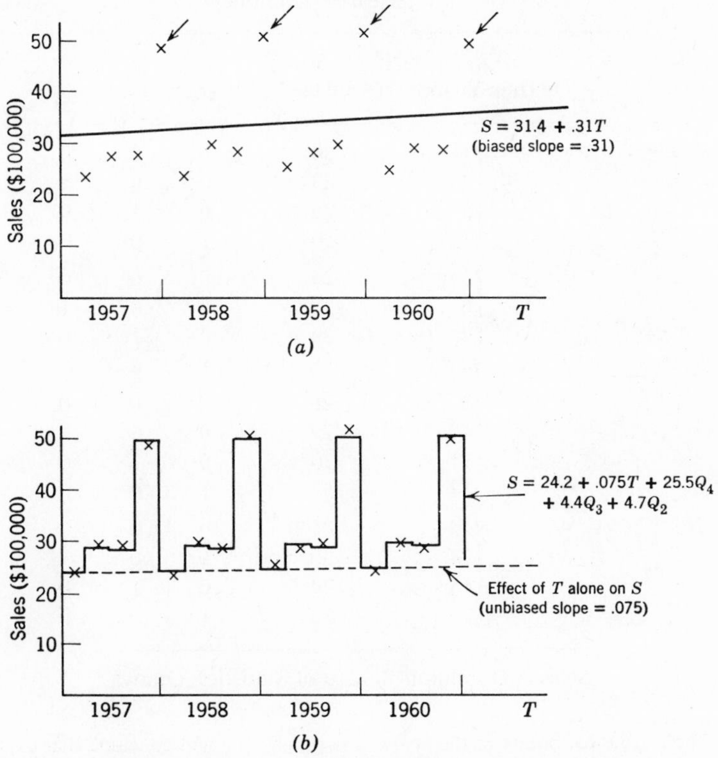

FIG. 3-9 Secular growth in Canadian jewelry sales, with and without seasonal adjustment. (a) Inadequate simple regression of S on T alone. (b) Multiple regression of S on T, including seasonal adjustment.

[12] This is equivalent to a simple regression of B on W. Because of the peculiar scatter involved, this regression line would pass through these two means; thus their difference represents the effect of W on B.

(b) Seasonal Adjustment

To illustrate, consider a spectacular example from real life. Suppose we wish to examine how department store sales of jewelry increase over time. When we plot quarterly sales (in Table 3-4) against time as in Figure 3-9, we note how sales shoot up every fourth quarter because of Christmas. Since we are interested in the long-term secular increase in sales, these strange Christmas observations should be discounted. This calls for a dummy variable[13] Q_4 (for

TABLE 3-4 Department Store Jewelry Sales (S), and Seasonal Dummies

	T (Quarter Years)	S ($100,000's)	Q_4	Q_3	Q_2
1957	1	24	0	0	0
	2	29	0	0	1
	3	29	0	1	0
	4	50	1	0	0
1958	5	24	0	0	0
	6	30	0	0	1
	7	29	0	1	0
	8	51	1	0	0
1959	9	26	0	0	0
	10	29	0	0	1
	11	30	0	1	0
	12	52	1	0	0
1960	13	25	0	0	0
	14	30	0	0	1
	15	29	0	1	0
	16	50	1	0	0

Source. Dominion Bureau of Statistics, Ottawa.

[13] There are three points in the analysis at which we might conclude that explicit account should be taken of seasonal swings. We may expect a strong seasonal influence from prior theoretical reasoning. Or, such an influence may be discovered when we plot the scatter. Finally, it may be discovered by examining residuals after the regression is fitted. Clearly those observations indicated by arrows (in Figure 3-9*a*) will have consistently high residuals. To explain this, we look for something they have in common. Their common property is that they all occur in the fourth quarter. Hence, the fourth quarter is introduced as a dummy regressor. This technique of "squeezing the residuals until they talk" is important in every kind of regression, not just time series; used with discretion, it indicates which further regressors may be introduced in order to reduce bias and residual variance.

fourth quarter) so that our model is

$$S = \alpha + \beta_1 T + \beta_4 Q_4 + e \tag{3-23}$$

Even this model may not be adequate. If allowance should also be made for shifts in the other quarters, dummies Q_2 and Q_3 should be added. A dummy Q_1 is not needed for the first quarter, because Q_2, Q_3, and Q_4 measure the shift from a first quarter base. (Whether or not to include the various regressors Q_4, Q_3, Q_2, can be decided on statistical grounds, by testing for statistical significance. It is common to include them all in such a test, and reject or accept them as a group. But such a statistical test on data as extreme as ours would be superfluous.) Our modified model is now

$$S = \alpha + \beta_1 T + (\beta_4 Q_4 + \beta_3 Q_3 + \beta_2 Q_2) + e \tag{3-24}$$

The least squares fit[14] to the data in Table 3-4 is graphed in Figure 3-9*b*. Notice that our seasonal adjustment is exactly the same every year, e.g., each year there is the same upward shift ($\hat{\beta}_2$) in our fit between the first and second quarters. (These seasonal shift coefficients need not always be positive, as in our example.)

By contrast, the simple regression of S on T without quarterly adjustment is graphed in Figure 3-9*a*. It is a poor fit, with large residual variance. Even worse, the calculated slope showing the relation of S to T is biased, for the same reasons as in the bond example of subsection (a).

(c) Seasonal Adjustment Without Dummies (Moving Average)

Dummy variables are not the only means of seasonally adjusting data. Another common method is to take a moving average (over a whole year) of the time series, as shown in Table 3-5. Note how the wild seasonal swing at Christmas is ironed out in this averaging process. The desired relation of sales to time can now be estimated by a simple regression of seasonally adjusted S' on T.

It is interesting to compare this method with the dummy variable alternative. An apparent disadvantage is that a total of three observations are lost at the beginning and end of the time series, in order to get the moving average started and finished. However, although it is less evident, the same loss is involved in using dummy variables, since three degrees of freedom are lost in estimating the shift coefficients β_2, β_3, and β_4.

An advantage of the moving average method is that it is not necessary to assume a constant seasonal shift; thus the adjustment for any quarter

---

[14] The least squares fit to this model was calculated by a method similar to that of Table 3-3. Equation system (3-4) was extended to a system of five estimating equations for the five unknowns.

TABLE 3-5 Moving Average

Time		S (Unadjusted)	S′ (Adjusted by Four Quarter Moving Average)
1957	1	24	
	2	29	$\frac{1}{4}(24 + 29 + 29 + 50) = 33$
	3	29	$\frac{1}{4}(29 + 29 + 50 + 24) = 33$
	4	50	$\cdot \quad = 33.25$
	5	24	$\cdot \quad = 33.25$
1958	6	30	$\cdot \quad = 33.5$
	7	29	$\cdot$
	8	51	$\cdot$
	$\cdot$		$\cdot$
	$\cdot$		
	$\cdot$		

varies from year to year. The advantage of dummy variables is that both seasonal shifts *and* the relation of S to T are estimated simultaneously in the same regression. (A moving average adjustment is only the first stage in a two-step process; only after it is completed can S' be regressed on T.) Another advantage is that the dummy coefficients (β_2, β_3, and β_4) give an index of the average seasonal shift, and tests of significance on them can easily be undertaken using standard procedures.

PROBLEMS

3-5 Referring to the jewelry sales in Figure 3-9, predict the sales S for the next quarter ($T = 17$, the first quarter of 1961):
(a) Using the simple regression of S on T alone.
(b) Using the multiple regression of S on T, including seasonal adjustment. Is this any better than (a)?

3-6 Referring to the two years of jewelry sales in Table 3-5:
(a) Compute the simple regression of S' (adjusted) on T.
(b) Compute the simple regression of S (unadjusted) on T.
(c) Of the two slopes in (a) and (b),
(i) Which do you think better shows the time trend of sales?
(ii) Which agrees more closely with the slope $\hat{\beta}_1 = .075$, estimated by using seasonal dummies?

3-7 Referring to the jewelry sales in Table 3-4, consider the eight quarters from the fourth to the eleventh quarter. Supposing this were the only data available:

(a) Fit a simple regression line of S on T, without quarterly adjustment.

(b) Is your slope estimate (time trend) unbiased? Why?

3-8 Referring to Figures 3-6 and 3-8a, suppose the last four years were missing. If a simple regression of B on Y is calculated (ignoring W), will the bias of the slope be less or greater than before (when all the years were used)? Why?

3-7 REGRESSION, ANALYSIS OF VARIANCE, AND ANALYSIS OF COVARIANCE

Multiple regression is an extremely useful tool with many broad applications. We define three special cases, distinguished by the nature of the independent variables:

1. "*Standard regression*" is regression on only numerical variables.
2. *Analysis of Variance*[15] (*ANOVA*) is equivalent to regression on only categorical (dummy) variables.
3. *Analysis of Covariance* (*ANOCOVA*) is regression on both categorical and numerical variables.

These three techniques are compared using the hypothetical data of Figures 3-10 to 3-13, which show the possible ways that mortality may be analyzed.

The hypothetical data in Figure 3-10 shows a sample of observations of the mortality of American men. Applying standard regression, we would reject the hypothesis that the true slope $\beta = 0$; thus we conclude that age does affect the mortality rate. In the process, we derive a useful estimate $\hat{\beta}$, of *how* age affects mortality.

If the data is collected into three groups, the result is the scatter shown in Figure 3-11. Note that this is exactly the same set of mortality (Y) observations as in Figure 3-10. The only difference is that we are no longer as specific about the age (X) variable. But with the data now assembled in three classifications, ANOVA can be applied[16] to test whether the means of these three

[15] For students who have not already studied analysis of variance, an introduction to this topic (and to analysis of covariance and multiple comparisons mentioned below) may be found, for example, in T. H. Wonnacott and R. J. Wonnacott "Introductory Statistics," New York: John Wiley, 1969, Chapter 10. See also Section 13-7 of this same reference for a concrete illustration of how ANOVA is equivalent to regression using dummy variables only.

[16] Standard regression could also be applied, with a line fitted to the scatter in Figure 3-11. However, if this technique is to be applied, it is more efficient to use the ungrouped data of Figure 3-10.

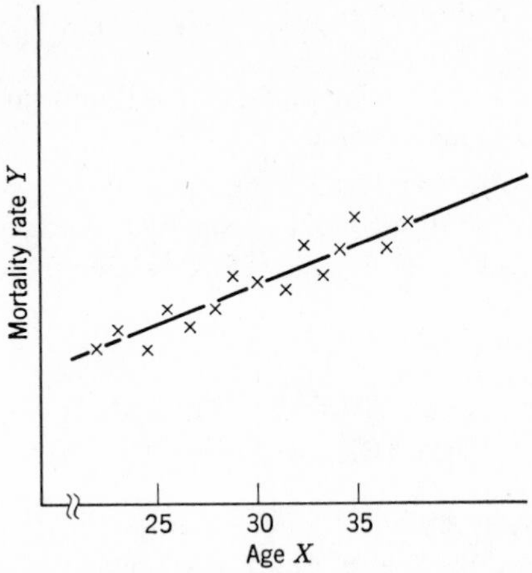

FIG. 3-10 "Standard regression," since X is numerical.

scatters are significantly different. Once again, the conclusion is that age affects mortality. However, ANOVA does not tell us *how* age affects mortality, unless we extend it to multiple comparisons.

So long as X is numerical, as in Figures 3-10 and 3-11, we conclude that standard regression can be applied and is often the preferred technique. But when X is categorical, it cannot be applied. For example, in Figure 3-12 we graph how mortality depends on nationality;[17] our X variable ranges over various categories, (American, British, etc.) and there is no natural way of

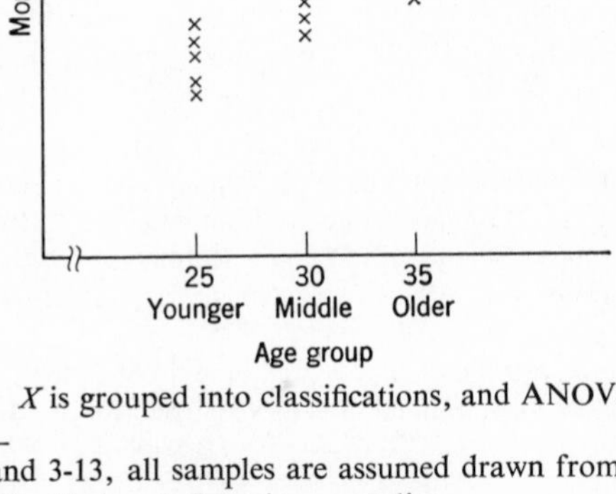

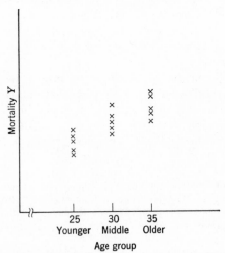

FIG. 3-11 X is grouped into classifications, and ANOVA may be used.

[17] In Figures 3-12 and 3-13, all samples are assumed drawn from a single age group; we consider only the other factors influencing mortality.

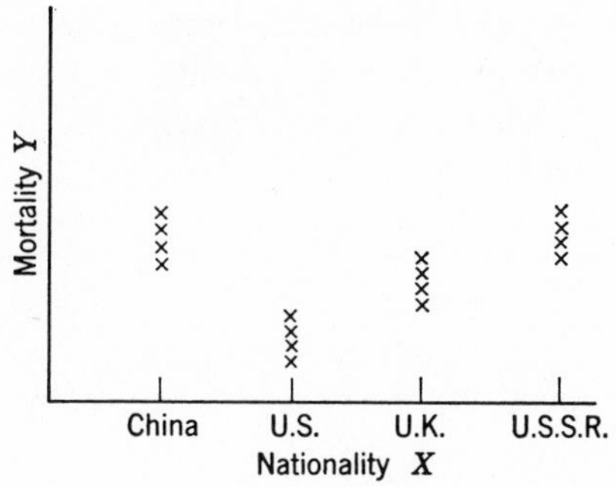

FIG. 3-12 *X* is categorical, and ANOVA must be used.

placing these on a numerical scale—or even ordering them. Hence, standard regression is out of the question,[18] and ANOVA must be used.

If mortality is dependent on income as well as nationality, the analysis of covariance shown in Figure 3-13 is appropriate. This uses nationality dummies, with the numerical variable income explicitly introduced to eliminate the error that it might otherwise cause. We confirm that this has greatly improved our analysis. Whereas it appeared in Figure 3-12 that a national characteristic of the British was a lower mortality rate than the Chinese, we see in Figure 3-13 that it is not this simple. The height of the fitted lines for China and the United Kingdom are practically the same. The lower U.K. mortality rate is explained solely by higher income.

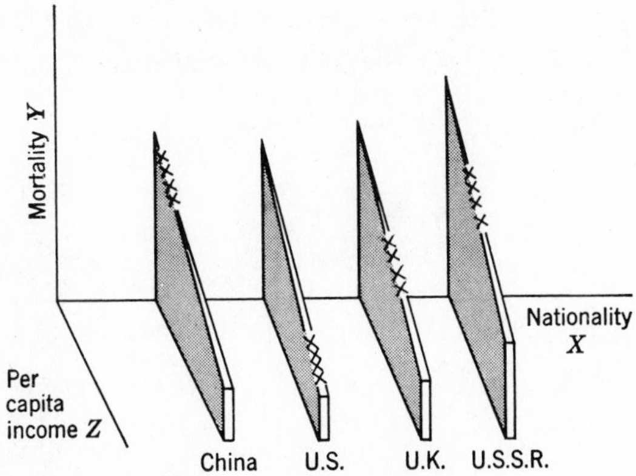

FIG. 3-13 Analysis of covariance for a categorical variable (nationality) and numerical variable (income).

[18] To confirm, note that a standard linear regression line fitted to the scatter in Figure 3-12 would yield $\hat{\beta} \approx 0$ (i.e., no evidence that nationality matters). Yet, if China is graphed last rather than first, $\hat{\beta} \not\approx 0$ and it would be concluded that nationality does matter. Thus, the conclusion would depend on the arbitrary ordering of the nationality variable.

In summary, standard regression is the more powerful tool whenever the independent variable X is numerical and the dependence of Y on X can be described by a simple function. Analysis of variance is appropriate if the independent variable is a set of unordered categories.

PROBLEMS

3-9 The following is the result of a test of gas consumption on a sample of 6 cars:

	Miles per gallon	Engine horsepower
Make A	21	210
	18	240
	15	310
Make B	20	220
	18	260
	15	320

(a) Determine the difference in the performance (miles per gallon) of the two makes, allowing for horsepower differences.
(b) Graph your results as in Figure 3-13.

3-10 (a) Based on the following sample information, use the analysis of covariance to describe how education is related to father's income and place of residence.
(b) Graph your results.

	Years of Formal Education (E)	Father's Income (F)
Urban sample	15	\$8,000
	18	11,000
	12	9,000
	16	12,000
Rural sample	13	\$5,000
	10	3,000
	11	6,000
	14	10,000

chapter 4

Regression Extensions

4-1 INTRODUCTION

The first three chapters have been devoted to the linear model. There are, of course, many other ways in which Y may depend on X; an example has already been given in Figure 2-10. In this chapter, we analyze some of the many forms nonlinearity may take. It will become evident, even from these few examples, that our standard regression procedure can often still be applied—provided the variables can be redefined, or the form of the equation appropriately transformed; but in many cases it cannot.

If it is argued that the simple linear relation ($Y = \alpha + \beta X$) does not apply, there are several broad possibilities. To illustrate, Y may be related to X as in:

$$Y = \alpha + \beta X^2 \tag{4-1}$$

or

$$Y = X^\beta \tag{4-2}$$

In both instances the relation of Y to X is no longer a straight line. But there is a fundamental difference in the two cases. In (4-1), the only nonlinearity is in the variable X; α and β appear in this equation in the same linear way as in Chapter 2, and as a consequence the techniques developed there can be applied without any difficulty. On the other hand, the nonlinearity in (4-2) directly involves β, the parameter to be estimated, and more serious estimating problems may arise. The most promising avenue is to search for a transformation that will make this equation linear, and hence amenable to the analysis we have already developed.

4-2 IF NONLINEARITY APPLIES ONLY TO THE VARIABLES, BUT NOT TO THE PARAMETERS

The regressions studied so far are of the form

$$Y = \alpha + \beta X \tag{4-3}$$

Although we don't write down the error explicitly, it is assumed throughout this section that the error term follows the assumptions of Chapter 2.

Equation (4-3) is linear in both the variable X and the parameters α and β. Now if we closely examine the least squares method in Chapter 1, we note that, as long as α and β appear in a linear way, the estimating equations (1-12) and (1-15) will be linear in the estimates of α and β. Hence, no problems are involved in their solution.

As an illustration, suppose our model is

$$Y = \alpha + \beta Z^2 \tag{4-4}$$

The student with calculus can easily derive the estimating equations appropriate to this model, and he will note that they are easily solved because they are linear in $\hat{\alpha}$ and $\hat{\beta}$. Equivalently, we could define a new variable

$$X = Z^2$$

When this is substituted into (4-4), our model is transformed into the standard form of (4-3), and least squares regression of Y on this new X variable gives us the solution.

This principle can best be shown with detailed examples; the first, with two parameters, is an extension of Chapter 1 and 2; the second, with several parameters, is an extension of the multiple regression of Chapter 3.

(a) Example: A Special Case of Liquidity Preference

Consider the model

$$Y = \alpha + \beta\left(\frac{1}{L - L^*}\right) \tag{4-5}$$

An economic illustration of this type of relationship might be the Keynesian liquidity preference function, showing how the interest rate Y is related to the quantity of money L. Within the context of this model, L^* might be a constant independent of the interest rate, representing the transactions demand for money; $L - L^*$ represents the speculative demand for money; and α is the liquidity trap, that is, the minimum level of interest. This function

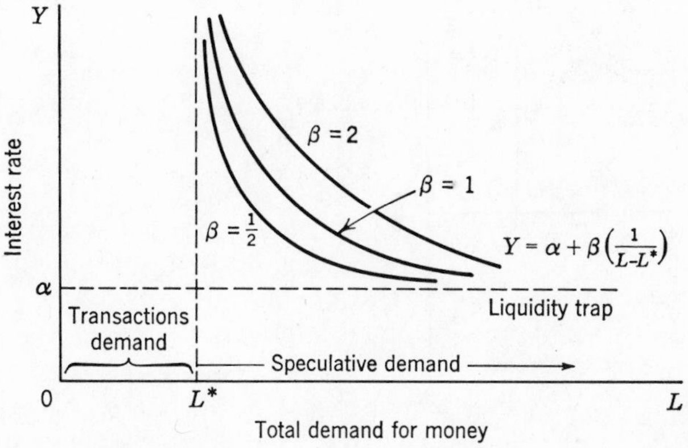

FIG. 4-1 Possible liquidity preferences—a family of rectangular hyperbolas.

is graphed in Figure 4-1; it is a rectangular hyperbola with curvature depending on β.

If L^* is known, then observations of Y and L can be used to estimate α and β. A hypothetical scatter of Y and L observations is shown in Figure 4-2*a* and in columns 1 and 2 of Table 4-1; (using a liquidity preference example, we might suppose that interest Y is measured in %, and the demand for money L is measured in units of \$50 billion). In addition, suppose we have prior information that $L^* = 2$. This scatter confirms our theoretical expectation that the relation between the variables is hyperbolic, rather than linear. The estimators $\hat{\alpha}$ and $\hat{\beta}$ are found in three steps.

Step 1. If, in (4-5) we let

$$X = \frac{1}{L - L^*} \tag{4-6}$$

then our model becomes the simple linear regression of Y on X given in (4-3). It can be fitted by our standard procedure. Therefore, the first step is to transform L into X according to (4-6). This is shown in columns 3 and 4 of Table 4-1; geometrically this transformation is shown below the baseline in Figure 4-2*a*.

In Figure 4-2*b*, the new X variable is measured left to right from a zero origin, and the same observed scatter is plotted, but this time in the new (X, Y) frame of reference. As expected, this transformation of L into X has transformed our scatter into a roughly linear relation.

Step 2. Y is now regressed on X by our standard procedures, shown in columns 5 to 7 of Table 4-1. The resulting fit is

$$Y = 2.54 + 1.50X \tag{4-7}$$

shown in Figure 4-2*b*.

Table 4-1

Fitting a Rectangular Hyperbola to a Set of Observations Generated By:

$$Y_i = \alpha + \beta\left(\frac{1}{L_i - L^*}\right) + e_i$$

Step 1 Transformation of L into X	Step 2 Regression of Y on X
	Step 3 Retransformation of X back into L

(1) Y_i	(2) L_i	(3) $L_i - L^*$	(4) $X_i = \frac{I}{L_i - L^*}$	(5) $x_i = X_i - \bar{X}$	(6) $Y_i x_i$	(7) x_i^2	(8) $\hat{Y}_i = \bar{Y} + \hat{\beta}x_i = 4.07 + 1.5x_i$	(9) $\hat{e}_i = Y_i - \hat{Y}_i$	(10) $\hat{e}_i^2 = (Y_i - \hat{Y}_i)^2$
6.0	2.5	0.5	2.00	0.98	5.88	0.96	5.54	0.46	0.2116
5.5	2.4	0.4	2.50	1.48	8.14	2.19	6.29	−0.79	0.6241
5.5	2.7	0.7	1.43	0.41	2.26	0.17	4.69	0.81	0.6561
4.8	2.6	0.6	1.67	0.65	3.12	0.42	5.05	−0.25	0.0625
4.4	3.0	1.0	1.00	−0.02	−0.09	0	4.04	0.36	0.1296
3.7	3.3	1.3	0.77	−0.25	−0.93	0.06	3.69	0.01	0.0001
3.5	3.7	1.7	0.59	−0.43	−1.51	0.18	3.42	0.08	0.0064
3.2	4.4	2.4	0.42	−0.60	−1.92	0.36	3.17	0.03	0.0009
2.7	4.9	2.9	0.34	−0.68	−1.84	0.46	3.05	−0.35	0.1225
3.0	5.6	3.6	0.28	−0.74	−2.22	0.55	2.96	0.04	0.0016
2.5	6.2	4.2	0.24	−0.78	−1.95	0.61	2.90	−0.40	0.1600

$\Sigma Y_i = 44.8$

$\bar{Y} = \frac{\Sigma Y_i}{n} = \frac{44.8}{11} = 4.07$

$\Sigma X_i = 11.24$

$\bar{X} = \frac{\Sigma X_i}{n} = 1.02$

$\Sigma x_i = 0$ $\quad \Sigma Y_i x_i = 8.94$ $\quad \Sigma x_i^2 = 5.96$

$\hat{\beta} = \frac{\Sigma Y_i x_i}{\Sigma x_i^2} = \frac{8.94}{5.96} = 1.50$

The fitted regression is

$Y = \bar{Y} + \hat{\beta}x$
$= 4.07 + 1.50x$

or, using capital X:

$Y = \bar{Y} + \hat{\beta}(X - \bar{X})$
$= 4.07 + 1.50(X - 1.02)$
$= 2.54 + 1.50X$ (4-7)

$\Sigma (Y_i - \hat{Y}_i)^2 = 1.9745$

$s^2 = \frac{\Sigma (Y_i - \hat{Y}_i)^2}{n - 2} = 0.219$

$s = 0.47$

or

$$Y = 2.54 + 1.5\left(\frac{1}{L - L^*}\right)$$

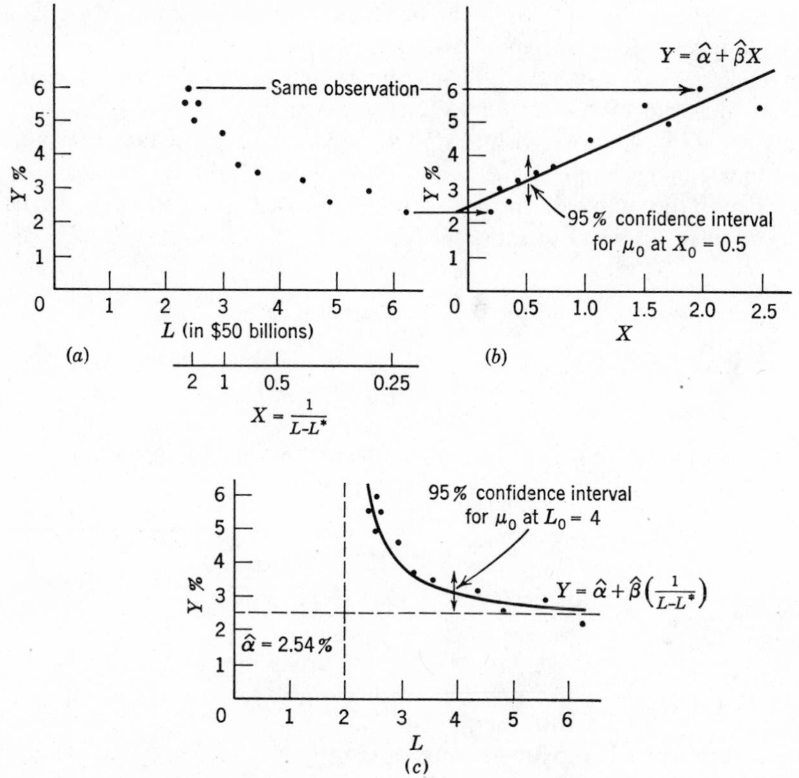

FIG. 4-2 Fitting a rectangular hyperbola. (*a*) Step 1: transformation of L into X. (*b*) Step 2: regression of Y on X. (*c*) Step 3: retransformation of X back into L.

Step 3. We finally need to retransform X back into L. Substituting (4-6) into (4-7)

$$Y = 2.54 + 1.50\left(\frac{1}{L - L^*}\right) \tag{4-8}$$

which is the hyperbola shown in Figure 4-2*c*; thus, our least squares fit of the scatter shown in Figure 4-2*a* is complete.

In summary, it may be concluded that because the relation (4-5) is linear in the parameters α and β, standard regression procedures may be applied without complication.[1] It is only necessary before proceeding to

[1] We have considered fitting a typical rectangular hyperbola, of which Keynesian liquidity preference *might* be a special case. But any attempt in practice to estimate liquidity preference would involve further complications. For example, the transactions demand for money L^* would have to be independently estimated, and it is by no means clear, as we have assumed, that it is independent of the interest rate. Furthermore, it could not normally be (*cont'd*)

define a new variable, and after the linear regression, to retransform. Confidence intervals, tests of hypothesis, etc., can be undertaken as outlined in Chapter 2; *it is only necessary to take great care in transforming variables.*

To illustrate: What is the 95% confidence interval for μ_0, the mean of Y when $L_0 = 4.0$? We wish to apply the standard procedure for calculating the confidence interval for a mean, set out in (2-40). But this can only be applied to the simple linear regression of Y on X given in (4-7). As a start, therefore, it is necessary to transform L_0 into X_0. From (4-6)

$$X_0 = \frac{1}{L_0 - L^*}$$

$$= \frac{1}{4.0 - 2.0} = .50$$

But we note that (2-40) requires that X_0 be expressed as a deviation

$$x_0 = X_0 - \bar{X}$$

$$= .50 - 1.02 = -.52$$

Now we can find the point estimate for μ_0. From (2-37)

$$\hat{\mu}_0 = \hat{\alpha} + \hat{\beta}x_0$$

$$= 4.07 + 1.50(-.52) = 3.29$$

And the interval estimate for μ_0 is, from (2-40),

$$\mu_0 = \hat{\mu}_0 \pm t_{.025}\, s \sqrt{\frac{1}{n} + \frac{x_0^2}{\sum x_i^2}}$$

$$= 3.29 \pm 2.26(.47)\sqrt{\frac{1}{11} + \frac{(-.52)^2}{5.96}}$$

$$= 3.29 \pm .39$$

$$2.90 < \mu_0 < 3.68 \tag{4-9}$$

This 95% confidence interval is shown in Figure 4-2*c*.

---

assumed that the relationship is exactly a rectangular hyperbola in shape—that is, it might be necessary to start with a more general form of relation, such as:

$$Y = \alpha + \beta\left(\frac{1}{L - L^*}\right)^{\gamma}$$

There are even more problems with liquidity preference, which we ignore, because our interest is in developing nonlinear econometric techniques rather than monetary theory.

(b) Example: The U-Shaped Cost Curve

As our second example, consider a polynomial model

$$Y = \alpha + \beta Q + \gamma Q^2 \tag{4-10}$$

This sort of model might occur in relating marginal cost Y to total output Q, for example. At various levels of output (Q_i), corresponding marginal costs (Y_i) are given in columns 1 and 2 of Table 4-2, and graphed in Figure 4-3. Since marginal cost decreases at first and then increases, the parabolic model in (4-10) seems appropriate.

To find the least-squares estimators $\hat{\alpha}$, $\hat{\beta}$, and $\hat{\gamma}$, we recognize from equation (4-10) that if we let

$$X = Q \tag{4-11}$$

and

$$Z = Q^2 \tag{4-12}$$

then our model is exactly that of Chapter 3. We note in passing that although Y is related to only one independent *variable* Q, our fit involves regressing Y on two *regressors*, Q and Q^2. This is the first time that it has been necessary to distinguish between independent variables and regressors, but the distinction is important. When one variable is used to obtain several regressors, as in this instance, we might wonder if multicollinearity becomes a problem.

Although Z_i and X_i are *functionally* dependent (i.e., one is the square of the other), they are not *linearly* dependent (i.e., one is not, say, three times the

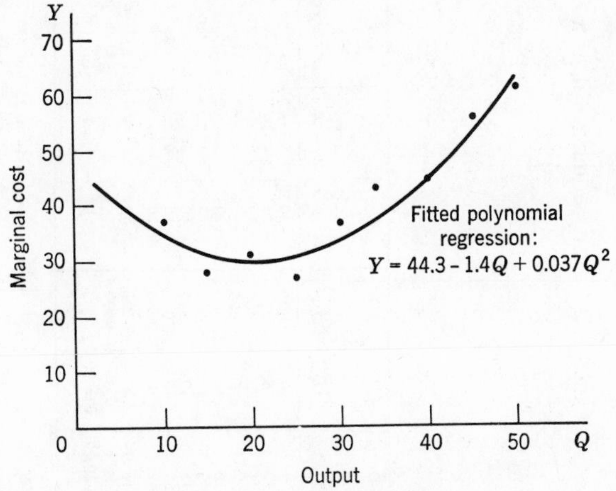

FIG. 4-3 Fitted parabola relating marginal cost to output.

Table 4-2 Least Squares Fit of a U-Shaped Marginal Cost Curve to a Set of Observations Generated by:

$$Y_i = \alpha + \beta Q_i + \gamma Q_i^2 + e_i$$

Transformation of Q and Q^2 into X and Z | Regression of Y on X and Z

Retransformation of X and Z back into Q and Q^2

(1)	(2)	(3)	(4)	(5)	(6)	(7)	(8)	(9)	(10)	(11)
Y_i	$X_i = Q_i$	$Z_i = Q_i^2$	$x_i = X_i - \bar{X}$	$z_i = Z_i - \bar{Z}$	$Y_i x_i$	$Y_i z_i$	x_i^2	z_i^2	$x_i z_i$	$\hat{Y}_i = 40.22 - 1.4376\, x_i + .03657\, z_i$
37	10	100	−20	−966.67	−740	−35,766.79	400	934,450.89	19333.40	33.63
27	15	225	−15	−841.67	−405	−22,725.09	225	708,408.39	12625.05	31.00
31	20	400	−10	−666.67	−310	−20,666.77	100	444,448.89	6666.70	30.22
27	25	625	−5	−441.67	−135	−11,925.09	25	195,072.39	2208.35	31.26
36	30	900	0	−166.67	0	−6,000.12	0	27,778.89	0	34.13
42	35	1225	5	158.33	210	6,649.86	25	25,068.39	791.65	38.82
45	40	1600	10	533.33	450	23,999.85	100	284,440.89	5333.30	45.35
55	45	2025	15	958.33	825	52,708.15	225	918,396.39	14374.95	53.70
62	50	2500	20	1433.33	1240	88,866.46	400	2,054,434.89	28666.60	63.89
$\Sigma Y = 362$	$\Sigma X = 270$	$\Sigma Z = 9600$	$\Sigma x_i = 0$	$\Sigma z_i = 0$	$\Sigma Y_i x_i = 1135$	$\Sigma Y_i z_i = 75{,}140.46$	$\Sigma x_i^2 = 1500$	$\Sigma z_i^2 = 5{,}592{,}500.00$	$\Sigma x_i z_i = 90000.00$	
$\bar{Y} = 40.22$	$\bar{X} = 30$	$\bar{Z} = 1066.67$								

$$Y = 40.22 - 1.4376(X - \bar{X}) + .03657\,(Z - \bar{Z})$$

or $Y = 44.34 - 1.4376X + .03657Z$

i.e. $Y = 44.34 - 1.4376Q + .03657Q^2$

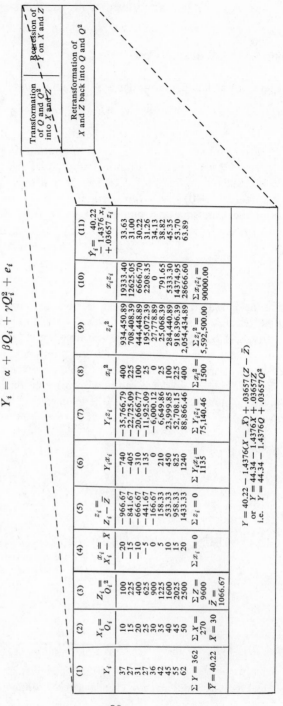

other). Geometrically, the points (X_i, Z_i) do lie on a curve (shown in Figure 4-4); the important point is, however, that they do not lie on a line. Thus, the problem of complete multicollinearity is avoided.[2] From a mathematical point of view, the physical or economic source of the X_i and Z_i values is irrelevant; just so long as X and Z are *linearly* independent, the mathematical model of Chapter 3 can be applied.

We therefore proceed with Table 4-2. Columns 2 and 3 set out the first step: the translation of Q into X and Z. The second step is the standard regression of Y on X and Z in columns 4 to 10. Our calculations are substituted into the last two estimating equations in (3-4), obtaining

$$1135 = \hat{\beta}(1500) + \hat{\gamma}(90{,}000)$$
$$75{,}140 = \hat{\beta}(90{,}000) + \hat{\gamma}(5{,}592{,}500)$$

These two may be solved:

$$\hat{\beta} = -1.4376$$

and

$$\hat{\gamma} = .03657$$

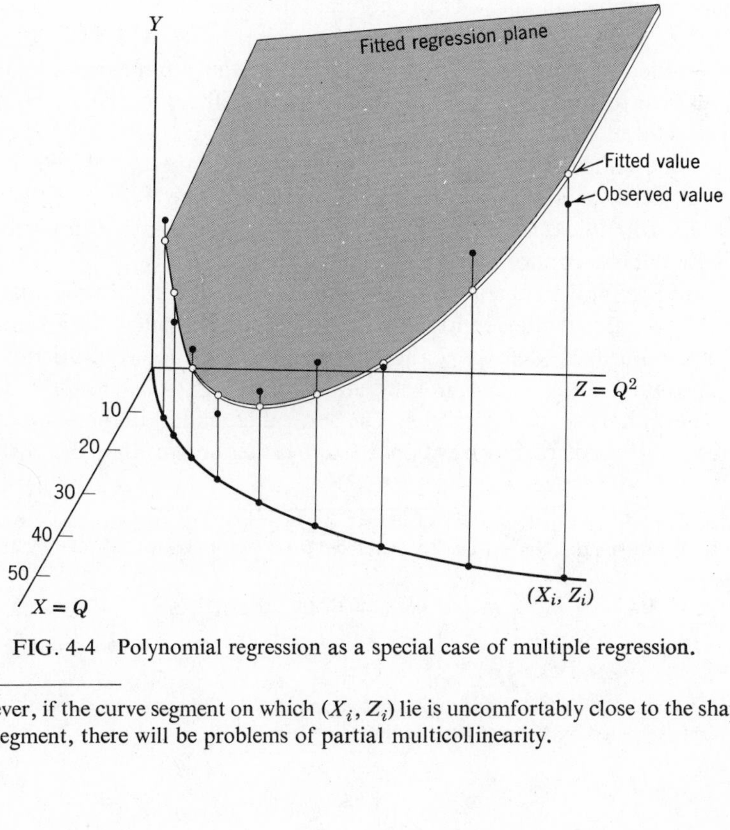

FIG. 4-4 Polynomial regression as a special case of multiple regression.

[2] However, if the curve segment on which (X_i, Z_i) lie is uncomfortably close to the shape of a line segment, there will be problems of partial multicollinearity.

The first estimating equation in (3-4) tells us that $\hat{\alpha} = \bar{Y} = 40.22$. Thus, the least squares fitted equation is

$$Y = 40.22 - 1.4376x + .03657z \tag{4-13}$$

This may be written

$$Y = 40.22 - 1.4376(X - \bar{X}) + .03657(Z - \bar{Z})$$

Substituting for $\bar{X}$ and $\bar{Z}$ from Table 4-2

$$Y = 44.34 - 1.4376X + .03657Z \tag{4-14}$$

Our final step is to express X and Z in terms of Q, as in equations (4-11) and (4-12),

$$\boxed{Y = 44.34 - 1.4376Q + .03657\,Q^2} \tag{4-15}$$

This is our fitted least squares regression of marginal cost Y on output[3] Q.

Fitted values for Y may be computed from equation (4-15), or its equivalent (4-13) as in column 11 of Table 4-2. These fitted Y values are plotted in Figures 4-3 and 4-4; when joined, they become our fitted U-shaped cost curve.

Confidence intervals and hypothesis tests on the parameters of this model are identical to those set out in Chapter 3. But there is one problem that deserves special attention: Is the parabolic model really necessary, or would a straight line suffice? One approach is to test the hypothesis H_0: $\gamma = 0$. If this can be rejected at a 5% level of significance, then the term in Q^2 plays an important role in explaining cost, and the parabolic model is indicated. But if this hypothesis cannot be rejected, there are no entirely satisfactory guidelines, and the analyst must rely to some extent on judgment. In the absence of prior knowledge to the contrary, this might be regarded as grounds for assuming a linear model; the $\hat{\alpha}$ and $\hat{\beta}$ of this linear model would then have to be recomputed, and will not, in general, be the same as the $\hat{\alpha}$ and $\hat{\beta}$ estimated from the first (parabolic) model. On the other hand, if there are strong theoretical grounds or prior evidence from earlier studies that the cost curve

[3] Students with integral calculus will note that this marginal cost curve is easily translated into a total cost (C) function, provided that fixed costs (F) are known. If $F = 25$, then

$$C = F + \int_0^Q (44.3 - 1.44Q + .037Q^2)\,dQ$$
$$= 25 + 44.3Q - .72Q^2 + .012Q^3 \tag{4-16}$$

The total cost curve of (4-16) will not generally be exactly the total cost curve that would have been estimated by a direct least squares fit of C on Q, Q^2, and Q^3.

is U-shaped, then the parabolic model may be retained. This is recognized as the argument that has recurred before in hypothesis testing: inability to reject H_0 does not necessarily imply that H_0 should be accepted.

PROBLEMS

4-1 (a) Fit C with a second degree polynomial in Q (parabola) for the following data:

Output Q (Thousands)	Marginal Cost C
1	32
2	20
3	20
4	28
5	50

(b) Graph the five points, and the fitted curve.
(c) What is the estimated C when $Q = 2.5$?

4-3 MODELS THAT ARE NONLINEAR IN THE PARAMETERS

When the nonlinearity in an equation is not restricted to the variables, but involves the parameters as in (4-2) then difficulties increase. The most promising approach in these circumstances is to search for a transformation that will linearize the equation. Failing this, regression analysis may be extremely difficult to apply. Again, we illustrate with examples.

(a) Transformation for the Cobb-Douglas Production Function

Economists often assume a Cobb-Douglas production function in relating output Q to quantity of labor L and capital K, as follows:

$$Q = AL^{\beta}K^{1-\beta} \tag{4-17}$$

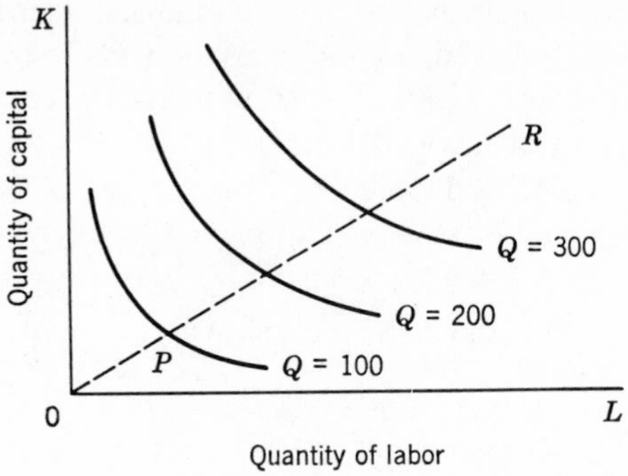

FIG. 4-5 The Cobb-Douglas production function.

For a specified value of A and β, this function is graphed in Figure 4-5; this diagram also illustrates how economists typically force a relation of three variables (L, K, and Q) into a two-dimensional space, by graphing the L-K curves (isoquants) corresponding to various fixed levels of Q. Thus, for example, the isoquant labeled $Q = 100$ represents all possible combinations of L and K resulting in 100 units of output. As we move from the origin to the northeast onto larger and larger isoquants, we can visualize moving up a three-dimensional surface, with output rising like a hill from a zero origin.

Economists are by now familiar with the economically attractive features of this model, which are briefly summarized below.

1. *Constant returns to scale.* If both L and K are doubled, output is also doubled; in other words, if we start at P and move out twice as far from the origin on the straight line path R, we will find ourselves on the 200 unit isoquant. Geometrically, we would be always facing exactly the same slope as we climb this output "hill"—provided that we always move in a straight line away from the origin. Mathematically, constant returns are ensured because the exponents of L and K (i.e., β and $1 - \beta$) sum to 1.[4] However, the model is easily adapted to other assumptions. For example, the exponent of K may be changed from $(1 - \beta)$ to another independent parameter γ; the exponents β and γ may then sum to more than 1 (increasing returns to scale), or less than 1 (decreasing returns).

2. *A changing rate of substitution between labor and capital.* As output is held constant and we move along an isoquant, its slope changes. Thus, the

[4] Formally, this means that the production function is homogeneous of degree one. If both inputs are increased by any factor λ, then output will also increase by λ. This is easily established. From (4-17) an increase in L and K to λL and λK results in an output of

$$A(\lambda L)^{\beta}(\lambda K)^{1-\beta} = \lambda^{\beta+1-\beta}AL^{\beta}K^{1-\beta} = \lambda AL^{\beta}K^{1-\beta} = \lambda Q$$

more we move to the southeast along the ($Q = 100$) isoquant, the flatter it becomes; that is, more and more labor must be added to compensate for a unit reduction in capital.

3. *An attractive theory of distribution.* This follows if the Cobb-Douglas production model is combined with the marginal productivity theory of wages. If each factor is paid its marginal product, total output will be just exhausted; hence, there will be no problem of how output should be distributed.[5]

So much for the model. Now let us turn to the problem of fitting it to a set of observations (Q_i, L_i, K_i). The first question is what we assume about the error term. If it can be argued that large errors are associated with large values of Q, then it may be appropriate to assume that our observations have been generated by:

$$Q = AL^{\beta}K^{1-\beta}v \tag{4-22}$$

where the errors v have a distribution that fluctuates around one.

It turns out that a logarithmic transformation will make this model linear. Take natural logarithms of both sides of equation (4-22)

$$\ln Q = \ln A + \beta \ln L + (1 - \beta) \ln K + \ln v \tag{4-23}$$

---

[5] This is a special case of Euler's theorem, which applies to any function that is homogeneous of degree one. In the Cobb-Douglas case, the marginal product of labor is

$$\frac{\partial Q}{\partial L} = \frac{\partial}{\partial L}(AL^{\beta}K^{1-\beta}) = \beta AL^{\beta-1}K^{1-\beta} \tag{4-18}$$

and of capital is

$$\frac{\partial Q}{\partial K} = \frac{\partial}{\partial K}(AL^{\beta}K^{1-\beta}) = (1 - \beta)AL^{\beta}K^{-\beta} \tag{4-19}$$

Now if each of the L units of labor is paid its marginal product as in (4-18), then the payment to labor R_L will be

$$R_L = L\frac{\partial Q}{\partial L} = L\beta AL^{\beta-1}K^{1-\beta} = \beta Q \tag{4-20a}$$

Thus labor's share of the product is βQ. Similarly, capital's share of the product is shown to be

$$(1 - \beta)Q \tag{4-20b}$$

Thus,

$$R_L + R_K = Q \tag{4-21}$$

That is, total factor payments exactly use up total output Q. (This argument has been developed in terms of physical units of output, but it also follows if factor payments and output are defined in value terms, and output price (P) is constant—as under pure competition. This is left as an exercise; it simply involves running through equations (4-20) and (4-21) once again, with all terms multiplied by P.)

Transformation of Q, L, K into Y and X	Linear regression of Y on X
Retransformation of model back into Q, L, K	

TABLE 4-3 Least Squares Fit of a Cobb-Douglas Function to Observations of Output, Labor, and Capital

(1) Q_i	(2) $\ln Q_i$	(3) L_i	(4) $\ln L_i$	(5) K_i	(6) $\ln K_i$	(7) $Y_i = \ln Q_i - \ln K_i$	(8) $X_i = \ln L_i - \ln K_i$	(9) $x_i = X_i - \bar{X}$	(10) x_i^2	(11) $Y_i x_i$	(12) $\hat{Y}_i = \bar{Y} + \hat{\beta} x_i = -.582 + .461 x_i$	(13) $(Y_i - \hat{Y}_i) = \hat{e}_i$	(14) $(Y_i - \hat{Y}_i)^2 = \hat{e}_i^2$
90	4.499	80	4.382	200	5.298	−.798	−.916	−.373	.139	.297	−.754	−.044	.00194
160	5.075	180	5.192	250	5.521	−.446	−.328	.214	.046	−.095	−.483	.036	.00135
210	5.347	180	5.192	460	6.131	−.784	−.938	−.395	.156	.309	−.764	−.019	.00038
250	5.521	300	5.703	400	5.991	−.470	−.287	.255	.065	−.120	−.464	−.005	.00003
300	5.703	430	6.063	430	6.063	−.360	0	.543	.295	−.195	−.331	−.028	.00082
350	5.857	300	5.703	660	6.492	−.634	−.788	−.245	.060	.155	−.695	.061	.00374
						$\Sigma Y_i = -3.493$ $\bar{Y} = -.582$	$\Sigma X_i = -3.259$ $\bar{X} = -.543$	$\Sigma x_i = 0$	$\Sigma x_i^2 = .761$	$\Sigma Y_i x_i = .351$			$\Sigma (Y_i - \hat{Y}_i)^2 = .00826$ $s^2 = \frac{\Sigma (Y_i - \hat{Y}_i)^2}{n-2} = .00206$ $s = .0454$

$$\hat{\beta} = \frac{\Sigma Y_i x_i}{\Sigma x_i^2} = .461$$

Therefore, the estimated linear regression is:

$$Y = \bar{Y} + \hat{\beta} x$$
$$Y = -.582 + .461x$$

Or, in terms of X:

$$Y = -.582 + .461(X - \bar{X})$$
$$Y = -.582 + .461X - .461(-.543)$$
$$Y = -.331 + .461X$$

The constant in this equation (−.331) is our estimate of α in (4-26). But from (4-25), $\alpha = \ln A$. Therefore, $A = \text{anti-ln}\,\alpha = 0.718$. Since β was not redefined, our estimate can be used directly. Substituting this estimate of A and our estimate of β into (4-17), we have the fitted Cobb-Douglas function:

$$Q = 0.718 L^{.46} K^{.54}$$

that is,

$$\ln Q - \ln K = \ln A + \beta[\ln L - \ln K] + \ln v \tag{4-24}$$

All that is necessary now is a simple renaming of the terms in this equation; let

$$\left.\begin{aligned} Y &= \ln Q - \ln K \\ \alpha &= \ln A \\ X &= \ln L - \ln K \\ e &= \ln v \end{aligned}\right\} \tag{4-25}$$

Let us assume that v is distributed[6] so that $e = \ln v$ satisfies the assumptions of Chapter 2. Then (4-24) turns out to be our familiar linear model,

$$Y = \alpha + \beta X + e \tag{4-26}$$

Thus, simple regression can be fully applied to these new variables.

This redefinition (4-25) has not been entirely arbitrary, since variables are redefined as variables, and parameters as parameters. It is this that has made the redefinition successful; in the next section, it will be evident that any term involving both variables *and* parameters cannot be successfully redefined in this way.

We note a second important requirement of this logarithmic transformation. It made the error term additive, rather than multiplicative. [Note how the error v was multiplied to the rest of the Cobb-Douglas function in (4-22); but after the transformation, e is added, as our model requires in (4-26).] To restate: the application of the simpler linear model (4-26) requires the assumption that the error term in the original equation (4-22) is multiplicative. If this assumption is unwarranted, then our model will require some sort of special treatment.

Example

In Table 4-3, a Cobb-Douglas function is fitted to the observed values of Q, L, and K shown in columns 1, 3, and 5. (These observations are also shown as the scatter of crosses in Figure 4-6; the K and L values for each observation are, of course, read off the K and L axes, while the Q value is written in beside the cross.) The important point to note here is that since

[6] For example, v might have median 1, so that $\ln v$ has median 0. We insist that $\ln v$ also have mean 0, and a finite variance. If $\ln v$ furthermore has a normal distribution, then v is said to have the lognormal distribution.

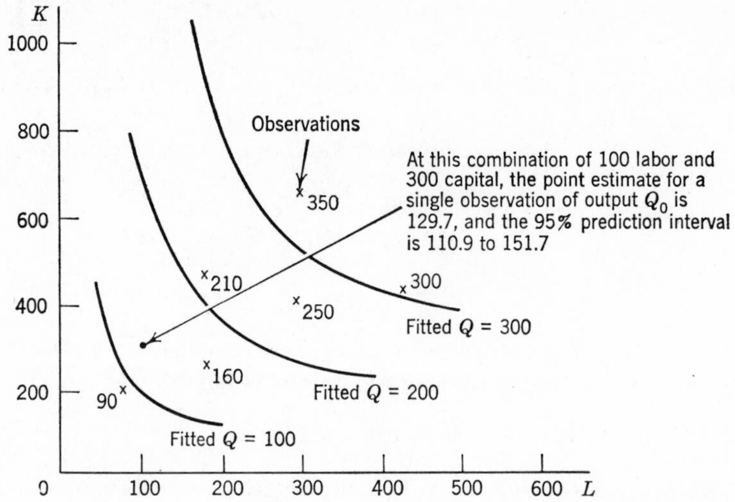

FIG. 4-6 A least squares Cobb-Douglas fit to observations of output, labor, and capital.

observed values of Q, L, and K are given, our new variables Y and X are completely defined, and are calculated in columns 7 and 8. Y is then regressed on X, and the results are retranslated into the Cobb-Douglas fit

$$Q = 0.718L^{.46}K^{.54} \tag{4-27}$$

If we wish to construct a 95% interval estimate for β, (2-30) can be applied to the linear regression model in the right half of Table 4-3, obtaining

$$\begin{aligned}\beta &= \hat{\beta} \pm t_{.025} \frac{s}{\sqrt{\sum x_i^2}} \\ &= .46 \pm 2.776 \frac{.0454}{\sqrt{.761}} \\ &= .46 \pm .14\end{aligned}$$

Thus,

$$.32 < \beta < .60 \tag{4-28}$$

Usually statistical conclusions require transformation back and forth from the original model to the linear model. For example, suppose the problem is to predict a single output Q_0 when $L_0 = 100$ and $K_0 = 300$. The prediction interval in (2-44) cannot be applied to our Cobb-Douglas function directly, but it can be applied to our linear model when Y was regressed on X.

Substituting (2-42) into (2-44) we have the 95% prediction interval

$$Y_0 = \hat{\alpha} + \hat{\beta} x_0 \pm t_{.025}\, s \sqrt{\frac{1}{n} + \frac{x_0^2}{\sum x_i^2} + 1} \tag{4-29}$$

First, calculate the x_0 value corresponding to $L_0 = 100$ and $K_0 = 300$. From (4-25)

$$X_0 = \ln L_0 - \ln K_0$$

$$X_0 = \ln 100 - \ln 300 = -1.098$$

and

$$x_0 = X_0 - \bar{X}$$

$$= -1.098 + .543 = -.555$$

(4-29) can now be written

$$Y_0 = -.582 + .461(-.555) \pm 2.776\,(.0454)\sqrt{\frac{1}{6} + \frac{(-.555)^2}{.761} + 1}$$

$$Y_0 = -.839 \pm .156 \tag{4-30}$$

which yields the 95% prediction interval for a single Y of

$$-.995 < Y_0 < -.683 \tag{4-31}$$

These two extreme values of Y need now only be translated into Q. From (4-25) we may write

$$Y_0 = \ln Q_0 - \ln K_0$$

$$\ln Q_0 = Y_0 + \ln K_0$$

$$Q_0 = \text{anti ln}\,(Y_0 + 5.703) \tag{4-32}$$

Substituting each of our extreme Y_0 values from (4-31)

$$\text{lower } Q_0 = \text{anti ln}\,(-.995 + 5.703) = 110.9$$

and

$$\text{upper } Q_0 = \text{anti ln}\,(-.683 + 5.703) = 151.7$$

Thus, our 95% prediction interval for Q_0 is

$$110.9 < Q_0 < 151.7 \tag{4-33}$$

To obtain a *point* prediction for Q_0, we similarly transform the point estimate for Y_0, which is

$$Y_0 = \hat{\alpha} + \hat{\beta} x_0 = -.838$$

This is transformed by (4-32)

$$Q_0 = \text{anti ln}\,(-.838 + 5.703) = 129.7 \tag{4-34}$$

This point prediction, and the interval prediction of (4-33), are shown in Figure 4-6.

(b) Intractable Nonlinear Models

There are many models that cannot be transformed into linear functions and solved by well-established means. Consider a hypothetical example that an economic historian might face. Suppose that he has uncovered a running annual asset statement (Y_t) over twenty years of a wealthy family (such as the Fuggers). Further suppose that additional fragmentary information becomes available: in the initial time period t_0 Jacob Fugger made a substantial loan (α_1) to the Hapsburg monarch, none of which was repaid over the twenty-year span; this sum was loaned at a "special" rate of interest (i_1), while the balance of the family's assets (α_2) was loaned out at the market rate of interest (i_2). The historian might be very interested in knowing how much of this family's assets were tied up in loans to the monarchy (α_1). Furthermore, he might wish to establish whether or not the state loan carried a lower interest rate (perhaps in exchange for licenses, mineral concessions, etc.); this would involve comparing estimates of i_1 and i_2.

The following model relating total assets to time would be appropriate:

$$Y_t = \alpha_1(1 + i_1)^t + \alpha_2(1 + i_2)^t + e \tag{4-35}$$

where t takes on values from 0 to 20, and Y_t represents the known total asset position at any time t; α_1, α_2, i_1, and i_2 are unknown. If there was also evidence that additions or withdrawals from this asset pool were negligible enough to be covered by the error term e, then the question is whether Y_t can be regressed on t in (4-35) to provide estimates of the parameters α_1, α_2, i_1, and i_2.

We have strong prior grounds for setting up the problem in the form (4-35); but this leaves us with several major difficulties in its estimation. First, there is no way of transforming (4-35) into a linear model. (For example, the transformation used to fit the Cobb-Douglas function is quite out of the question.) This does not mean it is hopeless; least squares estimates can still be derived. Since the fitted value for Y will be

$$\hat{Y}_t = \hat{\alpha}_1(1 + \hat{i}_1)^t + \hat{\alpha}_2(1 + \hat{i}_2)^t \tag{4-36}$$

the sum of the squared residuals between the observed Y_t and the fitted $\hat{Y}_t$ is

$$S(\hat{\alpha}_1, \hat{\alpha}_2, \hat{i}_1, \hat{i}_2) = \sum [Y_t - \hat{\alpha}_1(1 + \hat{i}_1)^t - \hat{\alpha}_2(1 + \hat{i}_2)^t]^2 \tag{4-37}$$

Our procedure now is the same as was used to derive estimating equations

(1-13) and (1-16). This sum of squares is minimized when the partial derivatives of S with respect to $\hat{\alpha}_1$, $\hat{\alpha}_2$, $\hat{\imath}_1$, and $\hat{\imath}_2$ are equal to zero:

$$\left.\begin{aligned}
\frac{\partial S}{\partial \alpha_1} &= \sum 2[-(1+\hat{\imath}_1)^t][Y_t - \hat{\alpha}_1(1+\hat{\imath}_1)^t - \hat{\alpha}_2(1+\hat{\imath}_2)^t] = 0 \\
\frac{\partial S}{\partial \alpha_2} &= \sum 2[-(1+\hat{\imath}_2)^t][Y_t - \hat{\alpha}_1(1+\hat{\imath}_1)^t - \hat{\alpha}_2(1+\hat{\imath}_2)^t] = 0 \\
\frac{\partial S}{\partial i_1} &= \sum 2[-\hat{\alpha}_1 t(1+\hat{\imath}_1)^{t-1}][Y_t - \hat{\alpha}_1(1+\hat{\imath}_1)^t - \hat{\alpha}_2(1+\hat{\imath}_2)^t] = 0 \\
\frac{\partial S}{\partial i_2} &= \sum 2[-\hat{\alpha}_2 t(1+\hat{\imath}_2)^{t-1}][Y_t - \hat{\alpha}_1(1+\hat{\imath}_1)^t - \hat{\alpha}_2(1+\hat{\imath}_2)^t] = 0
\end{aligned}\right\} \quad (4\text{-}38)$$

Given observed values of Y_t and t, this is a system of four equations in the four parameters to be estimated. The problem is that they are nonlinear. Even a single nonlinear equation in a single unknown may be difficult to solve, and this system of four nonlinear equations poses even greater computational problems. Moreover, there may no longer be a unique solution to (4-38). If several solutions were found, each solution (set of parameter values) would have to be plugged into the sum of squares (4-37) to find which yields a minimum. So great are the difficulties, however, that in practice there is often no attempt made to derive and solve estimating equations (4-38). Instead it is easier to use a computer minimization routine on (4-37) directly.

Thus, major computational problems are involved in fitting any model that cannot be linearized by a transformation or a redefinition of variables. But the additional difficulty of multicollinearity is encountered in our particular model. Even if i_1 and i_2 were known, then there would be two regressors that are similar functions of t, namely $(1 + i_1)^t$ and $(1 + i_2)^t$; the collinearity problem is immediately evident, especially if i_1 and i_2 are roughly equal. Moreover, the problem is compounded because i_1 and i_2 are not known, but must be estimated.

4-4 THE PHYSICAL AND SOCIAL SCIENCES CONTRASTED

In the physical sciences, there are often sound theoretical reasons for postulating a specific model. For example, an object dropping free of air resistance falls a distance Y in time t according to the quadratic function

$$Y = \tfrac{1}{2}gt^2 + vt \qquad (4\text{-}39)$$

where g is the gravitational constant, and v is the initial velocity. This mathematical model (hypothesis) is called a "law" because its adequacy has been empirically verified innumerable times (Galileo discovered it in the 17th century, and it is still used today); furthermore, it is consistent with the other laws of physics (in fact, it can be theoretically derived from Newton's laws of motion). By contrast, in economics there are neither empirical nor theoretical reasons to justify, for example, always using a quadratic, rather than a linear, marginal cost function. The physical sciences, therefore, are often more exact than the social sciences because the *form* of the function to be fitted is known.

A second reason that the physical sciences are more exact is that observations are often more precise. Consequently, statistical considerations become secondary. This is illustrated with the same model. Suppose that g is very precisely estimated ("known") from previous experimental results, and that time t and distance Y can be observed very precisely too. Then the hypothesis $H_0\colon v = 0$ (i.e., the object was dropped from rest) can be tested quite adequately by taking only *one* observational pair (t, Y). When these values (along with g) are plugged into (4-39), they determine v. The problem is primarily a mathematical one of solving for a unique value of v, rather than a statistical problem of computing the best estimate using some criterion such as least squares.

While the physical sciences usually have precise observations, at the same time their mathematical models are often very complex. Thus, even though problems may theoretically involve a statistical dimension, it is often ignored because of the difficulties involved in just getting a mathematical solution; in our example, if the unique mathematical estimate of v is close enough to zero to be explained by a small observational error in t and Y, then H_0 might be accepted without much explicit reference to statistical guidelines. It is not that the world of economics is simpler than the world of physics (indeed, many economic problems call for general equilibrium models of great mathematical complexity). The point is that there is a different trade-off. Economists usually must use models with a statistical dimension, and this necessarily restricts the mathematical complexity of their model. On the other hand, because their error of observation is small, physicists may often drop the statistical dimension in favor of using a more complicated mathematical model.

The third reason that the physical and social sciences differ is that experimental control can be introduced in the physical sciences.[7] The effect of

[7] Some people regard psychology research under experimental control as a branch of the physical rather than the social sciences. This implies that experimental control is a useful line of demarcation between the physical and social sciences.

nuisance variables (such as temperature) can often be eliminated by undertaking experiments under controlled conditions in which they are fixed. Even if they cannot be fixed, nuisance variables can have their effect neutralized by an unbiased randomized experiment. By contrast, the economist who examines, for example, the effect of interest on investment, finds it impossible to fix other variables such as consumption changes.[8] Hence, he must turn to multiple regression to try to neutralize their effects.

The best summary is a paradox. Because social behavior is less predictable than physical phenomena, mathematical models are a less accurate approximation of reality in the social sciences, hence statistical methods are more necessary.

A mathematical model provides a useful structure with which an economist may perhaps better understand and predict economic phenomena; it can hardly be regarded as ultimate truth. In fact, in certain instances a mathematical model may be used even when it is known not to be exactly right, if it is "good enough." (See Figure 2-1, where a curve is approximated by a straight line in the region of interest.) At our present level of knowledge, it is often better to use a simple, more tractable model rather than a complicated one—even though the latter provides a somewhat better fit. This is especially true if there are no prior grounds for expecting that the complicated model better describes the real world.

PROBLEMS

4-2

Time t (Years)	Population Y
0	1,570
20	1,810
40	2,250
50	2,510

(a) Graph.

(b) Which of the following models do you think would be most appropriate? (In making your judgment, take into consideration simplicity,

[8] As pointed out earlier, the economist may have other problems as well; it may not even be feasible to observe the interest rate at various possible values—and this is the independent variable whose effect is being measured.

closeness of fit, the nature of the error term, and validity of extrapolations into the recent past and future.)

(1) $Y = \alpha + \beta t$

(2) $Y = \alpha + \beta t + \gamma t^2$

(3) $Y = \alpha e^{\beta t}$

4-3 For each of the following models, outline the method you would use to estimate the parameters (Greek letters).

First, assume the errors are independent, and all have the same distribution.

(a) $Y = \alpha + \beta X^2$

(b) $Y = \alpha + \beta X + \gamma e^{\delta t}$

(c) $Y = \alpha + \beta t + \gamma \sin (2\pi t/12)$ (Linear growth with annual cycle.)

Next, in the following models assume that while the errors remain independent, they now have different distributions, with large errors in Y_i tending to occur when Y_i itself is large.

(d) $Y = \alpha e^{\beta t}$

(e) $Y = \alpha(1 + \beta)^t$ where β may be interpreted as a "growth rate."

(f) $Y = \alpha \beta^t \gamma^X$

(g) $Y = \alpha \beta^t + \delta^X$

4-4 Suppose that in 1950 a bank balance is left to accumulate at a constant interest rate i.

(a) Assuming no deposits or withdrawals, estimate the original balance B_0 in 1950, and the interest rate, from the following observations:

Time	Balance
1952	\$106.09
1953	\$109.27
1954	\$112.55
1955	\$115.92

(b) If bank calculations are error-free (i.e., there is no random disturbance e), would you need all four observations to calculate i and B_0? How many observations are necessary?

chapter 5 — *Know up to page 125 only*

Correlation

degree to which variables are related

5-1 SIMPLE CORRELATION

Regression analysis showed us *how* variables are related; correlation analysis will show us the *degree* to which variables are related. In regression analysis, a whole mathematical function is estimated (the regression equation); but simple correlation analysis yields only one number—an index designed to give an immediate picture of how closely two variables move together. In correlation analysis, we need not worry about cause and effect relations. Correlation between X and Y can be estimated regardless of whether: (a) X affects Y, or vice versa; (b) both affect each other; or (c) neither affects the other, but they move together because some third variable influences both. Because it is their business to define cause and effect relationships as specifically as possible, economists generally find correlation a less powerful technique. But because correlation and regression are so closely related mathematically, correlation often becomes a useful aid in regression analysis.

(a) The Sample Correlation Coefficient r

As an example, consider the marks on a verbal (Y) and mathematical (X) test scored by a sample of eight college students. Each student's performance is represented by a point in the scatter shown in Figure 5-1a; this information is set out in the first two columns of Table 5-1.

Since we are after a single measure of how closely these variables are related, our index should be independent of our choice of origin in Figure 5-1a. So we shift *both* axes in Figure 5-1b, just as we shifted one axis in Chapter 1. Both x and y are now defined as deviations from the mean; that is,

$$x = X - \bar{X}$$

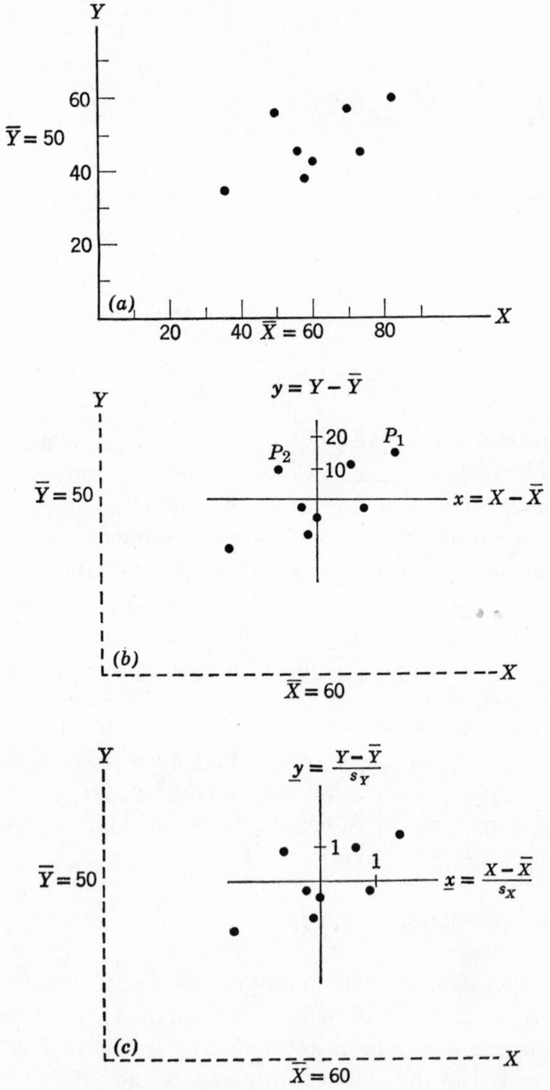

FIG. 5-1 Scatter of math and verbal scores. (*a*) Original observations. (*b*) Shift axes. (*c*) Change scale of axes to standard units.

TABLE 5-1 Math Score (X) and Corresponding Verbal Score (Y) of a Sample of Eight Students Entering College.

(1) X	(2) Y	(3) $x = X - \bar{X}$	(4) $y = Y - Y$	(5) xy	(6) x^2	(7) y^2	(8) $\hat{Y} = \bar{Y} + \hat{\beta}x$	(9) $Y - \hat{Y}$	(10) $(Y - \hat{Y})^2$	(11) $\hat{X} = \bar{X} + \hat{\beta}_* y$	(12) $X - \hat{X}$	(13) $(X - \hat{X})^2$
36	35	−24	−15	360	576	225	37.96	−2.96	8.76	48.27	−12.27	150.55
80	65	20	15	300	400	225	60.03	4.97	24.70	71.73	8.27	68.39
50	60	−10	10	−100	100	100	44.99	15.01	225.30	67.82	−17.82	317.55
58	39	−2	−11	22	4	121	49.00	−10.00	100.00	51.39	6.61	43.69
72	48	12	−2	−24	144	4	56.02	−8.02	64.32	58.44	13.56	183.87
60	44	0	−6	0	0	36	50.00	−6.00	36.00	55.31	4.69	22.00
56	48	−4	−2	8	16	4	47.99	.01	.0001	58.44	−2.44	5.95
68	61	8	11	88	64	121	54.01	6.99	48.86	68.61	−.61	.37
$\Sigma X = 480$	$\Sigma Y = 400$	$\Sigma x = 0$	$\Sigma y = 0$	$\Sigma xy = 654$	$\Sigma x^2 = 1304$	$\Sigma y^2 = 836$			$\Sigma (Y - \hat{Y})^2 = 508$			$\Sigma (X - \hat{X})^2 = 792.37$
$\bar{X} = 60$	$\bar{Y} = 50$			$\hat{\beta} = \dfrac{\Sigma xy}{\Sigma x^2} = .5015$	$s_X^2 = \dfrac{\Sigma x^2}{n-1} = \dfrac{1304}{7} = 186.3$	$s_Y^2 = \dfrac{\Sigma y^2}{n-1} = \dfrac{836}{7} = 119.4$			$s^2 = \dfrac{\Sigma (Y - \hat{Y})^2}{n-2} = \dfrac{508}{6} = 84.7$			$s_*^2 = \dfrac{\Sigma (X - \hat{X})^2}{n-2} = \dfrac{792}{6} = 132$
				$\hat{\beta}_* = \dfrac{\Sigma xy}{\Sigma y^2} = .782$	$s_X = 13.65$	$s_Y = 10.93$			$s = 9.20$			$s_* = 11.5$

and (5-1)

$$y = Y - \bar{Y}$$

Values of the translated variables are shown in columns 3 and 4 of Table 5-1.

Suppose we multiply the x and y coordinate values for each student, and sum them all. This ($\sum xy$) gives us a good measure of how math and verbal results tend to move together. Whenever an observation such as P_1 falls in the first quadrant in Figure 5-1*b* both its x and y coordinates will be positive, and their product xy positive. This also holds true for any observation in the third quadrant, with both coordinates negative. The product is negative only for observations such as P_2 in the second or fourth quadrant (one coordinate positive, the other negative). If X and Y move together, most observations will fall in the first and third quadrants; consequently, most products xy will be positive, as will their sum—a reflection of the positive relationship between X and Y. But if X and Y are negatively related (i.e., when one rises the other falls), the original scatter will run downhill rather than uphill; hence, most observations will fall in the second and fourth quadrants, yielding a negative value for our $\sum xy$ index. We conclude that as an index of correlation, $\sum xy$ at least carries the right sign. Moreover, when there is no observed relationship between X and Y, and our observations are distributed evenly over the four quadrants, positive and negative terms will cancel, and this index will be zero.

There are just two ways that $\sum xy$ can be improved. First, it depends on the units in which x and y are measured. (Suppose the math test had been marked out of 50 instead of 100; x values and our $\sum xy$ index would be only half as large—even though the degree to which verbal and mathematical performance is related would not have changed.) This difficulty is avoided by measuring both x and y in terms of standard units; that is, both x and y are divided by their observed standard deviations

$$x_i = \frac{X_i - \bar{X}}{s_X}$$

$$y_i = \frac{Y_i - \bar{Y}}{s_Y} \tag{5-2}$$

where, of course

$$s_X^2 = \frac{1}{n-1}\sum(X_i - \bar{X})^2,$$

and (5-3)

$$s_Y^2 = \frac{1}{n-1}\sum(Y_i - \bar{Y})^2$$

This step is shown in Figure 5-1*c*.

Our new index $\sum x_i y_i$ has only one remaining flaw: it is dependent on sample size. (Suppose we observed exactly the same sort of scatter from a sample of double the size; our index would also double, even though the picture of how these variables move together is the same.) To avoid this problem we divide by the sample size n—or rather $(n - 1)$, the divisor in (5-3). This yields the sample correlation coefficient:

$$r = \frac{1}{n - 1} \sum x_i y_i \qquad (5\text{-}4)$$

because $\sum x_i y_i$ dependent on size of sample

r may be expressed in terms of the original observations (X_i, Y_i), by substituting (5-2) and (5-3) into (5-4) and canceling $(n - 1)$:

$$r = \frac{\sum (X_i - \bar{X})(Y_i - \bar{Y})}{\sqrt{\sum (X_i - \bar{X})^2 \sum (Y_i - \bar{Y})^2}} \qquad (5\text{-}5)$$

Example

The data in Table 5-1 is applied to (5-5) to calculate the correlation coefficient between the math and verbal scores of our sample of eight students:

$$r = \frac{654}{\sqrt{(1304)(836)}} = .62 \qquad (5\text{-}6)$$

Some idea of how r behaves is given in Figure 5-2; especially note diagram (*b*). When there is a perfect linear association, the product of the coordinates in every case is postive; thus, their sum (and the resulting coefficient of correlation) is as large as possible. The same argument holds true for the perfect *inverse* relation of Y and X shown in diagram (*d*). This suggests that r has an upper limit of $+1$ and a lower limit of -1. (This is proved in subsection (f) below.)

Finally compare diagrams (*e*) and (*f*). Our calculation of r in either case is zero, because positive products of the coordinates are offset by negative ones. When we examine the two scatters, no relation between X and Y is confirmed in (*e*)—but a strong relation is evident in (*f*); in this case a knowledge of X will tell us a great deal about Y. A zero value for r, therefore, does not imply "no relation." Rather, it means "no *linear* relation." Thus correlation is a measure of *linear relation* only; it is of no use in describing nonlinear relations. This brings us to the next critical question: "In calculating r, what are we assuming about the underlying population?"

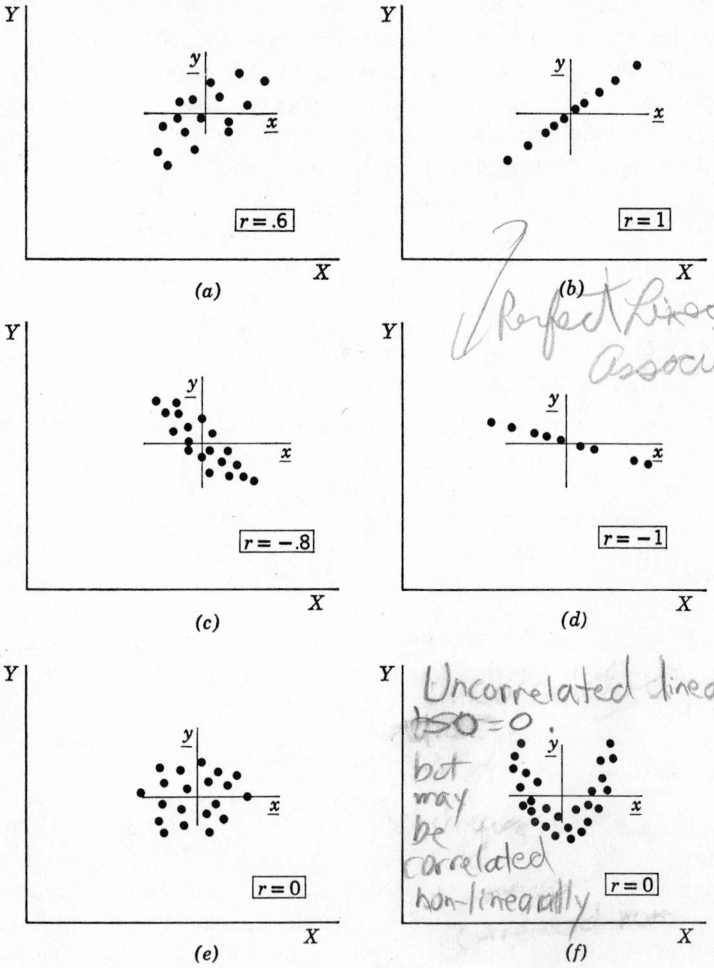

FIG. 5-2 Scatter diagrams and their associated correlation coefficients.

(b) Population Correlation ρ

Before we can draw any statistical inference from our sample statistic r, we must clarify our assumptions about the parent population from which our sample was drawn. In our example, this would be the math and verbal marks scored by *all* college entrants.

This population might appear as in Figure 5-3, except that there would, of course, be many more dots in this scatter, each representing another

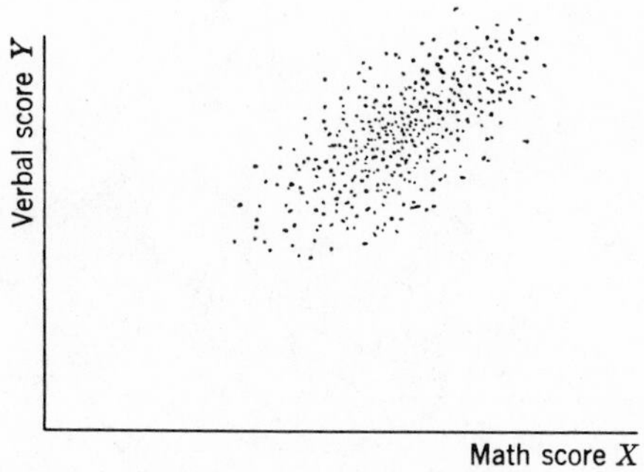

FIG. 5-3 Bivariate population scattergram (math and verbal scores).

student. If we subdivide both X and Y into class intervals, the space in our diagram will be divided up in a checkerboard pattern. From the relative frequency of observations in each of the "squares," the histogram in Figure 5-4 can be constructed. If this histogram is approximated by a smooth surface, the result is the continuous function shown in Figure 5-5, representing the relative frequency, or probability density of any X and Y combination.

A special kind of joint distribution of X and Y is assumed in making statistical inferences in simple correlation analysis—a bivariate normal distribution. Bivariate, because both X and Y are random variables; one is not fixed, as was the fertilizer in Chapter 1. Normal, because the conditional distribution of X or of Y is always normal. Specifically, if we select any Y value (say Y_0) and slice the surface in the X direction, the resulting cross section is normal. Similarly, if we select any X value (say X_0) and slice the surface in the Y direction, the resulting cross section is also normal.

For the population, the correlation coefficient ρ (rho) has the same definition and interpretation as the sample correlation r. Thus, by analogy with (5-4),

$$\rho \stackrel{\Delta}{=} \frac{1}{N}\sum_{i=1}^{N} x_i y_i \tag{5-7a}$$

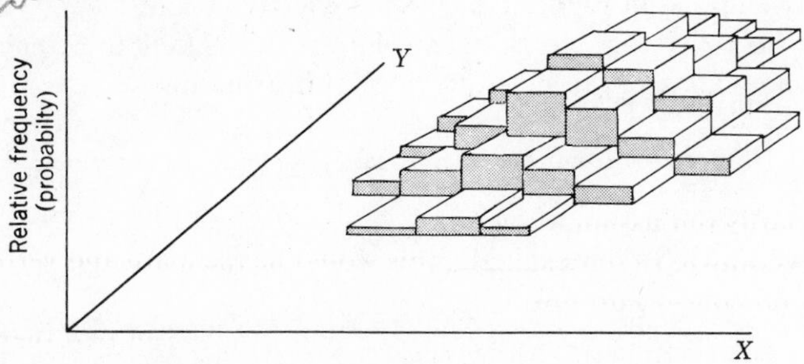

FIG. 5-4 Bivariate population histogram.

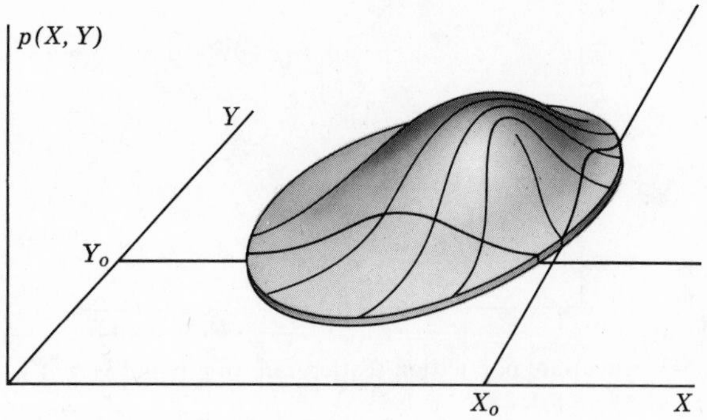

FIG. 5-5. Bivariate normal distribution.

where $\underline{x}_i$, $\underline{y}_i$ are appropriately standardized population values, and N is the population size. This may be written more briefly and precisely[1] as a mathematical expectation

$$\rho \triangleq E(\underline{x}\,\underline{y}) \triangleq E\left(\frac{X - \mu_X}{\sigma_X}\right)\left(\frac{Y - \mu_Y}{\sigma_Y}\right) \tag{5-7b}$$

It is worthwhile pausing briefly to consider the alternative way that the bivariate normal population shown in three dimensions in Figure 5-5 can be graphed in two dimensions. Instead of slicing the surface vertically as we did in that diagram, slice it horizontally as in Figure 5-6*a*. The resulting cross section is an ellipse, representing all X, Y combinations with the same probability density. This "isoprobability" curve is marked "c" in the two dimensional (X, Y) space in Figure 5-6*b*; isoprobability ellipses defined when this surface is sliced horizontally at higher and lower levels are also shown. (Once again, economists will recognize this as the familiar strategy of forcing a three-dimensional function into a two-dimensional space by showing one variable as a set of isoquants.) Special attention should be directed to isoprobability ellipse q in Figure 5-6*b*, which encloses about 85% of the distribution, and is called the "ellipse of concentration."[2] Often, this single curve is used to represent an entire bivariate normal distribution.

[1] Equation (5-7b) represents both the discrete case (5-7a) and the continuous case:

$$\rho \triangleq \int_{\underline{x}}\int_{\underline{y}} \underline{x}\,\underline{y}\,p(\underline{x}, \underline{y})\,d\underline{x}\,d\underline{y} \tag{5-7c}$$

[2] The ellipse of concentration is defined more precisely in H. Cramer, *Mathematical Methods of Statistics*, Princeton, 1946. It has the same first two bivariate moments as the normal distribution that it represents.

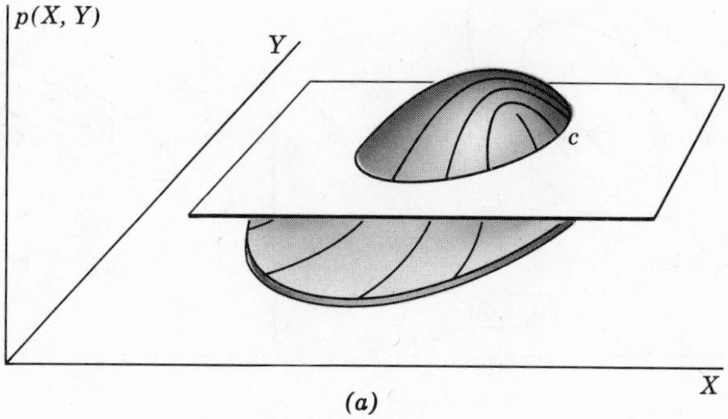

(a)

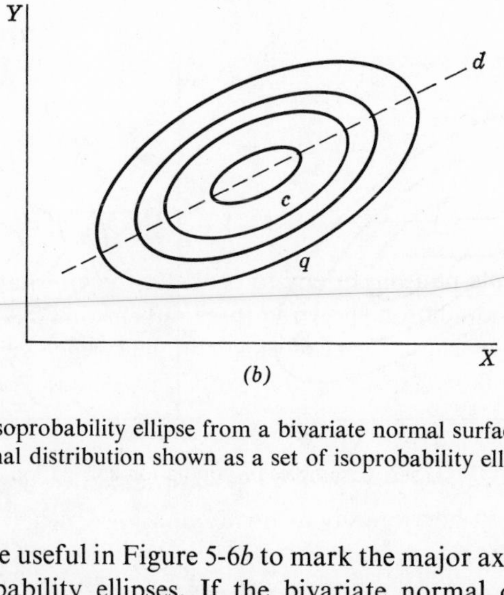

(b)

FIG. 5-6 (*a*) An isoprobability ellipse from a bivariate normal surface. (*b*) The bivariate normal distribution shown as a set of isoprobability ellipses.

It will also be useful in Figure 5-6*b* to mark the major axis (*d*) common to all these isoprobability ellipses. If the bivariate normal distribution concentrates about its major axis, ρ increases. Several examples of populations and their associated correlation coefficients ρ are shown in Figure 5-7.

Provided that the parent population is approximately bivariate normal (as assumed), inferences about the true population correlation ρ can easily be made from a sample correlation r. Whereas ρ is a fixed parameter, its estimator r is a random variable, fluctuating from sample to sample. Figure 5-8 shows how r is distributed around the true ρ, when the sample size $n = 10$.

The distribution of r for a ρ of .7 is shown in this diagram; it is a skewed distribution, with one tail longer than the other. The distribution of r for a ρ of 0 is also shown; this is the only instance in which the distribution of r is symmetric. Clearly, r does not generally have a normal distribution; however

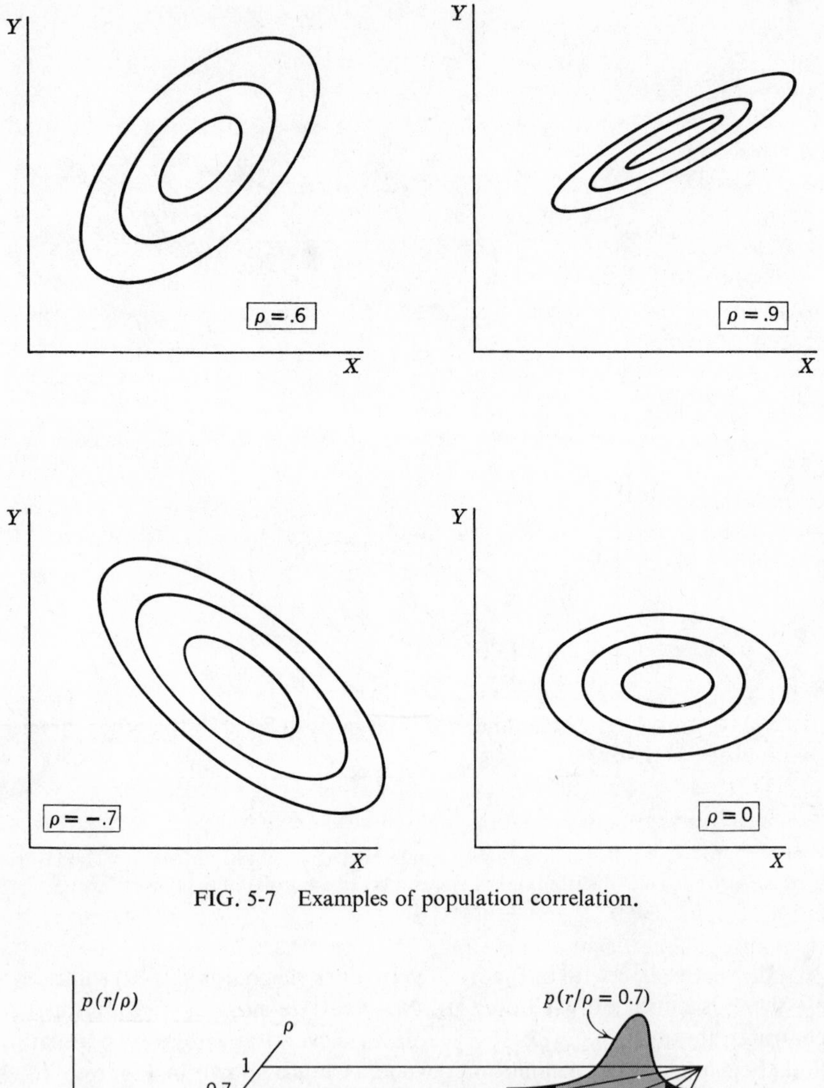

FIG. 5-7 Examples of population correlation.

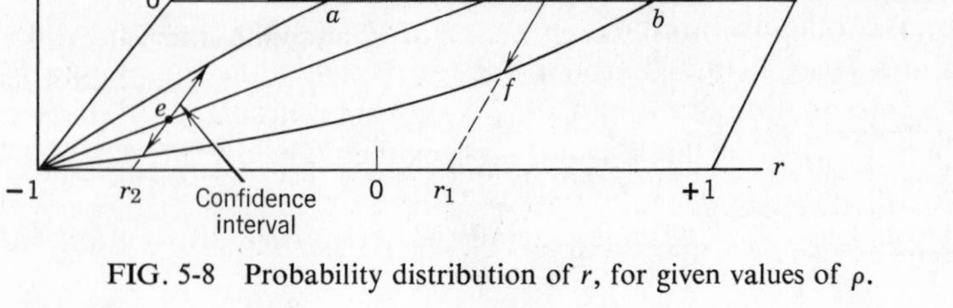

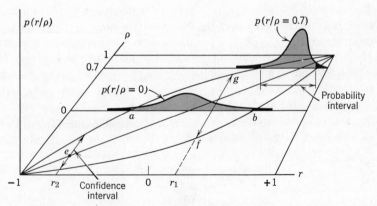

FIG. 5-8 Probability distribution of r, for given values of ρ.

the normal approximation becomes better and better for values of ρ close to 0, and as the sample size increases.[3]

The distribution of r has greater spread if $\rho = 0$ than if $\rho = .7$. Thus r becomes a more accurate estimator of ρ for values of ρ close to $+1$ or -1. In the limit, if the variables are perfectly correlated and $\rho = 1$, all sample combinations of X and Y must lie on a straight line, so that $r = 1$ and is thus an exact estimator.

For each possible value of ρ, such a probability function of r exists. For each function we plot the two critical points (such as a and b) which enclose 95% of its area (i.e., which leave $2\frac{1}{2}$% in each tail). When all such points similar to a and b are joined, the result is the two curves defining a 95% probability band.

This description of how the statistic r is related to the population ρ can, of course, be "turned around" to draw a statistical inference about ρ from an observed sample r. Thus, if we have observed a sample correlation r_1 (e.g., +.2 in our diagram), the 95% confidence interval for ρ is defined by fg, the probability band above r_1, that is, approximately

$$-.5 < \rho < +.7 \tag{5-8}$$

Whereas the probability interval is defined in a horizontal direction (i.e., parallel to the r axis), the confidence interval is defined in the other direction (parallel to the ρ axis).

This is, of course, the same logic we have used in defining confidence intervals before; we will, nevertheless, pause briefly to review, because this is a more general argument than we have previously encountered. Suppose the true value of ρ is 0. Then there is a probability of 95% that a sample r will fall between a and b. *If and only if* it does (e.g., r_1) will the confidence interval we construct bracket the true ρ of 0. We are, therefore, using an estimation procedure that is 95% probable to bracket the true value of ρ, and thus yield a correct statement. But we must recognize the 5% probability that the sample r will fall beyond a or b (e.g., r_2); in this case our interval estimate will not bracket $\rho = 0$, and our conclusion will be wrong. (The student can verify that in the case in which the sample r just barely falls within the probability interval, that is, at either a or b, the resulting confidence interval just barely brackets $\rho = 0$.)

Why is this a more general theory of confidence interval estimation? Among other things, our previous estimates (e.g. of a population β) have

---

[3] r is often transformed into a new variable called "Fisher's z" which is practically normal, and on which hypothesis tests and interval estimates can be constructed. But, as we see directly, there is often a simpler procedure available.

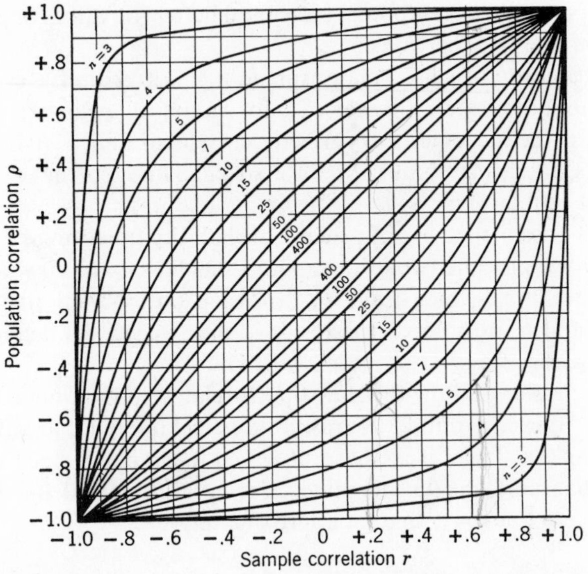

FIG. 5-9 95% confidence bands for correlation ρ in a bivariate normal population, for various sample sizes n. (This chart is reproduced with the permission of Professor E. S. Pearson from F. N. David, *Tables of the Ordinates and Probability Integral of the Distribution of the Correlation Coefficient in Small Samples*, Cambridge University Press, 1938.)

involved constructing a confidence interval symmetrically about our point estimate ($\hat{\beta}$). But in estimating ρ, no such symmetry is generally involved. For example, if our observed sample correlation is r_2, then the confidence interval we construct for ρ is *not* symmetrical about our point estimate e.

Our 95% probability band in Figure 5-8 is set out in Figure 5-9, along with the similar bands appropriate for other sample sizes. This diagram can be used both to construct interval estimates, and equivalently, run two-tailed tests of hypotheses. As an exercise, the student can verify our interval estimate shown for ρ in equation (5-8). He should also note that since this interval includes the hypothesis that $\rho = 0$, this hypothesis cannot be rejected. Also note that this table allows one-sided hypothesis tests at a $2\frac{1}{2}\%$ significance level, by examining the appropriate side of the 95% probability band.

Because of space limitations, we shall concentrate in the balance of this chapter on sample correlations, and ignore the corresponding population correlations. But each time a sample correlation is introduced, it should be recognized that an equivalent population correlation is defined in the same way, and inferences may be made about it from the sample correlation.

PROBLEMS

5-1

Son's Height (Inches)	Father's Height (Inches)
68	64
66	66
72	71
73	70
66	69

From the above random sample of five son and father heights, find
(a) The sample correlation r.
(b) The 95% confidence interval for the population correlation ρ.
(c) At the 5% significance level, can you reject the hypothesis that $\rho = 0$?

⇒5-2 (This problem is designated with an arrow; hence, it is important as an introduction to a section of the text that follows.) From the following sample of student grades:

Student	First Test X	Second Test Y
A	80	90
B	60	70
C	40	40
D	30	40
E	40	60

(a) Calculate r; find a 95% confidence interval for ρ.
(b) Calculate the regression of Y on X, and find a 95% confidence interval for β.
(c) Graph the five data points and the estimated regression line.
(d) At the 5% significance level, can you reject
  (i) the null hypothesis $\rho = 0$?
  (ii) the null hypothesis $\beta = 0$?

(c) Correlation and Regression

If regression and correlation analysis were both applied to the same scatter of math (X) and verbal (Y) scores, how would they be related? Specifically, consider the relation between the estimated correlation r, and the estimated regression slope $\hat{\beta}$. In Problem 1-4b, it was confirmed that

$$\hat{\beta} = b = \frac{\sum xy}{\sum x^2} \tag{5-9}$$

and from (5-5), noting that both x and y are defined as deviations,

$$r = \frac{\sum xy}{\sqrt{\sum x^2}\sqrt{\sum y^2}} \tag{5-10}$$

When (5-9) is divided by (5-10)

$$\frac{\hat{\beta}}{r} = \frac{\sqrt{\sum x^2}\sqrt{\sum y^2}}{\sum x^2} = \sqrt{\frac{\sum y^2}{\sum x^2}} \tag{5-11}$$

If we divide both the numerator and denominator inside the square root sign by $(n - 1)$,

$$\frac{\hat{\beta}}{r} = \sqrt{\frac{\sum y^2/(n-1)}{\sum x^2/(n-1)}} = \frac{s_Y}{s_X} \tag{5-12}$$

or

$$\hat{\beta} = r\frac{s_Y}{s_X} \tag{5-13}$$

This close correspondence of $\hat{\beta}$ and r will play an important role in the argument later. Note that if either r or $\hat{\beta}$ is zero, the other will also be zero.

(d) Explained and Unexplained Variation

In Figure 5-10, we reproduce our sample of math (X) and verbal (Y) scores, along with the fitted regression of Y on X, calculated in a straightforward way from the information set out in Table 5-1. Now, if we wished to predict a student's verbal score (Y) without knowing X, then the best prediction would be the average observed value ($\bar{Y}$). At x_i, it is clear from this diagram that we would make a very large error—namely ($Y_i - \bar{Y}$), the deviation in Y_i from its mean. However, once our regression equation has been calculated, we predict Y to be $\hat{Y}_i$. Note how this reduces our error,

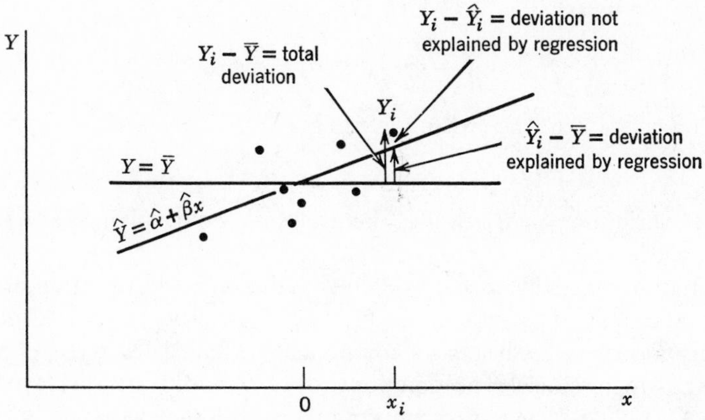

FIG. 5-10 The value of regression in reducing variation in Y.

since $(\hat{Y}_i - \bar{Y})$—a large part of our deviation—is now "explained." This leaves only a relatively small "unexplained" deviation $(Y_i - \hat{Y}_i)$. The total deviation of Y is the sum:

$$(Y_i - \bar{Y}) = (\hat{Y}_i - \bar{Y}) + (Y_i - \hat{Y}_i), \text{ for any } i \tag{5-14}$$

total deviation = explained deviation + unexplained deviation

It follows that

$$\sum (Y_i - \bar{Y}) = \sum (\hat{Y}_i - \bar{Y}) + \sum (Y_i - \hat{Y}_i) \tag{5-15}$$

What is surprising is that this same equality holds true when these deviations are squared,[4] that is,

$$\boxed{\sum (Y_i - \bar{Y})^2 = \sum (\hat{Y}_i - \bar{Y})^2 + \sum (Y_i - \hat{Y}_i)^2} \tag{5-16}$$

total variation = explained variation + unexplained variation

where variation is defined as the sum of squared deviations.

---

[4] For proof, square both sides of (5-14), and sum over all values of i

$$\begin{aligned}\sum (Y_i - \bar{Y})^2 &= \sum [(\hat{Y}_i - \bar{Y}) + (Y_i - \hat{Y}_i)]^2 \\ &= \sum (\hat{Y}_i - \bar{Y})^2 + \sum (Y_i - \hat{Y}_i)^2 + 2\sum (\hat{Y}_i - \bar{Y})(Y_i - \hat{Y}_i)\end{aligned} \tag{5-17}$$

The last term can be rewritten using (5-18)

$$2\hat{\beta} \sum x_i(Y_i - \hat{Y}_i)$$

But this sum vanishes; in fact, it was set equal to zero in equation (1-15) used to estimate our regression line. Thus, the last term in (5-17) disappears, and (5-16) is proved. This same theorem can similarly be proved in the general case of multiple regression.

A further justification of the least squares technique (not mentioned in Chapter 1) is that it results in this useful relation between explained, unexplained, and total variation.

Since we may write, according to Problem 1-4a,

$$(\hat{Y}_i - \overline{Y}) = \hat{y}_i = \hat{\beta} x_i \tag{5-18}$$

it is often convenient to rewrite (5-16) as

$$\sum (Y_i - \overline{Y})^2 = \hat{\beta}^2 \sum x_i^2 + \sum (Y_i - \hat{Y}_i)^2 \tag{5-19}$$

total variation = variation explained by X + unexplained variation

This equation makes clear that explained variation is the variation accounted for by the estimated regression coefficient $\hat{\beta}$. This procedure of decomposing total variation and analysing its components is called "analysis of variance applied to regression." The components of variance are displayed in the ANOVA Table 5-2; it is very important to note that variance is variation divided by degrees of freedom. From this, a null hypothesis test on β may be constructed; the question is whether the ratio of the explained variance to

TABLE 5-2 Analysis of Variance Table for Linear Regression

(a) General

Source of Variation	Variation	Degrees of Freedom (d.f)	Variance
Explained (by regression)	$\sum (\hat{Y}_i - \overline{Y})^2$ or $\hat{\beta}^2 \sum x_i^2$	1	$\dfrac{\hat{\beta}^2 \sum x_i^2}{1}$
Unexplained (residual)	$\sum (Y_i - \hat{Y}_i)^2$	$n - 2$	$s^2 = \dfrac{\sum (Y_i - \hat{Y}_i)^2}{n - 2}$
Total	$\sum (Y_i - \overline{Y})^2$	$n - 1$	

(b) For Sample of Verbal and Math Scores (Table 5-1)

Source of Variation	Variation	Degrees of Freedom (d.f.)	Variance	F
Explained (by regression)	328	1	328	3.87
Unexplained (residual)	508	6	84.7	
Total	836 ✓	7 ✓		

unexplained variance is sufficiently large to reject the hypothesis that Y is unrelated to X. Specifically, a test of the hypothesis

$$H_0: \beta = 0 \tag{5-20}$$

involves forming the ratio

$$F = \frac{\text{variance explained by regression}}{\text{unexplained variance}}$$

$$= \frac{\hat{\beta}^2 \sum x_i^2}{s^2} \tag{5-21}$$

A 5% significance test involves finding the critical F value that leaves 5% of the distribution in the right-hand tail. If the sample F value calculated in (5-21) exceeds this, reject the hypothesis.

We must emphasize that this is just an alternative way of testing the null hypothesis (5-20). The first method—using the t distribution to find the confidence interval for β (as in Section 2-7)—is usually preferable.

Note that the F and t distributions are related, in general, by

$$F = t^2 \tag{5-22}$$

where there is one degree of freedom in the numerator of F. Since the F calculated in (5-21) is just the t^2 of (2-36), the ANOVA F-test of this section is justified.

Example

In Table 5-2b, the ANOVA calculations are presented for our verbal and math score example. (The necessary computational details are shown at the bottom of Table 5-1.) To test $\beta = 0$, (5-21) is evaluated to be

$$F = \frac{328}{84.7} = 3.87 \tag{5-23}$$

Since this falls short of 5.99, the critical 5% point of F (see Appendix Table VII), we do not reject the null hypothesis.

Equivalently, $\beta = 0$ could be tested using (2-36):

$$t = \frac{\hat{\beta}}{s/\sqrt{\sum x_i^2}} = \frac{.50}{9.2/\sqrt{1304}} = 1.97 \tag{5-24}$$

Since this falls short of 2.45, the critical value (leaving a total of 5% in both tails of the t distribution), the null hypothesis is not rejected. Again note that $t^2 = F$ (both for the calculated and for the critical values) so that the same conclusion must follow from both tests.

Alternatively, a 95% confidence interval for β could be constructed from (2-30)

$$\beta = .50 \pm (2.45).254$$

$$= .50 \pm .62 \tag{5-25}$$

This includes the value $\beta = 0$, once more confirming that H_0 cannot be rejected.

(e) Interpretation of Correlation

The variations in Y will now be related to r. It follows from (5-11) that

$$\hat{\beta} = r\sqrt{\frac{\sum y_i^2}{\sum x_i^2}} \tag{5-26}$$

Substituting this value for $\hat{\beta}$ in (5-19)

$$\sum (Y_i - \bar{Y})^2 = r^2 \sum y_i^2 + \sum (Y_i - \hat{Y}_i)^2 \tag{5-27}$$

Noting that $\sum y_i^2$ is by definition $\sum (Y_i - \bar{Y})^2$, the solution for r^2 is

$$\frac{\sum (Y_i - \bar{Y})^2 - \sum (Y_i - \hat{Y}_i)^2}{\sum (Y_i - \bar{Y})^2} = r^2 \tag{5-28}$$

Finally, we can reexpress the numerator by noting (5-16). Thus:

$$\boxed{r^2 = \frac{\sum (\hat{Y}_i - \bar{Y})^2}{\sum (Y_i - \bar{Y})^2} = \frac{\text{explained variation of } Y}{\text{total variation of } Y}} \tag{5-29}$$

This equation provides a clear intuitive interpretation of r^2. (Note that this is the *square* of the correlation coefficient r, and is often called the coefficient of determination.) *It is the proportion of the total variation in Y explained by fitting the regression.* Since the numerator cannot exceed the denominator, the maximum value of the right-hand side of (5-29) is 1. Since the maximum value of r^2 is 1, the limits on r are ± 1. These two limits were illustrated in Figure 5-2: in part (*b*), $r = 1$ and all observations lie on a straight line running uphill; in part (*d*), $r = -1$ and this perfect inverse correlation reflects the fact that all observations lie on a straight line running downhill. In either case, a regression fit will explain all the variation in Y.

When $r = 0$ (and $r^2 = 0$), the explained variation of Y is zero and a regression line explains nothing; that is, the regression line will be parallel to the X axis, with $\hat{\beta} = 0$. Thus $r = 0$ and $\hat{\beta} = 0$ are seen to be equivalent ways of formally stating "no observed linear relation between X and Y."

(f) Regression Analysis Applied to a Bivariate Normal Population

In Table 5-1, a regression was calculated for sample values assumed taken from a bivariate normal population. We now ask: "Is the $\hat{\beta}$ we calculated an estimator of a population β, or does β even exist? For a bivariate normal population, does there exist a true regression line of Y on X?" It will now be shown that the answer is yes.

Our assumed bivariate normal population is shown in Figure 5-11 as a set of isoprobability ellipses, with major axis d. Now consider the straight line $Y = \alpha + \beta X$, defined by joining points of vertical tangency such as P_1 and P_3. Each of these vertical tangents defines a cross-section slice of Y which is normal. Concentrating on the slice through P_1Q_1, for example, we see that the mean of these Y values occurs at the point of tangency P_1; at this point our vertical line touches its highest isoprobability ellipse, and the

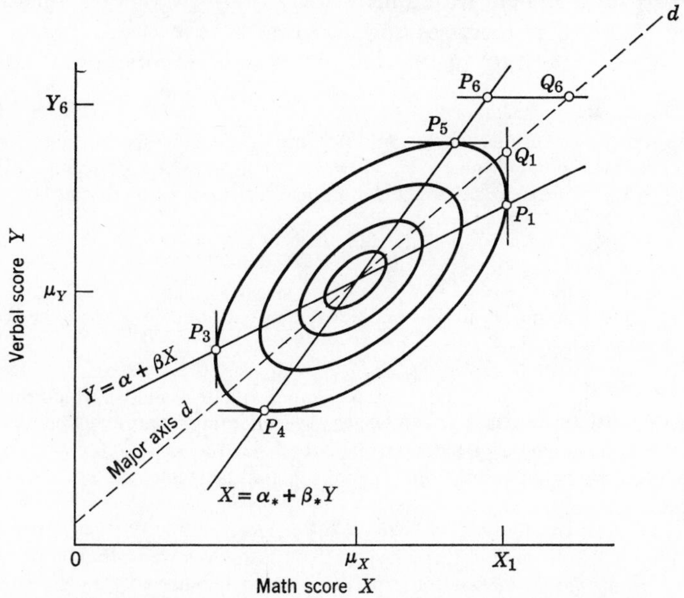

FIG. 5-11 The two regression lines in a bivariate normal population.

highest point on any normal curve is at the mean. Thus, we see that the means of the Y populations lie on the straight line $Y = \alpha + \beta X$. Next, the variance of the Y populations can be shown to be constant.[5] Thus, the assumptions of the *regression* model (2-2) are satisfied by a bivariate normal (*correlation*) population. The line $Y = \alpha + \beta X$ may, therefore, be regarded as a true linear regression of Y on X.

Thus, if we know a student's math score and we wish to predict his verbal score, this regression line would be appropriate, (e.g., if his math score were X_1, we would predict his verbal score to be P_1). It is important to fully understand why we would *not* predict Q_1; that is, we do *not* use the major axis of the ellipse (line d) for prediction, even though this represents "equivalent" performance on the two tests. Since this student is far above average in mathematics, an equivalent verbal score seems too optimistic a prediction. Recall that there is a large random element involved in performance. There are a lot of students who will do well in one exam, but poorly in the other; technically, ρ is less than 1 for this population. Therefore, instead of predicting at Q_1, we are more moderate and predict at P_1—a sort of average[6] of "equivalent" performance Q_1 and "average" performance μ_Y.

This is the origin of the term regression. Whatever a student's score in math, there will be a tendency for his verbal score to "regress" towards mediocrity (i.e., the average).[7] It is evident from Figure 5-11 that this is equally true for a student with a math score below average; in this case, the predicted verbal score regresses upward toward the average.

Another interesting observation is that the correlation coefficient

---

[5] This may seem like a curious conclusion, since in Figure 5-5 the size of each cross-section slice differs depending on the value of X_0. However, each slice $p(X_0, Y)$ must be adjusted by division by $p(X_0)$ in order to define the conditional distribution of Y, that is,

$$p(Y/X_0) = \frac{p(X_0, Y)}{p(X_0)}$$

In fact, this adjustment makes all the conditional distributions of Y "look alike," and thus have the same variance.

[6] P_1 is in fact a weighted average of Q_1 and μ_Y, with weights depending on ρ. Thus, in the limiting case in which $\rho = 1$, X and Y are perfectly correlated, and we would predict Y at Q_1. At the other limit, in which $\rho = 0$, we can learn nothing about likely performance on one test from the result of the other, and we would predict Y at μ_Y. But for all cases between these two limits, we predict using both Q_1 and μ_Y; and the greater the ρ, the more heavily Q_1 is weighted.

[7] The classical case, encountered by Pearson & Lee (*Biometrika*, 1903) involved trying to predict a son's height from his father's height. If the father is a giant, the son is likely to be tall; but there are good reasons for expecting him to be shorter than his father. (For example, how tall was his mother? And his grandparents? And so on.) So the prediction for the son was derived by "regressing" his father's height toward the population average.

between X and Y is unique (i.e. ρ_{XY} is identically ρ_{YX}); but there are two regressions, the regression of Y on X *and* the regression of X on Y. This is immediately evident if we ask how we would predict a student's math score (X) if we knew his verbal score (e.g., Y_6).

Exactly the same argument holds. Equivalent performance (point Q_6 on line d) is a bad predictor; since he has done very well in the verbal test, we would expect him to do less well in math, although still better than average. Thus, the best prediction is P_6 on the line $X = \alpha_* + \beta_* Y$, the regression of X(math) on Y(verbal). This is the direct analogue to our regression of Y on X, but in this case our regression is defined by joining points (P_5, P_4, etc.) of *horizontal*, rather than vertical tangency. Each of these horizontal tangents defines a normal conditional distribution of X, given Y; each of these distributions has the same variance, with its mean lying on this regression line, thus satisfying our conditions of a true regression of X on Y; hence, least squares values $\hat{\alpha}_*$ and $\hat{\beta}_*$ are used to estimate α_* and β_*.

Example

Our sample of eight student's scores shown in Figure 5-1 and Table 5-1 was, by assumption, drawn from a bivariate normal population as shown in Figure 5-11. We have already estimated ρ with

$$r = .62 \qquad \text{(5-6) repeated.}$$

And from Table 5-1, we estimated $Y = \alpha + \beta X$ with

$$\begin{aligned} Y &= 50 + .50x && \text{(5-30)} \\ &= 50 + .50(X - \bar{X}) \\ &= 20 + .50X && \text{(5-31)} \end{aligned}$$

We now estimate $X = \alpha_* + \beta_* Y$. The coefficients in this simple regression of X on Y are calculated in Table 5-1; this involves using the estimating equations (1-13) and (1-16), taking care to interchange X and Y throughout.

Thus

$$\begin{aligned} X &= 60 + .78y && \text{(5-32)} \\ &= 60 + .78(Y - \bar{Y}) \\ &= 21 + .78Y && \text{(5-33)} \end{aligned}$$

The two estimated regressions (5-31) and (5-33) are shown in Figure 5-12. Thus, for example, the predicted verbal score of a student with a math result of 90 is 65; and the predicted math score of a student with a verbal result of 30 is 44.4.

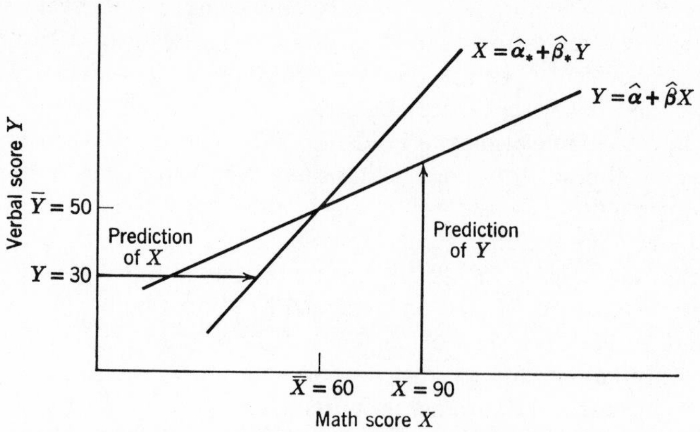

FIG. 5-12 The two regression lines estimated from a sample of verbal and math scores.

(g) When Correlation, When Regression?

Both the standard regression and correlation models require that Y be a random variable. But the two models differ in the assumptions made about X. The regression model makes few assumptions about X, but the more restrictive correlation model of this chapter requires that X be a random variable, having with Y a bivariate normal distribution. We, therefore, conclude that the standard regression model has wider application. It may be used for example to describe the fertilizer-yield problem in Chapter 1 where X was fixed, or the bivariate normal population of X and Y in this chapter; however, the standard correlation model describes only the latter. (It is true that r^2 can be *calculated* even when X is fixed, as an indication of how effectively regression reduces variation; but r cannot be used for inferences about ρ in Figure 5-9.)

In addition, regression answers more interesting questions. Like correlation, it indicates if two variables move together; but it also estimates how. Moreover, it can be shown that a key issue in correlation analysis—the test of the null hypothesis

$$H_0: \rho = 0 \tag{5-34}$$

can be answered directly from regression analysis by testing the equivalent null hypothesis

$$H_0: \beta = 0 \tag{5-35}$$

Thus, rejection of $\beta = 0$ implies rejection of $\rho = 0$, and the conclusion that correlation does exist between X and Y. If this is the only correlation question, then it can be answered by the regression test (5-35), and there is no need to introduce correlation analysis at all.

Since regression answers a broader and more interesting set of questions, (and some correlation questions as well), it becomes the preferred technique; correlation is useful primarily as an aid to understanding it, and as an auxiliary tool.

(h) "Nonsense" Correlations

In interpreting correlation, one must keep firmly in mind that absolutely no claim is made that this necessarily indicates cause and effect. For example, suppose that the correlation of teachers' salaries and the consumption of liquor over a period of years turns out to be .98. This would not prove that teachers drink; nor would it prove that liquor sales increase teachers' salaries. Instead, both variables moved together, because both are influenced by a third variable—long-run growth in national income. If only third factors of this kind could be kept constant—or their effects fully discounted—then correlation would become more meaningful. This is the objective of *partial correlation* in the next section.

Correlations such as the above are often called "nonsense" correlations. It would be more accurate to say that the observed mathematical correlation is real enough, but any naive inference of cause and effect is nonsense. Moreover, it should be recognized that the same charge can also be leveled at the conclusions sometimes drawn from regression analysis. For example, a regression applied to teachers' salaries and liquor sales would also yield a statistically significant $\hat{\beta}$ coefficient. Any inference of cause and effect from this would still be nonsense.

Although correlation and regression cannot be used as *proof* of cause and effect, these techniques are very useful in two ways. First, they may provide *further confirmation* of a relation that theory tells us should exist (e.g., prices depend on wages). Second, they are often helpful in *suggesting* causal relations that were not previously suspected. For example, when cigarette smoking was found to be highly correlated with lung cancer, possible links between the two were investigated further. This included more correlation studies in which third factors were more rigidly controlled, as well as extra-statistical studies such as experiments with animals and chemical analysis.

PROBLEMS

5-3 For the following random sample of five shoes, find:

(a) The proportion of the variation in Y explained by its regression on X.

(b) The proportion unexplained.

(c) Whether Y depends on X, at the 5% significance level. Answer this in three alternate ways using the F test, t test, and a 95% confidence interval.

X = Cost of Shoe	Y = Months of Wear
10	8
15	10
10	6
20	12
20	9

5-4 Suppose a bivariate normal distribution of scores is perfectly symmetric in X and Y, with $\rho = .50$ and with isoprobability ellipses as follows:

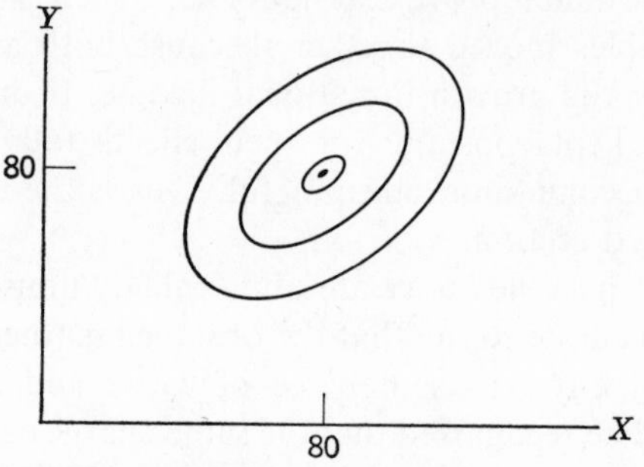

True or False? If false, correct it.

(a) The regression curve of Y on X is

$$Y = 80 + .5(X - 80)$$

(b) The regression line of Y on X has the following graph:

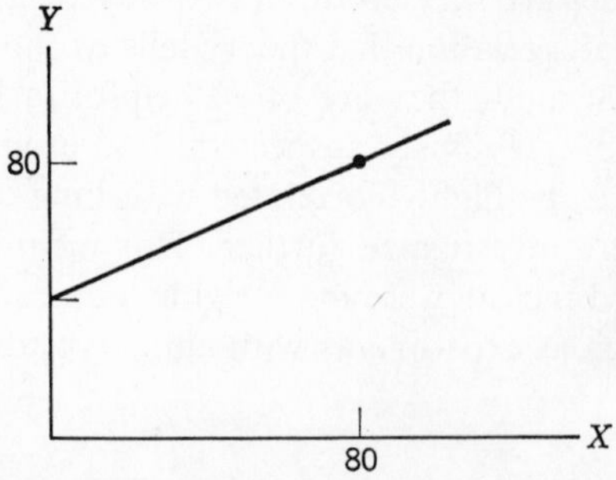

(c) The variance of Y is 1/4 the variance of X.

(d) The proportion of the Y variation explained by X is only 1/4.

(e) Thus, the residual Y values (after fitting X) would have 3/4 the variation of the original Y values.

(f) For a student with a Y score of 70, the predicted X score is also 70.

5-5 Let $\hat{\beta}$ and $\hat{\beta}_*$ be the sample regression slopes of Y on X, and X on Y, for any given scatter of points.
True or False? If false, correct it.

(a) $\hat{\beta} = r \dfrac{s_Y}{s_X}$

(b) $\hat{\beta}_* = r \dfrac{s_X}{s_Y}$

(c) $\hat{\beta}\hat{\beta}_* = r^2$

(d) If $\hat{\beta} > 1$, then $\hat{\beta}_* < 1$ necessarily.

(e) If $\hat{\beta} < 1$, then $\hat{\beta}_* > 1$ necessarily.

5-6 In the following graph of four students' marks, find geometrically (without doing any algebraic calculations):

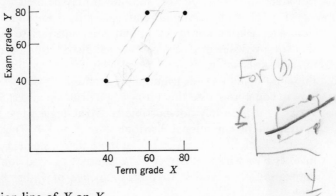

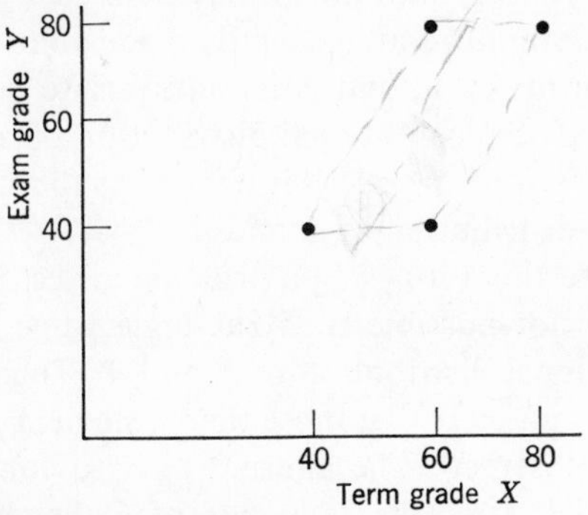

(a) The regression line of Y on X.

(b) The regression line of X on Y.

(c) The correlation r (*Hint:* Problem 5-5c).

(d) The predicted Y-score of a student with X-score of 70.

(e) The predicted X-score of a student with Y-score of 70.

5-2 PARTIAL CORRELATION

As soon as we move from the simple two-variable case to relations that involve more than two variables, complications arise. To illustrate, consider a simple three-variable example: suppose that yield of hay (Y) depends on spring temperature (X) and rainfall (Z).

Following the techniques of Chapter 3 we could fit the following regression plane to a scatter of observations of Y, X, and Z:

$$Y = \hat{\alpha} + \hat{\beta}X + \hat{\gamma}Z \tag{5-36}$$

Recall how we interpreted the multiple regression coefficient: $\hat{\beta}$ estimates how Y is related to X if Z were constant. The partial correlation coefficient $r_{XY.Z}$ is a similar concept. It estimates the degree to which X and Y move together if Z were held constant.

While the previous sections of this chapter correspond to the simple regression analysis of Chapter 2, the partial correlation analysis in this section corresponds to the multiple regression analysis of Chapter 3. Thus, we could embark here on a whole chapter on partial correlation, and a long one at that. However, since we have argued in the previous section that correlation is relatively less important, we confine ourselves to a brief intuitive introduction to this concept, and how it may be used.

The following assumptions are generally made about the parent population. The distribution of X, Y, and Z is multivariate normal. This implies that for any value of Z, the conditional distribution of Y and X is bivariate normal as shown in Figure 5-5. $\rho_{YX.Z}$ is defined as the simple correlation of this conditional joint distribution of X and Y.

In computing its estimator $r_{YX.Z}$ a problem arises. Since Z is a random variable, it is simply not possible to fix a single value Z_0 and sample the corresponding conditional distribution of X and Y. Thus, unless the sample is extremely large, it is unlikely that more than a single Y, X, Z_0 combination involving Z_0 will be observed. The alternative is to compute $r_{YX.Z}$ as the correlation of Y and X after the influence of Z has been removed from each.[8]

The resulting partial correlation $r_{XY.Z}$ can, after considerable manipulation, be expressed as the simple correlation of Y and X (r_{YX}), adjusted by applying the two simple correlations involving Z (namely r_{XZ} and r_{YZ}) as

[8] By the "influence" of Z on Y, we mean the fitted regression of Y on Z:

$$\hat{Y} = \hat{\alpha} + \hat{\beta}Z \tag{5-37}$$

By "removing the influence," we mean subtracting this fitted $\hat{Y}$ from the observed Y value, obtaining the residual deviation:

$$\hat{u} = Y - \hat{Y} = Y - \hat{\alpha} - \hat{\beta}Z \tag{5-38}$$

which is recognized to be that part of Y not explained by Z. Similarly we obtain $\hat{v}$, the residual deviation of X from its fitted value on Z. The partial correlation coefficient $r_{XY \cdot Z}$ is the simple correlation of $\hat{u}$ and $\hat{v}$, thus:

$$r_{XY \cdot Z} = r_{\hat{u}\hat{v}} \tag{5-39}$$

follows:

$$r_{YX.Z} = \frac{r_{YX} - r_{YZ}\, r_{XZ}}{\sqrt{1 - r_{XZ}^2}\sqrt{1 - r_{YZ}^2}} \tag{5-40}$$

This formula shows explicitly that there need be no close correspondence between the partial and simple correlation coefficient; however, in the special case that both X and Y are completely uncorrelated with Z (i.e., $r_{XZ} = r_{YZ} = 0$), then (5-40) reduces to

$$r_{YX.Z} = r_{YX} \tag{5-41}$$

and, as we would expect, the partial and simple correlation coefficients are the same.

It is instructive to note what happens at the other extreme when X becomes perfectly correlated with Z. In this case $r_{YX.Z}$ cannot be calculated since $r_{XZ} = 1$ and the denominator of (5-40) becomes zero as a consequence. This is recognized as the multicollinearity problem of Chapter 3, where the corresponding multiple regression estimate $\hat{\beta}$ could not be defined.

The parallel statistical properties of $\hat{\beta}$ and $r_{YX.Z}$ can be extended further: rejection of the hypothesis that $\beta = 0$ in Chapter 3 is equivalent to rejecting the null hypothesis that $\rho_{YX.Z} = 0$. Again, one reason for emphasizing regression analysis is confirmed: multiple regression will not only answer its own set of questions, but also partial correlation questions as well.

5-3 MULTIPLE CORRELATION

A partial correlation coefficient may be computed for each regressor in a multiple regression. In addition, one single overall index of the value of fitting the multiple regression equation can be defined:

Definition.

> the multiple correlation coefficient R is the simple correlation coefficient of the observed Y and the fitted $\hat{Y}$.

Thus, if our estimated regression is

$$\hat{Y} = \hat{\alpha} + \hat{\beta}X + \hat{\gamma}Z \tag{5-42}$$

then

$$\boxed{R \triangleq r_{Y\hat{Y}}} \tag{5-43}$$

This has all the nice algebraic properties of any simple correlation. In particular, we note (5-29), which takes the form

$$R^2 = \frac{\sum (\hat{Y}_i - \bar{Y})^2}{\sum (Y_i - \bar{Y})^2} = \frac{\text{explained variation of } Y}{\text{total variation of } Y} \tag{5-44}$$

Note that this is identical to r^2 if there is only one regressor (independent variable). If there is more than one regressor, then the numerator represents the variation of Y explained by all of them [with Y estimated from the full multiple regression, e.g. (5-42)]. Thus, as we add additional explanatory variables to our model, by watching how fast R^2 increases we can immediately see in (5-44) how helpful these variables are in improving our explanation of Y. Our conclusion is the same as in simple correlation: one of the major values of calculating R^2 is to clarify how successfully our regression explains the variation in Y.

It remains, finally, to relate this to our t test of multiple regression coefficients, using our example in (3-15). It will be proved (in Chapter 15) that (5-19) can be generalized in the multiple regression case to:

$$\text{total variation} = \text{variation explained by } (X_1 \cdots X_3) + \text{additional variation explained by } X_4 + \text{unexplained variation} \tag{5-45}$$

This can be used to construct the ratio

$$F = \frac{\text{additional variance explained by } X_4}{\text{unexplained variance}} \tag{5-46}$$

A test of significance of this observed value of F is thus seen to be a test of the significance of the (last included) regressor X_4. Similarly, we could construct an observed F ratio for each of the other regressors in turn. These F values translated into t values[9] appear under equation (3-15); it is these t values that are usually used to test the statistical significance of each regressor.

PROBLEMS

5-7 For the data of Problem 3-1 relating saving S to income Y and assets W, find:

(a) r_{SY}, the simple correlation of S and Y.

(b) $r_{SY.W}$, the partial correlation of S and Y, holding W fixed.

(c) R, the multiple correlation of S on Y and W.

(d) The proportion of the variation of S which is explained by

(i) Y alone,

(ii) by Y and W.

---

[9] Using, of course (5-22).

(e) Comparing (a) and (c), is R larger than r in this problem? Is R necessarily always larger than r?

(f) Is r_{SY} or $r_{SY.W}$ a better measure of "how S and Y are related, other things being equal"?

5-8 Repeat Problem 5-7, using the data of Problem 3-2 and substituting N for W throughout.

*5-9 Following Problem 5-7d, find:

(a) The proportion of the variation explained by the addition of W as a regressor.

(b) The proportion of the variation that is unexplained after regression of S on Y and W.

(c) How many degrees of freedom are there for the two components of variation in (a) and (b)?

(d) Using parts (a), (b), and (c), calculate the variance ratio F to test the statistical significance of adding W to the regression model.

(e) Calculate $t = -\sqrt{F}$. Could the t values in an equation such as (3-15) be found in this way?

*5-10 Repeat the steps of Problem 5-9 to find the t value to test the statistical significance of adding Y as a regressor after S is regressed on W.

chapter 6

Serial Correlation and Other Problems

This chapter is devoted to situations in which least squares estimation appears to be in question because the error term does not behave as assumed in (2-4). But it will be evident that with some ingenuity, these problems can often be transformed so that least squares (hereafter referred to as "ordinary least squares" or OLS) is justified after all.

6-1 CHANGING VARIANCE IN THE ERROR (HETEROSCEDASTICITY)

So far, all disturbance terms e_i have been assumed to have the same variance; that is,

$$\sigma_i^2 \text{ is constant} \tag{6-1}$$

When this assumption is unjustified, and the variance of the disturbance is not constant, we have

$$\text{heteroscedasticity: } \sigma_i^2 \text{ is not constant} \tag{6-2}$$

For now, we continue to assume the errors e_i are independent (and hence uncorrelated). An example is shown in the scatter in Figure 6-1; let us suppose that the Y_i have been generated by the simple regression model

$$Y_i = \alpha + \beta X_i + e_i \tag{6-3}$$

satisfying all the standard assumptions cited in Chapter 2, except that the errors are heteroscedastic: as X increases, so does the variance of the error. In such circumstances, "weighted" least squares (WLS) becomes the appropriate estimating technique.

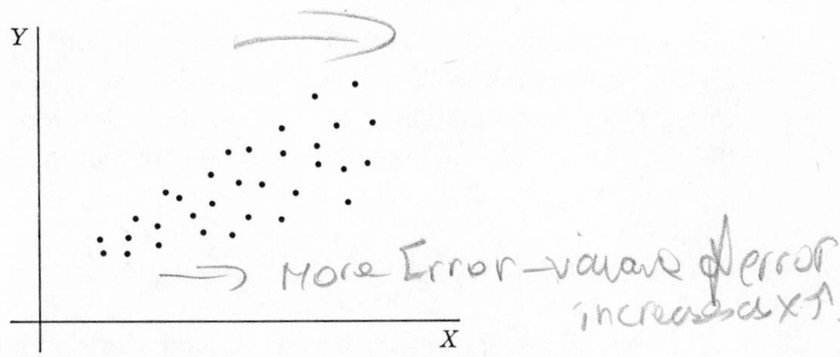

FIG. 6-1 Linear regression scatter when σ_i is proportional to X_i.

(a) Weighted Least Squares (WLS)

The underlying philosophy is simple enough. A greater error occurs in the observations on the right in this diagram; thus, these observations give a less precise indication of where the true regression line lies. Therefore, it is reasonable to pay less attention to these than to the more precise observations on the left. WLS provides a means of fitting a line by deflating the influence of the less precise observations.

Specifically, instead of minimizing the familiar

$$\sum (Y_i - \hat{\alpha} - \hat{\beta}X_i)^2 \tag{6-4}$$

we instead minimize[1]

$$\sum \frac{1}{\sigma_i^2}(Y_i - \hat{\alpha} - \hat{\beta}X_i)^2 \tag{6-5}$$

Thus, the only difference is that each squared deviation is weighted by a factor $1/\sigma_i^2$ before summing. Thus, when disturbance or error tends to be large (i.e., when σ_i^2 is large, as on the right-hand side of Figure 6-1), the weight $1/\sigma_i^2$ is relatively small; consequently these (unreliable) observations are discounted in fitting the line.

---

[1] This criterion is justified by maximum likelihood, assuming normal error. For any hypothetical α and β, the likelihood function of our set of sample observations $Y_1 \cdots Y_n$ is:

$$L = \frac{1}{(2\pi)^{n/2}\prod^{n}\sigma_i} e^{-(1/2)\Sigma(Y_i - \alpha - \beta X_i)^2/\sigma_i^2} \tag{6-6}$$

This likelihood is maximized when the negative exponent is minimized, that is, when we select α and β so that

$$\sum \frac{(Y_i - \alpha - \beta X_i)^2}{\sigma_i^2} \text{ is minimized} \tag{6-7}$$

Thus (6-5) yields MLE.

Formulas for the WLS estimators (corresponding to OLS estimators (1-13) and (1-16)) may be derived by applying the calculus of minimization to (6-5). Since these formulas are awkward to develop (especially if σ_i^2 are unknown), we turn to a common special case that is easily solved.

(b) Special Case

Suppose we are estimating (6-3), and the standard deviation of the disturbance σ_i increases proportionately with X_i. Specifically,

$$\sigma_i = kX_i$$

or

$$\frac{\sigma_i}{X_i} = k \tag{6-8}$$

This is the kind of heteroscedasticity illustrated in Figure 6-1. Then weighted least squares (6-5) requires us to minimize

$$\sum \frac{1}{k^2 X_i^2}(Y_i - \hat{\alpha} - \hat{\beta}X_i)^2 \tag{6-9}$$

Rather than grinding out partial derivatives, we shall develop an easier equivalent solution.

(c) Equivalent Solution, by Transforming the Equation

Equation (6-8) suggests that we should transform the original equation (6-3) by dividing by X_i:

$$\frac{Y_i}{X_i} = \alpha \frac{1}{X_i} + \beta + \frac{e_i}{X_i} \tag{6-10}$$

The disturbance term is now e_i/X_i, and from (6-8) its standard deviation is a constant, k; thus, it is now justified to apply OLS to this transformed equation. Not only is it justified; it is also highly useful, because it will yield results identical to applying WLS to the original equation (6-3). This follows because by definition, OLS on (6-10) involves selecting $\hat{\alpha}$ and $\hat{\beta}$ so as to minimize

$$\sum \left(\frac{Y_i}{X_i} - \hat{\alpha}\frac{1}{X_i} - \hat{\beta}\right)^2 = \sum \left(\frac{Y_i - \hat{\alpha} - \hat{\beta}X_i}{X_i}\right)^2$$

$$= \sum \frac{1}{X_i^2}(Y_i - \hat{\alpha} - \hat{\beta}X_i)^2 \tag{6-11}$$

or, equivalently,[2] to minimize

$$\sum \frac{1}{k^2X_i^2}(Y_i - \hat{\alpha} - \hat{\beta}X_i)^2 \tag{6-12}$$

(6–9) repeated

which is, of course, exactly what we minimized in applying WLS to the original equation.

We are simply finding $\hat{\alpha}$ and $\hat{\beta}$ in a more convenient way:

1. Transform the data by dividing Y_i and 1 by X_i.
2. Regress Y_i/X_i on $1/X_i$ using OLS. The estimated coefficient of $1/X_i$ is $\hat{\alpha}$, and the estimated constant term is $\hat{\beta}$.

PROBLEMS

*6-1

X	Y
2	4
6	7
10	4

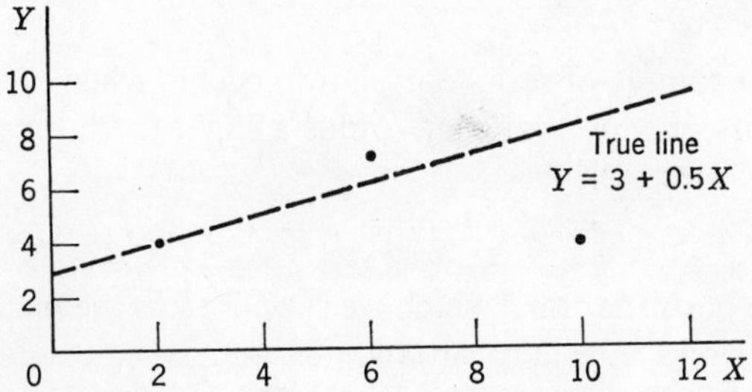

In this figure, suppose the three observations are drawn from three successive normal populations where the standard deviation increases proportionately with X.

(a) Using the transformation illustrated in the text, calculate the WLS estimate of β; then calculate the 90% confidence interval for β.

(b) Calculate the OLS estimate of β, and the subsequent 90% confidence interval.

(c) Comparing (a) and (b):

(i) Which gives an estimate $\hat{\beta}$ closer to the true β?

[2] Whatever minimizes $f(t)$ will also minimize $cf(t)$, where c is any constant.

(ii) Which (if any) gives a valid confidence interval? that is, will 90% of such confidence intervals calculated from many different samples be true?

6-2 SERIAL CORRELATION IN THE ERROR TERM

In this section and the next we consider some of the difficulties that may arise in any analysis involving time series data. Consider the following linear relation, defining the dependence of Y on X in any time period t:

$$Y_t = \alpha + \beta X_t + e_t \tag{6-13}$$

α and β are the parameters to be estimated. e_t is the disturbance term, which is often serially correlated, or autocorrelated. By this, we mean that the error e_t at any time t is correlated with one or more of its previous values (e_{t-1}, e_{t-2}, etc.). Thus, the disturbance term no longer satisfies the independence assumption of the first five chapters, and new methods of regression must be found.

(a) An Example

A simple example of serial correlation occurs when e_t is made up of two components: its previous value e_{t-1}, plus a slight further perturbation; more precisely,

$$e_t = e_{t-1} + v_t \qquad t = 1, 2, 3, \ldots n \tag{6-14}$$

where v_t is the perturbation,[3] which we suppose has the usual characteristics: it has mean 0 and constant variance σ^2 and is independent of the other perturbations v_{t-1}, v_{t-2}, etc. The initial value e_0 also has mean zero, and variance σ_0^2, say. We further assume that the X_t are fixed, or independent of the e_t.

To illustrate equation (6-14), we drew a sample of 20 independent values of v_t from a table of standard normal deviates (Appendix Table II-b). Then, starting with a random $e_0 = 5$ for example, we used equation (6-14) to generate $e_1, e_2, e_3 \cdots e_{20}$ as shown in Figure 6-2. The positive nature of the autocorrelation is clear; e_t tends to be high whenever the previous value e_{t-1} is high. This phenomenon is called "tracking." (There are many examples of tracking series outside of economics. For example, a machine gun fired

[3] "Perturbation" is an awkward term, but we use it in describing v_t in order to clearly distinguish it from our error or residual e_t.

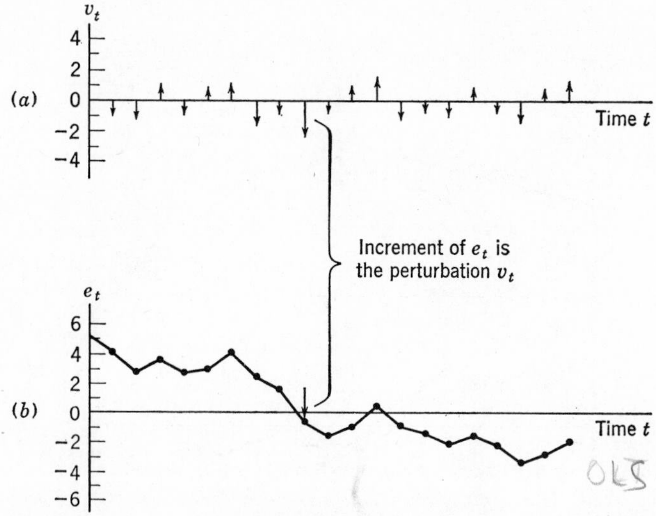

FIG. 6-2 The construction of a serially correlated error term. (*a*) Independent perturbation v_t. (*b*) Generated error: $e_t = e_{t-1} + v_t$.

along a wall will leave a tracking path of bullets; similarly, an aircraft on a bombing run will leave a tracking path of bombs.)

Suppose the true regression line (defined by α and β) is as shown in Figure 6-3*a*. Suppose further that the disturbance terms $e_1, e_2, \ldots$ are those generated in Figure 6-2; they are reproduced in Figure 6-3*b*. Any observed Y (e.g., Y_2) is the sum of its expected value ($\alpha + \beta X_2$) as given by the true regression, plus the corresponding error term (e_2). Since this error e is tracking over time, once our observations are above this true regression, they will tend to stay above it (i.e., once e is positive, it will be more likely to take on a positive value in the following time period). Similarly, whenever e becomes negative, it tends to stay negative.

In Figure 6-3*a* we can immediately see the difficulties that this serial correlation causes, by observing how badly an ordinary regression through this scatter would estimate the true regression.[4] Specifically, in this sample, β would be underestimated and α overestimated. But in another sample we might have observed precisely the opposite pattern of residuals, with e initially taking on negative values, followed by positive ones. In this case, we

[4] To simplify the argument, it has been assumed in Figure 6-3*a* that X is increasing over time regularly. The argument still holds true even if X just tends to increase over time. On the other hand, if X alternates between low and high values, then our analysis would be complicated; in particular, our later conclusion about the efficiency of OLS would have to be modified.

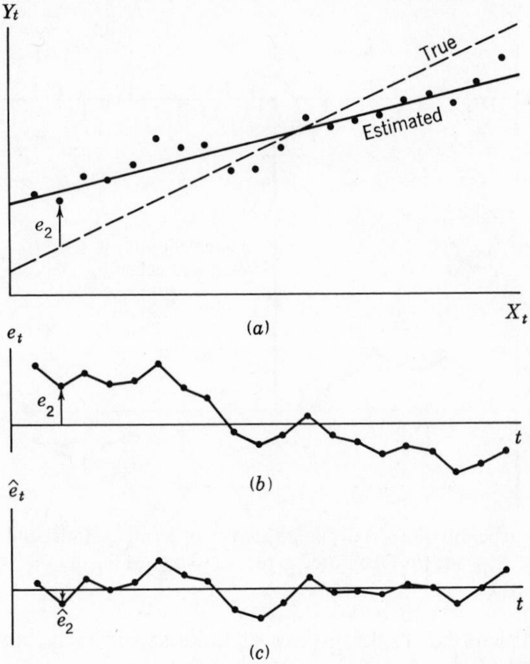

FIG. 6-3 Regression with serially correlated error. (*a*) True and estimated regression lines. (*b*) True error terms. (*c*) Estimated error terms.

would overestimate β and underestimate α. Either of these two types of estimation error seems equally likely; and there are other possibilities as well. Intuitively, it seems that the problem is not bias, since we are as likely to get an overestimate as an underestimate. Rather, the problem is that estimates may be badly wide of the target. Although unbiased, the estimates have a large variance. Nor is this primarily the fault of the least squares estimating procedure; any other estimating procedure (such as fitting by eye) would fit the "tilted" data about the same way. In fact, despite the large variance of its estimators, OLS may still be quite efficient; although there is another more sophisticated technique (Generalized Least Squares) that is more efficient, the improvement it provides over OLS may be quite small.

We are now in a position to draw our first conclusions; (for a more precise development, see Chapter 16):

1. Ordinary least squares estimates $\hat{\alpha}$ and $\hat{\beta}$ are unbiased. (6-15)
2. When the X_t increase regularly, OLS may be relatively efficient (6-16)

However, for an *interval* estimate of β (or α), ordinary least squares (OLS) would be grossly deceptive. There are two reasons for this, which will

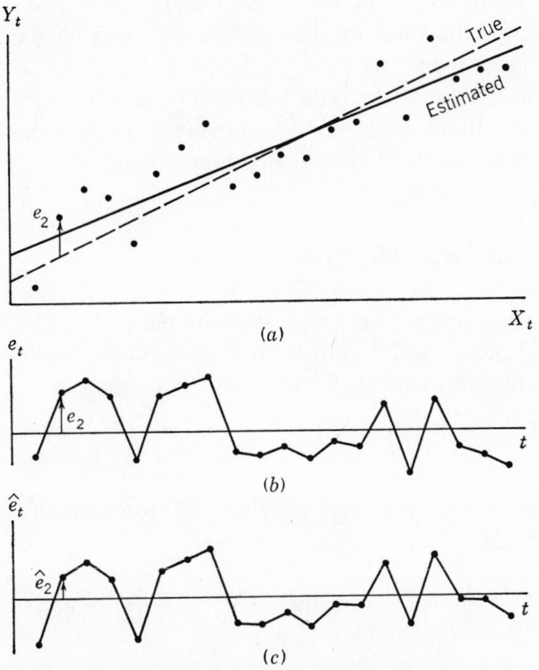

FIG. 6-4 Regression with independent error (yet same variance as in Figure 6-3). (*a*) True and estimated regression lines. (*b*) True error terms. (*c*) Estimated error terms.

be seen in comparing the serial correlation of Figure 6-3 to the case of no serial correlation in Figure 6-4. These two figures are alike in all respects other than the serial correlation; in particular, we emphasize that they have the same variance for the error e_t.

Since Figure 6-4 satisfies the assumptions of OLS, it will provide a valid confidence interval. But this is not so for the serially correlated data of Figure 6-3; in this case the standard confidence interval

$$\beta = \hat{\beta} \pm t_{.025} \frac{s}{\sqrt{\sum x_i^2}} \qquad \text{(6-17)}$$
(2-30) repeated

will err for two reasons:

1. It is likely to be centered at a more erroneous value of $\hat{\beta}$. We might hope that it would allow for this greater error by providing a wider confidence interval.

2. Yet it has a *narrower* confidence interval, because it has a smaller value of s. To establish this, we recall that the variance s^2 is calculated from

the observed residuals $\hat{e}_t$. In the case of serial correlation, the estimated regression line fits the tracking data rather well, leaving the small residuals $\hat{e}_t$ shown in Figure 6-3*c*.

To sum up, because the data is tracking, an OLS estimate of β is, in fact, less reliable. But it appears to the statistician to be *more* reliable because tracking data tends to yield smaller observed residuals.

(b) Regression of First Differences

To estimate β in the linear regression model (6-13), the remedy for this special case of serial correlation is to transform the data so that it does satisfy the assumptions of OLS. Since (6-13) holds true for any time t, it holds for time $(t - 1)$:

$$Y_{t-1} = \alpha + \beta X_{t-1} + e_{t-1} \tag{6-18}$$

We can now examine the change over time of our variables, by subtracting (6-18) from (6-13),

$$(Y_t - Y_{t-1}) = \beta(X_t - X_{t-1}) + (e_t - e_{t-1}) \tag{6-19}$$

Note from (6-14) that

$$e_t - e_{t-1} = v_t$$

and define

$$\left.\begin{aligned} Y_t - Y_{t-1} &\triangleq \Delta Y_t \\ X_t - X_{t-1} &\triangleq \Delta X_t \end{aligned}\right\} \tag{6-20}$$

which are called "first differences." Then (6-19) can be written:

$$\boxed{\Delta Y_t = \beta \Delta X_t + v_t} \tag{6-21}$$

In this form, the error v_t has all the properties assumed in OLS. Thus, β may be validly estimated by OLS regression of ΔY on ΔX.

(c) Generalized Differences

The model for the error term (6-14) may be modified to conform more realistically to economic situations:

$$e_t = \rho e_{t-1} + v_t \tag{6-22}$$

where[5]

$$|\rho| < 1$$

The error e_t is again the sum of two components: its previous value *attenuated* by the factor ρ, plus the further perturbation v_t.

We continue to assume the linear regression model

$$Y_t = \alpha + \beta X_t + e_t \qquad (6\text{-}24)$$

(6-13) repeated

To estimate β, we transform the data in much the same way as before. Equation (6-24) for time $(t - 1)$ is multiplied by ρ:

$$\rho Y_{t-1} = \rho\alpha + \rho\beta X_{t-1} + \rho e_t \qquad (6\text{-}25)$$

Subtracting (6-25) from (6-24)

$$Y_t - \rho Y_{t-1} = \alpha(1 - \rho) + \beta(X_t - \rho X_{t-1}) + (e_t - \rho e_{t-1}) \qquad (6\text{-}26)$$

We define

$$\left.\begin{aligned} Y_t - \rho Y_{t-1} &\triangleq \tau Y_t \\ X_t - \rho X_{t-1} &\triangleq \tau X_t \end{aligned}\right\} \qquad (6\text{-}27)$$

These transformed values are sometimes called "generalized differences." Then (6-26) can be written:

$$\boxed{\tau Y_t = \alpha(1 - \rho) + \beta\tau X_t + v_t} \qquad (6\text{-}28)$$

---

[5] If $\rho = 1$ as in (6-14), a major problem arises because the error becomes "explosive"; that is, the variance of e_t increases infinitely with time. This is proved as follows. We note that

$$\begin{aligned} e_t &= v_t + e_{t-1} \\ &= v_t + (v_{t-1} + e_{t-2}) \\ &\ \ \vdots \\ &= v_t + v_{t-1} + v_{t-2} + \cdots + v_1 + e_0 \end{aligned}$$

Because of independence

$$\begin{aligned} \text{var}\, e_t &= \sigma^2 + \sigma^2 + \cdots + \sigma^2 + \sigma_0^2 \\ &= t\sigma^2 + \sigma_0^2 \to \infty \end{aligned} \qquad (6\text{-}23)$$

This means that if the relation (6-13) has been in operation over many past time periods, any Y that is now observed may be completely dominated by the explosive error e_t; thus, the relation of Y to X in (6-13) cannot be ascertained.

The specification that $|\rho| < 1$ ensures a stationary error, with finite variance independent of t, as given in (16-43).

In this form the error v_t has all the properties required by OLS. Thus, with this transformation we may regress τY_t on τX_t to estimate β.

However, prior to this regression one additional adjustment must be made to the data. The *first* observed values Y_1 and X_1 cannot be transformed by (6-28), since their previous values are not available; instead the appropriate transformation is

$$\left.\begin{aligned} \sqrt{1-\rho^2}\, Y_1 &\triangleq \tau Y_1 \\ \sqrt{1-\rho^2}\, X_1 &\triangleq \tau X_1 \end{aligned}\right\} \tag{6-29}$$

This final adjustment is very important, as shown in Chapter 16-4; without it, the regression (6-28) may be no better than OLS on (6-13), and perhaps not even as good.[6]

To sum up, if ρ is known, the data is transformed by (6-27) and (6-29), with the regression of τY_t on τX_t in (6-28) providing the estimate of β. The problem with this approach, of course, is that ρ is generally not known, and must be estimated.

(d) Statistical Estimation of ρ

For this estimate, equation (6-22) would be ideal if the true residuals e_t could be observed. Since they cannot, we are forced to use the fitted residuals $\hat{e}_t$ that fall out of the OLS regression of Y_t on X_t, as in Figure 6-3*c*. Thus ρ is estimated by applying OLS to

$$\hat{e}_t = \rho \hat{e}_{t-1} + \text{error} \tag{6-30}$$

With this regression, we obtain an estimate r for ρ which is consistent. Yet r has a bias, which can be seen from Figure 6-3*c*. The estimated residuals $\hat{e}_t$ fluctuate around zero more (and hence have a smaller serial correlation) than do the true residuals[7] e_t. Thus r underestimates ρ on the average.

• There are ways to allow for this underestimation; the most popular is *the Durbin-Watson test* for $\rho = 0$, against the alternative $\rho > 0$. Obviously

[6] See Chapter 16-6(c). The transformation (6-29) must be used with some care. It is appropriate if and only if the process (6-22) generating the error has been going on undisturbed for a long time previous to collecting the data. In practice, however, the first observation often is taken just after a war or some other catastrophe, which seriously disturbs the error. In this case, the transformation (6-29) of the first observation should be dropped.

[7] In Figure 6-3*b*, the true residuals e_t cross the zero axis only three times. Yet in Figure 6-3*c* the estimated residuals $\hat{e}_t$ bounce around the zero axis, crossing it eight times. Hence, they appear to have very little serial correlation; in fact, in this respect they behave like the uncorrelated residuals in Figure 6-4*b*, which also cross the zero axis eight times.

H_0 should be rejected when r is high. What is the critical value of r? Durbin and Watson obtained an equivalent test of $\rho = 0$ by using the statistic

$$D = \frac{\sum_{t=2}^{n} (\hat{e}_t - \hat{e}_{t-1})^2}{\sum_{t=1}^{n} \hat{e}_t^2} \approx 2(1 - r) \tag{6-31}$$

which was originally called the "Von Neumann ratio." When r is high, then D is low. Durbin and Watson tabulated the critical value of D, rather than r. This is reproduced in Appendix Table IX. As well as allowing for the bias of r in estimating ρ, Durbin and Watson allowed for the dependence of r upon the configuration of X. Thus, there are two limiting values of D tabulated (D_L and D_U), corresponding to the two most extreme configurations of X; for any other configuration, the critical value of D will be somewhere between D_L and D_U.

(e) Conclusions

When facing time series with an unknown amount of serial correlation, one possible practical procedure is:

1. Apply OLS to (6-13), obtaining estimates $\hat{\alpha}$, $\hat{\beta}$ and also a time series of estimated residuals $\hat{e}_t$; then
2. Estimate ρ from (6-30). If this estimate r is close to 0, there is little evidence that serial correlation is a major problem, and the OLS estimates calculated in 1 can be viewed with considerable confidence.

On the other hand, if r is high, a problem exists and a warning of the possible unreliability of the OLS estimates in 1 is in order. But unfortunately, it may not be possible to come up with anything better. If r is quite high, generalized differencing (6-28) and (6-29) may be applied, substituting r for ρ. But so little is known about the resulting estimates that this becomes a matter of judgment, and there is no guarantee that the result is any better than the OLS result in 1.

Thus, this section has been primarily a theoretical, rather than a practical, exercise; it is justified as an aid to understanding both the estimation problem introduced by serial correlation and the better methods of treating it that hopefully may be introduced in the future.

(f) Further Difficulties

Of the remaining problems, space permits us to mention only a few:

1. The serial correlation of the errors may be of a more complicated

type than (6-22), following the so-called "general autoregressive scheme,"

$$e_t = \rho_1 e_{t-1} + \rho_2 e_{t-2} + \cdots \rho_k e_{t-k} + v_t \tag{6-32}$$

For example, suppose the error e_t depends on its previous *pair* of values, that is,

$$e_t = \rho_1 e_{t-1} + \rho_2 e_{t-2} + v_t \tag{6-33}$$

where v_t has all the usual properties of a residual. As before, our problem is to estimate β in

$$Y_t = \alpha + \beta X_t + e_t \tag{6-34}$$

The treatment here is similar to that used in our earlier, simpler case (6-22). Since (6-34) holds true for any time t, it also holds for $(t - 1)$ and $(t - 2)$:

$$Y_{t-1} = \alpha + \beta X_{t-1} + e_{t-1}$$

$$Y_{t-2} = \alpha + \beta X_{t-2} + e_{t-2} \tag{6-35}$$

Multiplying the first equation by ρ_1 and the second by ρ_2

$$\rho_1 Y_{t-1} = \rho_1 \alpha + \rho_1 \beta X_{t-1} + \rho_1 e_{t-1} \tag{6-36}$$

$$\rho_2 Y_{t-2} = \rho_2 \alpha + \rho_2 \beta X_{t-2} + \rho_2 e_{t-2} \tag{6-37}$$

Subtracting (6-36) and (6-37) from (6-34)

$$Y_t - \rho_1 Y_{t-1} - \rho_2 Y_{t-2} = (1 - \rho_1 - \rho_2)\alpha + \beta(X_t - \rho_1 X_{t-1} - \rho_2 X_{t-2}) + (e_t - \rho_1 e_{t-1} - \rho_2 e_{t-2}) \tag{6-38}$$

If we define

$$\tau Y_t \triangleq Y_t - \rho_1 Y_{t-1} - \rho_2 Y_{t-2} \tag{6-39}$$

$$\tau X_t \triangleq X_t - \rho_1 X_{t-1} - \rho_2 X_{t-2} \tag{6-40}$$

$$\tau \alpha \triangleq (1 - \rho_1 - \rho_2)\alpha \tag{6-41}$$

and noting (6-33), we may rewrite (6-38):

$$\tau Y_t = \tau \alpha + \beta \tau X_t + v_t \tag{6-42}$$

Because v_t has the desirable properties of a residual, τY_t may be regressed on τX_t in (6-42) to estimate β provided ρ_1 and ρ_2 are known beforehand.

If ρ_1 and ρ_2 are not known—as is generally the case—then they must be estimated. An ordinary least squares regression of Y_t on X_t in (6-34) will yield $\hat{e}_t$; then a multiple regression of $\hat{e}_t$ on its previous two values will yield estimates ρ_1 and ρ_2. But again the regression of Y_t on X_t in (6-34) will make the error term appear less autocorrelated than it really is; as before, this introduces a downward bias in the estimates of ρ_1 and ρ_2.

In the simple model in the previous section, we concluded that if ρ is unknown, taking generalized differences is no longer necessarily helpful.

The conclusion remains the same in this more complicated case, if ρ_1 and ρ_2 are not known, but must be estimated; or for that matter, this conclusion still holds if ρ_1 is known, but ρ_2 is not. Thus, the problem of a serially correlated error is seen to involve not only estimating the ρ's, but also knowing how many nonzero ρ's there are (i.e., how many previous values influence e_t).

2. Serial correlation in the errors may occur along with other problems, such as the problem of lagged variables in the next section, which are more serious and take precedence. It is beyond the scope of this text to handle these problems simultaneously.

6-3 LAGGED VARIABLES

(a) Distributed Lags

Now suppose that Y_t is dependent, not only on X_t, but also on previous values of X:

$$Y_t = \alpha + \beta X_t + \beta_1 X_{t-1} + \beta_2 X_{t-2} \cdots + e_t \tag{6-43}$$

An economic example might be dividend payments by a corporation (Y_t); these depend not only on earnings in the present period (X_t), but also on earnings in previous periods.

As it stands (6-43) is very difficult to deal with. There are many regressors; moreover, they may be closely related, with multicollinearity a serious problem. Therefore, it is natural to search for some simplifying assumption. Since distant history has less effect than the present, the coefficients β_j in (6-43) may be expected to decrease over time. Suppose we assume that they decrease exponentially

$$\beta_j = \beta\lambda^j \qquad j = 1, 2, \ldots \tag{6-44}$$

with λ being any value in the range $0 < \lambda < 1$. Now our model can be completely defined by estimating α, β, and λ, rather than the whole string of parameters in (6-43). This can be made more explicit. Using (6-44), the model (6-43) becomes

$$Y_t = \alpha + \beta X_t + \beta\lambda X_{t-1} + \beta\lambda^2 X_{t-2} + \cdots + e_t \tag{6-45}$$

and for the previous t, of course

$$Y_{t-1} = \alpha + \beta X_{t-1} + \beta\lambda X_{t-2} + \beta\lambda^2 X_{t-3} + \cdots + e_{t-1} \tag{6-46}$$

If (6-46) is multiplied by λ, and subtracted from (6-45), most of the terms drop out and we obtain

$$Y_t - \lambda Y_{t-1} = \alpha(1 - \lambda) + \beta X_t + (e_t - \lambda e_{t-1}) \tag{6-47}$$

or

$$\boxed{Y_t = \alpha^* + \lambda Y_{t-1} + \beta X_t + e_t^*} \tag{6-48}$$

where

$$\begin{aligned} \alpha^* &= \alpha(1 - \lambda) \\ e_t^* &= e_t - \lambda e_{t-1} \end{aligned} \tag{6-49}$$

Now a regression of Y_t on Y_{t-1} and X_t in (6-48) will yield the desired estimates of β, λ, and[8] α, if e_t^* is serially uncorrelated.

With the simplifying assumption (6-44), the intractable model (6-43) has been brought into the manageable form (6-48); the number of regressors has been reduced to two, and the problem of multicollinearity largely overcome. Many further difficulties remain, however, if e_t^* is autocorrelated—but possible solutions to this problem are beyond the scope of this book.

*(b) Serial Correlation in the Dependent Variable

Now consider a model[9] where Y depends on its *own* previous value:

$$Y_t = \alpha + \beta Y_{t-1} + e_t \tag{6-50}$$

where e_t are independent, and are normally distributed with mean 0 and variance σ^2; briefly we may write

$$e_t \sim N(0, \sigma^2) \tag{6-51}$$

Possible assumptions other than (6-51) might be more realistically made about the disturbance. For example, e_t may follow the autocorrelated pattern (6-43). Although such a complication can be very serious, we shall not pursue it. The simplifying assumption (6-51) at first seems to fit the model into the theory of Chapter 2. But we must examine more closely one assumption there—equation (2-2) says that all the variables on the left-hand side of the equation (in this case, Y_t, $Y_{t+1}, \ldots$) should be independent. This assumption is obviously violated, since Y_t depends on its previous value, according to (6-50). Therefore, it cannot automatically be concluded that OLS on (6-50) is appropriate.

Specifically, we ask: "Is OLS equivalent to maximum likelihood (MLE)?" The answer is: almost, but not quite. To see why, we show that

---

[8] Of course, the regression will yield an estimate not of α, but of α^*. But from this and the estimate of λ, α is easily estimated from (6-49).

[9] In fact, the model in (6-50) may be viewed as a special case of the model in the preceding section; that is, if in (6-48) $\beta = 0$ and the e_t^* are independent, then this reduces to (6-50).

least squares is the MLE for a model very similar to (6-50): let us change the nature of only the first observation, by assuming that Y_1 is fixed, rather than a random variable determined by its previous value and a disturbance term. With Y_1 fixed, (6-50) shows how Y_1 and e_2 determine Y_2, then Y_2 and e_3 determine Y_3, etc. Thus, the complete set of observations is generated by $Y_1, e_2, e_3, \ldots, e_n$. With Y_1 fixed, the likelihood of observing this set of sample observations is

$$p(e_2, \ldots e_n) = p(e_2)\,p(e_3) \cdots p(e_n)$$

From (6-51)
$$= \prod_{t=2}^{n} \left[\frac{1}{\sqrt{2\pi\sigma^2}} e^{-(1/2\sigma^2)e_t^2} \right]$$

$$= \frac{1}{(\sqrt{2\pi\sigma^2})^{n-1}} e^{-(1/2\sigma^2)\Sigma e_t^2}$$

From (6-50)
$$= \frac{1}{(\sqrt{2\pi\sigma^2})^{n-1}} e^{-(1/2\sigma^2)\Sigma(Y_t - \alpha - \beta Y_{t-1})^2} \tag{6-52}$$

This is maximized where the (negative) exponent is of smallest magnitude; that is, select α and β so that

$$\sum_{t=2}^{n} (Y_t - \hat{\alpha} - \hat{\beta} Y_{t-1})^2 \tag{6-53}$$

is minimized. This is recognized as the least squares estimate.[10]

Thus, if Y_1 were fixed,[11] OLS would be the MLE. The question, therefore, becomes "How important is this restriction that Y_1 is fixed?" For a small sample over a short time period, this may make a difference; but this tends to disappear as sample size increases. Thus, OLS approaches MLE, and is a consistent estimator.

PROBLEMS

6-2 As in Figure 6-2 and equation (6-14), construct a string of ten serially correlated disturbances e_t. (For v_t, use the table of standard normal

---

[10] The student will recognize that this argument is parallel to (2-47) to (2-52). The only difference is that here we consider the likelihood of a set of e's, whereas in (2-47) we considered the likelihood of a set of Y's. In this single equation model, these are just two alternative ways of looking at the same thing.

[11] Or if Y_1 were independent of α, β, and the process generating the errors $e_2, e_3, \ldots e_n$. This example of a peculiar first observation Y_1 is somewhat similar to the peculiar first error e_1 referred to in the footnote to (6-29).

numbers of Appendix Table IIb, rounded. Start with $e_0 = 0$ for simplicity.) By graphing, guess whether your particular string of disturbances causes $\hat{\beta}$ to be an underestimate or overestimate of β.

6-3 (a) Construct a sequence of 20 Y's according to the autoregressive scheme (6-50). Suppose $\alpha = 0$ and $\beta = .8$. For e_t, use the random normal numbers of Appendix Table IIb. Start with $Y_0 = 0$ for simplicity.

(b) Graph the time series Y_t as a function of t.

(c) Graph Y_t versus Y_{t-1}, and draw in by eye the fitted line to estimate β.

(d) What justification would there be for an OLS fit in part (c)?

chapter 7

Simultaneous Equations, and Other Examples of Correlated Regressor and Error

In this chapter, we introduce a new method of estimation—the "covariance" or "instrumental variable" technique. The reader may view this as an annoying digression. However, he should consider it as an investment—and an important one at that, since it will provide one single means of analyzing a whole array of problems taken up in the next three chapters. Our hope is to develop one plot, rather than write a whole set of unconnected short stories.

7-1 A NEW LOOK AT OLS

(a) Covariance Operator

For a moment, let us look back to our calculation of the correlation of X and Y in Chapter 5; this involved three steps:

1. Expressing both X and Y as deviations, x and y.
2. Dividing x by s_X and y by s_Y to obtain the fully standardized x and y.
3. Calculating $\sum xy$ and dividing by $(n - 1)$.

The covariance of X and Y (s_{XY}) is defined in precisely the same way, except that the second step is omitted. Thus,

$$s_{XY} \triangleq \frac{\sum xy}{n - 1}$$

Note — Cov. of X+Y is $\sum xy$

Def'n of covariance (similar to s technique) of X+Y

If we compare this with the correlation coefficient r in (5-4), we confirm that the only difference is that x and y are defined as deviations, rather than the fully standardized $\underline{x}$ and $\underline{y}$. Moreover s_{XY} is zero if r_{XY} is zero.

Now, reconsider the model of Chapter 2,

$$Y = \alpha + \beta X + e \tag{7-1}$$

Taking covariances of X with each of the variables in this equation

$$s_{XY} = \beta s_{XX} + s_{Xe} \tag{7-2}$$

To justify this, we recall that the n sample observations of X and Y are assumed in (7-1) to be generated in the following way:

$$\left.\begin{aligned} Y_1 &= \alpha + \beta X_1 + e_1 \\ Y_2 &= \alpha + \beta X_2 + e_2 \\ &\cdot \\ &\cdot \\ &\cdot \\ Y_n &= \alpha + \beta X_n + e_n \end{aligned}\right\} \tag{7-3}$$

We can easily show[1] that with an appropriate translation of both the X and Y axes, the intercept term disappears and we may write

$$\left.\begin{aligned} y_1 &= \beta x_1 + e_1' \\ y_2 &= \beta x_2 + e_2' \\ &\cdot \\ &\cdot \\ &\cdot \\ y_n &= \beta x_n + e_n' \end{aligned}\right\} \tag{7-6}$$

where the y_i, x_i, and e_i' represent deviations from the sample mean. The first equation may be multiplied by x_1, the second by x_2, and so on:

$$\left.\begin{aligned} x_1 y_1 &= \beta x_1 x_1 + x_1 e_1' \\ x_2 y_2 &= \beta x_2 x_2 + x_2 e_2' \\ &\cdot \\ &\cdot \\ &\cdot \\ x_n y_n &= \beta x_n x_n + x_n e_n' \end{aligned}\right\} \tag{7-7}$$

---

[1] Since

$$Y_i = \alpha + \beta X_i + e_i$$

Taking averages,

$$\bar{Y} = \alpha + \beta \bar{X} + \bar{e}$$

Subtracting

$$y_i = \beta x_i + e_i' \tag{7-4}$$

where

$$e_i' = e_i - \bar{e} \tag{7-5}$$

When we sum all these equations, and divide by $(n - 1)$:

$$\frac{\sum xy}{n-1} = \frac{\beta \sum xx}{n-1} + \frac{\sum xe'}{n-1} \tag{7-8}$$

Recalling from (7-5) that e' is just e expressed as deviations from the mean, (7-8) may be written

$$s_{XY} = \beta s_{XX} + s_{Xe} \qquad \text{(7-2) proved}$$

(b) The OLS Estimate

In order to estimate β, we divide (7-2) by s_{XX} (the variance of X):

$$\frac{s_{XY}}{s_{XX}} = \beta + \frac{s_{Xe}}{s_{XX}} \tag{7-9}$$

From the observations of X and Y, s_{XY} and s_{XX} are easily calculated. But e is unobservable, so that s_{Xe} cannot be evaluated. However, if we can assume that s_{Xe} is small enough to neglect, we obtain the estimator

$$\frac{s_{XY}}{s_{XX}} = \hat{\beta} \tag{7-10}$$

We recognize this[2] as the OLS estimator (1-16).

In Chapter 2, when X was assumed fixed at various levels, the OLS estimator was justified on several grounds. Moreover, in Chapter 2-11 we concluded that even if X is random, so long as it is independent of the error e, the OLS estimator is still justified. Now we see from (7-10) that the OLS estimator is justified under conditions that are even broader; OLS is still a consistent estimator, provided

$$s_{Xe} \xrightarrow{p} 0 \tag{7-11a}$$

while

$$s_{XX} \xrightarrow{p} \text{nonzero} \tag{7-12a}$$

---

[2] Noting that it was called b in Chapter 1, the OLS estimator in (1-16) may be written:

$$\frac{\sum Yx}{\sum x^2}$$

Using Problem 1-4b

$$= \frac{\sum xy}{\sum xx} = \frac{\sum xy/(n-1)}{\sum xx/(n-1)} = \frac{s_{XY}}{s_{XX}}$$

where $\xrightarrow{p}$ means, "approaches in probability as $n \to \infty$," as defined in (2-81a) and (2-81b). To restate verbally:

the sample covariance s_{Xe} asymptotically approaches zero (7-11b)

while s_{XX} approaches a nonzero limit[3] (7-12b)

To keep the argument simple, we shall henceforth always assume that (7-12) is satisfied; this is recognized as the condition that the x's be spread out (i.e., perfect multicollinearity avoided) already discussed in Chapter 3-4.

Turning to condition (7-11), we note that the independence of X and e would, of course, ensure this. In fact, even the (population) uncorrelation of X and e is sufficient; hence, we shall abbreviate (7-11) roughly[4] by saying "X and e are uncorrelated."

7-2 INCONSISTENCY OF OLS WHEN e AND X CORRELATED

(a) Problem

When e is correlated with X, we see from (7-9) that the OLS estimator is no longer consistent, because s_{Xe} no longer approaches zero.

This issue is important enough to illustrate graphically. To be concrete, suppose e and X are positively correlated, as in Figure 7-1. Then positive values of e tend to be associated with positive values of the deviation x. Consequently, the OLS fit will have too large a slope. This bias in $\hat{\beta}$

---

[3] To be precise, we need not require s_{XX} to approach a limit; it is enough that s_{XX} be bounded away from zero (in probability), that is, there exists some fixed number $\delta > 0$ for which

$$\Pr\,(s_{XX} < \delta) \to 0 \quad \text{as } n \to \infty \tag{7-13}$$

[4] The condition (7-11) includes other cases besides the case where a random sample of X and e are drawn from a population with covariance $\sigma_{Xe} = 0$. For example:

1. (7-11) will hold if X_t and e_t are stationary time series, with e_t having zero autocorrelation, and the (population) covariance of X_t and e_t is zero for every t. An example of such "contemporaneously uncorrelated" X_t and e_t is found in Chapter 6-3(b).

2. (7-11) will also hold true even if X_t and e_t are nonstationary time series, just as long as $\sigma_e^2 \to 0$ while σ_X^2 is bounded. This can happen even while X_t and e_t maintain high correlation; according to the definition of ρ,

$$\sigma_{Xe} = \rho_{Xe}\sigma_X\sigma_e \tag{7-14}$$

so that if $\sigma_e \to 0$, it will force $\sigma_{Xe} \to 0$, no matter what ρ_{Xe} may be.

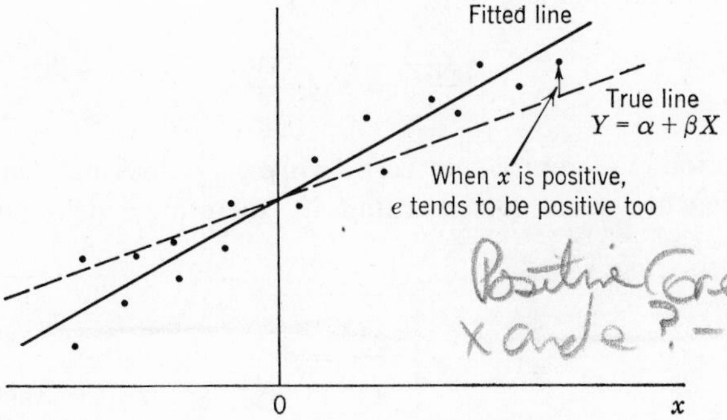

FIG. 7-1 How correlation of e and X makes $\hat{\beta}$ biased and inconsistent.

will persist even with a very large sample (and, in fact, approaches σ_{Xe}/σ_{XX}).

Intuitively, the reason for this inconsistency is clear. In explaining Y, OLS gives as little credit as possible to the error, and as much credit as possible to the regressor. When the error and regressor are correlated, then some of the effect of the error is wrongly attributed to the regressor.

(b) Solution, Using Instrumental Variables (IV)

We have seen that taking covariances with X in (7-2) led us in (7-9) to the OLS estimator, which is inconsistent when X and e are correlated. If there were some random variable Z that is uncorrelated with e, then we might hope to use it instead of X to avoid the inconsistency.

To work this out in detail, we shall call a random variable Z an "instrumental variable" if it satisfies the following two requirements:

(1) Z and e are uncorrelated, or more precisely, (7-15)

$$s_{Ze} \xrightarrow{p} 0$$

(2) Z and X are correlated, or more precisely, (7-16)

$$s_{ZX} \xrightarrow{p} \text{nonzero}$$

If we take covariances of Z with each of the variables in (7-1),

$$s_{ZY} = \beta s_{ZX} + s_{Ze} \tag{7-17}$$

(This may be justified just as (7-2) was justified earlier.)

To obtain an estimate of β, divide by s_{ZX}

$$\frac{s_{ZY}}{s_{ZX}} = \beta + \frac{s_{Ze}}{s_{ZX}}$$

By assumption, s_{Ze} approaches zero, while s_{ZX} does not, so that the last term approaches zero. Disregarding it, therefore, yields the consistent estimator

$$\boxed{\frac{s_{ZY}}{s_{ZX}} = \hat{\beta}} \tag{7-18}$$

OLS is recognized to be just the special case of instrumental variable estimation, when X itself is used as the instrumental variable.

7-3 IV EXTENDED TO MULTIPLE REGRESSION

We illustrate with two regressors, although the case of n regressors is entirely similar. The problem is to estimate the parameters of

$$Y = \beta_0 + \beta_1 X_1 + \beta_2 X_2 + e \tag{7-19}$$

In order to estimate the two unknown slope coefficients β_1 and β_2 we shall need two estimating equations, which in turn requires two instrumental variables Z_1 and Z_2. Each of these two instrumental variables, of course, must satisfy the requirements of (7-15), that is, be uncorrelated with the error e, yet correlated with the regressors. In addition, the instrumental variables should avoid linear dependence among themselves, in order to avoid the problem of multicollinearity.

When we apply the first instrumental variable Z_1, that is, take covariances of Z_1 with the variables of (7-19), we obtain

$$s_{Z_1Y} = \beta_1 s_{Z_1X_1} + \beta_2 s_{Z_1X_2} + s_{Z_1e} \tag{7-20}$$

When the last term (which tends to zero) is dropped

$$s_{Z_1Y} \triangleq \beta_1 s_{Z_1X_1} + \beta_2 s_{Z_1X_2} \tag{7-21}$$

where $\triangleq$ means "equals in the limit." Similarly, by applying the second instrumental variable Z_2 we obtain

$$s_{Z_2Y} \triangleq \beta_1 s_{Z_2X_1} + \beta_2 s_{Z_2X_2} \tag{7-22}$$

These two equations are then solved for the estimators $\hat{\beta}_1$ and $\hat{\beta}_2$. If the constant β_0 needs to be estimated, it can easily be recovered at the end, as shown in Chapter 3, and illustrated again in Section 7-4(b).

It is interesting to note what happens if the regressors X_1 and X_2 themselves are uncorrelated with e. Then they are the best possible instrumental variables, and the estimating equations (7-21) and (7-22) become

$$s_{X_1Y} \mathrel{\hat{=}} \beta_1 s_{X_1X_1} + \beta_2 s_{X_1X_2} \tag{7-23}$$

$$s_{X_2Y} \mathrel{\hat{=}} \beta_1 s_{X_2X_1} + \beta_2 s_{X_2X_2} \tag{7-24}$$

Except for notational changes, these are the OLS estimating equations (3-4); confirming this is left as an exercise. Hence, the IV estimators coincide exactly with the OLS estimators. Thus, we confirm in multiple regression the conclusion first encountered in simple regression: when OLS is valid, it is just a special case of IV.

7-4 SIMULTANEOUS EQUATIONS—THE CONSUMPTION FUNCTION

(a) The Problem

The most common example of correlation between error and regressor occurs when the equation to be estimated is part of a whole system of simultaneous equations. We illustrate in detail with the simplest possible example: a consumption function, embedded in a very simple national income model of two equations

$$C = \alpha + \beta Y + e \tag{7-25}$$

$$Y = C + I \tag{7-26}$$

Equation (7-25) is the standard form of the consumption function that relates consumption C to income Y. The parameters of this function that must be estimated are α (the intercept) and β (the slope, or marginal propensity to consume). The successive values of the error term e are assumed to be independent and identically distributed, with 0 mean and finite variance. Equation (7-26) is an identity, which states that national income is defined as the sum of consumption and investment. Since both sides of this equation are, by definition, equal, no error term appears in this equation. Moreover, the simple equality sign can be replaced by the identity sign ($\equiv$), although in the argument that follows the more familiar equality is used.

An important distinction must be made between two kinds of variables in our system. By assumption, I is an exogenous variable. Since its value is determined *outside* the system of equations, it will often be referred to as "predetermined"; however it should be recognized that a predetermined variable may be either fixed *or* random. The essential point is that its values are determined elsewhere, and are not influenced by C, Y, or e. In particular, we emphasize that

$$I \text{ and } e \text{ are statistically independent} \tag{7-27}$$

On the other hand, Y and C are endogenous variables; their values are determined *within* the model and thus are influenced by I and e. Since there are two equations to determine these two endogenous variables, the model is mathematically complete.[5]

The economist will immediately recognize certain oversimplifications in this model. For example, it describes a closed economy with no government sector. The assumption that I is exogenous is also an oversimplification. In fact, I is likely to depend on C or Y. You are invited to experiment in setting up a three-equation model in Y, C, and I; such a system would involve an additional endogenous variable I and an additional equation relating I to another variable that might more reasonably be regarded as exogenous (e.g., the interest rate). Economic assumptions can be made more realistic in this way by increasing the size of the model—but then its mathematical complexity also increases. Econometricians constantly must make decisions that involve this sort of trade-off between economic realism and mathematical manageability. A larger model would also be more difficult to show geometrically. Since this is our next objective, we shall stick to our original two-equation model.

A diagram will be useful in illustrating the statistical difficulties encountered. To highlight the problems the statistician will face, let us suppose that we have some sort of omniscient knowledge, so that we know the true consumption function $C = \alpha + \beta Y$ as shown in Figure 7-2. And let us watch what happens to the statistician—a mere mortal—who does not have this knowledge but must try to estimate this function by observing only C and Y. Specifically, let us show how badly things will turn out if he estimates α and β by fitting an OLS regression of C on Y. To find the sort of scatter of C and Y he will observe, we must remember that all observations must satisfy both equations (7-25) and (7-26).

Consider (7-25) first. Whenever e takes on a zero value, the observation of C and Y must fall somewhere along the true consumption function $C = \alpha + \beta Y$, shown in Figure 7-2. If e takes on a value greater than zero (say + \$50 billion), then consumption is greater as a consequence, and the observed C, Y combination will fall somewhere along $C = \alpha + \beta Y + 50$. Similarly, if e takes on a value of -50, he will observe a point on the line $C = \alpha + \beta Y - 50$. According to the standard assumptions, e is distributed about a

[5] While there must be as many linear equations as unknowns to yield a unique solution, this is not always sufficient; these equations must also be linearly independent.

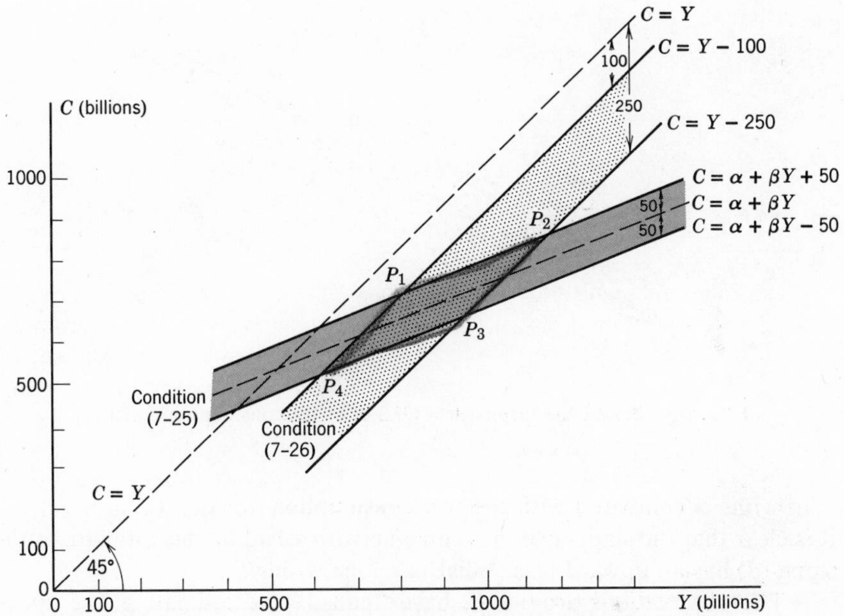

FIG. 7-2 The consumption function, and the scatter of observed points around it.

zero mean. To keep the geometry simple, we further assume that e is equally likely to take on any value between $+50$ and -50. Thus the statistician will observe C and Y falling within this band around the consumption function, shaded in Figure 7-2.

Any observed combination of C and Y must also satisfy (7-26). What does this imply? This condition can be rewritten as

$$C = Y - I$$

If I were zero, then C and Y would be equal, and any observation would fall on the familiar 45° line where $C = Y$. Let us suppose that when I is determined by outside factors it is distributed uniformly through a range of 100 to 250. If $I = 100$, then an observation of C and Y would fall along $C = Y - 100$, which is simply the line lying 100 units below the 45° line. Similarly, when $I = 250$, an observation of C and Y would fall along the line $C = Y - 250$. These two lines define the stippled band within which observations must fall to satisfy (7-26).

Since any observed combination of C and Y must satisfy *both* conditions, all observations will fall within the parallelogram $P_1P_2P_3P_4$. To clarify, this parallelogram of observations is reproduced in Figure 7-3. When the statistician regresses C on Y using OLS, the result is shown as $C = \hat{\alpha} + \hat{\beta}Y$.

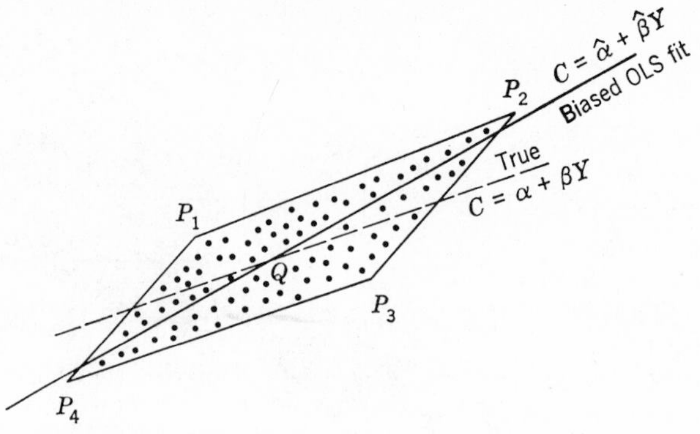

FIG. 7-3 Biased and inconsistent OLS fit of the consumption function.

When this is compared with the true consumption function ($C = \alpha + \beta Y$), it is clear that the statistician has come up with a bad fit; his estimate of the slope ($\hat{\beta}$) has an upward bias. What has gone wrong?

The observations around P_2 have "pulled" the estimating line above the true regression; similarly, the observations around P_4 have pulled the estimating line below the true regression. It is the pull on both ends that has tilted this estimated line. Moreover, increasing sample size will not help to reduce this bias. If the number of observations in this parallelogram is doubled, this bias will remain intact.[6] Hence, OLS is inconsistent.

We notice the similarity of Figures 7-3 and 7-1. In both cases the error term is correlated with the regressor (plotted along the horizontal axis),[7] and causes the inconsistency in OLS.

---

[6] With an increase in sample size, the reliability of $\hat{\beta}$ as an estimator will be increased somewhat, because its variance will decrease toward zero. But its bias will not be reduced.

It is curious that the OLS fit does not pass exactly through the tips of the parallelogram, P_2 and P_4. Although this can be verified computationally, as in Problem 7-1, we shall also give an intuitive reason: the OLS line provides a good fit on *all* observations. To be concrete, suppose we are fitting a line through Q, with slope to be determined. Now if P_2 were the only observation, then the line would be more tilted in order to pass right through P_2. On the other hand, if the vertical slice through P_3 were the only set of observations, then the line would be less tilted; (in fact, the line would be tilted down to the position of the true line $C = \alpha + \beta Y$). As a compromise, the OLS line fits both kinds of observations by passing somewhere between these two extremes.

[7] Although Figure 7-3 makes clear the correlation of e and the regressor Y, it could also have been deduced from the algebra of equation (7-34): as long as $\beta < 1$, the coefficient of e is positive; hence Y and e are positively correlated.

(b) Solution by Instrumental Variable (IV)

We can obtain a consistent estimator of β if we can find an instrumental variable. The exogenous variable I is just what we need, since it satisfies the two requirements of an instrumental variable:

From (7-27), I is uncorrelated with e, and (7-15) is satisfied.

From (7-26), I affects Y, thus the two are correlated and (7-16) is satisfied.

To use I as an instrumental variable involves taking covariances in the consumption function, obtaining

$$s_{IC} = \beta s_{IY} + s_{Ie} \tag{7-28}$$

To estimate β divide by s_{IY}

$$\frac{s_{IC}}{s_{IY}} = \beta + \frac{s_{Ie}}{s_{IY}} \tag{7-29}$$

Since the last term tends to zero, we disregard it to obtain the consistent estimator:

$$\boxed{\frac{s_{IC}}{s_{IY}} = \hat{\beta}} \tag{7-30}$$

If desired, we can derive an estimator of α, the other parameter in the consumption function. Taking expected values of all terms in the consumption function

$$\begin{aligned} E(C) &= \alpha + \beta E(Y) + E(e) \\ &= \alpha + \beta E(Y) \end{aligned} \tag{7-31}$$

A consistent estimator $\hat{\alpha}$ is obtained by substituting consistent estimators for all other terms in (7-31)

$$\bar{C} = \hat{\alpha} + \hat{\beta}\bar{Y}$$

Solving

$$\hat{\alpha} = \bar{C} - \hat{\beta}\bar{Y} \tag{7-32}$$

(c) The Relevance of an Instrumental Variable

It is now appropriate to reconsider in detail the second requirement of the instrumental variable I, namely, correlation with the regressor Y. As is evident in (7-29), the higher the covariance s_{IY}, the smaller will be the term s_{Ie}/s_{IY}, which is the source of estimation error; hence, the better will be the estimator.

As our instrumental variable, therefore, we should look for the most relevant variable (i.e., the instrumental variable most highly correlated with Y) to get the most "statistical leverage." Thus, the exogenous variable I was a natural choice. Rainfall in California or even the price of haircuts in Denver might satisfy the theoretical requirements of an instrumental variable; yet either would lack statistical leverage. To state this mathematically, if California rainfall R were used as an instrumental variable, its correlation with Y would be so small that the error term s_{Re}/s_{RY} would be large. Only in extremely large samples would this ratio settle down to zero. The consistency of $\hat{\beta}$ in huge samples would be cold comfort for an economist faced with a small sample. Or, to look at it from another point of view, suppose the price of haircuts in Denver were alternatively used as an instrumental variable; since this would also involve a large estimating error, the two small-sample estimates of β might vary widely—even though in an infinitely large sample they would coincide.

In view of this relevancy requirement for an instrument, we shall confine ourselves for the rest of the text[8] to a "conservative" instrumental variable approach: hereafter, *we concede as instrumental only those exogenous variables that explicitly appear in our model*—that is, which appear in at least one of the equations in the system.

It is evident that neither this conservative approach, nor any other, entirely overcomes our difficulties; the decision on which variables may be used as instrumental variables is just pushed onto the econometrician who specifies the model, and in particular the exogenous variables that are included. Specification of the model remains arbitrary to a degree, and this gives rise to some arbitrariness in statistical estimation. But this cannot be avoided. It can only be concluded that the first task of specifying the original structure of the model is a very important one, since it involves a prior judgment of which variables are "close to" C and Y, and which variables are relatively "far away."

Finally, it is important to distinguish between the term "instrument" as used by economists, and "instrumental variable" as used by statisticians. "Instruments" refer to variables (such as the interest rate) that are determined by policy makers with a view toward influencing "targets" (such as national income). "Instrumental variable" is a broader term describing *any* predetermined variable (including instruments such as the interest rate, which is determined by the policy maker, and the weather, which is not). While only instruments can be manipulated by the policy maker, all instrumental variables can be used for estimation by the statistician.

[8] With the single exception of Section 7-5(c).

(d) Solution by Indirect Least Squares (ILS)

Indirect Least Squares is another way of deriving consistent estimates, identical to those derived by IV in this example. This alternative method is introduced because it has a very useful economic and statistical interpretation. If the problem with regressing C on Y is that Y is correlated with e, why not regress C on a variable that is not correlated with e, namely I? This is the strategy of ILS.

The first step is to take the original set of equations, called the "*structural form*" and transform it into its "*reduced form*." This means solving the system of equations for the endogenous variables explicitly in terms of the exogenous variables and error terms.

For example, consider the original system (or structural form) (7-25) and (7-26) with structural coefficients (or parameters) α, β, etc. When it is solved for C and Y, the result is the reduced form:

$$C = \left(\frac{\alpha}{1-\beta}\right) + \left(\frac{\beta}{1-\beta}\right)I + \left(\frac{1}{1-\beta}\right)e \tag{7-33}$$

$$Y = \left(\frac{\alpha}{1-\beta}\right) + \left(\frac{1}{1-\beta}\right)I + \left(\frac{1}{1-\beta}\right)e \tag{7-34}$$

the reduced form coefficients of course being $[\alpha/(1-\beta)]$, $[\beta/(1-\beta)]$, etc.

The reduced form equations show explicitly how exogenous investment I affects consumption C and income Y. For example, from (7-34) we see that a \$1 increase in investment causes an increase in income of $1/(1-\beta)$. This reduced form coefficient is recognized as the familiar investment multiplier, with β being the marginal propensity to consume. Similarly, the coefficient of I in (7-33) is the multiplier showing how consumption is affected by a \$1 increase in investment. In general, the reduced form shows the equilibrium impact of a change in any exogenous variable on each endogenous variable. Thus, both the statistician and the economist are interested in the reduced form. The statistician appreciates the advantages of transforming a system into its reduced form as a means of estimating the original structure, as we shall see directly; but even though the original structure may be estimated in some other way, the economist often finds it useful to transform it into its reduced form in order to answer policy questions.

We return to the statistical problem of estimating α and β from (7-33).[9] First, the error term, being just a constant multiple of e, is independent of I

[9] Although we choose to work with equation (7-33), it would be equally valid to work with the other reduced form equation (7-34). In fact, we would arrive at exactly the same estimators.

[according to (7-27)]. Therefore, OLS on this equation yields consistent estimates. That is, an OLS fit of (7-33), namely

$$C = a + bI \tag{7-35}$$

will yield computed coefficients a and b that are consistent estimates of the corresponding reduced form coefficients in (7-33), that is,

$$a \mathrel{\hat{=}} \frac{\alpha}{1-\beta} \tag{7-36}$$

$$b \mathrel{\hat{=}} \frac{\beta}{1-\beta} \tag{7-37}$$

where $\hat{=}$ means "is a consistent estimator of," or "equals in the limit." Our conclusion can be stated even more strongly: since the requirements of OLS are met (in particular, e and I are independent), a and b are Gauss-Markov estimators; thus, they are unbiased, minimum variance estimators.

These two equations (7-36) and (7-37), can be solved for estimates of α and β. For simplicity, we shall confine our attention to β, which can be consistently estimated by solving the last equation (7-37):

$$\hat{\beta} = \frac{b}{1+b} \tag{7-38}$$

This solution can be written more explicitly by noting from Chapter 1 that the OLS estimator b in (7-35) would be

$$b = \frac{s_{IC}}{s_{II}} \tag{7-39}$$

Substituting (7-39) into (7-38)

$$\hat{\beta} = \frac{s_{IC}/s_{II}}{1 + s_{IC}/s_{II}}$$

$$\hat{\beta} = \frac{s_{IC}}{s_{II} + s_{IC}} \tag{7-40}$$

To simplify the denominator, we return to the identity

$$Y = C + I \qquad \text{(7-26) repeated}$$

and take covariances of I with all these variables, obtaining

$$s_{IY} = s_{IC} + s_{II} \tag{7-41}$$

When this is substituted into (7-40), we obtain

$$\hat{\beta} = \frac{s_{IC}}{s_{IY}} \tag{7-42}$$

As promised, this is exactly the same as the IV estimator (7-30). This is not just a coincidence. If we had taken the trouble to estimate the other parameter α, the ILS estimator would again coincide with the IV estimator. This, in fact, is always true: whenever ILS is feasible,[10] it will coincide with IV.

A final warning: although b is an unbiased estimator of $\beta/(1-\beta)$ in (7-37), $b/(1+b)$ in (7-38) is a biased estimator of β, because unbiasedness is preserved only by linear transformations.[11] However, consistency is preserved, so $\hat{\beta}$ is a consistent estimator and, therefore, *asymptotically* unbiased.

To recapitulate: ILS involves transforming the original structure (7-25) and (7-26) into its reduced form (7-33) and (7-34). OLS estimation of the parameters of the reduced form (such as $[\beta/(1-\beta)]$) is fully justified, and provides unbiased, consistent estimates. When these are transformed back into estimates of the structural parameters (such as β), the resulting estimates are consistent, despite small-sample bias. It is not surprising that these estimates coincide with the IV estimates, since the same exogenous variable I is used as the regressor in ILS and the instrumental variable in IV.

PROBLEMS

7-1 Suppose that the true consumption function is $C = 10 + .6Y$ and the following combinations of C, Y, and I have been observed:

C	Y	I
46	60	14
31	45	14
61	75	14
58	80	22
43	65	22
73	95	22
70	100	30
55	85	30
85	115	30

[10] Cases where ILS estimation is not feasible are considered in the next chapter.

[11] To illustrate: since $6 + 2b$ is a linear transformation of b [and b is an unbiased estimator of $\beta/(1-\beta)$], it follows that $6 + 2b$ is an unbiased estimator of $6 + 2[\beta/(1-\beta)]$. On the other hand, $b/(1+b)$ is *not* a linear transformation of b, hence $b/(1+b)$ is a biased estimator of $[\beta/(1-\beta)]/\{1 + [\beta/(1-\beta)]\} = \beta$.

(a) Graph the true consumption function and the scatter of C and Y observations.

(b) Regress C on Y using OLS, and graph the estimated consumption function. Is it consistent?

(c) Estimate the consumption function:

(i) Using I as an instrumental variable (IV). Graph this estimated consumption function. Is it consistent?

(ii) Using indirect least squares (ILS).

(d) Explain why this small sample is a lucky one. What would you expect if your small sample is less lucky?

*7-2 Prove the footnote preceding equation (7-35).

7-3 To estimate the consumption model (7-25), suppose the covariance matrix (or table) of Y, C, I has been computed for a sample as follows:

$$\begin{bmatrix} s_{YY} & s_{CY} & s_{IY} \\ s_{YC} & s_{CC} & s_{IC} \\ s_{YI} & s_{CI} & s_{II} \end{bmatrix} = \begin{bmatrix} 130 & 100 & 30 \\ 100 & 80 & 20 \\ 30 & 20 & 10 \end{bmatrix}$$

(a) Find consistent estimates for the marginal propensity to consume, and the investment multiplier.

(b) Estimate the marginal propensity to consume by applying OLS to the consumption function directly. Is this estimate consistent? Using a diagram, explain this to an economics student whose statistics is limited to understanding OLS.

(c) Which of the above estimators are:

(i) Biased asymptotically?

(ii) Biased (even slightly) in small samples?

0411

*7-5 ERRORS IN BOTH VARIABLES

While systems of simultaneous equations provide the commonest example of correlation between regressor and error, we consider another important example in this section.

(a) The Problem

Since this section has nothing to do with simultaneous equations, consider the simple single-equation model

$$Y = \alpha + \beta X + e \tag{7-43}$$

Until now it has been assumed that there is a disturbance term e associated with only Y, the dependent variable or "regressand." In our previous analysis, e has included both error in measuring Y, and any stochastic element in Y. At the same time, it has been assumed that there is no such disturbance associated with the regressor X. In many economic models this must be questioned. X as well as Y is often measured with error; moreover, a stochastic disturbance in X must often be explicitly recognized.

When X, as well as Y, is subject to error, how does this complicate our problem of estimating the relation of Y to X? If the exactly related values are denoted by X_0 and Y_0, then we are supposing

$$Y_0 = \alpha + \beta X_0 \tag{7-44}$$

where α and β are the parameters to be estimated.[12] As before, we continue to assume that the Y_0 value is perturbed by an error e, yielding the measured value

$$Y = Y_0 + e \tag{7-45}$$

The new feature is that the X_0 value is also perturbed,[13] by an error v, yielding the measured value

$$X = X_0 + v \tag{7-46}$$

Substituting (7-45) and (7-46) into (7-44):

$$\begin{aligned} (Y - e) &= \alpha + \beta(X - v) \\ Y &= \alpha + \beta X + (e - \beta v) \end{aligned} \tag{7-47}$$

The problem is to consistently estimate α and β, in terms of the measured variables X and Y.

Before developing an estimation technique when both variables are in error, consider the two limiting cases in which only one variable is subject to error.

---

[12] It is very important to realize that this discussion is concerned with *estimation of parameters*. If we are only concerned with *prediction* (e.g., of Y from X), then there is no need to go to all this trouble. The OLS estimator of Y on X would be the optimal predictor.

[13] There are two possible interpretations of X_0. If, as frequently occurs, Y_0 is exactly related to whatever value the regressor takes (including stochastic element), then any stochastic element is included in X_0 in (7-44), and hence is not included in v in (7-46); v in this case represents only measurement error, and is often negligibly small.

But in some instances, Y_0 may be exactly related to the regressor *exclusive* of stochastic disturbances. Then X_0 is defined to exclude stochastic disturbances, which are therefore included (along with measurement error) in v. For example, in Friedman's permanent income model, permanent income is related to permanent consumption. Although he argues that this relation is precise, neither of these variables can be measured. When, as the best alternative, total income and total consumption are measured as proxies, *each* includes a stochastic disturbance (which he refers to as "transient" income and "transient" consumption).

The familiar case occurs when only Y is subject to error, and v, the error in X, is zero; then equation (7-47) reduces to the familiar model of Chapter 2:

$$Y = \alpha + \beta X + e \tag{7-48}$$

and an OLS regression of Y on X is the appropriate way of estimating α and β.

At the other extreme, suppose that only X is subject to error. Then e (the error in Y) is zero, with neither a measurement nor stochastic error in Y; then (7-47) becomes

$$Y = \alpha + \beta(X - v) \tag{7-49}$$

Or

$$X = -\frac{\alpha}{\beta} + \frac{1}{\beta} Y + v$$

which may be written

$$X = \alpha_* + \beta_* Y + v$$

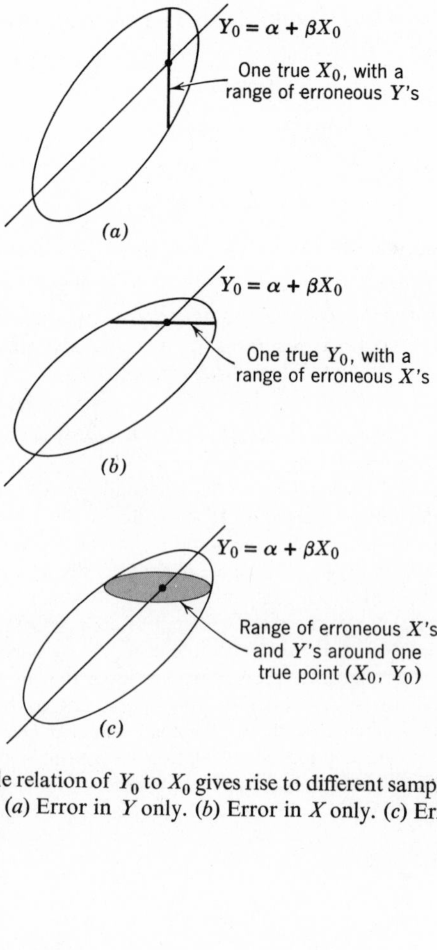

FIG. 7-4 How a single relation of Y_0 to X_0 gives rise to different sample scatters, depending on errors in variables. (*a*) Error in Y only. (*b*) Error in X only. (*c*) Error in both variables.

In this case, an OLS regression of X on Y is the appropriate way of estimating α_* and β_*, thence estimating α and β.

These conclusions are reviewed in Figure 7-4, which shows how a single true relation of Y_0 to X_0 may generate quite different sample scatters. In Figure 7-4*a*, the error is in Y alone, and a regression of Y on X is required. On the other hand, in Figure 7-4*b*, the error is in X alone; it is easy to see that a regression of Y on X fitted to this scatter would be inappropriate, since it would underestimate[14] β. Instead, a regression of X on Y is required.

Finally, the general case in which both variables are in error is shown in Figure 7-4*c*; intuitively, it follows from parts *a* and *b* that the greater the error in Y relative to the error in X, the closer will the OLS regression of Y on X lie to the true line; and the greater the error in X relative to the error in Y, the closer will the OLS regression of X on Y lie to the true line. Clearly, if we have prior knowledge of the ratio of these errors (σ_e^2/σ_v^2, which we denote as λ), then we can use this (in subsection (b) below) in order to obtain the proper compromise between the two OLS regressions.

(b) Solution when the Error Ratio is Known

Suppose we know the ratio of error variances

$$\lambda = \frac{\sigma_e^2}{\sigma_v^2} \tag{7-50}$$

We emphasize, as in the footnote immediately following (7-45), that e includes both stochastic and measurement errors in Y; but v may be only measurement error in X, depending on how Y is judged to depend on X. We assume further that

$$e \text{ and } v \text{ are uncorrelated} \tag{7-51}$$

and

$$e \text{ and } v \text{ are each uncorrelated with the true values } X_0 \text{ and } Y_0 \tag{7-52}$$

It is not necessary to assume that e and v are normal.

To derive a consistent estimate of β, first take covariances of X with all variables in (7-47)

$$s_{XY} = \beta s_{XX} + s_{X(e-\beta v)} \tag{7-53}$$

Now the sample covariance is approximately equal (in the limit, exactly equal) to the population covariance, σ, that is,

$$s_{X(e-\beta v)} \hat{=} \sigma_{X(e-\beta v)} \tag{7-54}$$

[14] As an exercise, sketch in freehand a fitted regression of Y on X, observing that its slope is substantially less than the true slope β. Then in Figure 7-4*c*, sketch in the two OLS fits, noting how both are off target.

From (7-46)

$$s_{X(e-\beta v)} \mathrel{\hat{=}} \sigma_{(X_0+v)(e-\beta v)}$$

From (7-51) and (7-52)

$$\mathrel{\hat{=}} \sigma_{v(-\beta v)}$$

$$\mathrel{\hat{=}} -\beta\sigma_{vv}$$

Thus

$$s_{X(e-\beta v)} \mathrel{\hat{=}} -\beta\sigma_v^2 \tag{7-55}$$

When (7-55) is substituted into (7-53)

$$s_{XY} \mathrel{\hat{=}} \beta s_{XX} - \beta\sigma_v^2 \tag{7-56}$$

Here we explicitly see how the correlation of the error with the regressor has produced the extra term $\beta\sigma_v^2$; this explicitly confirms that OLS regression of Y on X (which ignores this last term) would produce a biased estimator of β. To correctly estimate β, we need a second estimating equation because there are two unknowns, β and σ_v^2. We therefore take covariances of Y with all variables in (7-47), obtaining

$$s_{YY} \mathrel{\hat{=}} \beta s_{XY} + s_{Y(e-\beta v)} \tag{7-57}$$

Just as (7-53) was reduced to (7-56), we can now reduce (7-57) to

$$s_{YY} \mathrel{\hat{=}} \beta s_{XY} + \sigma_e^2 \tag{7-58}$$

From (7-50)

$$s_{YY} \mathrel{\hat{=}} \beta s_{XY} + \lambda\sigma_v^2 \tag{7-59}$$

Equations (7-56) and (7-59) are our two estimating equations in two unknowns β and σ_v^2. (We now see why λ must be known; if it is not, we are stuck with (7-56) and (7-58)—two equations in three unknowns, with no solution.) Before proceeding, we pause to recall the special cases diagrammed in Figure 7-4.

1. If $\sigma_v^2 = 0$ (no error in X), then $\lambda = \infty$. In this case, (7-56) can be used alone to estimate β, since the last term disappears. The solution corresponds, as expected, to the OLS regression of Y on X

$$\hat{\beta} = \frac{s_{XY}}{s_{XX}}$$

2. If $\sigma_e^2 = 0$ (no error in Y), $\lambda = 0$ and (7-59) can be used alone to estimate β, since its last term disappears. As an exercise, it may be shown that the solution

$$\hat{\beta} = \frac{s_{YY}}{s_{XY}}$$

corresponds, as expected, to the OLS regression of X on Y.

3. For intermediate values of λ, it may be proved that intermediate values of $\hat{\beta}$ are obtained. Thus, an economist who doesn't know λ may at least be confident that the correct solution for β is bounded by the above two estimates. An important case occurs when the stochastic error in Y dominates the other errors in (7-50); in this case, λ becomes very large, with the appropriate estimate approaching the OLS regression of Y on X given in 1.

If λ is known, the only problem is to solve (7-56) and (7-59)—our two estimating equations in two unknowns (β and σ_v^2). Unfortunately, they are nonlinear, so their solution will be a little complicated. Let us eliminate σ_v^2 (the nuisance unknown) by first solving (7-59)

$$\sigma_v^2 \mathrel{\hat{=}} \frac{1}{\lambda}(s_{YY} - \beta s_{XY}) \tag{7-60}$$

When this is substituted into (7-56)

$$s_{XY} \mathrel{\hat{=}} \beta s_{XX} - \frac{\beta}{\lambda}(s_{YY} - \beta s_{XY}) \tag{7-61}$$

which is a quadratic equation in β. By multiplying through by λ and collecting terms, we find

$$-s_{XY}\beta^2 + (s_{YY} - \lambda s_{XX})\beta + \lambda s_{XY} \mathrel{\hat{=}} 0$$

Finally, dividing by $-s_{XY}$,

$$\beta^2 - \left(\frac{s_{YY} - \lambda s_{XX}}{s_{XY}}\right)\beta - \lambda \mathrel{\hat{=}} 0$$

or

$$\beta^2 - (2\theta)\beta - \lambda \mathrel{\hat{=}} 0 \tag{7-62}$$

where

$$\theta = \frac{s_{YY} - \lambda s_{XX}}{2s_{XY}} \tag{7-63}$$

The solution to (7-62) is given by the standard quadratic formula,[15]

$$\boxed{\hat{\beta} = \theta \pm \sqrt{\theta^2 + \lambda}} \tag{7-64}$$

Which of the two solutions is appropriate? Since λ is positive, $\sqrt{\theta^2 + \lambda}$ is greater, in absolute value, than θ. Thus, the selection of the $\pm$ sign in (7-64)

[15] With the additional assumption that the errors e and v are normal, the MLE solution coincides with (7-64). (For details, see J. Johnston, *Econometric Methods*, New York: McGraw-Hill, 1963, pp. 152–154, noting that he uses a different notation for our λ and s_{XY}.)

determines the sign of $\hat{\beta}$. This indicates choosing the $\pm$ sign to agree with the sign of s_{XY}. For example, when s_{XY} is positive, that is, a positive relationship is observed between X and Y, then $\hat{\beta}$ is chosen to be positive too.

(c) Solution by IV

In the fortunate circumstance that an instrumental variable Z is available, this will provide an alternative, simpler solution.

Specifically, we suppose that Z is uncorrelated with both errors e and v. Then it will be uncorrelated with the error term of (7-47). Assuming as required that Z is correlated with X, it then provides a consistent estimator of β; taking covariances of all terms in (7-47) with Z yields

$$\hat{\beta} = \frac{s_{ZY}}{s_{ZX}} \tag{7-65}$$

Once an adequate instrumental variable Z has been found, this is a very simple, straightforward method. The problem is finding an instrumental variable that is not only free of correlation with e and v, but also highly correlated with X (if its correlation with X is low, then the denominator of (7-65) will be close to zero, and the resulting estimate will be unstable). There may also, of course, be the problem of selecting between several equally good (or bad) instruments, with the resulting estimate being highly sensitive to the one arbitrarily chosen. In summary, all our earlier reservations against instrumental variables apply here. Their major justification is consistency; but this is a large sample property that may provide little comfort in small sample estimation. If only questionable instrumental variables are available (with low correlation with X), then it may be better to use the technique of subsection (b), using an arbitrary but reasonable value for λ. At least this technique guarantees an estimate bounded by the regressions of X on Y and Y on X, whereas IV does not.

PROBLEMS

*7-4 In Figure 7-4, it was shown how one true relation of Y to X gave rise to three different observed scatters. Draw a diagram to show how three different true relations might yield the same observed scatter. (To reemphasize: in Figure 7-4, the three lines are the same, and the scatters differ; in this problem the scatters are the same, thus the three lines must differ.)

*7-5 Assuming no error in Y, what is wrong with this analysis? "First, we may write (7-49) as

$$Y = \alpha + \beta X + (-\beta v)$$

where the error $(-\beta v)$ is just a multiple of v; hence it has zero mean, etc. We therefore take OLS regression of Y on X to estimate α and β consistently."

*7-6 Suppose that from a scatter of observations:

$$s_{XY} = 60$$

$$s_{XX} = 50$$

$$s_{YY} = 100$$

In each of the following circumstances, estimate β in the model (7-47) as well as you can. Assume, from (a) through (e), that e and v are independent.

(a) $\sigma_v^2 = 0$

(b) $\sigma_e^2 = 0$

(c) $\sigma_e^2 = \sigma_v^2$

(d) $\sigma_e^2 = 2\sigma_v^2$

(e) σ_e^2 and σ_v^2 are completely unknown

Now suppose that e and v are correlated, in (f) and (g).

(f) $\sigma_e^2 = 2\sigma_v^2$

(g) A random variable Z is observable, which is uncorrelated with both errors e and v, yet correlated with X and Y. In fact, $s_{ZX} = 100$ and $s_{ZY} = 150$.

chapter 8

The Identification Problem

The previous chapter sets out the difficulties encountered by an economist fitting a consumption function to a scatter of observations of consumption and income. Even worse difficulties may be encountered if he attempts to fit a demand curve to a scatter of price and quantity observations, as we shall see.

8-1 UNIDENTIFICATION[1]: A SUPPLY AND DEMAND EXAMPLE

In order to show how badly things may go wrong, let us again assume that we are omniscient. Thus, we can distinguish between what is really going on, and what the statistician can observe. Suppose that the price P and quantity Q demanded and supplied in a competitive market are determined by the simple model:

$$\text{Demand:} \quad Q = \alpha + \beta P + e \tag{8-1}$$

$$\text{Supply:} \quad Q = \gamma + \delta P + v \tag{8-2}$$

For simplicity, we assume that the error terms e and v have the characteristics set out in Chapter 2-1. Moreover, for the moment (in Section 8-1), we also assume that e and v are known to be independent, and symmetrically distributed around zero.

Before we become involved in identification problems, we must ask whether this model is mathematically complete, that is, whether there are

[1] An unidentified equation is customarily called "underidentified," as explained in Section 8-5.

enough equations to get a unique solution for the two endogenous variables (P, Q). To solve for these two unknowns requires two equations,[2] which we have. It is important to recognize and dispose of this issue before proceeding, because—as we shall soon see—the problem of identification requires a similar mathematical analysis: it, too, involves comparing equations and unknowns, although in an entirely different context. In the discussion that follows we deal only with models that are mathematically complete; that is, there are enough equations so that the endogenous variables are uniquely determined (in terms of exogenous variables and errors).

In Figure 8-1, economists are warned that their familiar Q and P axes have been switched. This is convenient so long as it is assumed (as we have for both demand and supply) that Q is a function of P. Figure 8-1*a* shows true demand D and supply S (which we assume to know through omniscience), and the ellipse of concentration for the population of generated observations. If the errors e and v are normal, then P and Q are bivariate normal[3] and the ellipse of concentration may be interpreted as a horizontal slice of the probability density function—like slice q in Figure 5-6*b*.

The orientation of the P, Q distribution has many possibilities, depending not only on the slopes β and δ of the supply and demand curves, but also on the variances of the errors v and e. But the orientation of the P, Q distribution does have one restriction—the ellipse must be cut into four equal quarters by the D and S lines. For if one quarter, for example, the upper quarter, were more probable, that would mean that positive v and positive e occurred together more than one quarter of the time, which violates the independence assumption.[4]

We show the whole population in Figure 8-1*a* in order to distinguish between two problems. The first we may refer to as the "statistical" problem

---

[2] In general, the model will be complete if there are as many equations as unknowns. These equations, of course, must be linearly independent; in our example, β and δ must be unequal (i.e., in Figure 8-1*a* the demand and supply lines must have different slopes so that they intersect).

[3] To prove this, we look ahead to the reduced form equations (8-3b) and (8-4b):

$$P = P_0 + u_1$$
$$Q = Q_0 + u_2$$

where the errors u_1 and u_2 are linear combinations of the structural errors v and e, and hence are jointly normal with zero mean. Thus, P and Q are jointly normally distributed about the mean (P_0, Q_0).

[4] If u and v are independent, then

$$\begin{aligned}\Pr(e > 0 \text{ and } v > 0) &= \Pr(e > 0)\Pr(v > 0)\\ &= (\tfrac{1}{2})(\tfrac{1}{2})\\ &= \tfrac{1}{4}\end{aligned}$$

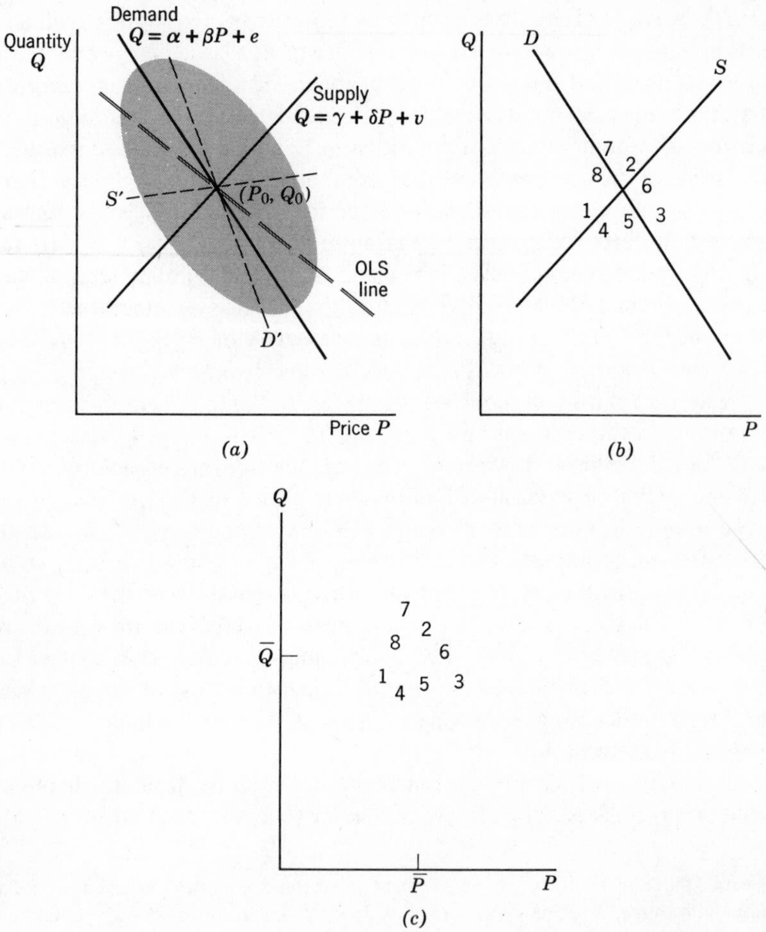

FIG. 8-1 (*a*) Population of price and quantity determined by true D and S; or equally well by bogus D' and S'. (*b*) Sample of eight prices and quantities determined by true D and S. (*c*) The sample that the statistician observes.

of estimating the population from a sample. But even if this problem were solved (i.e., even if the population ellipse in Figure 8-1*a* were known), the quite different problem of "identification" would remain. For we see that a bogus demand D' and supply S' could generate exactly the same population ellipse: note that S' and D' also cut the ellipse into four equal quarters. Furthermore, there are an unlimited number of bogus demand and supply systems that we could draw in—all of which would generate this same population ellipse. And there is no way of distinguishing between bogus systems and the true one. Thus, even if the statistician knew the population, he could not reconstruct the true D and S curves. He must have further information.

If the statistician were to fit an OLS line in Figure 8-1a, he would obtain a curve that was neither D nor S, but rather a combination of the two.[5]

In order to simplify the figures, from now on we shall show only a sample of a few observations that are representative of the population. This is the kind of data that an economist observes. But it must be remembered that even if the economist were blessed with an infinite amount of data (and thus knew the population distribution of P, Q as given by the ellipse in Figure 8-1a), the problem of identification would remain exactly the same: there are many demand/supply systems that could generate this population, and how can the true one be discovered?

8-2 IDENTIFICATION USING PRIOR INFORMATION

A typical sample of eight observations is shown in Figure 8-1b. Demand and supply have generated observations in four segments, with an observation in a specific segment the result of a specific combination of signs of e and v. Thus, for example, observations 1 and 8 were the result of a negative e (dropping these observations below the demand curve) and a positive v (raising these observations above the supply curve). Similarly, observations 2 and 7 were the result of a positive e and a positive v, and so on. Note that since e and v are independent, the eight observations are distributed evenly, with two falling in each of the four segments. This is a typical pattern; although it is not guaranteed for such a small sample, it is guaranteed for the population.

The statistician will be able to estimate one or both of the D and S lines if he is lucky enough to have certain kinds of prior information. We shall give three examples.

1. Suppose he has prior knowledge of the slope β of demand. In this case, he would be able to distinguish between the true demand and bogus demands. He could estimate the intercept α of demand from his scatter in Figure 8-1c by taking a line with slope β and raising it to just the right level so as to split the eight observed points into two equal halves with four in each. (The error e in demand was assumed to be positive and negative equally often.)

[5] Since the error e in demand is less than the error v in supply, the population of observations is oriented fairly close to the demand D. Since the OLS line is fairly close to the D line, the statistician might be tempted to erroneously call his OLS fit a demand curve.

It is very interesting that the supply line can be identified too. It would be placed so that supply, along with the known demand, would split the eight observations into four equal quarters. (This equal division follows, since e and v are assumed independent.) Although there is not a unique way to do this in a small sample, there is a unique way in the population, as can be seen in Figure 8-1a. Thus, we have seen how prior knowledge of β allowed us to identify demand; and the further prior knowledge that e and v are independent allowed us to identify supply also.

2. The independence of the error terms is a useful piece of prior information for identification purposes, just like knowledge of a specific parameter. However, for the balance of this discussion, we no longer assume that e and v are independent. Identification will then require some other element of prior information. Suppose that our second piece of prior information is knowledge of δ, the slope of supply; (we continue to assume prior knowledge of β). Demand can now be identified, just as before, by raising a line with slope β to split our observations into two equal halves. Moreover, supply can also now be identified in exactly the same way, by raising a line with slope δ to split our observation into halves. (Note that this does not generally divide our observations into four equal quarters; there is no necessity for doing this, since we are no longer assuming that e and v are independent.)

This is easily verified algebraically by examining the two reduced form equations in P and Q. Substitute (8-2) into (8-1)

$$\gamma + \delta P + v = \alpha + \beta P + e$$

$$P = \frac{\gamma - \alpha}{\beta - \delta} + \frac{v - e}{\beta - \delta} \tag{8-3a}$$

or, in simpler notation,

$$P = P_0 + u_1 \tag{8-3b}$$

Similarly

$$Q = \frac{\beta\gamma - \alpha\delta}{\beta - \delta} + \frac{\beta v - \delta e}{\beta - \delta} \tag{8-4a}$$

or

$$Q = Q_0 + u_2 \tag{8-4b}$$

Equations (8-3a) and (8-4a) comprise the reduced form of (8-1) and (8-2). Since e and v are on average zero, u_1 and u_2 (being a linear combination of e and v) must also be on average zero. Thus, the average values of (8-3a) and (8-4a) provide the two estimating equations

$$\bar{P} \mathrel{\hat{=}} \frac{\gamma - \alpha}{\beta - \delta} \tag{8-5}$$

$$\bar{Q} \mathrel{\hat{=}} \frac{\beta\gamma - \alpha\delta}{\beta - \delta} \tag{8-6}$$

The statistician has no difficulty in calculating $\bar{P}$ and $\bar{Q}$ from his observations in Figure 8-1*c*; thus, he can estimate the two reduced form coefficients $[(\gamma - \alpha)/(\beta - \delta)]$ and $[(\beta\gamma - \alpha\delta)/(\beta - \delta)]$. But without further information he cannot transform these back into corresponding estimates of the four structural coefficients α, β, γ, and δ, since there is an infinite number of values for these that correspond. This is the essence of the identification problem, and it is easy to see why this problem remains even if the statistical problem of estimating the reduced form coefficients could be perfectly solved. Even if the two reduced form coefficients were known exactly, unique values for the four structural coefficients could still not be determined.

To put the problem in another way, (8-5) and (8-6) are two equations that cannot be solved for the four unknown structural coefficients. But if the statistician has prior knowledge of any two (say β and δ), he can solve for the other two (α and γ).

3. Prior information about error variance can also be used to identify. Suppose that one error is known to be zero (or, in practice, that one error is very much smaller than another). For example, suppose the statistician knows a priori that the error e in demand has a variance much smaller than the variance of the error v in supply. Observations typically generated by such a system are shown in Figure 8-2*a*; and the statistician who fits a line to what he observes in Figure 8-2*b* will generally come up with a good

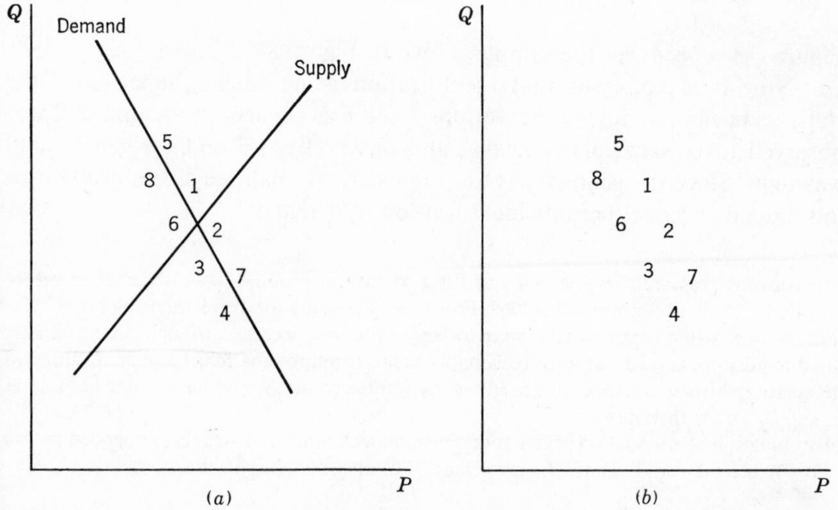

FIG. 8-2 (*a*) How demand and supply determine a sample of eight P, Q points when supply has a much larger error variance than demand. (*b*) The sample that the statistician observes.

approximation to the demand curve.[6] If there is no error in demand (σ_e^2 is known to be zero), then all observations in Figure 8-2a will fall exactly on the demand curve, which is, therefore, identified by the disturbances in supply. But supply remains unidentified; this would require another piece of prior information.

8-3 IDENTIFICATION USING PRIOR INFORMATION ABOUT EXOGENOUS VARIABLES

Although very useful, the kinds of prior knowledge illustrated in the previous section are seldom available to economists. We therefore turn now to a more realistic type of prior knowledge.

To begin untangling the problem of unidentification in Figure 8-1, the economist might ask about the nature of the supply error. For example, if the product is agricultural, its supply is sensitive to variations in rainfall R. Thus[7] it may be reasonable to redefine our model to explicitly include this exogenous variable:

$$\text{Demand:} \quad Q = \alpha + \beta P + e \qquad \begin{matrix}(8\text{-}8)\\(8\text{-}1)\text{ repeated}\end{matrix}$$

$$\text{Supply:} \quad Q = \gamma + \delta P + \theta R + u \qquad \begin{matrix}(8\text{-}9)\\(8\text{-}2)\text{ modified}\end{matrix}$$

Figure 8-3 reproduces the sample shown in Figure 8-1.

Now it is apparent that identification is no longer hopeless, if the statistician can pin down observations 7 and 8 as occurring when rainfall was observed to be particularly heavy, and observations 3 and 5 when rainfall was light. Since the geometry is not too clear, we shall see algebraically how this extended model permits identification of demand.

---

[6] Historically, research on the demand for agricultural products was undertaken before knowledge of identification difficulties. Fortunately demand for these necessities was relatively stable, while supply was subject to large shifts with weather. In such circumstances, fitted regressions turned out to be reasonably accurate approximations to demand. But had the relative shifts in the functions been reversed, these studies would have yielded estimates of supply rather than demand.

[7] Examination of residual error is a sound general technique that was recommended before —in Chapters 2 and 3. Thus, the error v of (8-2) may be thought of as

$$\begin{aligned} v &= \theta R + u \\ &= \text{part explained systematically by rainfall} + \text{residual} \end{aligned} \qquad (8\text{-}7)$$

When (8-7) is substituted into (8-2), we obtain (8-9).

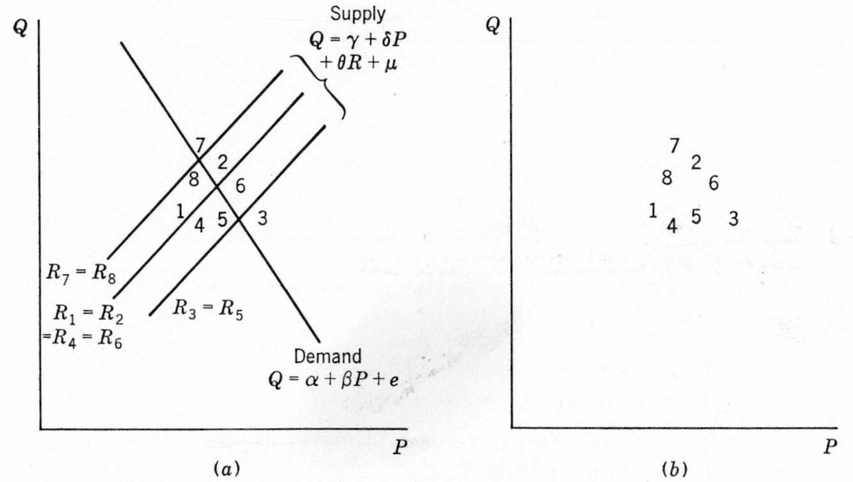

FIG. 8-3 The same data as Fig. 8-1, generated by an extended model that includes exogenous rainfall. (a) How demand and supply generate sample. (b) The sample the statistician observes.

Since R is an exogenous variable and uncorrelated with e, we may use it as an instrumental variable on the demand equation (8-8), obtaining

$$s_{QR} = \hat{\beta}s_{PR} \qquad (8\text{-}10)$$

Thus

$$\hat{\beta} = \frac{s_{QR}}{s_{PR}} \qquad Demand$$

$$can\ be\ identified$$

Thus, knowledge of R, as we hoped, allows us to identify and estimate demand.

When we similarly use R as an instrument on the supply equation (8-9), we obtain

$$s_{QR} = \hat{\delta}s_{PR} + \hat{\theta}s_{RR} \qquad Supply\ not\ identified\quad(8\text{-}11)$$

$$since\ don't\ know\ \theta$$

Since R is the only exogenous variable available as an instrumental variable, we are confined to this single equation in the two unknowns $\hat{\delta}$ and $\hat{\theta}$, which do not have a unique solution. Thus, supply is not identified.

We can now review how the exogenous variable R helps in identification. For each of the demand and supply equations, R provided an estimating equation when used as an instrumental variable. Yet in the case of the supply equation, R appeared with an additional parameter θ that had to be estimated, in a sense canceling its benefit. Thus, R could be used to identify only demand—the equation from which it was excluded.

From another point of view, we might say that the demand equation was identified because the coefficient of R in that equation was known to be zero. Thus, we see again that it is *prior* knowledge that identifies an equation.

8-4 REQUIREMENT FOR IDENTIFICATION, IN GENERAL

We have seen how identification of an equation is made possible by an exogenous variable that is excluded from that equation. Thus, we may guess the condition required to identify an equation in general, when the only kind of prior knowledge is the exclusion of certain variables by virtue of a zero coefficient:

> *Order Condition Necessary to Identify an Equation*
>
> The number of *exogenous*[8] variables *excluded* from the equation must at least equal the number of *endogenous* variables *included* on the right-hand side of the equation. (8-12)

We shall illustrate (8-12) with two more examples, followed by an informal proof. (A formal proof is given in Chapter 18-2.)

Example 1

In Figure 8-4, supply shifts with rainfall R, and demand with national income Y. (We are careful to specify that in this model, unlike the model of the previous chapter, Y is exogenous; that is, Y affects demand for this good, but the market for this particular good does not noticeably affect Y.) Note the unpromising scatter of Q and P observations facing the statistician; it seems unlikely he can identify either demand or supply. Yet from the estimating equations shown just below the diagram, it is clear that he can generally identify *both*. For example, to identify demand both Y and R may be used as instrumental variables. The two resulting equations are sufficient to solve for estimates of the two parameters β and η. We note that condition (8-12) is satisfied: in the demand equation, there is one excluded exogenous variable R that was instrumental in estimating the parameter of the one included endogenous variable P on the right-hand side. A similar argument shows that the supply equation can be identified.

[8] Strictly speaking, in this chapter "exogenous" should be replaced by the broader term "predetermined," which includes lagged endogenous variables as well as exogenous variables.

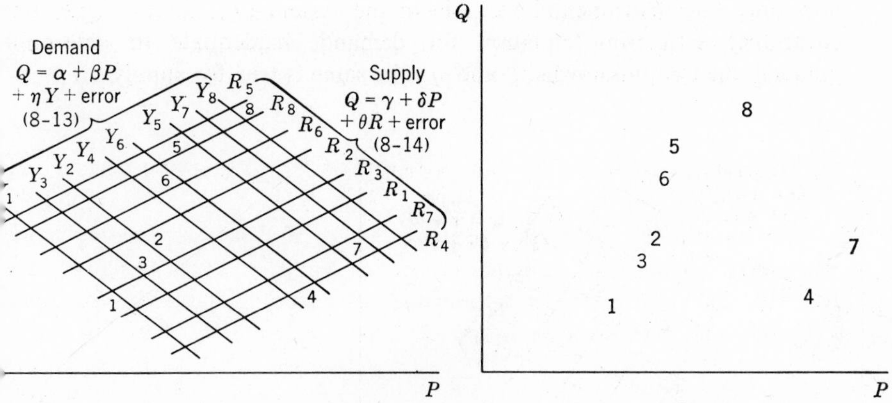

FIG. 8-4 Supply and demand shifting with different exogenous variables. (*a*) Model generating the sample. (*b*) The sample that the statistician observes.

Estimating equations

Demand

Using Y as an instrumental variable: $s_{QY} = \hat{\beta} s_{PY} + \hat{\eta} s_{YY}$ (8-15)

Using R as an instrumental variable: $s_{QR} = \hat{\beta} s_{PR} + \hat{\eta} s_{YR}$ (8-16)

Two equations in two unknowns; solvable.

Supply

Using R as an instrumental variable: $s_{QR} = \hat{\delta} s_{PR} + \hat{\theta} s_{RR}$ (8-17)

Using Y as an instrumental variable: $s_{QY} = \hat{\delta} s_{PY} + \hat{\theta} s_{RY}$ (8-18)

Again, two equations in two unknowns; solvable.

Example 2

In Figure 8-5, both supply and demand shift with the same exogenous variable time (T). The scatter the statistician observes is a clearly defined one, and there seems to be some message in it. It turns out, however, that it is insufficient information; since it tells us too little about the shape of supply or demand, both remained unidentified. This is confirmed by examining the covariance equations written in directly below the diagram. Since there is now only one instrumental variable in the system (T), there is only one covariance estimating equation for demand, inadequate to determine uniquely the two unknowns, $\hat{\beta}$ and $\hat{\eta}$. The same is true for supply.

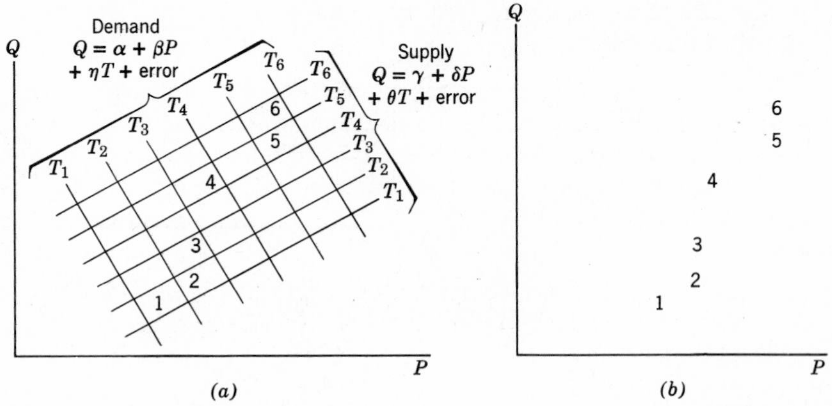

FIG. 8-5 Supply and demand shifting with the same exogenous variable T. (a) Model generating the sample. (b) The sample that the statistician observes.

Estimating equations

Demand

Only instrumental variable available is T: $s_{QT} = \hat{\beta}s_{PT} + \hat{\eta}s_{TT}$

Only one equation in two unknowns; not uniquely solvable.

Supply

Only instrumental variable available is T: $s_{QT} = \hat{\delta}s_{PT} + \hat{\theta}s_{TT}$

Again, only one equation in two unknowns; not uniquely solvable.

To confirm statement (8-12) in general, we note that each exogenous variable included in the equation gives rise to an estimating covariance equation that will just "take care of" its parameter. But we still need an estimating equation for each parameter attached to the endogenous variables on the right-hand side of the equation. The only way to generate these estimating equations is by using *excluded* exogenous variables as instrumental variables; therefore, the number of these must at least equal the number of endogenous variables on the right-hand side.

We have now illustrated the identification problem from two points of view:

1. The reduced form was used in Section 8-2; however this algebra would have been far too cumbersome in the more complicated examples that followed; hence, in succeeding sections we have
2. Applied instruments.

We now pause to review the equivalence of these two approaches. It is always possible, given observations on the endogenous and exogenous variables, to estimate the coefficients of the reduced form. Unidentification means that this reduced form cannot be transformed back into a unique structure; instead there is a whole set of corresponding structures. The equivalent view of unidentification using the IV approach is that there are not enough prespecified zero coefficients in the equation being estimated; that is, there are not enough instrumental variables to estimate the nonzero coefficients.

PROBLEMS

8-1 Use the order condition (8-12) to determine which equations may be identified in this model. We denote the three exogenous variables by X_i, and the endogenous variables by Y_i.

$$Y_1 = \alpha_0 + \alpha_2 Y_2 + \alpha_3 Y_3 + \beta_1 X_1 + e_1$$
$$Y_2 = \gamma_0 + \gamma_1 Y_1 + \delta_1 X_1 + \delta_2 X_2 + \delta_3 X_3 + e_2$$
$$Y_3 = \theta_0 + \theta_1 Y_1 + \theta_2 Y_2 + \eta_1 X_1 + \eta_2 X_2 + e_3$$

8-2 Repeat Problem 8-1 using the following model:

$$Y_1 = \alpha_0 + \alpha_2 Y_2 + \beta_2 X_2 + e_1$$
$$Y_2 = \gamma_0 + \delta_1 X_1 + \delta_2 X_2 + \delta_3 X_3 + e_2$$

8-3 (a) In Problems 8-1 and 8-2, was it the long or short equations (equations with many or few terms) which were identified?

(b) True or False? If false, correct.

(i) Prior knowledge is required to identify (pin down) the parameters of an equation. The absence of a variable from an equation may be regarded as the prior knowledge that its coefficient is zero. Thus, the short equations that have many zero coefficients are identified, while the long equations are not. To be precise, an equation may be identified if the number of terms (or number of coefficients) on the right-hand side is no more than the number of exogenous variables.

(ii) If one equation in a system can be identified, all equations can.

8-4 Referring to the model (8-8) and (8-9), suppose the following four observations have been collected.

P	Q	R
5	3	-1
4	4	1
3	3	1
4	2	-1

(a) Is demand identified?
(b) Calculate the deviations $p_i = P_i - \bar{P}$ and $q_i = Q_i - \bar{Q}$.
(c) Estimate β with the instrument R.
(d) Estimate β with ordinary least squares.
(e) Graph the four sample values of P, Q and show the two slopes of (c) and (d). Which slope is appropriate?
(f) What is the sample correlation between R and the fitted residuals $\hat{e}$, when we use:
(i) The instrumental variable R.
(ii) Ordinary least squares.
(g) What is the population correlation between R and e assumed to be? Which answer to part (f) does this match?

8-5 Suppose true D and S are given by:

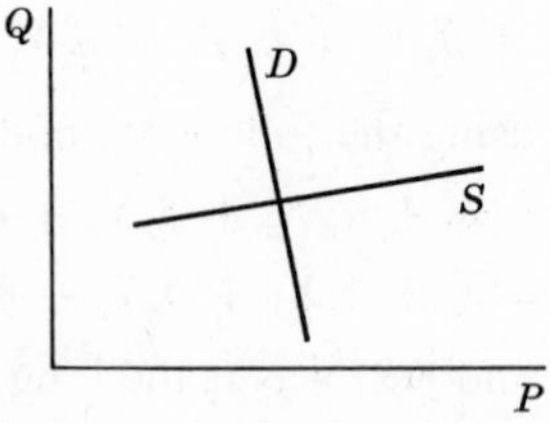

(a) Further suppose that the errors e and v are independent, with rectangular distributions with equal variance. As in the consumption function example in the previous chapter, draw in the parallelogram within which the population observations must fall. Note how this parallelogram is oriented along the demand line—even though error variances are equal. Why?
(b) If e and v were normal with equal variance, sketch in the ellipse of concentration of P and Q.

8-5 OVER IDENTIFICATION

So far we have investigated primarily the algebraic problem of how many prior restrictions are necessary to identify the parameters of an equation. Suppose that we have established that a given equation is identified.[9] Thus, we know that its statistical estimation is possible. How should we proceed?

We first review some of our previous work with some additional geometry.

(a) An Unidentified Equation Reconsidered

In Section 8-3, we saw that supply was not identified, because there was only one estimating equation (8-11) for the two unknowns $\hat{\delta}$ and $\hat{\theta}$. This is illustrated in Figure 8-6*a*.

(b) Identified Equation

(i) Exactly Identified Equation. In Figure 8-4, supply was identified because there were two estimating equations (8-17) and (8-18) for the two unknowns $\hat{\delta}$ and $\hat{\theta}$. This is illustrated in Figure 8-6*b*(i).

(ii) Over Identified Equation. Now consider a model where there is one more exogenous variable than we need to identify supply:

$$\text{Demand:} \quad Q = \alpha + \beta P + \eta T + \xi Y + e \tag{8-19}$$

$$\text{Supply:} \quad Q = \gamma + \delta P + \theta R + v \tag{8-20}$$

When we use the three exogenous variables T, Y, and R as instrumental

[9] Here we must be very careful. Equation (8-12) is only a necessary condition and, therefore, does not guarantee identification. The sufficient condition must also be fulfilled; but this is so complicated that it is deferred to Chapter 18.

For illustration, however, we can show how an equation may remain unidentified, even though the necessary condition (8-12) is just barely satisfied (so that there are exactly as many excluded exogenous variables as there are coefficients of endogenous variables to be estimated). Suppose two of the excluded exogenous variables are linearly related (e.g., one is a variable measured in feet, the other is the same variable measured in inches, as in Chapter 3). In this case, we get information essentially from only one of these instrumental variables, not both, and as a consequence we don't have enough information to identify.

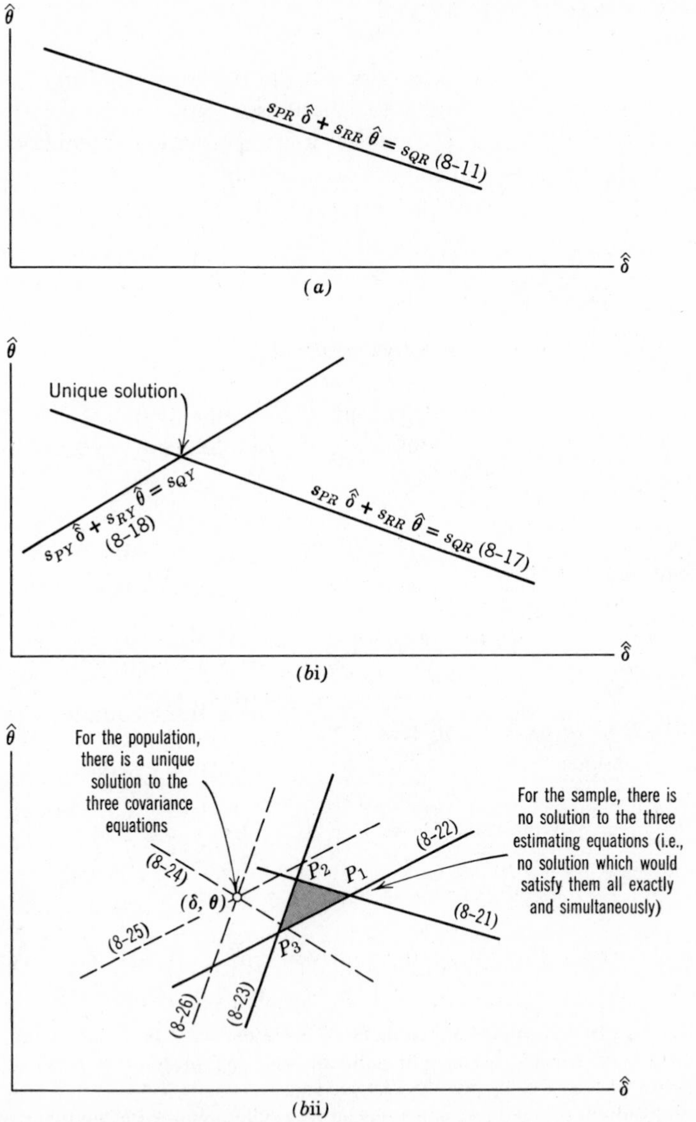

FIG. 8-6 Graphs of estimating equations for the two unknown parameters in the supply equation. (*a*) Unidentified case, equation (8-11). (*b*) Identified cases: (i) Exactly identified case, equations (8-17) and (8-18); (ii) Over identified case, equations (8-21) to (8-23).

variables on the supply equation (8-20), we obtain

$$s_{QT} = \hat{\delta} s_{PT} + \hat{\theta} s_{RT} \tag{8-21}$$

$$s_{QY} = \hat{\delta} s_{PY} + \hat{\theta} s_{RY} \tag{8-22}$$

$$s_{QR} = \hat{\delta} s_{PR} + \hat{\theta} s_{RR} \tag{8-23}$$

We must remember that identification is not primarily a statistical issue. If an equation is unidentified, even an infinite sample won't help; on the other hand, if an equation is identified, δ and θ can be estimated—approximately if the sample is small, or exactly if it is infinite. Consider this latter case where the population (i.e., the set of σ's) is known. The three equations for $\hat{\delta}$ and $\hat{\theta}$ become

$$\sigma_{QT} = \hat{\delta} \sigma_{PT} + \hat{\theta} \sigma_{RT} \tag{8-24}$$

$$\sigma_{QY} = \hat{\delta} \sigma_{PY} + \hat{\theta} \sigma_{RY} \tag{8-25}$$

$$\sigma_{QR} = \hat{\delta} \sigma_{PR} + \hat{\theta} \sigma_{RR} \tag{8-26}$$

These three equations will have a unique solution[10]—the true parameters (δ, θ), designated by the empty dot in Figure 8-6*b*(ii).

So far, cases (i) and (ii) seem similar—they both are identified equations. But when we ask about *statistical* estimation, we see a difference. In case (ii) there are three statistical estimating equations (8-21) to (8-23) for only two unknowns; generally they will not have a unique solution because of statistical fluctuation; that is, the three lines in Figure 8-6*b*(ii) will not have a common intersection point.

What should the statistician do with these three equations (remember that he is not omniscient; he does not know σ_{QT}, but only the sample s_{QT}, etc.)? A naive answer is to use the first two equations (8-21) and (8-22), ignoring the information given by the third instrumental variable R. This means using solution P_1. It is the simplest answer to the "embarrassment of riches—more than enough instrumental variables." Yet another statistician might choose to use two different equations—(8-21) and (8-23)—and so obtain the estimate P_2. A third statistician might argue for point P_3.

Which of these three points is the best estimate? Or is there yet another point in or near the triangle $P_1P_2P_3$ that is even better? This is a tough problem to answer; it takes up most of Chapters 9 and 19, and has been the area of a vast amount of recent econometric research.

---

[10] *Proof.* Applying the *population* covariance operator for the instrumental variable T, to (8-20),

$$\sigma_{QT} = \delta \sigma_{PT} + \theta \sigma_{RT} + \sigma_{vT} \tag{8-24}$$

But the instrumental variable T and error v, by definition, have $\sigma_{vT} = 0$, so that

$$\sigma_{QT} = \delta \sigma_{PT} + \theta \sigma_{RT}$$

This equation states that (δ, θ) satisfies (8-24). Similarly, (δ, θ) satisfies (8-25) and (8-26), and so is a solution to the system.

We finally must explain the terms "exactly" identified and "over" identified. In Figure 8-6*b*(ii) we have just shown that two instrumental variables would have been enough to get some kind of estimate of the two parameters. In a naive sense, the third instrumental variable might be called "more than enough" or "too much."[11] For this reason, this case is called the over identified case. By contrast, the case in Figure 8-6*b*(i) is called the exactly identified case. Finally, the case in Figure 8-6*a* is sometimes called under identified as well as unidentified.

PROBLEMS

8-6 Of the equations in Problem 8-2, which are exactly identified, and which are over identified?

8-6 SUMMARY: IDENTIFICATION IN CONTEXT

There are three distinct issues facing an economist in model-building:

1. Mathematical completeness of the model.
2. Identification of the parameters of an equation in the model.
3. Statistical estimation of the parameters of the equation.

Each issue must be settled satisfactorily before going on to the next. Whereas the first issue of completeness is pretty trivial, the second issue of identification takes up most of this chapter and Chapter 18, while the third issue of statistical estimation is just introduced in this chapter and is developed in detail in Chapters 9, 19, and 20.

We shall illustrate these issues by referring again to the supply-demand model of Chapter 8-5:

$$\text{Demand:} \quad Q = \alpha + \beta P + \eta T + \xi Y + e \qquad \text{(8-19) repeated}$$

$$\text{Supply:} \quad Q = \gamma + \delta P + \theta R + v \qquad \text{(8-20) repeated}$$

It will be useful to describe this system with the flow diagram shown in Figure 8-7. Values of the exogenous variables and disturbances are fed into the structural system, and yield values for the endogenous variables.

[11] Yet, in a truer sense, all sample information is helpful in estimation, so that the third instrument is not "too much." It is only too much for someone who is unprepared to use it wisely.

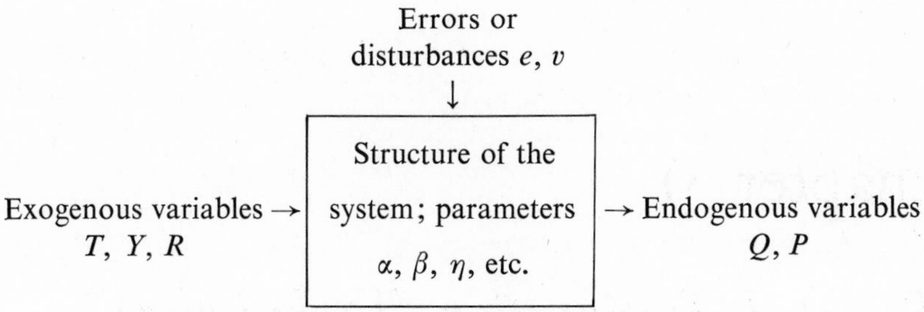

FIG. 8-7 A schematic view of an econometric system.

1. *Mathematical completeness* means that, if the errors, exogenous variables, and structural parameters are known, the endogenous variables are uniquely determined. It requires that the model have as many independent equations as endogenous variables.

2. *Identification* means that if the errors, exogenous variables, and endogenous variables are known, the structural parameters are uniquely determined. Unidentification occurs when a given set of disturbances and exogenous variables may be "passed through" several different structures, each yielding the same values for the endogenous variables. In this case, the true structure cannot be identified from a whole set of bogus structures.[12]

Identification of a single structural equation requires that there be enough prior information that some parameters are zero[13] to "pin down" the other parameters of the equation uniquely. Specifically, the order condition (8-12) for identification is that there must be at least as many omitted exogenous variables as there are endogenous variables included on the right-hand side.

3. Finally, suppose realistically that only a *sample* of the values of the exogenous and endogenous variables is known. *Statistical estimation* is the problem of estimating the structural parameters in such a way as to minimize the (observed) errors in some sense; (compare to the estimation of parameters in Chapter 2—the objective is the same in either case).

Statistical estimation is simple if there are exactly as many estimating covariance equations as unknown parameters (the exactly identified case). However, when we have more estimating covariance equations (the over identified case), there remains a major problem of how to use all this information effectively.

[12] This issue is clarified in Chapter 18-2(a).

[13] Or, alternatively, prior information about the error terms.

chapter 9

Selected Estimating Techniques

9-1 TWO-STAGE LEAST SQUARES (2SLS)

Two-Stage Least Squares is perhaps the simplest solution to the problem of overidentification. It provides estimators in the situation described in Figure 8-6*b*(ii), where use of all available instrumental variables results in a set of estimating equations with no unique solution.

A precise explanation of 2SLS must be left to the more advanced analysis in Chapter 19; however, in this section we illustrate the main ideas. Consider again the demand-supply model of Section 8-5:

$$\text{Demand:} \quad Q = \alpha + \beta P + \eta T + \xi Y + e \tag{9-1}$$

(8-19) repeated

$$\text{Supply:} \quad Q = \gamma + \delta P + \theta R + v \tag{9-2}$$

(8-20) repeated

where P, Q are endogenous, and T, Y, R are exogenous, hence independent of the errors e, v. Suppose we wish to estimate the second equation, which has the overidentified parameters. But suppose we had missed the whole point that supply is one equation in a simultaneous system, and had applied OLS to (9-2). What would happen? As shown in Chapter 7, we would get inconsistent estimates of γ, δ, and θ because one of our regressors (P) is an endogenous variable, hence is dependent on v. However, we can eliminate this problem if we can purge P of its dependence on v. This is the first stage, and it allows us then, in the second stage, to apply OLS.

First Stage

Find a modified regressor $\hat{P}$ that resembles P, yet is independent of v. To find $\hat{P}$, regress P on all the exogenous variables (T, Y, R), obtaining the fitted value

$$\hat{P} = b_0 + b_1 T + b_2 Y + b_3 R \tag{9-3}$$

Since T, Y, and R are exogenous, each is independent of the error v; hence any function of them (in particular, the linear combination $\hat{P}$) will also be independent[1] of v.

Second Stage

Substituting $\hat{P}$ for P in equation (9-2), *estimate the parameters* (γ, δ, θ) *by applying OLS to this equation*, which now becomes

$$Q = \gamma + \delta\hat{P} + \theta R + v^* \tag{9-4}$$

This procedure is now legitimate, since $\hat{P}$ is uncorrelated with the adjusted error term v^*. (This can be proved following Chapter 15-2.)

Figure 8-6*b*(ii) provides an intuitive view of what two-stage least squares involves. Recall that this diagram showed how the use of instrumental variables Y, T, and R would result in three estimating equations for the two parameters δ and θ. There was no unique solution for this overdetermined system, because there were no guidelines for discarding one of these equations, or for attaching relative weights to them. But suppose one of our instrumental variables (T) cannot properly be regarded as an exogenous variable affecting this system, that is, suppose it does not enter the demand equation and, hence, has no effect on either P or Q. Therefore, its covariance with either P or Q is zero,[2] and it makes no sense to estimate (8-21) in Figure 8-6*b*(ii). With this equation eliminated, a unique estimate for δ and θ exists at P_3. This instrumental variable technique now does yield a unique solution, with T disappearing entirely from the calculations.

Under these circumstances, P_3 can also be shown to be the 2SLS solution: since T has no effect on P (nor on Q), T should not be included in the first stage (9-3), nor does T appear in the second stage (9-4); thus T disappears from 2SLS calculations also.

---

[1] Not quite independent. Since the coefficients b_i in (9-3) are not absolute constants, but are estimates depending on v, $\hat{P}$ depends slightly on v. This reservation holds true in small sample estimation. But with an infinite sample, any dependence of the b_i on the error terms disappears, making 2SLS a consistent estimator.

[2] Strictly speaking, it is only the population covariances σ_{QT} and σ_{PT} that are zero. There is no reason to expect that their sample estimators s_{QT} and s_{PT} will be precisely zero, especially if the sample is very small. But if they are not zero, this is a reflection only of sampling error, and our conclusion that it makes no sense to evaluate equation (8-21) still holds.

This limiting case is not of great interest in itself because with T disqualified as an instrumental variable, supply becomes exactly identified. But it does illustrate what occurs in the less extreme case in which T has some effect on the system, but much less than Y or R. Supply is again overidentified. In these circumstances the 2SLS solution will not be P_3, but some point close to it. Thus 2SLS may be regarded as a method of selecting a unique solution point in Figure 8-6*b*(ii), with the exact position of this point depending on the relative effect of the instrumental variables T, Y, and R on the endogenous variables.

An important conclusion (proved in Chapter 19) is that 2SLS is, in fact, instrumental variable estimation, with $\hat{P}$ being used as an instrumental variable along with R. These are the two instrumental variables required to estimate (9-2), and the problem of oversupply of instrumental variables is solved. In the general case where the equation to be estimated includes several endogenous variables (on the right-hand side), the instrumental variables used are the fitted values of each of these endogenous variables (along with the exogenous variables in the equation, of course). It is evident that this always provides just the right number of instrumental variables for estimation purposes.

To sum up, overidentification means an oversupply of instrumental variables. 2SLS reduces this to just the right number, by taking linear combinations of the original instrumental variables.

9-2 OTHER PROCEDURES: EQUATION VERSUS SYSTEM ESTIMATION

There are many other procedures available for estimating an equation in a simultaneous system, such as Limited Information/Maximum Likelihood and Least Generalized Variance. Since these require more formidable mathematics, they are developed in Chapter 19. Like 2SLS, they are called "limited information" techniques since they involve estimating only one equation; hence, they do not require observing all variables in all equations in the system.

It is true, of course, that these techniques can be used to estimate a whole system, one equation at a time. But if the whole system is to be estimated, there are other—even more complicated—procedures available for *simultaneously* estimating all equations. These are called "full information" methods, since they require observations on all variables in the system. Some of these methods, such as Three-Stage Least Squares and Full Information/Maximum Likelihood, are described in Chapter 20.

9-3 RECURSIVE SYSTEMS

As a final topic, consider the much easier problem when the equations in a system are not simultaneous, but recursive.

(a) The Simple Recursive System

In such a system, the endogenous variables are determined one at a time, in sequence. Thus, the first endogenous variable is determined from the first equation, independent of the other endogenous variables; its solution then appears in the second equation to determine the value of the second endogenous variable, and so on.

The successive or sequential nature of this solution is illustrated in the following recursive system:

$$\left.\begin{aligned}
Y_1 \qquad\qquad\qquad\qquad &= a_{11}X_1 + a_{12}X_2 + \cdots + a_{1M}X_M + e_1 \\
b_{21}Y_1 + Y_2 \qquad\qquad\qquad &= a_{21}X_1 + \cdots \qquad\quad + a_{2M}X_M + e_2 \\
b_{31}Y_1 + b_{32}Y_2 + Y_3 \qquad &= a_{31}X_1 + \cdots \qquad\quad + a_{3M}X_M + e_3 \\
&\ \vdots \\
b_{Q1}Y_1 + \cdots \qquad + Y_Q &= a_{Q1}X_1 + \cdots \qquad\quad + a_{QM}X_M + e_Q
\end{aligned}\right\} \tag{9-5}$$

where X_i = exogenous variables
Y_i = endogenous variables

and, most important,

e_i = *independent* error terms[4]

From given values of the exogenous variables (X_i), and a randomly determined value for e_1, the first equation yields a solution for Y_1; note that

[4] This is the crucial assumption that defines a recursive system. *Any* system can have its left side put into triangular form (9-5) by simple manipulations of linear algebra. But these same manipulations usually will so entangle the errors on the right side that the errors will no longer be independent. When this happens, we will call the system nonrecursive, because the recursive OLS solution to be discussed is no longer valid.

this value of Y_1 is logically independent of all the other Y_i values in the system. With the value of Y_1 thus determined, the second equation yields a solution for Y_2.[5] And as we move through successive steps, each equation yields one more Y in terms of the previously determined Y's and the exogenous variables.

A recursive system is easier to deal with than a simultaneous system: in particular, ordinary least squares can be used to estimate its parameters. To justify its application, recall that OLS is appropriate if the error term in the equation is independent of the regressors. Clearly, it can be applied to the first equation, since the only regressors are exogenous variables, which are—by assumption—independent of e_1. Moreover, OLS can be applied to the second equation, where Y_2 is regressed on Y_1, and the exogenous X's; all these regressors are independent of e_2. Specifically, the X's are independent of e_2 because they are exogenous. Y_1 is also independent of e_2 since, from the first equation, the only error term affecting Y_1 is e_1. Because e_1 and e_2 are assumed independent, it follows that Y_1 and e_2 are independent.[6] The justification of OLS on each succeeding equation follows a similar argument.

(b) Bloc Recursive Systems

A system of equations becomes bloc recursive if any of the individual endogenous variables in (9-5) is replaced with a whole bloc of simultaneously determined endogenous variables. The simple example in Figure 9-1 will illustrate. The first bloc is made up of Y_1 and Y_2; these are simultaneously determined by the first two equations. These solved values are then conceptually plugged into the last three equations to determine the solution for Y_3, Y_4, and Y_5—the second bloc of endogenous variables. Errors e_1 and e_2 associated with the first bloc are assumed independent of errors e_3, e_4, and e_5 associated with the second bloc; (however, the errors within a bloc may be dependent—i.e., e_1 and e_2 may be dependent). OLS is no longer valid, because the system now involves elements of simultaneity.[7] Hence, a more sophisticated, bloc-by-bloc approach is required: in each bloc, the Y variables from the previous blocs are treated as exogenous (predetermined), and the bloc

[5] That is, $Y_2 = -b_{21}Y_1 + a_{21}X_1 + \cdots + a_{2M}X_M + e_2$

[6] Contrast this with a simultaneous system in which both Y_1 and Y_2 appear in the first equation, as well as the second. Thus, Y_1 and Y_2 depend on both e_1 and e_2. In particular, the dependence of the regressor Y_1 on e_2 would mean that OLS applied to the second equation would result in biased and inconsistent estimates.

[7] Specifically, OLS cannot be used on the first equation to (consistently) regress Y_1 on $Y_2, X_1 \cdots X_M$, because the regressor Y_2 is not independent of e_1.

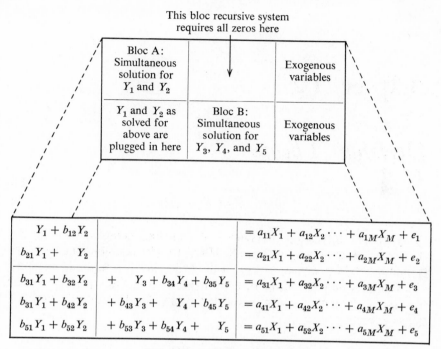

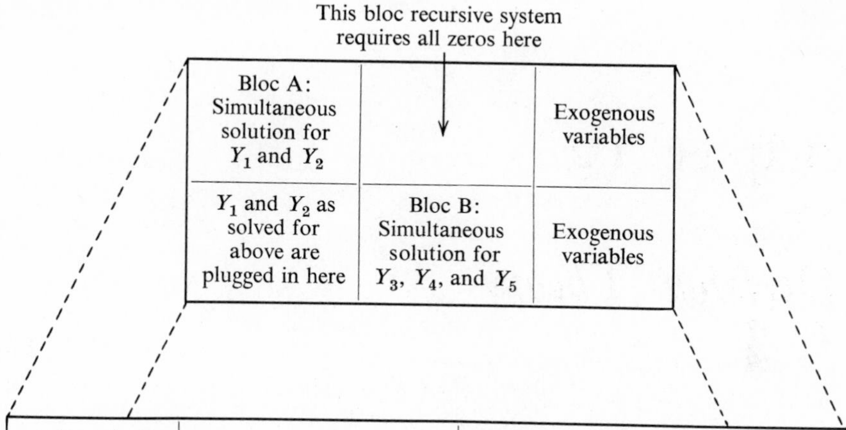

$Y_1 + b_{12}Y_2$		$= a_{11}X_1 + a_{12}X_2 \cdots + a_{1M}X_M + e_1$
$b_{21}Y_1 + \quad Y_2$		$= a_{21}X_1 + a_{22}X_2 \cdots + a_{2M}X_M + e_2$
$b_{31}Y_1 + b_{32}Y_2$	$+ \quad Y_3 + b_{34}Y_4 + b_{35}Y_5$	$= a_{31}X_1 + a_{32}X_2 \cdots + a_{3M}X_M + e_3$
$b_{31}Y_1 + b_{42}Y_2$	$+ b_{43}Y_3 + \quad Y_4 + b_{45}Y_5$	$= a_{41}X_1 + a_{42}X_2 \cdots + a_{4M}X_M + e_4$
$b_{51}Y_1 + b_{52}Y_2$	$+ b_{53}Y_3 + b_{54}Y_4 + \quad Y_5$	$= a_{51}X_1 + a_{52}X_2 \cdots + a_{5M}X_M + e_5$

FIG. 9-1 A bloc recursive system.

coefficients are estimated by 2SLS (described in Section 9-1) equation by equation, or by some similar method.

In summary, a bloc recursive system is one that has a very special combination of zero coefficients attached to the endogenous variables, and the assumption that every error term is independent of errors in another bloc.

chapter 10

Decision Theory

With our discussion of systems of equations completed in the last chapter, we now turn to an entirely different topic: decision making in the face of uncertainty. A large part of the discussion involves Bayesian methods, which are not only useful for their own sake, but also sharpen our understanding of the limitations of classical statistics. The best introduction is a simple example.

10-1 AN EXAMPLE: THE PRIOR AND POSTERIOR DISTRIBUTION

In a certain country, it rains 40% of the days and shines 60% of the days. A barometer manufacturer, in testing his instrument, has found that it sometimes errs: on rainy days it erroneously predicts "shine" 10% of the time, and on shiny days it erroneously predicts "rain" 20% of the time.

The best prediction of tomorrow's weather *before* looking at the barometer[1] would be the prior distribution in Table 10-1. But *after* looking at

TABLE 10-1 Prior Probabilities, $p(\theta)$

State θ	Rain (θ_1)	Shine (θ_2)
Prior probability $p(\theta)$	.40	.60

the barometer and seeing it predict "rain," what is the posterior distribution? That is, with this new information in hand, can't we quote better odds on rain than Table 10-1?

[1] In this analysis, it is assumed that there is no other available information (such as a weather report, or visual observation of how the weather is developing).

The answer is, of course, yes. To see why, we first formally set out the reliability of the barometer in Table 10-2. This information is combined with

TABLE 10-2 Conditional Probabilities, $p(x/\theta)$

Prediction x \ State θ	Rain (θ_1)	Shine (θ_2)
"Rain" (x_1)	.90	.20
"Shine" (x_2)	.10	.80
$\sum$	1.00	1.00

the prior probabilities in Table 10-1 to define the sample space shown as the entire large rectangle in Figure 10-1. It has four subdivisions, each representing the probability of a specific state of nature, and a barometric prediction. Thus, for example, the probability of the state of nature θ being rain and the barometric prediction (x) being "rain" is[2]

$$p(\theta_1, x_1) = p(\theta_1) \cdot p(x_1/\theta_1) \tag{10-1}$$

$$= (.4)(.9) = .36 \tag{10-2}$$

Similarly, the probability of the state shine, and the prediction "rain" is

$$p(\theta_2, x_1) = p(\theta_2) \cdot p(x_1/\theta_2) \tag{10-3}$$

$$= (.6)(.2) = .12 \tag{10-4}$$

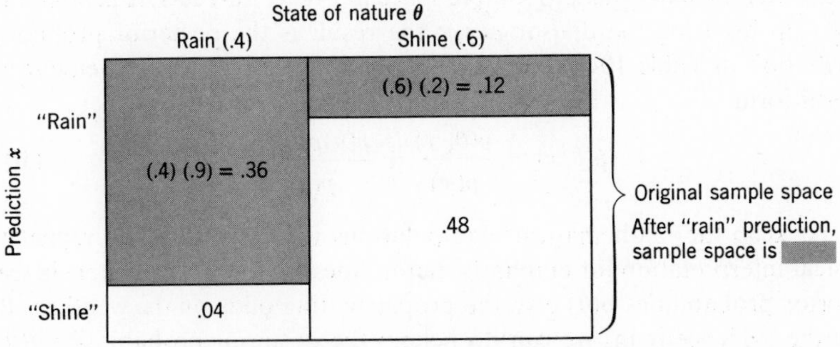

FIG. 10-1 How posterior probabilities are determined.

[2] We use the conditional probability theorem

$$p(y, z) = p(y) \cdot p(z/y) \tag{10-5}$$

For reference, see for example Wonnacott and Wonnacott, *op. cit.*, Chapter 3.

Of course, after "rain" has been predicted, this sample space is no longer relevant. It is replaced by the new, shaded sample space; now rain is seen to be three times as probable as shine (.36 versus .12). This leads us directly to our posterior distribution in Table 10-3. Comparing this with Table 10-1, we

TABLE 10-3 Posterior Probabilities, $p(\theta/x)$

State θ	Rain (θ_1)	Shine (θ_2)
Posterior probability $p(\theta/\text{"rain"})$	.75	.25

see, as expected, just how the odds on rain improve once the barometer has predicted it.

Since this is so important, we now write down its full formal confirmation. From (10-2) and (10-4)

$$p(\text{prediction "rain"}) = p(x_1) = .36 + .12 = .48 \tag{10-6}$$

Using (10-5) again

$$p(\theta_1/x_1) = \frac{p(\theta_1, x_1)}{p(x_1)} = \frac{.36}{.48} = .75$$

Similarly (10-7)

$$p(\theta_2/x_1) = \frac{p(\theta_2, x_1)}{p(x_1)} = \frac{.12}{.48} = .25$$

In this way, the new (shaded) sample space in Figure 10-1 has its probabilities blown up by using the divisor $p(x_1)$; the result is the posterior probability distribution in Table 10-3. This is often written in the more convenient and general form

$$p(\theta/x) = \frac{p(\theta, x)}{p(x)} = \frac{p(\theta)p(x/\theta)}{p(x)} \tag{10-8}$$

To keep the mathematical manipulations in perspective, we repeat the physical interpretation for emphasis. Before the evidence (barometer) is seen, the prior probabilities $p(\theta)$ give the proper betting odds on the weather. But after the evidence is in, we can do better; the posterior probabilities $p(\theta/x)$ now give the proper betting odds. (This may be intuitively grasped by appealing to the relative frequency interpretation. Of all the times the barometer registers "rain," in what proportion will rain actually occur? The answer: 75%.) As a simple summary, we note that the prior probability distribution is adjusted by the empirical evidence to yield the posterior distribution. Schematically:

Prior probabilities	and	probability of empirical evidence	yields →	posterior probabilities	(10-9)
$p(\theta)$		$p(x/\theta)$		$p(\theta/x)$	

PROBLEMS

10-1 Suppose another barometer is used: on shiny days it erroneously predicts "rain" 30% of the time, but on rainy days it always correctly predicts "rain."

(a) With the prior probabilities in Table 10-1, calculate the posterior probability of rain, once this barometer has predicted "rain." What is the posterior probability of shine?

(b) What do you think of this argument: "Since the barometer always predicts 'rain' when it does rain, a 'rain' prediction means that it is dead certain that it will rain."

(c) Explain why the posterior probability of rain is now *less* than in Table 10-3, even though this new barometer is a better predictor when it rains.

10-2 In a population of workers, suppose 40% are grade school graduates, 50% are high school graduates, and 10% are college graduates. Among the grade school graduates, 10% are unemployed, among the high school graduates, 5% are unemployed, and among the college graduates 2% are unemployed. If a worker is chosen at random and found to be unemployed, what is the probability that he is:

(a) A grade school graduate?

(b) A high school graduate?

(c) A college graduate?

10-3 A factory has three machines (θ_1, θ_2, and θ_3) making bolts. The newer the machine, the larger and more accurate it is, according to the following table:

Machine →	θ_1 (Oldest)	θ_2	θ_3 (Newest)
Proportion of total output produced by this machine	10%	40%	50%
Rate of defective bolts it produces	5%	2%	1%

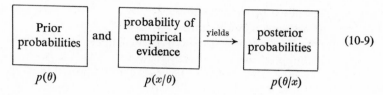

Thus, for example, θ_3 produces half of the factory's output, and of all the bolts it produces, 1% are defective.

(a) Suppose a bolt is selected at random; *before* it is examined, what is the chance it was produced by machine θ_1? by θ_2? by θ_3?

(b) Suppose the bolt is examined and found to be defective; *after* this examination, what is the chance it was produced by machine θ_1? by θ_2? by θ_3?

⇒10-4 Suppose a man is drawn at random from a group of ten people, whose heights θ have the following distribution:

θ (Inches)	$p(\theta)$
70	.1
71	.3
72	.2
73	.2
74	.1
75	.1

(a) Graph this (prior) distribution of θ.

(b) Suppose also that a crude measuring device is available that makes errors with the following distribution:

e (Error in Inches)	$p(e)$
−2	.1
−1	.2
0	.4
1	.2
2	.1

Surely this can help us a little in estimating the man's height. For example, suppose his measured height using this crude device is $x = 74''$. We now have further information about θ; that is, this measurement changes the probabilities for θ from the prior distribution $p(\theta)$ to a posterior distribution $p(\theta/x = 74)$. Calculate and graph this posterior distribution.

10-2 OPTIMAL DECISIONS

(a) Example

Suppose a salesman regularly sells umbrellas or lemonade on Saturday afternoons at football games. To keep matters simple, suppose he has just three possible options (actions, a_i):

a_1 = sell only umbrellas.

a_2 = sell some umbrellas, some lemonade.

a_3 = sell only lemonade.

If he chooses a_1 and it rains, his profit is \$20; but if it shines, he loses \$10. It will be more convenient to describe everything as a loss (negative profit); thus his losses will be -20 or $+10$ respectively.

If he chooses action a_2 or a_3, there will also be certain losses. All this information may be assembled conveniently in the following loss table:

TABLE 10-4 Loss Function $l(a, \theta)$

Action a \ State θ	Rain (θ_1)	Shine (θ_2)
a_1	−20	10
a_2	5	5
a_3	25	−7

Suppose further that the probability distribution (long-run relative frequency) of the weather is as follows:

TABLE 10-5 Probability Distribution of θ

State θ	Rain (θ_1)	Shine (θ_2)
Probability $p(\theta)$	.20	.80

What is the best action for the salesman to take? (You are urged to work this out, before reading on; it will be easier that way.)

Solution. If he chooses a_1, what could he expect his loss to be, on average? Intuitively, we calculate the average (expected) loss if he chooses a_1

$$L(a_1) = -20\,(.20) + 10\,(.80) = 4 \tag{10-10}$$

Formally[3]

$$L(a_1) = l(a_1, \theta_1)\, p(\theta_1) + l(a_1, \theta_2)\, p(\theta_2) = \sum_{\theta} l(a_1, \theta)\, p(\theta) \tag{10-11}$$

Similarly, we evaluate

$$L(a_2) = 5(.20) + 5(.80) = 5 \tag{10-12}$$

and

$$L(a_3) = 25(.20) - 7(.80) = -.6 \tag{10-13}$$

In general

$$L(a) = \sum_{\theta} l(a, \theta)\, p(\theta) \tag{10-14}$$

The optimal action is seen to be a_3, which minimizes the expected loss; in fact, this is the only option that allows any expected profit. All our information and calculations are summarized in Table 10-6.

TABLE 10-6 Calculation of the Optimal Action a

$p(\theta)$	.20	.80	
a \ θ	θ_1	θ_2	$L(a)$ = expected loss
a_1	−20	10	4
a_2	5	5	5
a_3	25	−7	−.6 ← minimum

(The θ_1, θ_2 columns: Loss function $l(a, \theta)$)

(b) Generalization

It hardly seems necessary to state that this problem can be generalized to any number of states θ or actions a (even an infinite number, as in the next

[3] This is just an application of the concept of expected value. It has the following justification. In, say, 100 days the salesman would get about 20 rainy days at \$−20 each, yielding \$−400; and about 80 shiny days, at \$+10 each, yielding \$+800—for a sum of about \$+400 in 100 days, or an average of \$4 per day.

section). The objective remains the same: to minimize expected loss. We now pause to reconsider in detail:

1. The probabilities $p(\theta)$.
2. The loss function $l(a, \theta)$.

1. *The probabilities* $p(\theta)$, of course, should represent the best possible intelligence on the subject. For example, suppose the salesman moves to another state, with weather probabilities as given in Table 10-1. If he has no barometer, he will have to use the (prior) probabilities in this table. But if he can consult the barometer (described in Table 10-2), then of course the posterior probabilities $p(\theta/x)$ in Table 10-3 should be used. (See Problem 10-5 below.)

The logic of Bayesian inference is laid out in the block diagram, Figure 10-2. Incidentally, in the calculation of the average loss $L(a)$ in (10-14) it would not hurt to use $kp(\theta)$ instead of $p(\theta)$ as weights, where k is any constant (independent of θ and a). For $kp(\theta)$ would generate losses $kL(a)$, which would rank in the same order as the true losses $L(a)$ and, hence, point to the same correct optimizing action. This is a very useful observation. Thus, for example, our umbrella salesman need not undertake the last step in calculating the posterior probabilities of rain in (10-7); he can forget about

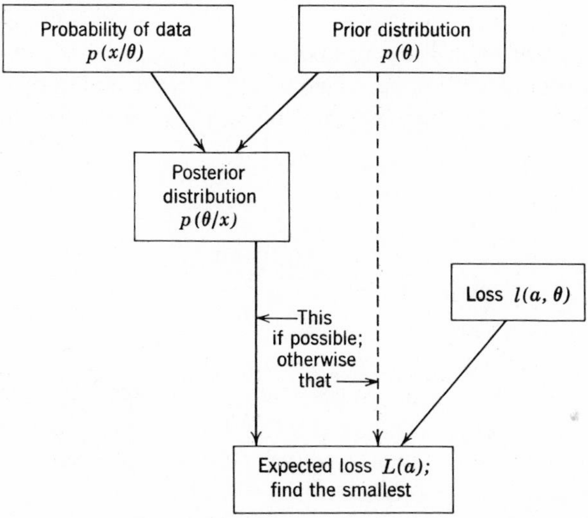

FIG. 10-2 The logic of Bayesian decisions to minimize expected loss.

the denominator $p(x_1)$, and use (10-2) and (10-4) instead—without affecting his decision.[4]

2. *The loss function*, $l(a, \theta)$. In our example, we assumed that monetary loss is the appropriate consideration. This may be valid enough if the decision is made ("game is played") over and over again: whatever minimizes the expected loss in each game will minimize total expected loss in the long run.

Yet there are some decisions that are made only once, and then expected monetary loss may not be the right criterion. To illustrate: suppose you were offered (tax-free) a choice between

$$\left.\begin{array}{l}\text{(a) \$100,000 for sure, or}\\ \text{(b) a 1/2 chance (lottery ticket) on a \$210,000 prize.}\end{array}\right\} \qquad (10\text{-}15)$$

Most people would prefer choice (a), even though its expected monetary value

$$\$100{,}000\,(1) = \$100{,}000$$

is less than that of choice (b): (10-16)

$$\$210{,}000\,(1/2) = \$105{,}000$$

The reason is that most people value the first hundred thousand more than the second. (You can easily speculate on how you would spend the first hundred thousand. Once these purchases have been made, there would be less exciting opportunities for spending the second hundred thousand; the sports car has already been bought, and so on.) Such a decision should be

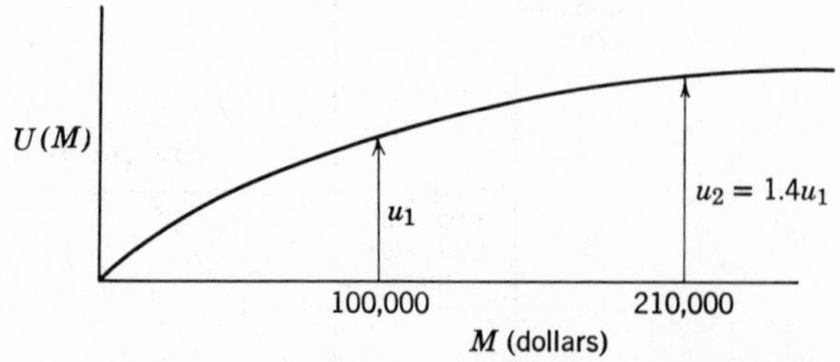

FIG. 10-3 Author's subjective evaluation of money.

[4] That is, attaching weights of .36 and .12 to his losses would yield the same result as weights of .75 and .25.

based not on money itself as in (10-16), but rather on a subjective valuation of money, or the "utility" of money. As an illustration, Figure 10-3 shows one author's subjective evaluation[5] $U(M)$. Since utility is the more appropriate measure, the decision should be based on *expected utility*, rather than expected money. Using Figure 10-3, the expected utilities of the two choices are:

$$\begin{aligned} &\text{(a)} \quad u_1(1) = u_1 \\ &\text{(b)} \quad u_2(\tfrac{1}{2}) = 1.4u_1(\tfrac{1}{2}) = .7u_1 \end{aligned} \tag{10-17}$$

which is a clear victory for choice (a). In decision situations, a *loss-of-utility* function of this kind should typically be used as our loss function $l(a, \theta)$; hereafter we shall interpret losses in this way.

PROBLEMS

10-5 Using the losses of Table 10-4, calculate the optimal action if:

(a) The only available probabilities are the prior probabilities of Table 10-1.

(b) The barometer reads "rain" (so that the posterior probabilities of Table 10-3 are relevant).

(c) The barometer reads "shine."

(d) Is the following a true or false summary of questions (a) to (c) above? If false, correct it.

If the salesman must choose his action (order his merchandise) before consulting a barometer, then a_2 (umbrellas and lemonade) is best.

However, if the barometer can be consulted first, then the salesman should

Choose a_1 (umbrellas) if the barometer predicts "rain."
Choose a_3 (lemonade) if the barometer predicts "shine."

But a bright salesman could have seen this obvious solution without going to all the trouble of learning about Bayesian decisions.

10-6 A farmer has to decide whether to sell his corn for use A or use B. His losses depend on its water content, (determined by the mill during processing, after the farmer's decision has been made) according

[5] This utility curve is highly personal, and temporary. It is defined empirically for an individual by asking him which bets he prefers. In other words, many bets like (10-15) are used to define utility.

to the following table:

Action a \ State θ	Dry	Wet
Use A	-10	30
Use B	20	10

(a) If his only additional information is that, through long past experience his corn has been classified as dry one third of the time, what should his decision be?
(b) Suppose he has developed a rough-and-ready means of determining whether it is wet or dry—a method which is correct 3/4 of the time regardless of the state of nature. If this indicates that his corn is "dry" what should his decision be?
(c) How much is the method of part (b) worth, that is, how much does it reduce his expected loss?

⇒ 10-7 A school is to be built to serve 125 students, who live along a single road.

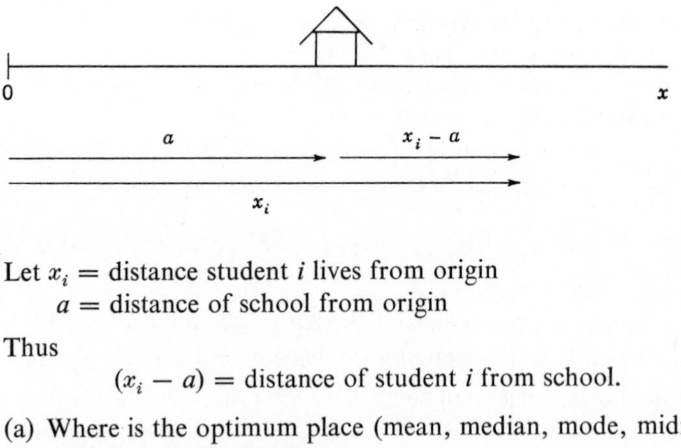

Let x_i = distance student i lives from origin
a = distance of school from origin

Thus

$$(x_i - a) = \text{distance of student } i \text{ from school.}$$

(a) Where is the optimum place (mean, median, mode, midrange?) to build the school in order to
1. Minimize the distance that the farthest student has to walk.
2. Minimize the total walking done, that is, minimize the sum of the absolute deviations:

$$\sum |x_i - a|$$

*3. Minimize the sum of the squared deviations:

$$\sum (x_i - a)^2$$

(*Hint.* Calculus suggests differentiating with respect to a, setting the result equal to zero.)

4. Maximize the number of students who live where the school is built, and do not have to walk at all.

(b) Does the following accurately reflect your conclusions in question (a) above? If not, correct it.

In (2) we are concerned only about the total walking done; walking is considered a loss, no matter who does it. In (1), on the other hand, only the walking done by the two extreme people is considered a loss; walking done by any others is of no concern whatsoever. (3) is a compromise; we imply that although all walking is some kind of loss, the more a student has walked, the greater his loss in walking one more mile. Thus the person who walks 3 miles ($x_i - a = 3$) contributes 9 to the loss function, whereas the person who walks 1 mile contributes only 1.

10-3 ESTIMATION AS A DECISION

In our earlier example the states θ (rain and shine) and actions a were categorical (i.e., nonnumerical). But this was not an essential part of the theory; in this section we consider a numerical example.

Example

Suppose the judge at a beauty contest is asked to guess the height θ of the first contestant, whom he has never seen. Yet he is not in complete ignorance; suppose he knows that the heights of contestants follow the probability distribution $p(\theta)$ shown in Figure 10-4.

(i) Suppose, in order to encourage an intelligent guess, the judge is to be fined \$1 if he makes a mistake (no matter how large or small); "a miss is as good as a mile." What should the rational judge guess?

θ (inches)	$p(\theta)$
64	.1
65	.1
66	.2
67	.2
68	.3
69	.1

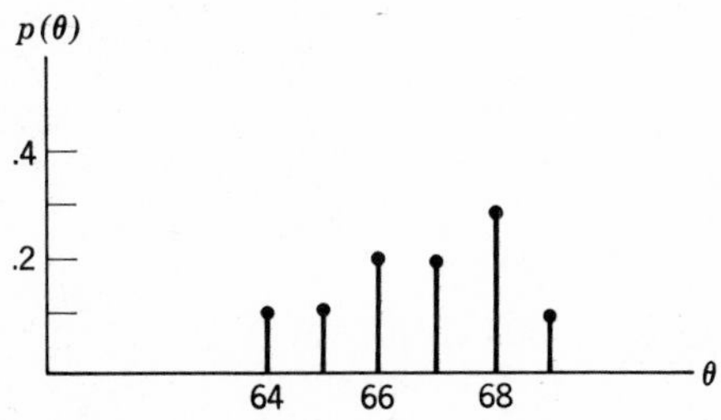

FIG. 10-4 Prior distribution of heights θ.

(ii) Suppose the rules become more severe, by fining the judge $\$x$ for an error of x inches; the greater his error, the greater his loss. What is his rational guess?

(iii) Suppose the rules are made even more severe, by fining the judge $\$x^2$ for an error of x inches; this is the same as (b), except that the loss becomes more severe as his error increases. What is his rational guess now?

TABLE 10-7 How the Optimal Estimator of θ Depends on the Loss Function

If the Loss Function $l(a, \theta)$ is:	Then the Corresponding Optimal Estimator a is:
(i) 0 if $a = \theta$ exactly, 1 otherwise ("the 0–1 loss function")	Mode of $p(\theta)$
(ii) $\lvert a - \theta\rvert$	Median
(iii) $(a - \theta)^2$	Mean

Solution. (i) The most likely (modal) value 68.
(ii) The median value 67.
(iii) The mean value 66.8.

Thus (i), (ii), and (iii) are like (4), (2), and (3) in the schoolhouse Problem 10-7, with the same solution.

To translate this into the familiar language of decision theory, the girl's height is the state of nature θ, and the guessed height (estimate) is the action a to be taken. The fine the judge must pay is the loss function $l(a, \theta)$; since a and θ are numerical, the loss function is most conveniently given by a formula, rather than a table. Each of the three loss functions, along with its corresponding optimal estimator, is shown in Table 10-7.

The quadratic loss function (iii) is the one that is usually used in decision theory. It is graphed in Figure 10-5. It is justified not only by its

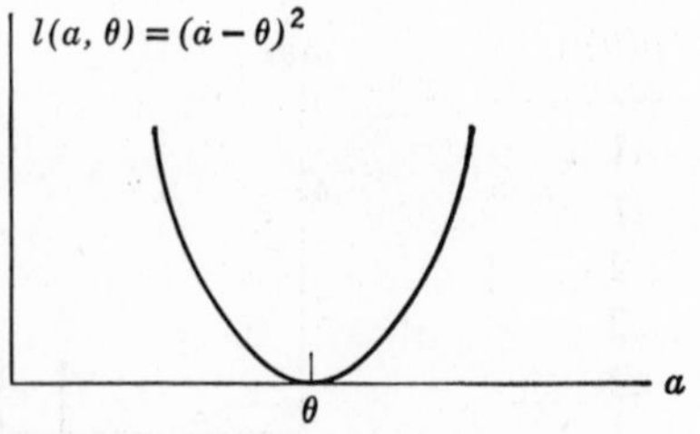

FIG. 10-5 The quadratic loss function.

intuitive appeal, but also by its attractive mathematical properties. For example, it is easily differentiated (an important requirement in minimization problems); on the other hand (i) obviously cannot be differentiated, nor can (ii), since it is an absolute value function.

We reemphasize that the probability distribution $p(\theta)$ used in the decision process ought to reflect the best available information. Thus we may be forced to use the prior distribution $p(\theta)$ if we have not yet collected any data. but after data is collected, the posterior distribution $p(\theta/x)$ is appropriate.

PROBLEMS

These are extensions of Problem 10-4.

10-8 Suppose you have to guess the height of the man drawn in Problem 10-4, with only the prior distribution $p(\theta)$ known. Find the optimal estimate of θ

(a) Assuming
$$l(a, \theta) = 0 \quad \text{if } a = \theta$$
$$= 1 \quad \text{otherwise.} \tag{10-18}$$

(b) Assuming
$$l(a, \theta) = |a - \theta|. \tag{10-19}$$

(c) Assuming
$$l(a, \theta) = (a - \theta)^2. \tag{10-20}$$

10-9 Repeat Problem 10-8, *after* the man's height has been crudely measured as $x = 74$, so that the posterior distribution $p(\theta/x)$ is relevant.

10-4 ESTIMATION FOR NORMAL DISTRIBUTIONS: BAYESIAN VERSUS CLASSICAL

This comparison is best shown with an extended example, illustrated in Figure 10-6; from this we shall draw conclusions later.

(a) Example

Suppose it is essential to estimate the length θ of a beetle accidentally caught in a delicate piece of machinery. A measurement x is possible, using a device which is subject to some error; suppose x is normally distributed about the true value θ, with $\sigma = 1$. Suppose x turns out to be 20 mm.

Question (a). What is the classical 95% confidence interval for θ?

Solution. Our information on the sampling distribution of x, that is,

$$p(x/\theta) = N(\theta, \sigma^2), \quad \text{specifically } N(\theta, 1) \tag{10-21}$$

can be "turned around" to construct the following confidence interval for θ:

$$\theta = 20 \pm 1.96(1)$$
$$= 20 \pm 1.96 \tag{10-22}$$

and, of course,

$$\text{point estimate of } \theta = 20 \tag{10-23}$$

Question (b). Suppose we take the effort to find out from a biologist that the population of all beetles has a normally distributed length, with mean $\theta_0 = 25$ mm and variance $\sigma_0^2 = 4$. How can this be used to define a posterior distribution of θ?

Solution. It will be useful to develop a general formula applying for any θ_0, σ_0, etc., and then solve it for our specific example. Since our prior distribution is

$$p(\theta) = N(\theta_0, \sigma_0^2) \tag{10-24}$$

and the distribution of our empirical evidence x is

$$p(x/\theta) = N(\theta, \sigma^2) \qquad \text{(10-21) repeated}$$

it can be shown[6] that the posterior distribution is also normal; specifically:

$$p(\theta/x) = N(ab, a) \tag{10-36}$$

[6] (10-24) and (10-21) may be written

$$p(\theta) = K_1\, e^{-(1/2\sigma_0^2)(\theta-\theta_0)^2} \tag{10-25}$$

$$p(x/\theta) = K_2\, e^{-(1/2\sigma^2)(x-\theta)^2} \tag{10-26}$$

where K_1 and K_2 and other similar constants introduced in this footnote are of a form not critical to the argument. Since

$$p(x, \theta) = p(\theta)\, p(x/\theta) \tag{10-27}$$

we can use (10-25) and (10-26) to write

$$p(x, \theta) = K_1 K_2\, e^{-(1/2)\,[(1/\sigma_0^2)(\theta^2-2\theta\theta_0+\theta_0^2)+(1/\sigma^2)(x^2-2x\theta+\theta^2)]} \tag{10-28}$$

Now consider only the exponent, which may be rearranged to

$$-\tfrac{1}{2}\left[\theta^2\left(\frac{1}{\sigma_0^2} + \frac{1}{\sigma^2}\right) - 2\theta\left(\frac{\theta_0}{\sigma_0^2} + \frac{x}{\sigma^2}\right) + K_3\right] \tag{10-29}$$

Let

$$\frac{1}{\sigma_0^2} + \frac{1}{\sigma^2} = \frac{1}{a} \tag{10-30}$$

$$\frac{\theta_0}{\sigma_0^2} + \frac{x}{\sigma^2} = b \tag{10-31}$$

(cont'd)

where

$$\frac{1}{a} = \frac{1}{\sigma_0^2} + \frac{1}{\sigma^2} \tag{10-37}$$

$$b = \frac{\theta_0}{\sigma_0^2} + \frac{x}{\sigma^2} \tag{10-38}$$

Now apply this to our example. Since

$$\sigma_0^2 = 4$$
$$\sigma^2 = 1$$
$$\theta_0 = 25$$
$$x = 20$$

it follows that

$$\frac{1}{a} = \frac{1}{4} + \frac{1}{1} = \frac{5}{4}$$

and

$$b = \frac{25}{4} + \frac{20}{1} = \frac{105}{4}$$

Thus

$$\text{mean} = ab = 21.0$$
$$\text{variance} = a = .8$$

Hence the posterior distribution may be formally written

$$p(\theta/x = 20) = N(21, .8) \tag{10-39}$$

compared with the prior

$$p(\theta) = N(25, 4) \tag{10-40}$$

Using these definitions, the exponent (10-29) can be written

$$-\frac{1}{2a}[\theta^2 - 2ab\theta + K_4] \tag{10-32}$$

$$= -\frac{1}{2a}[(\theta - ab)^2 + K_5] \tag{10-33}$$

Finally we use this to write (10-28) as

$$p(x, \theta) = K_6 e^{-(1/2a)(\theta - ab)^2} \tag{10-34}$$

and

$$p(\theta/x) = \frac{p(x, \theta)}{p(x)} = K_7 e^{-(1/2a)(\theta - ab)^2} \tag{10-35}$$

This means that θ, given x, is a normal variable with mean ab and variance a, provided a appears appropriately in K_7. But it must, since $p(\theta/x)$ is a bona fide probability function (integrating to 1), and K_7 is just the scale factor necessary to ensure this.

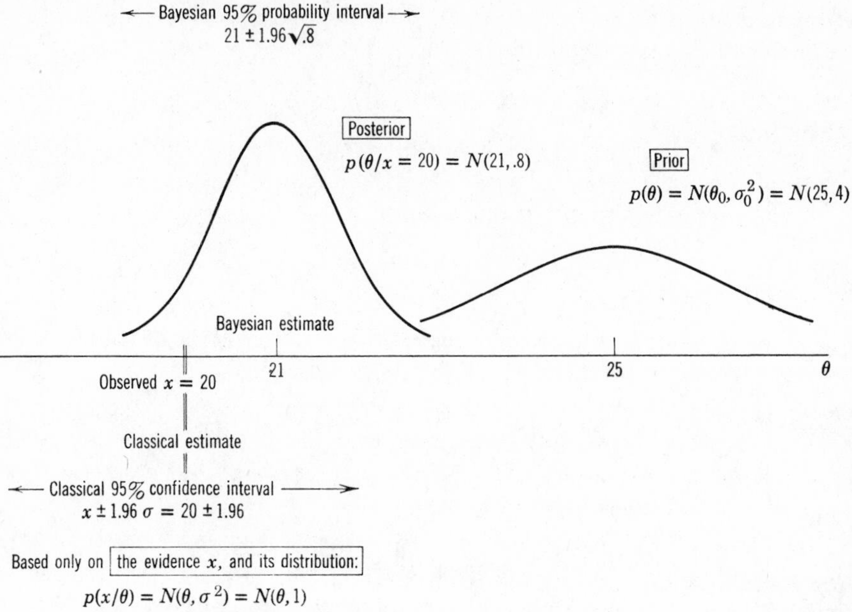

FIG. 10-6 Bayesian versus classical estimation.

The Bayesian logic is shown in Figure 10-6. A prior distribution is adjusted to take account of observed data (x), with the weight attached to the observed x depending on its probability $p(x/\theta)$. The result is the posterior distribution, with mean (21) falling, as expected, between the prior mean (25) and the observed value (20). (As a bonus, variance is reduced in the posterior distribution. Although this does not always happen, it is evident that it must happen for normal distributions; for (10-37) shows that the posterior variance a is less than σ_0^2, and also less than σ^2 incidentally.)

***Question* (c).** With the posterior distribution (10-39) now in hand, defining a Bayesian estimate of θ requires only a loss function. Suppose this is the quadratic loss function; what is the Bayesian point estimator of θ? Find also the 95% probability interval for θ.

Solution. For the quadratic loss function, the posterior mean (21) is the optimum estimator. (Note that because $p(\theta/x)$ is normal, this is also the posterior median and mode, so that all the loss functions in Table 10-7 yield the same answer. This is reassuring, and frequently happens in practice.)

To construct a 95% probability interval, we know from (10-39) that, given the observation $x = 20$, there is a 95% probability that θ will fall in the interval

$$21 \pm 1.96\sqrt{.8}$$
$$= 21 \pm 1.76$$

Note that this is narrower (more precise) than the classical interval (10-22), reflecting the value of the prior information $p(\theta)$.

PROBLEMS

10-10 As our method of measuring (beetles) becomes more and more precise ($\sigma^2 \to 0$), show that in the posterior distribution $p(\theta/x)$,

$$\begin{aligned}\text{the mean} &\to x \\ \text{variance} &\to 0\end{aligned} \tag{10-41}$$

In other words, if we use an errorless measuring device, we can be certain that the true θ will be its measured value x.

$\Rightarrow$ 10-11 Using Figure 10-6, what would you expect intuitively of the posterior mean if two independent measurements of the beetle had yielded an average of 20 mm? (For an extension of your answer, see the section immediately following.)

(b) Generalization

Suppose that a sample of n independent measurements $x_1, x_2, \ldots, x_n$ can be taken rather than just a single x. Using the sample mean $\bar{x}$, what now is the Bayesian estimate of θ? In particular, what happens as we get more and more observations ($n \to \infty$)?

This problem may be solved, using (10-36) to (10-38) with one important change. Since our data now is $\bar{x}$ instead of x we must make this substitution in (10-38), and also substitute

$$\sigma_{\bar{x}}^2 = \frac{\sigma^2}{n} \tag{10-42}$$

for σ^2 in (10-37) and (10-38). [Of course, (10-42) is just the variance of a sample mean when σ^2 is the variance of a single observation.] Thus, our generalized definition of a and b in (10-36) is

$$\frac{1}{a} = \frac{1}{\sigma_0^2} + \frac{n}{\sigma^2} \qquad \text{for } n = 1, \text{ this reduces to (10-37)} \tag{10-43}$$

$$b = \frac{\theta_0}{\sigma_0^2} + \frac{n\bar{x}}{\sigma^2} \qquad \text{for } n = 1, \text{ this reduces to (10-38)} \tag{10-44}$$

In the limit, as sample size $n \to \infty$:

$$\frac{1}{a} \simeq \frac{n}{\sigma^2} \tag{10-45}$$

$$b \simeq \frac{n\bar{x}}{\sigma^2} \tag{10-46}$$

Incidentally, exactly these same results follow, whether $n \to \infty$, or

$$\sigma_0^2 \to \infty \tag{10-47}$$

Thus, evaluating (10-36)

$$\text{posterior mean} = ab \simeq \bar{x} \tag{10-48}$$

$$\text{posterior variance} = a \simeq \frac{\sigma^2}{n} \tag{10-49}$$

Again the normality of this posterior distribution ensures that its mean, mode, and median coincide. Hence, regardless of which loss function we may use:

$$\text{Bayesian estimator of } \theta \simeq \bar{x} \tag{10-50}$$

$$95\% \text{ probability interval} \simeq \bar{x} \pm 1.96 \frac{\sigma}{\sqrt{n}} \tag{10-51}$$

We conclude that, as $n \to \infty$, Bayesian estimation approaches the classical. This is exactly as it should be: as more and more data are collected, less and less weight need be attached to prior information; and with an unlimited sample, prior information is completely disregarded, as in classical estimation. The classical and Bayesian approaches are compared in more detail in Table 10-8.

We now turn to the other condition that leads to the same result. Bayes estimators also approach the classical if prior information is very vague (i.e., if $\sigma_0^2 \to \infty$, as stated in (10-47)). Thus the less the prior distribution tells us,

TABLE 10-8 Relation of Classical and Bayesian Estimation. (Although Normality is Assumed, Results are Instructive for Other Cases Too)

Procedure to Estimate θ	Point and Interval Estimates	Requires, Along With Observed x	And Gets the Answer: In Our Example ($n = 1$)	In the Limit, as $n \to \infty$ or $\sigma_0^2 \to \infty$
Classical	Point estimate		20	$\bar{x}$
	Confidence interval	$p(x/\theta)$	20 ± 1.96	$\bar{x} \pm 1.96 \frac{\sigma}{\sqrt{n}}$
Bayesian	Point estimate	$p(x/\theta)$, $p(\theta)$ and loss function	21	Same as classical
	Probability interval	$p(x/\theta)$, $p(\theta)$	21 ± 1.76	Same as classical

the less weight we attach to it. To sum up, the two reasons for completely disregarding prior information are (1) if present data is in unlimited supply, or (2) if prior information is useless.

(c) Is θ Fixed or Variable?

In this chapter we regard the target to be estimated as a random variable—for example, the beetle's length θ in Figure 10-6. Yet in all preceding chapters, we have regarded the target as a fixed parameter—for example, the true regression coefficient β. Nevertheless, we may often find it useful to think of β as having a *subjective* probability distribution—with this being a description of the betting odds we would give that β is bracketed by any two given values. It may be helpful to boil down our best prior knowledge of β into a prior subjective distribution of β. Then the posterior subjective distribution of β would reflect how the sampling data changed the betting odds.

PROBLEMS

10-12 Following the beetle example in Section 10-4(b), suppose that:

$$\sigma_0^2 = 100$$
$$\theta_0 = 25$$
$$\sigma^2 = 1$$

and a sample of four independent observations on the trapped beetle yields an average length $\bar{x}$ of 20 mm.
(a) Calculate the Bayesian point estimate for θ, the length of the beetle. For two reasons this estimate is closer to the observed value of 20 than the Bayesian estimate (21) in Figure 10-6. Explain.
(b) Calculate the Bayesian 95% probability interval for θ.

⇒ 10-13 Suppose that, in a random sample of ten students on an American college campus, you find only one is a Democrat. Which would you rather quote as your "best estimate" of the proportion π of Democrats in the population (whole campus):
(a) The classical estimate,

$$P = \frac{x}{n} = \frac{1}{10} = .10$$

or
(b) The Bayesian estimate which, assuming this subjective prior

distribution:

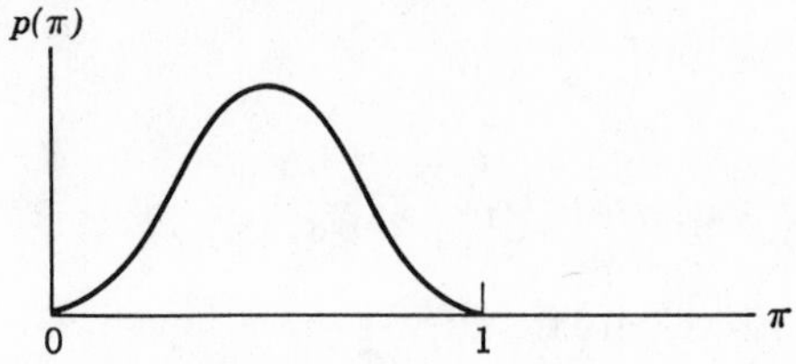

and a quadratic loss function, yields[7] the estimate

$$\frac{x+3}{n+6} = \frac{4}{16} = .25$$

10-5 CRITIQUE OF BAYESIAN METHODS

(a) Strength

Bayesian inference is the optimal statistical method (in the sense of minimizing loss of utility) if there is a known prior distribution $p(\theta)$ and loss function $l(a, \theta)$. Compared to classical methods, Bayesian methods often yield shorter interval estimates (e.g. Table 10-8), more credible point estimates (e.g. Problem 10-13), and more appropriate hypothesis tests (e.g. Problem 10-15 below). Bayesian methods may be increasingly useful in economics because sample size is often very small.

(b) Weakness

The major criticism of Bayesian estimation is that it is highly subjective. The prior $p(\theta)$ and loss function $l(a, \theta)$ are usually not known[8]—nor is there often any hope at all of specifying them exactly. For example, what is the loss function for an economist measuring a population's unemployment rate, with inevitable statistical error? We have already seen that this is not as serious a difficulty as it seems at first glance, since in many problems any of the three loss functions of Table 10-7 lead to the same Bayesian estimator. Hence, selecting the "wrong" one involves no error in the final estimate.

[7] For proof, see for example, B. W. Lindgren, *Statistical Theory*, 2nd Ed. New York: Macmillan, 1967.

[8] The other required information for Bayesian inference is $p(x/\theta)$, the distribution of sample data x. But this can often be borrowed from classical statistics. [For example, recall how we borrowed a classical deduction in (10-42).]

The other information required—the prior distribution $p(\theta)$—usually remains unknown too. Moreover, there are often difficulties in interpreting θ as a random variable; an economist cannot regard the unemployment rate θ as a random variable (as though it were drawn from a bowlful of chips). Instead, he must think of $p(\theta)$ as a subjective distribution reflecting his prior betting odds on θ. But he may not view even this as entirely satisfactory.

(c) Compromise

These issues may be clarified by considering the dilemma an economist may face. Suppose he is estimating β, the marginal propensity to consume.

At hand is a good deal of prior knowledge (drawn from economic theory, previous studies, or the like) before he collects data. For example, previous studies may indicate β to be close to .75; moreover, he may be almost certain that $.5 < \beta < 1$. He now has several options:

1. Ignore this prior knowledge, and opt for the classical estimate regardless.
2. Use prior knowledge informally to truncate his classical estimate at .5 and 1. For example, if he gets an estimate $\hat{\beta} = .23$, quote instead $\hat{\beta} = .5$; if he gets an estimate $\hat{\beta} = .52$, quote it as is.
3. A variant on this truncation option is simply to ignore the result if the estimated $\hat{\beta}$ exceeds 1, or is less than .5.
4. Use prior knowledge formally by postulating a subjective prior distribution such as:

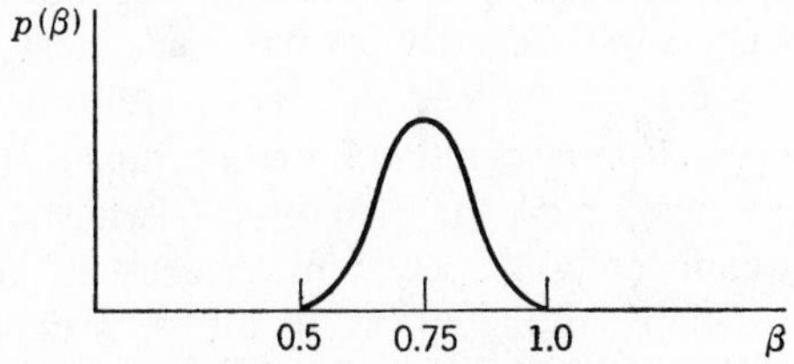

Possible prior distribution of β.

It is evident that none of these options is entirely satisfactory; yet one option must be chosen [just doing nothing with the prior knowledge is a decision—decision (1) in fact]. Judgment on which of these options is best involves examining the consequence of each.

Option (1) implies that if the data are particularly unreliable, so that for example $\hat{\beta} = .23$, this implausible answer would be used regardless. This seems to be the least attractive option.

Option (2) implies that an unfortunate estimate like $\hat{\beta} = .23$ would be pulled up to the more "respectable" value of .5. Furthermore, any estimate less than .5 is handled in exactly the same way; thus, $\hat{\beta} = .47$ would be pulled up to .5. This raises two questions: (a) Should not the estimate .47 be pulled up higher than the estimate .23? (b) Should not an estimate $\hat{\beta} = .51$ be pulled up some also, toward our prior expectation .75? It is evident that truncation is in the spirit of Bayesian inference, since it does use prior information. The difficulty is that it is bad Bayesian inference, because it involves a "switching" decision procedure:

(a) If $.5 < \hat{\beta} < 1$, it completely ignores the prior restriction, placing complete faith in the data; on the other hand,

(b) If $\hat{\beta} > 1$ or $\hat{\beta} < .5$, it completely ignores the data, placing complete faith in the prior restriction. In this case, there is just a playback of an arbitrary assumption, without adjustment.

Option (3) involves discarding an estimate that your judgment (prior information) tells you is unreliable. This is a better approach than (2) in the sense that you avoid using a figure[9] that *appears* to be the product of statistical analysis, but is in fact just an arbitrary initial assumption.

Option (4) is the Bayesian compromise: in *all* instances the final estimate reflects both prior information and the statistical evidence; thus the unfortunate switching decision procedure in (2) or (3) is avoided. Like these other methods, (4) does involve a (somewhat arbitrary) prior specification—using a functional form that may make some economists uncomfortable. Yet it is less arbitrary than the prior restriction used in (2) or (3).

The two "lesser evils" among these four options seem to be (3) or (4). Which is more appropriate in any specific case will depend on both the outlook of the statistician and the use to which the result must be put. Thus, a conservative statistician may be inclined to bury a result out of line with his good judgment, while publishing unaltered a result that is in line. Thus, he can let his statistical results "speak for themselves" (while still reserving the right to muzzle them completely in special instances). On the other hand, a less conservative statistician will incline to (4) on the grounds that all new statistical information should be presented, rather than buried—even though it may be misleading (after all, maybe it is *not* misleading). While both agree that a statistical result should be restricted in *some* way by prior information, this statistician will feel that the Bayesian approach is more reasonable and better justified mathematically.

A final, and often very important, reason for choosing (4) rather than (3) is if the statistician cannot "opt out" of estimating β. For example, an econometrician building a many-equation model of an economy must use

[9] For example, .23 adjusted to .5.

some consumption function. Thus, if he estimates an implausible value of β, he cannot just forget about it. He must use some $\hat{\beta}$, in the same way that an auto manufacturer must use some carburetor, even though he feels none is fully satisfactory. The model won't run without it.

In such circumstances there is one additional option. The econometrician may choose to discard the implausible $\hat{\beta}$, in favor of reestimating it. This may be a reasonable enough approach in certain circumstances; but it raises the practical difficulty of where he will find another sample in the nonexperimental world of economics. There is also a major theoretical difficulty: if his estimator has a substantial spread (variance), the econometrician may be able to confirm a preconceived notion of what the marginal propensity to consume should be, simply by reestimating until such a $\hat{\beta}$ turns up. This, of course, would represent an even more rigid application of prior knowledge.

Again we conclude: statistical analysis *must* be tempered by good common sense. Moreover, there is no single approach, infallible in all circumstances. But if an estimate must be derived, the two most reasonable options seem to be: the Bayesian method, with the problem it raises of specifying a prior distribution; or simply reestimating an implausible $\hat{\beta}$, recognizing that this procedure tends to lose its statistical validity as it is repeated.

*(d) Classical Methods as Bayesian Methods in Disguise

Suppose a Bayesian wishes to estimate θ with no prior knowledge. In desperation he might use the "equiprobable" prior

$$p(\theta) = c, \text{ a constant} \tag{10-52}$$

Further suppose that, rather than using the familiar and attractive quadratic loss function, he opts for the 0-1 loss function. He thus will estimate θ with the mode of the posterior distribution

$$p(\theta/x) = \frac{p(\theta)\, p(x/\theta)}{p(x)} \tag{10-53}$$

(10-8) repeated

But because of (10-52)

$$= \left[\frac{c}{p(x)}\right] p(x/\theta) \tag{10-54}$$

To find the mode, he finds the value of θ which makes $p(\theta/x)$ largest. But since the bracketed term $[c/p(x)]$ doesn't depend on θ, he only needs to find:

$$\text{the value of } \theta \text{ that makes } p(x/\theta) \text{ largest} \tag{10-55}$$

But this statement is recognized as just the definition of the classical MLE.

From this, we conclude that a classical statistician who uses MLE is getting the same result as a Bayesian using the 0-1 loss function and an "equiprobable" prior. This seems a very unflattering description of MLE, since neither this prior nor this loss function is easy to justify. But in many cases, MLE is not nearly this restrictive. If $p(\theta/x)$ is unimodal and symmetric, as it often is, then its mean, mode and median coincide; in such circumstances MLE is equivalent to Bayesian estimation using *any* of our three loss functions.

As if the discussion of MLE above has not been damaging enough, we consider an even more questionable application. Suppose we are estimating a population proportion π (as in Problem 10-13). It has been proved[10] that a classical statistician using MLE will arrive at the same result (estimating π with x/n) as a Bayesian using the quadratic loss function and the prior distribution shown in Figure 10-7.

This prior distribution is obviously hopeless, the worst we have yet encountered. (It means that a huge majority of students are Republican, or a huge majority are Democratic.) We recall that we may have been uncomfortable about the prior distribution graphed in Problem 10-13; but it was vastly better than this. This explains why MLE can occasionally give a very strange result in a small sample; our intuition was correct in leading us to reject it in Problem 10-13.

In conclusion, although MLE has many attractive characteristics,

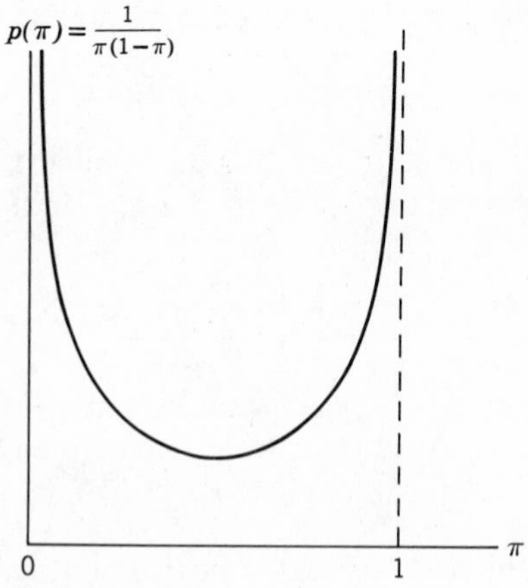

FIG. 10-7

[10] Again, see for example, B. W. Lindgren, *Statistical Theory*, 2nd Ed., New York: Macmillan 1967.

these are large sample properties; in small sample estimation, it should be used with great caution.

*10-6 HYPOTHESIS TESTING AS A BAYESIAN DECISION

(a) Example

Suppose there are two species of beetle. Species S_0 is harmless, while species S_1 is a serious pest, requiring an expensive insecticide. A beetle is sighted in a new, as yet uninfested territory; but this sighting provides no information useful in establishing whether the beetle was S_0 or S_1. Should insecticide be used or not?

TABLE 10-9 Probabilities of States of Nature, and Loss Function

$p(\theta)$	.7	.3
State θ / Action a	S_0 (Harmless Species)	S_1 (Harmful Species)
a_0 (don't spray)	5	100
a_1 (spray)	15	15

To answer this question, we need to know the costs $l(a, \theta)$ of a wrong decision, and the probabilities $p(\theta)$ of it being one species or the other; these are given in Table 10-9. Obviously action a_0 (don't spray) is appropriate if the state of nature is S_0 (harmless beetle) while a_1 is appropriate if the state is S_1.

Question (a). Should we spray, or not?

Solution. It will be convenient to generalize the loss table, calling $l(a_i, \theta_j) = l_{ij}$, for short. As always, we calculate the expected losses $L(a)$, by weighting elements in each row of this table by their appropriate probabilities:

$$\begin{aligned} L(a_0) &= p(\theta_0)\, l_{00} + p(\theta_1)\, l_{01} \\ &= (.7)\, 5 + (.3)\, 100 = 33.5 \end{aligned} \tag{10-56}$$

and

$$L(a_1) = (.7)\, 15 + (.3)\, 15 = 15 \leftarrow \text{min}$$

Thus the optimal action is a_1: spray.

We see that this problem may be expressed in terms of hypothesis testing: action a_0 (don't spray) may be interpreted as accepting H_0 (harmless beetle), while action a_1 (spray) may be interpreted as accepting H_1 (harmful beetle).

***Question* (b).** Suppose that prior information about the beetles is that species S_0 is 9 times as common as S_1. Given this new information about $p(\theta)$, what is the optimum action?

Solution. Don't spray, as shown in Table 10-10.

TABLE 10-10 Calculation of Optimal Action, a priori

$p(\theta)$	.9	.1	
State θ / Action a	S_0 (H_0)	S_1 (H_1)	$L(a)$
a_0 (don't spray)	5	100	14.5 ← min
a_1 (spray)	15	15	15

In this case the harmful species is so rare, that it is better to "take the risk," that is, assume the beetle is harmless as our working hypothesis.

***Question* (c).** So far we have assumed no statistical information on the beetle that has been sighted. Now suppose it has been captured, with its length measured as 27 mm. Suppose further that the two species are distinguishable by their lengths, which are normal random variables with $\sigma = 4$, and means $\theta_0 = 25$ and $\theta_1 = 30$ respectively. What now is the best action, a posteriori? [Assume $p(\theta)$ and losses given in Table 10-9.]

Solution. It will be most instructive to develop a general solution, leaving substitution of particulars to the end. Losses are calculated as in (10-56), substituting the appropriate posterior probabilities $p(\theta/x)$ for $p(\theta)$:

$$L(a_0) = p(\theta_0/x)\, l_{00} + p(\theta_1/x)\, l_{01} \tag{10-57}$$

Similarly

$$L(a_1) = p(\theta_0/x)\, l_{10} + p(\theta_1/x)\, l_{11} \tag{10-58}$$

We choose action a_0 iff (if and only if)

$$L(a_0) < L(a_1) \tag{10-59}$$

Substituting (10-57) and (10-58) into (10-59), and collecting like terms, we obtain the criterion: choose a_0 iff

$$p(\theta_1/x)\,[l_{01} - l_{11}] < p(\theta_0/x)\,[l_{10} - l_{00}] \tag{10-60}$$

The bracketed quantities

$$r_0 \triangleq l_{10} - l_{00} \tag{10-61}$$

and

$$r_1 \triangleq l_{01} - l_{11} \tag{10-62}$$

are called regrets. It is easy to see why: the regret if the beetle is harmless (r_0) is the extra loss incurred if we used the wrong action—that is, sprayed (a_1), rather than not sprayed (a_0). Evaluating (10-61) we see that r_0 is $15 - 5 = 10$, the difference in column elements in Table 10-9. Our much larger regret $r_1 = 100 - 15$ represents our net loss if we employ the wrong action (don't spray) on a beetle that turns out to be harmful.

Returning to (10-60), it may now be written in terms of regrets:

$$p(\theta_1/x)\, r_1 < p(\theta_0/x)\, r_0 \tag{10-63}$$

that is

$$\frac{p(\theta_1/x)}{p(\theta_0/x)} < \frac{r_0}{r_1} \tag{10-64}$$

The posterior probabilities in this equation can now be expressed in full using (10-8), and noting that $p(x)$ cancels,

$$\frac{p(\theta_1)\, p(x/\theta_1)}{p(\theta_0)\, p(x/\theta_0)} < \frac{r_0}{r_1} \tag{10-65}$$

Recall that this is our criterion for action a_0 (don't spray), interpreted as acceptance of H_0: (beetle harmless, $\theta = \theta_0$). An appropriate cross-multiplication of (10-65) leads us to an important theorem, called the

Bayesian Likelihood-Ratio Criterion:

Accept H_0 iff

$$\frac{p(x/\theta_1)}{p(x/\theta_0)} < \frac{r_0\, p(\theta_0)}{r_1\, p(\theta_1)} \tag{10-66}$$

where r_i is the regret if θ_i is true, $p(\theta_i)$ is the prior distribution, and $p(x/\theta_i)$ is the distribution of the observed data.

As stated earlier, $p(x/\theta_i)$ is often borrowed directly from classical deduction, and is the distribution of the estimator x, given the parameter θ_i. Specifically, it appears in maximum likelihood estimation as the likelihood function. Thus the left-hand side of (10-66) is called the "likelihood ratio."

This criterion is certainly reasonable. If θ_1 is a sufficiently implausible explanation of the data [i.e., $p(x/\theta_1)$ is sufficiently less than $p(x/\theta_0)$], then the likelihood ratio will be small enough to satisfy this inequality. Thus H_0 will be accepted, as it should be.

To illustrate further, consider the very simple case in which the regrets (penalties for error) are assumed equal, and the prior probabilities $p(\theta_0)$ and $p(\theta_1)$ are also assumed equal. The right-hand side of (10-66) becomes 1; thus H_0 is accepted if the likelihood of θ_0 generating the sample $[p(x/\theta_0)]$ is greater than the likelihood of θ_1 generating the sample $[p(x/\theta_1)]$. Otherwise, the alternative H_1 is accepted. In simplest terms: we select the hypothesis which is more likely to generate the observed x. In this sense, this could be viewed as hypothesis testing, within a maximum likelihood context, shown in Figure 10-8*a*. In *b* we make the further assumption that the two likelihood functions (centered on θ_0 and θ_1 respectively) have the same normal[11]

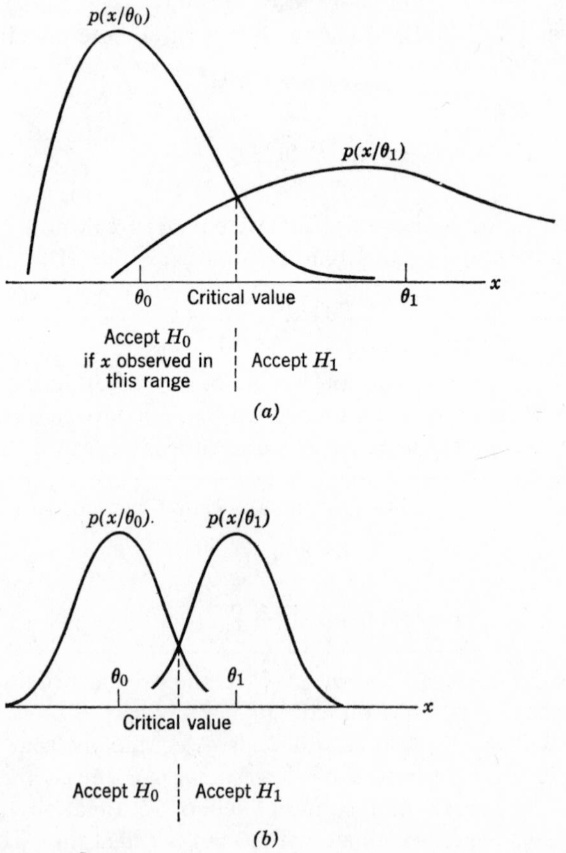

FIG. 10-8 Hypothesis testing, using the Bayesian likelihood ratio [special case when $r_0 = r_1$ and $p(\theta_2) = p(\theta_1)$]. (*a*) For any $p(x/\theta_i)$. (*b*) If $p(x/\theta_i) = N(\theta_i, \sigma)$.

[11] In fact, normality is not required; the two distributions need only be unimodal and symmetric.

distribution. Then criterion (10-66) reduces to

$$\text{Accept } H_0 \text{ iff } x \text{ is observed closer to } \theta_0 \text{ than } \theta_1 \tag{10-67}$$

Again, a very reasonable result.

Evaluating (10-66) when $r_0 \neq r_1$ or $p(\theta_0) \neq p(\theta_1)$ is obviously a more complicated matter. To keep things simple, we assume that $\theta_0 < \theta_1$, and that $p(x/\theta_0)$ and $p(x/\theta_1)$ are normal with a common σ. Then (10-66)—our criterion for accepting H_0—becomes

$$\frac{e^{-(1/2\sigma^2)(x-\theta_1)^2}}{e^{-(1/2\sigma^2)(x-\theta_0)^2}} < \frac{r_0\, p(\theta_0)}{r_1\, p(\theta_1)} \tag{10-68}$$

This may be reduced[12] to: accept H_0 iff

$$x < \frac{\sigma^2}{\theta_1 - \theta_0} \log \left[\frac{r_0\, p(\theta_0)}{r_1\, p(\theta_1)}\right] + \frac{\theta_1 + \theta_0}{2} \tag{10-69}$$

(The logarithms used throughout this section are natural logarithms, to the base e. The common logarithms of Appendix Table VIII can be converted to natural logarithms by multiplying by 2.30.) We note that the right-hand side of (10-69) is independent of x; as in all hypothesis tests, this can be evaluated prior to observing x. At the same time it does depend, as expected, on background information $p(\theta)$ and regrets. Moreover, when $r_0 = r_1$ and $p(\theta_0) = p(\theta_1)$, then the log term disappears and this reduces to the special case (10-67).

Finally, the particular problem of the beetle spray can now be solved. Substituting the information given in question (c) and Table 10-9 into

---

[12] Details: taking logarithms of (10-68):

$$-\frac{1}{2\sigma^2}(x - \theta_1)^2 + \frac{1}{2\sigma^2}(x - \theta_0)^2 < K \tag{10-70}$$

where

$$K = \log \left[\frac{r_0\, p(\theta_0)}{r_1\, p(\theta_1)}\right] \tag{10-71}$$

Rearranging (10-70):

$$\frac{1}{2\sigma^2}(2\theta_1 x - 2\theta_0 x - \theta_1^2 + \theta_0^2) < K \tag{10-72}$$

$$2(\theta_1 - \theta_0)x - (\theta_1^2 - \theta_0^2) < 2\sigma^2 K \tag{10-73}$$

that is, accept H_0 iff:

$$x < \frac{\sigma^2}{\theta_1 - \theta_0} K + \frac{(\theta_1^2 - \theta_0^2)}{2(\theta_1 - \theta_0)} \tag{10-74}$$

Using the definition of K in (10-71), (10-74) may be written as (10-69).

(10-69) yields: accept H_0 iff

$$x < \frac{16}{5} \log \left[\frac{10(.7)}{85(.3)}\right] + 27.5 \tag{10-75}$$

$$< 3.2 \log \left(\frac{7}{25.5}\right) + 27.5 \tag{10-76}$$

$$< 3.2(-1.29) + 27.5 \tag{10-77}$$

$$< 23.4 \tag{10-78}$$

Since we observed a 27 mm beetle, this condition is violated, and we reject H_0. But what does seem strange is the critical value in (10-78): even if the beetle were 25 mm—exactly θ_0, the length we would expect of a *harmless* beetle—we would still spray. With further thought we see that this answer is, after all, reasonable. The heavy damage involved if the beetle turns out to be harmful induces us to spray to avoid this risk. [From (10-75) we confirm that it is in fact the relative size of the two regrets that explains this result.]

(b) Comparison with Classical Methods

Bayesian testing is more complicated than classical testing, yet often more satisfactory. Classical testing uses only the probability function $p(x/\theta)$, while the Bayesian method also exploits the prior distribution $p(\theta)$ and regrets (the loss function); we have seen in the last section how important both these can be in setting up an appropriate test. Restated, the classical method sets the level of significance (probability of type I error) at 5% or 1%—sometimes arbitrarily, sometimes with implicit reference to vague considerations of loss and prior belief. Bayesians would argue that these considerations should be explicitly introduced—with all the assumptions exposed, and open to criticism and improvement.

PROBLEMS

10-14 Using $p(\theta)$ and losses given in Table 10-10:

(a) Reconstruct the hypothesis test of question (c) above. With your measurement of 27 mm, what would you do? Why does our previous argument (spray even if beetle is 25 mm) no longer hold?

(b) Suppose that species S_0 and S_1 were equally frequent. Would that alter your decision?

(c) How frequent would species S_0 have to be in order to alter your decision?

10-15 Suppose a psychiatrist has to classify people as sick or well (hospitalized or not) on the basis of a psychological test. The test scores are normally distributed, with $\sigma = 8$, and mean $\theta_0 = 100$ if they are well or $\theta_1 = 120$ if they are sick. The losses (regrets) of a wrong classification are obvious: if a healthy person is hospitalized, resources are wasted and the person himself may even be hurt by the treatment. Yet the other loss is even worse: if a sick person is not hospitalized, he may do damage, conceivably fatal. Suppose this second loss is considered roughly five times as serious. From past records it has been found that of the people taking the test, 60% are sick and 40% are healthy.

(a) (1) What should be the critical score above which the person is classified as sick? Then

(2) What is α? (Probability of type I error).

(3) What is β? (Probability of type II error).

(b) (1) If a classical test is used, arbitrarily setting $\alpha = 5\%$, what will be the critical score? Then

(2) What is β?

(3) By how much has the average loss increased by using this less-than-optimal method?

(c) What would we have to assume the ratio of the two regrets to be in order to arrive at a Bayesian test having $\alpha = 5\%$? Do you think it is reasonable?

*10-7 GAME THEORY

Although it is often irrelevant to the econometrician's immediate needs, we shall include game theory because it provides a fascinating analysis of conflict situations. These may arise, for example, in poker, business, or politics; thus our conflicting parties might be card players playing for insignificant stakes, oligopolists playing to remain in business, or military leaders engaged in a desperate set of moves and countermoves.

(a) Strictly Determined Games

The players employ strategies. Because a player can choose his strategy, he has some control over the outcome of the game. But he is not in complete control; the outcome will also depend on the strategy of his opponent.

The way the outcome of the game is related to the strategy of both

TABLE 10-11 An Example of a Payoff Matrix for A (Loss Function for B)

		B's Strategies		
		1	2	3
A's Strategies	1	25	6	11
	2	20	10	18
	3	11	7	5

players is shown in Table 10-11; this is called the "payoff matrix," and defines the payoff going to player A. Thus if A selects strategy 2 and B strategy 1, A receives 20. There might also be a payoff matrix for B, similarly dependent on the strategies selected by the two players. However, to keep the discussion simple, suppose that this is a "zero-sum" game—that is, what A gains, B loses. Thus, Table 10-11 defines not only the gain matrix for A, but also the loss matrix (or loss function) for B. A should be selecting a strategy to make the outcome as large as possible, while B should be trying to keep the outcome as small as possible.

Obviously B will have no interest in playing the game shown in Table 10-11 since he can do nothing but lose. So we might think of a payoff matrix normally involving some positive elements (where B pays A) and some negative ones (where A pays B). Alternatively, in order to induce B to play the game shown in Table 10-11, A might bribe B \$12 for each time he plays. This is the assumption we now make, in order to keep our payoff matrix all-positive for easier geometric interpretation. The question is "With this \$12 side payment, is it in B's interest to play this game?"

If a player can select his strategy after he knows how his opponent has committed himself, his appropriate strategy is obvious and the game becomes a trivial one. For example, if it is known that B has chosen strategy 3, A will just scan column 3, select the largest payoff (18) and then play that strategy 2. The essence of game theory, however, is that each player must commit himself without knowledge of his opponent's decision; he only knows the payoff matrix. We further assume that the game is repeated many times. The only clues a player has about his opponent's strategy must come from observing his past pattern of play.

In these circumstances A finds the continuous play of strategy 1 unattractive. It is true that this row has the largest possible payoff (\$25). But this requires B's cooperation in playing his strategy 1, and it is clearly not in B's interest to cooperate. Indeed if B observes that A is continuously playing strategy 1, he will select strategy 2, thus keeping the payoff down to 6. *A* finds strategy 3 similarly unattractive; *B* will counter with strategy 3, reducing *A*'s payoff to only 5. *A* chooses strategy 2; the very best play by *B* will still yield *A* a payoff of 10. Now review why *A* chose strategy 2. He calculated the minimum value in each row—and then selected the largest of these minimum values. This *maxi*mum of the row *min*ima is called the "maximin."

Now consider the problem from *B*'s point of view. Recall that he wants to keep the payoff as low as possible. Strategy 1 is ill-advised; when *A* observes him playing this, he will counter with 1, leaving *B* with a loss of \$25. Strategy 3 is also rejected—it may cost him \$18. He selects strategy 2; the most it can cost him is \$10. Note that *B* calculates the maximum value of each column, and then selects the smallest of these. This *mini*mum of the column *max*ima is called the "minimax." Note that in this special case minimax occurs at the same point as maximin, with a payoff of 10. In this game, *A* will play his strategy 2, and *B* will play his strategy 2; this is called a "strictly determined" game—because minimax and maximin coincide.

This is illustrated in Figure 10-9, a diagram of the payoff matrix with each payoff measured vertically. At *X* we note a "saddle point," which is

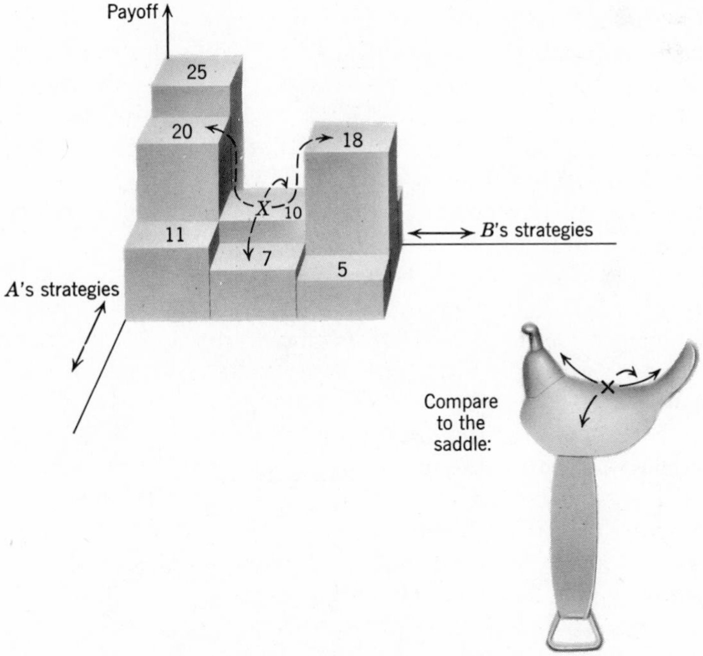

FIG. 10-9 Payoff matrix in Table 10-11.

both the largest element in its column and the smallest element in its row. When such a saddle point exists, it is both maximin and minimax.

Summary. In this strictly determined game, both A and B will play strategy 2. The payoff (from B to A) is always 10, so that it is clearly a game B will wish to play if he is bribed \$12 to do so.

PROBLEMS

10-16 What is the appropriate strategy for each opponent, in the following games; in each case decide which player the game favors.

(a)

		B 1	2	3	4
	1	3	−1	0	−2
A	2	2	2	1	3
	3	−2	0	−1	−3

(b)

		B 1	2	3
A	1	10	−2	10
	2	20	−1	5

(c)

		B 1	2
	1	−20	−4
A	2	−6	−2
	3	1	0

(b) Mixed Strategies

Let us now try to apply the theory of part (a) to the following game:

TABLE 10-12

		B 1	B 2	B 3
A	1	3	6	2
A	2	5	4	8

Minimax (5) Maximin (4)

A would select his strategy 2; this is the row with the largest minimum value (maximin = 4); at the same time *B* would select his strategy 1; this is the column with the smallest maximum value (minimax = 5). But now problems arise; because minimax and maximin do not coincide, there is no saddle point. Such a game is not strictly determined, with each playing only one strategy; it is easy to see why. *B* begins by playing column 1, while *A* plays row 2; the payoff is 5. Now *B* observes, that as long as *A* is playing row 2, he can do better by playing column 2, thus reducing the payoff to 4. But when *B* switches to column 2, it is now in *A*'s interest to switch to row 1, raising the payoff to 6. As an exercise the student should confirm that a whole series of such moves and countermoves are set into play—eventually drawing the players in a circle around to the initial position. Then a new cycle begins.

This will continue until the players recognize a fundamental point. Once a player allows his strategy to be predicted, he will be hurt. Thus, for example, when *A*'s strategy becomes clear, he can be hurt by *B*. What is his defense?

A's best plan is to keep *B* guessing. Thus if *A* determines his strategy by a chance process, *B* will be unable to predict what he will do. For example, *A* might toss a coin, playing row 1 if heads, or row 2 if tails. He is using a "mixed strategy," weighting each row with a probability of .50. Now *B* doesn't know what to expect; the only question left for *A* is whether this 50/50 mix is the best set of odds to use.

The best mix of strategies for *A* is determined in Figure 10-10. Along the horizontal axis we consider various probabilities that *A* may attach to

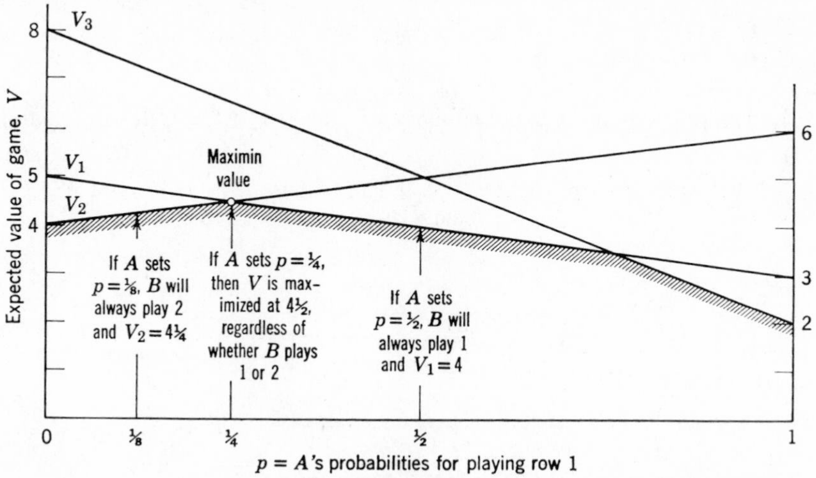

FIG. 10-10 Determination of A's mixed strategy (for game shown in Table 10-12).

playing row 1. This is all A has to select; once this is determined (e.g., if A sets $p = 1/3$), then the probability attached to playing row 2 is also determined ($1 - 1/3 = 2/3$).

Vertically, we plot the expected value of the game—which, of course, not only depends on the probabilities A may select, but also on what B may do. If B plays *only* column 1, then the expected value of the game is a function only of the probability A may select; this appears in this diagram as the line V_1. It is worth examining in detail.

At the extreme left, if A sets $p = 0$ (i.e., never plays row 1, but always plays row 2) then the value of the game V_1 is 5. On the other hand, at the extreme right, if A sets $p = 1$ (and always plays row 1), then $V_1 = 3$. Or if A sets $p = 1/2$, then

$$V_1 = 3(1/2) + 5(1/2) = 4 \tag{10-79}$$

Generally, for any probability p that A may select

$$V_1 = 3(p) + 5(1 - p) = 5 - 2p \tag{10-80}$$

The form of (10-80) confirms that V_1 is a straight line function of p, the probability A selects. Similarly, if B plays only column 2, then

$$V_2 = 6p + 4(1 - p) = 4 + 2p \tag{10-81}$$

Or, if B plays only column 3, then

$$V_3 = 2p + 8(1 - p) = 8 - 6p \tag{10-82}$$

These last two equations are also graphed in Figure 10-10.

The game is now laid out for A to analyze, with his problem being to select p. If he selects $p = 1/8$, his opponent will counter by always playing 2, and keep the expected value of the game at $4\frac{1}{4}$. [This is shown geometrically, and confirmed by evaluating (10-81) setting $p = 1/8$.] Or if A selects $p = 1/2$, B will counter with 1, thus keeping the expected value of the game down to 4. Since A is dealing with an opponent who will be selecting strategies to keep V *low*, the expected value of the game from A's point of view is shown as the hatched line in Figure 10-10. The best A can do, therefore, is to select $p = 1/4$. This guarantees $V = 4\frac{1}{2}$; moreover, note that this is the intersection of V_1 and V_2. Thus this is the value of the game regardless of whether B plays 1 or 2. This geometric solution may be read from Figure 10-10, or determined algebraically by setting $V_1 = V_2$; using (10-80) and (10-81):

$$5 - 2p = 4 + 2p \tag{10-83}$$

$$p = \tfrac{1}{4} \tag{10-84}$$

Finally, this value of p is substituted back into (10-81) for the value of the game

$$V_2 = 4 + 2(\tfrac{1}{4}) = 4\tfrac{1}{2} \tag{10-85}$$

Thus A decides to attach a probability of 1/4 to playing row 1. How does he put this into practice? There are several possibilities; for example, he might toss 2 coins. If they both come up heads (probability 1/4), then he plays row 1; if not, he plays row 2. If this game is repeated many times, A will insure that he receives an average payoff which will tend towards $4\frac{1}{2}$—and there is nothing B can do to reduce this. All B can hope for is that A has bad luck; (e.g., by the luck of the toss, A plays row 1 when B is playing column 1). This sort of bad luck can reduce A's average winning below $4\frac{1}{2}$ if the game is played only a few times (or A's good luck can raise his average winnings above $4\frac{1}{2}$); but as the game is played over and over, the element of bad luck tends to fade out.

PROBLEMS

⇒ 10-17 (a) Let's play a variation on matching coins. Each of us will choose heads or tails, independently and secretly. I'll pay you \$30 if I show tails and you show heads. I'll pay you \$10 if I show heads and you show tails. Finally, to make it fair, you pay me \$20 if we match (i.e., both show heads, or both show tails). Do you want to play? Why?
(b) What are the optimal strategies of the two players in an *ordinary* game of matching pennies? (Recall that in this game, one player gets the pennies if they match, the other gets them if they don't match.)

Would you still toss your penny in such a game, rather than secretly selecting a head or tail? Why?

10-18 You find yourself on a long sea voyage. You wish to match pennies, but your companion wants to play cards. He therefore suggests a compromise. You choose heads or tails while he selects an ace. If you select a head he pays you \$15, \$4, \$−5, and \$1 respectively, depending on whether he's chosen the spade, heart, diamond or club ace. If you select a tail, he pays you \$−10, \$−2, \$1, and \$−5, again depending on which ace he's chosen.

(a) Do you agree to play? Why? What strategies?

(b) If you were to play this game five times and found you had won \$5, what would you conclude?

(c) Are there any two lines in your diagram that do *not* intersect? From both the diagram and the payoff matrix, show that, no matter what the circumstances, it is always preferable for him to select the club ace instead of the heart ace (i.e., the heart strategy is "dominated by" the club strategy). By initially examining the payoff matrix, couldn't he have dropped the heart strategy from all further consideration?

(c) Conclusions

In solving for the best game strategy, the first step is to test whether maximin and minimax coincide. If they do, this is a strictly determined game, and the single strategy to be used by each player is determined.

If minimax and maximin do not coincide, the game is not strictly determined. Mixed strategies are called for, and are determined in simple cases geometrically or algebraically as we have illustrated. In more complex cases, more advanced mathematical techniques such as linear programming are required; but rather than extending the mechanical solution, it is more important to consider the fundamental philosophy and assumptions underlying game theory:

1. A player using his best mixed strategy can guarantee a certain expected value for the game, regardless of what his opponent may do. However, this is only the value towards which the average of many games will tend. If the game is only played a few times, luck may raise or lower this payoff.

2. Once the optimal mixed strategy is determined (e.g., $p = 1/2$), the play is dictated by a random process (tossing a coin). It is simply not good enough to decide to play each strategy half the time—for example, alternating

1, then 2, then 1, then 2, and so on. Once the opponent observes this pattern, he can predict your next play, and hurt you. Note in the simplest game of matching pennies (Problem 10-17b), how badly a player would be hurt if he alternated heads and tails rather than tossed the coin. Once an intelligent opponent observed this pattern, he could win every time. Each player must be unpredictable, by deciding his play by chance.

3. The theory of games is a very conservative strategy. It is appropriate if a game is being replayed many times against an intelligent strategist, who is out to get you, knows the payoff matrix, and can observe your strategy mix. If these conditions are not met, chances are you can find a better strategy than game play. To illustrate, consider an extreme example. Your payoff is:

		Opponent 1	Opponent 2	
You	1	\$4,000	\$1	
	2	\$4	\$2	→ minimax = maximin.

Since maximin and minimax coincide, both you and your opponent should play strategy 2 every time. But suppose on the first play, your opponent plays strategy 1! This means either that he is a fool, or unaware of the payoff matrix (and that \$4,000 debacle that he faces). It doesn't matter which; in these circumstances you drop game strategy, play row 1 and punish your opponent for his stupidity or ignorance.

Game theory also should not be used in games against nature. As an example, suppose you are trying to decide whether to hold a picnic indoors or outdoors.

		Nature: Rain 1	Nature: Not Rain 2
You hold picnic:	Indoors 1	100	0
	Outdoors 2	0	1,000

Your profit depends on both where the picnic is held, and the weather. You can easily confirm that game theory means selecting $p = 10/11$, with an expected profit of just over \$90. These odds mean that you will probably hold the picnic indoors.

Something clearly has gone wrong. An intuitive glance at the payoff matrix suggests you should go outdoors, providing there is a reasonable expectation that it won't rain. Game strategy is inappropriate because it is based on the false premise that nature is an opponent—determining the weather with the sole objective of ruining your picnic (i.e., minimizing V). Instead, nature's odds are determined independently; and let us suppose that the probability is 4/5 that it will *not* rain. With these odds, you should be holding the picnic outdoors, with an expected profit of:

$$0(\tfrac{1}{5}) + 1000(\tfrac{4}{5}) = 800 \tag{10-86}$$

The more complicated game solution is dead wrong in this case, because one of the key game theory assumptions (nature is intelligent and out to get you) simply does not hold. The student will immediately see that the simpler solution (10-86) is required; and this of course is the Bayesian, or expected value, solution outlined in Section 10-2.

In conclusion, if a prior distribution $p(\theta)$ does not exist independently, but rather is determined by a hostile opponent, then game theory is appropriate; but even under these conditions it may be too conservative a line of play, unless the opponent is highly intelligent and informed. On the other hand, if $p(\theta)$ is determined independently (e.g., rain versus shine), then Bayesian methods are required.

Part II

More Advanced Econometrics

chapter 13

Multiple Regression Using Matrices (A Generalization of Chapters 1, 2, and 3)

In Part II we now change gears: the rest of this book is a much more mathematical treatment of the material in earlier chapters. It is assumed before proceeding that readers will have had a solid college course in calculus, and another in matrix algebra. We make no attempt to teach these; it is our view that this background should not be rushed, and can be learned most effectively in courses given by math departments from good existing tests.

However, from time to time we shall build on these prerequisites. For example, see the vector geometry developed in Chapter 15, and the vector differentiation in the next section.

Although Part II generalizes the material in earlier chapters, and hence provides a reasonably self-contained introduction to more advanced econometrics, it is by no means a comprehensive survey of this very broad area. Students specializing in this field will also wish to consult textbooks like Goldberger, *Econometric Theory* (Wiley, 1964) and Malinvaud, *Statistical Methods of Econometrics* (Rand-McNally, 1966), as well as the extensive reading lists detailed in these texts. Although a course in mathematical statistics is not a prerequisite, it may be valuable to have at hand a text such as Lindgren, *Statistical Theory*, 2nd edition (Macmillan, 1967), or Hoel, *Mathematical Statistics* (Wiley, 1962). A review of statistical distributions is given in Chapter 14.

13-1 PARTIAL DERIVATIVES OF LINEAR AND QUADRATIC FORMS

This is important for developing the MLE for $\boldsymbol{\beta}$ in later sections.

(a) Linear Form

Consider the linear form in the variables β_i (where a_i are constants),

$$L = a_1\beta_1 + a_2\beta_2 + \cdots a_k\beta_k \tag{13-1}$$

If in this section we let an undesignated vector be a column vector and its prime be a row vector, (13-1) may be written as

$$L = \mathbf{a}'\boldsymbol{\beta} \quad \text{or} \quad \boldsymbol{\beta}'\mathbf{a} \tag{13-2}$$

i.e.

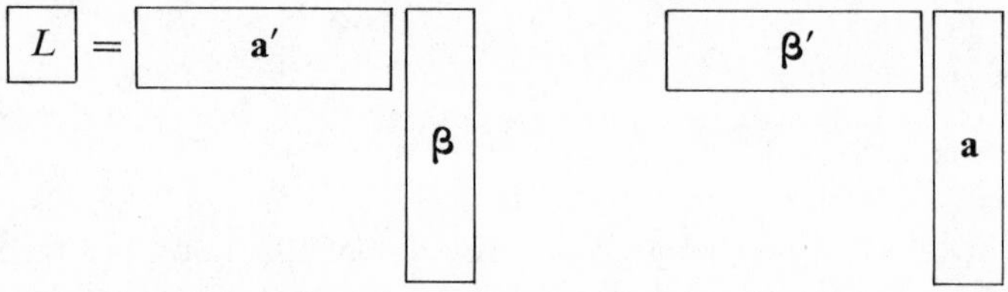

The partial derivatives of (13-1) with respect to each variable are

$$\begin{aligned} \frac{\partial L}{\partial \beta_1} &= a_1 \\ \frac{\partial L}{\partial \beta_2} &= a_2 \\ &\ \vdots \\ \frac{\partial L}{\partial \beta_k} &= a_k \end{aligned} \tag{13-3}$$

Let us stack these partial derivatives in a column vector denoted by $\dfrac{\partial L}{\partial \boldsymbol{\beta}}$ or $\dfrac{\partial}{\partial \boldsymbol{\beta}}(\mathbf{a}'\boldsymbol{\beta})$. Then (13-3) may be written more concisely as

$$\boxed{\frac{\partial}{\partial \boldsymbol{\beta}}(\mathbf{a}'\boldsymbol{\beta}) = \mathbf{a}} \tag{13-4}$$

Note the similarity to the formula in ordinary calculus

$$\frac{d}{dx}(ax) = a \tag{13-5}$$

(b) Quadratic Form

Consider next the quadratic form in the same variables β_i (where a_{ij} are constants)

$$Q = a_{11}\beta_1^2 + a_{12}\beta_1\beta_2 + \cdots + a_{21}\beta_2\beta_1 + a_{22}\beta_2^2 + \cdots \\ + a_{ij}\beta_i\beta_j \cdots + a_{k1}\beta_k\beta_1 + \cdots a_{kk}\beta_k^2 \tag{13-6}$$

where $a_{ij} = a_{ji}$ without loss of generality. In matrix notation, this may be rewritten as

$$Q = \boldsymbol{\beta}'\mathbf{A}\boldsymbol{\beta} \tag{13-7}$$

i.e.

$$\boxed{Q} = \begin{bmatrix} \beta_1 & \cdots & \beta_k \end{bmatrix} \begin{bmatrix} a_{11} & \cdots & a_{1k} \\ \vdots & & \\ a_{k1} & \cdots & a_{kk} \end{bmatrix} \begin{bmatrix} \beta_1 \\ \vdots \\ \beta_k \end{bmatrix}$$

where $\mathbf{A} = \mathbf{A}'$ without loss of generality.

If we take the partial derivatives of (13-6) with respect to each variable, and remember $a_{21} = a_{12}$ etc., then

$$\frac{\partial Q}{\partial \beta_1} = 2a_{11}\beta_1 + a_{12}\beta_2 + \cdots a_{1k}\beta_k \\ + a_{21}\beta_2 + \cdots a_{k1}\beta_k$$

Similarly

$$\left.\begin{aligned} &= 2(a_{11}\beta_1 + a_{12}\beta_2 + \cdots a_{1k}\beta_k) \\ \frac{\partial Q}{\partial \beta_2} &= 2(a_{21}\beta_1 + a_{22}\beta_2 + \cdots a_{2k}\beta_k) \\ &\vdots \\ \frac{\partial Q}{\partial \beta_k} &= 2(a_{k1}\beta_1 + \cdots \quad a_{kk}\beta_k) \end{aligned}\right\} \tag{13-8}$$

As before, these partial derivatives stacked in a column are denoted by $\partial Q/\partial \boldsymbol{\beta}$ or $(\partial/\partial\boldsymbol{\beta})(\boldsymbol{\beta}'\mathbf{A}\boldsymbol{\beta})$. Since the right side of (13-8) is the matrix product $2\mathbf{A}\boldsymbol{\beta}$, (13-8) may be written concisely as

$$\boxed{\frac{\partial}{\partial\boldsymbol{\beta}}(\boldsymbol{\beta}'\mathbf{A}\boldsymbol{\beta}) = 2\mathbf{A}\boldsymbol{\beta}} \tag{13-9}$$

Note again the similarity to the formula in ordinary calculus

$$\frac{d}{dx}(ax^2) = 2ax \tag{13-10}$$

13-2 INTRODUCTION TO THE GENERAL LINEAR MODEL

Before embarking on the vector and matrix algebra of the general case, it is wise to clarify our notation. A boldface capital letter, such as **A** or **X** represents a matrix; a boldface small letter is a vector; to avoid too many transpose signs, a vector may be either row *or* column, depending on the context in which it is introduced. Thus, a set of observations on one variable is introduced as a column, for example,

$$\mathbf{y} = \boxed{\begin{matrix} y_1 \\ y_2 \\ \cdot \\ \cdot \\ \cdot \\ y_n \end{matrix}}$$

while a set of variables is introduced as a row, for example,

$$\mathbf{x} = \boxed{x_1, x_2, \ldots x_k}$$

A single entry in a matrix or vector is designated by an ordinary small letter. The reader is warned that from now on, the variables x and y may refer to *either* their actual observed values or deviations from their mean. Following Chapters 2 and 3, it is recommended that the reader regard the y's as actual observed values, and all the x's as deviations from the mean. But this is not absolutely necessary. Both sets of variables could be treated as original observed variables or, for that matter, both could be treated as deviations from their means—provided that the different definition of the intercept constant is kept in mind (as in Figure 1-7), and other minor adjustments are made.

During the course of this chapter, the reader is advised to consult Table 13-1 frequently, since it lays out the results from the univariate and multivariate cases side by side for easy comparison.

TABLE 13-1 Comparison of Univariate and Multivariate Regression

Univariate		*Multivariate*	
1. *Model*			
$Y_i = \alpha + x_i\,\beta + e_i$	(2-3)	$y_i = \mathbf{x}_i\,\boldsymbol{\beta} + e_i$	(13-12)
		so that altogether	
		$\mathbf{y} = \mathbf{X}\boldsymbol{\beta} + \mathbf{e}$	(13-13)
2. *Least squares maximum likelihood estimates*			
$\hat{\beta} = (\sum x_i^2)^{-1}(\sum x_i y_i)$	(1-16)	$\hat{\boldsymbol{\beta}} = (\mathbf{X}'\mathbf{X})^{-1}\mathbf{X}'\mathbf{y}$	(13-24)
3. *Distribution of* $\hat{\beta}$			
$\hat{\beta}$ is normal		$\hat{\boldsymbol{\beta}}$ is multivariate normal	
with $E(\hat{\beta}) = \beta$	(2-7)	with $E(\hat{\boldsymbol{\beta}}) = \boldsymbol{\beta}$	(13-30)
and var $(\hat{\beta}) = \sigma^2(\sum x_i^2)^{-1}$	(2-8)	and cov $(\hat{\boldsymbol{\beta}}) = \sigma^2(\mathbf{X}'\mathbf{X})^{-1}$	(13-32)
$= \sigma^2 v$		$= \sigma^2\mathbf{V}$	(13-34)
4. *Standardized distribution*			
$z = \dfrac{\hat{\beta} - \beta}{\sqrt{\sigma^2 v}}$	(2-23)		
or $z^2 = (\hat{\beta} - \beta)(\sigma^2 v)^{-1}(\hat{\beta} - \beta)$ has χ^2 distribution with 1 d.f.		$\chi^2 = (\mathbf{C}\hat{\boldsymbol{\beta}} - \mathbf{C}\boldsymbol{\beta})'(\sigma^2\mathbf{CVC}')^{-1}(\mathbf{C}\hat{\boldsymbol{\beta}} - \mathbf{C}\boldsymbol{\beta})$ has χ^2 distribution with r d.f.	(13-38)
5. *Quasi-standardized distribution, using* s^2 *for* σ^2			
$t = \dfrac{(\hat{\beta} - \beta)}{\sqrt{s^2 v}}$	(2-26)		
has t distribution on $(n - 2)$ d.f. or $t^2 = (\hat{\beta} - \beta)(s^2 v)^{-1}(\hat{\beta} - \beta)$ has F distribution on $(1, n - 2)$ d.f.		$F = \dfrac{1}{r}(\mathbf{C}\hat{\boldsymbol{\beta}} - \mathbf{C}\boldsymbol{\beta})'(s^2\mathbf{CVC}')^{-1}(\mathbf{C}\hat{\boldsymbol{\beta}} - \mathbf{C}\boldsymbol{\beta})$ has F distribution on $(r, n - k)$ d.f. where k is the number of regressors, and r the number being simultaneously tested	(13-39)

13-3 THE MATHEMATICAL MODEL

If y is a linear function of the independent variables $x_2, x_3 \cdots x_k$, plus error, then the ith observation y_i can be written as

$$y_i = \beta_1 + \beta_2 x_{i2} \cdots + \beta_k x_{ik} + e_i \tag{13-11}$$

where the subscript i refers to the ith observation. Notice that β_1 is not a slope, but is, in fact, the constant term in the equation—that is, what we have called α in earlier chapters. One of the great virtues of matrices is that this constant term will no longer require special treatment. In vector notation, (13-11) is

$$y_i = \mathbf{x}_i \boldsymbol{\beta} + e_i \tag{13-12}$$

that is,

$$\boxed{y_i} = \boxed{1 \; x_{i2} \; \cdots \; x_{ik}} \begin{bmatrix} \beta_1 \\ \beta_2 \\ \cdot \\ \cdot \\ \cdot \\ \beta_k \end{bmatrix} + \boxed{e_i}$$

If we stack all y observations into a column vector, we have

$$\mathbf{y} = \mathbf{X}\boldsymbol{\beta} + \mathbf{e} \tag{13-13}$$

$$\begin{bmatrix} y_1 \\ y_2 \\ \cdot \\ \cdot \\ \cdot \\ y_i \\ \cdot \\ \cdot \\ \cdot \\ y_n \end{bmatrix} = \begin{bmatrix} 1 & x_{12} & \cdots & x_{1k} \\ 1 & x_{22} & \cdots & x_{2k} \\ & \cdot & & \cdot \\ & \cdot & & \cdot \\ & \cdot & & \cdot \\ 1 & x_{i2} & & x_{ik} \\ & \cdot & & \cdot \\ & \cdot & & \cdot \\ & \cdot & & \cdot \\ 1 & x_{n2} & \cdots & x_{nk} \end{bmatrix} \begin{bmatrix} \beta_1 \\ \beta_2 \\ \cdot \\ \cdot \\ \cdot \\ \beta_k \end{bmatrix} + \begin{bmatrix} e_1 \\ e_2 \\ \cdot \\ \cdot \\ \cdot \\ e_i \\ \cdot \\ \cdot \\ \cdot \\ e_n \end{bmatrix}$$

We assume the e_i are independent errors, with mean 0 and variance σ^2, so that

$$E(\mathbf{e}) = \mathbf{0} \tag{13-14}$$

and the covariance matrix of $\mathbf{e}$ is

$$\text{cov}(\mathbf{e}) \triangleq E(\mathbf{e}\mathbf{e}') = \sigma^2 \mathbf{I} \tag{13-15}$$

i.e.

$$\begin{bmatrix} E(e_1e_1) & E(e_1e_2) & \cdots & E(e_1e_n) \\ E(e_2e_1) & E(e_2e_2) & \cdots & \cdot \\ \cdot & & & \cdot \\ \cdot & & & \cdot \\ \cdot & & & \\ E(e_ne_1) & E(e_ne_2) & \cdots & E(e_ne_n) \end{bmatrix} = \begin{bmatrix} \sigma^2 & & & & 0 \\ & \sigma^2 & & & \\ & & \cdot & & \\ & & & \cdot & \\ & & & & \cdot \\ 0 & & & & \sigma^2 \end{bmatrix} \tag{13-16}$$

Since the e distribution is, in fact, the y distribution translated onto a zero mean, the only difference in these two sets of variables is their mean value. Thus:

$$\boxed{\begin{aligned} E(\mathbf{y}) &= \mathbf{X}\boldsymbol{\beta} \qquad (13\text{-}17) \\ \text{and } \operatorname{cov}(\mathbf{y}) &= \sigma^2\mathbf{I} \qquad (13\text{-}18) \end{aligned}}$$

Note that the covariance matrix of $\mathbf{e}$ in (13-15) and of $\mathbf{y}$ in (13-18) are identical.

At this point, we come to the choice of the weak or strong assumption about the distribution of the error term $\mathbf{e}$, as discussed in Chapter 2. In the interests of a speedy development, we defer our generalization of the Gauss-Markov theorem based on the weak assumption to Chapter 16, and proceed here immediately to the strong assumption, that is,

$$\mathbf{e} \text{ is normally distributed} \tag{13-19}$$

Example

In the wheat yield model, we assume that our seven observations of y were generated as follows:

$$\begin{bmatrix} y_1 \\ y_2 \\ y_3 \\ y_4 \\ y_5 \\ y_6 \\ y_7 \end{bmatrix} = \begin{bmatrix} 1 & -300 & 1 \\ 1 & -200 & -2 \\ 1 & -100 & 2 \\ 1 & 0 & 2 \\ 1 & 100 & -1 \\ 1 & 200 & -3 \\ 1 & 300 & 1 \end{bmatrix} \begin{bmatrix} \beta_1 \\ \beta_2 \\ \beta_3 \end{bmatrix} + \begin{bmatrix} e_1 \\ e_2 \\ e_3 \\ e_4 \\ e_5 \\ e_6 \\ e_7 \end{bmatrix} \tag{13–20}$$

in which the β's are unknowns to be estimated, and the error terms are drawn from the normal distribution described in (13-14) and (13-15).

13-4 MAXIMUM LIKELIHOOD ESTIMATES (MLE)

These are derived by trying out all possible values for $\boldsymbol{\beta}$ and σ and selecting that set which maximizes the likelihood of our observed sample. For any $\boldsymbol{\beta}$ and σ we consider, the likelihood of our observed sample $\mathbf{y}$ is

$$L(\boldsymbol{\beta}, \sigma^2) = \frac{1}{(2\pi\sigma^2)^{n/2}} e^{-(1/2\sigma^2)(\mathbf{y}-\mathbf{X}\boldsymbol{\beta})'(\mathbf{y}-\mathbf{X}\boldsymbol{\beta})} \tag{13-21}$$

This is simply a generalization of (2-48), with the mean $\alpha + \beta x_i$ being replaced by the mean $\beta_1 + \beta_2 x_{i2} \cdots + \beta_k x_{ik}$ of (13-11), and dressed up in matrix notation.

As remarked after equation (2-48), whatever the value of σ we try, we can maximize (13-21) with respect to $\boldsymbol{\beta}$ by minimizing the exponent

$$(\mathbf{y} - \mathbf{X}\boldsymbol{\beta})'(\mathbf{y} - \mathbf{X}\boldsymbol{\beta}) \tag{13-22}$$

This is simply the sum of squared deviations, expressed in matrix form; hence, MLE is equivalent to least squares. We expand[1] (13-22),

$$\mathbf{y}'\mathbf{y} - 2\mathbf{y}'\mathbf{X}\boldsymbol{\beta} + \boldsymbol{\beta}'\mathbf{X}'\mathbf{X}\boldsymbol{\beta} \tag{13-23}$$

The minimum occurs where the partial derivatives with respect to $\boldsymbol{\beta}$ are zero. The vector of partial derivatives may be obtained by applying the results of Section 13-1 to equation (13-23) since its three terms in $\boldsymbol{\beta}$ are constant, linear, and quadratic. Thus, the vector of partial derivatives is

$$\mathbf{0} - 2\mathbf{X}'\mathbf{y} + 2\mathbf{X}'\mathbf{X}\boldsymbol{\beta}$$

Setting this equal to zero yields[2] the MLE, or least squares estimate:

$$\boxed{\hat{\boldsymbol{\beta}} = (\mathbf{X}'\mathbf{X})^{-1}\mathbf{X}'\mathbf{y}} \tag{13-24}$$

[1] The expansion of (13-22) into (13-23) is analogous to the expansion of the scalar quantity $(y - xb)^2$ into $y^2 - 2y(xb) + (xb)^2$. The details are as follows:
(13-22) may be written

$$\{\mathbf{y}' - (\mathbf{X}\boldsymbol{\beta})'\}\{\mathbf{y} - \mathbf{X}\boldsymbol{\beta}\} = \mathbf{y}'\mathbf{y} - \mathbf{y}'\mathbf{X}\boldsymbol{\beta} - (\mathbf{X}\boldsymbol{\beta})'\mathbf{y} + (\mathbf{X}\boldsymbol{\beta})'\mathbf{X}\boldsymbol{\beta}$$

But since $\mathbf{y}'\mathbf{X}\boldsymbol{\beta}$ is a 1×1 matrix, it is identical to its transpose $(\mathbf{X}\boldsymbol{\beta})'\mathbf{y}$. Thus, the two middle terms may be collected together and (13-23) follows.

[2] We assume that $\mathbf{X}$ is of full rank (complete multicollinearity is avoided) so that $\mathbf{X}'\mathbf{X}$ is invertible. We might be tempted to rewrite (13-24) as

$$\hat{\boldsymbol{\beta}} = (\mathbf{X}^{-1}\mathbf{X}'^{-1})\mathbf{X}'\mathbf{y} = \mathbf{X}^{-1}\mathbf{y}$$

This is *only* justified however, when $\mathbf{X}$ is *square* so that $\mathbf{X}^{-1}$ exists. In this case, where $k = n$, there are as many parameters as observations, and the problem is no longer a statistical problem of best fit, but rather a mathematical problem of the *only* fit. This idea is used later, in equation (20-3).

As in Appendix 2-4, it can be shown that the MLE of σ^2 (the variance of e), is simply the average of the squared residuals between the observed and fitted values of y:

$$\hat{\sigma}^2 = \frac{1}{n}(\mathbf{y} - \hat{\mathbf{y}})'(\mathbf{y} - \hat{\mathbf{y}}) \tag{13-25}$$

where $\hat{\mathbf{y}} = \mathbf{X}\hat{\boldsymbol{\beta}}$. However, in the development below, we prefer to use the unbiased estimator:

$$\boxed{s^2 = \frac{1}{n-k}(\mathbf{y} - \hat{\mathbf{y}})'(\mathbf{y} - \hat{\mathbf{y}})} \tag{13-26}$$

The ratio s^2/σ^2 has a C^2 (modified Chi squared) distribution with only $(n - k)$ degrees of freedom, since k degrees of freedom out of the total n have been used in deriving the k estimators $\hat{\boldsymbol{\beta}}$. The details of this, and other distributions, will be given in Chapter 14.

Example

In the wheat yield example, $\hat{\boldsymbol{\beta}}$ is estimated from (13-24) by

$$\begin{bmatrix} \hat{\beta}_1 \\ \hat{\beta}_2 \\ \hat{\beta}_3 \end{bmatrix} = (\mathbf{X}'\mathbf{X})^{-1}\mathbf{X}'\mathbf{y}$$

$$= \left(\begin{bmatrix} 1 & 1 & \cdots & 1 \\ -300 & -200 & \cdots & 300 \\ 1 & -2 & \cdots & 1 \end{bmatrix} \begin{bmatrix} 1 & -300 & 1 \\ 1 & -200 & -2 \\ & \cdot & \\ & \cdot & \\ & \cdot & \\ 1 & 300 & 1 \end{bmatrix} \right)^{-1} \begin{bmatrix} 1 & 1 & \cdots & 1 \\ -300 & -200 & \cdots & 300 \\ 1 & -2 & \cdots & 1 \end{bmatrix} \begin{bmatrix} 40 \\ 45 \\ \cdot \\ \cdot \\ \cdot \\ 80 \end{bmatrix}$$

$$= \begin{bmatrix} 7 & 0 & 0 \\ 0 & 28_4 & -500 \\ 0 & -500 & 24 \end{bmatrix}^{-1} \begin{bmatrix} 420 \\ 19_3 \\ -20 \end{bmatrix} = \begin{bmatrix} 1/7 & 0 & 0 \\ 0 & ._5371 & ._4773 \\ 0 & ._4773 & .0433 \end{bmatrix} \begin{bmatrix} 420 \\ 19_3 \\ -20 \end{bmatrix} = \begin{bmatrix} 60.0 \\ .0689 \\ .603 \end{bmatrix}$$

where the subscript represents the number of omitted zeros; for example, 28_4 means 280000, while $._5371$ means .00000371.

Note how the measurement of x values as deviations has resulted in zeros in all but one of the elements of the first row and column of $\mathbf{X}'\mathbf{X}$. This greatly simplifies its inversion. $\hat{\boldsymbol{\beta}}$ now defines our estimated regression plane, from which fitted y values can be calculated:

$$\hat{\mathbf{y}} = \mathbf{X}\hat{\boldsymbol{\beta}} \tag{13-27}$$

In our example:

$$\begin{bmatrix} \hat{y}_1 \\ \hat{y}_2 \\ \cdot \\ \cdot \\ \cdot \\ \\ \hat{y}_7 \end{bmatrix} = \begin{bmatrix} 1 & -300 & 1 \\ 1 & -200 & -2 \\ 1 & -100 & 2 \\ 1 & 0 & 2 \\ 1 & 100 & -1 \\ 1 & 200 & -3 \\ 1 & 300 & 1 \end{bmatrix} \begin{bmatrix} 60.0 \\ .0689 \\ .603 \end{bmatrix} = \begin{bmatrix} 39.9 \\ 45.0 \\ 54.3 \\ 61.2 \\ 66.3 \\ 72.0 \\ 81.3 \end{bmatrix}$$

These estimated values of y, along with the observed values of y, allow us to estimate the variance of our error from (13-26):

$$s^2 = \frac{1}{(7-3)} \begin{bmatrix} .1 & 0 & -4.3 & \cdots & -1.3 \end{bmatrix} \begin{bmatrix} .1 \\ 0 \\ -4.3 \\ 3.8 \\ 3.7 \\ -2.0 \\ -1.3 \end{bmatrix}$$

$$= 13.08$$

13-5 DISTRIBUTION OF $\hat{\boldsymbol{\beta}}$

Because $\mathbf{X}$ is fixed, $\hat{\boldsymbol{\beta}}$ estimated in (13-24) is just a linear transformation of normal, independent variables $\mathbf{y}$. To emphasize this, we rewrite (13-24) as

$$\hat{\boldsymbol{\beta}} = \mathbf{M}\mathbf{y} \tag{13-28}$$

where

$$\mathbf{M} = (\mathbf{X}'\mathbf{X})^{-1}\mathbf{X}' \tag{13-29}$$

As stated in Table 13-2, such a linear transformation keeps $\hat{\boldsymbol{\beta}}$ normal,

TABLE 13-2 Linear Transformations and Their Distributions (Extension of Appendix 2-1)

	Variable	Mean	Variance	Distribution
(a) *Univariate case*				
Original variable	y	μ	σ^2	normal
				↓
Its transformation	$z = my$	$m\mu$	$m^2\sigma^2$	normal
(b) *Bivariate case*				
Original variables	y_1 y_2	μ_1 μ_2	σ_1^2 σ_2^2 and covariance σ_{12}	normal normal ↓
Transformation	$z = m_1 y_1 + m_2 y_2$	$m_1\mu_1 + m_2\mu_2$	$m_1^2\sigma_1^2 + m_2^2\sigma_2^2 + 2m_1 m_2 \sigma_{12}$	normal
(In matrix notation)	$\boxed{z} = \boxed{m_1 \;\; m_2} \begin{bmatrix} y_1 \\ y_2 \end{bmatrix}$	$\boxed{m_1 \;\; m_2} \begin{bmatrix} \mu_1 \\ \mu_2 \end{bmatrix}$	$\boxed{m_1 \;\; m_2} \begin{bmatrix} \sigma_1^2 & \sigma_{12} \\ \sigma_{12} & \sigma_2^2 \end{bmatrix} \begin{bmatrix} m_1 \\ m_2 \end{bmatrix}$	
(c) *Multivariate case*			covariance matrix	
Original variables	$\mathbf{y}$	$\boldsymbol{\mu}$	$\boldsymbol{\Sigma}$	normal
Transformation				↓
(In matrix notation)	$\mathbf{z} = \mathbf{My}$	$\mathbf{M}\boldsymbol{\mu}$	$\mathbf{M\Sigma M}'$	normal
	$\boxed{\mathbf{z}} = \boxed{\mathbf{M}} \boxed{\mathbf{y}}$	$\boxed{\mathbf{M}} \boxed{\boldsymbol{\mu}}$	$\boxed{\mathbf{M}} \boxed{\boldsymbol{\Sigma}} \boxed{\mathbf{M}'}$	

with mean

$$E(\hat{\boldsymbol{\beta}}) = E(\mathbf{My}) = \mathbf{M}E(\mathbf{y})$$

Noting (13-29) and (13-17)

$$= \{(\mathbf{X}'\mathbf{X})^{-1}\mathbf{X}'\}\mathbf{X}\boldsymbol{\beta}$$

$$\boxed{E(\hat{\boldsymbol{\beta}}) = \boldsymbol{\beta}} \tag{13-30}$$

Thus, $\hat{\boldsymbol{\beta}}$ is a normal, unbiased estimator of $\boldsymbol{\beta}$. The covariance matrix of $\hat{\boldsymbol{\beta}}$ is also found from Table 13-2, and is

$$\text{cov}\,(\hat{\boldsymbol{\beta}}) = \mathbf{M}\,(\text{cov}\,\mathbf{y})\mathbf{M}'$$

Noting[3] (13-29) and (13-18)

$$= \{(\mathbf{X}'\mathbf{X})^{-1}\mathbf{X}'\}\sigma^2\mathbf{I}\{(\mathbf{X}'\mathbf{X})^{-1}\mathbf{X}'\}' \tag{13-31}$$

$$\boxed{\text{cov}\,(\hat{\boldsymbol{\beta}}) = \sigma^2(\mathbf{X}'\mathbf{X})^{-1}} \tag{13-32}$$

Note how the inverse $(\mathbf{X}'\mathbf{X})^{-1}$ keeps reappearing. Since it will continue to be of fundamental importance in our estimating procedures, we introduce the abbreviation

$$\mathbf{V} \triangleq (\mathbf{X}'\mathbf{X})^{-1} \tag{13-33}$$

Thus

$$\text{cov}\,\hat{\boldsymbol{\beta}} = \sigma^2\mathbf{V} \tag{13-34}$$

13-6 CONFIDENCE REGIONS AND HYPOTHESIS TESTING: A GENERALIZED APPROACH

With the distribution of the estimator $\hat{\boldsymbol{\beta}}$ in hand, we are now in a position to develop confidence intervals and hypothesis tests for $\boldsymbol{\beta}$. But we choose instead to slow down, and generalize our argument. In the following section, we consider a general linear transformation of $\hat{\boldsymbol{\beta}}$, which will be useful in constructing a whole array of confidence intervals about some or all of the β's. The student who finds this concept a bit difficult is advised that this is a high-return investment. From this general procedure, many specific confidence intervals and tests will be easily derived.

---

[3] Also noting that the transpose of an inverse equals the inverse of the transpose, and that $(\mathbf{X}'\mathbf{X})' = \mathbf{X}'\mathbf{X}$, that is, $\mathbf{X}'\mathbf{X}$ is symmetric.

Let us consider the distribution of $\hat{\boldsymbol{\gamma}}$, a general linear transformation of $\hat{\boldsymbol{\beta}}$:

$$\hat{\boldsymbol{\gamma}} = \mathbf{C}\hat{\boldsymbol{\beta}}$$

$$\begin{bmatrix} \hat{\gamma}_1 \\ \cdot \\ \cdot \\ \cdot \\ \hat{\gamma}_r \end{bmatrix} = \begin{bmatrix} c_{11} & \cdots & c_{1k} \\ \cdot & & \\ \cdot & & \\ \cdot & & \\ c_{r1} & & c_{rk} \end{bmatrix} \begin{bmatrix} \hat{\beta}_1 \\ \cdot \\ \cdot \\ \cdot \\ \hat{\beta}_k \end{bmatrix} \tag{13-35}$$

where **C** is any arbitrary matrix of constants, subject only to the restriction that it be of rank r. This means that the rows must be linearly independent, and in particular, that $r \leq k$. Looking ahead, we see that if we let **C** be the identity, for example, (13-35) will enable us to find the distribution of $\hat{\boldsymbol{\beta}}$ itself; or if we let $\mathbf{C} = (1\ 0\ 0 \cdots 0)$, the result is the distribution of a single variable $\hat{\beta}_1$. While k is the total number of regressors in the model, r is the number we will be testing.

To find the distribution of $\mathbf{C}\hat{\boldsymbol{\beta}}$, we appeal once more to the theory of linear transformations described in Table 13-2. Also noting (13-30), it follows that

$$E(\mathbf{C}\hat{\boldsymbol{\beta}}) = \mathbf{C}E(\hat{\boldsymbol{\beta}}) = \mathbf{C}\boldsymbol{\beta} \tag{13-36}$$

and from (13-34)

$$\text{cov}\,(\mathbf{C}\hat{\boldsymbol{\beta}}) = \mathbf{C}(\text{cov}\,\hat{\boldsymbol{\beta}})\mathbf{C}' = \sigma^2\mathbf{CVC}' \tag{13-37}$$

Just as we found a standardized normal variable (z) in the univariate case, so we shall standardize in this multivariate case. It may be shown that

$$\chi^2 = (\mathbf{C}\hat{\boldsymbol{\beta}} - \mathbf{C}\boldsymbol{\beta})'(\sigma^2\mathbf{CVC}')^{-1}(\mathbf{C}\hat{\boldsymbol{\beta}} - \mathbf{C}\boldsymbol{\beta}) \tag{13-38}$$

has a χ^2_r distribution (Chi-square with r degrees of freedom).

We remind the reader again that the distributions in this chapter are discussed more systematically in Chapter 14, which may be read concurrently with Chapter 13. Note that our standardization procedure, as in the single variable case, involves measuring the variables as deviations from their means $(\mathbf{C}\hat{\boldsymbol{\beta}} - \mathbf{C}\boldsymbol{\beta})$, and expressing them in terms of standard units by dividing by their variance,[4] that is, multiplying by $(\sigma^2\mathbf{CVC}')^{-1}$.

---

[4] We divide by the variance rather than the standard deviation because we have "squared" all our r normal variables $(\mathbf{C}\hat{\boldsymbol{\beta}} - \mathbf{C}\boldsymbol{\beta})$ in (13-38). This complicated quadratic function involves r normal variables—but they are correlated because each $\hat{\gamma}_i$ is a linear function of $\hat{\boldsymbol{\beta}}$. Nevertheless, the distribution of (13-38) is equivalent to a simple sum of r squared uncorrelated normal variates, which sum by definition is a χ^2 variate with r degrees of freedom. The reason for this equivalence is that the correlation of $\hat{\gamma}_1 \cdots \hat{\gamma}_r$ is compensated for, or "undone," by the complexity of the matrix $(\sigma^2\mathbf{CVC}')^{-1}$.

If we divide (13-38) by r (degrees of freedom), the χ^2 variable becomes a C^2 variable (d.f. $= r$). Since σ^2 is unknown, its unbiased estimator s^2 (d.f. $= n - k$) is substituted; in the process (13-38) becomes a ratio of two independent C^2 variables, that is, an F variable. Note again the similarity to the univariate case, where replacement of σ^2 by s^2 changed a normal variable to a t variable. Thus the quantity

$$F = \frac{1}{r}(\mathbf{C}\hat{\boldsymbol{\beta}} - \mathbf{C}\boldsymbol{\beta})'(\mathbf{CVC}')^{-1}(\mathbf{C}\hat{\boldsymbol{\beta}} - \mathbf{C}\boldsymbol{\beta})/s^2 \tag{13-39}$$

has an F distribution, with r and $(n - k)$ degrees of freedom. F is the basic quantity we shall be using for constructing confidence intervals or for testing hypotheses about $\boldsymbol{\beta}$. Furthermore, we can construct any number of diverse tests from this fundamental result—simply by using an appropriately specified $\mathbf{C}$ matrix.

The F statistic has a well-tabulated distribution, whose critical 5% point is denoted by $F_{.05}$ (Table VII of Appendix). Thus, from (13-39), the following probability statement can be made:

$$\Pr\left[\frac{1}{r}(\mathbf{C}\hat{\boldsymbol{\beta}} - \mathbf{C}\boldsymbol{\beta})'(\mathbf{CVC}')^{-1}(\mathbf{C}\hat{\boldsymbol{\beta}} - \mathbf{C}\boldsymbol{\beta})/s^2 \leq F_{.05}\right] = 95\% \tag{13-40}$$

13-7 CONFIDENCE REGIONS

From the quantity within brackets in (13-40), we obtain a 95% confidence region for $\mathbf{C}\boldsymbol{\beta}$:

$$\boxed{(\mathbf{C}\boldsymbol{\beta} - \mathbf{C}\hat{\boldsymbol{\beta}})'(\mathbf{CVC}')^{-1}(\mathbf{C}\boldsymbol{\beta} - \mathbf{C}\hat{\boldsymbol{\beta}}) \leq s^2\, r\, F_{.05}} \tag{13-41}$$

(a) For all β_i

To obtain a simultaneous (joint) confidence region for all the β_i, set $\mathbf{C} = \mathbf{I}$. In this special case the 95% confidence region (13-41) becomes:

$$\boxed{(\boldsymbol{\beta} - \hat{\boldsymbol{\beta}})'(\mathbf{V})^{-1}(\boldsymbol{\beta} - \hat{\boldsymbol{\beta}}) \leq s^2\, k\, F_{.05}} \tag{13-42}$$

Since $\mathbf{V} = (\mathbf{X}'\mathbf{X})^{-1}$, it follows that $\mathbf{V}^{-1}$ is simply $(\mathbf{X}'\mathbf{X})$.

In (13-42) of course everything is known except $\boldsymbol{\beta}$. The values of $\boldsymbol{\beta}$ which satisfy this inequality form a k-dimensional ellipsoid.

Example

In the wheat yield example, the right side of (13-42) is (13.08)(3)(6.59) = 258.6. Thus (13-42) in full is:

$$\begin{bmatrix} \beta_1 - 60.0 & \beta_2 - .0689 & \beta_3 - .603 \end{bmatrix} \begin{bmatrix} 7 & 0 & 0 \\ 0 & 280{,}000 & -500 \\ 0 & -500 & 24 \end{bmatrix} \begin{bmatrix} \beta_1 - 60.0 \\ \beta_2 - .0689 \\ \beta_3 - .603 \end{bmatrix} \leq 258.6 \qquad (13\text{-}43)$$

which is an ellipsoid in three-dimensional space, with center (60.0, .0689, .603).

Since we haven't estimated a joint confidence region before, it may be a bit difficult for the reader to get an intuitive grasp of what is going on; so let's consider the simpler example of Chapter 2 in which yield is related to fertilizer only. In this case there are only two parameters to simultaneously estimate—β_1 (which we denoted in Chapter 2 as α) and β_2 (which we denoted in Chapter 2 simply as β). The 95% confidence region equivalent to (13-43) in this case would be a two-dimensional ellipse, something like the ellipse in Figure 13-1*a*. This ellipse could have fallen in any one—or any combination—of the four quadrants in the (β_1, β_2) space.

In Figure 13-1*b*, this 95% confidence region is translated into our original (Y, x) space. Since β_1 represents the Y intercept, the limiting restrictions on its values are easily translated, using dotted horizontal lines. Since β_2 is a slope parameter, the restrictions on its possible values cannot be so easily translated. However, the reader will note from the left-hand diagram that β_2 is limited to positive values—and he can confirm that the only regressions that can be fitted into the confidence band in the right hand diagram are those with a positive slope. This suggests the appropriate way of thinking about the joint confidence band in Figure 13-1*b*; at a 95% level of confidence it can be stated that this band will cover the true regression line *throughout its entire length.*[5]

[5] The relation between this confidence band and the shaded band in Figure 2-9*c* is quite subtle. It may be proved that they are not identical. In fact, this confidence band in Figure 13-1*b* contains the shaded band in Figure 2-9*c*, and a little more area as well.

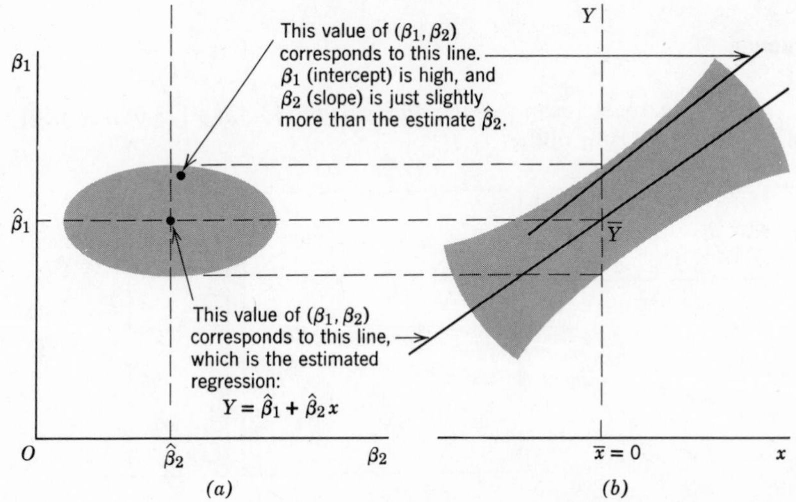

FIG. 13-1 Interpretation of joint confidence region in simple regression. (*a*) (β_1, β_2) space. (*b*) (x, Y) space.

There are several important observations in this special two-dimensional case, which also apply in the general case. The advantage of measuring x as deviations from the mean is that this ensures that the axes of the ellipse in Figure 13-1*a* will be parallel to the β_1 and β_2 axes. Formally, measuring in terms of deviations makes the x vector (associated with β_2) orthogonal to the unit vector (associated with β_1); it is this that guarantees that these axes will be parallel. This equally implies that the estimates of β_1 and β_2 will be statistically independent. This attractive property is an additional important reason for measuring the independent variable as deviations.

(b) For Several β_i

Without loss of generality, we can rearrange our x variables so that the ones of interest are put last; let us suppose there are r of these, and we wish to obtain a simultaneous confidence region for them: Let $\boldsymbol{\beta}_r$ be the column vector of the last r β's and

$$\mathbf{C} = \left[\begin{array}{c|cccc} & 1 & & & \\ & & 1 & & \\ 0 & & & \ddots & \\ & & 0 & & \\ & & & & 1 \end{array}\right] \tag{13-44}$$

so that

$$\mathbf{C}\boldsymbol{\beta} = \boldsymbol{\beta}_r \tag{13-45}$$

The estimator for these r β's, of course, is

$$\mathbf{C}\hat{\boldsymbol{\beta}} = \hat{\boldsymbol{\beta}}_r \tag{13-46}$$

The final step necessary before we can apply (13-41) is to compute the ovariance matrix $\mathbf{CVC}'$ which is designated $\mathbf{V}_r$:

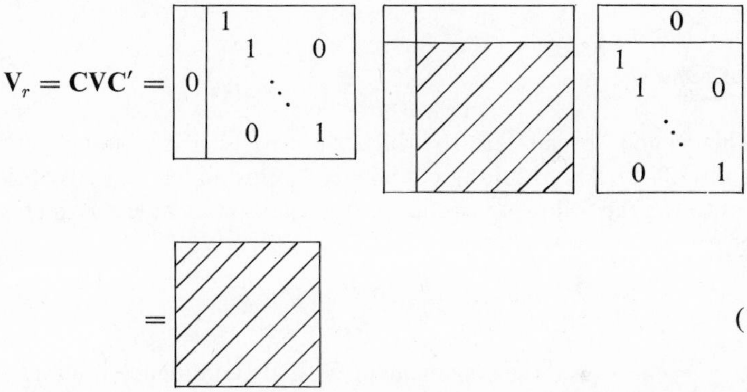

(13-47)

Thus $\mathbf{V}_r$ is the lower right-hand $r \times r$ block of $\mathbf{V}$. This is just what we feel intuitively: only the covariances of the last r β's are relevant. Substituting into (13-41), we derive the 95% joint confidence region for the last r β's:

$$\boxed{(\boldsymbol{\beta}_r - \hat{\boldsymbol{\beta}}_r)'(\mathbf{V}_r)^{-1}(\boldsymbol{\beta}_r - \hat{\boldsymbol{\beta}}_r) \le s^2\, r\, F_{.05}} \tag{13-48}$$

Example

Suppose in the wheat yield problem we are interested in a joint confidence region for only the two slope parameters β_2 and β_3 (i.e., we are interested only in the marginal effects of fertilizer and rainfall on yield). Then the two-dimensional 95% confidence ellipse, from (13-48) is:

$$\begin{bmatrix} \beta_2 - .0689 & \beta_3 - .603 \end{bmatrix} \begin{bmatrix} ._5371 & ._4773 \\ ._4773 & .0433 \end{bmatrix}^{-1} \begin{bmatrix} \beta_2 - .0689 \\ \beta_3 - .603 \end{bmatrix} \le 181.2 \tag{13-49}$$

In passing, we note that the development of the previous section (a) and the next section (c) are, in fact, just two interesting special cases of this analysis. Thus, if we set $r = k$ in (13-48), we obtain equation (13-42) of section (a). This special case was treated separately not only because it is the limiting case in which all β_i are simultaneously estimated, but also because the central matrix $\mathbf{V}^{-1}$ was so easy to deal with. [Since it is the inverse of $(\mathbf{X}'\mathbf{X})^{-1}$, it is simply $\mathbf{X}'\mathbf{X}$ itself, that is, no inversion or reinversion is necessary. The same is not true for $\mathbf{V}_r^{-1}$ in this section, unfortunately.]

(c) For One β_i

The second special case to which we now turn is obtained by setting $r = 1$ in (13-48). The resulting confidence "ellipsoid" is one dimensional; it reduces to the the following confidence interval for a single β (which without loss of generality we take as β_k)

$$(\beta_k - \hat{\beta}_k)^2 \frac{1}{v_k} \leq s^2 F_{.05} \tag{13-50}$$

where v_k = the lower right element of $\mathbf{V}$. This confidence interval may be reexpressed to bring it into more familiar form:

$$(\beta_k - \hat{\beta}_k)^2 \leq v_k\, s^2 F_{.05} \tag{13-51}$$

$$|\beta_k - \hat{\beta}_k| \leq \sqrt{v_k\, s^2 F_{.05}} \tag{13-52}$$

We may further reexpress this in terms of the t distribution, if we like, by noting that $F_{.05}$ with 1 and $(n - k)$ degrees of freedom is just the square of the $t_{.025}$ value on $(n - k)$ degrees of freedom:

$$F_{.05} = t_{.025}^2 \tag{13-53}$$

Thus, (13-52) becomes

$$|\beta_k - \hat{\beta}_k| \leq \sqrt{v_k}\, s\, t_{.025} \tag{13-54}$$

or the confidence interval

$$\beta_k = \hat{\beta}_k \pm \sqrt{v_k}\, s\, t_{.025} \tag{13-55}$$

The quantity $\sqrt{v_k}\, s$ is sometimes called s_k, the standard deviation estimate of $\hat{\beta}_k$. In this notation, (13-55) may be rewritten

$$\beta_k = \hat{\beta}_k \pm s_k\, t_{.025} \tag{13-56}$$

As an exercise, the student may confirm that for $k = 2$, this is simply equation (2-30) in disguise.

Example

Suppose we are interested in the marginal effect of rainfall on wheat yield—that is, a 95% confidence interval for β_3. From (13-55) this is

$$\begin{aligned} \beta_3 &= .603 \pm \sqrt{.0433}(3.62)(2.776) \\ &= .603 \pm 2.09 \\ &= -1.49 \text{ to } 2.69 \end{aligned} \tag{13-57}$$

A two-sided test of a hypothesis is equivalent to asking whether or not the hypothetical value for β_3 falls within this interval. Since the null hypothesis $\beta_3 = 0$ does fall in this interval, it cannot be rejected. In other words, the marginal effect of water on yield is not statistically significant. Alternatively, we could substitute zero (the hypothetical value for β_3) into (13-54); rearranging this, would yield the inequality

$$\left| \frac{\hat{\beta}_3}{\sqrt{v_3}\, s} \right| \leq t_{.025} \tag{13-58}$$

It is no surprise that the statistic on the left-hand side has a t distribution. For recall that $\hat{\beta}_3$ is normal, and by hypothesis has a zero mean. When it is standardized by dividing by its estimated standard deviation $s_3 = \sqrt{v_3}\, s$, then of course it has the t distribution.

H_0 will be "acceptable at the 5% level" if $\hat{\beta}_3$ satisfies the inequality (13-58). To see whether this is so, we substitute the observed data:

$$\left| \frac{.603}{\sqrt{.0433}\,(3.62)} \right| \leq 2.776 \tag{13-59}$$

$$.80 \leq 2.776 \tag{13-60}$$

Thus, H_0 is indeed acceptable; or more precisely, the result is statistically not significant.

Estimated regressions are usually set out in a form that facilitates this sort of hypothesis test or confidence interval for each of the β_i. Thus, in the example we are working through, our regression equation might appear in the form:

$$\left.\begin{array}{ccccc} Y = \quad 60 & + & .0689x_2 & + & .603x_3 \\ (\pm 3.8) & & (\pm .0194) & & (\pm 2.09) \\ (s_1 = 1.36) & & (s_2 = .0070) & & (s_3 = .75) \\ (t_1 = 44) & & (t_2 = 9.8) & & (t_3 = .80) \end{array}\right\} \tag{13-61}$$

where the standard errors of each of the β coefficients are found as follows:

$$\begin{aligned} s_1 &= \sqrt{v_1}\, s = \sqrt{1/7}\ (3.62) &&= 1.36 && \text{(a)} \\ s_2 &= \sqrt{v_2}\, s = \sqrt{.{}_5 371}\ (3.62) &&= .0070 && \text{(b)} \\ s_3 &= \sqrt{v_3}\, s = \sqrt{.0433}\ (3.62) &&= .75 && \text{(c)} \end{aligned} \tag{13-62}$$

Each of the t values shown is the estimated regression coefficient $\hat{\beta}_i$ divided by its standard error s_i, as in (13-58). Each of the confidence limits shown is calculated as in (13-56).

For further interpretations of (13-61), the reader is referred back to (3-15), where this sort of regression analysis was first introduced.

13-8 TESTING HYPOTHESES

We have already considered testing an hypothesis about a single coefficient in the example above. Now we shall generalize, by considering a joint hypothesis test on several coefficients. Suppose we wish to test the hypothesis

$$H_0 : \mathbf{C}\boldsymbol{\beta} = \boldsymbol{\gamma}_0 \tag{13-63}$$

against the hypothesis

$$H_1 : \mathbf{C}\boldsymbol{\beta} \neq \boldsymbol{\gamma}_0$$

$\boldsymbol{\gamma}_0$ is a column of specified (null) values, often zero. It turns out, as usual, that there are two equivalent ways to make the test:

1. Construct a confidence region for $\mathbf{C}\boldsymbol{\beta}$, as in (13-41) and see whether it contains the null vector $\boldsymbol{\gamma}_0$. If it does not, reject the null hypothesis.
2. In equation (13-40) substitute for $\mathbf{C}\boldsymbol{\beta}$ its null value $\boldsymbol{\gamma}_0$, and calculate the value of the F statistic. Then reject H_0 iff (13-40) is violated, that is, iff F is calculated to be more than the critical value $F_{.05}$.

Example

Suppose we wish to test the hypothesis that average wheat yield is 65 bu/acre, and is not influenced by either fertilizer or rainfall. Thus, we wish to test the null hypothesis:

$$H_0: \begin{bmatrix} 1 & 0 & 0 \\ 0 & 1 & 0 \\ 0 & 0 & 1 \end{bmatrix} \begin{bmatrix} \beta_1 \\ \beta_2 \\ \beta_3 \end{bmatrix} = \begin{bmatrix} 65 \\ 0 \\ 0 \end{bmatrix} \tag{13-64}$$

against the hypothesis that at least one β is not as specified. Note that the matrix **C** is the identity matrix for this particular test. The first way to test is simply to observe that the null vector on the right-hand side of (13-64) falls outside the joint confidence region in (13-43); therefore, H_0 can be rejected. Alternatively, if we had to start from scratch to test this hypothesis, we could go back to (13-40); the quantity inside the bracket becomes:

$$\left(\frac{1}{3}\right)\left(\frac{1}{13.08}\right)\begin{bmatrix} 60-65 & .0689 & .603 \end{bmatrix}\begin{bmatrix} 7 & 0 & 0 \\ 0 & 28_4 & -500 \\ 0 & --500 & 24 \end{bmatrix}\begin{bmatrix} 60-65 \\ .0689 \\ .603 \end{bmatrix} \overset{?}{\leq} 6.59 \qquad (13\text{-}65)$$

noting that $\mathbf{V}^{-1}$ is $\mathbf{X}'\mathbf{X}$. Since this inequality is violated, we reject H_0.

13-9 MULTICOLLINEARITY

Multicollinearity occurs, for example, if the variables x_2 and x_3 measure nearly the same thing; in terms of the matrix

$$\mathbf{X} = \begin{bmatrix} 1 & x_{12} & x_{13} & \cdots & x_{1k} \\ 1 & x_{22} & x_{23} & \cdots & x_{2k} \\ \cdot & & & & \cdot \\ \cdot & & & & \cdot \\ \cdot & & & & \cdot \\ 1 & x_{n2} & x_{n3} & \cdots & x_{nk} \end{bmatrix} \qquad (13\text{-}66)$$

this means that the second and third columns are almost linearly dependent. If, as another example, the variable x_4 is almost the sum of x_2 and x_3, then the second, third, and fourth columns of **X** will be almost linearly dependent. Such multicollinearity results in the inverse matrix $(\mathbf{X}'\mathbf{X})^{-1}$ having some extremely large entries. (In the limiting case of perfect collinearity, the determinant of $\mathbf{X}'\mathbf{X}$ is zero, and its inverse does not exist.) Since $\sigma^2(\mathbf{X}'\mathbf{X})^{-1}$ is the covariance matrix of $\hat{\boldsymbol{\beta}}$, we therefore obtain some very large variances and covariances, and hence broad confidence intervals. In such circumstances, it becomes very difficult to establish that an individual regressor influences y. Intuitively, when two regressors are nearly the same, the influence on y of one of them may be erroneously attributed to the other.

This can be shown more rigorously by examining in detail the joint confidence region for two parameters, β_k and β_{k-1} let us say. If the two corresponding regressors are almost linearly dependent, then $\hat{\beta}_k$ and $\hat{\beta}_{k-1}$ have very large variances and covariance. Geometrically, this means that the elliptical confidence region given by (13-48) is very tilted, as in Figure 13-2. This is a striking contrast to the level confidence region of Figure 13-1*a*.

In Figure 13-2 we see the ambiguity that results. Since the point P is in the confidence region, an acceptable hypothesis is $\beta_{k-1} = 0$, while $\beta_k = 2$. On the other hand, since Q also is in the confidence region, another acceptable hypothesis is $\beta_k = 0$, while $\beta_{k-1} = 3$. Which parameter is zero, β_{k-1} or β_k (or neither)? There is no good way to resolve this ambiguity. We can say, however, that the hypothesis $\beta_{k-1} = 0$ *and* $\beta_k = 0$ is unacceptable, because the origin (0, 0) is not in the confidence region. Thus, we establish that one of these coefficients is nonzero, even though it is not clear whether it is β_k or β_{k-1}— or both.

In Figure 13-2 we can also see the broad confidence intervals for the parameters[6] if they are tested one at a time. This vagueness about an individual parameter results from the possibility of one regressor being "robbed of its influence" by the other collinear regressor.

Multicollinearity is avoided if the regressors differ as much as possible, that is, are statistically uncorrelated. In Figure 3-3, this means that the points in the x-z plane are not clustered near line L. Algebraically, it means that the columns of $\mathbf{X}$ are orthogonal;[7] that is, the product $\mathbf{X'X}$ is diagonal. Of course,

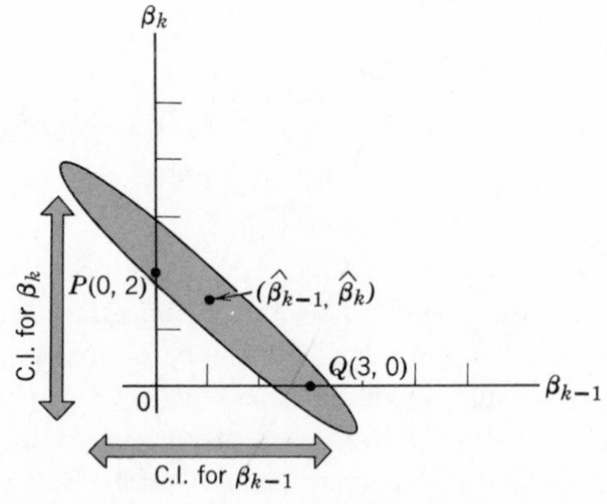

FIG. 13-2 Confidence region for the coefficients of two highly collinear regressors.

[6] It can be proved that the confidence interval for one parameter, say β_k, is almost equal to the projection of the joint confidence ellipse onto the β_k axis.
[7] For an extended discussion of orthogonality, see Chapter 15-3.

economists often have to take the data as it comes, even if it is multicollinear. But scientists who have the freedom to design their experiments (and this sometimes includes computer simulators of economic models) make their regressors orthogonal, in order to exploit the following advantages:

1. In avoiding multicollinearity, they get more precise confidence intervals and more certainty about which regressors are relevant.

2. If a smaller model with only j independent variables (rather than the original k) is appropriate, then the coefficients $\hat{\beta}_1 \cdots \hat{\beta}_j$ of this new model will be exactly the same as the coefficients in the old extended model. In other words, coefficients of included variables do not change as some variables are dropped from the model. This is more satisfactory, philosophically as well as computationally.

3. The matrix $(\mathbf{X}'\mathbf{X})^{-1}$ being diagonal, is very easy to compute. Thus, the estimators $\hat{\boldsymbol{\beta}}$ and their covariance matrix are easily computed.

13-10 INTERPOLATION AND PREDICTION

If we consider a new set of values for the independent variables $\mathbf{x}_0 = (1, x_{02}, x_{03} \cdots x_{0k})$, what will be (a) the confidence interval for the *mean* value of the corresponding y_0? (b) the prediction interval for a *single* corresponding y_0?

(a) Confidence Interval for the Mean of y_0

We use

$$\hat{\mu}_0 \triangleq \mathbf{x}_0\hat{\boldsymbol{\beta}} \tag{13-67}$$

to estimate the mean of y_0:

$$\mu_0 \triangleq \mathbf{x}_0\boldsymbol{\beta} \tag{13-68}$$

To find its confidence interval, we simply set

$$\mathbf{C} = \mathbf{x}_0$$

so that (13-35) reduces to (13-67). Continuing with this substitution, we obtain from (13-41) a 95% confidence interval for $\mathbf{x}_0\boldsymbol{\beta}$:

$$(\mathbf{x}_0\boldsymbol{\beta} - \mathbf{x}_0\hat{\boldsymbol{\beta}})'(\mathbf{x}_0\mathbf{V}\mathbf{x}_0')^{-1}(\mathbf{x}_0\boldsymbol{\beta} - \mathbf{x}_0\hat{\boldsymbol{\beta}}) \leq s^2F_{.05}$$

Noting (13-67) and (13-68), this 95% confidence interval reduces to

$$(\mu_0 - \hat{\mu}_0)^2 \leq s^2F_{.05}(\mathbf{x}_0\mathbf{V}\mathbf{x}_0')$$

If we substitute $t^2_{.025}$ for $F_{.05}$, and take the square root

$$|\mu_0 - \hat{\mu}_0| \leq t_{.025}\, s \sqrt{\mathbf{x}_0 \mathbf{V} \mathbf{x}_0'}$$

In other words:

> The 95% confidence interval for the mean of y_0 is:
>
> $$\mu_0 = \hat{\mu}_0 \pm t_{.025}\, s \sqrt{\mathbf{x}_0 \mathbf{V} \mathbf{x}_0'} \tag{13-69}$$

where $\hat{\mu}_0 = \hat{\beta}_1 + \hat{\beta}_2 x_{02} + \cdots \hat{\beta}_k x_{0k}$ and $t_{.025}$ is the critical t value with $(n - k)$ d.f.

Example

What is the 95% confidence interval for the average or expected value of yield at a fertilizer application of 550 pounds and 38 inches of rainfall? Note that this problem involves both interpolation (of fertilizer), and extrapolation (of rainfall).

Noting that both independent variables are measured as deviations from their means, $x_2 = 150$ and $x_3 = 3$. Thus, from (13-69), the 95% confidence interval for the mean of y_0 is

$$\mu_0 = 60 + (.0689)\,150 + (.603)\,3$$

$$\pm\, 2.776\,(3.62)\sqrt{\begin{bmatrix} 1 & 150 & 3 \end{bmatrix}\begin{bmatrix} 1/7 & 0 & 0 \\ 0 & ._{5}371 & ._{4}773 \\ 0 & ._{4}773 & .0433 \end{bmatrix}\begin{bmatrix} 1 \\ 150 \\ 3 \end{bmatrix}}$$

$$= 72.1434 \pm 8.32 \tag{13-70}$$

or[8] $63.8 \leq \mu_0 \leq 80.5$

---

[8] The student may question why we have a less precise prediction of yield than in the case of (2-41) in which we ignored rainfall, and related yield only to fertilizer. The main reason is that we are extrapolating with the unreliable regressor rainfall. See (13-57). In addition, of course, a degree of freedom in the residuals was lost to the additional estimate $\hat{\beta}_3$—and this increased the t value.

(b) Prediction Interval for y_0

This is the same as the confidence interval for the mean of y_0, except that the variance term must be augmented because of the estimated dispersion (s^2) of an individual y value about its mean. Thus, we obtain:

95% prediction interval for an individual y_0:

$$y_0 = \hat{\mu}_0 \pm s\, t_{.025}\sqrt{\mathbf{x}_0 \mathbf{V} \mathbf{x}_0' + 1} \tag{13-71}$$

where $\hat{\mu}_0$, s, and t are as in (13-69).

Example

The prediction interval of a single observation of yield with 550 pounds of fertilizer and 38 inches of rainfall is

$$y_0 = 60 + (.0689)\,150 + (.603)\,3$$

$$\pm\, 2.776\,(3.62)\sqrt{\begin{bmatrix} 1 & 150 & 3 \end{bmatrix} \begin{bmatrix} 1/7 & 0 & 0 \\ 0 & ._5371 & ._4773 \\ 0 & ._4773 & .0433 \end{bmatrix} \begin{bmatrix} 1 \\ 150 \\ 3 \end{bmatrix} + 1}$$

$$= 72.14 \pm 13.05$$

or $59.1 \leq y_0 \leq 85.2$

PROBLEMS

13-1 Referring to Problem 3-1, we are now in a position to find confidence intervals for the model

$$S = \beta_1 + \beta_2 y + \beta_3 w$$

where y and w are income and wealth, measured as deviations from the mean. Let us also measure y and w in thousands, and S in hundreds, to reduce the number of zeros in our computations. Then you may verify that, in the notation of this chapter,

$$\mathbf{X}'\mathbf{X} = \begin{bmatrix} 5 & 0 & 0 \\ 0 & 18 & -18 \\ 0 & -18 & 144 \end{bmatrix}$$

and

$$\mathbf{X}'\mathbf{y} = \begin{bmatrix} 38 \\ 26 \\ -63 \end{bmatrix}$$

where $\mathbf{y}$ of course is the vector of the dependent variable (savings). Then

$$\mathbf{V} = (\mathbf{X}'\mathbf{X})^{-1} = \begin{bmatrix} 1/5 & 0 & 0 \\ 0 & 8/126 & 1/126 \\ 0 & 1/126 & 1/126 \end{bmatrix}$$

$$= \begin{bmatrix} .2 & 0 & 0 \\ 0 & .0635 & .00794 \\ 0 & .00794 & .00794 \end{bmatrix}$$

finally

$$s^2 = \frac{1}{n-k} (\mathbf{y} - \hat{\mathbf{y}})'(\mathbf{y} - \hat{\mathbf{y}}) = .39$$

(a) Construct a 95% confidence region for:
1. β_2 and β_3 simultaneously.
2. β_3.
3. β_2.
4. β_1 and β_2 simultaneously.

(b) Write out the estimated regression equation in standard form, as in Problem 3-4; (i.e., for each coefficient, write the confidence limits, the standard deviation, and the t value). Then check to see that you agree with the answer given in Problems 5-9 and 5-10.

(c) Test the following hypotheses at the 5% significance level:
1. $\beta_2 = 0$ and $\beta_3 = 0$ simultaneously.
2. $\beta_3 = 0$ (i.e., wealth is irrelevant).
3. $\beta_2 = 0$ (i.e., income irrelevant).
4. $\beta_2 = 1.0$. (This may be a colleague's prior claim, which you happen to question.)
5. $\beta_2 = 1.57$ (This may be the well-established coefficient for another country, and you wonder whether the two countries are the same.)
6. $\beta_2 = -5\beta_3$. (i.e., the income effect is opposite to the wealth effect, and five times as strong).

(d) For a family earning $Y = \$6{,}000$ and having assets $W = \$10{,}500$:
1. What would you predict savings to be?
2. In what sense is this family an average of families D and E (in the data of Problem 3-1). Why then is the predicted value of savings not equal to the average of \$300 and \$700?
3. Construct an interval that is 95% sure of correctly predicting this family's savings.

13-2 Referring to Problem 3-10, we are now in a position to find confidence intervals for the model

$$E = \beta_1 + \beta_2 f + \beta_3 d$$

where f is father's income measured in thousands, and d is the dummy. Again, f and d are in deviation form. Then you may verify that

$$(\mathbf{X'X}) = \begin{bmatrix} 8 & 0 & 0 \\ 0 & 68 & -8 \\ 0 & -8 & 2 \end{bmatrix}$$

and

$$\mathbf{X'y} = \begin{bmatrix} 109 \\ 47 \\ -6.5 \end{bmatrix}$$

hence

$$\mathbf{V} = (\mathbf{X'X})^{-1} = \begin{bmatrix} 1/8 & 0 & 0 \\ 0 & 1/36 & 4/36 \\ 0 & 4/36 & 34/36 \end{bmatrix} = \begin{bmatrix} .125 & 0 & 0 \\ 0 & .0278 & .111 \\ 0 & .111 & .944 \end{bmatrix}$$

Finally

$$s^2 = \frac{1}{n-k}(\mathbf{y} - \hat{\mathbf{y}})'(\mathbf{y} - \hat{\mathbf{y}}) = 3.30$$

(a) Construct a 90% confidence interval for:
1. β_2 and β_3 simultaneously. (In more extended tables than Appendix Table VII, $F_{.10}$ with 2 and 5 d.f. is found to be 3.78.)
2. β_3.
3. β_2.

(b) Test the following hypotheses at the 10% significance level:
1. $\beta_2 = \beta_3 = 0$.
2. $\beta_3 = 0$ (i.e., urban-rural factor is irrelevant).
3. $\beta_2 = 0$ (i.e., father's income is irrelevant)

(c) In part (b), how can you reconcile the answers to parts (2) and (3) with the answer to part (1)?

(d) Write out the estimated regression equation in standard form, as in Problem 3-4.

(e) For a rural resident whose father's income is \$6500, find a 90% prediction interval for his education E.

(f) For *all* rural residents whose father's income is \$6500, find a 90% confidence interval for their mean education.

* (g) For a man picked at random, on whom no information is available, construct a 90% prediction interval for his education E. (Assume that the data of Problem 3-10 is a random sample from the same population from which the man is picked). Compare to part (e).

13-3 Prove that the confidence interval

$$\beta_k = \hat{\beta}_k \pm \sqrt{v_k}\, s\, t_{.025} \tag{13-55}$$

reduces, in the case of simple regression (on one independent variable), to the familiar formula

$$\beta = \hat{\beta} \pm t_{.025} \frac{s}{\sqrt{\sum x^2}} \tag{2-30}$$

(Hint: you should remember that x represents deviations, not original values.)

chapter 14

Distribution Theory: How the Normal, t, χ^2, and F Distributions are Related

14-1 INTRODUCTION

The reader is advised to frequently consult Tables 14-1 and 14-2 at the end of the chapter, since they provide a guide to the relations among the variables.

The distribution of the standard normal variable z is assumed to be well known to the reader. (It is discussed in every elementary statistics text; for example, *Introductory Statistics* by T. H. Wonnacott and R. J. Wonnacott, Chapter 4.) Normal variables are the building blocks of the other variables in this Chapter. The first of these is the χ^2, to which we now turn.

14-2 χ^2, THE CHI-SQUARE DISTRIBUTION

(a) Definition

If n independent standard normal variables are squared and added, we obtain a random variable that appears in many applications (though in slightly disguised form). It is denoted χ^2_n, and is called "a Chi-square variable with n degrees of freedom." Thus

$$\chi^2_n \triangleq z_1^2 + z_2^2 + \cdots + z_n^2 \tag{14-1}$$

$$= \sum_{i=1}^{n} z_i^2$$

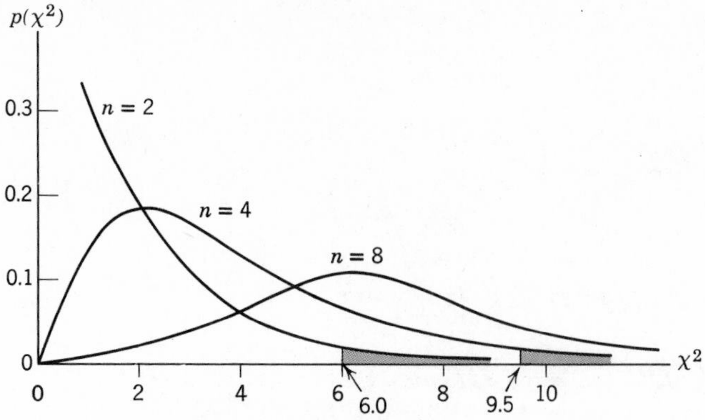

FIG. 14-1 Probability distribution of χ^2_n.

where the z_i's are independent variables, with distributions that are standard normal and therefore identical.

The probability distribution of χ^2_n is shown in Figure 14-1. Of course, for each different n we get a different probability distribution; the larger the n, the larger will this χ^2 sum of n terms tend to be. Although the χ^2 distribution requires sophisticated mathematics to derive in detail, its most important general features are easily deduced. Since χ^2 is a sum of squares, it must be positive. Moreover, we note from (14-1) that it is a sum of independent and identically distributed variables (the sum of what may be regarded as a sample from the z^2 population). Thus, the formulas for sample sums can be applied (alternatively Table 13-2(b) can be extended):

$$E(\chi^2_n) = nE(z^2)$$

Since z is standard, its variance is one. That is,

$$E(z^2) = 1 \tag{14-2}$$

Thus

$$E(\chi^2_n) = n \tag{14-3}$$

Similarly

$$\text{var } \chi^2_n = n \text{ var } (z^2) \tag{14-4}$$

It may be proved with advanced calculus that

$$\text{var } (z^2) = 2 \tag{14-5}$$

Thus

$$\text{var } \chi^2_n = 2n \tag{14-6}$$

Finally, the Central Limit theorem assures us that as n grows large, the distribution of χ^2_n approaches the normal. This can be seen in Figure 14-1.

(b) Other Views and Uses of χ^2

(i) If we take a sample from a normal distribution, $y_1, y_2, \ldots, y_n$, and standardize,

$$z_i = \frac{y_i - \mu}{\sigma}$$

then from (14-1)

$$\sum_{i=1}^{n} \left(\frac{y_i - \mu}{\sigma}\right)^2 \sim \chi_n^2 \tag{14-7}$$

$$\frac{\sum_{i=1}^{n} (y_i - \mu)^2}{\sigma^2} \sim \chi_n^2 \tag{14-8}$$

where the symbol $\sim$ means "is distributed as." Thus $\sim\chi_n^2$ is read, "is distributed as Chi-square with n d.f."

(ii) We may generalize (14-8). First, we reexpress it in vector notation:

$$\frac{1}{\sigma^2}(\mathbf{y} - \boldsymbol{\mu})'(\mathbf{y} - \boldsymbol{\mu}) \sim \chi_n^2$$

$$(\mathbf{y} - \boldsymbol{\mu})'(\sigma^2\mathbf{I})^{-1}(\mathbf{y} - \boldsymbol{\mu}) \sim \chi_n^2 \tag{14-9}$$

The middle factor $\sigma^2\mathbf{I}$ represents the covariance matrix of the y_i's, which were assumed to be independent and identically distributed with variance σ^2 (as, for example, in a sample). We now wonder what can be done if we relax this assumption about the y_i's. Suppose, in fact, that there are r normal variates in the vector $\mathbf{y}$, having a mean vector $\boldsymbol{\mu}$ with perhaps different components, and a covariance matrix, no longer based on the identity, but now the more general $\sigma^2\mathbf{W}$. We shall prove that:

$$\boxed{(\mathbf{y} - \boldsymbol{\mu})'(\sigma^2\mathbf{W})^{-1}(\mathbf{y} - \boldsymbol{\mu}) \sim \chi_r^2} \tag{14-10}$$

where the r variates[1] $\mathbf{y} \sim N(\boldsymbol{\mu}, \sigma^2\mathbf{W})$

Proof of (14-10). Without loss of generality, assume $\boldsymbol{\mu} = \mathbf{0}$. In linear algebra, it may be proved that since $\sigma^2\mathbf{W}$ is a covariance matrix, and hence $\mathbf{W}$ is positive definite, there exists a "square root" matrix $\mathbf{R}$ that satisfies

$$\mathbf{R}\mathbf{R}' = \mathbf{W} \tag{14-11}$$

[1] Since we no longer interpret the y_i's as a sample, we use r instead of n for the number of y_i's.

Now let

$$\mathbf{q} = \mathbf{R}^{-1}\mathbf{y} \tag{14-12}$$

The covariance matrix of $\mathbf{q}$ is obtained by the theory of linear transformations of Table 13-2, and is

$$\begin{aligned} \text{cov}\,(\mathbf{q}) &= \mathbf{R}^{-1}(\text{cov}\,\mathbf{y})\mathbf{R}^{-1'} \\ &= \mathbf{R}^{-1}(\sigma^2\mathbf{W})\mathbf{R}^{-1'} \end{aligned}$$

Substituting[2] for $\mathbf{W}$ as given by (14-11),

$$= \sigma^2\mathbf{I} \tag{14-13}$$

This proves $\mathbf{q}$ is an independent set of variables, with variance σ^2. Moreover, since $\mathbf{q}$ is the linear transformation (14-12) of the normal $\mathbf{y}$, it has the same $\mathbf{0}$ mean (recall that we assumed $\boldsymbol{\mu} = \mathbf{0}$), and it is normal. Hence $\frac{1}{\sigma}\mathbf{q}$ is a set of fully standardized normal variates, and

$$\frac{1}{\sigma^2}\mathbf{q}'\mathbf{q} \sim \chi_r^2 \tag{14-14}$$

Substituting (14-12) into (14-14)

$$\frac{1}{\sigma^2}(\mathbf{y}'\mathbf{R}^{-1'})(\mathbf{R}^{-1}\mathbf{y}) \sim \chi_r^2$$

$$\frac{1}{\sigma^2}\mathbf{y}'(\mathbf{R}^{-1'}\mathbf{R}^{-1})\mathbf{y} \sim \chi_r^2$$

$$\frac{1}{\sigma^2}\mathbf{y}'(\mathbf{R}\mathbf{R}')^{-1}\mathbf{y} \sim \chi_r^2$$

By (14-11),

$$\mathbf{y}'(\sigma^2\mathbf{W})^{-1}\mathbf{y} \sim \chi_r^2$$

This establishes (14-10) for $\boldsymbol{\mu} = \mathbf{0}$, and there are no problems involved in translating this into the general case where $\boldsymbol{\mu}$ is nonzero.

The primary example of (14-10) is the vector of k regression estimators $\hat{\boldsymbol{\beta}}$ that occurs in (13-42); from (14-10) and (13-34) it follows that

$$(\hat{\boldsymbol{\beta}} - \boldsymbol{\beta})'(\sigma^2\mathbf{V})^{-1}(\hat{\boldsymbol{\beta}} - \boldsymbol{\beta}) \sim \chi_k^2 \tag{14-15}$$

and, more generally, following (13-36) and (13-37):

$$(\mathbf{C}\hat{\boldsymbol{\beta}} - \mathbf{C}\boldsymbol{\beta})'(\sigma^2\mathbf{C}\mathbf{V}\mathbf{C}')^{-1}(\mathbf{C}\hat{\boldsymbol{\beta}} - \mathbf{C}\boldsymbol{\beta}) \sim \chi_r^2 \tag{14-16}$$

(13-38) proved

[2] Noting also that $\mathbf{R}^{-1'} = \mathbf{R}'^{-1}$.

(iii) Going back to the idea of the sample of y_i that occur in (14-8), we may ask what happens when we substitute $\bar{y}$ for the unknown μ. It was remarked in Section 2-5 that $\bar{y}$ is the "best fit" to the sample, in the least squares sense. Thus, the squared deviations measured from $\bar{y}$ are less than from any other value, even slightly less than from μ; that is, $\sum_{i=1}^{n} (y_i - \bar{y})^2$ is slightly less than $\sum_{i=1}^{n} (y_i - \mu)^2$. Thus, the distribution of $\sum (y_i - \bar{y})^2/\sigma^2$ is a little below the χ_n^2 distribution of $\sum (y_i - \mu)^2/\sigma^2$. In fact, it turns out[3] to be

---

[3] Equation (14-17) and its generalization (14-23) are proved in advanced texts in mathematical statistics, such as Cramer, or Kendall and Stuart. The proof is simple and instructive enough in the special case when $n = 2$, that we give it in this footnote:

In the left side of (14-17)

$$\begin{aligned}\sum_{i=1}^{2} (y_i - \bar{y})^2 &= (y_1 - \bar{y})^2 + (y_2 - \bar{y})^2 \\ &= \left(y_1 - \frac{y_1 + y_2}{2}\right)^2 + \left(y_2 - \frac{y_1 + y_2}{2}\right)^2 \\ &= \left(\frac{y_1 - y_2}{2}\right)^2 + \left(\frac{y_2 - y_1}{2}\right)^2 \\ &= \frac{(y_1 - y_2)^2}{2} \qquad (14\text{-}18)\end{aligned}$$

Dividing by σ^2

$$\frac{\sum_{i=1}^{2} (y_i - \bar{y})^2}{\sigma^2} = \frac{(y_1 - y_2)^2}{2\sigma^2} \qquad (14\text{-}19)$$

Since $y_i \sim N(\mu, \sigma^2)$ and are independent, then the variable $(y_1 - y_2)$ is normal,

with mean $\quad \mu - \mu = 0$

and variance $\quad \sigma^2 + \sigma^2 = 2\sigma^2$

so that its standardized value is

$$z = \frac{(y_1 - y_2) - 0}{\sqrt{2\sigma^2}}$$

that is,

$$z^2 = \frac{(y_1 - y_2)^2}{2\sigma^2} \qquad (14\text{-}20)$$

Substituting (14-20) into (14-19)

$$\begin{aligned}\frac{\sum_{i=1}^{2} (y_i - \bar{y})^2}{\sigma^2} &= z^2 \\ &= \chi_1^2 = \chi_{n-1}^2 \qquad (14\text{-}21)\end{aligned}$$

the distribution of χ^2_{n-1}; that is,

$$\frac{\sum_{i=1}^{n}(y_i - \bar{y})^2}{\sigma^2} \sim \chi^2_{n-1} \tag{14-17}$$

(iv) In the previous section, we used $\bar{y}$ as the "best fit" to a simple sample. Regression theory extended this same concept of "best fit" to the case in which there are k explanatory variables, or regressors. (We include the dummy regressor (1, 1, 1, 1, . . . 1), so that there are altogether k parameters to be estimated in the linear regression.) In equation (13-25) the residual sum of squares was given as

$$(\mathbf{y} - \hat{\mathbf{y}})'(\mathbf{y} - \hat{\mathbf{y}}) = \sum_{i=1}^{n}(y_i - \hat{y}_i)^2 \tag{14-22}$$

By definition, the least squares estimators made the sum of squared deviations from $\hat{y}_i$ less than from any other value, even less than from μ_i. Thus the distribution of $\sum (y_i - \hat{y}_i)^2/\sigma^2$ is below the χ^2_n distribution of $\sum (y_i - \mu_i)^2/\sigma^2$. In fact, there was so much freedom of choice in selecting all k estimates, that $\sum_{i=1}^{n} (y_i - \hat{y}_i)^2/\sigma^2$ has the distribution of χ^2_{n-k}, that is,

$$\frac{\sum (y_i - \hat{y}_i)^2}{\sigma^2} \sim \chi^2_{n-k} \tag{14-23}$$

(c) C^2, the Modified χ^2

Let χ^2_r be a Chi-square variable with r d.f. The "modified χ^2_r" is defined by dividing by the d.f.:

$$\boxed{C^2_r \triangleq \frac{\chi^2_r}{r}} \tag{14-24}$$

Just as χ^2_r may be regarded as a sample sum, so C^2_r may be regarded as a sample mean from the z^2 population. Thus, its expectation is the population mean $E(z^2)$ given by (14-2) as 1. Thus

$$E(C^2_r) = 1 \tag{14-25a}$$

Similarly, from (14-5)

$$\text{var } C^2_r = \frac{2}{r} \tag{14-25b}$$

These two equations establish that C^2_r has zero bias and a variance that approaches zero; by (2-83), therefore, its probability limit is the population mean

$$C^2_r \xrightarrow{p} 1 \tag{14-25c}$$

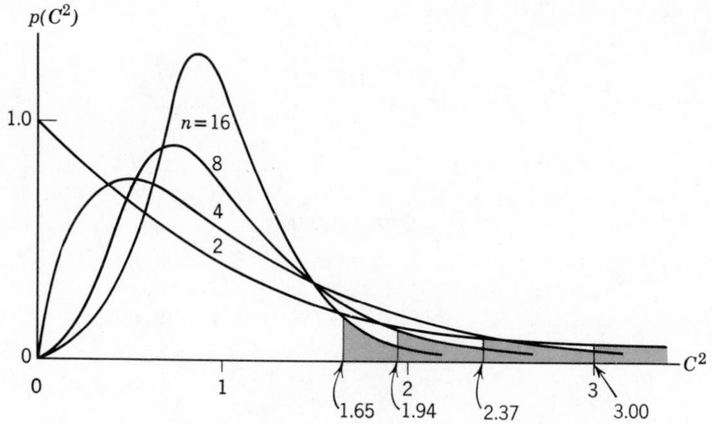

FIG. 14-2 Probability distribution of C_n^2 (modified χ_n^2).

Equation (14-25c) may alternatively be derived by noting that it is a special case of Problem 2-9: the sample mean is a consistent estimator of the population mean. This is shown in Figure 14-2.

The value of modifying χ_r^2 to C_r^2 is to simplify formulas (14-17) and (14-23). If we divide (14-17) by $(n - 1)$ on both sides, we obtain

$$\boxed{\frac{s^2}{\sigma^2} \sim C_{n-1}^2} \tag{14-26}$$

where s^2 is the residual variance after fitting the sample mean.

Similarly, if we divide (14-23) by $(n - k)$ on both sides, we obtain

$$\boxed{\frac{s^2}{\sigma^2} \sim C_{n-k}^2} \tag{14-27}$$

where s^2 is the residual variance after fitting k parameters in the regression analysis. This is a generalization of (14-26).

(d) χ^2-Estimators

We shall show that s^2 is a consistent and unbiased estimator of σ^2. In view of its distribution, it is appropriate to call it a χ^2-estimator of σ^2.

To establish its consistency, we consider a fixed number of regressors

(k), and let $n \to \infty$; hence, $(n - k) \to \infty$. Then from (14-25c)

$$C^2_{n-k} \xrightarrow{p} 1,$$

and from (14-27), therefore,

$$\frac{s^2}{\sigma^2} \xrightarrow{p} 1$$

that is,

$$\boxed{s^2 \xrightarrow{p} \sigma^2} \tag{14-28}$$

Next, to establish its unbiasedness, we begin with the fact that C^2 is scaled to have a mean of 1; from (14-25a)

$$E(C^2_{n-k}) = 1$$

From (14-27)

$$E\left(\frac{s^2}{\sigma^2}\right) = 1$$

Since σ^2, the population variance, is constant,

$$\frac{1}{\sigma^2} E(s^2) = 1$$

$$\boxed{E(s^2) = \sigma^2} \tag{14-29}$$

This unbiasedness, of course, is the reason for using $(n - k)$ instead of n as the divisor for s^2.

14-3 t DISTRIBUTION

(a) Definition

The mathematical definition of "student's" t with r d.f. is

$$\boxed{t_r \triangleq \frac{z}{C_r}} \tag{14-30}$$

where z is a standard normal variable, and

$$C_r = \sqrt{C_r^2} \tag{14-31}$$

It is also assumed that the modified Chi-square variable C_r^2 is *statistically independent of* z. C_r is called a modified chi variable.

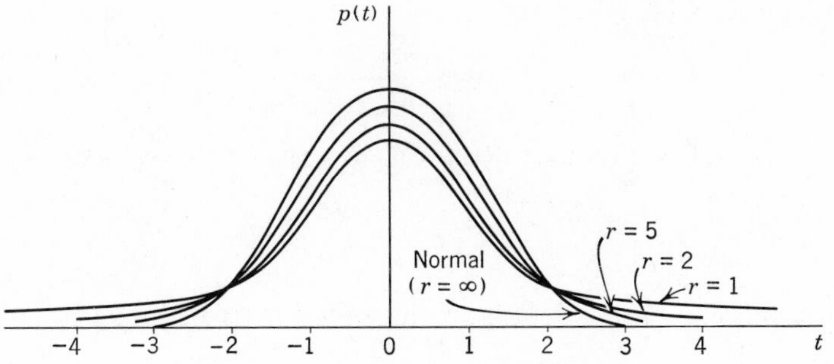

FIG. 14-3 Probability distribution of t_r.

The probability distribution of t_r is shown in Figure 14-3. Of course, for each different r there is a different C_r^2, hence a different t_r. The critical values of the t distribution for each r are given in Table V in the Appendix. Although the t distribution requires sophisticated mathematics to derive in detail, we can easily deduce its most important features. From (14-25c) as $r \to \infty$

$$C_r \xrightarrow{p} 1$$

hence, from (14-30)

$$t_r \xrightarrow{p} z \tag{14-32}$$

This is seen in Figure 14-3; the t distribution gradually approaches the normal as r increases. This is also verified in Appendix Table V; as r gets very large, the t percentiles get very close to the z percentiles (given in the last row, for reference). In fact, if $r > 30$, there is very little error in approximating t with z.

On the other hand, as long as r is finite, C_r is not equal to 1; instead, it is distributed around 1. It is this variability of C_r in the denominator of (14-30) that spreads the t distribution out more than the normal. In Figure 14-2, the student will note that the smaller is r, the greater is the variability of C_r^2 (hence C_r); this causes greater variability in the corresponding t distribution in Figure 14-3.

(b) Uses of *t*

(i) Sample Mean. In practice, the t distribution occurs in quasi-standardizing a normal variate. As the commonest example, we consider a sample mean $\bar{y}$.

If $y \sim N(\mu, \sigma^2)$, then the sample mean $\bar{y} \sim N(\mu, \sigma^2/n)$ and in its standardized form is

$$z = \frac{\bar{y} - \mu}{\sigma/\sqrt{n}} \tag{14-33}$$

Moreover, when s was substituted for σ, we called it the *quasi*-standardized

$$z^* = \frac{\bar{y} - \mu}{s/\sqrt{n}} \tag{14-34}$$

To prove this has a t distribution, we introduce two canceling occurrences of σ into (14-34)

$$\begin{aligned} z^* &= \frac{\bar{y} - \mu}{(s/\sigma)(\sigma/\sqrt{n})} \\ &= \frac{(\bar{y} - \mu)/(\sigma/\sqrt{n})}{(s/\sigma)} \end{aligned}$$

by (14-33) and (14-26)

$$z^* = \frac{z}{C_{n-1}} \tag{14-35}$$

By (14-30) this has the t distribution, provided that the numerator and denominator are independent, that is, that $\bar{y}$ and s are independent. At first glance there seems to be doubt about this independence, because s and $\bar{y}$ are calculated from the same sample; indeed, $\bar{y}$ occurs explicitly in the formula $s^2 = \sum (y_i - \bar{y})^2/(n - 1)$. Yet there is a surprising theorem that proves that s and $\bar{y}$ in fact are independent,[4] and this completes our argument.

---

[4] This is proved in advanced texts such as Cramer, or Kendall and Stuart. The proof is simple and instructive enough in the special case when $n = 2$, that we give it in this footnote:

From (14-18) it follows that

$$s^2 = \frac{(y_1 - y_2)^2}{2}$$

while, by definition:

$$\bar{y} = \frac{y_1 + y_2}{2}$$

Since constants can be ignored without loss of generality, it is enough to prove that $(y_1 - y_2)$ is independent of $(y_1 + y_2)$.

We therefore consider the covariance of these variables, obtaining

$$\begin{aligned} E(y_1 - y_2)(y_1 + y_2) &= E(y_1^2 - y_2^2) \\ &= E(y_1^2) - E(y_2^2) \\ &= 0 \end{aligned} \tag{14-36}$$

since (by assumption) y_1 and y_2 have identical distributions. Moreover, since both y_1 and y_2 are normal, $(y_1 - y_2)$ and $(y_1 + y_2)$ are also normal. Hence, their zero covariance in (14-36) establishes their independence.

(ii) General Case. It is not only the sample mean that can be quasi-standardized to produce a t statistic. It may be similarly proved that whenever any normal variate is quasi-standardized, it becomes a t variable rather than a z variable. The estimated regression coefficients $\hat{\beta}_i$ are prime examples. The substituted s, being a random variable, makes the t distribution a little more widespread than the z distribution. This causes confidence intervals to be a little wider (vaguer)—the price paid for not knowing σ exactly.

14-4 THE F DISTRIBUTION

(a) Definition

The mathematical definition of an F variable with m and n d.f. is rather like the definition of t

$$\boxed{F_{m,n} \triangleq \frac{C_m^2}{C_n^2}} \tag{14-37}$$

where C_m^2, C_n^2 are *independent* modified Chi-square variables. This is the same sort of independence of numerator and denominator specified in the definition of t. As an extreme example of what could conceivably happen were this independence not assured, suppose $m = n$, and C_m^2 and C_n^2 are perfectly dependent by being identical; then their ratio must be 1 exactly, and this is not a very interesting random variable.

Some of the limiting properties of the F distribution are obvious from the limiting properties of C^2. From (14-25), as $n \to \infty$,

$$C_n^2 \xrightarrow{p} 1$$

Thus, from (14-37), as $n \to \infty$

$$\boxed{F_{m,n} \xrightarrow{p} C_m^2} \tag{14-38}$$

Figure 14-4 shows how the F distribution approaches the corresponding C_m^2 distribution as n increases. This is also borne out in Appendix Table VII; as n gets large, the percentiles of $F_{m,n}$ get close to the percentiles of C_m^2 (given in the last row, for reference).

Finally, as $m \to \infty$ as well as $n \to \infty$,

$$F_{m,n} \xrightarrow{p} 1 \tag{14-39}$$

This means that the critical values of F approach 1 as both m and n become

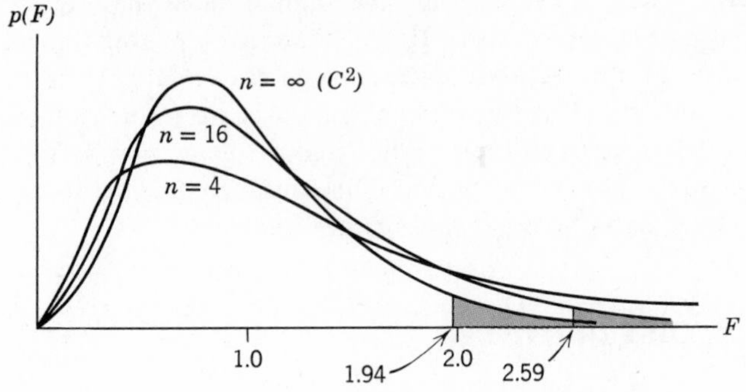

FIG. 14-4 Probability distribution of $F_{m,n}$ for $m = 8$, and various n.

very large, that is, as we move towards the lower right-hand corner of Appendix Table VII.

(b) Use of F in Regression

When σ^2 is known, regression tests may be made using the modified Chi-square statistic:

$$C_r^2 = \frac{1}{r}(\mathbf{C}\hat{\boldsymbol{\beta}} - \mathbf{C}\boldsymbol{\beta})'(\mathbf{CVC}')^{-1}(\mathbf{C}\hat{\boldsymbol{\beta}} - \mathbf{C}\boldsymbol{\beta})/\sigma^2 \tag{14-40}$$

(14-16) modified

But in the usual case, s^2 must be substituted for the unknown σ^2. We shall establish that the resulting

$$F = \frac{1}{r}(\mathbf{C}\hat{\boldsymbol{\beta}} - \mathbf{C}\boldsymbol{\beta})'(\mathbf{CVC}')^{-1}(\mathbf{C}\hat{\boldsymbol{\beta}} - \mathbf{C}\boldsymbol{\beta})/s^2 \tag{14-41}$$

(13-39) repeated

does have an F distribution according to the definition (14-37). We merely introduce canceling occurrences of σ^2 into (14-41)

$$F = \frac{(\mathbf{C}\hat{\boldsymbol{\beta}} - \mathbf{C}\boldsymbol{\beta})'(\sigma^2\mathbf{CVC}')^{-1}(\mathbf{C}\hat{\boldsymbol{\beta}} - \mathbf{C}\boldsymbol{\beta})/r}{s^2/\sigma^2} \tag{14-42}$$

The numerator and denominator have already [in (14-16) and (14-27) respectively] been shown to be C^2 variates. Their independence can be proved in advanced texts (such as Cramer, *op. cit.*) so that (14-41) indeed does follow the F distribution, with r and $(n - k)$ degrees of freedom.

In conclusion, the substitution of s for σ changed a C^2 variable in (14-40) into an F variable (14-41), just as it changed a z into a t in Section 14-3.

14-5 COMPARISON AND REVIEW

A summary is presented in Table 14-1.

A briefer summary is given in Table 14-2, where we note that each variable in column (1) is just a special case ($r = 1$) of the corresponding variable in column (2). Thus

$$z^2 = C_1^2 \tag{14-43}$$

and

$$t_{n-k}^2 = F_{1,n-k} \tag{14-44}$$

It is also interesting to note that in a sense each variable in row (1) is a special case ($n = \infty$) of the corresponding variable in row 2. Thus

$$z = t_\infty \tag{14-45}$$

and

$$C_r^2 = F_{r,\infty} \tag{14-46}$$

This information is summarized in Figure 14-5, which shows how the F table includes these other distributions as well.

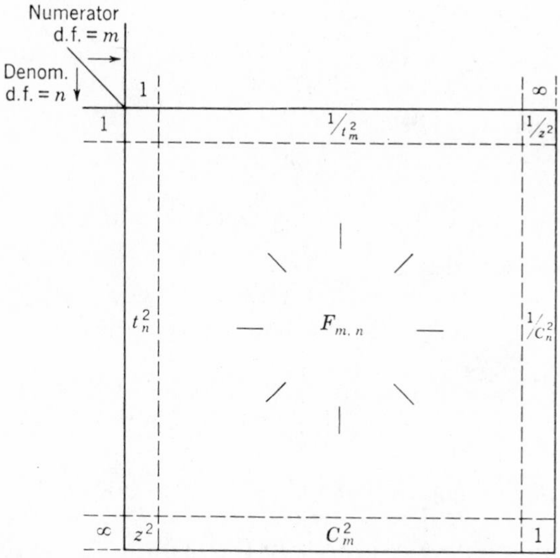

FIG. 14-5 Relation of the F distribution to C^2, t^2, and z^2 (as found in Appendix Table VII).

TABLE 14-1 Summary of How Variables in this Chapter are Distributed

(a) *Chi-square* (χ_r^2)

Definition:

$$\sum_{i=1}^{n} z_i^2 = \frac{\sum (y_i - \mu)^2}{\sigma^2} \sim \chi_n^2 \qquad (14\text{-}1)$$

or, in matrix terms,

$$(\mathbf{y} - \boldsymbol{\mu})'(\sigma^2 \mathbf{I})^{-1}(\mathbf{y} - \boldsymbol{\mu}) \sim \chi_n^2 \qquad (14\text{-}9)$$

This holds true even if we consider an entirely different set of variables that are not independent, with cov $\mathbf{y} = \sigma^2\mathbf{W}$. Then

$$(\mathbf{y} - \boldsymbol{\mu})'(\sigma^2 \mathbf{W})^{-1}(\mathbf{y} - \boldsymbol{\mu}) \sim \chi_n^2 \qquad (14\text{-}10)$$

Now suppose that in (14-1) μ is unknown and is replaced with $\bar{y}$

$$\sum_{i=1}^{n} \frac{(y_i - \bar{y})^2}{\sigma^2} \sim \chi_{n-1}^2 \qquad (14\text{-}17)$$

and in the general case with k regressors

$$\sum_{i=1}^{n} \frac{(y_i - \hat{y}_i)^2}{\sigma^2} \sim \chi_{n-k}^2 \qquad (14\text{-}23)$$

(b) *Modified Chi-square* (C_r^2)

Definition:

$$\frac{\chi_r^2}{r} \sim C_r^2 \qquad (14\text{-}24)$$

In the single (dummy) regressor case, when μ is estimated by $\bar{y}$

$$\frac{s^2}{\sigma^2} \sim C_{n-1}^2 \qquad (14\text{-}26)$$

In the general case, with k regressors

$$\frac{s^2}{\sigma^2} \sim C_{n-k}^2 \qquad (14\text{-}27)$$

s^2 is used to estimate σ^2, below.

(c) *Student's t*

Definition:

$$\frac{z}{C_r} \sim t_r \qquad (14\text{-}30)$$

Used in quasi-standardizing:

$$\frac{\bar{y} - \mu}{s/\sqrt{n}} \sim t_{n-1} \qquad (14\text{-}34)$$

(d) *F*

Definition:

$$\frac{C_m^2}{C_n^2} \sim F_{m,n} \qquad (14\text{-}37)$$

Also used for quasi-standardizing, in regression:

$$\frac{(\mathbf{C}\hat{\boldsymbol{\beta}} - \mathbf{C}\boldsymbol{\beta})'(\mathbf{C}\mathbf{V}\mathbf{C}')^{-1}(\mathbf{C}\hat{\boldsymbol{\beta}} - \mathbf{C}\boldsymbol{\beta})/r}{s^2} \sim F_{r,n-k} \qquad (14\text{-}41)$$

TABLE 14-2 Relation of Various Distributions for Practical Work[a]

Available knowledge ↓ / Purpose →	(1) Confidence Interval or Test for *One* Parameter	(2) Confidence Interval or Test for *Several* (r) Parameters
(1) σ^2 known	Use z (or z^2)	C_r^2
(2) σ^2 unknown, s^2 used instead	t_{n-k} (or t_{n-k}^2)	$F_{r,n-k}$

[a] n = sample size, k = number of regressors, and r = number of parameters to be simultaneously tested.

PROBLEMS

14-1 It is possible to find the critical points of C_1^2 using only the z table. In this way, find the critical point of C_1^2 which

(a) marks off 5% in the upper tail

(b) marks off 1% in the upper tail.

14-2 Using only the F table, find the critical point of C_r^2 which

(a) when $r = 5$, marks off 5% in the upper tail

(b) when $r = 15$, marks off 5% in the upper tail.

14-3 Construct a 90% confidence interval for σ^2 from this sample of n observations from $N(\mu, \sigma^2)$: 28, 31, 21, 28, 22

(a) Assume μ is known to be 25. [*Hint:* (14-8)]

(b) Assume, more realistically, that μ is unknown. [*Hint:* (14-26)]

chapter 15

The Vector Geometry of Regression and Correlation (A Generalization of Chapters 3 and 5)

15-1 THE GEOMETRIC INTERPRETATION OF VECTORS

(a) Introduction

Assuming the reader is familiar with vector algebra, we develop its corresponding geometric interpretation in this chapter; this is then used to reinterpret regression and correlation theory. Readers with matrix algebra will have simultaneously taken varying amounts of geometry; hence, some may be able to pick up this argument at a midway point. But for the sake of those who have very little background, this geometry is developed from first principles. For simplicity, we begin by showing vectors in only two or three dimensions. However, interpretations in any number of dimensions are equally valid; thus, we can drop explicit reference to the dimension of the space later on.

Consider the vector

$$\mathbf{x} = (x_1, x_2, \ldots, x_n) \tag{15-1}$$

For example,

$$\mathbf{x} = (2, 4, 3) \tag{15-2}$$

which may be plotted as a point in three dimensions (Figure 15-1). Sometimes it is more convenient to represent it as an arrow from the origin to the point. If a vector is designated as an arrow, it may be shifted, provided its length and

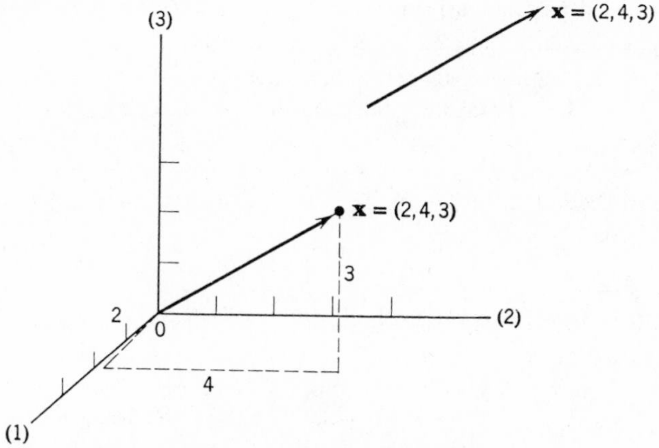

FIG. 15-1 A three-dimensional vector. This vector is the direction and distance defined by moving two units in the first direction, four units in the second direction, and three units in the third direction.

direction are maintained—that is, it may be shifted in a parallel way. But if a vector is designated as a point only, then of course this point may *not* be shifted.

The simple algebraic manipulations of vectors are set out in Table 15-1, along with the corresponding geometric interpretation. In addition, each geometric operation is detailed in Figures 15-2 to 15-4.

In review, in Figure 15-5 we see that the sum $(\mathbf{x} + \mathbf{y})$ is one diagonal of the parallelogram formed from $\mathbf{x}$ and $\mathbf{y}$, while the difference $(\mathbf{x} - \mathbf{y})$ is the other diagonal.

(b) Dot Product

(i) Definition and Properties. The dot product (also called inner product or scalar product) of two vectors is defined as a simple kind of matrix multiplication

$$\mathbf{x} \cdot \mathbf{y} = \mathbf{x}\mathbf{y}' = \begin{bmatrix} x_1 & x_2 & \cdots & x_n \end{bmatrix} \begin{bmatrix} y_1 \\ y_2 \\ \cdot \\ \cdot \\ \cdot \\ y_n \end{bmatrix} = x_1y_1 + x_2y_2 + \cdots x_ny_n \quad (15\text{-}3)$$

For example,

$$(3, 1, -1) \cdot (2, -3, 0) = 3$$

TABLE 15-1 Comparison of the Algebra and Geometry of Vectors

	Since each manipulation is defined algebraically in this way:	It follows that it has this geometric interpretation:
Scalar multiplication by a positive constant	$2(3, 1) = (6, 2)$	Changes length (Figure 15-2)
Scalar multiplication by -1	$-1(3, 1) = (-3, -1)$	Changes direction (Figure 15-2)
Addition	$(3, 1) + (1, 2) = (4, 3)$	Shifts the arrow **y** to follow the arrow **x** (Figure 15-3); this is seen to yield the diagonal of the parallelogram constructed from **x** and **y**
Subtraction	$(3, 1) - (1, 2)$ $= (2, -1)$	Is equivalent to summing **x** + (−**y**), i.e., shifting the arrow (−**y**) to follow the arrow **x** in Figure 15-4*a*. This is also seen to be the arrow obtained in Figure 15-4*b* by moving from the *point* **y** to the *point* **x**

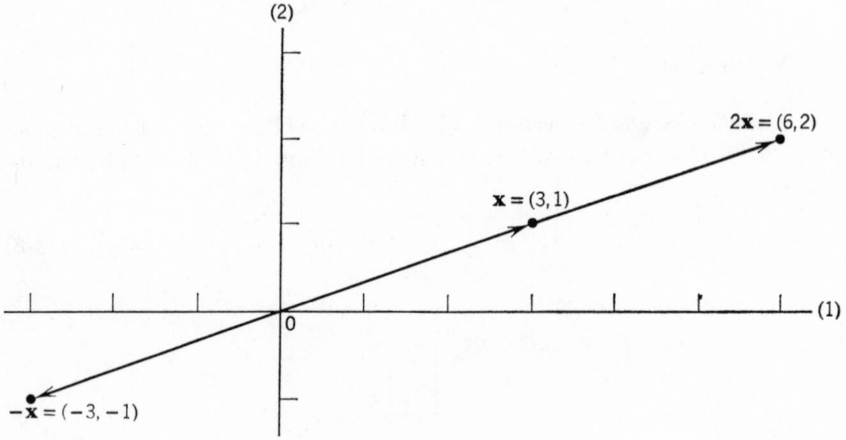

FIG. 15-2 Scalar multiplication.

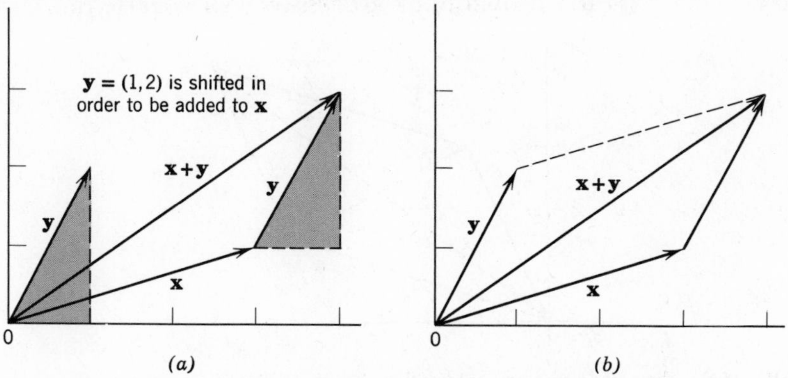

FIG. 15-3 Vector addition, which in (*b*) is seen to be equivalent to constructing a diagonal of the parallelogram defined by **x** and **y**.

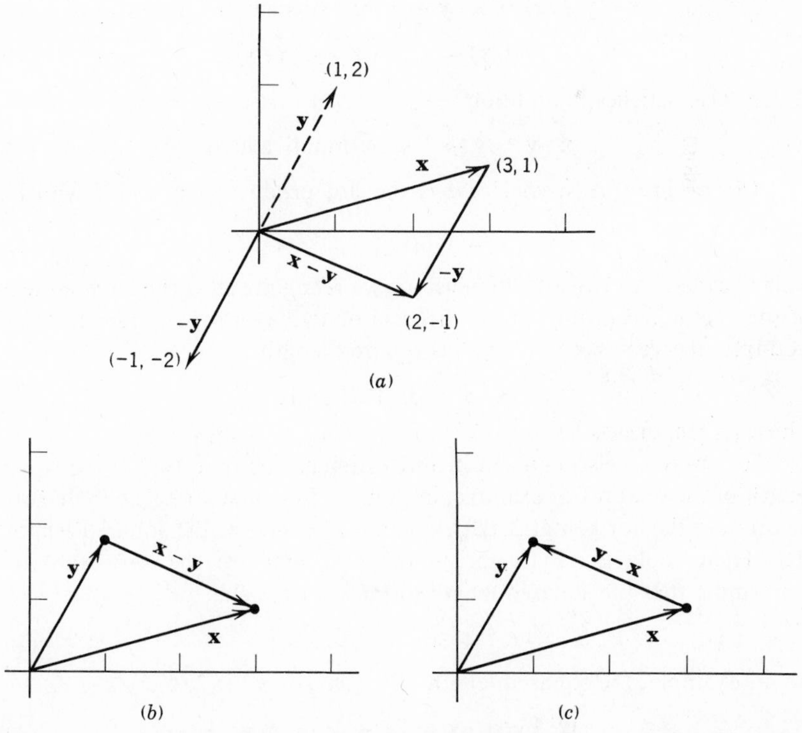

FIG. 15-4 Vector subtraction (**x** − **y**), which in (*b*) is seen to be equivalent to moving from point **y** to point **x**. (*c*) The reader can confirm that (**y** − **x**) is similarly obtained by moving from point **x** to point **y**.

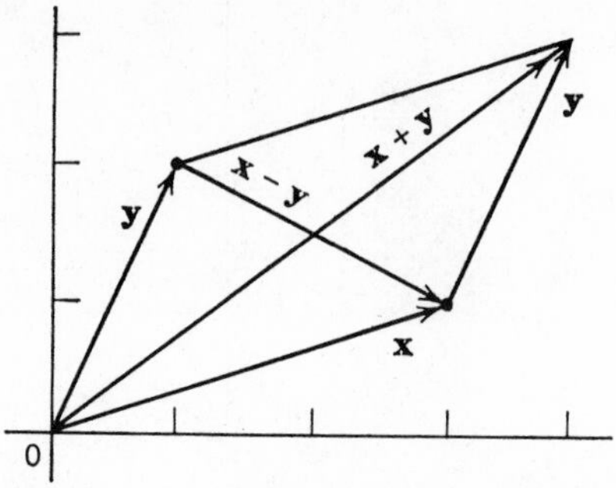

FIG. 15-5 Vector addition and subtraction compared. Addition is the diagonal obtained by shifting the arrow **y** to follow the arrow **x**; subtraction is the diagonal obtained by moving from the point **y** to the point **x**.

The dot product, of course, obeys all the rules of matrix multiplication; for example,

$$\mathbf{x} \cdot (\mathbf{y} + \mathbf{z}) = \mathbf{x} \cdot \mathbf{y} + \mathbf{x} \cdot \mathbf{z} \quad \text{(distributive law)} \tag{15-4}$$

$$\mathbf{x} \cdot (c\mathbf{y}) = (c\mathbf{x}) \cdot \mathbf{y} = c(\mathbf{x} \cdot \mathbf{y}) \tag{15-5}$$

But, it also satisfies in addition

$$\mathbf{x} \cdot \mathbf{y} = \mathbf{y} \cdot \mathbf{x} \quad \text{(commutative law)} \tag{15-6}$$

(ii) Length. A special case is the dot product of a vector with itself

$$\mathbf{x} \cdot \mathbf{x} = x_1^2 + x_2^2 + \cdots + x_n^2 \tag{15-7}$$

This is called $\|\mathbf{x}\|^2$. In two dimensions we recognize it as the squared length of the vector, according to the theorem of Pythagoras in Figure 15-6*a*. For example, the vector $\mathbf{x} = (3, 1)$ has squared length

$$\mathbf{x} \cdot \mathbf{x} = 3^2 + 1^2 = 10$$

Thus, its length is $\sqrt{10}$.

It is easy to also confirm in three dimensions that $\|\mathbf{x}\|^2$ is the squared length of the vector. For example, in Figure 15-6*b*, first apply the Pythagorean theorem to the horizontal ΔABC, obtaining $x_1^2 + x_2^2$ as the squared length of AC. Then apply the Pythagorean theorem again to the vertical ΔACD, confirming that the squared length of the vector AD is

$$(x_1^2 + x_2^2) + x_3^2 = \|\mathbf{x}\|^2 \tag{15-8}$$

As an example, the squared length of the vector $\mathbf{x} = (2, 4, 3)$ is

$$\|\mathbf{x}\|^2 = \mathbf{x} \cdot \mathbf{x} = 2^2 + 4^2 + 3^2 = 29$$

Thus, its length is

$$\|\mathbf{x}\| = \sqrt{29} \tag{15-9}$$

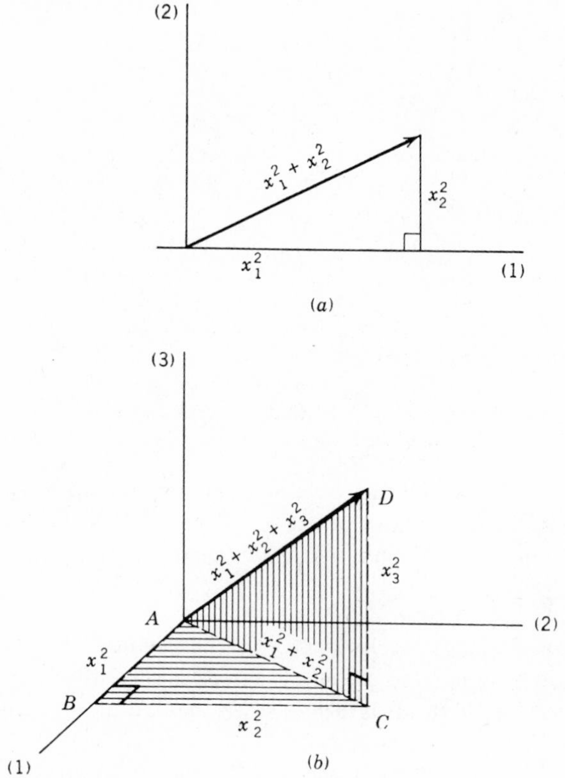

FIG. 15-6 Squared lengths of vectors, related by the theorem of Pythagoras. (*a*) In two dimensions. (*b*) In three dimensons.

$\|\mathbf{x}\|$ has turned out to be length wherever it is physically meaningful (in 1, 2, or 3 dimensions). We shall use a little mathematical imagination and call $\|\mathbf{x}\|$ the length (or "norm") in any number of dimensions.

To review:

$$\|\mathbf{x}\|^2 = \mathbf{x} \cdot \mathbf{x} \tag{15-10}$$

$$= x_1^2 + x_2^2 \cdots + x_n^2 = \text{squared length} \tag{15-11}$$

while

$$\|\mathbf{x}\| = \text{length, or norm}$$

One of the most frequently used facts about length is that, if c is positive,

$$\|c\mathbf{x}\| = c\,\|\mathbf{x}\| \tag{15-12a}$$

This is obvious from Figure 15-2, and may be proved more rigorously in n

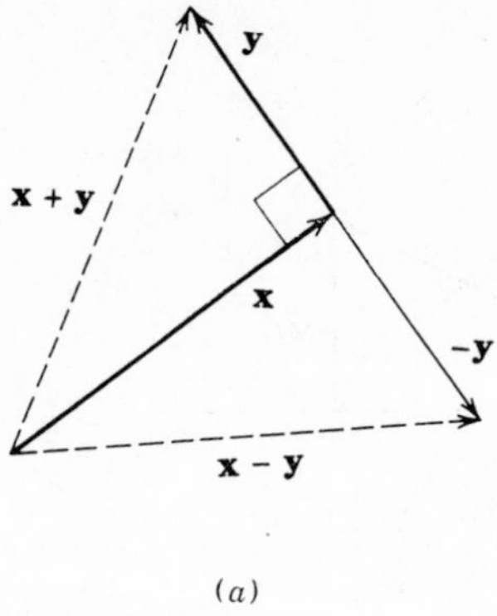

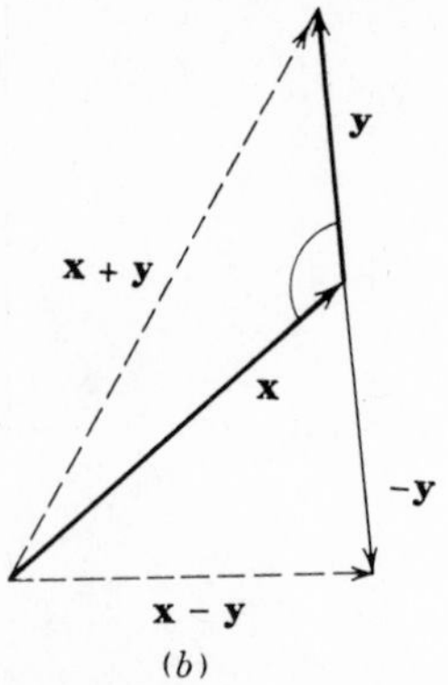

FIG. 15-7 $\mathbf{x} \perp \mathbf{y}$ iff $\|\mathbf{x} + \mathbf{y}\| = \|\mathbf{x} - \mathbf{y}\|$. (Note that the diagrams are valid in any number of dimensions.) (*a*) $\mathbf{x} \perp \mathbf{y}$. (*b*) $\mathbf{x}$ not $\perp \mathbf{y}$.

dimensions.[1] When c is negative, equation (15-12a) cannot be correct because the right side is negative while the left side is positive. By taking the absolute value (magnitude) of c, we may write a generally correct form of (15-12a):

$$\|c\mathbf{x}\| = |c| \, \|\mathbf{x}\| \tag{15-12b}$$

(iii) Perpendicularity. Also called "orthogonality," and symbolized by $\perp$, this is easily expressed in terms of vector length. From Figure 15-7, it is evident that $\mathbf{x} \perp \mathbf{y}$ iff the length of $(\mathbf{x} + \mathbf{y})$ equals the length of $(\mathbf{x} - \mathbf{y})$, that is, iff

$$\|\mathbf{x} + \mathbf{y}\|^2 = \|\mathbf{x} - \mathbf{y}\|^2$$

$$(\mathbf{x} + \mathbf{y}) \cdot (\mathbf{x} + \mathbf{y}) = (\mathbf{x} - \mathbf{y}) \cdot (\mathbf{x} - \mathbf{y})$$

$$\mathbf{x} \cdot \mathbf{x} + 2\mathbf{x} \cdot \mathbf{y} + \mathbf{y} \cdot \mathbf{y} = \mathbf{x} \cdot \mathbf{x} - 2\mathbf{x} \cdot \mathbf{y} + \mathbf{y} \cdot \mathbf{y}$$

$$4\mathbf{x} \cdot \mathbf{y} = 0$$

$$\boxed{\mathbf{x} \perp \mathbf{y} \text{ iff } \mathbf{x} \cdot \mathbf{y} = 0} \tag{15-13}$$

In words, two vectors are perpendicular if and only if their dot product is zero.

---

[1] **Proof of (15-12a)**

Since $c\mathbf{x} = (cx_1, cx_2, \ldots)$, from definition (15-11),

$$\|c\mathbf{x}\|^2 = (cx_1)^2 + (cx_2)^2 + \cdots$$
$$= c^2(x_1^2 + x_2^2 + \cdots)$$

Thus

$$\|c\mathbf{x}\| = \sqrt{c^2(x_1^2 + x_2^2 + \cdots)}$$
$$= c\sqrt{x_1^2 + x_2^2 + \cdots}$$
$$= c \, \|\mathbf{x}\|.$$

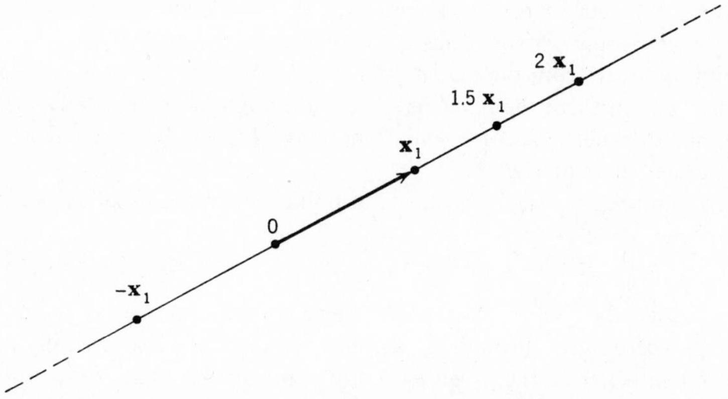

FIG. 15-8 The line L generated by $\mathbf{x}_1$. (The diagram may be pictured in either two or three dimensions.) L is $c_1\mathbf{x}_1$, where c_1 takes on all values, so that the line extends to infinity.

(c) Subspaces

(i) Generation of Subspaces. In Figure 15-8, we show that when a fixed vector $\mathbf{x}_1$ is multiplied by every possible scalar c_1, a straight line is generated running through $\mathbf{x}_1$ and the origin. Each vector $c_1\mathbf{x}_1$ may be represented as an arrow or a point, but the picture is less cluttered if we simply use a point. In summary we write

$$L: \quad c_1\mathbf{x}_1 \qquad -\infty < c_1 < \infty \tag{15-14}$$

In Figure 15-9, we increase dimension by one. In this figure, we use for the first time two conventions about arrowheads. First, arrows within the

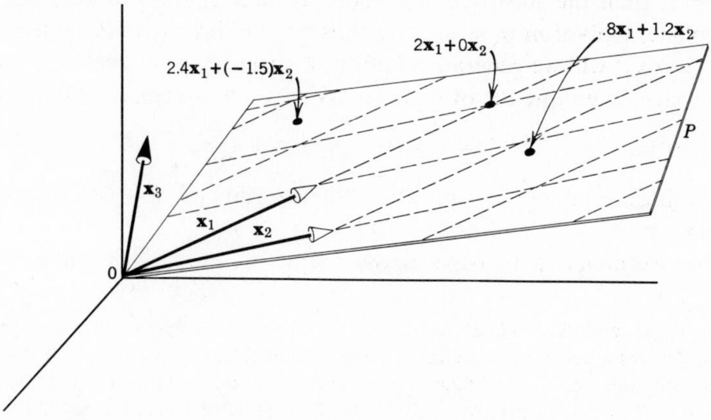

FIG. 15-9 The plane P generated by $\mathbf{x}_1$ and $\mathbf{x}_2$. P is $c_1\mathbf{x}_1 + c_2\mathbf{x}_2$, where c_1, c_2 take on all values, so that the plane extends to infinity.

plane have a light arrowhead, and arrows outside the plane have a dark arrowhead. Second, arrowheads are shown as cones so that when the arrow is pointing away from the reader, the circular base of the cone can be seen. Finally, we represent the plane as a slab, although mathematically speaking, it has no thickness. These conventions make higher dimensional geometry much easier to visualize.

In Figure 15-9, we show the set of points generated by two fixed vectors in 3-space,

$$P: \quad c_1\mathbf{x}_1 + c_2\mathbf{x}_2 \qquad -\infty < c_1, c_2 < \infty \tag{15-15}$$

This is called the "set of all possible linear combinations of $\mathbf{x}_1$ and $\mathbf{x}_2$," and is the plane running through $\mathbf{x}_1$, $\mathbf{x}_2$, and the origin.[2] Geometrically, we see that we can generate (i.e., "get to") any point on this plane P by taking the appropriate linear combination of $\mathbf{x}_1$ and $\mathbf{x}_2$, that is, by appropriately selecting c_1 and c_2 in (15-15); but we cannot generate any point above or below this plane.

To generate the whole 3-space requires a third independent vector, such as $\mathbf{x}_3$, to take us off the plane P. Thus, the whole set of points in this 3-space could be generated by

$$c_1\mathbf{x}_1 + c_2\mathbf{x}_2 + c_3\mathbf{x}_3 \qquad -\infty < c_i < \infty \tag{15-16}$$

This is often stated as, "$\mathbf{x}_1$, $\mathbf{x}_2$, and $\mathbf{x}_3$ generate (or span) this 3-space." Or, "$\mathbf{x}_1$, $\mathbf{x}_2$, and $\mathbf{x}_3$ are a basis of this 3-space."

This generalizes into n-space; consider the set of points

$$c_1\mathbf{x}_1 + c_2\mathbf{x}_2 + \cdots + c_m\mathbf{x}_m \qquad -\infty < c_i < \infty \tag{15-17}$$

This set of all possible linear combinations of these m fixed vectors is called an m-dimension "subspace." If $m = 1$, then the subspace is a straight line. If $m = 2$, then the subspace is a plane. If $m > 2$, the subspace is called a hyperplane. Only if $m = n$, and we thus have n linearly independent vectors $(\mathbf{x}_1, \mathbf{x}_2 \cdots \mathbf{x}_n)$ will we generate all of our n-space. For any vector or point $\mathbf{y}$ in this n-space, a unique set of coefficients $c_1, c_2 \cdots c_n$ can be found such that

$$\mathbf{y} = c_1\mathbf{x}_1 + c_2\mathbf{x}_2 \cdots + c_n\mathbf{x}_n \tag{15-18}$$

These values $\langle c_1, c_2 \cdots c_n \rangle$ are called "the coordinates of $\mathbf{y}$ with respect to the basis $(\mathbf{x}_1, \mathbf{x}_2 \cdots \mathbf{x}_n)$."

For example, in two-space, the vectors $\mathbf{x}_1 = (1, -1)$ and $\mathbf{x}_2 = (2, 1)$

[2] Unless $\mathbf{x}_1$, $\mathbf{x}_2$, and the origin all lie on a straight line, in which case we can generate only this line. Or worse yet, if $\mathbf{x}_1$, $\mathbf{x}_2$, and the origin all coincide, (i.e., $\mathbf{x}_1 = \mathbf{x}_2 = \mathbf{0}$) then we can generate only one point—the origin. These degenerate cases are called "linear dependence of $\mathbf{x}_1$ and $\mathbf{x}_2$." For simplicity, we shall assume throughout this chapter that linear dependence does not occur.

will generate or span the whole space. We now use (15-18) to find the coordinates (with respect to this basis $\mathbf{x}_1, \mathbf{x}_2$) of a given vector, say $\mathbf{y} = (4, -1)$; this involves selecting c_1 and c_2 so that

$$c_1\mathbf{x}_1 + c_2\mathbf{x}_2 = \mathbf{y} \tag{15-19}$$

that is[3]

$$c_1 \begin{bmatrix} 1 \\ -1 \end{bmatrix} + c_2 \begin{bmatrix} 2 \\ 1 \end{bmatrix} = \begin{bmatrix} 4 \\ -1 \end{bmatrix} \tag{15-20}$$

that is,

$$c_1 + 2c_2 = 4$$
$$-c_1 + c_2 = -1$$

The algebraic solution to this set of equations is $c_1 = 2$, $c_2 = 1$. We have expressed $\mathbf{y}$ as a linear combination of $\mathbf{x}_1$ and $\mathbf{x}_2$, with the coefficients $\langle 2, 1\rangle$ being the coordinates of $\mathbf{y}$ with respect to $\mathbf{x}_1$ and $\mathbf{x}_2$.

This is seen geometrically in Figure 15-10: the line (subspace) L_1 generated by $\mathbf{x}_1$ is shown, along with the subspace L_2 generated by $\mathbf{x}_2$. Then we complete the parallelogram, confirming that c_1 must be 2, and c_2 must be 1.

In other words, to find the coordinates of $\mathbf{y}$, we project; to find c_1, we project $\mathbf{y}$ onto L_1 in the direction parallel to L_2; or, more briefly, we "project $\mathbf{y}$ onto $\mathbf{x}_1$ along $\mathbf{x}_2$." Similarly, to find c_2 we project $\mathbf{y}$ onto $\mathbf{x}_2$ along $\mathbf{x}_1$.

The simplest kind of projection occurs when $\mathbf{x}_1 \perp \mathbf{x}_2$; this is called an "orthogonal projection," as in Figure 15-11.

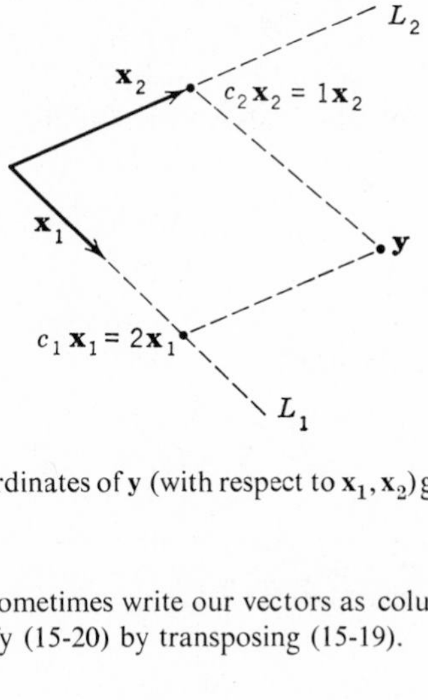

FIG. 15-10 Finding the coordinates of $\mathbf{y}$ (with respect to $\mathbf{x}_1, \mathbf{x}_2$) geometrically by projection.

[3] For convenience, we shall sometimes write our vectors as columns instead of rows. More formally, we can easily justify (15-20) by transposing (15-19).

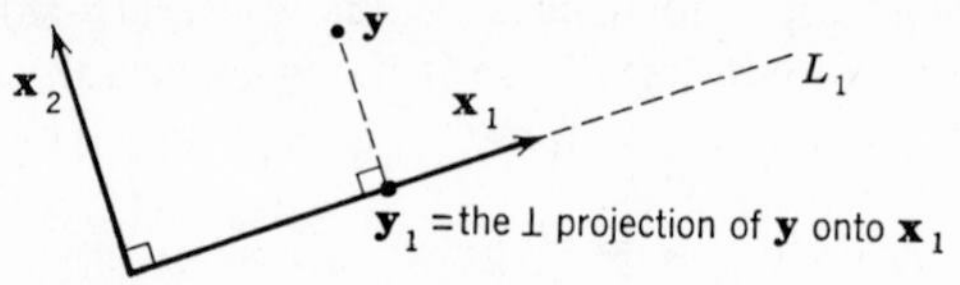

FIG. 15-11 The orthogonal projection of $\mathbf{y}$ onto $\mathbf{x}_1$.

(d) Perpendicular Projections and Least Distance

Perpendicular projections are particularly easy to calculate, because the condition for perpendicularity (15-13) is so simple. To work out $\mathbf{y}_1$, the $\perp$ projection of $\mathbf{y}$ onto $\mathbf{x}_1$, consider Figure 15-12, which is valid in any dimension. Of course, since the projection vector $\mathbf{y}_1$ lies on L_1, it is just a (scalar) multiple of $\mathbf{x}_1$; that is,

$$\mathbf{y}_1 = c\mathbf{x}_1 \tag{15-21}$$

with the problem being to determine c. Moreover, we note (Figure 15-5) that $\mathbf{y} - \mathbf{y}_1$ is the vector defined by moving from $\mathbf{y}_1$ to $\mathbf{y}$. But we must keep this perpendicular to $\mathbf{x}_1$, that is, we must find c, so that

$$(\mathbf{y} - \mathbf{y}_1) \perp \mathbf{x}_1 \tag{15-22}$$

Substitute (15-21) into (15-22) and use (15-13)

$$(\mathbf{y} - c\mathbf{x}_1) \cdot \mathbf{x}_1 = 0$$

$$(\mathbf{y} \cdot \mathbf{x}_1) - c(\mathbf{x}_1 \cdot \mathbf{x}_1) = 0$$

$$\boxed{c = \frac{\mathbf{y} \cdot \mathbf{x}_1}{\mathbf{x}_1 \cdot \mathbf{x}_1}} \tag{15-23}$$

Substituting (15-23) into (15-21) establishes that

$$\boxed{\mathbf{y}_1 = \left(\frac{\mathbf{y} \cdot \mathbf{x}_1}{\mathbf{x}_1 \cdot \mathbf{x}_1}\right)\mathbf{x}_1} \tag{15-24}$$

where $\mathbf{y}_1$ is the $\perp$ projection of $\mathbf{y}$ onto $\mathbf{x}_1$.

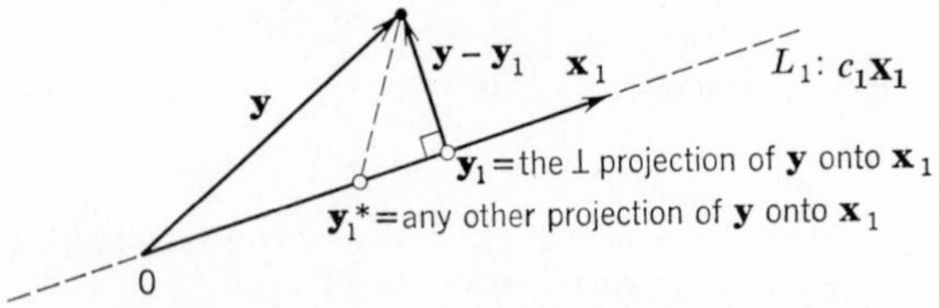

FIG. 15-12 Orthogonal projection in two dimensions: $\mathbf{y}$ projected onto $\mathbf{x}_1$.

The length of this projected vector has a simple formula too:

$$\begin{aligned}\|\mathbf{y}_1\|^2 &= \mathbf{y}_1 \cdot \mathbf{y}_1\\ &= c^2\mathbf{x}_1 \cdot \mathbf{x}_1\\ &= \left[\frac{\mathbf{y} \cdot \mathbf{x}_1}{\mathbf{x}_1 \cdot \mathbf{x}_1}\right]^2 \mathbf{x}_1 \cdot \mathbf{x}_1\end{aligned}$$

$$\boxed{\|\mathbf{y}_1\|^2 = \frac{(\mathbf{y} \cdot \mathbf{x}_1)^2}{\mathbf{x}_1 \cdot \mathbf{x}_1}} \tag{15-25}$$

Hence, the norm or length of $\mathbf{y}_1$ is

$$\|\mathbf{y}_1\| = \frac{|\mathbf{y} \cdot \mathbf{x}_1|}{\|\mathbf{x}_1\|} \tag{15-26}$$

Referring again to Figure 15-12, we see that the *perpendicular* projection $\mathbf{y}_1$ is the point on L_1 closest to $\mathbf{y}$; any nonperpendicular projection, say $\mathbf{y}_1^*$, is farther from $\mathbf{y}$. The proof is simple: the distance $\|\mathbf{y} - \mathbf{y}_1^*\|$ must be greater than the distance $\|\mathbf{y} - \mathbf{y}_1\|$, because the hypotenuse of a right-angled triangle is greater than either side.

This theorem is important enough for regression and correlation theory that it is shown in the three-dimension case in Figure 15-13.

The perpendicular projection of $\mathbf{y}$ onto the subspace $c_1\mathbf{x}_1 + c_2\mathbf{x}_2 \cdots + c_m\mathbf{x}_m$ is the one point on this subspace closest to $\mathbf{y}$.	(15-27)

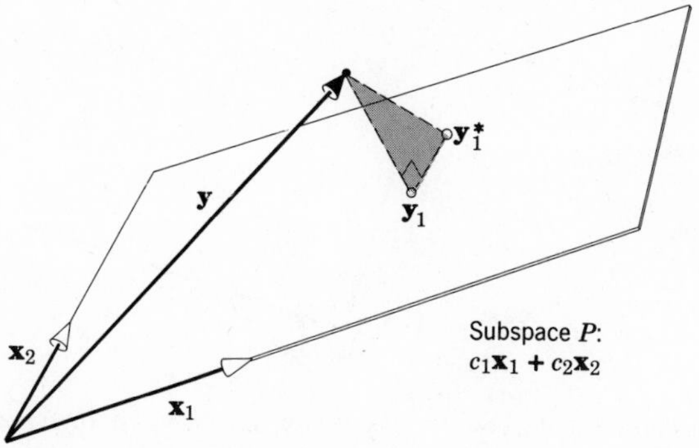

FIG. 15-13 Orthogonal projection in three dimensions: $\mathbf{y}$ projected onto $(\mathbf{x}_1, \mathbf{x}_2)$ subspace.

(e) Cos θ

We can now obtain a simple formula for the cosine of the angle between any two vectors $\mathbf{x}_1$ and $\mathbf{y}$. Referring to Figure 15-14, we first $\perp$ project $\mathbf{y}$ onto $\mathbf{x}_1$; then, by definition from trigonometry

$$\cos\theta = \pm\frac{\|\mathbf{y}_1\|}{\|\mathbf{y}\|} \tag{15-28}$$

Moreover, from Figure 15-14, it is clear that the sign of $\cos\theta$ agrees with the sign of the coefficient c in (15-21). Using this equation, we may rewrite (15-28) as

$$\cos\theta = \frac{c\,\|\mathbf{x}_1\|}{\|\mathbf{y}\|} \tag{15-29}$$

Substituting (15-23)

$$\cos\theta = \frac{\mathbf{y}\cdot\mathbf{x}_1}{\|\mathbf{x}_1\|^2}\,\frac{\|\mathbf{x}_1\|}{\|\mathbf{y}\|} \tag{15-30}$$

$$\cos\theta = \frac{\mathbf{y}\cdot\mathbf{x}_1}{\|\mathbf{x}_1\|\;\|\mathbf{y}\|} \tag{15-31}$$

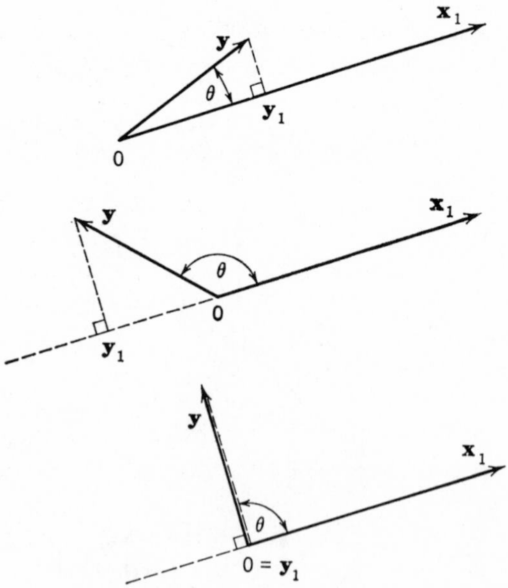

FIG. 15-14 Cos θ. (*a*) θ acute, $\cos\theta > 0$; $\mathbf{y}_1 = c\mathbf{x}_1$, where $c > 0$. (*b*) θ obtuse, $\cos\theta < 0$; $\mathbf{y}_1 = c\mathbf{x}_1$, where $c < 0$. (*c*) θ is 90° ($\mathbf{y} \perp \mathbf{x}_1$), $\cos\theta = 0$; $\mathbf{y}_1 = c\mathbf{x}_1$, where $c = 0$.

To free our notation somewhat, we rename $\mathbf{x}_1$ by $\mathbf{x}$:

$$\boxed{\cos\theta = \frac{\mathbf{x}\cdot\mathbf{y}}{\|\mathbf{x}\|\,\|\mathbf{y}\|}} \tag{15-32}$$

where θ is the angle between $\mathbf{x}$ and $\mathbf{y}$.

PROBLEMS

15-1 Let $\mathbf{x} = (1, -2)$ and $\mathbf{y} = (3, 1)$. Graph as arrows $\mathbf{x}$ and $\mathbf{y}$ and the following:
(a) $2\mathbf{x}$.
(b) $\mathbf{x} + \mathbf{y}$.
(c) $\mathbf{x} - \mathbf{y}$.
(d) $(\mathbf{x} + \mathbf{y}) + (\mathbf{x} - \mathbf{y})$. Check that this equals $2\mathbf{x}$.
(e) $(\mathbf{x} + \mathbf{y}) - (\mathbf{x} - \mathbf{y})$. Check that this equals $2\mathbf{y}$.
(f) $-3\mathbf{x} + 2\mathbf{y}$.

15-2 Which of the following pairs are orthogonal?
(a) $(1, 3)$ and $(-6, 2)$.
(b) $(1, -2)$ and $(1, 2)$.
(c) $(1, 2, -2)$ and $(2, 3, 2)$.
(d) $(1, -2, 1, 0, 1)$ and $(2, 0, 1, -1, -1)$; call these $\mathbf{x}_1$ and $\mathbf{x}_2$.

15-3 Find c so that $(\mathbf{x}_2 - c\mathbf{x}_1)$ will be perpendicular to $\mathbf{x}_1$ in Problem 15-2(d) above.

15-4 Using the basis $\mathbf{x}_1 = (1, -1)$, $\mathbf{x}_2 = (2, 1)$, find algebraically the coordinates of each of the following points. Then verify your result geometrically (work approximately).
(a) $(-1, -2)$.
(b) $(0, 3)$.
(c) $(-1, 1)$.
(d) $(3, -1)$.

15-5 Find the coordinates of the point $(1.2, .3)$ with respect to
(a) the basis $\mathbf{x}_1 = (.5, .1)$, $\mathbf{x}_2 = (.1, .2)$
(b) the orthogonal basis $\mathbf{x}_1 = (-.4, .2)$, $\mathbf{x}_2 = (.1, .2)$
(c) the orthonormal basis $\mathbf{x}_1 = (-.6, -.8)$, $\mathbf{x}_2 = (-.8, .6)$, where each vector is normalized, that is, of length 1. Which basis is easiest?

15-6 Consider the basis $\mathbf{x}_1 = (1, 0, 2)$ and $\mathbf{x}_2 = (2, -1, 1)$ which generates a plane P in three-space. For each point below, find whether it lies on the plane; if it does, then find its coordinates with respect to $(\mathbf{x}_1, \mathbf{x}_2)$.
(a) $(5, -1, 7)$.
(b) $(4, 0, 1)$.
(c) $(3, -2, 0)$.

15-7 Consider vectors $\mathbf{x}_1$, $\mathbf{x}_2$ in the two-space: $c_1\mathbf{x}_1 + c_2\mathbf{x}_2$

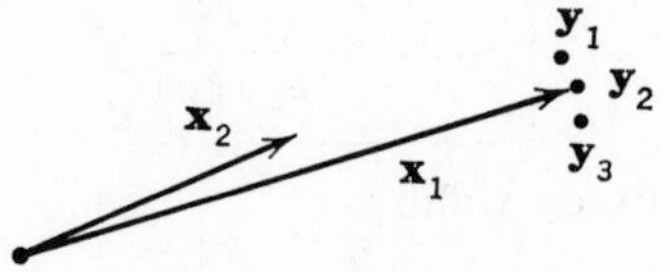

(a) Match the point with the correct pair of coordinates with respect to $(\mathbf{x}_1, \mathbf{x}_2)$. Work geometrically, and roughly.

$\mathbf{y}_1$	$\langle 1,\ 0\rangle$
$\mathbf{y}_2$	$\langle \frac{1}{2},\ 1\rangle$
$\mathbf{y}_3$	$\langle 1\frac{1}{2},\ -1\rangle$

(b) The three points are close together. Are their coordinates close? Give an intuitive reason why.

15-8

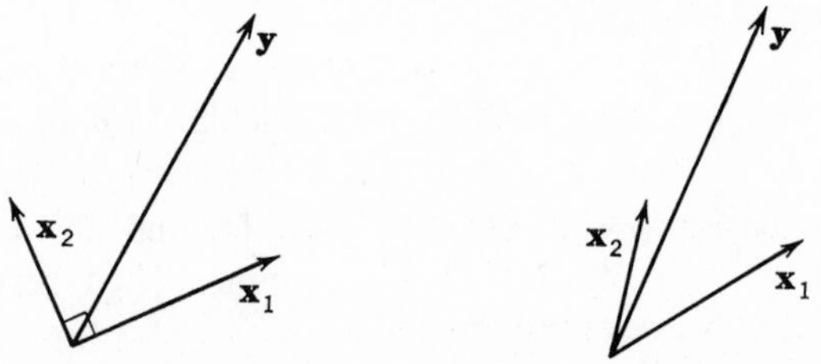

(a) (b)

Work geometrically in two-space. In each case, find the $\perp$ projection of $\mathbf{y}$ onto $\mathbf{x}_1$, and $\mathbf{y}$ onto $\mathbf{x}_2$. Call them $\mathbf{y}_1$ and $\mathbf{y}_2$. Under what circumstances does $\mathbf{y} = \mathbf{y}_1 + \mathbf{y}_2$?

15-2 LEAST SQUARES FIT

With this geometry in hand, we now turn to its application to regression. First, consider the problem of fitting a line, as in Chapter 1. To keep the geometry simple, our example in Figure 15-15 consists of only three observed points. The values of x are centered at 0; this can always be achieved by using deviations from the mean (y may or may not be also translated to a zero mean). The mathematical model may be written out in matrix notation,

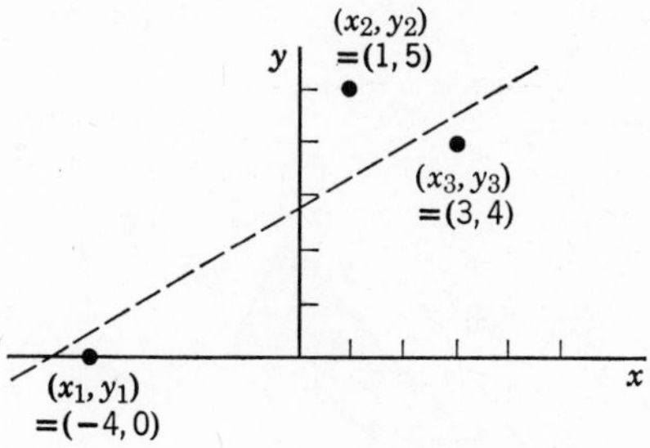

FIG. 15-15 Regression scatter: points are observations, axes are variables.

as in (13-13)

$$\text{Observed vector} = \text{Mean vector} + \text{Error vector}$$

$$\begin{bmatrix} y_1 \\ y_2 \\ y_3 \end{bmatrix} = \begin{bmatrix} 1 & x_1 \\ 1 & x_2 \\ 1 & x_3 \end{bmatrix} \begin{bmatrix} \beta_1 \\ \beta_2 \end{bmatrix} + \begin{bmatrix} e_1 \\ e_2 \\ e_3 \end{bmatrix} \qquad (15\text{-}33)$$

The problem of least squares fit may be similarly displayed

$$\text{Observed vector} \approx \text{Fitted vector}$$

$$\begin{bmatrix} y_1 \\ y_2 \\ y_3 \end{bmatrix} \approx \begin{bmatrix} 1 & x_1 \\ 1 & x_2 \\ 1 & x_3 \end{bmatrix} \begin{bmatrix} \hat{\beta}_1 \\ \hat{\beta}_2 \end{bmatrix} \qquad (15\text{-}34)$$

where $\begin{bmatrix} \hat{\beta}_1 \\ \hat{\beta}_2 \end{bmatrix}$ is the set of estimators of $\begin{bmatrix} \beta_1 \\ \beta_2 \end{bmatrix}$, chosen to make the fitted values on the right as close as possible (in the sense of least squares) to the observed values on the left. Equation (15-34) may be rewritten

$$\begin{bmatrix} y_1 \\ y_2 \\ y_3 \end{bmatrix} \approx \hat{\beta}_1 \begin{bmatrix} 1 \\ 1 \\ 1 \end{bmatrix} + \hat{\beta}_2 \begin{bmatrix} x_1 \\ x_2 \\ x_3 \end{bmatrix} \qquad (15\text{-}35)$$

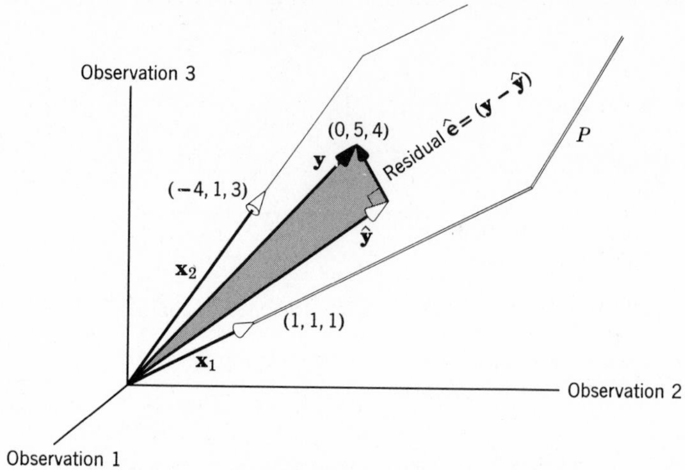

FIG. 15-16 Same information as in Figure 15-15; but here points (vectors) are variables, axes are observations.

or, in the notation of column vectors,

$$\mathbf{y} \approx \hat{\beta}_1\mathbf{x}_1 + \hat{\beta}_2\mathbf{x}_2 \tag{15-36}$$

where

$$\mathbf{y} = \begin{bmatrix} y_1 \\ y_2 \\ y_3 \end{bmatrix}, \quad \mathbf{x}_1 = \begin{bmatrix} 1 \\ 1 \\ 1 \end{bmatrix}, \quad \mathbf{x}_2 = \begin{bmatrix} x_1 \\ x_2 \\ x_3 \end{bmatrix} \tag{15-37}$$

In Figure 15-15, we have graphed each of our three observations in a two-space, with one dimension for each variable x and y. In Figure 15-16, we now switch around our terms of reference, plotting each *variable* in a three-space, with one dimension for each *observation.* Referring to the specific example shown in Figure 15-15, (15-34) becomes

$$\begin{bmatrix} 0 \\ 5 \\ 4 \end{bmatrix} \approx \begin{bmatrix} 1 & -4 \\ 1 & 1 \\ 1 & 3 \end{bmatrix} \begin{bmatrix} \hat{\beta}_1 \\ \hat{\beta}_2 \end{bmatrix} \tag{15-38}$$

Each point plotted in Figure 15-15 was drawn from a row of (15-38) [e.g., the first point (−4, 0) was drawn from the first row]. On the other hand each point or vector in Figure 15-16 is a column of (15-38). In general:

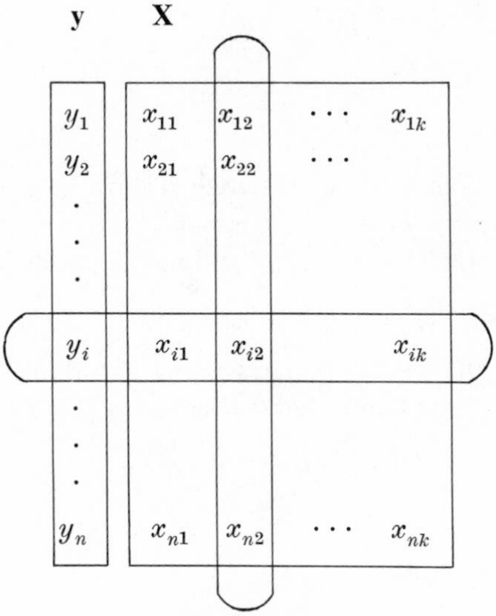

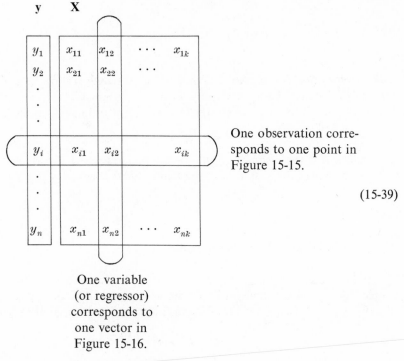

One observation corresponds to one point in Figure 15-15.

(15-39)

One variable (or regressor) corresponds to one vector in Figure 15-16.

In our example we also note that $\mathbf{x}_1$ and $\mathbf{x}_2$ are perpendicular. This follows because:

$$\begin{aligned}\mathbf{x}_1 \cdot \mathbf{x}_2 &= (1, 1, 1) \cdot (x_1, x_2, x_3)\\ &= x_1 + x_2 + x_3\\ &= n\bar{x}\end{aligned}$$

Recall that x was translated so that $\bar{x} = 0$; therefore:

$$\mathbf{x}_1 \cdot \mathbf{x}_2 = 0 \tag{15-40}$$

This establishes that $\mathbf{x}_1 \perp \mathbf{x}_2$. This was the motive for translating x onto a zero mean.

Algebraically in (15-36) our problem is to find a fitted value of $\mathbf{y}$ that is a linear combination of $\mathbf{x}_1$ and $\mathbf{x}_2$. Geometrically, in Figure 15-16, this means that we must select a fit somewhere on the plane P generated by $\mathbf{x}_1$ and $\mathbf{x}_2$. If we wish to determine the point or vector on this plane P that "best fits," or is "closest to" the observed $\mathbf{y}$, we should drop a perpendicular from $\mathbf{y}$ onto P obtaining a vector we shall call $\hat{\mathbf{y}}$. This turns out to be the least squares method in disguise. For recall that least squares involves minimizing

$$\sum (y_i - \hat{y}_i)^2 \tag{15-41}$$

In vector notation, according to (15-11),

$$= \|\mathbf{y} - \hat{\mathbf{y}}\|^2 \tag{15-42}$$

That is, least squares involves minimizing the squared distance (i.e., minimizing the distance) between $\mathbf{y}$ and $\hat{\mathbf{y}}$.

It is also important to note that the vector of estimated residuals

$$\hat{\mathbf{e}} = (\mathbf{y} - \hat{\mathbf{y}})$$

is perpendicular (orthogonal) to the $(\mathbf{x}_1, \mathbf{x}_2)$ plane; hence $\hat{\mathbf{e}}$ is orthogonal to each of the regressors $\mathbf{x}_1$ and $\mathbf{x}_2$ in the plane. This means

$$\mathbf{x}_1 \cdot \hat{\mathbf{e}} = 0, \qquad \text{and} \qquad \mathbf{x}_2 \cdot \hat{\mathbf{e}} = 0$$

15-3 ORTHOGONAL REGRESSORS

If the regressors are orthogonal, as in Figure 15-16, we can then find simple formulas for $\hat{\beta}_1$ and $\hat{\beta}_2$. Referring to Figure 15-17, for notation, we find that $\hat{\mathbf{y}}$ is just the sum of $\hat{\mathbf{y}}_1$ and $\hat{\mathbf{y}}_2$, the individual $\perp$ projections of $\mathbf{y}$ onto $\mathbf{x}_1$ and $\mathbf{x}_2$ respectively. That is,

$$\hat{\mathbf{y}} = \hat{\mathbf{y}}_1 + \hat{\mathbf{y}}_2 \tag{15-43}$$

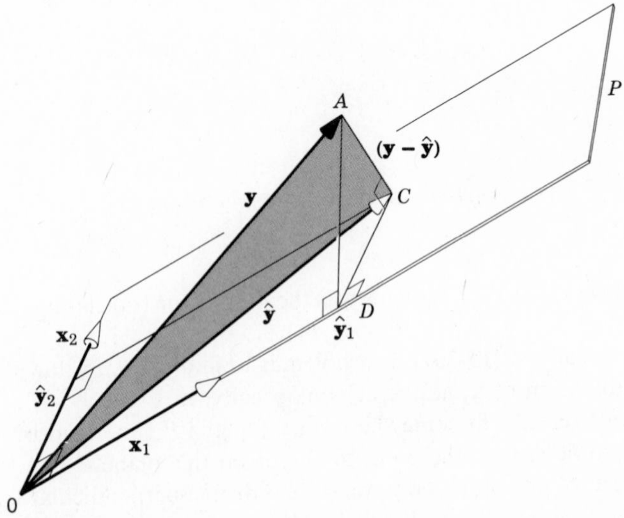

FIG. 15-17 The projected $\hat{\mathbf{y}}$ is the sum of the individual projections $\hat{\mathbf{y}}_1$ and $\hat{\mathbf{y}}_2$, because $\mathbf{x}_1 \perp \mathbf{x}_2$.

From (15-24)

$$\hat{\mathbf{y}} = \left(\frac{\mathbf{y}\cdot\mathbf{x}_1}{\|\mathbf{x}_1\|^2}\right)\mathbf{x}_1 + \left(\frac{\mathbf{y}\cdot\mathbf{x}_2}{\|\mathbf{x}_2\|^2}\right)\mathbf{x}_2 \tag{15-44}$$

Comparing (15-44) with (15-36), we conclude that the coefficient

$$\hat{\beta}_1 = \frac{\mathbf{y}\cdot\mathbf{x}_1}{\|\mathbf{x}_1\|^2} \tag{15-45}$$

Now recall from (15-37) that $\mathbf{x}_1$ is just the unit vector. Thus

$$\mathbf{y}\cdot\mathbf{x}_1 = y_1 + y_2 + y_3, \qquad \text{and in general} = \sum_{i=1}^{n} y_i$$

$$\|\mathbf{x}_1\|^2 = 1 + 1 + 1, \qquad \text{and in general} = n$$

Thus (15-45) reduces to

$$\hat{\beta}_1 = \bar{y} \tag{15-46}$$

(1-13) confirmed

Similarly, we conclude that

$$\hat{\beta}_2 = \frac{\mathbf{x}_2\cdot\mathbf{y}}{\|\mathbf{x}_2\|^2} \tag{15-47}$$

and noting that $\mathbf{x}_2$ is, in fact, the variable $\mathbf{x}$ appearing in Chapter 1

$$\hat{\beta}_2 = \frac{\sum x_i y_i}{\sum x_i^2} \tag{15-48}$$

(1-16) confirmed

15-4 SIMPLE ANOVA (ANALYSIS OF VARIANCE)

If we apply the Pythagorean theorem to Figure 15-17, it turns out to be the ANOVA table in disguise. Specifically, consider ΔADC, reproduced again in Figure 15-18 (noting that the vector $DC = \hat{\mathbf{y}}_2 = \hat{\beta}_2\mathbf{x}_2$). From the

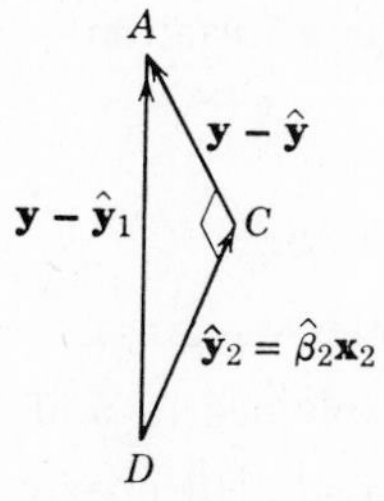

FIG. 15-18 Pythagorean theorem and ANOVA, for the little triangle of Figure 15-17.

theorem of Pythagoras

$$\|\mathbf{y} - \hat{\mathbf{y}}_1\|^2 = \|\hat{\beta}_2\mathbf{x}_2\|^2 + \|\mathbf{y} - \hat{\mathbf{y}}\|^2 \tag{15-49}$$

When we recognize that $\mathbf{x}_2$ here is just the x in Chapter 5, this equation begins to look suspiciously like equation (5-19) expressed in vector notation. This can easily be verified; since

$$\hat{\mathbf{y}}_1 = \hat{\beta}_1\mathbf{x}_1 \tag{15-50}$$

by (15-46) and (15-37)

$$= \bar{y}\begin{bmatrix} 1 \\ 1 \\ 1 \end{bmatrix}$$

$$= \begin{bmatrix} \bar{y} \\ \bar{y} \\ \bar{y} \end{bmatrix}$$

Thus

$$(\mathbf{y} - \hat{\mathbf{y}}_1) = \begin{bmatrix} y_1 - \bar{y} \\ y_2 - \bar{y} \\ y_3 - \bar{y} \end{bmatrix} \tag{15-51}$$

Thus fitting $\mathbf{y}$ on the dummy regressor $\mathbf{x}_1$ is just expressing $\mathbf{y}$ in terms of deviations from its mean. It follows from (15-51) that

$$\|\mathbf{y} - \hat{\mathbf{y}}_1\|^2 = \text{total variation, as in (5-19)} \tag{15-52}$$

Similarly we can express the right side of (15-49)

$$\|\hat{\beta}_2\mathbf{x}_2\|^2 = \hat{\beta}_2^2 \|\mathbf{x}_2\|^2$$
$$= \text{explained variation, as in (5-19)} \tag{15-53}$$

and

$$\|\mathbf{y} - \hat{\mathbf{y}}\|^2 = \text{unexplained (residual) variation, as in (5-19)}$$

Thus, (15-49) becomes

$$\text{total variation} = \text{explained variation} + \text{unexplained variation} \tag{15-54}$$

(5-19) proved

More formally, this can be written:

total variation after $\mathbf{y}$ regressed on $\mathbf{x}_1$

= variation explained by adding regressor $\mathbf{x}_2$

+ variation still left unexplained (15-55)

15-5 THE STATISTICAL MODEL

In applying statistical tests, we use a mathematical model, that is, a set of assumptions about the parent population of all possible outcomes. Referring to (15-33), we note that the population consists of all possible observed $\mathbf{y}$ vectors, generated by all possible errors. This is shown schematically in Figure 15-19. If errors are assumed normal, the possible $\mathbf{y}$'s we might observe would be spread out in a boundless cloud, thick around $E(\mathbf{y})$, but thinning out in the distance. But to make the geometry manageable, it is necessary to draw an ellipsoid that delimits most of the observed $\mathbf{y}$'s, the so-called "ellipsoid of concentration". For the independent errors specified in (13-15), the ellipsoid is simply a sphere. This sphere of y observations (vectors, points) is centered at the mean $E(\mathbf{y})$, which is in the plane P generated by $\mathbf{x}_1$ and $\mathbf{x}_2$. In the example shown in Figure 15-19, our observed $\mathbf{y}$ involves substantial error; that is, $\mathbf{y}$ is quite distant from $E(\mathbf{y})$.

Least squares estimation consists of projecting orthogonally this observed vector $\mathbf{y}$ onto the plane P, the resulting $\hat{\mathbf{y}}$ becoming the estimate of $E(\mathbf{y})$. To derive $\hat{\beta}_1$, the estimate of the true population coefficient β_1, we project $\hat{\mathbf{y}}$ along $\mathbf{x}_2$ onto[4] $\mathbf{x}_1$; similarly, $\hat{\beta}_2$ is derived by projecting $\hat{\mathbf{y}}$ along $\mathbf{x}_1$

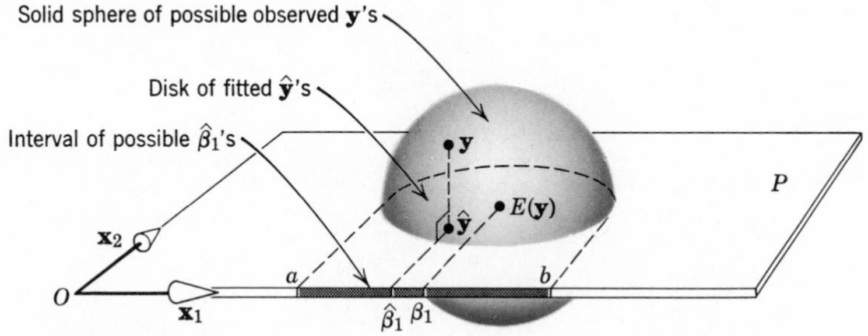

FIG. 15-19 The distributions of $\mathbf{y}$, $\hat{\mathbf{y}}$, and $\hat{\beta}_1$ (assuming $\mathbf{x}_1 \perp \mathbf{x}_2$).

---

[4] To be precise, such a projection gives us, for example, $\beta_1\mathbf{x}_1$, rather than the β_1 shown in Figure 15-19. But to keep things simple, we have cheated a little and assumed $\mathbf{x}_1$ is of *unit* length, so that $\beta_1\mathbf{x}_1$ is a vector of length β_1. Thus β_1 may be easily interpreted as the distance along $\mathbf{x}_1$. The estimator $\hat{\beta}_1$ is similarly interpreted.

But suppose $\mathbf{x}_1$ is not of unit length. (Usually it will not be; indeed in our example, $\mathbf{x}_1$ is the dummy regressor of 1's, so that its length is $\sqrt{n}$.) Then to be precise we must interpret β_1 and β_2 as the coordinates of $E(\mathbf{y})$ on the plane P [i.e., the solution to $E(\mathbf{y}) = \beta_1\mathbf{x}_1 + \beta_2\mathbf{x}_2$]. Thus β_1 is found by projecting $E(\mathbf{y})$ along $\mathbf{x}_2$ onto $\mathbf{x}_1$, and seeing how many times longer than $\mathbf{x}_1$ this is. The estimator $\hat{\beta}_1$ is similarly interpreted.

onto $\mathbf{x}_2$. We note in this example, that $\hat{\beta}_1$ happened to underestimate β_1, because of the particular error in the observed vector $\mathbf{y}$.

Our more general observations on Figure 15-19 are: $E(\mathbf{y})$ is fixed, while the disk around it, lying in P, represents possible fitted values of $\hat{\mathbf{y}}$, corresponding to the possible observed $\mathbf{y}$'s falling in the sphere. ab is the projection of this whole disk along $\mathbf{x}_2$ onto $\mathbf{x}_1$. This is the interval of $\hat{\beta}_1$'s around the fixed true β_1. This "sampling distribution" of $\hat{\beta}_1$ intuitively seems to be unbiased and normal, since the possible observed $\mathbf{y}$'s are normally distributed in the sphere centered on $E(\mathbf{y})$; these properties in fact have already been rigorously established in Chapter 13-5.

15-6 SKEWED REGRESSORS

Figure 15-19 showed what happens when the regressors $\mathbf{x}_1$ and $\mathbf{x}_2$ are orthogonal; then the projection of $\hat{\mathbf{y}}$ along $\mathbf{x}_2$ onto $\mathbf{x}_1$ is just the $\perp$ projection. On the other hand, Figure 15-20a shows what happens when $\mathbf{x}_1$ and $\mathbf{x}_2$ are not orthogonal; the skewed projection of the disk of possible $\hat{\mathbf{y}}$'s along $\mathbf{x}_2$ onto $\mathbf{x}_1$ "spreads out" the interval of $\hat{\beta}_1$'s.

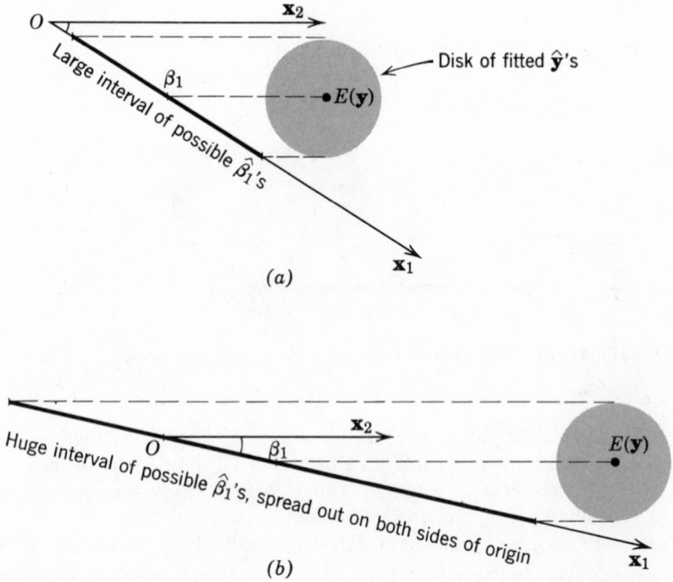

FIG. 15-20 The plane P from Figure 15-19 is laid flat on the paper, and viewed from above. (a) The distributions of $\hat{\mathbf{y}}$ and $\hat{\beta}_1$ when $\mathbf{x}_1$ and $\mathbf{x}_2$ are not $\perp$. (b) When $\mathbf{x}_1$ and $\mathbf{x}_2$ are highly collinear.

As the vectors $\mathbf{x}_1$ and $\mathbf{x}_2$ become more collinear, the problem gets worse, as in Figure 15-20*b*; here the interval of $\hat{\beta}_1$'s is dispersed on both sides of the origin. The point estimate $\hat{\beta}_1$ may be positive—but there is now a good chance it may be negative. Moreover, although we see from Figure 15-20*b* that the true β_1 is *not* zero, this is very difficult to establish statistically; usually $H_0(\beta_1 = 0)$ will not be rejected because of the huge standard deviation of $\hat{\beta}_1$.

Although collinearity causes a huge spread in $\hat{\beta}_1$, the other attractive properties of $\hat{\beta}_1$ (normality, unbiasedness) are not affected.

15-7 CORRELATION AND COS θ

In Section 15-4 it was established that

$$(\mathbf{y} - \hat{\mathbf{y}}_1) = \boxed{\begin{matrix} y_1 - \bar{y} \\ y_2 - \bar{y} \\ y_3 - \bar{y} \end{matrix}} \qquad \text{(15-56)} \quad \text{(15-51) repeated}$$

$$= \text{deviations of } \mathbf{y} \qquad \text{(15-57)}$$

Throughout the rest of the chapter, we shall be interested only in this deviation form for every vector.

If we consider two such deviation vectors, $\mathbf{x}$ and $\mathbf{y}$, it would be interesting to measure how closely these deviations correspond. The standard geometric measure of the closeness of the direction of two vectors is

$$\cos\theta = \frac{\mathbf{x} \cdot \mathbf{y}}{\|\mathbf{x}\|\ \|\mathbf{y}\|} \qquad \text{(15-58)}$$

Writing the dot product explicitly in terms of components,

$$\cos\theta = \frac{\sum x_i y_i}{\sqrt{\sum x_i^2}\sqrt{\sum y_i^2}} \qquad \text{(15-59)}$$

Since the x_i and y_i values are deviations, we recognize this as the correlation coefficient of (5-5). Thus,

$$\boxed{r = \cos\theta} \qquad \text{(15-61)}$$

where θ is the angle between the deviation vectors $\mathbf{x}$ and $\mathbf{y}$. In other words, the geometric interpretation of correlation is the closeness of the angle θ. This is shown in Figure 15-21.

Thus, for every geometrical statement about cos θ, there is an equivalent statistical statement about r. A few such examples are given in Table 15-2.

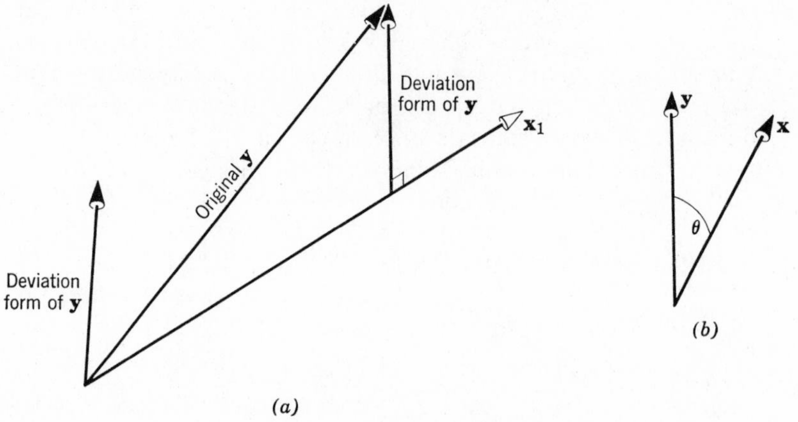

FIG. 15-21 (*a*) Relation of a vector **y** to its deviation form. (*b*) Correlation = $\cos\theta$, where **x** and **y** are in deviation form.

TABLE 15-2 Comparison of the Geometrical Interpretation of Cos θ and the Statistical Interpretation of Correlation r (All variables are in deviation form)

Geometry	Statistics
$\cos\theta$	r
$-1 \leq \cos\theta \leq 1$	$-1 \leq r \leq 1$
$\cos\theta = +1$ iff **x** and **y** agree perfectly in direction.	$r = +1$ iff x and y move together perfectly
$\cos\theta = -1$ iff **x** and **y** are in perfectly opposite directions	$r = -1$ iff x and y move together perfectly, but in opposite directions.
$\cos\theta = 0$ iff **x** and **y** are $\perp$	$r = 0$ iff x and y have no linear relation; iff x and y are uncorrelated

TABLE 15-3 Comparison of the Geometry and Statistics of Regression and ANOVA (All variables are in deviation form).

Geometry	Statistics
Squared length of $\mathbf{y}$	Variation of y
Length of $\mathbf{y}$	Standard deviation of y (except for the divisor $\sqrt{n-1}$)
$\perp$ projection, yielding $\mathbf{y} - \hat{\mathbf{y}}$ of minimum length	Statistical least squares fit, yielding minimum sum of squared deviations.
Pythagorean theorem: $\lVert\mathbf{y} - \hat{\mathbf{y}}_1\rVert^2 = \lVert\hat{\beta}_2\mathbf{x}_2\rVert^2 + \lVert\mathbf{y} - \hat{\mathbf{y}}\rVert^2$	ANOVA: Total variation = explained variation + unexplained variation

Similarly, the equivalence of the geometry and statistics of regression is given in Table 15-3.

15-8 CORRELATIONS—SIMPLE, MULTIPLE AND PARTIAL

We reiterate that in the rest of this chapter, we shall express all vectors in deviation form. It is important to realize that $\mathbf{x}_1$ and $\mathbf{x}_2$ are not the same as the original two regressors of Section 15-2. In particular, $\mathbf{x}_1$ can no longer be the constant regressor $(1, 1, \ldots)$; it is a variable regressor, reduced to deviation form—the same sort of regressor as $\mathbf{x}_2$. Also, we are not assuming that $\mathbf{x}_1 \perp \mathbf{x}_2$.

With this changed notation in mind, we see in Figure 15-22 that the correlation r_{YX_2} is just $\cos\theta_2$. To distinguish it from the multiple and partial correlations, r_{YX_2} is sometimes called the "simple" or "ordinary" correlation.

The multiple correlation coefficient R is defined as the simple correlation between $\mathbf{y}$ and $\hat{\mathbf{y}}$—that is, $\cos\lambda$ in Figure 15-22. This provides an index of how well $\mathbf{y}$ can be explained by both regressors $\mathbf{x}_1$ and $\mathbf{x}_2$.

The partial correlation of $\mathbf{y}$ and $\mathbf{x}_2$, designated $r_{YX_2 \cdot X_1}$, is the simple correlation of $\mathbf{y}$ and $\mathbf{x}_2$ after the influence of $\mathbf{x}_1$ has been removed from each. The influence of $\mathbf{x}_1$ on $\mathbf{y}$ is the fitted value ($\hat{\mathbf{y}}_1$) when $\mathbf{y}$ is regressed on $\mathbf{x}_1$. When this influence is removed, or subtracted from $\mathbf{y}$, the result is the residual vector $(\mathbf{y} - \hat{\mathbf{y}}_1)$. Similarly, $\mathbf{x}_2$ is regressed on $\mathbf{x}_1$ (at A), and when this

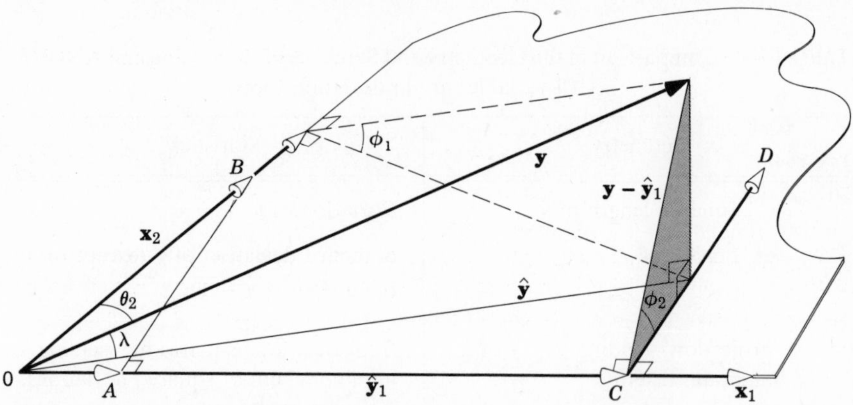

FIG. 15-22 Multiple correlation coefficient ($R = \cos \lambda$) compared with simple correlation coefficient ($r_{YX_2} = \cos \theta_2$) and partial correlation coefficient ($r_{XY_2 \cdot X_1} = \cos \phi_2$).

influence is removed from $\mathbf{x}_2$, the result is the vector AB; this is shifted to CD, forming the angle ϕ_2. Then $\cos \phi_2$ is the partial correlation $r_{YX_2 \cdot X_1}$. Similarly, we could show that $\cos \phi_1$ is $r_{YX_1 \cdot X_2}$.

In Table 15-4, we extend Table 15-2 to a comparison of the geometry and statistics of multiple and partial correlation.

TABLE 15-4 Comparison of the Geometry and Statistics of Correlations—Simple, Partial, and Multiple (An Extension of Table 15-2. Also refer to Figure 15-22.)

Geometry	Statistics
$\cos \theta_2$	Simple correlation r_{YX_2}
$\cos \phi_2$	Partial correlation $r_{YX_2 \cdot X_1}$
$\cos \lambda$	Multiple correlation R
$\cos \lambda = 1$ iff $\mathbf{y}$ and $\hat{\mathbf{y}}$ coincide; iff $\mathbf{y}$ lies in the $(\mathbf{x}_1, \mathbf{x}_2)$ subspace	$R = 1$ iff x_1 and x_2 explain y exactly, leaving no residual
$\cos \lambda = 0$ iff $\mathbf{y}$ orthogonal to the $(\mathbf{x}_1, \mathbf{x}_2)$ subspace	$R = 0$ iff $\hat{y} = 0x_1 + 0x_2 = 0$ i.e., x_1 and x_2 do not explain y at all
$\|\cos \theta_2\| \leq \|\cos \lambda\|$	$r_{YX_2} \leq R$
$\|\cos \phi_2\| \leq \|\cos \lambda\|$	$r_{YX_2 \cdot X_1} \leq R$

15-9 GENERALIZATION TO k REGRESSORS

With a little imagination, we can think of replacing $\mathbf{x}_1$ by a set of regressors $\mathbf{x}_1, \mathbf{x}_2, \ldots, \mathbf{x}_{k-1}$. Then the last regressor is no longer $\mathbf{x}_2$, but rather $\mathbf{x}_k$. The only major change this causes in the theory of the previous section is that the line generated by $\mathbf{x}_1$ is replaced by a $(k - 1)$ dimensional subspace generated by $\mathbf{x}_1 \cdots \mathbf{x}_{k-1}$. This is impossible to draw, and so will still be represented in the figures by a line, doubly marked in Figure 15-23. In this diagram $\cos \phi$ is the partial correlation of $\mathbf{y}$ and $\mathbf{x}_k$; it is obtained by removing the influence of $\mathbf{x}_1 \cdots \mathbf{x}_{k-1}$ from both $\mathbf{y}$ and $\mathbf{x}_k$.

15-10 ANOVA TO TEST THE LAST REGRESSOR

In Figure 15-23, we can also show the analysis of variance to test the statistical significance of the last regressor $\mathbf{x}_k$. This will generalize the ANOVA of Section 15-4.

The Pythagorean theorem can be applied to the shaded triangle of Figure 15-23, which is reproduced in Figure 15-24. From the right-angled triangle we obtain the ANOVA identity:

$$\begin{aligned}&\text{unexplained variation after } \mathbf{y} \text{ is regressed on } \mathbf{x}_1 \cdots \mathbf{x}_{k-1}\\ &\quad = \text{variation explained by introducing } \mathbf{x}_k + \text{unexplained variation}\\ &\qquad\qquad \text{remaining after } \mathbf{y} \text{ is regressed on } \mathbf{x}_1 \cdots \mathbf{x}_{k-1}, \mathbf{x}_k \end{aligned} \tag{15-62}$$

The two variations on the right side of (15-62) are statistically independent χ^2 variables, with 1 and $(n - 1 - k)$ d.f. respectively.[6] Thus the ratio,

$$F = \frac{\text{additional variation explained by introducing } \mathbf{x}_k/1}{\text{residual variation}/(n - 1 - k)} \tag{15-63}$$

follows the F distribution and can be used to test the statistical significance of the last regressor $\mathbf{x}_k$.

---

[6] For proof, see for example, H. Scheffé, *The Analysis of Variance*, New York: John Wiley, 1959, p. 42–45. Of course, we are assuming that the true coefficient of $\mathbf{x}_k$ is zero, since this is the null hypothesis being tested. The k regressors of chapter 13 include the constant regressor, which is not included among the k of this analysis. This is why the degrees of freedom in this test and the test in chapter 13 appear to differ, even though they are of course the same.

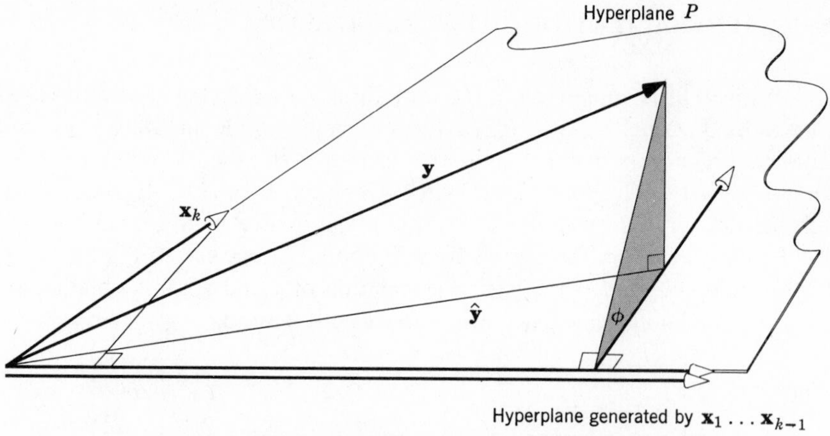

FIG. 15-23 Partial correlation. (Compare with Figure 15-22.)

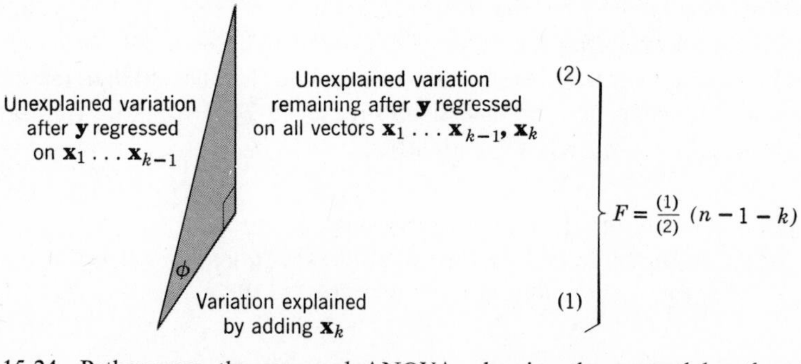

FIG. 15-24 Pythagorean theorem and ANOVA, showing the squared lengths of the vectors in the shaded triangle of Figure 15-23.

ADDITIONAL NOTES

1. Alternatively the last regressor $\mathbf{x}_k$ may be tested with the t test; taking the square root of (15-63)

$$t = \pm \sqrt{F} = \pm \sqrt{\frac{\text{variation explained by adding } \mathbf{x}_k}{\text{residual variation}/(n - 1 - k)}} \tag{15-64}$$

has the t distribution with $(n - 1 - k)$ d.f. (The sign of t is chosen to agree with the sign of the regression coefficient $\hat{\beta}_k$.)

2. As a final alternative, the F test (15-63) may be expressed in terms of the partial correlation $r_{YX_k \cdot X_1 X_2 \cdots X_{k-1}}$, which we shall abbreviate to r in this discussion. Recall from Figure 15-24 that

$$r = \cos \phi \tag{15-65}$$

Furthermore, using this diagram we can reexpress (15-63) as

$$F = (\cot \phi)^2 (n - 1 - k) \tag{15-66}$$

By trigonometry

$$(\cot \phi)^2 = \frac{(\cos \phi)^2}{1 - (\cos \phi)^2} \tag{15-67}$$

$$= \frac{r^2}{1 - r^2} \tag{15-68}$$

Thus,

$$F = \frac{r^2(n - 1 - k)}{1 - r^2} \tag{15-69}$$

We note in Figure 15-23, that if $\mathbf{x}_k$ adds more than a random amount to our explanation of $\mathbf{y}$, then $\mathbf{y}$ will lie close to the hyperplane P generated by $\mathbf{x}_1 \cdots \mathbf{x}_{k-1}$ and $\mathbf{x}_k$. Then the angle ϕ will be close, making r large and F in (15-69) large, thus statistically significant.

Finally, noting (15-64) and (15-69)

$$t = \pm \sqrt{\frac{r^2}{1 - r^2}(n - 1 - k)} \tag{15-70}$$

*15-11 FORWARD STEPWISE REGRESSION

In this section we shall discuss a kind of "forward" stepwise regression, where we start from scratch, adding one significant regressor at a time. In practice, the forward procedure is typically used by computer programs in the interest of cost, since alternative stepwise procedures[7] involve fitting regressions of larger dimension.

But first, in Figure 15-25 we show the result of applying the standard multiple regression of $\mathbf{y}$ on $\mathbf{x}_1$ and $\mathbf{x}_2$. (Although our remarks are illustrated for two regressors, they are easily generalized to k regressors.) Although the true coefficients β_1 and β_2 are not shown, they must be kept in mind as the targets; we suppose that β_1 and β_2 are both nonzero, so that $\mathbf{y}$ depends on both $\mathbf{x}_1$ and $\mathbf{x}_2$. The near collinearity between $\mathbf{x}_1$ and $\mathbf{x}_2$ results in large

[7] See Draper and Smith, "Applied Regression Analysis," New York: John Wiley, 1967.

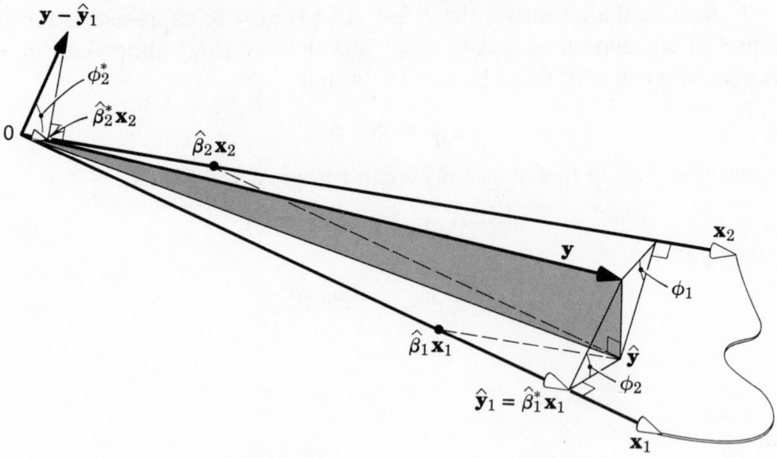

FIG. 15-25 Problems in stepwise regression.

standard errors for the estimators $\hat{\beta}_1$ and $\hat{\beta}_2$; but at least $\hat{\beta}_1$ and $\hat{\beta}_2$ are unbiased, and the residual $\mathbf{y} - \hat{\mathbf{y}}$ is minimized.

Forward stepwise regression is easily shown to yield a less satisfactory result. The first step is to regress $\mathbf{y}$ on $\mathbf{x}_1$ alone, yielding the fit $\hat{\mathbf{y}}_1 = \hat{\beta}_1^* \mathbf{x}_1$. Clearly, so long as the regressors $\mathbf{x}_1$ and $\mathbf{x}_2$ are not orthogonal, $\hat{\beta}_1^*$ will be a biased estimate of β_1. (In the case shown in Figure 15-25 it is larger than the unbiased $\hat{\beta}_1$.)

The second step is to consider the second regressor $\mathbf{x}_2$. If we are not careful we may follow the natural temptation, now that $\mathbf{x}_1$ has been "netted out," to regress the residual $(\mathbf{y} - \hat{\mathbf{y}}_1)$ on $\mathbf{x}_2$. In Figure 15-25 we shift this residual vector to the origin, and show the resulting estimate $\hat{\beta}_2^*$. Again, as long as $\mathbf{x}_1$ and $\mathbf{x}_2$ are not orthogonal, $\hat{\beta}_2^*$ will be a biased estimator of β_2; (in the case shown it is smaller than the unbiased $\hat{\beta}_2$). In this example, any common influence of the two regressors on $\mathbf{y}$ has been attributed to $\mathbf{x}_1$, thus "robbing" $\mathbf{x}_2$ of its effect. But there is even more damage, beyond the biased coefficients. The final residual $\mathbf{y} - \hat{\beta}_1^* \mathbf{x}_1 - \hat{\beta}_2^* \mathbf{x}_2$ will not be as small as in the standard multiple regression.[8] Furthermore, a test of significance on $\hat{\beta}_2^*$ would be based on the partial correlation coefficient $\cos \phi_2^*$, which is nearly zero.[9]

We have earlier concluded that with collinear regressors, it is difficult

[8] The standard least squares regression coefficients $\hat{\beta}_1$ and $\hat{\beta}_2$ were chosen, by definition, to make $\mathbf{y} - \hat{\beta}_1 \mathbf{x}_1 - \hat{\beta}_2 \mathbf{x}_2$ a minimum, thus smaller than $\mathbf{y} - \hat{\beta}_1^* \mathbf{x}_1 - \hat{\beta}_2^* \mathbf{x}_2$. (Unless, of course, $\mathbf{x}_1$ and $\mathbf{x}_2$ are orthogonal, in which case the two residuals coincide.)

[9] Reason: Since the residual $\mathbf{y} - \hat{\mathbf{y}}_1$ is perpendicular to $\mathbf{x}_1$, and since $\mathbf{x}_1$ and $\mathbf{x}_2$ are nearly parallel, $\mathbf{y} - \hat{\mathbf{y}}_1$ will be nearly perpendicular to $\mathbf{x}_2$, i.e., ϕ_2^* will be nearly 90°.

in any case to establish statistical significance; here we are using a biased method that makes it even more difficult to establish the significance of regressors that are tested last.

The correct unbiased test of the relationship between $\mathbf{y}$ and $\mathbf{x}_2$ involves a test of $r_{YX_2 \cdot X_1}$, or $\cos \phi_2$. But this is the angle between the residual $\mathbf{y} - \hat{\mathbf{y}}_1$ and $\mathbf{x}_2^{\perp}$, *not* $\mathbf{x}_2$—where $\mathbf{x}_2^{\perp}$ is a vector in the $(\mathbf{x}_1, \mathbf{x}_2)$ plane, perpendicular to $\mathbf{x}_1$, $(\mathbf{x}_2^{\perp} = \hat{\mathbf{y}} - \hat{\mathbf{y}}_1)$. This, in fact, is the way most computer programs proceed. In addition, they adjust the $\hat{\beta}^*$ coefficients until they coincide with the correct $\hat{\beta}$ coefficients. Most computer programs also give the squared multiple correlation R^2 at each step, so the economist can see how well the variation in $\mathbf{y}$ is being explained.[10]

In summary, we restate two major problems involved in stepwise regression when regressors are not orthogonal.

1. Biased estimates of correlation (or regression) coefficients will result if the $\mathbf{y}$ residuals are regressed on an excluded regressor $\mathbf{x}_k$. Instead, residuals must be regressed[11] on $\mathbf{x}_k^{\perp}$.

2. The second problem may be encountered even if we avoid the first problem, and correctly use $\mathbf{x}_k^{\perp}$. Suppose we have tested $\mathbf{x}_1$ and included it[12] in the first step; then we test the significance of $\mathbf{x}_2$ by examining $\cos \phi_2$ in Figure 15-25. Although the multiple correlation of $\mathbf{y}$ on $\mathbf{x}_1$ and $\mathbf{x}_2$ is high, the partial correlation ($\cos \phi_2$) may be statistically insignificant because of collinearity. Then the final regression fit would include only $\mathbf{x}_1$. On the other hand, consider what would happen if we took up the regressors in the other order. In the first step we would include $\mathbf{x}_2$; then, in testing the significance of $\mathbf{x}_1$, we might find the partial correlation ($\cos \phi_1$) statistically insignificant. In this case, the final regression equation would include only $\mathbf{x}_2$. Thus, the variables appearing in our final model may depend on the order in which they are brought into consideration. In practice, most computer programs automatically pick up first the regressor that is most highly correlated with $\mathbf{y}$.

---

[10] Since the inclusion of even an irrelevant variable will amost certainly increase R^2 because of chance fluctuation, it is sometimes wise to correct for this, by reducing R^2 appropriately. If there are k regressors (not counting the constant regressor), the corrected R^2 is defined as

$$\bar{R}^2 \triangleq R^2 - \frac{k}{n-k-1}(1 - R^2)$$

[11] In general $\mathbf{x}_k^{\perp}$ is defined as a vector perpendicular to $\mathbf{x}_1, \mathbf{x}_2 \cdots \mathbf{x}_{k-1}$, (the included regressors previously picked up by the stepwise procedure), and lying in the subspace generated by $\mathbf{x}_1, \mathbf{x}_2 \cdots \mathbf{x}_{k-1}, \mathbf{x}_k$.

[12] In the first step of regressing $\mathbf{y}$ on $\mathbf{x}_1$ only, the test of $\mathbf{x}_1$ involves examining $\cos \theta_1$, where θ_1 is the angle between $\mathbf{y}$ and $\mathbf{x}_1$ in Figure 15-25. This close angle leads us to conclude that $\mathbf{x}_1$ is a statistically significant regressor.

In conclusion, if there are clear prior guidelines indicating that a few specific regressors are appropriate, then they should all be used right away in a full multiple regression, rather than tested one at a time with any sort of stepwise approach. If there are no such prior guidelines, but the number of regressors must be kept small to provide a more manageable model, then a stepwise technique may be reasonable. But it must be recognized that this procedure tends to discriminate against regressors tested last, even if correctly applied; and if incorrectly applied, it discriminates even more.

*15-12 SPECIFICATION ERROR

An important econometric problem is "How much do estimates err when the model is misspecified?" We shall consider two possible misspecifications. First, suppose that $\mathbf{y}$ is dependent on $\mathbf{x}_1$ and $\mathbf{x}_2$. But through ignorance $\mathbf{y}$ is specified to be a function of $\mathbf{x}_1$ only. In such circumstances, we would run a simple regression of $\mathbf{y}$ on $\mathbf{x}_1$, yielding the biased estimate $\hat{\beta}_1^*$. This is exactly the same biased estimate encountered in the first stage of the stepwise procedure of the preceding section. Therefore, unless regressors are orthogonal, ignoring some will bias estimates of the others. (Exactly the same bias would, of course, occur if $\mathbf{x}_2$ were originally included in the model, but then dropped because of a too casual acceptance of $H_0: \beta_2 = 0$ in a small sample, with $\mathbf{y}$ then fitted on $\mathbf{x}_1$ alone.)

On the other hand, we could err by including regressors that are irrelevant. To illustrate, suppose that $\mathbf{y}$ is related to $\mathbf{x}_1$, but *not* to $\mathbf{x}_2$, that is,

$$\mathbf{y} = \beta_1 \mathbf{x}_1 + 0\mathbf{x}_2 + \mathbf{e} \tag{15-71}$$

Now if we erroneously regress $\mathbf{y}$ on both $\mathbf{x}_1$ and $\mathbf{x}_2$, our estimator $\hat{\beta}_2$ will generally not equal zero exactly because of chance fluctuation. If we test $\hat{\beta}_2$ at the 5% significance level, 5% of the time we will be unlucky enough to keep $\hat{\beta}_2$ in the model. (This is not a serious risk perhaps, if our misspecification is limited to including just one irrelevant variable. But if we are "trying on" a whole set of such variables, the risk increases, perhaps to a prohibitive degree). Then there will be three unfortunate consequences:

1. The inclusion of $\hat{\beta}_2$ itself will be erroneous, of course. In addition, any test of $\hat{\beta}_1$ will be weakened for the following two separate reasons.
2. The estimator $\hat{\beta}_1$ will be more variable than it would be under the proper specification, as shown in Figure 15-26.
3. There will be fewer degrees of freedom in the residuals to estimate σ^2.

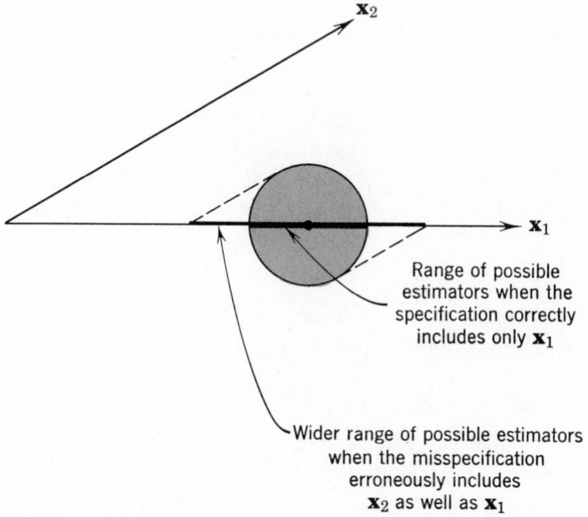

FIG. 15-26 When model is misspecified by erroneously including $\mathbf{x}_2$, the coefficient of $\mathbf{x}_1$ is made more variable. Figure is reduced to the two dimensions of the $(\mathbf{x}_1, \mathbf{x}_2)$ plane.

In conclusion, it cannot be emphasized too strongly that sound prior specification of the model is very important—in many ways more important than the details of the statistical techniques to which this book is devoted. Note how this strengthens our earlier conclusions in Chapters 3-5 and 7-4(c).

PROBLEMS

15-9 In the model

$$\mathbf{y} = \beta_0 + \beta_1\mathbf{x}_1 + \beta_2\mathbf{x}_2 + \text{error}$$

suppose we wish to test the null hypothesis $H_0: \beta_2 = 0$.

If a sample of 48 observations gives $\hat{\beta}_2 = 1.32$, with a partial correlation $r_{X_2Y \cdot X_1} = .30$,

(a) Calculate the t value from (15-70).

(b) If the alternate hypothesis H_1 is $\beta_2 \neq 0$,

  (i) Test H_0 at the 5% level of significance.

  (ii) Test H_0 at the 1% level of significance.

  (iii) What is the prob-value for H_0?

(c) Assuming the alternate hypothesis H_1 is $\beta_2 > 0$, repeat part (b).

(d) Assuming the alternate hypothesis H_1 is $\beta_2 < 0$, repeat (b)(i).

15-10 Referring to Figure 15-22, suppose the regressors $\mathbf{x}_1$ and $\mathbf{x}_2$ were more correlated, so that the picture was like this:

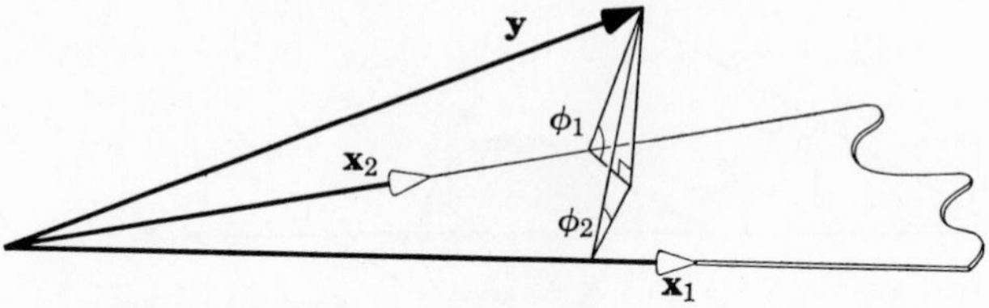

Suppose two economists, using the same sample of 24 observations, made the following two different analyses of the model:

$$\mathbf{y} = \beta_0 + \beta_1\mathbf{x}_1 + \beta_2\mathbf{x}_2 + \text{error} \tag{15-72}$$

1. The first economist makes a test of the null hypothesis $\beta_2 = 0$ against the alternate hypothesis $\beta_2 > 0$. Following the method of Problem 15-9, the t value was calculated, and turned out to be only 1.1 (reflecting a small partial correlation, i.e., a wide angle ϕ_2). At the 5% level, the null hypothesis is not rejected, and so he recommends using the model:

$$\mathbf{y} = \beta_0 + \beta_1\mathbf{x}_1 + \text{error} \tag{15-73}$$

The estimated coefficients turn out to be

$$\mathbf{y} = 1.70 + 1.3\mathbf{x}_1 + \text{residual} \tag{15-74}$$

with the coefficient 1.3 being statistically significant.

2. In the model (15-72), the second economist makes a test of the null hypothesis $\beta_1 = 0$ against the alternative $\beta_1 > 0$.

Following the method of Problem 15-9, the t value was calculated, and turned out to be only 1.6 (reflecting a small partial correlation, i.e., a wide angle ϕ_1). At the 5% level, the null hypothesis is not rejected, and so he recommends the model:

$$\mathbf{y} = \beta_0 + \beta_2\mathbf{x}_2 + \text{error} \tag{15-75}$$

The estimated coefficients turn out to be

$$\mathbf{y} = 1.70 + 4.7\mathbf{x}_2 + \text{error} \tag{15-76}$$

with the coefficient 4.7 being statistically significant.

(a) Is it possible that the two economists could validly arrive at such different conclusions as (15-74) and (15-76), or can the discrepancy be explained away as a computational error?

(b) Which economist has the better model? Or is there an even better model than these two? If you cannot answer this categorically, list the possible criteria for choosing between models.

15-11 (a) In a sample of 30 observations, suppose the multiple correlation of $\mathbf{y}$ with $\mathbf{x}_1 \cdots \mathbf{x}_6$ is .72, where $\mathbf{x}_1$ is the constant regressor. Including another variable $\mathbf{x}_7$ increases the multiple correlation to .75.

Test the hypothesis $\beta_7 = 0$ ($\mathbf{x}_7$ is irrelevant) at the 5% level.

(b) If $R = .75$ does not achieve statistical significance, what value of R would?

(c) When $R = .75$, what proportion of the variation remains unexplained? (i.e., what is the ratio of residual variation to total variation?)

(d) What is the partial correlation of $\mathbf{y}$ with $\mathbf{x}_7$?

15-12 Refer to Figure 15-23. Suppose that instead of observing $\mathbf{x}_k$, an economist observed a variable $\mathbf{z}_k$ that was more closely correlated to the previous variables $\mathbf{x}_1 \cdots \mathbf{x}_{k-1}$, yet still generated the same hyperplane P. Suppose further that there is no doubt that the previous variables $\mathbf{x}_1 \cdots \mathbf{x}_{k-1}$ belong in the model. The only question is whether the last variable ($\mathbf{x}_k$ or $\mathbf{z}_k$) belongs.

True or false? If false, correct it.

(a) $\mathbf{z}_k$ would be statistically significant iff $\mathbf{x}_k$ is statistically significant; that is, they would have the same t values (15-64).

(b) The multiple correlation of $\mathbf{y}$ with $\mathbf{x}_1 \cdots \mathbf{x}_{k-1}, \mathbf{z}_k$ would equal the multiple correlation of $\mathbf{y}$ with $\mathbf{x}_1 \cdots \mathbf{x}_{k-1}, \mathbf{x}_k$.

(c) The partial correlation of $\mathbf{y}$ with $\mathbf{z}_k$ would equal the partial correlation of $\mathbf{y}$ with $\mathbf{x}_k$.

15-13 True or false? If false, correct it.

(a) In studying the relation of three variables, if $\mathbf{x}$ and $\mathbf{y}$ are each uncorrelated with $\mathbf{z}$, then $r_{XY \cdot Z} = r_{XY}$, that is, the partial and simple correlations coincide.

(b) In studying the relation of many variables, if $\mathbf{x}$ and $\mathbf{y}$ are each uncorrelated with all the others, then the partial correlation of $\mathbf{x}$ and $\mathbf{y}$ equals their simple correlation.

(c) If the multiple correlation of $\mathbf{y}$ with $\mathbf{x}_1 \cdots \mathbf{x}_k$ is zero, then the partial correlation of $\mathbf{y}$ with $\mathbf{x}_1$ is also zero, as is the simple correlation of $\mathbf{y}$ with $\mathbf{x}_1$.

*15-14 Suppose we wish to explain a time series y_t by a linear regression on another time series x_t, and an annual cycle z_t. (z_t may be a cyclical time series such as $0\ 1\ 0\ -1\ 0\ 1\ 0\ -1 \cdots$ for quarterly data, or z_t may be a collection of three dummy variables representing the three seasonal changes, as in Chapter 3. This latter case is more complicated, but would give a better adjustment than the former.) Three methods are proposed by three different economists, to obtain a fitted time series $\hat{y}_t$:

1. Use a straightforward multiple regression of y_t on z_t and x_t.
2. First regress y_t on z_t; the residual is called the "seasonally adjusted y_t" or "y_t^a." Then regress y_t^a on x_t.
3. Seasonally adjust x_t as well as y_t. Then regress y_t^a on x_t^a.

Will these three methods all give the same final residual? If not, which method gives the smallest residual, and hence the best fit? (*Hint:* Let y_t be represented by $\mathbf{y}$ in Figure 15-23. Also let x_t be represented by $\mathbf{x}_k$, and z_t be represented by $\mathbf{x}_1$ . . . . If you still have difficulty, it may help to reread Section 15-11.)

*15-15 In Problem 15-14, suppose that in method 1 we obtain the fit

$$y_t = \hat{\beta}_0 + \hat{\beta}_1 z_t + \hat{\beta}_2 x_t + \text{residual}$$

and in the last stage of method 2 we obtain

$$y_t^a = \hat{\alpha}_0 + \hat{\alpha}_2 x_t + \text{residual}$$

(a) Are $\hat{\alpha}_2$ and $\hat{\beta}_2$ the same? If not, is one necessarily larger than the other?

(b) Prove that $\hat{\alpha}_2 = (1 - r_{XZ}^2)\hat{\beta}_2$.

*15-16 As in Figure 15-25 suppose $\mathbf{x}_1$ and $\mathbf{x}_2$ are highly collinear. In addition, suppose that the true (as opposed to observed) $\mathbf{y}$ has a perfect positive correlation with $\mathbf{x}_2$, that is, the true model is: $\mathbf{y} = 0\mathbf{x}_1 + \beta_2\mathbf{x}_2$. Moreover, suppose that we are lucky enough in our sample to observe $\mathbf{y}$ being perfectly correlated with $\mathbf{x}_2$, that is, $\mathbf{y}$ is perfectly explained by this single regressor. Hence, the fitted standard multiple regression of $\mathbf{y}$ on $\mathbf{x}_1$ and $\mathbf{x}_2$ is

$$\mathbf{y} = 0\mathbf{x}_1 + \hat{\beta}_2\mathbf{x}_2 \tag{15-77}$$

(a) Show this geometrically.

(b) Is $\hat{\beta}_2$ unbiased?

(c) What is the vector of residuals?

Now, to show how badly a stepwise analysis can go wrong if applied carelessly, suppose an erroneous stepwise procedure is undertaken and in the first step $\mathbf{y}$ is regressed on $\mathbf{x}_1$ as follows:

$$\mathbf{y}_1 = \hat{\beta}_1^*\mathbf{x}_1$$

(d) Is $\hat{\beta}_1^*$ biased? Is it possible for us to conclude that $\hat{\beta}_1^*$ is significantly different from zero?

(e) Suppose after erroneously including $\mathbf{x}_1$ as a regressor, we further err by regressing the residual vector $(\mathbf{y} - \hat{\mathbf{y}}_1)$ on $\mathbf{x}_2$ rather than $\mathbf{x}_2^{\perp}$.

Is the resulting estimate of β_2 biased? Is it possible that we will, therefore, reject $\mathbf{x}_2$ as a regressor (even though $\mathbf{x}_2$ in fact perfectly explains $\mathbf{y}$)?

(f) How does the resulting fitted equation compare with (15-77)?

(g) How does the final residual vector resulting from this stepwise procedure compare with the residual vector in (c)?

(h) Could this disastrous result have occurred if, in the first step, we had asked "which regressor is most highly correlated with $\mathbf{y}$?" and then brought in this regressor first? (This is how a good computer stepwise routine would operate.)

15-17 Using Figure 15-23, prove equation (5-45).

15-18 Interpret all of the following in one diagram: a fitted regression of $\mathbf{y}$ on $\mathbf{x}_1$ and $\mathbf{x}_2$, showing the estimated coefficients for $\mathbf{x}_1$ and $\mathbf{x}_2$; the residual vector, orthogonal to the regressor plane; the multiple correlation coefficient; the partial correlation coefficients; the F test of significance on the first regressor; the bias introduced if the model is misspecified by excluding $\mathbf{x}_2$; the desirability of orthogonal regressors.

15-19 An economist fitted the simple regression

$$\mathbf{y} = a + b\mathbf{x} + \hat{\mathbf{e}} \text{ (residual)}$$

The next day he decided that he should include another explanatory variable $\mathbf{z}$, for the same data; he therefore fitted the multiple regression

$$\mathbf{y} = a' + b'\mathbf{x} + c'\mathbf{z} + \hat{\mathbf{e}}'$$

The letters a, b, a', etc., refer to the fitted (OLS) values, not the true (population) values. Under what circumstances will the following be true? (Answer very carefully; for example, "never," or "always," or "usually, except when . . . ," or "rarely; only when . . .")

(a) $b' = b$

(b) $\sum_{i=1}^{n} (\hat{e}'_i)^2 \leq \sum_{i=1}^{n} (\hat{e}_i)^2$

(c) b' is statistically significant at the 5% level, yet b is not.

(d) b is statistically significant at the 5% level, yet b' is not.

chapter 16

Generalized Least Squares (GLS) (A Generalization of Chapter 6)

16-1 MAXIMUM LIKELIHOOD ESTIMATES

We begin this chapter by generalizing the linear model in Chapter 13. Suppose

$$\mathbf{y} = \mathbf{X}\boldsymbol{\beta} + \mathbf{e} \tag{16-1}$$

where

$$\mathbf{e} \text{ has mean zero} \tag{16-2}$$

and

$$\text{known covariance matrix } \mathbf{U} \tag{16-3}$$

$\mathbf{U}$ may be *any* covariance matrix, rather than the special covariance matrix $\sigma^2\mathbf{I}$ previously assumed in (13-15). If we assume that $\mathbf{e}$ has a multivariate normal distribution, the likelihood of the sample is the multivariate normal probability function

$$L(\boldsymbol{\beta}) = \frac{1}{(2\pi)^{n/2}\,|\mathbf{U}|^{1/2}}\, e^{-(1/2)(\mathbf{y}-\mathbf{X}\boldsymbol{\beta})'\mathbf{U}^{-1}(\mathbf{y}-\mathbf{X}\boldsymbol{\beta})} \tag{16-4}$$

This is a maximum when the magnitude of the negative exponent is a minimum, that is, when the generalized sum of squares (quadratic form)

$$(\mathbf{y} - \mathbf{X}\boldsymbol{\beta})'\mathbf{U}^{-1}(\mathbf{y} - \mathbf{X}\boldsymbol{\beta}) \tag{16-5}$$

is a minimum. Thus, we see that "generalized least squares" provides maximum likelihood estimates. Using an argument similar to that used in Chapter 13, we set the partial derivatives (with respect to $\boldsymbol{\beta}$) equal to zero to obtain the MLE:

$$\boxed{\hat{\boldsymbol{\beta}} = (\mathbf{X}'\mathbf{U}^{-1}\mathbf{X})^{-1}\mathbf{X}'\mathbf{U}^{-1}\mathbf{y}} \tag{16-6}$$

We can further verify that $\hat{\boldsymbol{\beta}}$ is normally distributed with:

$$E(\hat{\boldsymbol{\beta}}) = \boldsymbol{\beta} \tag{16-7}$$

$$\text{cov}\,(\hat{\boldsymbol{\beta}}) = (\mathbf{X}'\mathbf{U}^{-1}\mathbf{X})^{-1} \tag{16-8}$$

Equation (16-7) states that $\hat{\boldsymbol{\beta}}$ is unbiased. In the next section we shall see that its variance in (16-8) is optimal too, in a certain sense.

PROBLEMS

16-1 The model for OLS assumes that e_i are uncorrelated and of constant variance. This means

$$\mathbf{U} = \begin{bmatrix} \sigma^2 & & & & & 0 \\ & \sigma^2 & & & & \\ & & \sigma^2 & & & \\ & & & \cdot & & \\ & & & & \cdot & \\ 0 & & & & & \sigma^2 \end{bmatrix} = \sigma^2\mathbf{I}$$

(a) Show that the likelihood function (16-4) reduces to the likelihood function for OLS in (13-21).

(b) Show that the GLS estimators (16-6) reduce to the OLS estimators (13-24).

16-2 Prove (16-6) through (16-8), using methods analogous to Chapter 13.

16-2 GAUSS-MARKOV THEOREM

Now we shall generalize the theory of Chapter 2-5, establishing that even without the normality assumption, the estimators (16-6) are justified on the grounds of the:

Gauss-Markov Theorem.

Within the class of linear unbiased estimators of the parameters, it is the generalized least squares estimators (16-6) that minimize the variance of each[1] estimator.	(16-9)

Proof. Denote the estimators (16-6) by

$$\hat{\boldsymbol{\beta}} = \mathbf{A}\mathbf{y} \tag{16-10}$$

where

$$\mathbf{A} = (\mathbf{X}'\mathbf{U}^{-1}\mathbf{X})^{-1}\mathbf{X}'\mathbf{U}^{-1} \tag{16-11}$$

To prove that the vector **Ay** is indeed the minimum variance estimator, we shall consider whether it could possibly be improved. That is, we shall try to find a better linear estimator

$$(\mathbf{A} + \mathbf{C})\mathbf{y} \tag{16-12}$$

with **C** the "improvement" to be determined.

Our objective is to choose **C** to minimize variance; but our choice is restricted. Specifically, the condition of unbiasedness puts some limitation on **C**; the addition of **Cy** (to hopefully reduce variance) must not change the expected value of our unbiased[2] estimator **Ay**, that is,

$$E(\mathbf{C}\mathbf{y}) = \mathbf{0} \tag{16-13}$$

But

$$E(\mathbf{C}\mathbf{y}) = \mathbf{C}E(\mathbf{y})$$

by (16-2)

$$= \mathbf{C}\mathbf{X}\boldsymbol{\beta}$$

Thus, we must have

$$\mathbf{C}\mathbf{X}\boldsymbol{\beta} = \mathbf{0} \text{ for all possible vectors } \boldsymbol{\beta} \tag{16-14}$$

Hence, we must set

$$\mathbf{C}\mathbf{X} = \mathbf{0} \tag{16-15}$$

---

[1] That is, which minimize each of the diagonal elements in the covariance matrix of $\hat{\boldsymbol{\beta}}$. But because of the multivariate nature of $\hat{\boldsymbol{\beta}}$, we perhaps should be concerned with minimizing the "generalized variance"—defined as the determinant $|\text{cov } \hat{\boldsymbol{\beta}}|$. From (16-18) it follows that the generalized least squares estimators also minimize this generalized variance. For proof, see Goldberger, *Econometric Theory*, New York: John Wiley, 1964, Chapters 2 and 4.

In fact, an even stronger conclusion is possible. If we consider any linear transformation of $\boldsymbol{\beta}$, say $\mathbf{L}\boldsymbol{\beta}$ [as in equation (13-35)], we would naturally be interested in the unbiased linear estimator of $\mathbf{L}\boldsymbol{\beta}$ that has minimum generalized variance. The answer is $\mathbf{L}\hat{\boldsymbol{\beta}}$, where $\hat{\boldsymbol{\beta}}$ is the GLS estimator in (16-6).

[2] **Ay** is unbiased by (16-7)

This is the restriction on $\mathbf{C}$ that keeps (16-12) unbiased.

Now we turn to the crucial calculation of the variance of the new estimator. From Table 13-2

$$\begin{aligned}\text{cov}\,(\mathbf{A}+\mathbf{C})\mathbf{y} &= (\mathbf{A}+\mathbf{C})\,(\text{cov}\,\mathbf{y})(\mathbf{A}+\mathbf{C})' \\ &= (\mathbf{A}+\mathbf{C})\mathbf{U}(\mathbf{A}+\mathbf{C})' \\ &= \mathbf{AUA}' + \mathbf{CUA}' + \mathbf{AUC}' + \mathbf{CUC}' \qquad (16\text{-}16)\end{aligned}$$

Now consider just the second term; substituting (16-11)

$$\begin{aligned}\mathbf{CUA}' &= \mathbf{CU}\{(\mathbf{X}'\mathbf{U}^{-1}\mathbf{X})^{-1}\mathbf{X}'\mathbf{U}^{-1}\}' \\ &= \mathbf{CU}\{\mathbf{U}^{-1\prime}\mathbf{X}(\mathbf{X}'\mathbf{U}^{-1}\mathbf{X})^{-1\prime}\} \qquad (16\text{-}17)\end{aligned}$$

Because it is a covariance matrix, $\mathbf{U}' = \mathbf{U}$. It follows from this[3] that $\mathbf{U}^{-1\prime} = \mathbf{U}^{-1}$ and $(\mathbf{X}'\mathbf{U}^{-1}\mathbf{X})^{-1\prime} = (\mathbf{X}'\mathbf{U}^{-1}\mathbf{X})^{-1}$. Equation (16-17) can, therefore, be rewritten

$$\mathbf{CUA}' = \mathbf{CX}(\mathbf{X}'\mathbf{U}^{-1}\mathbf{X})^{-1}$$

Noting (16-15)

$$= \mathbf{0}$$

Of course, the third term of (16-16), being the transpose of the second term, is also zero, so that (16-16) becomes

$$\text{cov}\,(\mathbf{A}+\mathbf{C})\mathbf{y} = \mathbf{AUA}' + \mathbf{CUC}' \qquad (16\text{-}18)$$

To see if $\mathbf{C}$ may reduce the variance of a single (say the ith) estimator, we look at the ith diagonal term in the covariance matrix. It will be the sum of the diagonal term from $\mathbf{AUA}'$ (the old variance[4] for $\hat{\beta}_i$) and the diagonal term from $\mathbf{CUC}'$. Since $\mathbf{CUC}'$ is positive indefinite,[5] however, its diagonal term will be positive or zero, and hence will *increase* the variance at worst, or leave it unchanged at best.

Since we wish to keep the variance to a minimum, we set $\mathbf{CUC}'$ equal to zero. This can be accomplished by setting

$$\mathbf{C} = \mathbf{0} \qquad (16\text{-}19)$$

that is, the "improvement" $\mathbf{C}$ is zero. Thus, there is no improvement possible in the GLS estimator, and the Gauss-Markov theorem is established: GLS is the "best linear unbiased estimator" (BLUE).

---

[3] We also use the matrix theorem that the transpose of an inverse equals the inverse of the transpose.

[4] When the original (unaugmented) $\mathbf{Ay}$ was used to estimate $\boldsymbol{\beta}$.

[5] Since $\mathbf{U}$ is itself positive definite, being a covariance matrix. For details, see Goldberger, *op. cit.*, Chapter 2.

Let us review the GLS estimator (16-6). By definition, it is the set of estimators that minimized the "generalized sum of squares" (16-5). These are the maximum likelihood estimators, if the errors **e** have a multivariate normal distribution. Even without the normality assumption, however, the Gauss-Markov theorem states that they are the estimators with the smallest variance, in the class of linear unbiased estimators.

As a special case, we may set $\mathbf{U} = \sigma^2\mathbf{I}$ to obtain the classical OLS estimators, thus proving their attractive properties (BLUE, MLE).

In the next two sections, we shall develop two other special cases—heteroscedasticity and serial correlation.

16-3 HETEROSCEDASTICITY

(a) WLS Solution

This section is a generalization of Chapter 6-1. We assume as usual that each observation is generated by the model:

$$y_i = \mathbf{x}_i\boldsymbol{\beta} + e_i \qquad i = 1, 2, \ldots n \tag{16-20a}$$

that is,

$$\mathbf{y} = \mathbf{X}\boldsymbol{\beta} + \mathbf{e} \tag{16-20b}$$

But the components e_i of **e** have

$$\text{unequal variances } \sigma_i^2 \tag{16-21}$$

We still assume, however, that the e_i are uncorrelated with each other and with the x_i. Thus **e** has a diagonal covariance matrix

$$\mathbf{U} = \begin{bmatrix} \sigma_1^2 & & & & 0 \\ & \sigma_2^2 & & & \\ & & \cdot & & \\ & & & \cdot & \\ & & & & \cdot \\ 0 & & & & \sigma_n^2 \end{bmatrix} \tag{16-22}$$

The GLS estimator by definition minimizes

$$(\mathbf{y} - \mathbf{X}\boldsymbol{\beta})'\mathbf{U}^{-1}(\mathbf{y} - \mathbf{X}\boldsymbol{\beta}) \tag{16-23}$$

(16-5) repeated

Because $\mathbf{U}$ is diagonal, so is $\mathbf{U}^{-1}$:

$$\mathbf{U}^{-1} = \begin{bmatrix} \frac{1}{\sigma_1^2} & & & 0 \\ & \frac{1}{\sigma_2^2} & & \\ & & \ddots & \\ 0 & & & \frac{1}{\sigma_n^2} \end{bmatrix} \tag{16-24}$$

Thus (16-23) reduces to minimizing

$$\sum_{i=1}^{n} \frac{(y_i - \mathbf{x}_i \boldsymbol{\beta})^2}{\sigma_i^2} \tag{16-25}$$

(6-5) generalized

This is just the generalization of the weighted least squares (WLS) criterion (6-5) to the case of multiple regression.

The explicit WLS solution is given by (16-6)

$$\hat{\boldsymbol{\beta}} = (\mathbf{X}'\mathbf{U}^{-1}\mathbf{X})^{-1}\mathbf{X}'\mathbf{U}^{-1}\mathbf{y} \tag{16-26}$$

(16-6) repeated

where $\mathbf{U}^{-1}$ is given by (16-24) above. Since these WLS estimators are a special case of GLS, they are Gauss-Markov estimators, as well as MLE when normality is assumed.

(b) Equivalent Solution by Transformation

Alternatively, we may transform the system of equations (16-20) so that the errors have constant variance, and hence satisfy the OLS model. This may be achieved by dividing the ith equation by σ_i, that is, multiplying the system (16-20) by the "dividing matrix"

$$\mathbf{D} = \begin{bmatrix} \frac{1}{\sigma_1} & & & 0 \\ & \frac{1}{\sigma_2} & & \\ & & \ddots & \\ 0 & & & \frac{1}{\sigma_n} \end{bmatrix} \tag{16-27}$$

Then we have

$$(\mathbf{Dy}) = (\mathbf{DX})\boldsymbol{\beta} + (\mathbf{De}) \tag{16-28}$$

where

$$\mathbf{De} = \begin{bmatrix} e_1/\sigma_1 \\ e_2/\sigma_2 \\ \cdot \\ \cdot \\ \cdot \\ e_n/\sigma_n \end{bmatrix} \quad \text{has covariance matrix } \mathbf{I} \tag{16-29}$$

$$\mathbf{Dy} = \begin{bmatrix} y_1/\sigma_1 \\ y_2/\sigma_2 \\ \cdot \\ \cdot \\ \cdot \\ y_n/\sigma_n \end{bmatrix} \tag{16-30}$$

and

$$\mathbf{Dx} = \begin{bmatrix} x_{11}/\sigma_1 & x_{12}/\sigma_1 & \cdots \\ x_{21}/\sigma_2 & x_{22}/\sigma_2 & \\ \cdot & & \\ \cdot & & \\ \cdot & & \\ x_{n1}/\sigma_n & \cdots x_{nk}/\sigma_n & \end{bmatrix} \tag{16-31}$$

Now because of (16-29), OLS may be applied to (16-28); this solution is given by substituting **Dy** and **DX** for **y** and **X** in (13-24)

$$\begin{aligned} \hat{\boldsymbol{\beta}} &= \{(\mathbf{DX})'\mathbf{DX}\}^{-1}(\mathbf{DX})'(\mathbf{Dy}) \\ &= \{\mathbf{X}'(\mathbf{D}'\mathbf{D})\mathbf{X}\}^{-1}\mathbf{X}'(\mathbf{D}'\mathbf{D})\mathbf{y} \end{aligned} \tag{16-32}$$

Now

$$\mathbf{D'D} = \begin{bmatrix} \dfrac{1}{\sigma_1^2} & & & 0 \\ & \dfrac{1}{\sigma_2^2} & & \\ & & \ddots & \\ 0 & & & \dfrac{1}{\sigma_n^2} \end{bmatrix}$$

which is the same as $\mathbf{U}^{-1}$ in (16-24). Thus, (16-32) is exactly the same as the WLS solution (16-26). But this latter method is usually simpler: first transform as in (16-28) so that the error term behaves, then apply OLS.

PROBLEMS

16-3

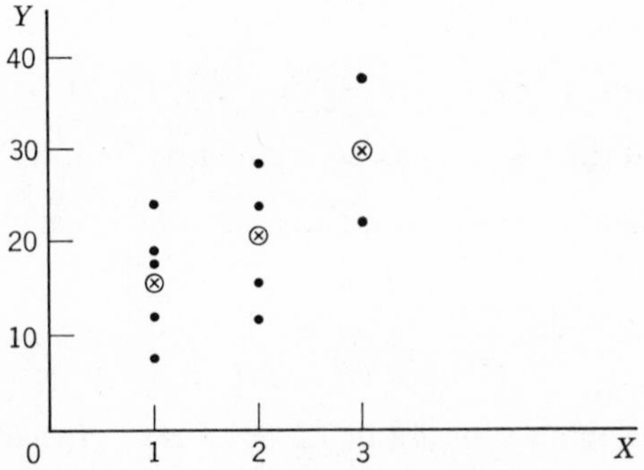

Suppose we have collected data as in the graph above. For each X, there are several sample values of Y, and their mean $\overline{Y}$ is graphed. Suppose that each conditional distribution of Y has the same variance σ^2, as in the model (2-2). We give a summary of this data in table form:

X_i	n_i	$\overline{Y}_i$
1	5	15
2	4	20
3	2	30

Suppose the individual observations Y_i have been lost, and only the $\overline{Y}_i$ retained.

(a) What is the variance of each of the $\bar{Y}_i$?
(b) Find the GLS estimate of the slope β.
(c) Estimate β by applying OLS to the values of $\bar{Y}_i$.
(d) Which estimator is better, (b) or (c)?
(e) Can you describe briefly why the OLS estimate is slightly higher than the GLS estimate?

16-4 SERIAL CORRELATION

(a) GLS Solution

In the linear regression model

$$y_t = \mathbf{x}_t\boldsymbol{\beta} + e_t \qquad t = 1, 2, \ldots n \tag{16-33}$$

that is,

$$\mathbf{y} = \mathbf{X}\boldsymbol{\beta} + \mathbf{e} \tag{16-34}$$

let us assume that the errors e_t are no longer uncorrelated. In fact, we assume that e_t are serially correlated in the simplest type of autoregressive scheme (or so-called Markov chain):

$$e_t = \rho e_{t-1} + v_t \qquad (t = \cdots -2, -1, 0, 1, 2, \ldots) \tag{16-35}$$

where $|\rho| < 1$, and the process has been going on for a long time.[6] (16-36)

Also, the "perturbation" v_t is assumed to have the usual characteristics

$$E(\mathbf{v}) = \mathbf{0} \tag{16-37}$$

and

$$\text{cov}\,(\mathbf{v}) = \sigma^2\mathbf{I} \tag{16-38}$$

These assumptions about $\mathbf{v}$ ensure that $\mathbf{e}$ has a zero expected value[7]

$$E(\mathbf{e}) = \mathbf{0} \tag{16-39}$$

[6] If the data start after a catastrophe, this assumption is not true of course, and our subsequent analysis is invalid. For the same issue from a slightly different viewpoint, see also the footnotes to (6-29) and (16-72).

[7] Use equation (16-35) over and over, reexpressing e_t in terms of present and past v_t:

$$\begin{aligned} e_t &= \rho e_{t-1} + v_t \\ &= \rho[\rho e_{t-2} + v_{t-1}] + v_t \\ &= \rho[\rho(\rho e_{t-3} + v_{t-2}) + v_{t-1}] + v_t \\ e_t &= v_t + \rho v_{t-1} + \rho^2 v_{t-2} + \rho^3 v_{t-3} + \cdots \end{aligned} \tag{16-40}$$

Therefore

$$\begin{aligned} E(e_t) &= E(v_t) + \rho E(v_{t-1}) + \cdots \\ &= 0 + 0 + 0 \cdots \\ E(e_t) &= 0, \text{ and is independent of } t \end{aligned} \tag{16-41}$$

but its covariance matrix is[8]

$$\mathbf{U} = \sigma_e^2 \begin{bmatrix} 1 & \rho & \rho^2 & \cdot & \cdot & \cdot \\ \rho & 1 & \rho & & & \\ \rho^2 & \rho & 1 & & & \\ \cdot & & & \cdot & & \\ \cdot & & & & \cdot & \\ \cdot & & & & & \cdot \\ \cdot & & & & & 1 \end{bmatrix} \tag{16-42}$$

where

$$\sigma_e^2 = \frac{\sigma^2}{1-\rho^2} \tag{16-43}$$

---

[8] From (16-40) and (16–38) it follows that:

$$\begin{aligned} \text{var}\,(e_t) &= \text{var}\, v_t + \rho^2 \,\text{var}\, v_{t-1} + \rho^4 \,\text{var}\, v_{t-2} + \cdots \\ &= \sigma^2 + \rho^2\sigma^2 + \rho^4\sigma^2 + \cdots \\ &= \sigma^2(1 + \rho^2 + \rho^4 + \rho^6 + \cdots) \end{aligned}$$

So long as $|\rho| < 1$ (i.e., so long as e_t is stationary), we may sum this infinite geometric series, obtaining

$$\boxed{\text{var}\, e_t = \frac{\sigma^2}{1-\rho^2}, \text{ and is independent of } t} \tag{16-43}$$

$$\begin{aligned} \text{cov}\,(e_t, e_{t+1}) = E(e_t\, e_{t+1}) &= E[e_t(\rho e_t + v_{t+1})] \\ &= E(\rho e_t^2) + E(e_t v_{t+1}) \end{aligned}$$

By (16–40) and (16–38),

$$= \rho \,\text{var}\, e_t + 0 \tag{16-44}$$

Since

$$\begin{aligned} e_{t+2} &= \rho e_{t+1} + v_{t+2} \\ &= \rho(\rho e_t + v_{t+1}) + v_{t+2} \end{aligned}$$

it follows that

$$\begin{aligned} \text{cov}\,(e_t, e_{t+2}) = E(e_t e_{t+2}) &= E[e_t(\rho^2 e_t + \rho v_{t+1} + v_{t+2})] \\ &= \rho^2 E(e_t^2) + \rho E(e_t v_{t+1}) + E(e_t v_{t+2}) \\ &= \rho^2 \,\text{var}\, e_t + 0 + 0 \end{aligned} \tag{16-45}$$

(16-43) to (16-45) may be generalized: for any $\tau = 0, 1, 2 \cdots$

$$\boxed{\text{cov}\,(e_t, e_{t+\tau}) = \rho^\tau \,\text{var}\, e_t} \quad \text{and is independent of } t \tag{16-46}$$

If equations (16-43) and (16-46) are put into matrix form, the result is (16-42).

σ^2 being the variance of the perturbation v_t. It may be easily verified, by multiplying $\mathbf{U}^{-1}\mathbf{U} = \mathbf{I}$, that

$$\mathbf{U}^{-1} = \frac{1}{\sigma_e^2}\left(\frac{1}{1-\rho^2}\right)\begin{bmatrix} 1 & -\rho & & & & \\ -\rho & 1+\rho^2 & -\rho & & & 0 \\ & -\rho & 1+\rho^2 & -\rho & & \\ & & \cdot & \cdot & \cdot & \\ & & & \cdot & \cdot & \cdot \\ & & & & \cdot & \cdot & \cdot \\ 0 & & & -\rho & 1+\rho^2 & -\rho \\ & & & & -\rho & 1 \end{bmatrix} \tag{16-47}$$

Thus, the GLS solution is

$$\hat{\boldsymbol{\beta}} = (\mathbf{X}'\mathbf{U}^{-1}\mathbf{X})^{-1}\mathbf{X}'\mathbf{U}^{-1}\mathbf{y} \tag{16-48}$$

(16-6) repeated

where $\mathbf{U}^{-1}$ is given by (16-47) above.

(b) Equivalent Solution by Transformation

Alternatively, we would like to transform the system of equations (16-34) so that the errors become uncorrelated, and hence satisfy the OLS model. In view of (16-35), which may be reexpressed as

$$-\rho e_{t-1} + e_t = v_t \tag{16-49}$$

we are motivated to multiply the system (16-34) by the "differencing matrix"

$$\mathbf{D} = \begin{bmatrix} \sqrt{1-\rho^2} & & & & \\ -\rho & 1 & & & 0 \\ & \cdot & \cdot & & \\ & & \cdot & \cdot & \\ 0 & & & \cdot & \cdot \\ & & & -\rho & 1 \end{bmatrix} \tag{16-50}$$

(The first row is exceptional, and will be explained later. For the moment, we shall just accept the fact that some such first row is necessary to keep the matrix square, $n \times n$.)

Then we have (16-34) transformed to

$$(\mathbf{Dy}) = (\mathbf{DX})\boldsymbol{\beta} + (\mathbf{De}) \tag{16-51}$$

where

$$\mathbf{De} = \begin{bmatrix} \sqrt{1-\rho^2}\, e_1 \\ -\rho e_1 + e_2 \\ -\rho e_2 + e_3 \\ \cdot \\ \cdot \\ \cdot \\ -\rho e_{n-1} + e_n \end{bmatrix} \tag{16-52}$$

According to (16-49)

$$\mathbf{De} = \begin{bmatrix} \sqrt{1-\rho^2}\, e_1 \\ v_2 \\ v_3 \\ \cdot \\ \cdot \\ \cdot \\ v_n \end{bmatrix} \tag{16-53}$$

which is an uncorrelated set of errors, as we intended. **Dy** and **DX** are defined like (16-52); for example:

$$\mathbf{Dy} = \begin{bmatrix} \sqrt{1-\rho^2}\, y_1 \\ -\rho y_1 + y_2 \\ \cdot \\ \cdot \\ \cdot \\ -\rho y_{n-1} + y_n \end{bmatrix} \tag{16-54}$$

The OLS solution of (16-51) is given by substituting **Dy** and **DX** for **y** and **X** in (13-24),

$$\begin{aligned} \hat{\boldsymbol{\beta}} &= \{(\mathbf{DX})'\mathbf{DX}\}^{-1}(\mathbf{DX})'\mathbf{Dy} \\ &= \{\mathbf{X}'(\mathbf{D}'\mathbf{D})\mathbf{X}\}^{-1}\mathbf{X}'(\mathbf{D}'\mathbf{D})\mathbf{y} \end{aligned} \tag{16-55}$$

Now from (16-50),

$$\mathbf{D}'\mathbf{D} = \begin{bmatrix} 1 & -\rho & & & & \\ -\rho & 1+\rho^2 & -\rho & & 0 & \\ & -\rho & 1+\rho^2 & -\rho & & \\ & & \cdot & \cdot & \cdot & \\ & & & \cdot & \cdot & \cdot \\ & & & & \cdot & \cdot & \cdot \\ & 0 & & -\rho & 1+\rho^2 & -\rho \\ & & & & -\rho & 1 \end{bmatrix} \tag{16-56}$$

which is the same as[9] $\mathbf{U}^{-1}$ in (16-47). Thus (16-55) is exactly the same as the GLS solution (16-48). In fact, it was precisely for this reason that the first row of **D** was defined as it was; it made $\mathbf{D}'\mathbf{D} = \mathbf{U}^{-1}$ essentially.

(c) Generalized Differencing

Our solution (16-55) using the **D** transformation is recognized to be the method of generalized differencing introduced in Chapter 6-2(c). It involves the following steps.

1. Use (16-54) to calculate the generalized differences

$$\left.\begin{aligned} \tau y_t &= y_t - \rho y_{t-1} \\ \text{and} \qquad \tau \mathbf{x}_t &= \mathbf{x}_t - \rho \mathbf{x}_{t-1} \end{aligned}\right\} \quad t = 2, 3, 4, \ldots n \tag{16-57}$$

(6-27) generalized

2. Adjust the first observed **x** and y values

$$\left.\begin{aligned} \tau y_1 &= \sqrt{1-\rho^2}\, y_1 \\ \text{and} \qquad \tau \mathbf{x}_1 &= \sqrt{1-\rho^2}\, \mathbf{x}_1 \end{aligned}\right\} \tag{16-58}$$

(6-29) generalized

Now we see why this adjustment—which may have been a bit of a mystery when introduced in (6-29)—must be made. It makes this procedure equivalent to GLS, with all its attractive properties.

3. Apply OLS to the set of all n generalized differences, regressing $\tau\mathbf{y}$ on $\tau\mathbf{X}$.

---

[9] Except for a scalar that cancels out in the reciprocal appearances of $\mathbf{U}^{-1}$ in (16-48).

16-5 GENERALIZATION: GLS EQUIVALENT TO A TRANSFORMATION AND OLS

In the last two sections we have seen two examples of how GLS estimates could be obtained by first transforming in order to make the error satisfy the standard assumptions of Chapter 13, then applying OLS. This approach will be generalized in this section.

Recall that the GLS model is

$$\mathbf{y} = \mathbf{X}\boldsymbol{\beta} + \mathbf{e} \tag{16-1}$$

repeated

where

$$\text{cov } \mathbf{e} = \mathbf{U} \tag{16-3}$$

repeated

Whatever the covariance matrix $\mathbf{U}$ may be, it is possible to linearly transform the errors $\mathbf{e}$ by a matrix $\mathbf{M}$ so that

$$\text{cov } (\mathbf{Me}) = \mathbf{I} \tag{16-59}$$

Proof. Since $\mathbf{U}$ is a covariance matrix, it is positive definite and symmetric;[10] therefore there exists an invertible matrix $\mathbf{M}$ such that

$$\mathbf{MUM}' = \mathbf{I} \tag{16-60}$$

(The proof is given in standard linear algebra texts. The matrix $\mathbf{M}$ is not unique, but this does not cause any difficulty.) It is easily verified that[11]

$$\mathbf{M}'\mathbf{M} = \mathbf{U}^{-1} \tag{16-61}$$

Thus $\mathbf{M}$ is sometimes denoted by $\mathbf{U}^{-1/2}$.

From Table 13-2,

$$\begin{aligned} \text{cov } (\mathbf{Me}) &= \mathbf{M}(\text{cov } \mathbf{e})\mathbf{M}' \\ &= \mathbf{MUM}' \\ &= \mathbf{I} \end{aligned} \tag{16-62}$$

and (16-59) is proved.

---

[10] For details on the properties of a covariance matrix, see Goldberger, *op. cit.*, p 87.

[11] From (16-60), $\mathbf{U} = \mathbf{M}^{-1}\mathbf{I}\mathbf{M}'^{-1} = \mathbf{M}^{-1}\mathbf{M}'^{-1}$

Therefore,

$$\mathbf{U}^{-1} = \mathbf{M}'\mathbf{M}$$

We therefore transform (16-1) by premultiplying by $\mathbf{M}$:

$$(\mathbf{My}) = (\mathbf{MX})\boldsymbol{\beta} + (\mathbf{Me})$$

that is,

$$\mathbf{y}^* = \mathbf{X}^*\boldsymbol{\beta} + \mathbf{e}^* \tag{16-63}$$

obtaining a model where the error $\mathbf{e}^*$ satisfies the assumptions of OLS.

The OLS estimates are given by (13-24) as

$$\begin{aligned}\hat{\boldsymbol{\beta}} &= (\mathbf{X}^{*\prime}\mathbf{X}^*)^{-1}\mathbf{X}^{*\prime}\mathbf{y}^* \\ &= \{(\mathbf{MX})'\mathbf{MX}\}^{-1}(\mathbf{MX})'(\mathbf{My}) \\ &= \{\mathbf{X}'(\mathbf{M}'\mathbf{M})\mathbf{X}\}^{-1}\mathbf{X}'(\mathbf{M}'\mathbf{M})\mathbf{y} \qquad (16\text{-}64a)\end{aligned}$$

by (16-61)

$$= (\mathbf{X}'\mathbf{U}^{-1}\mathbf{X})^{-1}\mathbf{X}'\mathbf{U}^{-1}\mathbf{y} \tag{16-64b}$$

(16-6) repeated

which are just the GLS estimates.

In conclusion, an $\mathbf{M}$ must always exist, such that this transformation followed by OLS will yield the GLS result; in fact, GLS is often referred to as the "Aitken transformation." Thus GLS may be viewed as simply an extension of OLS. (This also means that the text and problems in Section 16-1 were really not essential; but they were included to provide an initial intuitive understanding of GLS.)

16-6 HOW MUCH IS GLS WORTH?

(a) In General

Whenever our data follow the model (16-1) to (16-3) we have shown that GLS estimates have certain desirable properties. They are

1. Unbiased.
2. MLE, if normality assumed.
3. BLUE even if normality is not assumed; that is, within the class of linear unbiased estimators they have the smallest variance (Gauss-Markov theorem).

We now ask how much damage would be done if OLS were applied directly to the data,[12] even though it may not be theoretically justified.

First of all, we are pleasantly surprised to find that OLS estimators would be unbiased. To prove this, we merely repeat the argument that

[12] In other words, suppose we apply OLS directly to (16-1), rather than *after* the GLS transformation $\mathbf{M}$.

established (13-30). This argument is still valid because the covariance matrix $\mathbf{U}$ does not appear anywhere in this computation of expected values; the crucial issue is that $\mathbf{E}(\mathbf{e}) = 0$, and this is still true in our model, by (16-2).

However (by Gauss-Markov), GLS estimators have smaller variance than other linear unbiased estimators, including OLS. How much variance would OLS have?

To derive the actual formula for the variance of the OLS estimators, we recall that the OLS estimator is

$$\hat{\boldsymbol{\beta}}_0 = (\mathbf{X}'\mathbf{X})^{-1}\mathbf{X}'\mathbf{y} \tag{16-65}$$

(13-24) repeated

From Table 13-2

$$\text{cov}\,(\hat{\boldsymbol{\beta}}_0) = (\mathbf{X}'\mathbf{X})^{-1}\mathbf{X}'(\text{cov}\,\mathbf{y})\{(\mathbf{X}'\mathbf{X})^{-1}\mathbf{X}'\}'$$

From (16-3), and noting that $(\mathbf{X}'\mathbf{X})$ is symmetric

$$\text{cov}\,(\hat{\boldsymbol{\beta}}_0) = (\mathbf{X}'\mathbf{X})^{-1}\mathbf{X}'\,\mathbf{U}\mathbf{X}(\mathbf{X}'\mathbf{X})^{-1} \tag{16-66}$$

We shall show in some special cases how much this exceeds the optimal variance of the GLS estimator

$$\text{cov}\,(\hat{\boldsymbol{\beta}}) = (\mathbf{X}'\mathbf{U}^{-1}\mathbf{X})^{-1} \tag{16-67}$$

(16-8) repeated

To be simple and concrete, we shall consider the case of simple regression (2-1), where the independent variable x takes on five successive values.

(b) Heteroscedasticity

Suppose the values of x_i are 1, 2, 3, 4, 5, and that the standard deviation[13] of y_i is proportional to x_i. The optimal GLS estimators have covariance computed in (16-67):

$$\text{cov}\,\hat{\boldsymbol{\beta}} = \boxed{\begin{matrix} 2.4 & -1.1 \\ -1.1 & 0.7 \end{matrix}} \tag{16-68}$$

whereas from (16-66), the OLS estimators have

$$\text{cov}\,\hat{\boldsymbol{\beta}}_0 = \boxed{\begin{matrix} 6.2 & -2.5 \\ -2.5 & 1.2 \end{matrix}} \tag{16-69}$$

which is far worse. In this case, GLS is worth a great deal.

---

[13] It is also assumed that the standard deviation of y_1 is 1, for simplicity. Furthermore, the x_i are not shifted to a zero mean, that is, x_i are not in deviation form.

(c) Serial Correlation

Suppose the values of x_i are $-2, -1, 0, 1, 2$, and that the errors in y follow a simple autocorrelated process (16-35) with[14] $\rho = 1/2$. Then for GLS

$$\text{cov}\,\hat{\boldsymbol{\beta}} = \begin{bmatrix} .57 & 0 \\ 0 & .154 \end{bmatrix} \tag{16-70}$$

whereas for OLS,

$$\text{cov}\,\hat{\boldsymbol{\beta}}_0 = \begin{bmatrix} .59 & 0 \\ 0 & .160 \end{bmatrix} \tag{16-71}$$

which is only slightly worse. Thus, in this example with x increasing regularly and ρ positive, OLS is quite efficient. [Note that this provides support for our statement (6-16).]

Finally, suppose we calculated GLS by transformation; but after calculating all generalized differences (16-57), we forgot to adjust the first observations as in (16-58). The result is:

$$\text{cov}\,\hat{\boldsymbol{\beta}}_* = \begin{bmatrix} 2.80 & -1.20 \\ -1.20 & .80 \end{bmatrix} \tag{16-72}$$

which is worse than OLS.[15] This confirms our earlier statement [following (6-29)] that this adjustment in the first observation may be crucial; without it, the result may be far worse than OLS.

This discussion of serial correlation must be kept in perspective with the following three observations.

(i) In concluding that OLS is often a reasonably good estimation procedure for serial correlation, we emphasize that we have only considered its efficiency in *point* estimation. OLS *interval* estimates may be highly misleading (see the discussion of Figures 6-3 and 6-4).

(ii) Chapter 16 has been devoted exclusively to the case where ρ is known. But it almost always must be estimated. In such circumstances, the

[14] And var $(v_t) = 1$, for simplicity.

[15] This spectacular result is, of course, in part due to the small sample. With a larger sample, the effect of an adjustment in the first observation tends to fade out. We should also keep in mind the possibility that the first observation occurs after a discontinuity in the process generating the error, as described in the footnote to (6-29). Then the GLS transformation (16-58) is not valid.

case for using OLS is strengthened, not because it becomes a better estimating technique, but rather because the application of alternative more complicated techniques becomes less justified.

(iii) Finally, there may be other problems involved in using time series data—such as lagged variables. These are difficult to treat simultaneously with autocorrelated error; but they will often be more serious problems, and hence take precedence.

PROBLEMS

16-4*(a) Verify (16-68) and (16-69). Note footnote 13 below (16–68).

(b) What is the efficiency of OLS relative to GLS for the slope estimate, in this example?

(c) Calculate the covariance matrices as in (16-68) and (16-69), assuming just three x values (1, 2, 3).

*16-5 Referring to Section 16-5, suppose the data were transformed by premultiplying by a matrix **M**; but let us now suppose that **M** is no longer the optimizing matrix satisfying (16-60). Then the estimator $\hat{\boldsymbol{\beta}}$ in (16-64a) cannot be further simplified. Prove that its covariance matrix is

$$\text{cov}\,\hat{\boldsymbol{\beta}} = (\mathbf{X}'\mathbf{M}'\mathbf{M}\mathbf{X})^{-1}\mathbf{X}'\mathbf{M}'\mathbf{M}\mathbf{U}\mathbf{M}'\mathbf{M}\mathbf{X}(\mathbf{X}'\mathbf{M}'\mathbf{M}\mathbf{X})^{-1} \quad (16\text{-}73)$$

*16-6 (a) Verify (16-70) to (16-72).

(b) Calculate the covariance matrices as in (16-70) to (16-72), assuming just three x values $(-1, 0, 1)$.

(c) Repeat (b), using $\rho = .9$ instead of .5

*16-7 Suppose the following four points were observed in a time series, whose errors e_t form a simple autocorrelated process with $\rho = -.9$. Suppose also that $e_t \sim N(0, 1.5^2)$.

t	x_t	y_t	e_t
1	0	0	
2	0	−1	
3	0	0	
4	1	0	

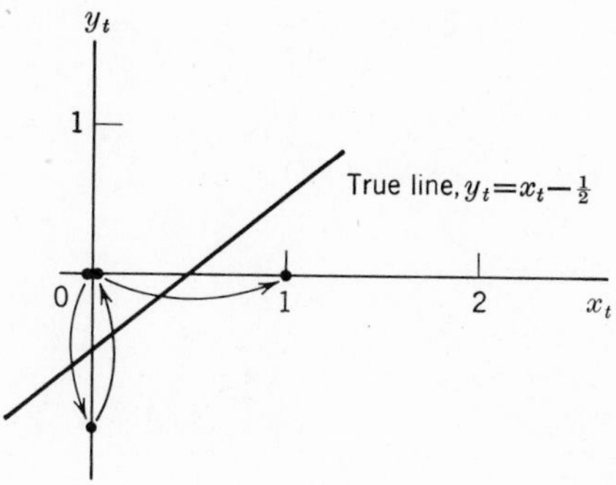

(a) Fill out the table of e_t. Are these errors very negatively correlated?
(b) Calculate the slope estimate using
  (i) OLS
  (ii) GLS
  (iii) Which is nearer the correct value $\beta = 1$?
(c) What is the theoretical variance of the slope estimate using
  (i) OLS
  (ii) GLS?
  (iii) What is the efficiency of OLS relative to GLS?

chapter 17

Instrumental Variables (IV) (A Generalization of Chapter 7)

17-1 REVIEW OF OLS GEOMETRY

In Figure 15-19 we showed how a least squares fit corresponded geometrically to a perpendicular projection. In order to simplify this review, we shall consider the regression of **y** on just one regressor **x**, according to the model

$$y_t = \beta x_t + e_t, \qquad (t = 1, 2, \ldots n) \tag{17-1}$$

that is,

$$\mathbf{y} = \beta\mathbf{x} + \mathbf{e} \tag{17-2}$$

where the e_t are independent and identically distributed with zero mean and variance σ^2. We regard **x** as fixed, or else independent of **e**, so that when we look at the conditional distribution of **e**, for a given **x**,

$$E(\mathbf{x} \cdot \mathbf{e}) = 0 \tag{17-3}$$

The expected value of **y** is $\beta\mathbf{x}$, shown in Figure 17-1 as a multiple of the vector **x** ($\beta = 2/3$). The possible errors **e** are delimited by the sphere of concentration, centered at the origin [since $E(\mathbf{e}) = \mathbf{0}$]. A typical observed error **e** is shown. Its correlation with **x**, which is cos θ, happens to be positive. But other errors such as $\mathbf{e}^*$ would have a negative correlation with **x**, so that if we averaged over all possible errors, the correlation of **x** and **e** would be zero, as stated in (17-3).

The typical observed **y** is given algebraically by (17-2); geometrically, we add **e** to $\beta\mathbf{x}$ to obtain **y** in Figure 17-1. Now OLS is the technique that $\perp$ projects **y** onto **x** at $\hat{\beta}\mathbf{x}$. Although this happens to slightly overestimate the target $\beta\mathbf{x}$, this procedure is just as likely to underestimate; on the average, $\hat{\beta}\mathbf{x}$ exactly equals $\beta\mathbf{x}$, that is, $\hat{\beta}$ is an unbiased estimator of β.

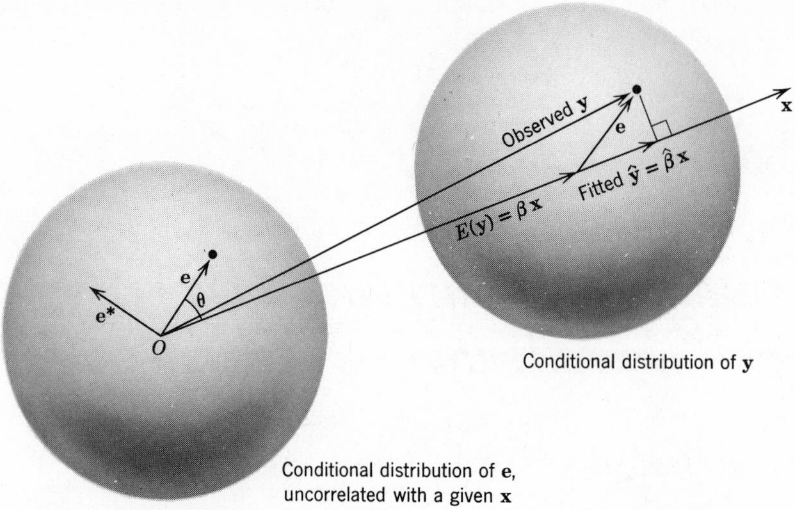

FIG. 17-1 OLS gives an unbiased estimator when **x** and **e** are uncorrelated.

17-2 GEOMETRY OF INSTRUMENTAL VARIABLES (IV)

We next consider the model

$$\mathbf{y} = \beta \mathbf{x} + \mathbf{e} \tag{17-4}$$

where the error vector is different; now **e** is correlated with **x**. As shown in Figure 17-2, for a given **x** the distribution of **e** will tend to be in the same direction as **x**. The conditional $E(\mathbf{e})$, at the center of the ellipsoid of concentration of **e**, will be no longer **0**.

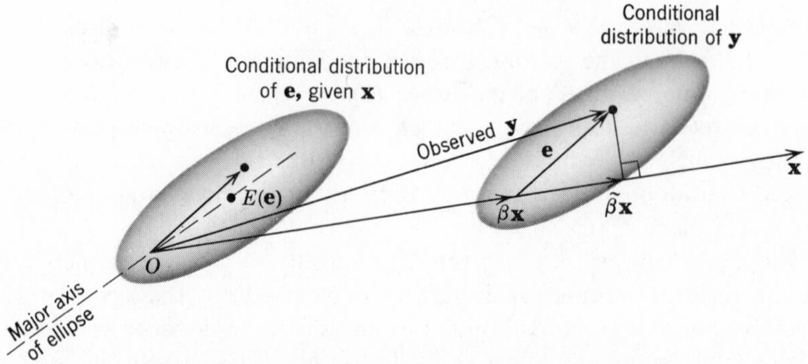

FIG. 17-2 OLS gives a biased estimator when **x** and **e** are correlated.

The OLS or $\perp$ projection of **y** onto **x** yields an estimate $\tilde{\beta}\mathbf{x}$, which happens to be too large. Furthermore, most of such estimates will be too large, because of the eccentric disposition of the errors (which is due, in turn, to the correlation of **e** with **x**). Thus $\tilde{\beta}$ is a biased estimator of β.

An unbiased estimator $\hat{\beta}$ could be obtained if we projected **y** onto **x** *in the direction of the major axis of the ellipse*, instead of the $\perp$ direction. For then our estimates would be distributed evenly above and below the target, making the estimator unbiased. In Figure 17-3 we shall see that application of an instrument gives us just exactly this skewed projection.

But first we review the algebraic conditions of an instrumental variable **z** as given in equations (7-15) and (7-16). Their geometric equivalents as shown in Figure 17-3, are roughly

1. **z** and **e** are perpendicular, in an infinite sample, and on average.[1]
2. **z** and **x** are not perpendicular, in an infinite sample, and on average.

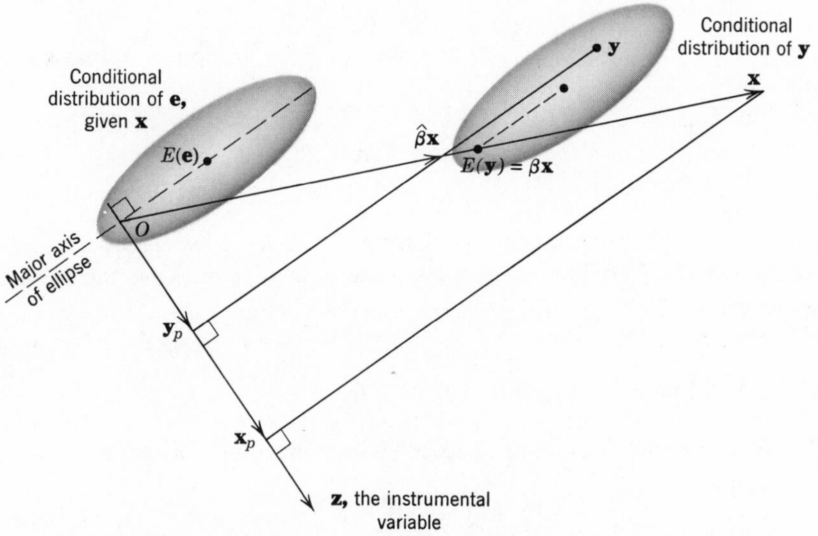

FIG. 17-3 Instrumental variable gives an unbiased estimator when **e** and **x** are correlated.

[1] To illustrate the geometry easily, we have imposed this stronger condition; requiring **z** and **e** to be perpendicular *on average* is slightly stronger than the condition of (7-15). It means that, over all the possible samples shown as the ellipse of concentation in Figure 17-3, **z** and **e** are perpendicular on average. Thus, an individual error **e** may not be $\perp$ to **z**, that is, the enclosed angle does not have $\cos\theta = 0$; however, the distribution on **e** on both sides of its major axis makes $\cos\theta$ sometimes positive, and sometimes negative, so that average $\cos\theta = 0$.

We now examine the estimate that results when $\mathbf{y}$ is $\perp$ projected onto such an instrument, i.e., when $\mathbf{y}$ is correctly projected in the direction of (the major axis of) the error, to the point $\hat{\beta}\mathbf{x}$ on $\mathbf{x}$, and to the point $\mathbf{y}_p$ on $\mathbf{z}$ itself. (Also, $\mathbf{x}$ is projected to $\mathbf{x}_p$ on $\mathbf{z}$.)

The unbiased estimate $\hat{\beta}$ is given, according to (15-12b), by

$$|\hat{\beta}| = \frac{\|\hat{\beta}\mathbf{x}\|}{\|\mathbf{x}\|} \tag{17-5}$$

Because of similarity of triangles, it is equally well given by

$$|\hat{\beta}| = \frac{\|\mathbf{y}_p\|}{\|\mathbf{x}_p\|} \tag{17-6}$$

from (15-26),

$$= \frac{|\mathbf{y}\cdot\mathbf{z}|/\|\mathbf{z}\|}{|\mathbf{x}\cdot\mathbf{z}|/\|\mathbf{z}\|}$$

$$= \frac{|\mathbf{y}\cdot\mathbf{z}|}{|\mathbf{x}\cdot\mathbf{z}|} \tag{17-7}$$

It is easily confirmed that $\hat{\beta}$ will be given correctly, in sign as well as magnitude, by

$$\boxed{\hat{\beta} = \frac{\mathbf{y}\cdot\mathbf{z}}{\mathbf{x}\cdot\mathbf{z}}} \tag{17-8}$$

But this is just the instrumental variable estimate in (7-18). Thus, the instrumental variable technique is seen to be a projection of $\mathbf{y}$ onto $\mathbf{x}$ in the direction of the error.

17-3 ALGEBRAIC GENERALIZATION

Now consider extending the use of instruments to the general case of k regressors

$$\mathbf{y} = \mathbf{X}\boldsymbol{\beta} + \mathbf{e} \tag{17-9}$$

(13-13) repeated

where $\mathbf{X}$ is the full matrix of n observations, $\mathbf{X} = [\mathbf{x}_1, \mathbf{x}_2, \ldots \mathbf{x}_k]$. Now estimation of the k parameters[2] in $\boldsymbol{\beta}$ requires k instruments, say $\mathbf{z}_1, \mathbf{z}_2, \ldots \mathbf{z}_k$. Let the n observations on these instruments be marshalled into the matrix $\mathbf{Z}$, which we note has the same dimension as $\mathbf{X}$. We shall now show that, to

[2] Hereafter, whenever instruments are used, we shall express all variables in deviation form. Thus, there is no intercept term, and all k regressors are variables. In any case, there is no problem in estimating the intercept at the end.

provide consistent estimates of $\boldsymbol{\beta}$, it is sufficient that the set of instrumental variables $\mathbf{Z}$ satisfy the following two conditions, which generalize (7-15) and (7-16)

1. z_i and e are uncorrelated, or more precisely, $s_{Z_ie} \xrightarrow{p} 0$ (17-10)

that is,

$$\frac{1}{n}\mathbf{z}_i'\mathbf{e} \xrightarrow{p} 0 \qquad \text{for} \qquad i = 1, 2, \ldots k$$

that is,

$$\boxed{\frac{1}{n}\mathbf{Z}'\mathbf{e} \xrightarrow{p} \mathbf{0}} \tag{17-11}$$

2. z_i and the x's are correlated, or more precisely

$$\boxed{\frac{1}{n}\mathbf{Z}'\mathbf{X} \xrightarrow{p} \text{a nonsingular limit } \mathbf{\Sigma}} \tag{17-12}$$

This condition implies that the $\mathbf{x}$ variables must be linearly independent, and the $\mathbf{z}$ variables also.

To obtain consistent estimators of $\boldsymbol{\beta}$ we apply all k instruments to (17-9), obtaining

$$\frac{1}{n}\mathbf{Z}'\mathbf{y} = \frac{1}{n}\mathbf{Z}'\mathbf{X}\boldsymbol{\beta} + \frac{1}{n}\mathbf{Z}'\mathbf{e} \tag{17-13}$$

Because of (17-11), as n increases

$$\frac{1}{n}\mathbf{Z}'\mathbf{y} \xrightarrow{p} \left(\frac{1}{n}\mathbf{Z}'\mathbf{X}\right)\boldsymbol{\beta} \tag{17-14}$$

Because of the invertibility specified in (17-12), we may solve (17-14)

$$\left(\frac{1}{n}\mathbf{Z}'\mathbf{X}\right)^{-1}\left(\frac{1}{n}\mathbf{Z}'\mathbf{y}\right) \xrightarrow{p} \boldsymbol{\beta} \tag{17-15}$$

It follows that the estimator

$$\hat{\boldsymbol{\beta}} = (\mathbf{Z}'\mathbf{X})^{-1}(\mathbf{Z}'\mathbf{y}) \xrightarrow{p} \boldsymbol{\beta} \tag{17-16}$$

that is, $\hat{\boldsymbol{\beta}}$ is consistent.

If $\mathbf{X}$ is asymptotically uncorrelated with $\mathbf{e}$ (condition 1) and not multicollinear (condition 2), $\mathbf{X}$ qualifies as the instrument set $\mathbf{Z}$. Substituting into (17-16) yields the consistent estimator

$$\hat{\boldsymbol{\beta}} = (\mathbf{X}'\mathbf{X})^{-1}(\mathbf{X}'\mathbf{y}) \tag{17-17}$$

which is, of course, the OLS estimator in (13-24).

Finally, now that this procedure is justified, we notice that by multiplying by n our original covariance estimating equations (17-13) can be written in the simpler form

$$\mathbf{Z}'\mathbf{y} = \mathbf{Z}'\mathbf{X}\boldsymbol{\beta} + \mathbf{Z}'\mathbf{e} \tag{17-18}$$

17-4 NOTATION

In Table 17-1, we review the different notations for instrumental variables used in Chapters 7 and 17. Once central idea stands out. Whether we

TABLE 17-1

Section	"Application" of the Instrument to the Model Equation (7-1) or Its Generalization Means:	Which in Turn Yields the Estimator:
Chapter 7 (simple algebra)	Taking covariances with Z, $s_{ZY} = \beta s_{ZX} + s_{Ze}$ (7-17)	$\hat{\beta} = \dfrac{s_{ZY}}{s_{ZX}}$ (7-18)
Chapter 17-2	Taking dot product with $\mathbf{z}$, $\mathbf{z} \cdot \mathbf{y} = \beta \mathbf{z} \cdot \mathbf{x} + \mathbf{z} \cdot \mathbf{e}$	$\hat{\beta} = \dfrac{\mathbf{z} \cdot \mathbf{y}}{\mathbf{z} \cdot \mathbf{x}}$ (17-8)
Chapter 17-3	Premultiplying by $\mathbf{z}'$, to estimate one parameter β $\mathbf{z}'\mathbf{y} = \beta\mathbf{z}'\mathbf{x} + \mathbf{z}'\mathbf{e}$	$\hat{\beta} = \dfrac{\mathbf{z}'\mathbf{y}}{\mathbf{z}'\mathbf{x}}$
	Premultiplying by $\mathbf{Z}'$, to estimate k parameters $\boldsymbol{\beta}$ $\mathbf{Z}'\mathbf{y} = \mathbf{Z}'\mathbf{X}\boldsymbol{\beta} + \mathbf{Z}'\mathbf{e}$ (17-18)	$\hat{\boldsymbol{\beta}} = (\mathbf{Z}'\mathbf{X})^{-1}(\mathbf{Z}'\mathbf{y})$ (17-16)

call it "taking covariances," "taking dot product," etc., we are doing the same calculation and obtaining exactly the same estimator in each case.

PROBLEMS

17-1 (a) What does the geometry of Figure 17-1 look like when the e_t are serially correlated, although e_t and x_t are still uncorrelated?
(b) Is the OLS estimate still unbiased?
*(c) What is wrong with the OLS confidence interval?

chapter 18

Identification (A Generalization of Chapter 8)

This chapter will consider what form the mathematical model (i.e., the system of equations) must take in order to identify the parameters of an equation. Before beginning it must be recognized, as in Chapter 8-2, that prior knowledge of the relative variance of the error terms—or more generally, prior knowledge of the covariance matrix of the error terms—can help identify an equation. While readers are referred to extensive analysis of this elsewhere,[1] it is not analyzed here. Instead, we limit ourselves to a discussion of the conditions for identification in the absence of prior information on covariance structure, where the only prior knowledge is that certain parameters are zero (i.e., certain terms in the equation are missing).

We begin by comparing the structural and reduced forms of the model.

18-1 STRUCTURAL AND REDUCED FORMS

(a) The Structural Form

This is diagrammed in Figure 18-1; it consists of a system of linear equations relating the current endogenous variables $\mathbf{y}$ to the errors $\mathbf{e}$ and the predetermined variables[2] $\mathbf{x}$. These latter must be defined broadly to include

[1] See, for example, Fisher, Franklin M., *The Identification Problem in Econometrics*. New York: McGraw-Hill, 1966.

[2] The constant term is accounted for by a dummy exogenous variable that always takes on the value 1, or else the constant term may be ignored. Either convention is satisfactory for this chapter, if followed consistently. That is, if the constant term is kept in, then there will also be associated with it the dummy exogenous variable, as the instrument to "just take care of" estimating the constant term.

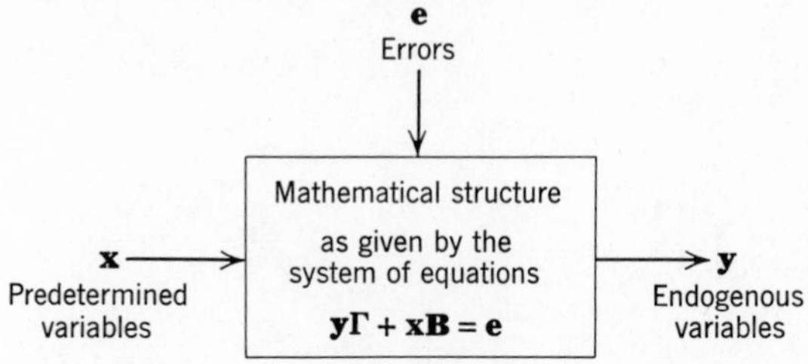

FIG. 18-1 A schematic view of an econometric model.

both exogenous variables with values determined outside the system, *and* lagged endogenous variables, whose values are, of course, also predetermined. (In the rest of this book, we will often loosely use "exogenous variables" when we mean more accurately "predetermined variables.") Thus, our model is:

$$\mathbf{y}\boldsymbol{\Gamma} + \mathbf{x}\mathbf{B} = \mathbf{e} \qquad \text{Structural form} \tag{18-1}$$

$$\boxed{\mathbf{y}}\,\boxed{\boldsymbol{\Gamma}} + \boxed{\mathbf{x}}\,\boxed{\mathbf{B}} = \boxed{\mathbf{e}}$$

Mathematical completeness requires that there be as many linearly independent equations as endogenous variables; hence the matrix $\boldsymbol{\Gamma}$ must be square and invertible.

An example will illustrate. In Chapter 8, we considered the following demand and supply equations:

$$\begin{aligned} &\text{Demand} \quad \nu Q = \alpha + \beta P + \eta T + \xi Y + e_1 \\ &\text{Supply} \quad \lambda Q = \gamma + \delta P + \theta R + e_2 \end{aligned} \tag{18-2a}$$

where the exogenous variables T, Y, and R determine the endogenous variables P and Q. The notation of (18-2a) is a little different from that used in (8-19) and (8-20). The errors are denoted e_1 and e_2. The coefficients ν and λ have been introduced to emphasize that an equation can be identified only up to a factor of proportionality; that is, we can only hope to identify the *ratios* α/ν, β/ν, etc. This idea of uniqueness up to a factor of proportionality will persist as far as equation (18-11). Equation (18-2a) in matrix form is:

$$\begin{bmatrix} P & Q \end{bmatrix} \begin{bmatrix} -\beta & -\delta \\ \nu & \lambda \end{bmatrix} + \begin{bmatrix} 1 & T & Y & R \end{bmatrix} \begin{bmatrix} -\alpha & -\gamma \\ -\eta & 0 \\ -\xi & 0 \\ 0 & -\theta \end{bmatrix} = \begin{bmatrix} e_1 & e_2 \end{bmatrix} \tag{18-2b}$$

The specification of this model involves setting three elements in $\mathbf{B}$ equal to zero a priori.

(b) The Reduced Form

This is the explicit solution of the structural form (18-1) for $\mathbf{y}$. Since $\mathbf{\Gamma}$ is invertible, this solution is obtained by postmultiplying (18-1) by $\mathbf{\Gamma}^{-1}$,

$$\mathbf{y} = -\mathbf{x}\mathbf{B}\mathbf{\Gamma}^{-1} + \mathbf{e}\mathbf{\Gamma}^{-1}$$

This is written simply as:

$$\boxed{\mathbf{y} = \mathbf{x}\mathbf{\Pi} + \mathbf{v} \qquad \text{Reduced form}} \tag{18-3}$$

in which

$$\mathbf{v} = \mathbf{e}\mathbf{\Gamma}^{-1}$$

and

$$\mathbf{\Pi} = -\mathbf{B}\mathbf{\Gamma}^{-1} \tag{18-4a}$$

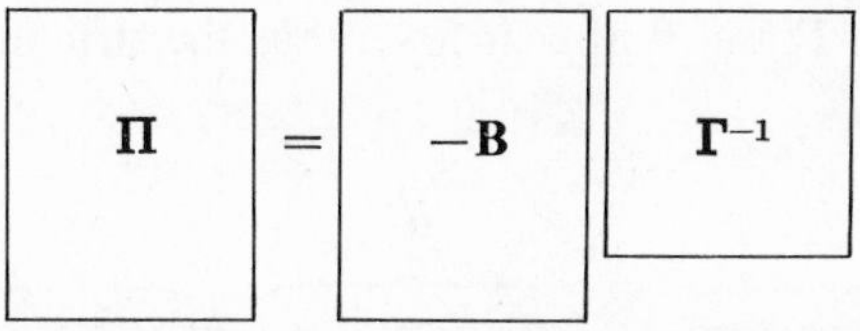

Postmultiplying (18-4a) by $-\mathbf{\Gamma}$, the relation may be written

$$-\mathbf{\Pi}\,\mathbf{\Gamma} = \mathbf{B} \tag{18-4b}$$

18-2 IDENTIFICATION—NECESSARY AND SUFFICIENT CONDITIONS

(a) Introduction

Consider the identification problem as stated in Chapter 8-6. We supposed that we know how the endogenous variables are related to the predetermined variables, that is, the reduced form (18-3). (In assuming the true reduced form is known, we emphasize that identification precedes statistical problems.) Without prior restrictions, that is, without adequate specification, there would be many possible corresponding structures (18-1);

that is, $\mathbf{y} = \mathbf{x\Pi} + \mathbf{v}$ would not correspond to a unique $\mathbf{y\Gamma} + \mathbf{xB} = \mathbf{e}$. For a single known $\mathbf{\Pi}$, there would be many ways to select $\mathbf{\Gamma}$ and $\mathbf{B}$.[3]

Identification means that there should be enough prior restrictions to leave no ambiguity in the structural form (18-1), that is, to ensure that $\mathbf{\Gamma}$ and $\mathbf{B}$ are uniquely determined, thus can be recovered once $\mathbf{\Pi}$ is known (or estimated). We shall find it convenient to answer the identification question one equation at a time. To summarize:

Definition.

> An equation of the structure (18-1) is identified if there are unique (up to a factor of proportionality) values of its parameters corresponding to a given reduced form, (and satisfying the prior restrictions, of course). (18-6)

(b) Condition on the Reduced Form

Without loss of generality, we can suppose that it is the first equation we wish to identify. We thus concentrate on the first column of $\mathbf{\Gamma}$ and $\mathbf{B}$ in (18-1). Furthermore, we order the variables so that the zero coefficients in the first column of $\mathbf{\Gamma}$ and $\mathbf{B}$ appear first; thus the structure is

$$\mathbf{y\Gamma} + \mathbf{xB} = \mathbf{e} \tag{18-7}$$

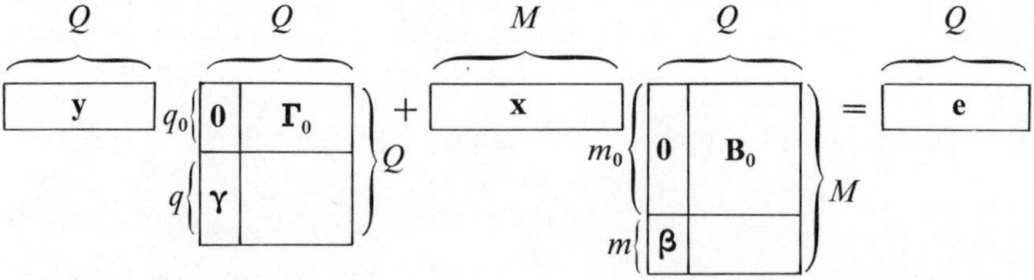

[3] We neglect the error term, because we made the basic assumption in this chapter that there was no prior information about its distribution that could help in identification.

It is easily shown that without prior restrictions many possible $\mathbf{\Gamma}$ and $\mathbf{B}$ correspond to the single given $\mathbf{\Pi}$. Suppose that one possible structure is

$$\mathbf{y}(\mathbf{\Gamma}_0) + \mathbf{x}(\mathbf{B}_0) = \mathbf{e} \tag{18-5}$$

If we postmultiply by any invertible matrix $\mathbf{M}$ (of appropriate dimension), then

$$\mathbf{y}(\mathbf{\Gamma}_0\mathbf{M}) + \mathbf{x}(\mathbf{B}_0\mathbf{M}) = \mathbf{eM}$$

is another possible structure, if *there are no prior restrictions*. However, if the coefficient matrix of $\mathbf{y}$ *does* have prior restrictions (such as 1, 0, 0, 0, 0 in the first row, for example), then $\mathbf{\Gamma}_0\mathbf{M}$ might violate these restrictions and be inadmissible. In fact, if the coefficient matrices of $\mathbf{y}$ and $\mathbf{x}$ have enough prior restrictions, so that every multiplier $\mathbf{M}$ produces inadmissible matrix coefficients (every multiplier except $\mathbf{M} = \mathbf{I}$, of course), then the only possible structure is (18-5), and the model is identified.

m_0 is the number of predetermined variables excluded from the first equation, while q is the number of endogenous variables included.[4] We shall soon see the important way in which they are related.

The form of $\mathbf{\Gamma}$ and $\mathbf{B}$ as given in (18-7) is now substituted into (18-4b)

$$-\mathbf{\Pi}\,\mathbf{\Gamma} = \mathbf{B} \tag{18-8}$$

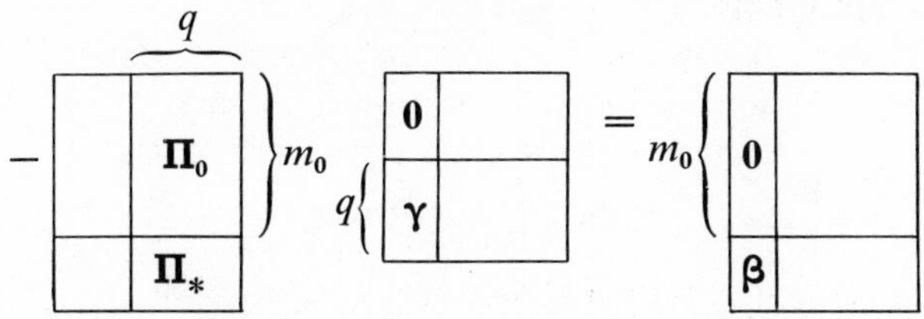

When the first column on the left side is equated to the first column on the right side, we obtain[5] the two matrix equations

$$-\mathbf{\Pi}_0\boldsymbol{\gamma} = \mathbf{0} \tag{18-9}$$

$$-\mathbf{\Pi}_*\boldsymbol{\gamma} = \boldsymbol{\beta} \tag{18-10}$$

For a given reduced form $\mathbf{\Pi}$, under what conditions will these equations yield a unique (up to a factor of proportionality) solution for $\boldsymbol{\gamma}$ and $\boldsymbol{\beta}$? Answering first the question for $\boldsymbol{\gamma}$, we note that (18-9) is a homogeneous system of equations in q unknowns. The theory of linear equations tells[6] us that the necessary and sufficient condition for a unique solution is:

rank $\mathbf{\Pi}_0 = q - 1$ (necessary and sufficient condition for identifying the first equation)	(18-11)

Of course, once $\boldsymbol{\gamma}$ is uniquely determined, then $\boldsymbol{\beta}$ is uniquely determined according to (18-10), and the first equation is identified.

---

[4] Other terms in (18-7) are defined in a straightforward way. Thus, $\mathbf{0}$ is an appropriately dimensioned zero vector, $\boldsymbol{\gamma}$ is the set of q nonzero coefficients in the first column of $\mathbf{\Gamma}$, etc.

[5] Because of the zeros in the first column of $\mathbf{\Gamma}$, only the last q elements ($\boldsymbol{\gamma}$) come into play.

[6] Outline of the argument:

If $\mathbf{\Pi}_0$ were of full rank q, then an invertible $q \times q$ submatrix $\mathbf{\Pi}_s$ could be found that would give the absolutely unique solution $\boldsymbol{\gamma} = -\mathbf{\Pi}_s^{-1}\mathbf{0} = \mathbf{0}$ for (18-9). But this is no use. Instead, we want to be able to specify one γ (usually $\gamma_1 = 1$ is the specification) and then solve uniquely for the other γ's in terms of it (uniqueness up to a factor of proportionality). This means the rank of $\mathbf{\Pi}_0$ must be $q - 1$.

(c) Condition on the Structural Form

It is more useful to reexpress condition (18-11) in terms of the structural form. Looking back to (18-7) we see that $\mathbf{\Gamma}_0$ and $\mathbf{B}_0$ are the coefficient matrices for the variables omitted from the first equation, and for all equations except the first.

We shall show that when these two matrices are combined, a necessary and sufficient condition for the identification of the first equation is

$$\boxed{\begin{array}{c}\text{rank}\begin{bmatrix}\mathbf{\Gamma}_0\\ \mathbf{B}_0\end{bmatrix} = Q - 1\\ \text{(necessary and sufficient condition for}\\ \text{identifying the first equation)}\end{array}} \tag{18-12}$$

that is, $\begin{bmatrix}\mathbf{\Gamma}_0\\ \mathbf{B}_0\end{bmatrix}$ is of full rank.[7]

To prove this, we note that rank will be unchanged if we augment this combined matrix with the corresponding zero coefficients in the first equation. Moreover, rank remains unchanged if the result is postmultiplied by the invertible matrix $\mathbf{\Gamma}^{-1}$. Thus, we obtain

$$\begin{array}{r} q_0\{ \\ m_0\{ \end{array}\left[\begin{array}{c|c} \mathbf{0} & \mathbf{\Gamma}_0 \\ \hline \mathbf{0} & \mathbf{B}_0 \end{array}\right]\left[\;\mathbf{\Gamma}^{-1}\;\right] \quad \text{which reduces}^{8} \text{ to} \quad \begin{array}{r} q_0\{ \\ m_0\{ \end{array}\overset{\quad q_0 \qquad q}{\left[\begin{array}{c|c} \mathbf{I} & \mathbf{O} \\ \hline * & -\mathbf{\Pi}_0 \end{array}\right]} \tag{18-13}$$

---

[7] It is impossible that rank $\begin{bmatrix}\mathbf{\Gamma}_0\\ \mathbf{B}_0\end{bmatrix} > Q - 1$, because this matrix has only $Q - 1$ columns.

[8] The star indicates a submatrix whose form is unimportant in the subsequent argument.

We establish (18-13) in two parts—top and bottom. To prove the top part, express $\mathbf{\Gamma}$ as in (18-7), and write

$$\mathbf{\Gamma}\mathbf{\Gamma}^{-1} = \mathbf{I}$$

$$q_0\{\left[\begin{array}{c|c} \mathbf{0} & \mathbf{\Gamma}_0 \\ \hline & \end{array}\right]\left[\;\mathbf{\Gamma}^{-1}\;\right] = q_0\{\overset{\quad q_0 \qquad q}{\left[\begin{array}{c|c} \mathbf{I} & \mathbf{O} \\ \hline & \end{array}\right]} \tag{18-14}$$

The shaded top part of (18-14) is exactly the top part of (18-13).

(cont'd)

Because the rank of $\mathbf{I}$ is obviously q_0, the rank of the right-hand matrix in (18-13) is $q_0 + \text{rank}\,\mathbf{\Pi}_0$. Therefore,

$$\text{rank}\begin{bmatrix}\mathbf{\Gamma}_0\\ \mathbf{B}_0\end{bmatrix} = q_0 + \text{rank}\,\mathbf{\Pi}_0 \tag{18-16}$$

We finally substitute the condition (18-11) for identifiability

$$\begin{aligned}\text{rank}\begin{bmatrix}\mathbf{\Gamma}_0\\ \mathbf{B}_0\end{bmatrix} &= q_0 + (q-1)\\ &= Q - 1\end{aligned} \tag{18-17}$$

and (18-12) is proved.

We shall next prove the order condition required for identification, first given in Chapter 8-4:

$$\boxed{\begin{gathered}m_0 \geq q - 1\\ \text{(the order condition necessary for}\\ \text{identifying the first equation)}\end{gathered}} \qquad \begin{gathered}\text{(18-18)}\\ \text{(8-12) repeated}\end{gathered}$$

To prove this, we go back to (18-11) to see that identification requires

$$\text{rank}\,\mathbf{\Pi}_0 = q - 1 \qquad \begin{gathered}\text{(18-19)}\\ \text{(18-11) repeated}\end{gathered}$$

But the rank of a matrix cannot exceed the number of its rows; thus,

$$\text{rank}\,\mathbf{\Pi}_0 \leq m_0 \tag{18-20}$$

Combining these last two equations, we see that identification requires

$$q - 1 \leq m_0 \qquad \text{(18-18) proved}$$

To prove the bottom part of (18-13), express $\mathbf{B}$ as in (18-7) and $\mathbf{\Pi}$ as in (18-8), and write (18-4*a*)

$$\mathbf{B}\mathbf{\Gamma}^{-1} = -\mathbf{\Pi}$$

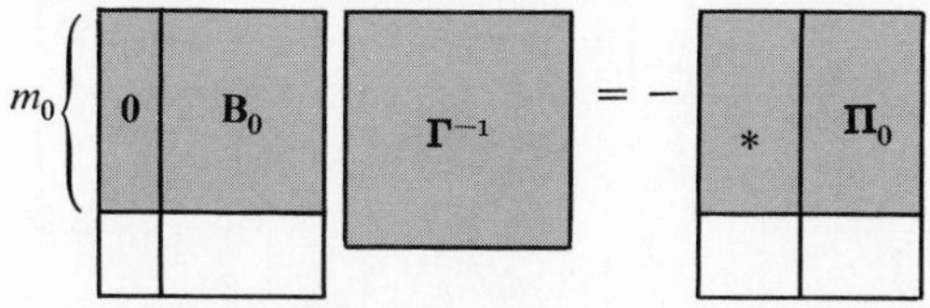

(18-15)

The shaded top part of (18-15) is exactly the bottom part of (18-13), and the proof is complete.

(d) Interpretation

We can use the rank condition (18-12) to investigate when the first equation is not identified. This occurs if

$$\operatorname{rank}\begin{bmatrix}\boldsymbol{\Gamma}_0\\ \mathbf{B}_0\end{bmatrix} < Q - 1 \tag{18-21}$$

In practice, there are several ways this can occur:

1. When $\begin{bmatrix}\boldsymbol{\Gamma}_0\\ \mathbf{B}_0\end{bmatrix}$ has too few rows; that is,

$$m_0 + q_0 < Q - 1$$

that is,

$$m_0 < (Q - q_0) - 1$$

that is,

$$m_0 < q - 1$$

This is merely stating that the order condition (18-18) has been violated—there are too few excluded exogenous variables (instrumental variables) to identify the first equation.

In the other cases to which we now turn, the necessary order condition (18-18) is satisfied, but the sufficient rank condition (18-12) is not.

2. When some specific column of $\begin{bmatrix}\boldsymbol{\Gamma}_0\\ \mathbf{B}_0\end{bmatrix}$ is identically zero.

This means that this specific equation of the system can confuse the first equation; referring to (18-7) for example, if this specific equation is added to the first, a bogus first equation is created that destroys the identity of the first equation.

For example, for our structural model we might take the following extension of the demand-supply system (18-2b); (we indicate nonzero parameters with an * to avoid proliferation of letters):

$$\begin{bmatrix} P & Q & S\end{bmatrix}\begin{bmatrix} * & * & * \\ * & * & 0 \\ 0 & \boxed{0 & *} \end{bmatrix} + \begin{bmatrix}1 & T & Y & R & Z\end{bmatrix}\begin{bmatrix} * & * & * \\ * & 0 & 0 \\ * & 0 & * \\ 0 & \boxed{0 & *} \\ * & 0 & * \end{bmatrix} = \begin{bmatrix} e_1 & e_2 & e_3\end{bmatrix} \tag{18-22}$$

To investigate the identification of the first equation, we have indicated by dotted lines the matrix

$$\begin{bmatrix} \boldsymbol{\Gamma}_0 \\ \mathbf{B}_0 \end{bmatrix} = \begin{array}{|cc|} \hline 0 & * \\ 0 & * \\ \hline \end{array} \tag{18-23}$$

This matrix has property (2)—a zero column—and hence the first equation is not identified. We see how reasonable this is; if the second equation were added to the first, a bogus first equation would be created. In terms of which variables are specified to be zero, this bogus equation would "look like" the first equation; only S and R are excluded. Were the first equation to be estimated, there would be no way of knowing whether the resulting fit was an estimate of the first equation, or a bogus combination of the first two equations.

3. When the columns of $\begin{bmatrix} \boldsymbol{\Gamma}_0 \\ \mathbf{B}_0 \end{bmatrix}$ are linearly dependent in some more subtle way, making the rank $< Q - 1$. We illustrate with an example:

$$\begin{array}{|cccc|} \hline y_1 & y_2 & y_3 & y_4 \\ \hline \end{array} \begin{array}{|cccc|} \hline * & * & 0 & 0 \\ * & * & 0 & * \\ * & 0 & * & * \\ 0 & 0 & * & 0 \\ \hline \end{array} + \begin{array}{|ccc|} \hline x_1 & x_2 & x_3 \\ \hline \end{array} \begin{array}{|cccc|} \hline 0 & * & 0 & * \\ 0 & 0 & * & 0 \\ * & * & * & * \\ \hline \end{array} = \begin{array}{|cccc|} \hline e_1 & e_2 & e_3 & e_4 \\ \hline \end{array} \tag{18-24}$$

To investigate the identifiability of the first equation, we have indicated by dotted lines the matrix

$$\begin{bmatrix} \boldsymbol{\Gamma}_0 \\ \mathbf{B}_0 \end{bmatrix} = \begin{array}{|ccc|} \hline 0 & * & 0 \\ * & 0 & * \\ 0 & * & 0 \\ \hline \end{array} \tag{18-25}$$

which has linearly dependent columns,[9] so that

$$\operatorname{rank} \begin{bmatrix} \boldsymbol{\Gamma}_0 \\ \mathbf{B}_0 \end{bmatrix} < 3$$
$$< Q - 1$$

which violates (18-12).

---

[9] *Proof.* If we denote the columns by c_1, c_2, and c_3, we see that

$$c_1 = kc_3$$

i.e., $$c_1 + 0c_2 - kc_3 = 0$$

This result is also reasonable. When the three columns (c_1, c_2, c_3) of (18-25) are linearly dependent, this means that some linear combination of the columns,

$$k_1c_1 + k_2c_2 + k_3c_3 = 0$$
$$\text{for some } k_i \neq 0$$

Then if the same linear combination of the last three equations is added to the first equation, a bogus first equation would result, just as before.

(e) A Final Subtlety

The rank requirement (18-12) depends on the matrix $\begin{bmatrix}\mathbf{\Gamma}_0\\ \mathbf{B}_0\end{bmatrix}$, some of whose elements (parameters) are known to be zero. The remaining elements are not known (in fact, their estimation is precisely the task of the econometrician). For example, we may have, in estimating the third equation of (18-24)

$$\begin{bmatrix}\mathbf{\Gamma}_0\\ \mathbf{B}_0\end{bmatrix} = \boxed{\begin{matrix}\gamma_{11} & \gamma_{12} & 0\\ \gamma_{21} & \gamma_{22} & \gamma_{24}\\ 0 & \beta_{12} & \beta_{14}\end{matrix}} \tag{18-26}$$

Although prespecified zeros no longer ensure it, it is still logically possible that the parameters are so related[10] as to make the matrix less than full rank, that is, rank $< Q - 1$. However, we consistently suppose throughout this chapter that no such relation between the parameters is known to exist a priori. And for such a relation to hold by coincidence would be practically impossible; it happens "almost nowhere," in mathematical language. The reader can appreciate this by giving the parameters of (18-26) values at random (taking the values out to two or three decimal places), and noting that condition (18-27) fails, that is, the matrix is indeed of full rank.

In conclusion, the cases where rank could "collapse by coincidence" are so rare, that they are ignored in practice.

---

[10] To be specific, the relation

$$\gamma_{11}\gamma_{22}\beta_{14} - \gamma_{21}\gamma_{12}\beta_{14} - \gamma_{11}\beta_{12}\gamma_{24} = 0 \tag{18-27}$$

makes the determinant zero, hence the rank <3.

PROBLEMS

18-1 Find which equations are identified. Of those equations that are identified, classify them as exactly identified or over identified.

$$
\boxed{\mathbf{y}}\begin{bmatrix} 0 & * & * \\ * & * & * \\ * & * & * \end{bmatrix} + \boxed{\mathbf{x}}\begin{bmatrix} * & * & * \\ * & 0 & 0 \\ * & 0 & 0 \\ 0 & * & 0 \\ * & * & * \\ * & * & 0 \end{bmatrix} = \boxed{\mathbf{e}}
$$

18-2 Repeat for

$$
\boxed{\mathbf{y}}\begin{bmatrix} * & * & * & 0 \\ * & * & 0 & * \\ * & * & * & * \\ * & * & * & * \end{bmatrix} + \boxed{\mathbf{x}}\begin{bmatrix} * & 0 & * & * \\ 0 & 0 & * & 0 \\ 0 & * & 0 & * \\ 0 & 0 & * & 0 \\ * & * & * & 0 \\ * & * & * & * \end{bmatrix} = \boxed{\mathbf{e}}
$$

18-3 ESTIMATION REQUIREMENTS: INDEPENDENCE OF VARIABLES

The conditions for identification are strictly algebraic, and apply to the *parameters* in the system. These conditions must be satisfied prior to looking at any statistical information. Statistical estimation of the parameters then requires overcoming another hurdle: in the case of exact identification the *variables* must be linearly independent. To illustrate, consider the following system:

$$
\begin{bmatrix} y_1 & y_2 & y_3 \end{bmatrix}\begin{bmatrix} 1 & 0 & \gamma_{13} \\ \gamma_{21} & 1 & \gamma_{23} \\ 0 & \gamma_{32} & 1 \end{bmatrix} + \begin{bmatrix} x_1 & x_2 \end{bmatrix}\begin{bmatrix} 0 & \beta_{12} & \beta_{13} \\ \beta_{21} & 0 & \beta_{23} \end{bmatrix} = \begin{bmatrix} e_1 & e_2 & e_3 \end{bmatrix} \tag{18-28}
$$

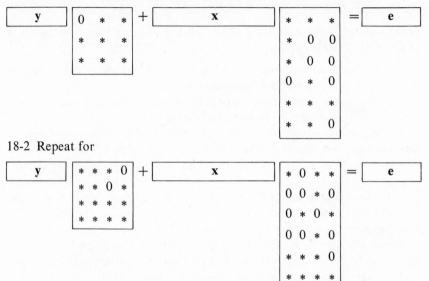

We have set one coefficient in each equation equal to one, so that we can discuss simple uniqueness, rather than uniqueness up to a factor of proportionality. The first equation is exactly identified; therefore, we may use our instrumental variables x_1 and x_2 on the first equation to obtain estimating equations:

$$\begin{bmatrix} s_{X_1Y_2} & s_{X_1X_2} \\ s_{X_2Y_2} & s_{X_2X_2} \end{bmatrix} \begin{bmatrix} \hat{\gamma}_{21} \\ \hat{\beta}_{21} \end{bmatrix} = - \begin{bmatrix} s_{X_1Y} \\ s_{X_2Y_1} \end{bmatrix} \tag{18-29}$$

There will be a unique solution iff the left-hand matrix **S** of covariances is of full rank, 2. This requires:

1. No linear dependence among the rows of **S**, caused by the exogenous variables[11] (x_1, x_2) being linearly dependent.

2. No linear dependence among the columns in **S**, caused by the included variables[12] (y_2, x_2) being linearly dependent.

Thus, once again we encounter the familiar problem of multicollinearity first discussed in Chapter 3. The condition that **S** be of full rank, is simply the condition that collinearity does not exist. However, in estimating systems of equations it may appear in either of the two above forms. It is interesting to note that these two conditions reduce to a single condition in multiple regression in the single equation model. In this special case, the requirement (see Chapter 3) that there be no collinearity between exogenous variables automatically satisfies conditions (1) and (2) above. Condition (1) is clearly met since the only exogenous variables in a single equation model are those that appear in that equation; and (2) is satisfied since the only included variables on the right-hand side of a single equation model are all the exogenous variables. Hence, the two collinearity conditions in multiple equation estimation reduce to a single collinearity condition in a single equation model.

18-4 SUMMARY: COMPLETENESS, IDENTIFICATION, AND ESTIMATION PROBLEMS

Formulating and estimating an econometric model requires that three successive conditions be met; each involves examining the rank of a different matrix. The three requirements are set out in Table 18-1.

---

[11] Both included in *and* excluded from the first equation. If, for example

$$x_1 = kx_2$$

then, in (18-27),

$$s_{X_1Y_2} = ks_{X_2Y_2}$$
$$s_{X_1X_2} = ks_{X_2X_2}$$

and the rows of **S** are linearly dependent.

[12] Both endogenous and exogenous. Here we define included variables as all those variables appearing in the equation *except* the variable determined by this equation—i.e., in this case, y_1. This definition is equivalent to the definition used in Chapter 8 of "included variables on the right-hand side."

TABLE 18-1 Conditions for Completeness, Identification, and Estimation

	Mathematical Completeness	Identification	Estimation
Question	Does the system of equations provide a unique solution for the endogenous variables?	Do the prior restrictions on parameters of the model allow us to identify the first equation?	Assuming exact identification, are problems of multicollinearity avoided?
I System of equations	*Necessary and sufficient condition* $\mathbf{\Gamma}$ is of full rank, i.e., $\boxed{\text{Rank } \mathbf{\Gamma} = Q}$	(In the absence of prior restrictions on the covariance of the error terms, or on the nonzero coefficients), the *necessary condition* is: Enough zero coefficients in the first equation; i.e., $\boxed{m_0 \geq q - 1}$ The *necessary and sufficient* condition is: $\boxed{\text{rank} \begin{bmatrix} \mathbf{\Gamma}_0 \\ \mathbf{B}_0 \end{bmatrix} = Q - 1}$ i.e., this matrix is of full rank.	*Necessary and Sufficient condition* Estimating covariance matrix [**S** in (18-29)] must be of full rank, i.e., $\boxed{\text{rank } \mathbf{S} = m + q - 1}$ This implies (a) no linear dependence between exogenous variables, included *and* excluded from first equation.[1] (b) no linear dependence between endogenous and exogenous variables included in the first equation.[2]
II Single equation model	Completeness and identification problems do not exist, provided of course that the equation is correctly specified as one endogenous variable as a function of several exogenous variables.		(a) and (b) above reduce to the single condition that there be no linear dependence among the exogenous variables in the equation.

[1] If the equation is over identified, some linear dependence between the exogenous variables (instruments) is allowed, since there is a surplus of instrumental variables.

[2] Except the endogenous variable determined by this equation, on the left-hand side.

1. First, the model must be mathematically complete. If this requirement is not met, then the model provides no solution for the endogenous variables, that is, the model cannot tell us how changes in exogenous variables influence endogenous variables; hence it is not an interesting economic model. Therefore, throughout this chapter we have tacitly assumed that this completeness condition was met.

2. The second requirement is identification; this also is an algebraic condition that should be established prior to any examination of statistical evidence. If this condition is not met, then there is no hope of estimating a specific equation, since there will be no way of knowing whether we are estimating this equation or some bogus combination of equations in the model. The condition

$$\text{rank}\begin{bmatrix}\mathbf{\Gamma}_0\\ \mathbf{B}_0\end{bmatrix} = Q - 1 \qquad \text{(18-12) repeated}$$

is the necessary and sufficient condition for identification, when the only prior knowledge is that certain variables have a zero coefficient.

3. Finally, in the exactly identified case, estimation of the parameters of a given equation requires that there be no statistical problem of multicollinearity among the relevant observed variables.

For emphasis we reiterate that the problems of mathematical completeness and identification relate only to the parameters to be estimated, and are problems that must be disposed of prior to any estimation. On the other hand, the problem of multicollinearity involves the observed variables (rather than the parameters) and, therefore, does not arise until the actual estimation is undertaken.

To summarize the identification issue as simply as possible, let us return to the order condition (18-18) relating the number of excluded exogeneous variables (m_0) to the number of included endogeneous variables (q). We distinguish several cases:

(a) If $m_0 < q - 1$, the equation is unidentified (also called "under identified")

(b) If the equation is identified, we distinguish two subcases:

(i) If $m_0 = q - 1$, the equation is called "exactly identified."

(ii) If $m_0 > q - 1$, the equation is called "over identified," because there are more instrumental variables available than is absolutely necessary. Thus, a statistical problem occurs as to how to use them all effectively. Some solutions are given in Chapter 19.

chapter 19

Single Equation Estimation (An Extension of Chapter 9)

19-1 INTRODUCTION

Certain sections of this chapter are starred, since they may be more difficult, and may be omitted. However, students who like geometry will find in these starred sections the motivation for the austere algebraic arguments in the other sections.

This chapter describes methods to estimate the parameters of a single over identified equation within a simultaneous system. (Recall that if an equation is unidentified, it cannot be estimated. If it is exactly identified, it can be estimated without difficulty using the exogenous variables as instrumental variables, or equivalently using ILS.) Without loss of generality, we place the single equation of interest first. The other equations now matter only insofar as they specify the other exogenous variables.

Consider, for example, the estimation of the first equation in the following simple system,

$$y_1 = \gamma_1 y_2 + e_1 \tag{19-1}$$

$$y_2 = \gamma_2 y_1 + \beta_1 x_1 + \beta_2 x_2 + e_2 \tag{19-2}$$

where

$$y_i = \text{endogenous variables}$$

$$x_i = \text{exogenous variables}$$

$$e_i = \text{errors}$$

To emphasize that the importance of the second equation is the exogenous variables that it specifies, we could write the system as

$$y_1 = \gamma_1 y_2 + e_1 \tag{19-3}$$

$$x_1, x_2 \text{ are the exogenous variables in the system} \tag{19-4}$$

We note that the subscripts on γ and e could be omitted in (19-3), since this is the only equation that will be considered henceforth. We further realize that for each variable, for example either of the y's, there is a column of observed values $\mathbf{y} = (y_1, y_2, \ldots y_t \ldots y_n)'$, often a time series. Thus, we finally write the system as

$$\mathbf{y}_1 = \gamma \mathbf{y}_2 + \mathbf{e} \tag{19-5}$$

$$\mathbf{x}_1 \text{ and } \mathbf{x}_2 \text{ are the exogenous variables in the system} \tag{19-6}$$

We assume as usual that every exogenous variable x is uncorrelated with e, so that the conditions in Chapter 17 for using x as an instrumental variable are satisfied. This means the *population* correlation of x and e is zero. The sample correlation, of course, will likely be slightly different from zero, because of sampling fluctuation; yet the sample correlation will be zero on the average, and in an infinite sample.

In fact, for our instrumental variables we can use *any* variables that are uncorrelated with e, including sometimes the lagged endogenous variables as well as the exogenous variables; these variables altogether constitute the "predetermined" variables.

19-2 TWO-STAGE LEAST SQUARES (2SLS)

*(a) Geometry

We shall show geometrically, in the simple system (19-5) and (19-6), that the two stages of 2SLS are:

1. Selection of the best instrumental variable.
2. The application of this IV.

1. Equation (19-5) is over identified, since there are two extra exogenous variables to use as instrumental variables, but only one is needed to estimate γ. It may be estimated by selecting either $\mathbf{x}_1$ or $\mathbf{x}_2$ as an instrumental variable and disregarding the other. This alternative is shown in Figure 19-1. On the one hand, the use of $\mathbf{x}_1$ as an instrumental variable (shown by shading) involves the projection[1] of the observed vectors $\mathbf{y}_1$ and $\mathbf{y}_2$ onto $\mathbf{x}_1$—at A and B. As in Chapter 17, the estimator is just the ratio of distances along this instrumental variable, that is,

$$\hat{\gamma} = \frac{0A}{0B} \tag{19-7}$$

On the other hand, use of $\mathbf{x}_2$ as an instrumental variable involves the projection

[1] From now on, to simplify, "projection" is used to designate "$\perp$ projection," unless stated otherwise.

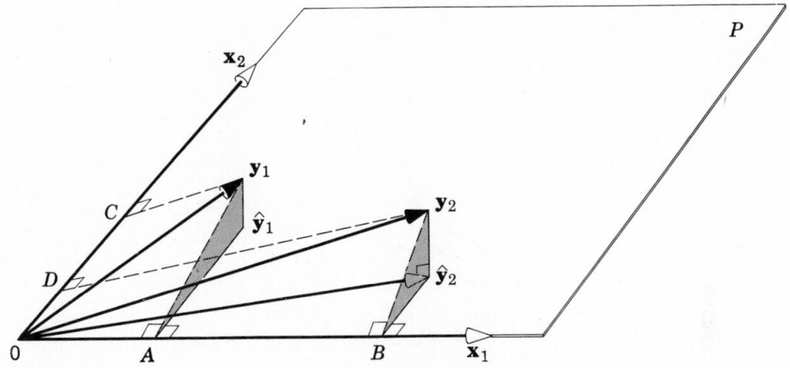

FIG. 19-1 How alternative instrumental variables can be used to estimate γ in (19-5).

of $\mathbf{y}_1$ and $\mathbf{y}_2$ onto $\mathbf{x}_2$; this yields a different estimator:

$$\hat{\gamma} = \frac{0C}{0D} \tag{19-8}$$

Since we assumed the error term $\mathbf{e}$ is perpendicular (on the average) to both $\mathbf{x}_1$ and $\mathbf{x}_2$, either of the above estimates is consistent. There is one other important observation: $\mathbf{x}_1$ and $\mathbf{x}_2$ generate a whole plane P of vectors perpendicular to $\mathbf{e}$. Hence, we could have used *any vector in P* as an instrumental variable.

If we had to choose between the two estimates (19-7) and (19-8), it would be reasonable to select the former (using $\mathbf{x}_1$ as the instrumental variable), since $\mathbf{y}_2$ is more correlated to $\mathbf{x}_1$ than to $\mathbf{x}_2$. (The desirability of a high correlation between $\mathbf{y}_2$ and the instrumental variable has already been established in Chapter 7.) Now it is immediately evident that we can find an even better instrumental variable than $\mathbf{x}_1$—namely the vector in P closest to $\mathbf{y}_2$. This is, of course $\hat{\mathbf{y}}_2$, the projection (i.e., least squares fit) of $\mathbf{y}_2$ onto P. This regression of $\mathbf{y}_2$ on the exogenous variables $\mathbf{x}_1$ and $\mathbf{x}_2$ is the first step in the two-stage procedure; it involves selecting as the new instrumental variable that linear combination of the original instrumental variables that best fits $\mathbf{y}_2$. In selecting a better instrumental variable, we also eliminate our "over" supply of instrumental variables.

2. The second stage, shown in Figure 19-2, is to apply this instrument $\hat{\mathbf{y}}_2$ to the equation (19-5) to be estimated. Thus, we obtain $\hat{\gamma}$ as the ratio of distances along the instrumental variable when $\mathbf{y}_1$ and $\mathbf{y}_2$ are projected onto $\hat{\mathbf{y}}_2$.

We shall now prove that the IV approach given above coincides with the 2SLS of Chapter 9-1 ($\hat{\mathbf{y}}_2$ substituted into (19-5), followed by OLS). We first write out the IV solution $\hat{\gamma}$ explicitly: in the notation of (17-8), when we

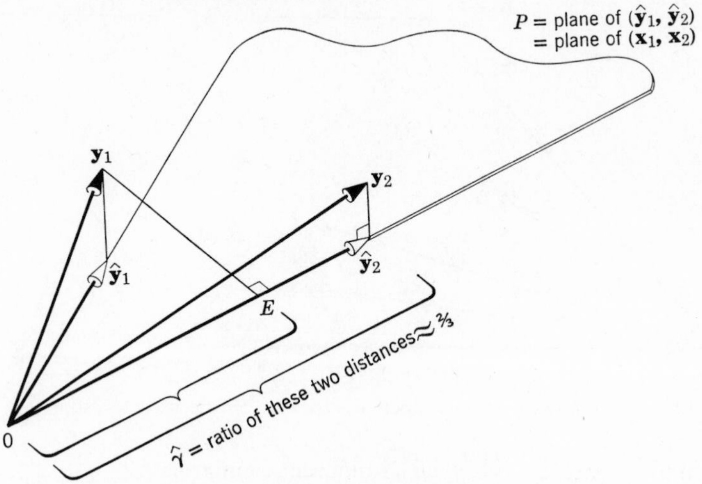

FIG. 19-2 2SLS estimate of γ in equation (19-5).

use $\hat{\mathbf{y}}_2$ as an instrumental variable on (19-5),

$$\hat{\mathbf{y}}_2 \cdot \mathbf{y}_1 = \gamma \hat{\mathbf{y}}_2 \cdot \mathbf{y}_2 + \hat{\mathbf{y}}_2 \cdot \mathbf{e} \tag{19-9}$$

which yields the estimator

$$\hat{\gamma} = \frac{\hat{\mathbf{y}}_2 \cdot \mathbf{y}_1}{\hat{\mathbf{y}}_2 \cdot \mathbf{y}_2} \tag{19-10}$$

But it may be seen geometrically[2] that

$$\hat{\mathbf{y}}_2 \cdot \mathbf{y}_2 = \hat{\mathbf{y}}_2 \cdot \hat{\mathbf{y}}_2 \tag{19-11}$$

2

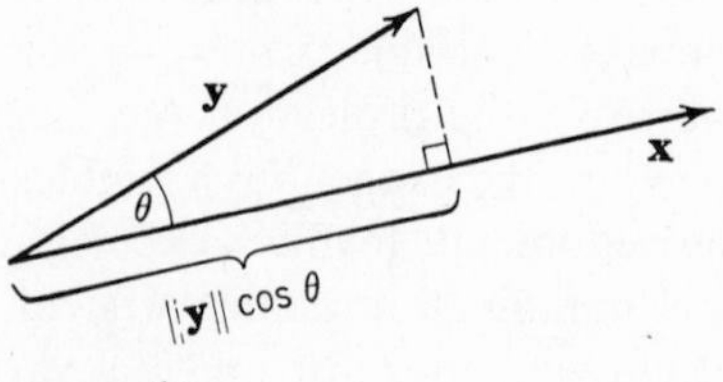

From (15-32), for any two vectors $\mathbf{x}$ and $\mathbf{y}$,

$$\begin{aligned} \mathbf{x} \cdot \mathbf{y} &= \|\mathbf{x}\| \, (\|\mathbf{y}\| \cos\theta) \\ &= (\text{length of } \mathbf{x}) \, (\text{length of projection of } \mathbf{y} \text{ on } \mathbf{x}). \end{aligned}$$

This is a very useful interpretation of the dot product. If we put $\mathbf{y}_2$ in the role of $\mathbf{y}$, and $\hat{\mathbf{y}}_2$ in the role of $\mathbf{x}$, we obtain

$$\begin{aligned} \hat{\mathbf{y}}_2 \cdot \mathbf{y}_2 &= (\text{length of } \hat{\mathbf{y}}_2) \, (\text{length of projection of } \mathbf{y}_2 \text{ on } \hat{\mathbf{y}}_2) \\ &= (\text{length of } \hat{\mathbf{y}}_2) \, (\text{length of } \hat{\mathbf{y}}_2) \\ &= \|\hat{\mathbf{y}}_2\|^2 \\ &= \hat{\mathbf{y}}_2 \cdot \hat{\mathbf{y}}_2 \end{aligned} \qquad \text{(19-11) proved}$$

When this is substituted into the denominator of (19-10)

$$\hat{\gamma} = \frac{\hat{\mathbf{y}}_2 \cdot \mathbf{y}_1}{\hat{\mathbf{y}}_2 \cdot \hat{\mathbf{y}}_2} \tag{19-12}$$

which is the OLS coefficient of regression of $\mathbf{y}_1$ on $\hat{\mathbf{y}}_2$. $\hat{\gamma}$ is, therefore, the 2SLS estimate of Chapter 9-1.

As a second example, we change (19-5) slightly by introducing a third exogeneous variable $\mathbf{x}_3$ into the first equation, obtaining

$$\mathbf{y}_1 = \gamma \mathbf{y}_2 + \beta_3 \mathbf{x}_3 + \mathbf{e} \tag{19-13}$$

$\mathbf{x}_1$, $\mathbf{x}_2$, and $\mathbf{x}_3$ are the exogenous variables in the system.

Except for notation, this is exactly the supply-demand system of (9-2) and (9-1) of Chapter 9.

In the first stage, we fit $\mathbf{y}_2$ to the ($\mathbf{x}_1$, $\mathbf{x}_2$, $\mathbf{x}_3$) subspace generated by all the exogenous variables in the system regardless of whether or not they appear in the equation to be estimated,[3] obtaining the instrumental variable $\hat{\mathbf{y}}_2$. In the second stage, $\hat{\mathbf{y}}_2$, along with $\mathbf{x}_3$, are used as instrumental variables on (19-13), to obtain estimates of γ and β_3.

In part (b) we shall prove in general that this IV approach coincides with the 2SLS described in Chapter 9-1.

(b) Algebraic Generalization

To generalize (19-13), we shall first make some notational changes. Remembering that there is a vector of n observations for each variable, we let:

(19-14)

$\mathbf{y}$ = the endogenous variable on the left-hand side (which is determined by the first equation, and was formerly denoted in (19-13) by $\mathbf{y}_1$).

$\mathbf{Y}_1$ = the other endogenous variables in the first equation, on the right-hand side (formerly a single variable denoted by $\mathbf{y}_2$).

$\mathbf{X}_1$ = the exogenous variables included in the first equation (formerly a single variable denoted by $\mathbf{x}_3$).

$\mathbf{X}_1^*$ = the exogenous variables in the system that are excluded from the first equation (formerly [$\mathbf{x}_1$, $\mathbf{x}_2$]). Thus $\mathbf{X} \triangleq [\mathbf{X}_1, \mathbf{X}_1^*]$ = all the exogenous variables in the whole system of equations.

[3] The student may wonder why $\mathbf{x}_3$ is used in the first stage, since it also appears later in the second stage. A simple answer is: because it is required in order to fit an adequate proxy

(cont'd)

Then the generalization of (19-13) may be written:

$$\mathbf{y} = \mathbf{Y}_1\boldsymbol{\gamma}_1 + \mathbf{X}_1\boldsymbol{\beta}_1 + \mathbf{e} \tag{19-15}$$

which may alternatively be written in partitioned matrix notation as

$$\mathbf{y} = [\mathbf{Y}_1, \mathbf{X}_1]\begin{bmatrix}\boldsymbol{\gamma}_1 \\ \boldsymbol{\beta}_1\end{bmatrix} + \mathbf{e} \tag{19-16}$$

The stages of 2SLS, as described in Chapter 9-1, are:

Stage 1. Regress each variable in $\mathbf{Y}_1$ on $\mathbf{X}$ (all the exogenous variables in the system). We let the theoretical relation be denoted

$$\mathbf{Y}_1 = \mathbf{X}\boldsymbol{\Pi}_1 + \mathbf{V}_1 \tag{19-17}$$

like (18-3)

Note that since we are fitting a *set* of variables $\mathbf{Y}_1$, we have a *matrix* of coefficients $\boldsymbol{\Pi}_1$. Then the OLS estimator is

$$\hat{\mathbf{Y}}_1 = \mathbf{X}\hat{\boldsymbol{\Pi}}_1 \tag{19-18a}$$

where

$$\hat{\boldsymbol{\Pi}}_1 = (\mathbf{X}'\mathbf{X})^{-1}\mathbf{X}'\mathbf{Y}_1 \tag{19-18b}$$

Stage 2. Substituting this $\hat{\mathbf{Y}}_1$ for $\mathbf{Y}_1$ in (19-16), we have

$$\mathbf{y} = [\hat{\mathbf{Y}}_1, \mathbf{X}_1]\begin{bmatrix}\boldsymbol{\gamma}_1 \\ \boldsymbol{\beta}_1\end{bmatrix} + \mathbf{e}^* \tag{19-19}$$

We now apply OLS to this equation[4], obtaining

2SLS solution:

$$\begin{bmatrix}\hat{\boldsymbol{\gamma}}_1 \\ \hat{\boldsymbol{\beta}}_1\end{bmatrix} = ([\hat{\mathbf{Y}}_1, \mathbf{X}_1]'[\hat{\mathbf{Y}}_1, \mathbf{X}_1])^{-1}[\hat{\mathbf{Y}}_1, \mathbf{X}_1]'\mathbf{y} \tag{19-20}$$

which is a generalization of (19-12).

---

for $\mathbf{y}_2$. Elaborating on this idea, we realize that in the reduced form, $\mathbf{y}_2$ will be a linear combination of *all* the x's, plus an error term. The first stage of 2SLS yields a consistent estimate of this linear combination.

Another viewpoint may be useful. If, in the first stage, we regress all the variables on the right side of the equation (both $\mathbf{y}_2$ and $\mathbf{x}_3$) on all the exogenous variables, then we obtain all the instrumental variables we need for the second stage: $\hat{\mathbf{y}}_2$, and $\hat{\mathbf{x}}_3 = \mathbf{x}_3$ itself.

[4] Noting, of course, that the $[\hat{\mathbf{Y}}_1, \mathbf{X}_1]$ and $\begin{bmatrix}\boldsymbol{\gamma}_1 \\ \boldsymbol{\beta}_1\end{bmatrix}$ in (19-19) correspond to the $\mathbf{X}$ and $\boldsymbol{\beta}$ in (13-24).

We also note in (19-19) that $\mathbf{e}^*$ is the error term $\mathbf{e}$ adjusted for the substitution of $\hat{\mathbf{Y}}_1$ for $\mathbf{Y}_1$.

We shall now prove its consistency by showing that it is equivalent to using the instruments $[\hat{\mathbf{Y}}_1, \mathbf{X}_1]$ on (19-16), which would yield

$$[\hat{\mathbf{Y}}_1, \mathbf{X}_1]'\mathbf{y} = [\hat{\mathbf{Y}}_1, \mathbf{X}_1]'[\mathbf{Y}_1, \mathbf{X}_1]\begin{bmatrix} \hat{\boldsymbol{\gamma}}_1 \\ \hat{\boldsymbol{\beta}}_1 \end{bmatrix} \tag{19-21}$$

which is a generalization of (19-9). When solved by matrix inversion, it yields

IV solution, using $\hat{\mathbf{Y}}_1$ and $\mathbf{X}_1$ as instrumental variables:

$$\begin{bmatrix} \hat{\boldsymbol{\gamma}}_1 \\ \hat{\boldsymbol{\beta}}_1 \end{bmatrix} = ([\hat{\mathbf{Y}}_1, \mathbf{X}_1]'[\mathbf{Y}_1, \mathbf{X}_1])^{-1}[\hat{\mathbf{Y}}_1, \mathbf{X}_1]'\mathbf{y} \tag{19-22}$$

which is a generalization of (19-10). We note that (19-22) corresponds exactly to (19-20), except for a single appearance of $\mathbf{Y}_1$ in place of $\hat{\mathbf{Y}}_1$. Equivalence of these two procedures thus hinges on showing that

$$[\hat{\mathbf{Y}}_1, \mathbf{X}_1]'[\hat{\mathbf{Y}}_1, \mathbf{X}_1] = [\hat{\mathbf{Y}}_1, \mathbf{X}_1]'[\mathbf{Y}_1, \mathbf{X}_1] \tag{19-23}$$

that is, that

$$\hat{\mathbf{Y}}_1'\hat{\mathbf{Y}}_1 = \hat{\mathbf{Y}}_1'\mathbf{Y}_1 \tag{19-24}$$

which is a generalization of (19-11), and

$$\mathbf{X}_1'\hat{\mathbf{Y}}_1 = \mathbf{X}_1'\mathbf{Y}_1 \tag{19-25}$$

To establish these, we return to our first stage solution for $\hat{\mathbf{Y}}_1$; from (19-18*a*) and (19-18*b*)

$$\hat{\mathbf{Y}}_1 = \mathbf{X}(\mathbf{X}'\mathbf{X})^{-1}\mathbf{X}'\mathbf{Y}_1 \tag{19-26}$$

Thus the left side of (19-24) can be written

$$\hat{\mathbf{Y}}_1'\hat{\mathbf{Y}}_1 = \{\mathbf{Y}_1'\mathbf{X}(\mathbf{X}'\mathbf{X})^{-1}\mathbf{X}'\}\,\{\mathbf{X}(\mathbf{X}'\mathbf{X})^{-1}\mathbf{X}'\mathbf{Y}_1\} \tag{19-27}$$

$$= \mathbf{Y}_1'\mathbf{X}(\mathbf{X}'\mathbf{X})^{-1}\mathbf{X}'\mathbf{Y}_1 \tag{19-28}$$

Again noting (19-26):

$$= \hat{\mathbf{Y}}_1'\mathbf{Y}_1 \qquad \text{(19-24) proved}$$

To establish (19-25), we note from (19-26) that

$$\mathbf{X}'\hat{\mathbf{Y}}_1 = \mathbf{X}'\{\mathbf{X}(\mathbf{X}'\mathbf{X})^{-1}\mathbf{X}'\mathbf{Y}_1\} \tag{19-29}$$

$$= \mathbf{X}'\mathbf{Y}_1 \tag{19-30}$$

From (19-14) we substitute for $\mathbf{X}$

$$[\mathbf{X}_1, \mathbf{X}_1^*]'\,\hat{\mathbf{Y}}_1 = [\mathbf{X}_1, \mathbf{X}_1^*]'\mathbf{Y}_1 \tag{19-31}$$

whose first component is

$$\mathbf{X}_1'\hat{\mathbf{Y}}_1 = \mathbf{X}_1'\mathbf{Y}_1 \qquad \text{(19-25) proved}$$

Thus, the 2SLS solution in (19-20) is proven equivalent to the IV solution in (19-22). The final question is: Are $[\hat{\mathbf{Y}}_1, \mathbf{X}_1]$ bona fide instrumental variables to use on (19-16), that is, do they satisfy the conditions of relevancy, and uncorrelation with the error?

Since the instrumental variables are the fitted values of the right-hand variables in (19-16), the condition of relevancy (17-12) is satisfied. The other condition (17-11) is that the instrumental variables be uncorrelated[5] with the error. Since, by assumption, $\mathbf{X}_1$ satisfies this requirement, we need only ensure that $\hat{\mathbf{Y}}_1$ also qualifies, that is, we must prove

$$\frac{1}{n}\hat{\mathbf{Y}}_1'\mathbf{e} \xrightarrow{p} \mathbf{0} \qquad \text{(19-32)}$$

To prove this, we first substitute for $\hat{\mathbf{Y}}_1'$ as given by (19-18*a*):

$$\begin{aligned} \frac{1}{n}\hat{\mathbf{Y}}_1'\mathbf{e} &= \frac{1}{n}(\mathbf{X}\hat{\mathbf{\Pi}}_1)'\mathbf{e} \\ &= \hat{\mathbf{\Pi}}_1'\left(\frac{1}{n}\mathbf{X}'\mathbf{e}\right) \end{aligned} \qquad \text{(19-33)}$$

Since the exogenous variables are uncorrelated with the error

$$\frac{1}{n}\mathbf{X}'\mathbf{e} \xrightarrow{p} \mathbf{0} \qquad \text{(19-34)}$$

and the OLS estimate (19-18*b*) from the first stage is consistent, that is,

$$\hat{\mathbf{\Pi}}_1 \xrightarrow{p} \mathbf{\Pi}_1 \qquad \text{(19-35)}$$

Substituting (19-35) and (19-34) into (19-33)

$$\frac{1}{n}\hat{\mathbf{Y}}_1\mathbf{e} \xrightarrow{p} \mathbf{\Pi}_1'\,\mathbf{0} = \mathbf{0} \qquad \text{(19-32) proved}$$

Thus $[\hat{\mathbf{Y}}_1, \mathbf{X}_1]$ is established as a bona fide set of instrumental variables, and it follows that 2SLS can be regarded as a special application of IV.

---

[5] We remind the reader that *asymptotic* uncorrelation is understood throughout this chapter, even when the word "asymptotic" is omitted.

*19-3 THE GEOMETRY OF LEAST WEIGHTED VARIANCE (LWV)

(a) Introduction

To illustrate the basic ideas as easily as possible, we return to the simple model of the introduction

$$\mathbf{y}_1 = \gamma \mathbf{y}_2 + \mathbf{e} \tag{19-37}$$

(19-5) repeated

$\mathbf{x}_1$ and $\mathbf{x}_2$ are the exogenous variables in the system (19-38)

(19-6) repeated

The 2SLS solution in Figure 19-2 is reproduced in Figure 19-3. Note how the projection of $\mathbf{y}_1$ onto $\hat{\mathbf{y}}_2$ (at E) is equivalent to

1. regressing $\mathbf{y}_1$ onto P, obtaining $\hat{\mathbf{y}}_1$; then
2. regressing $\hat{\mathbf{y}}_1$ onto $\hat{\mathbf{y}}_2$ (19-39)

We now ask: Suppose we had expressed the first equation differently, with $\mathbf{y}_2$ rather than $\mathbf{y}_1$ on the left-hand side? Then

$$\mathbf{y}_2 = \left(\frac{1}{\gamma}\right)\mathbf{y}_1 + \left(\frac{-1}{\gamma}\right)\mathbf{e}$$

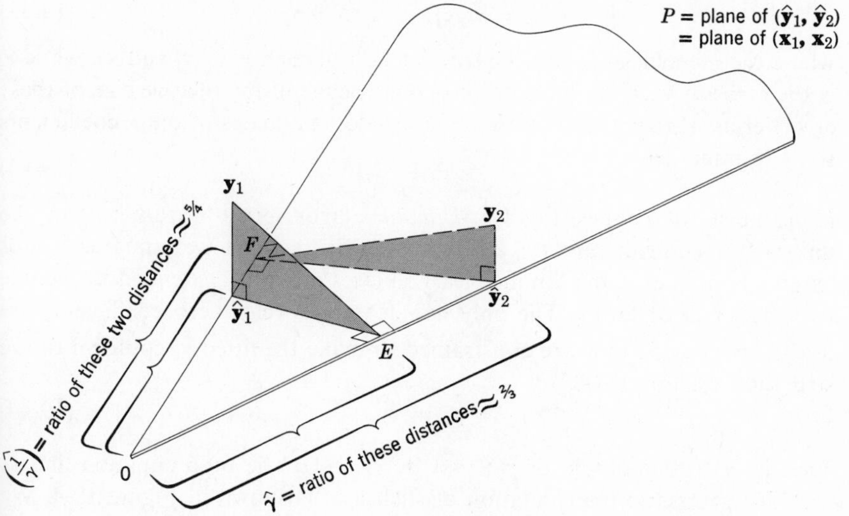

FIG. 19-3 Alternative 2SLS solutions.

that is,

$$\mathbf{y}_2 = \left(\frac{1}{\gamma}\right)\mathbf{y}_1 + \mathbf{u} \tag{19-40}$$

Of course, just as in Problem 5-5, we find that although $(1/\gamma)$ is the reciprocal of γ, the estimator $(\widehat{1/\gamma})$ need not be the reciprocal of $\hat{\gamma}$. This is shown in Figure 19-3. Whereas γ in (19-37) is estimated by 2SLS by projecting $\mathbf{y}_1$ onto $\hat{\mathbf{y}}_2$, $(1/\gamma)$ in (19-40) is estimated by projecting $\mathbf{y}_2$ onto $\hat{\mathbf{y}}_1$. In the special case shown in the diagram, the resulting $\hat{\gamma}$ is about 2/3; but $(\widehat{1/\gamma})$ is about 5/4, implying an estimate of γ of 4/5. Which estimate is preferable? Or would some other estimate somewhere between (e.g., 3/4) be better?

We recognize this to be similar to the problem of errors in variables, first discussed in Chapter 5; those conclusions may now be translated into this more complicated case. Thus, if $\mathbf{y}_1$ is subject to error, but $\mathbf{y}_2$ is not, then the equation should be written in the form (19-37) and we should regress $\mathbf{y}_1$ on $\hat{\mathbf{y}}_2$. On the other hand, if only $\mathbf{y}_2$ is subject to error, then (19-40) is the appropriate form, and we should regress $\mathbf{y}_2$ on $\hat{\mathbf{y}}_1$. But if both $\mathbf{y}_1$ and $\mathbf{y}_2$ are subject to error, we should seek an estimate somewhere between.

(b) Minimizing the Variances of Several Estimated Errors

To resolve this dilemma, we cast the system (19-37) and (19-38) into reduced form

$$\mathbf{y}_1 = \pi_{11}\mathbf{x}_1 + \pi_{12}\mathbf{x}_2 + \mathbf{v}_1 \tag{19-41}$$

$$\mathbf{y}_2 = \pi_{21}\mathbf{x}_1 + \pi_{22}\mathbf{x}_2 + \mathbf{v}_2 \tag{19-42}$$

where the π coefficients give the true relation of each $\mathbf{y}_i$ to $\mathbf{x}_1$ and $\mathbf{x}_2$, while $\mathbf{v}_i$ is the error in $\mathbf{y}_i$. If we have no prior knowledge of the relative size of these error terms, it might seem reasonable to select estimates of the π coefficients so as to minimize

$$\|\hat{\mathbf{v}}_1\|^2 + \|\hat{\mathbf{v}}_2\|^2 \tag{19-43}$$

(This must, of course, involve *estimated* error terms $\hat{\mathbf{v}}_i$ rather than the unknown true error terms $\mathbf{v}_i$.) Minimizing this sum of two squared vector lengths is similar to the familiar least squares criterion, extended to include two sets of error terms. The only new feature is that the π coefficients are not freely chosen; they are constrained to make the fitted $\hat{\hat{\mathbf{y}}}_i$ conform to the structural relation (19-37)

$$\hat{\hat{\mathbf{y}}}_1 = \hat{\gamma}\hat{\hat{\mathbf{y}}}_2 \tag{19-44}$$

That is, $\hat{\hat{\mathbf{y}}}_1$ is a multiple of $\hat{\hat{\mathbf{y}}}_2$; that is, $\hat{\hat{\mathbf{y}}}_1$ and $\hat{\hat{\mathbf{y}}}_2$ lie on a common line $\hat{L}$.

The geometric interpretation of such a fit is shown in Figure 19-4. We consider all possible lines $\hat{L}$ in the plane P generated by $\mathbf{x}_1$ and $\mathbf{x}_2$ (or equally well by $\hat{\mathbf{y}}_1$ and $\hat{\mathbf{y}}_2$).

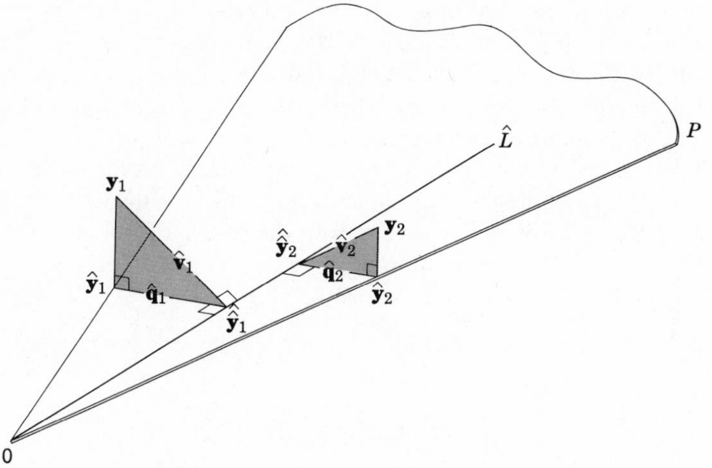

FIG. 19-4 Minimizing the estimated errors in the reduced form, subject to the constraint of the structural form.

The projection of the observed $\mathbf{y}_i$ onto $\hat{L}$ provides the estimate[6] $\hat{\hat{\mathbf{y}}}_i$. The estimated error $\hat{\mathbf{v}}_i$ is the difference between these observed and estimated vectors, $i = 1, 2$. We select the $\hat{L}$ that minimizes the sum of these squared lengths, as specified in (19-43). The estimate $\hat{\gamma}$ is, of course, the ratio of lengths along $\hat{L}$—specifically, the ratio of the lengths of $\hat{\hat{\mathbf{y}}}_1$ and $\hat{\hat{\mathbf{y}}}_2$. As we had hoped, this does yield $\hat{\gamma}$ between the pair of 2SLS estimates (i.e., between 2/3 and 4/5).

Because of the form of the equation (19-37), we had to restrict the estimate $\hat{\hat{\mathbf{y}}}_1$ to be a multiple of $\hat{\hat{\mathbf{y}}}_2$; thus both estimates fall on $\hat{L}$, simplifying the analysis. But if (19-37) included another exogenous variable $\mathbf{x}_3$ then $\hat{\hat{\mathbf{y}}}_1$ and $\hat{\hat{\mathbf{y}}}_2$ would have to be selected in a more complicated way. But the principle of minimizing (19-43) would remain the same.[7]

---

[6] The vector $\hat{\hat{\mathbf{y}}}_1$ is denoted with two "hats" to indicate that it has two contraints: (1) it must be a linear combination of the $\mathbf{x}_j$, and (2) it must be a linear combination (multiple) of $\hat{\hat{\mathbf{y}}}_2$. Geometrically, in Figure 19-4 this means that $\hat{\hat{\mathbf{y}}}_1$ must not only lie in P, but on $\hat{L}$ as well.

[7] Note that minimizing (19-43) is equivalent to minimizing

$$\|\hat{\mathbf{q}}_1\|^2 + \|\hat{\mathbf{q}}_2\|^2 \tag{19-45}$$

where $\hat{\mathbf{q}}_i$ in Figure 19-4 is the projection of $\mathbf{v}_i$ onto P.

Proof. Because the critical two triangles in Figure 19-4 have right angles, minimizing (19-43) is equivalent to minimizing

$$\|\hat{\mathbf{q}}_1\|^2 + \|\mathbf{y}_1 - \hat{\mathbf{y}}_1\|^2 + \|\hat{\mathbf{q}}_2\|^2 + \|\mathbf{y}_2 - \hat{\mathbf{y}}_2\|^2 \tag{19-46}$$

But the second and fourth terms in this equation remain constant for all possible $\hat{L}$. Therefore, minimizing (19-46) is equivalent to minimizing (19-45).

Finally, before leaving Figure 19-4, we emphasize that $\hat{\hat{\mathbf{y}}}_1$ and $\hat{\hat{\mathbf{y}}}_2$ represent the restricted fit of $\mathbf{y}_1$ and $\mathbf{y}_2$ onto the $(\mathbf{x}_1, \mathbf{x}_2)$ subspace, that is, the least squares fit of the reduced form (19-41) and (19-42) *restricted* to satisfy the structural relation (19-44). On the other hand, $\hat{\mathbf{y}}_1$ and $\hat{\mathbf{y}}_2$ represent the least squares fit of the reduced form that is free and *unrestricted.*

We now pause to consider the underlying assumptions of this model. In Figure 19-5 we show the parent populations from which the observed $\mathbf{y}_1$ and $\mathbf{y}_2$ are assumed to be drawn. $\mathbf{x}_1$ and $\mathbf{x}_2$ and the reduced form parameters π_{ij} are fixed. $\mathbf{v}_1$ is a linear combination of the $\mathbf{e}$'s in the structural equations, so that $E(\mathbf{v}_1) = \mathbf{0}$. When we take expected values of (19-41), we therefore obtain

$$E(\mathbf{y}_1) = \pi_{11}\mathbf{x}_1 + \pi_{12}\mathbf{x}_2 \tag{19-47}$$

Similarly, from (19-42)

$$E(\mathbf{y}_2) = \pi_{21}\mathbf{x}_1 + \pi_{22}\mathbf{x}_2 \tag{19-48}$$

That is, $E(\mathbf{y}_1)$ and $E(\mathbf{y}_2)$ lie in the instrumental variable plane as shown in Figure 19-5. Moreover, taking expected values of the structural equation 19-37,

$$E(\mathbf{y}_1) = \gamma E(\mathbf{y}_2) \tag{19-49}$$

That is, $E(\mathbf{y}_1)$ and $E(\mathbf{y}_2)$ lie on the same line through the origin, designated L.

In Figure 19-5, individual observed $\mathbf{y}_1$ and $\mathbf{y}_2$ are also shown, differing from their expected values because of the errors $\mathbf{v}_1$ and $\mathbf{v}_2$. The distributions of $\mathbf{y}_1$ and $\mathbf{y}_2$ are shown schematically as the two spheres of concentration with equal size if we assume that the error terms ($\mathbf{v}_1$ and $\mathbf{v}_2$) have equal variance.

The statistician, of course, only knows the location of $\mathbf{y}_1$, $\mathbf{y}_2$, and the instrumental variable plane. He estimates L in Figure 19-5 with $\hat{L}$ in Figure

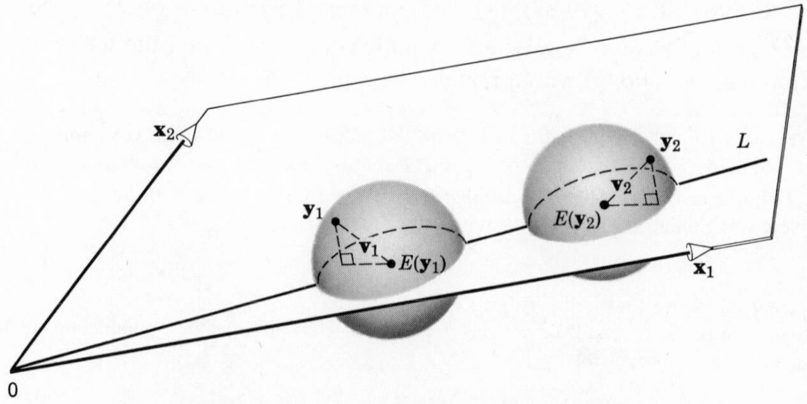

FIG. 19-5 Assumptions underlying Figure 19-4.

19-4. In the process, he estimates $\mathbf{v}_1$, $\mathbf{v}_2$, $E(\mathbf{y}_1)$ and $E(\mathbf{y}_2)$ with $\hat{\mathbf{v}}_1$, $\hat{\mathbf{v}}_2$, $\hat{\hat{\mathbf{y}}}_1$ and $\hat{\hat{\mathbf{y}}}_2$ respectively.[8]

To sum up, if we assume the variances of $\mathbf{v}_1$ and $\mathbf{v}_2$ are equal, the parent population is shown in Figure 19-5, with estimation shown in Figure 19-4. But if we assume $\mathbf{v}_2$ is nearly zero, then the true line L is near $\mathbf{y}_2$, and the 2SLS estimation, shown at E in Figure 19-3, would be more appropriate. Or if we assume instead that $\mathbf{v}_1$ is nearly zero, then the true line L is near $\mathbf{y}_1$, and the 2SLS estimation shown at F in Figure 19-3 would be more appropriate. It would seem desirable to avoid any arbitrary prior assumption about the relative size of $\mathbf{v}_1$ and $\mathbf{v}_2$. Instead, we shall *estimate* the relative size by observing how far $\mathbf{y}_1$ and $\mathbf{y}_2$ lie off the plane P, shown in Figure 19-6 as $\|\mathbf{w}_1\|$ and $\|\mathbf{w}_2\|$ respectively.

We thus arrive at the following criterion that generalizes (19-43). We shall choose the line $\hat{\hat{L}}$ (and with it $\hat{\hat{\mathbf{y}}}_1$, $\hat{\hat{\mathbf{y}}}_2$, and their ratio $\hat{\gamma}$) so as to minimize

$$\frac{\|\hat{\mathbf{v}}_1\|^2}{\|\mathbf{w}_1\|^2} + \frac{\|\hat{\mathbf{v}}_2\|^2}{\|\mathbf{w}_2\|^2} \tag{19-50}$$

We shall call this the criterion of *least weighted variance* (LWV). We must

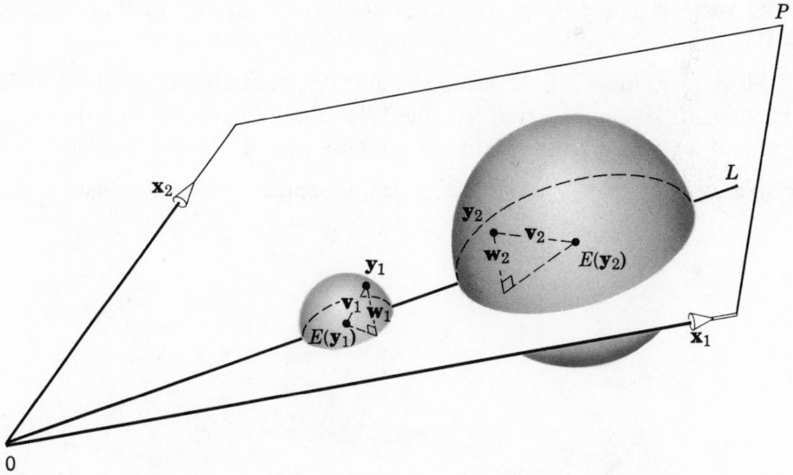

FIG. 19-6 Assumptions of least weighted variance (LWV) allowing errors of any relative size.

[8] We observe in passing that the assumption that $\mathbf{v}_1$ and $\mathbf{v}_2$ have the same variance does *not* generally lead to estimates $\mathbf{v}_1$ and $\hat{\mathbf{v}}_2$ that are equal. In fact minimizing (19-43) leads, in our example, to $\|\hat{\mathbf{v}}_1\| > \|\hat{\mathbf{v}}_2\|$. (This is similar to the result of chapter 2, that the assumed constant variance of the error in simple regression does not generally lead to estimated errors that are equal.)

examine how it solves the problems that motivated it. We note that when $\|\mathbf{w}_1\| = \|\mathbf{w}_2\|$, that is, when $\|\mathbf{v}_1\|$ seems about equal to $\|\mathbf{v}_2\|$, criterion (19-50) reduces to (19-43), as it should. When $\|\mathbf{w}_2\|$ is nearly zero, the second term of (19-50) becomes dominant. Then $\|\hat{\mathbf{v}}_2\|$ is minimized with little regard for $\|\hat{\mathbf{v}}_1\|$, so that the line $\hat{\hat{L}}$ is chosen below $\mathbf{y}_2$. Thus, the 2SLS solution is generated, as desired.

We note that LWV of (19-50) is very similar to the least weighted sum of squares of equation (6-5), which also arose out of heteroscedasticity assumptions. In both cases, our estimate is drawn toward the more reliable observation having less variance.

As shown in equation (19-45) of a previous footnote, minimizing (19-50) is equivalent to minimizing

$$\frac{\|\hat{\mathbf{q}}_1\|^2}{\|\mathbf{w}_1\|^2} + \frac{\|\hat{\mathbf{q}}_2\|^2}{\|\mathbf{w}_2\|^2} \tag{19-51}$$

The geometry is shown in Figure 19-7. The weights $\|\mathbf{w}_1\|$ and $\|\mathbf{w}_2\|$ are the observed distances of $\mathbf{y}_1$ and $\mathbf{y}_2$ from the instrumental variable plane, which provide the best indication of the relative size of the unknown $\|\mathbf{v}_1\|$ and $\|\mathbf{v}_2\|$. Once these fixed weights are found, $\hat{\hat{L}}$ is determined within the instrumental variable plane P, by selecting those vectors $\hat{\mathbf{q}}_1$ and $\hat{\mathbf{q}}_2$ that minimize (19-51).

Moreover, since $\hat{\hat{L}}$ is a vector in the instrumental variable plane, it is a bona fide instrumental variable. Thus, we obtain a consistent estimator $\hat{\hat{\gamma}}$, calculated as before from relative lengths measured along the instrumental variable $\hat{\hat{L}}$. Whereas $\hat{\mathbf{y}}_2$ was used in 2SLS because it was the instrumental

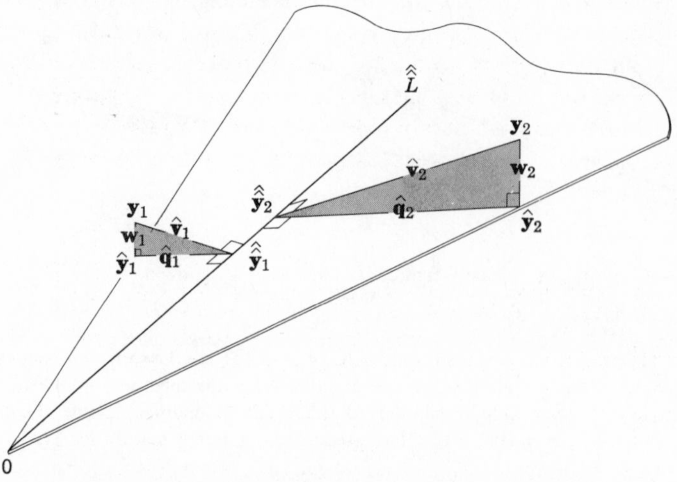

FIG. 19-7 Estimation, using least weighted variance (LWV).

variable closest to $\mathbf{y}_2$, we may regard $\hat{\hat{L}}$ in LWV as the instrumental variable closest, in some sense, to both $\mathbf{y}_1$ *and* $\mathbf{y}_2$. Otherwise our strategy remains the same: (1) find the appropriate instrumental variable; (2) use it. The next method we shall consider in Section 19-4 follows this same pattern, with L again being estimated closest to both $\mathbf{y}_1$ and $\mathbf{y}_2$, but in a somewhat different sense. But first, our progress in this chapter should be summarized.

(c) The Various Methods Compared

In Figure 19-8 we show how each method involves the selection of a different instrumental variable. (Since the specific solutions cannot be shown without hopelessly cluttering the diagram, we limit ourselves to the instrumental variable plane.)[9]

First, our single equation can be estimated using either $\mathbf{x}_1$ or $\mathbf{x}_2$ as an instrumental variable. By reviewing Figure 19-1, we can see the difficulties that arise. Using $\mathbf{x}_1$ as an instrumental variable yields the estimate

$$\hat{\gamma} = \frac{0A}{0B} \approx \frac{2}{5}$$

while $\mathbf{x}_2$ as an instrumental variable yields the quite different estimate

$$\frac{0C}{0D} \approx 2$$

Naive IV thus appears to be a very unstable estimating procedure, with the result very sensitive to the instrumental variable chosen. It is true that either estimator is consistent; in an infinite sample, $\hat{\mathbf{y}}_1$ and $\hat{\mathbf{y}}_2$ would both lie on the true line (L in Figure 19-5), and either instrumental variable would yield the same estimate. But in the small sample estimation in Figure 19-1, this is little comfort. Sample fluctuation has resulted in $\hat{\mathbf{y}}_1$ and $\hat{\mathbf{y}}_2$ lying off the true line. This, plus the fact that each instrumental variable is so far away from L, results in two widely differing estimates.

---

[9] Of course this instrumental variable plane is a fixed plane only while $\mathbf{x}_1$ and $\mathbf{x}_2$ are fixed. But since our instrumental variables are typically random variables, the instrumental variable plane takes on various random positions in space. Yet the geometry remains valid; whatever the position of the instrumental variable plane, the *conditional* distribution of $\mathbf{y}_1$ and $\mathbf{y}_2$ around it is validly shown in Figure 19-6. (This is similar to the argument of Chapter 2-11.)

Difficulties do arise, however, if there are errors in measuring the instrumental variables $\mathbf{x}_1$ and $\mathbf{x}_2$. Then the geometry no longer remains valid, and a whole new set of econometric problems is introduced. Throughout this book (except for Chapter 7-5), it is assumed that all instrumental variables are measured without error.

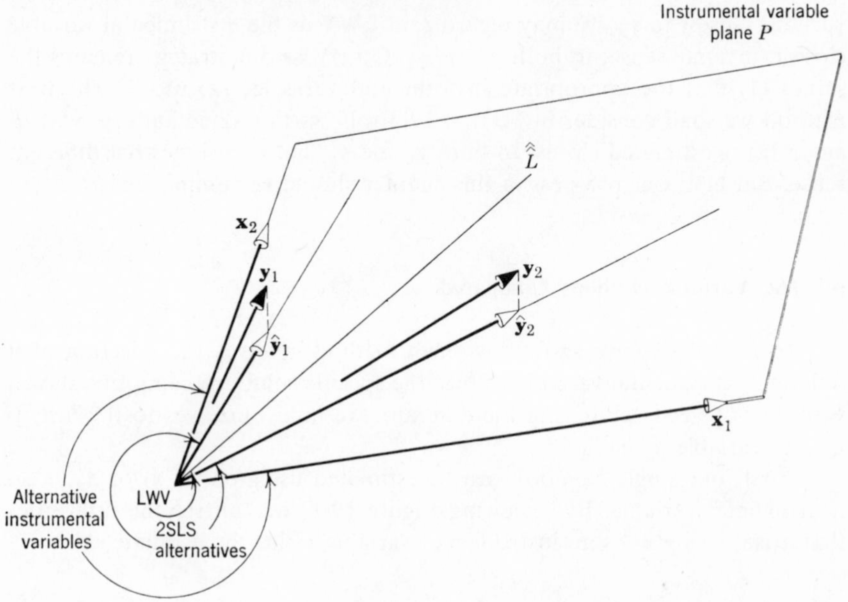

FIG. 19-8 Review of single equation solutions, defined on the instrumental variable subspace.

It also follows that although all the techniques we have discussed are consistent—they perform equally well in infinite samples—in small samples they do not. Therefore, rather than use either $\mathbf{x}_1$ or $\mathbf{x}_2$ alone, we prefer to combine them into a new instrumental variable. Specifically, either $\hat{\mathbf{y}}_1$ or $\hat{\mathbf{y}}_2$ are better (i.e., closer); in Figure 19-8, we show the pair of 2SLS estimators they generate.

Finally, LWV involves the selection of a unique instrument lying somewhere between.

19-4 LIMITED INFORMATION/LEAST GENERALIZED VARIANCE (LI/LGV); LIMITED INFORMATION/MAXIMUM LIKELIHOOD (LI/ML); LIMITED INFORMATION/LEAST VARIANCE RATIO (LI/LVR)

(a) Introduction

These three approaches all lead to exactly the same estimator (as proved in advanced texts). They share a common feature with LWV: we do not require a prior specification of whether $\mathbf{y}_1$ should be viewed as a function of $\mathbf{y}_2$, or $\mathbf{y}_2$ as a function of $\mathbf{y}_1$.

*(b) The Geometry of LI/LGV

We illustrate the first approach, LI/LGV, by considering the covariance matrix[10] of the estimated errors $\hat{\mathbf{v}}_1$ and $\hat{\mathbf{v}}_2$:

$$\hat{\mathbf{\Omega}} = \begin{bmatrix} \hat{\mathbf{v}}_1 \cdot \hat{\mathbf{v}}_1 & \hat{\mathbf{v}}_1 \cdot \hat{\mathbf{v}}_2 \\ \hat{\mathbf{v}}_2 \cdot \hat{\mathbf{v}}_1 & \hat{\mathbf{v}}_2 \cdot \hat{\mathbf{v}}_2 \end{bmatrix} \tag{19-52}$$

In LWV we minimized (19-43), which is recognized as the trace[11] of $\hat{\mathbf{\Omega}}$. On the other hand, LI/LGV which we now consider involves minimizing the determinant of $\hat{\mathbf{\Omega}}$, that is, minimizing

$$|\hat{\mathbf{\Omega}}| = \begin{vmatrix} \hat{\mathbf{v}}_1 \cdot \hat{\mathbf{v}}_1 & \hat{\mathbf{v}}_1 \cdot \hat{\mathbf{v}}_2 \\ \hat{\mathbf{v}}_2 \cdot \hat{\mathbf{v}}_1 & \hat{\mathbf{v}}_2 \cdot \hat{\mathbf{v}}_2 \end{vmatrix} = \tag{19-53}$$

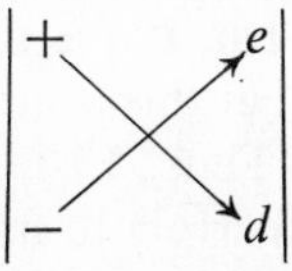

We might ask why anyone would want to minimize the determinant of $\hat{\mathbf{\Omega}}$ rather than its trace. The answer is that $|\hat{\mathbf{\Omega}}|$ takes account of the covariance as well as the variances of $\hat{v}_1$ and $\hat{v}_2$. The importance of this is shown in Figure 19-9, where we revert to a scatter diagram in which the axes refer to $\hat{v}_1$ and $\hat{v}_2$, rather than the n observations. We ask, "Would we prefer a fitting procedure that results in error pattern A, or error pattern B?" Our intuition tells us that pattern B might be preferred because it involves error spread over a smaller area.

Before proceeding, we note that the variances of the two *individual* errors are larger for B, since this scatter extends slightly farther in both the horizontal ($\hat{v}_2$) and vertical ($\hat{v}_1$) direction. Moreover, the covariance of $\hat{v}_1$ and $\hat{v}_2$ is also larger for B (in A the errors are uncorrelated, while in B they are highly correlated). In fact, it is the high covariance that tilts the ellipse and gives it smaller area.

Which estimation method would tell us to select B rather than A? If, as in LWV, we only minimize the variances of $\hat{v}_1$ and $\hat{v}_2$, we would select A with

[10] Except for the scalar divisor n. This constant can be ignored in the minimization procedures that will be discussed.

[11] This follows, since the trace is defined as the sum of the main diagonal elements, $\hat{\mathbf{v}}_1 \cdot \hat{\mathbf{v}}_1 + \hat{\mathbf{v}}_2 \cdot \hat{\mathbf{v}}_2 = \|\hat{\mathbf{v}}_1\|^2 + \|\hat{\mathbf{v}}_2\|^2$.

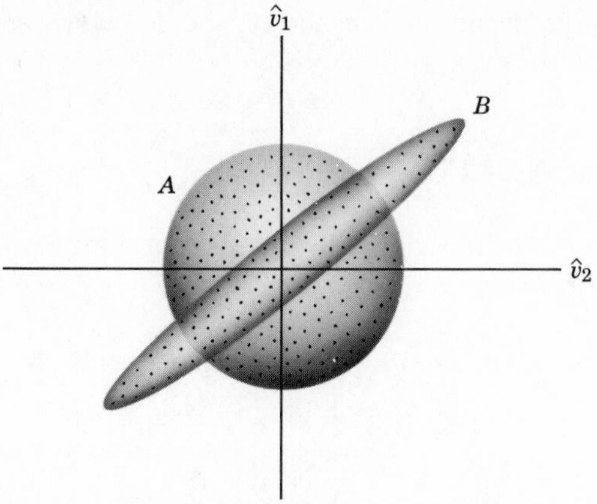

FIG. 19-9 Scatter diagram of alternative selections of $\hat{v}_1$ and $\hat{v}_2$. This is a scatter diagram in the variable space, rather than the observation space.

its smaller variances. But if, as in LI/LGV, we minimize the determinant of $\hat{\mathbf{\Omega}}$, we will select B. For in B it is true that the variances in the diagonal d in (19-53) are greater; but this is more than offset by the covariance terms in e that are subtracted. Thus, LI/LGV is a selection procedure that allows variances (of estimated error) to increase, provided this is more than offset by increased covariance. In conclusion, the idea is to select the error scatter in Figure 19-9 with the smallest area; and algebraically this is accomplished by minimizing $|\hat{\mathbf{\Omega}}|$.

This determinant is called the "generalized variance"; hence the name "least generalized variance." A possible solution that this criterion might yield is illustrated in Figure 19-10. The instrumental variable $\hat{\hat{\hat{L}}}$ is selected by choosing $\hat{\mathbf{v}}_1$ and $\hat{\mathbf{v}}_2$ to minimize $|\hat{\mathbf{\Omega}}|$; then, as before, we estimate $\hat{\gamma}$ from relative lengths along this instrumental variable; (in this example, $\hat{\gamma}$ is a little more than 1). Since we no longer minimize $\|\mathbf{v}_1\|^2$ and $\|\mathbf{v}_2\|^2$, these vectors are no longer selected perpendicular to $\hat{\hat{\hat{L}}}$.

Like LWV, LI/LGV may be regarded as a compromise between the two different 2SLS estimates; it is also similar in the sense that we fit $\mathbf{y}_1$ and $\mathbf{y}_2$ to the reduced form equations (19-41) and (19-42), while keeping in mind the restrictions imposed by the structural equation (19-37). LI/LGV differs from LWV only in using as its criterion of good fit the determinant rather than the weighted trace of $\hat{\mathbf{\Omega}}$. An advantage of LI/LGV is that it takes into account covariance[12] as well as variance terms; moreover, it provides a less restricted

[12] While LWV does not take account of the covariance of the errors $\mathbf{v}_1$ and $\mathbf{v}_2$ in the reduced form, it does reflect to some degree the covariance of the errors $\mathbf{e}_1$ and $\mathbf{e}_2$ in the original structure; this follows since each $\mathbf{v}_i$ depends on both $\mathbf{e}_1$ and $\mathbf{e}_2$.

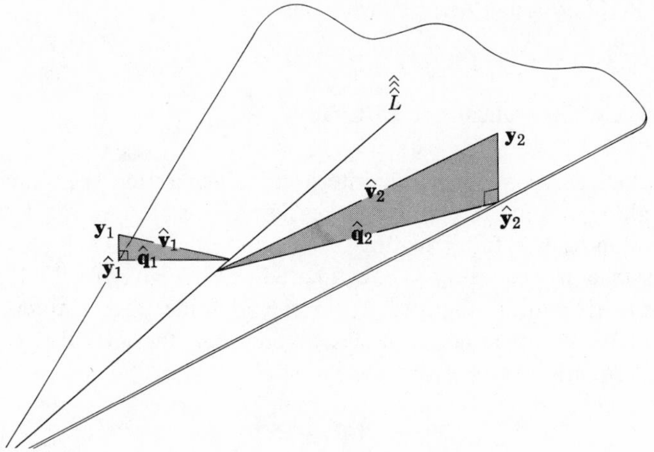

FIG. 19-10 Limited information/least generalized variance (LI/LGV). (We return to plotting vectors in the observation space.)

fit, since it does not require that $\hat{\mathbf{q}}_1$ be parallel to $\hat{\mathbf{q}}_2$. But we wonder whether this might prove a disadvantage. Once the vectors $\hat{\mathbf{v}}_1$ and $\hat{\mathbf{v}}_2$ are allowed to swing freely, may they not in special cases end up in odd directions? We notice in our example how this could result in a very strange estimate of γ, since this is defined by relative lengths along $\hat{\hat{\hat{L}}}$. Later on we shall see that this problem is not nearly as serious as this geometry suggests[13]; nevertheless, the occasional occurrence of estimates far off target remains a major weakness of LI/LGV, especially in small samples.

An algebraic development of LI/LGV is deferred to Chapter 20-3.

(c) LI/ML

We recall that in the exactly identified system, we could estimate the reduced form, and then infer the structural form (indirect least squares). If we attempt this procedure in the overidentified case, we would find that after estimating the reduced form, there would be no corresponding structural form that satisfies the constraints (zero coefficients in specified places). A natural solution is to estimate the reduced form, subject to constraints specified by the structural equations. Geometrically, we have shown that this is precisely what LI/LGV involves. If we assume that the errors are multivariate normal, then the criterion of maximum likelihood (LI/ML) would give

[13] In some other contexts as well, the three-dimensional geometry of LI/LGV may be misleading.

exactly the same estimates as LI/LGV. The proof would be similar to that of Chapter 2-10, although much more complex.

(d) Algebraic Generalization, LI/LVR

We turn finally to a third criterion for generating the same estimate of a single equation. It permits the easiest algebraic treatment, which we shall develop now in full generality.

The structural equation to be estimated was first given in (19-15); now we shall change notation slightly. As in the identification chapter, we shall collect all the endogenous variables together on the left side, so that the structural equation to be estimated is

$$\mathbf{Y}\boldsymbol{\gamma} = \mathbf{X}_1\boldsymbol{\beta}_1 + \mathbf{X}_1^*\mathbf{0} + \mathbf{e} \tag{19-54}$$

where $\mathbf{Y}$ includes all endogenous variables in the first equation ($\mathbf{Y} = [\mathbf{y}, -\mathbf{Y}_1]$ in our previous notation). By writing a zero coefficient, we emphasize that certain exogenous variables $\mathbf{X}_1^*$ are specifically excluded.

Let us consider some estimator $\hat{\boldsymbol{\gamma}}$, and the corresponding linear combination

$$\tilde{\mathbf{y}} = \mathbf{Y}\hat{\boldsymbol{\gamma}} \tag{19-55}$$

This we shall call the composite endogenous variable, which will be our estimate of $\mathbf{Y}\boldsymbol{\gamma}$ in (19-54). Referring to that equation, we hope to choose $\hat{\boldsymbol{\gamma}}$ so that $\tilde{\mathbf{y}}$ depends on $\mathbf{X}_1$ alone, not on all of $\mathbf{X} = [\mathbf{X}_1, \mathbf{X}_1^*]$. In terms of regression analysis, $\tilde{\mathbf{y}}$ should be explained by $\mathbf{X}_1$ just about as well as by $\mathbf{X}$. (Not *quite* as well, because the addition of more regressors $\mathbf{X}_1^*$ will improve the explanation *slightly* even when $\mathbf{X}_1^*$ is irrelevant.) Putting this algebraically, we would expect the ratio

$$\frac{\text{the residual variation, using } \mathbf{X}_1 \text{ only}}{\text{the residual variation, using all } \mathbf{X}} \tag{19-56}$$

to be only slightly greater than unity. Thus we have motivated a precise definition of the least-variance ratio (LI/LVR) estimator:

$$\boxed{\begin{array}{c}\hat{\boldsymbol{\gamma}} \text{ is chosen to make the variance ratio} \\ \text{(19-56) a minimum}\end{array}} \tag{19-57}$$

In order to develop the formula for $\hat{\boldsymbol{\gamma}}$, we first express the ratio (19-56) algebraically. Using (19-61) in the footnote below,[14] the denominator becomes

$$\text{residual variation (using } \mathbf{X}) = \tilde{\mathbf{y}}'\{\mathbf{I} - \mathbf{X}(\mathbf{X}'\mathbf{X})^{-1}\mathbf{X}'\}\tilde{\mathbf{y}} \tag{19-62}$$

Substituting (19-55)

$$= \hat{\boldsymbol{\gamma}}'\mathbf{Y}'\{\mathbf{I} - \mathbf{X}(\mathbf{X}'\mathbf{X})^{-1}\mathbf{X}'\}\mathbf{Y}\hat{\boldsymbol{\gamma}}$$

$$= \hat{\boldsymbol{\gamma}}'\mathbf{R}\hat{\boldsymbol{\gamma}} \tag{19-63}$$

where

$$\mathbf{R} = \mathbf{Y}'\{\mathbf{I} - \mathbf{X}(\mathbf{X}'\mathbf{X})^{-1}\mathbf{X}'\}\mathbf{Y} \tag{19-64}$$

Similarly, the numerator is

$$\text{residual variation (using } \mathbf{X}_1 \text{ only)} = \hat{\boldsymbol{\gamma}}'\mathbf{R}_1\hat{\boldsymbol{\gamma}} \tag{19-65}$$

where

$$\mathbf{R}_1 = \mathbf{Y}'\{\mathbf{I} - \mathbf{X}_1(\mathbf{X}_1'\mathbf{X}_1)^{-1}\mathbf{X}_1'\}\mathbf{Y} \tag{19-66}$$

Thus (19-56), the variance ratio to be minimized, may be written

$$\text{residual variance ratio} = \frac{\hat{\boldsymbol{\gamma}}'\mathbf{R}_1\hat{\boldsymbol{\gamma}}}{\hat{\boldsymbol{\gamma}}'\mathbf{R}\hat{\boldsymbol{\gamma}}} \tag{19-67}$$

We shall now show that the minimization of any such ratio of two quadratic forms requires only that we solve

$$\mathbf{R}_1\hat{\boldsymbol{\gamma}} = \lambda\mathbf{R}\hat{\boldsymbol{\gamma}} \tag{19-68}$$

that is,

$$\boxed{(\mathbf{R}_1 - \lambda\mathbf{R})\hat{\boldsymbol{\gamma}} = \mathbf{0}} \tag{19-69}$$

---

[14] Applying the Pythagorean theorem to $\triangle OAC$ in Figure 15-18,

$$\|\mathbf{y} - \hat{\mathbf{y}}\|^2 = \|\mathbf{y} - \hat{\mathbf{y}}_1\|^2 - \|\hat{\beta}_2\mathbf{x}_2\|^2 \tag{15-49}$$

repeated

This also holds true in higher dimensions, regardless of how many regressors are used. When deviations from the mean are denoted by **y** (rather than $\mathbf{y}\text{-}\hat{\mathbf{y}}_1$), then

$$\text{residual variation} = \text{total variation in } \mathbf{y} - \text{variation explained by all regressors} \tag{19-59}$$

$$= \mathbf{y}'\mathbf{y} - (\mathbf{X}\hat{\boldsymbol{\beta}})'(\mathbf{X}\hat{\boldsymbol{\beta}}) \tag{19-60}$$

Substituting (13-24) for $\hat{\boldsymbol{\beta}}$, and noting the canceling occurrences of $(\mathbf{X}'\mathbf{X})$,

$$= \mathbf{y}'\mathbf{y} - \mathbf{y}'\mathbf{X}(\mathbf{X}'\mathbf{X})^{-1}\mathbf{X}'\mathbf{y}$$

that is,

$$\text{residual variation} = \mathbf{y}'\{\mathbf{I} - \mathbf{X}(\mathbf{X}'\mathbf{X})^{-1}\mathbf{X}'\}\mathbf{y} \tag{19-61}$$

for the smallest eigenvalue[15] λ, and corresponding eigenvector $\hat{\boldsymbol{\gamma}}$.

Proof. To minimize (19-67) we could just as well minimize

$$\hat{\boldsymbol{\gamma}}'\mathbf{R}_1\hat{\boldsymbol{\gamma}} \tag{19-71}$$

subject to the constraint

$$\hat{\boldsymbol{\gamma}}'\mathbf{R}\hat{\boldsymbol{\gamma}} = c \tag{19-72}$$

where c is any constant. Solving by Lagrange multiplier, we form

$$g(\hat{\boldsymbol{\gamma}}) = \hat{\boldsymbol{\gamma}}'\mathbf{R}_1\hat{\boldsymbol{\gamma}} - \lambda(\hat{\boldsymbol{\gamma}}'\mathbf{R}\hat{\boldsymbol{\gamma}} - c) \tag{19-73}$$

$$= \hat{\boldsymbol{\gamma}}'(\mathbf{R}_1 - \lambda\mathbf{R})\hat{\boldsymbol{\gamma}} - \lambda c \tag{19-74}$$

and partially differentiate with respect to each component of $\hat{\boldsymbol{\gamma}}$. According to (13-9), we find the vector of partial derivatives

$$\frac{\partial g}{\partial \hat{\boldsymbol{\gamma}}} = 2(\mathbf{R}_1 - \lambda\mathbf{R})\hat{\boldsymbol{\gamma}} = \mathbf{0} \qquad \text{(19-69) almost proved}$$

We need now only show why the *smallest* value of λ is chosen. Substitute (19-68) into (19-67)

$$\text{residual variance ratio} = \frac{\hat{\boldsymbol{\gamma}}'(\lambda\mathbf{R}\hat{\boldsymbol{\gamma}})}{\hat{\boldsymbol{\gamma}}'\mathbf{R}\hat{\boldsymbol{\gamma}}} = \lambda \tag{19-75}$$

Clearly, to minimize this ratio, the *smallest* value of λ should be selected, and our proof is complete.

As we argued in (19-56), this variance ratio λ will generally exceed 1 and cannot in any case fall below it. Thus, minimization of λ involves selecting the λ closest to 1. We have designated this variance ratio as λ, since it appears as both a Lagrange multiplier and a latent root (eigenvalue). However, in the econometrics literature it is frequently referred to as $\hat{l}$.

In conclusion, to find the LI/LVR estimator:

1. Calculate the "residual matrices" $\mathbf{R}_1$ and $\mathbf{R}$, given by (19-66) and (19-64). (Recall that $\mathbf{R}_1$ uses only those $\mathbf{x}$'s appearing in the structural equation to be estimated, whereas $\mathbf{R}$ uses *all* the $\mathbf{x}$'s.)

---

[15] One way to solve is to set the determinant of the coefficient matrix of (19-69) equal to zero (a necessary and sufficient condition for nontrivial solutions for $\hat{\boldsymbol{\gamma}}$); i.e., set

$$|\mathbf{R}_1 - \lambda\mathbf{R}| = 0 \tag{19-70}$$

The solution of this polynomial yields various values of λ, with the smallest being selected. This is substituted into (19-69), which is then solved for $\hat{\boldsymbol{\gamma}}$, noting, of course, that $\hat{\boldsymbol{\gamma}}$ can be solved only up to a scale factor (i.e., fix one $\hat{\gamma}_i$, and solve for the rest).

2. Solve the characteristic equation (19-69), thus obtaining $\hat{\boldsymbol{\gamma}}$. But $\hat{\boldsymbol{\gamma}}$ can be determined only up to a scale factor; hence it must be "normalized" by setting some appropriate component (usually the first) equal to 1. Thus, we determine our composite endogenous variable to be

$$\tilde{\mathbf{y}} = \mathbf{y}_1 + \hat{\gamma}_2\mathbf{y}_2 + \hat{\gamma}_3\mathbf{y}_3 + \cdots \tag{19-76}$$

3. Using (19-76), calculate the vector of values of the "composite" endogenous variable $\tilde{\mathbf{y}}$, substitute this for $\mathbf{Y}\boldsymbol{\gamma}$ in (19-54), and use OLS on this equation to regress $\tilde{\mathbf{y}}$ on $\mathbf{X}_1$. Since the regressors $\mathbf{X}_1$ and error $\mathbf{e}$ satisfy all the OLS requirements, this will yield a consistent estimator $\hat{\boldsymbol{\beta}}_1$. This, along with the previously calculated $\hat{\boldsymbol{\gamma}}$, completes the estimation of the equation.

We shall hereafter designate any of the equivalent LI/LVR, LI/ML, LI/LGV as simply LI, although strictly speaking, *all* the methods developed in this chapter are "limited information," in the sense that they estimate one equation at a time.

19-5 *k*-CLASS ESTIMATORS

This is simply a new view of the estimators considered so far, again using the instrumental variable technique. In estimating the single equation

$$\mathbf{y} = \mathbf{Y}_1\boldsymbol{\gamma}_1 + \mathbf{X}_1\boldsymbol{\beta}_1 + \mathbf{e} \tag{19-77}$$

(19-15) repeated[16]

we recall that

1. OLS used the illegitimate instrumental variables $[\mathbf{Y}_1, \mathbf{X}_1]$
2. 2SLS used the instrumental variables $[\hat{\mathbf{Y}}_1, \mathbf{X}_1]$

where $\hat{\mathbf{Y}}_1$ was the unrestricted reduced-form fit. Since $\mathbf{X}_1$ is common to both methods, the difference lies in the illegitimate use of $\mathbf{Y}_1$ in OLS versus the legitimate use of $\hat{\mathbf{Y}}_1$ in 2SLS.

We now generalize this, and take a weighted average of these two methods (with weights $1 - k$ and k); this yields the instrumental variables

$$(1 - k)\mathbf{Y}_1 + k\hat{\mathbf{Y}}_1 = \mathbf{Y}_1 + k(\hat{\mathbf{Y}}_1 - \mathbf{Y}_1) \tag{19-78}$$

---

[16] Note that we return to the definition of $\mathbf{y}$ and $\mathbf{Y}_1$ in (19-15).

Of course, we retain $\mathbf{X}_1$ as our second set of instruments.[17] We see that by definition,

1. When $k = 0$, we get OLS.
2. When $k = 1$, we get 2SLS.

The surprising thing is that[18]

3. When $k = \lambda$ of equation (19-75), we get LI.

Note how frequently this term ($k = \lambda = \hat{l}$) keeps reappearing. We now show another useful interpretation. Recall how λ (hereafter referred to as $\hat{l}$) appeared as the variance ratio in (19-75). Its closeness to 1 is interpreted as how well $\tilde{\mathbf{y}}$ is explained by $\mathbf{X}_1$, compared to how well $\tilde{\mathbf{y}}$ is explained by all the regressors $\mathbf{X}$. To restate: if we have correctly specified the model, in the sense of including all the relevant regressors in $\mathbf{X}_1$, then $\hat{l}$ will be very close to 1, exceeding it only because of random fluctuation. On the other hand, if we have misspecified the model, then $\hat{l}$ will exceed 1 both because of random fluctuation and because of misspecification.

This suggests a statistical test for correct specification. Letting l represent the true parameter[19] estimated by $\hat{l}$, and noting that $l = 1$ if the equation is correctly specified, we test

$$H_0: l = 1 \tag{19-82}$$

---

[17] For a more explicit description of k-class estimators, apply the k-class instruments $[\mathbf{Y}_1 + k(\hat{\mathbf{Y}}_1 - \mathbf{Y}_1), \mathbf{X}_1]$ on equation (19-77). Dropping the error term, and exchanging the two sides of the equation, we obtain

$$\begin{bmatrix} \mathbf{Y}_1' + k(\hat{\mathbf{Y}}_1 - \mathbf{Y}_1)' \\ \mathbf{X}_1' \end{bmatrix} (\mathbf{Y}_1\hat{\boldsymbol{\gamma}}_1 + \mathbf{X}_1\hat{\boldsymbol{\beta}}_1) = \begin{bmatrix} \mathbf{Y}_1' + k(\hat{\mathbf{Y}}_1 - \mathbf{Y}_1)' \\ \mathbf{X}_1' \end{bmatrix} \mathbf{y} \tag{19-79}$$

On the left side, we may reexpress

$$(\mathbf{Y}_1\hat{\boldsymbol{\gamma}}_1 + \mathbf{X}_1\hat{\boldsymbol{\beta}}_1) = [\mathbf{Y}_1, \mathbf{X}_1] \begin{bmatrix} \hat{\boldsymbol{\gamma}}_1 \\ \hat{\boldsymbol{\beta}}_1 \end{bmatrix} \tag{19-80}$$

Substitution of (19-80) into (19-79) and appropriate matrix multiplication yields the following "k-class normal equations":

$$\left[\begin{array}{c:c} \mathbf{Y}_1'\mathbf{Y}_1 + k(\hat{\mathbf{Y}}_1 - \mathbf{Y}_1)'\mathbf{Y}_1 & \mathbf{Y}_1'\mathbf{X}_1 + k(\hat{\mathbf{Y}}_1 - \mathbf{Y}_1)'\mathbf{X}_1 \\ \hdashline \mathbf{X}_1'\mathbf{Y}_1 & \mathbf{X}_1'\mathbf{X}_1 \end{array}\right] \begin{bmatrix} \hat{\boldsymbol{\gamma}}_1 \\ \hat{\boldsymbol{\beta}}_1 \end{bmatrix} = \begin{bmatrix} \mathbf{Y}_1'\mathbf{y} + k(\hat{\mathbf{Y}}_1 - \mathbf{Y}_1)'\mathbf{y} \\ \mathbf{X}_1'\mathbf{y} \end{bmatrix} \tag{19-81}$$

which may be solved for $\begin{bmatrix} \hat{\boldsymbol{\gamma}}_1 \\ \hat{\boldsymbol{\beta}}_1 \end{bmatrix}$ by matrix inversion.

[18] For proofs in this section, see Goldberger, *op. cit.*, p. 341–344.

[19] More precisely, let l be the ratio of population (as opposed to sample) variances.

versus the alternative (i.e., the misspecification)

$$H_1 : l > 1 \tag{19-83}$$

If H_0 is true, the estimator $\hat{l}$ follows an adjusted[20] Chi-square distribution. Thus, a sufficiently large observed $\hat{l}$ would lead us to reject H_0 and search for a better specification.

An interesting and related question is "How does the k-class estimate behave as we change the value of k?" Recent studies indicate that the estimator varies little as long as k does not greatly exceed 1. But if it does, then the estimator may assume quite unreasonable values. This means that if we are using LI, and $\hat{l}$ greatly exceeds 1 (because of, say, misspecification), then LI may yield a quite unreasonable estimate. Some insurance against this, of course, is to avoid LI estimation when we fear misspecification and/or $\hat{l}$ turns out to be quite large; thus, the desirability of the test given in (19-82) is confirmed.

As already pointed out, LI and 2SLS are both k-class estimators. There is another interesting way in which they are related. Recall the discussion leading up to the definition of LI/LVR in (19-56); in asking that the residual variation (using $\mathbf{X}_1$ only) be just about as small as the residual variation (using all $\mathbf{X}$), we minimized the ratio of these two variances. Alternatively, why not minimize their *difference*? It can be shown that this difference criterion yields the 2SLS estimator.

A review of single equation estimation is given in Table 19-1. LWV is not shown in this table since it has not yet been used in practical estimation; it was introduced into this discussion as a pedagogical device, useful in bridging the gap between 2SLS and LI.

TABLE 19-1 How Single Equation Methods Are Related

Estimate of γ in our example was, let us say,	.60	.67	.75	.80	.85
Estimator used:	OLS	2SLS	LI	2SLS	OLS
		on (19-37)		on (19-40)	
Corresponding k values:	0	1	→ $\hat{l}$ ←	1	0

[20] Not to be confused with modified Chi-square. For the adjustment required, see Goldberger, *op. cit.*

PROBLEMS

19-1 Can OLS be used to estimate (19-15)? Why, or why not?

*19-2 Show the equivalence of 2SLS and IV as techniques for estimating the exactly identified consumption function (7-25). What is the direction of bias if OLS is used? Answer two ways: (a) algebraically (b) using vector geometry.

*19-3 In estimating the exactly identified demand equation below, use vector geometry to guess the answer to the following questions:

$$Q = \alpha + \beta P + \eta Y + \text{error} \qquad \text{(demand)} \qquad \text{(8-13) repeated}$$
$$Q = \gamma + \delta P + \theta R + \text{error} \qquad \text{(supply)} \qquad \text{(8-14) repeated}$$

Y and R are the exogenous variables in the system.

(a) Do 2SLS and IV involve projecting P and Q onto the same instrumental variable subspace?

(b) Are $\hat{Q}$ and the residual vector the same in both techniques?

(c) Is $\hat{Q}$ the same in the supply equation (8-14) as it is in the demand equation (8-13)?

chapter 20

Systems Estimation

20-1 THREE-STAGE LEAST SQUARES (3SLS)

This is the first technique we consider for simultaneously estimating a whole system. In simplest terms, it involves using 2SLS to estimate each equation in the system—one at a time. Each estimated equation yields a set of observed errors; these are drawn together to estimate the covariance matrix of all the errors. All 2SLS estimates are now abandoned, and only this estimated covariance matrix is retained. It is used in the final stage in applying generalized least squares (GLS) to estimate the entire system simultaneously.

(a) Instrumental Variables Reconsidered

In developing 3SLS, we begin by looking at IV from a different point of view, with the specific objective of drawing GLS into the discussion. (Since it is important in this analysis, we shall illustrate dimension from time to time.)

We shall first prove a theorem about the single equation model, where we have n observations on k exogenous variables[1] and a single endogenous variable:

$$\mathbf{y} = \mathbf{X}\boldsymbol{\beta} + \mathbf{e} \tag{20-1}$$

(16-1) repeated

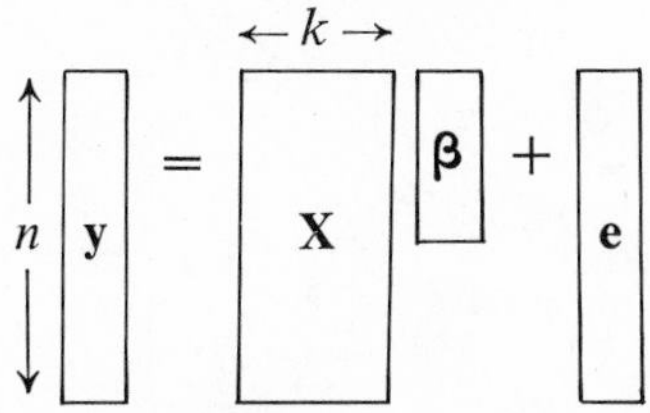

[1] To prevent us from becoming entangled in dimension difficulties, we assume prior knowledge that the intercept term in equation (20-1) is zero. Hence, we have k variable regressors included in $\mathbf{X}$, but no dummy.

Theorem.

> When $n = k$, the GLS and OLS estimates coincide with the estimates obtained by simply solving
>
> $$\mathbf{y} = \mathbf{X}\hat{\boldsymbol{\beta}} \tag{20-2}$$
>
> by matrix inversion,[2] obtaining
>
> $$\hat{\boldsymbol{\beta}} = \mathbf{X}^{-1}\mathbf{y} \tag{20-3}$$

Proof. The GLS estimates are

$$\hat{\boldsymbol{\beta}} = (\mathbf{X}'\mathbf{U}^{-1}\mathbf{X})^{-1}\mathbf{X}'\mathbf{U}^{-1}\mathbf{y} \qquad \text{(16-6) repeated}$$

When $\mathbf{X}$ as well as $\mathbf{U}$ is invertible, the bracketed quantity may be inverted by the standard rule, obtaining

$$\hat{\boldsymbol{\beta}} = (\mathbf{X}^{-1}\mathbf{U}\mathbf{X}'^{-1})\mathbf{X}'\mathbf{U}^{-1}\mathbf{y}$$

The four matrices in the middle cancel, leaving

$$\hat{\boldsymbol{\beta}} = \mathbf{X}^{-1}\mathbf{y} \qquad \text{(20-3) proved}$$

Finally, we note that OLS is just the special case of GLS where $\mathbf{U} = \mathbf{I}$ and, of course, yields the same result. Thus the proof is complete.

When $n = k$, that is, the number of observations exactly equals the number of parameters, then there is no information left over to estimate the error. In the language of Chapter 5, we say that there are "zero degrees of freedom to estimate the error," or more briefly that "the equation is estimated with zero d.f."

Of course, in the usual case of regression $n > k$, so that the error can be estimated and statistical tests made. In this case, we may estimate (20-1) by applying k instrumental variables $\mathbf{Z}$ (which may or may not be $\mathbf{X}$), obtaining,

$$\mathbf{Z}'\mathbf{y} = \mathbf{Z}'\mathbf{X}\boldsymbol{\beta} + \mathbf{Z}'\mathbf{e} \tag{20-4}$$

(17-18) repeated

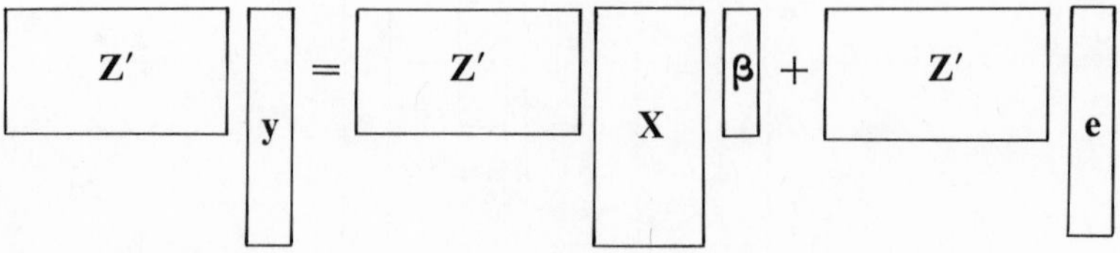

[2] Recall as in the footnote to (13-24), that $\mathbf{X}$ is assumed to be of full rank, so that $\mathbf{X}$ is invertible when square.

When (20-4) is solved for $\hat{\boldsymbol{\beta}}$, we obtain the standard IV solution (17-16). Alternatively, use of this instrumental variable set $\mathbf{Z}$ is viewed as transforming (20-1) into a system of just the right dimension—that is, a square system of k equations in k unknowns. Estimation of $\boldsymbol{\beta}$ now involves only solving these k equations. But according to our theorem, since the matrix $\mathbf{Z}'\mathbf{X}$ is square and invertible we can solve (20-4) just as we solved (20-2), that is, by applying OLS or GLS with zero degrees of freedom.

To sum up, "using just enough instrumental variables" may be thought of as the transformation of (20-1) with instrumental variables into (20-4), followed by the application of GLS.

(b) 2SLS Reconsidered

2SLS is the judicious use of an oversupply of instrumental variables, and may be thought of in the same way: transformation with the instrumental variables, followed by GLS. To prove this, we reconsider the equation to be estimated:

$$\mathbf{y} = [\mathbf{Y}_1, \mathbf{X}_1]\begin{bmatrix}\boldsymbol{\gamma}_1\\ \boldsymbol{\beta}_1\end{bmatrix} + \mathbf{e} \qquad \begin{matrix}(20\text{-}5)\\ (19\text{-}16) \text{ repeated}\end{matrix}$$

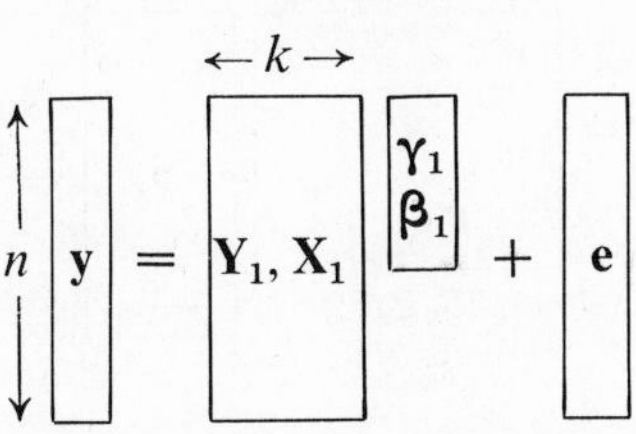

In the first stage, $\hat{\mathbf{Y}}_1$ is estimated. Then this is used, along with $\mathbf{X}_1$, as the set of instrumental variables in the second stage, that is,

$$\begin{bmatrix}\hat{\mathbf{Y}}_1'\\ \mathbf{X}_1'\end{bmatrix}\mathbf{y} = \begin{bmatrix}\hat{\mathbf{Y}}_1'\\ \mathbf{X}_1'\end{bmatrix}[\mathbf{Y}_1, \mathbf{X}_1]\begin{bmatrix}\boldsymbol{\gamma}_1\\ \boldsymbol{\beta}_1\end{bmatrix} + \begin{bmatrix}\hat{\mathbf{Y}}_1'\\ \mathbf{X}_1'\end{bmatrix}\mathbf{e}$$

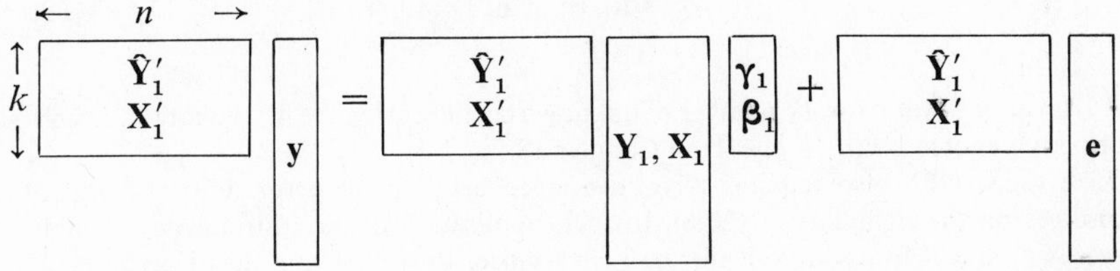

(20-6)

Since application of these instrumental variables has reduced the (row) dimension to k, GLS can be applied with zero degrees of freedom to estimate $\begin{bmatrix} \boldsymbol{\gamma}_1 \\ \boldsymbol{\beta}_1 \end{bmatrix}$. In summary, the 2SLS solution for (20-5) may be thought of as a transformation using $[\hat{\mathbf{Y}}_1, \mathbf{X}_1]'$, followed by GLS.

To reduce terminology, we define (20-5) as simply

$$\mathbf{y}_1 = \mathbf{S}_1\boldsymbol{\alpha}_1 + \mathbf{e}_1 \tag{20-7}$$

where $\mathbf{S}_1$ is made up of all the variables on the right side of the first equation, and $\boldsymbol{\alpha}_1$ is the vector of all coefficients attached to them. The subscript 1 has been added to $\mathbf{y}$ and $\mathbf{e}$ as a reminder that they belong to the first equation of a system.

There is another way we can arrive at the 2SLS solution: transform (20-7) with $\mathbf{X}$ (all M exogenous variables in all the equations), and then apply GLS. First, transforming (20-7) with $\mathbf{X}$:

$$\mathbf{X}'\mathbf{y}_1 = \mathbf{X}'\mathbf{S}_1\boldsymbol{\alpha}_1 + \mathbf{X}'\mathbf{e}_1 \tag{20-8}$$

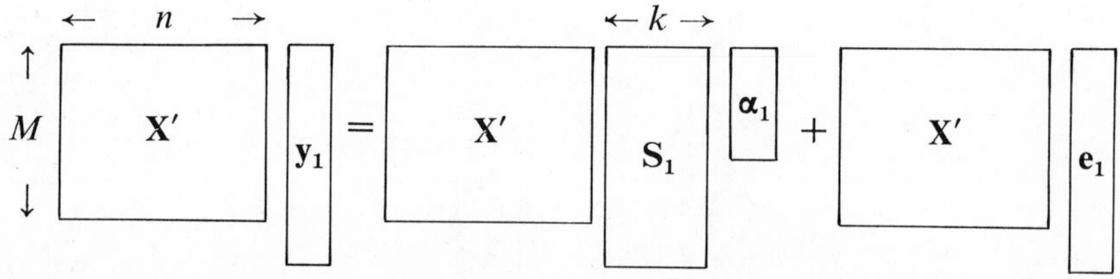

Since this equation is assumed to be identified, of course (and is usually overidentified), the number of instrumental variables M will usually exceed the number[3] of unknown parameters k. Therefore, there is no longer a simple solution with zero degrees of freedom. To apply GLS now requires[4] an estimate of the covariance of the error in (20-8); for simplicity we shall rename the error

$$\mathbf{u}_1 \triangleq \mathbf{X}'\mathbf{e}_1 \tag{20-9}$$

[3] k is an abbreviation for the number of unknown coefficients in the first equation, which was formerly denoted by $(m + q - 1)$ in Chapter 18.

[4] Like OLS, GLS also requires zero covariance between the error term and the other variables on the right side of (20-8). In fact, application of the instrumental variables $\mathbf{X}$ gives $\mathbf{X}'\mathbf{e}_1$ and $\mathbf{X}'\mathbf{S}_1$ asymptotically zero covariance, thus justifying this procedure.

If we make the standard assumption that

$$\text{cov}\,(\mathbf{e}_1) = \sigma_1^2\mathbf{I} \tag{20-10}$$

then, from Table (13-2),

$$\text{cov}\,(\mathbf{u}_1) = \text{cov}\,(\mathbf{X}'\mathbf{e}_1) = \mathbf{X}'(\text{cov}\,\mathbf{e}_1)\mathbf{X} \tag{20-11}$$

$$= \sigma_1^2\mathbf{X}'\mathbf{X} \tag{20-12}$$

With this in hand, the GLS estimate is given by applying (16-6) to (20-8); noting how reciprocal occurrences of σ_1^2 cancel, we obtain

$$\hat{\boldsymbol{\alpha}}_1 = \{(\mathbf{X}'\mathbf{S}_1)'(\mathbf{X}'\mathbf{X})^{-1}(\mathbf{X}'\mathbf{S}_1)\}^{-1}\{(\mathbf{X}'\mathbf{S}_1)'(\mathbf{X}'\mathbf{X})^{-1}(\mathbf{X}'\mathbf{y}_1)\} \tag{20-13}$$

By separating $\hat{\boldsymbol{\alpha}}_1$ into its two components we can verify that (20-13) is, in fact, just the 2SLS solution.[5]

---

[5] *Proof*. By bringing half the right side of (20-13) over to the left, and by expanding transposed products, we obtain

$$\mathbf{S}_1'\mathbf{X}(\mathbf{X}'\mathbf{X})^{-1}\mathbf{X}'\mathbf{S}_1\hat{\boldsymbol{\alpha}}_1 = \mathbf{S}_1'\mathbf{X}(\mathbf{X}'\mathbf{X})^{-1}\mathbf{X}'\mathbf{y}_1 \tag{20-14}$$

Recalling how $\mathbf{S}_1$ and $\boldsymbol{\alpha}_1$ were defined in (20-7), we may rewrite (20-14)

$$\begin{bmatrix}\mathbf{Y}_1'\\ \mathbf{X}_1'\end{bmatrix}\mathbf{X}(\mathbf{X}'\mathbf{X})^{-1}\mathbf{X}'\mathbf{S}_1\begin{bmatrix}\hat{\boldsymbol{\gamma}}_1\\ \hat{\boldsymbol{\beta}}\end{bmatrix} = \begin{bmatrix}\mathbf{Y}_1'\\ \mathbf{X}_1'\end{bmatrix}\mathbf{X}(\mathbf{X}'\mathbf{X})^{-1}\mathbf{X}'\mathbf{y}_1 \tag{20-15}$$

which partitions into

$$\mathbf{Y}_1'\mathbf{X}(\mathbf{X}'\mathbf{X})^{-1}\mathbf{X}'\mathbf{S}_1\begin{bmatrix}\hat{\boldsymbol{\gamma}}_1\\ \hat{\boldsymbol{\beta}}_1\end{bmatrix} = \mathbf{Y}_1'\mathbf{X}(\mathbf{X}'\mathbf{X})^{-1}\mathbf{X}'\mathbf{y}_1 \tag{20-16}$$

and

$$\mathbf{X}_1'\mathbf{X}(\mathbf{X}'\mathbf{X})^{-1}\mathbf{X}'\mathbf{S}_1\begin{bmatrix}\hat{\boldsymbol{\gamma}}_1\\ \hat{\boldsymbol{\beta}}_1\end{bmatrix} = \mathbf{X}_1'\mathbf{X}(\mathbf{X}'\mathbf{X})^{-1}\mathbf{X}'\mathbf{y}_1 \tag{20-17}$$

Similarly, the 2SLS solution in (19-20) may be written

$$\begin{bmatrix}\hat{\mathbf{Y}}_1'\\ \mathbf{X}_1'\end{bmatrix}[\hat{\mathbf{Y}}_1, \mathbf{X}_1]\begin{bmatrix}\hat{\boldsymbol{\gamma}}_1\\ \hat{\boldsymbol{\beta}}_1\end{bmatrix} = \begin{bmatrix}\hat{\mathbf{Y}}_1'\\ \mathbf{X}_1'\end{bmatrix}\mathbf{y}_1 \tag{20-18}$$

which partitions into

$$\hat{\mathbf{Y}}_1'[\hat{\mathbf{Y}}_1, \mathbf{X}_1]\begin{bmatrix}\hat{\boldsymbol{\gamma}}_1\\ \hat{\boldsymbol{\beta}}_1\end{bmatrix} = \hat{\mathbf{Y}}_1'\mathbf{y}_1 \tag{20-19}$$

(cont'd)

We conclude, then, that 2SLS can be interpreted as: (1) a transformation using all exogenous variables in the system as instruments, followed by (2) application of GLS.

(c) Three-Stage Least Squares

3SLS involves applying exactly this same procedure to estimate simultaneously *all* equations in the system, rather than just one. Just as in (20-8) we transformed the first equation, we now apply the instrumental variable **X**

---

and

$$\mathbf{X}_1'[\hat{\mathbf{Y}}_1, \mathbf{X}_1]\begin{bmatrix}\hat{\gamma}_1 \\ \hat{\beta}_1\end{bmatrix} = \mathbf{X}_1'\mathbf{y}_1 \tag{20-20}$$

We shall show the equivalence of (20-14) and 2SLS in (20-18) by establishing that (20-16) is equivalent to (20-19) and (20-17) to (20-20). To establish the first, we note that in the regression of $\mathbf{Y}_1$ on **X** in (19-18), we obtain the fitted values

$$\hat{\mathbf{Y}}_1 = \mathbf{X}(\mathbf{X}'\mathbf{X})^{-1}\mathbf{X}'\mathbf{Y}_1 \tag{20-21}$$

Transposing this, and noting that $(\mathbf{X}'\mathbf{X})$ is symmetric, (20-16) can be written

$$\hat{\mathbf{Y}}_1'\mathbf{S}_1\begin{bmatrix}\hat{\gamma}_1 \\ \hat{\beta}_1\end{bmatrix} = \hat{\mathbf{Y}}_1'\mathbf{y}_1 \tag{20-22}$$

Finally, noting that $\mathbf{S}_1 = [\mathbf{Y}_1, \mathbf{X}_1]$, and using (19-24) this is seen to be equivalent to (20-19).

To show the equivalence of (20-17) to (20-20) we let

$$\mathbf{X}(\mathbf{X}'\mathbf{X})^{-1}\mathbf{X}' = \mathbf{P} \tag{20-23}$$

and noting that $\mathbf{X}'\mathbf{P} = \mathbf{X}'$, we conclude that **P** acts like the identity matrix when post-multiplying $\mathbf{X}'$. (**P** is a projection operator onto the subspace generated by the columns of **X**). Furthermore, if we partition **X** into its parts that are included and excluded from the first equation, we obtain

$$\begin{bmatrix}\mathbf{X}_1' \\ \mathbf{X}_1^{*\prime}\end{bmatrix}\mathbf{X}(\mathbf{X}'\mathbf{X})^{-1}\mathbf{X}' = \begin{bmatrix}\mathbf{X}_1' \\ \mathbf{X}_1^{*\prime}\end{bmatrix} \tag{20-24}$$

Noting only the first part

$$\mathbf{X}_1'\mathbf{X}(\mathbf{X}'\mathbf{X})^{-1}\mathbf{X}' = \mathbf{X}_1' \tag{20-25}$$

This allows us to simplify (20-17) to

$$\mathbf{X}_1'[\mathbf{Y}_1, \mathbf{X}_1]\begin{bmatrix}\hat{\gamma}_1 \\ \hat{\beta}_1\end{bmatrix} = \mathbf{X}_1'\mathbf{y}_1 \tag{20-26}$$

which, using (19-25) reduces to (20-20).

to transform the whole system:

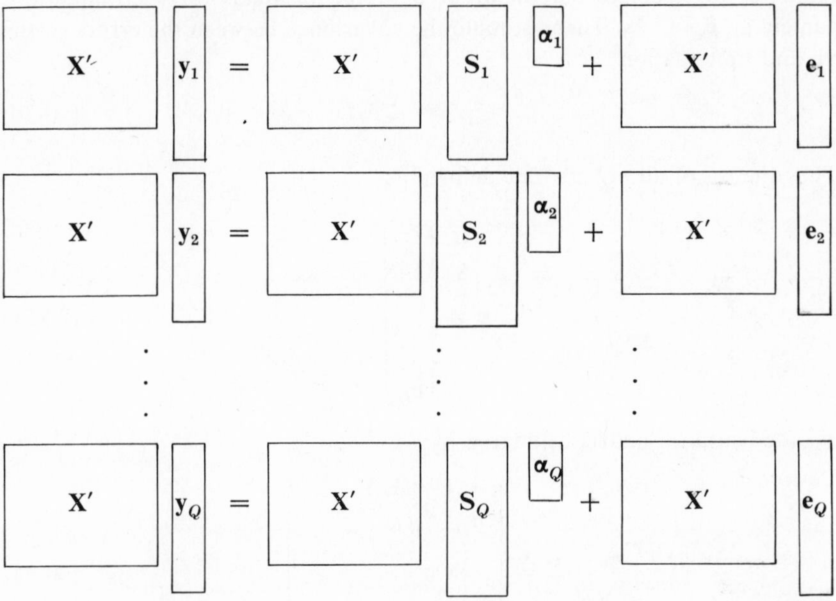

$$
\mathbf{X'}\,\mathbf{y_1} = \mathbf{X'}\,\mathbf{S_1}\,\boxed{\alpha_1} + \mathbf{X'}\,\mathbf{e_1}
$$

$$
\mathbf{X'}\,\mathbf{y_2} = \mathbf{X'}\,\mathbf{S_2}\,\boxed{\alpha_2} + \mathbf{X'}\,\mathbf{e_2}
$$

$$\vdots \qquad \vdots \qquad \vdots$$

$$
\mathbf{X'}\,\mathbf{y_Q} = \mathbf{X'}\,\mathbf{S_Q}\,\boxed{\alpha_Q} + \mathbf{X'}\,\mathbf{e_Q}
$$

$$(20\text{-}27)$$

We write this as a huge simultaneous system:

$$
\begin{bmatrix} \mathbf{X'y_1} \\ \mathbf{X'y_2} \\ \cdot \\ \cdot \\ \cdot \\ \mathbf{X'y_Q} \end{bmatrix} = \begin{bmatrix} \mathbf{X'S_1} & & \\ & \mathbf{X'S_2} & \mathbf{0} \\ & \cdot & \\ & \cdot & \\ \mathbf{0} & \cdot & \\ & & \mathbf{X'S_Q} \end{bmatrix} \begin{bmatrix} \alpha_1 \\ \alpha_2 \\ \cdot \\ \cdot \\ \cdot \\ \alpha_Q \end{bmatrix} + \begin{bmatrix} \mathbf{X'e_1} \\ \mathbf{X'e_2} \\ \cdot \\ \cdot \\ \cdot \\ \mathbf{X'e_Q} \end{bmatrix} \qquad (20\text{-}28)
$$

or, even more simply , as

$$\underline{\mathbf{y}} = \mathbf{S\alpha} + \mathbf{u} \qquad (20\text{-}29)$$

We now apply GLS to this system, which requires an estimate of the covariance of the error $\mathbf{u}$. This, in turn, requires knowledge of the covariance of the original unknown errors $\mathbf{e}$—and we seem to be stuck. But we follow the standard assumption that the errors *within* each equation [e.g., the components within the vector $\mathbf{e_1}$ in (20-27)] are uncorrelated and of constant variance; thus, we need concentrate only on the covariance of errors *between* equations, (e.g., the covariance of a component of $\mathbf{e_1}$ and a component of $\mathbf{e_2}$, which we designate σ_{12}). The critical question is: How do we estimate these covariance terms σ_{ij}?

The answer is to run a 2SLS estimate of each equation. Then use these estimates to calculate the vector of observed residuals for each equation, namely $\hat{\mathbf{e}}_1, \hat{\mathbf{e}}_2 \cdots \hat{\mathbf{e}}_Q$. Then estimate the covariance between the errors of the ith and jth equation

$$\hat{\sigma}_{ij} = \frac{1}{n} \hat{\mathbf{e}}_i' \hat{\mathbf{e}}_j \tag{20-30}$$

Thus the set of all nQ errors $\mathbf{e}$ defined as

$$\mathbf{e} \stackrel{\Delta}{=} \begin{bmatrix} \mathbf{e}_1 \\ \mathbf{e}_2 \\ \cdot \\ \cdot \\ \cdot \\ \mathbf{e}_Q \end{bmatrix} \tag{20-31}$$

has a covariance matrix estimated by

$$\hat{\boldsymbol{\Sigma}} = \begin{bmatrix} \hat{\sigma}_{11}\mathbf{I} & \hat{\sigma}_{12}\mathbf{I} & \cdots & \\ \hat{\sigma}_{21}\mathbf{I} & \cdot & & \\ \cdot & & \cdot & \\ \cdot & & & \cdot \\ \cdot & & & \\ & & & \hat{\sigma}_{QQ}\mathbf{I} \end{bmatrix} \tag{20-32}$$

Comparing (20-28) and (20-29) we note that $\mathbf{u}$ can be expressed with the following block multiplication:

$$\mathbf{u} = \begin{bmatrix} \mathbf{X}' & & & & 0 \\ & \mathbf{X}' & & & \\ & & \cdot & & \\ & & & \cdot & \\ & & & & \cdot \\ 0 & & & & \mathbf{X}' \end{bmatrix} \begin{bmatrix} \mathbf{e}_1 \\ \mathbf{e}_2 \\ \cdot \\ \cdot \\ \cdot \\ \mathbf{e}_Q \end{bmatrix} \tag{20-33}$$

From Table 13-2

$$\operatorname{cov} \mathbf{u} = \begin{bmatrix} \mathbf{X}' & & & & 0 \\ & \mathbf{X}' & & & \\ & & \cdot & & \\ & & & \cdot & \\ & & & & \cdot \\ 0 & & & & \mathbf{X}' \end{bmatrix} (\operatorname{cov} \mathbf{e}) \begin{bmatrix} \mathbf{X} & & & & 0 \\ & \mathbf{X} & & & \\ & & \cdot & & \\ & & & \cdot & \\ & & & & \cdot \\ 0 & & & & \mathbf{X} \end{bmatrix} \tag{20-34}$$

which it is reasonable to estimate by substituting $\hat{\boldsymbol{\Sigma}}$ of (20-32) for cov $\mathbf{e}$. We thus obtain

$$\hat{\mathbf{U}} = \begin{bmatrix} \mathbf{X}' & & & 0 \\ & \mathbf{X}' & & \\ & & \ddots & \\ 0 & & & \mathbf{X}' \end{bmatrix} \begin{bmatrix} \hat{\sigma}_{11}\mathbf{I} & \hat{\sigma}_{12}\mathbf{I} & \cdots & \\ \hat{\sigma}_{21}\mathbf{I} & & & \\ \vdots & \ddots & & \\ & & & \hat{\sigma}_{QQ}\mathbf{I} \end{bmatrix} \begin{bmatrix} \mathbf{X} & & & 0 \\ & \mathbf{X} & & \\ & & \ddots & \\ 0 & & & \mathbf{X} \end{bmatrix} \tag{20-35}$$

When multiplied out, this becomes

$$\hat{\mathbf{U}} = \begin{bmatrix} \mathbf{X}'\hat{\sigma}_{11}\mathbf{X} & \cdots & \\ \mathbf{X}'\hat{\sigma}_{21}\mathbf{X} & & \\ \vdots & \ddots & \\ & & \mathbf{X}'\hat{\sigma}_{QQ}\mathbf{X} \end{bmatrix} = \begin{bmatrix} \hat{\sigma}_{11}\mathbf{X}'\mathbf{X} & \cdots & \\ \hat{\sigma}_{21}\mathbf{X}'\mathbf{X} & & \\ \vdots & \ddots & \\ & & \hat{\sigma}_{QQ}\mathbf{X}'\mathbf{X} \end{bmatrix} \tag{20-36}$$

This then provides the missing link in applying GLS to (20-29); we now can calculate:

> The 3SLS solution:
> $$\hat{\boldsymbol{\alpha}} = (\mathbf{S}'\hat{\mathbf{U}}^{-1}\mathbf{S})^{-1}\,\mathbf{S}'\hat{\mathbf{U}}^{-1}\underline{\mathbf{y}} \tag{20-37}$$

where $\hat{\mathbf{U}}$ is given by (20-36), and $\mathbf{S}$ and $\underline{\mathbf{y}}$ are given by (20-29).

We have completed the chain of logic underlying 3SLS. The actual calculations typically proceed in a somewhat different sequence: 3SLS follows 2SLS through the first two stages, and the third stage is GLS estimation of the transformed system (20-29). These three stages, in detail, are:

1. Estimate the whole reduced form, to get fitted values corresponding to all the observed $\mathbf{Y}$. By obtaining all the $\hat{\mathbf{Y}}$ instrumental variables, we have completed the first stage of 2SLS—for *all* equations in the system.
2. Using the relevant instruments we proceed with the second stage of the 2SLS fit, again for each equation. So far, we have accomplished no more or no less than estimating the system by 2SLS, one equation at a time. These estimated equations then yield estimated errors $\hat{\mathbf{e}}_1, \hat{\mathbf{e}}_2, \ldots \hat{\mathbf{e}}_Q$, used to calculate $\hat{\mathbf{U}}$. (The 2SLS estimates are required only to calculate $\hat{\mathbf{U}}$; when this is done the 2SLS estimates are abandoned.)
3. Use $\hat{\mathbf{U}}$ to apply GLS to the transformed system (20-29), obtaining (20-37).

In this development, we have assumed that there are no identities in the system, and all equations are identified. If this assumption does not hold, then the analysis requires modification.

Finally, we emphasize again that the whole point of using 3SLS is to take account of observed correlation in errors between equations. When there is no such correlation, it can be shown that 3SLS reduces to a set of 2SLS estimates. This is as expected; in such circumstances, the picture is not obscured by correlation of errors between equations, and estimating them one at a time (2SLS) yields the same result as simultaneous estimation (3SLS).

20-2 SIMULTANEOUS LEAST SQUARES (SLS)

When we extend the 2SLS single equation method into system estimation, the result is 3SLS; similarly, LWV may be extended into systems estimation, with the result called Simultaneous Least Squares. As we would expect, this involves estimating all reduced form equations so as to minimize the weighted[6] trace of $\hat{\boldsymbol{\Omega}}$ in (19-52), subject to the restrictions in all structural equations. We note that $\hat{\boldsymbol{\Omega}}$ is now of dimension Q, since it is the covariance matrix of errors in all reduced form equations.

20-3 FULL INFORMATION/LEAST GENERALIZED VARIANCE (FI/LGV); FULL INFORMATION/MAXIMUM LIKELIHOOD (FI/ML)

The advantage of minimizing the determinant of $\hat{\boldsymbol{\Omega}}$ rather than its trace, applies in systems as well as single equation estimation; since this can be reviewed in Chapter 19-4, it is not repeated here. As expected, this procedure is called Least Generalized Variance (FI/LGV).

It can be shown to be equivalent to maximum likelihood estimation (FI/ML), assuming the errors are multivariate normal. Hereafter, we refer to either of these equivalent methods simply as FI.

FI shares with LI the sensitivity to misspecification, that is, it may give wild estimates when the structural equations do not have the variables correctly specified.

A detailed comparison of LI/LGV and FI/LGV will now be given, to provide an overview of the last two chapters.[7]

[6] In fact SLS originally involved minimizing the trace of $\hat{\boldsymbol{\Omega}}$, with all elements weighted equally. This raises difficulties, as we have seen in the single-equation case of Chapter 19-3. SLS was subsequently modified by rescaling all observed variables—a procedure that achieved some of the same objectives as weighting the trace.

[7] This will be our first explicit treatment of LI/LGV. Recall in Chapter 19-3 that, after the LI/LGV concept of minimizing $|\hat{\boldsymbol{\Omega}}|$ was introduced we dropped this procedure in favor of the equivalent but simpler LI/LVR approach.

Limited Information/Least Generalized Variance (LI/LGV)

The observations on the first equation are assembled:

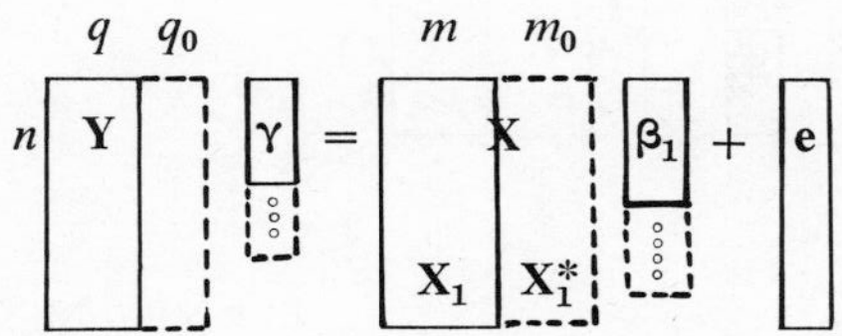

(20-38)
(19-54) repeated

where there are q endogenous and m exogenous variables included in this equation. Note how the last q_0 columns in **Y** and m_0 columns in **X** do not come into play because of the prior zero restrictions in $\boldsymbol{\gamma}$ and $\boldsymbol{\beta}_1$.

The corresponding reduced form is:

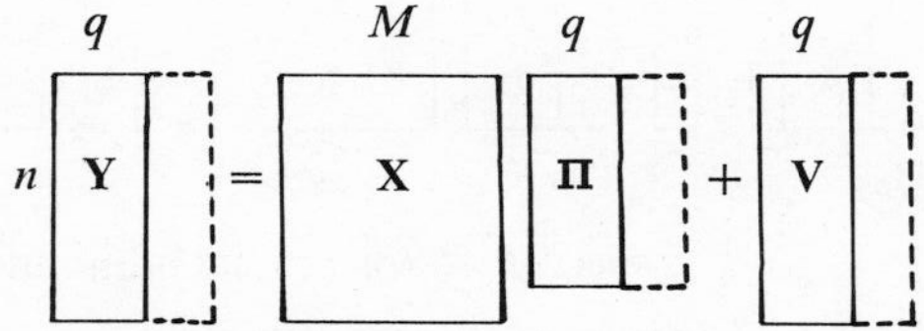

(20-40)

Note that we need concern ourselves only in the first q reduced form equations—that is, those equations corresponding to the q endogenous variables appearing in (20-38).

Full Information/Least Generalized Variance (FI/LGV)

The observations on all equations in the system are assembled:

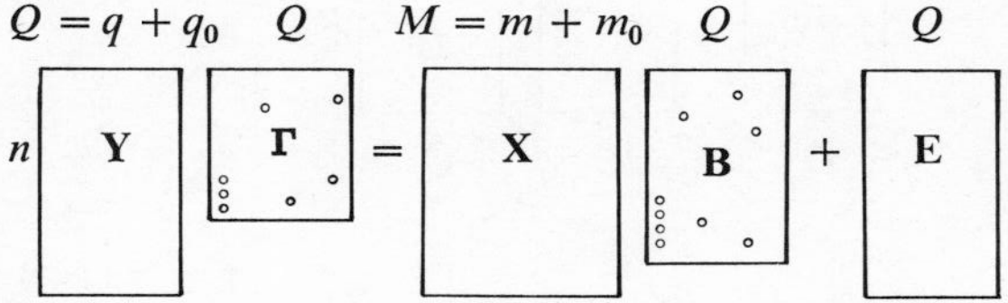

(20-39)

Note that all **Y**'s and **X**'s are included here; also note how the zero prior restrictions are scattered in $\boldsymbol{\Gamma}$ and **B**.

The corresponding reduced form is:

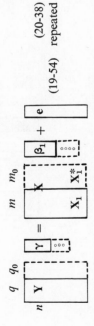

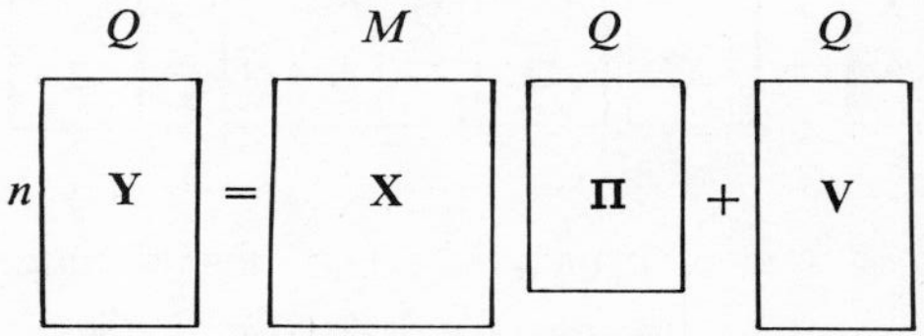

(20-41)

Here we are concerned with all reduced form equations.

LI/LGV (continued)

Postmultiplying (20-40) by γ yields:

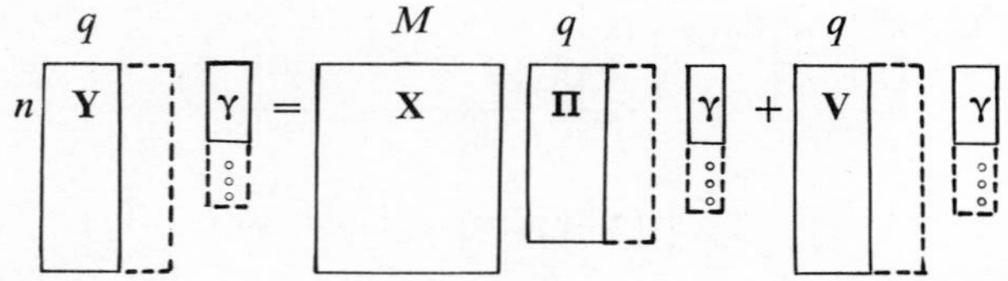

(20-42)

Comparing (20-42) with (20-38) we see that they are equivalent if:

(a) $\mathbf{V}\gamma = \mathbf{e}$, and

(b)

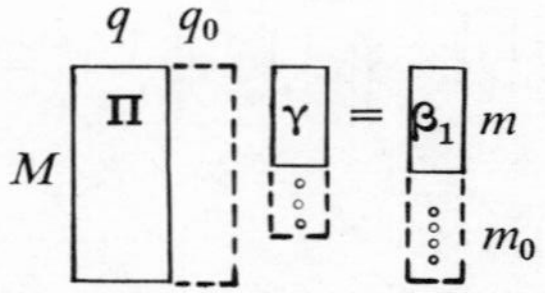

(20-44)

FI/LGV (continued)

Postmultiplying (20-41) by $\mathbf{\Gamma}$ yields:

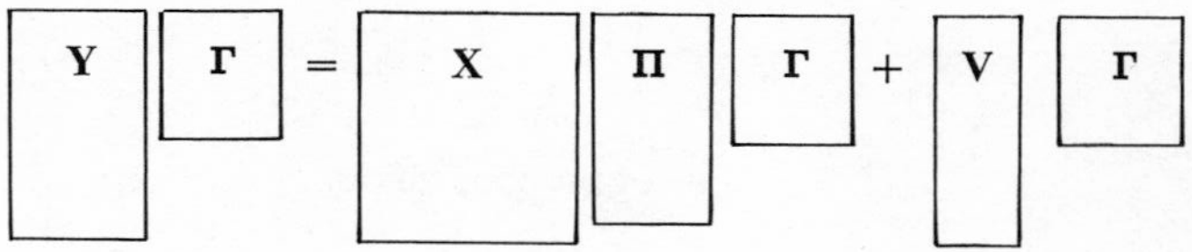

(20-43)

(20-43) and (20-39) are equivalent if

(a) $\mathbf{V\Gamma} = \mathbf{E}$, and

(b)

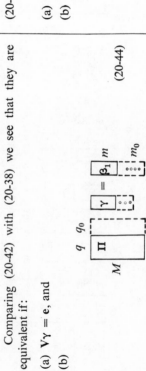

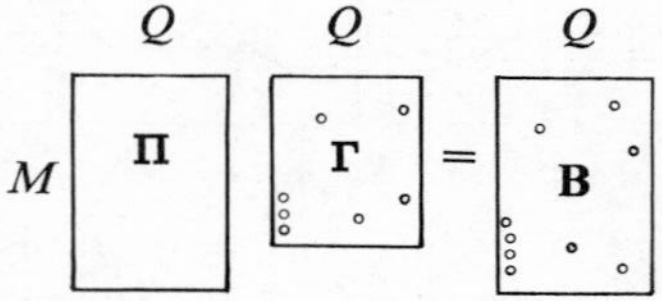

(20-45)

LI/LGV (continued)

We are not allowed a free, unrestricted fit of $\mathbf{\Pi}$ as in (20-40). Instead, we must estimate $\mathbf{\Pi}$ and $\boldsymbol{\gamma}$ subject to the restrictions in (20-44). But the first m equations provide no restraint on our selection of $\mathbf{\Pi}$ and $\boldsymbol{\gamma}$, since the first m elements in $\boldsymbol{\beta}$ are unrestricted. The only restraints, therefore, are the last m_0 equations, where $\boldsymbol{\beta}$ is set a priori at zero. Thus, the restraints in (20-44) reduce to:

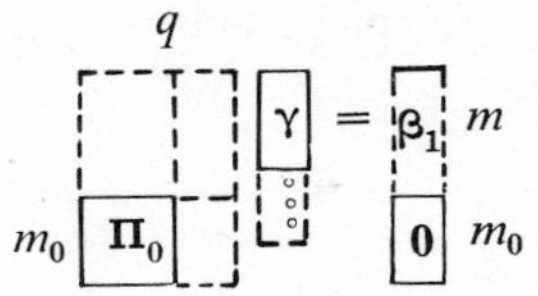

(20-46)

or

$$\mathbf{\Pi}_0 \boldsymbol{\gamma} = \mathbf{0} \tag{20-47}$$

(18-9)repeated

where $\mathbf{\Pi}_0$ is the lower left corner of $\mathbf{\Pi}$.

Note how the prior restrictions on $\boldsymbol{\gamma}$ and $\boldsymbol{\beta}$ appearing in (20-46) cause restrictions on $\mathbf{\Pi}_0$ and $\boldsymbol{\gamma}$ in (20-47).

FI/LGV (continued)

We must estimate $\mathbf{\Pi}$ and $\mathbf{\Gamma}$ subject to the restrictions given in (20-45). There are as many linear restrictions as there are zeros specified in $\mathbf{B}$. These restrictions reduce to:

$$\mathbf{\Pi}^0 \mathbf{\Gamma}^0 = \mathbf{0} \tag{20-48}$$

with these matrices being the appropriate segments of $\mathbf{\Pi}$, $\mathbf{\Gamma}$, and $\mathbf{B}$, as in the LI case. Again, the prior restrictions on $\mathbf{\Gamma}$ and $\mathbf{B}$ in the structure (20-39) cause restrictions on $\mathbf{\Pi}^0$ and $\mathbf{\Gamma}^0$ in (20-48).

LI/LGV (continued)

Subject to these constraints, we wish to minimize the determinant of $\hat{\mathbf{\Omega}}$, the q-dimension covariance matrix of $\hat{\mathbf{V}}$, the estimated errors in the reduced form. Noting that our fit of (20-40) will yield:

$$\hat{\mathbf{V}} = \mathbf{Y} - \mathbf{X}\hat{\mathbf{\Pi}} \qquad (20\text{-}49)$$

we therefore wish to minimize

$$|\hat{\mathbf{\Omega}}| = |\hat{\mathbf{V}}'\hat{\mathbf{V}}| = |(\mathbf{Y} - \mathbf{X}\hat{\mathbf{\Pi}})'(\mathbf{Y} - \mathbf{X}\hat{\mathbf{\Pi}})| \qquad (20\text{-}50)$$

subject to (20-47), that is,

$$\hat{\mathbf{\Pi}}_0\,\hat{\boldsymbol{\gamma}} = \mathbf{0} \qquad (20\text{-}51)$$

Minimization is accomplished by differentiating the Lagrange multiplier ($\boldsymbol{\lambda}$) function:

$$|(\hat{\mathbf{Y}} - \mathbf{X}\hat{\mathbf{\Pi}})'(\mathbf{Y} - \mathbf{X}\hat{\mathbf{\Pi}})| - \boldsymbol{\lambda}'(\hat{\mathbf{\Pi}}_0\hat{\boldsymbol{\gamma}}) \qquad (20\text{-}52)$$

with respect to its arguments $\hat{\mathbf{\Pi}}$, $\hat{\boldsymbol{\gamma}}$, $\boldsymbol{\lambda}$, setting these partial derivatives equal to zero, and solving for the estimates. With $\hat{\mathbf{\Pi}}$ and $\hat{\boldsymbol{\gamma}}$ thus determined, $\hat{\boldsymbol{\beta}}_1$ is found using (20-44).

To sum up: We have minimized $|\hat{\mathbf{\Omega}}|$, the generalized variance of the reduced form errors, subject to the zero restrictions on the first equation.

FI/LGV (continued)

Again, we minimize the determinant of $\hat{\mathbf{\Omega}}$, the estimated covariance matrix of errors $\hat{\mathbf{V}}$. But now $\hat{\mathbf{\Omega}}$ has dimension Q rather than q as in the LI case. We leave the rest of this argument as an exercise for the student, with these clues:

Same as (20-49), noting the greater dimension of $\hat{\mathbf{V}}$.

Same as (20-50), noting the greater dimension of $\hat{\mathbf{\Omega}}$.

Similar to LI.

Conclusions are the same, except that we minimize the generalized variance of *all* reduced form errors (rather than some), subject to the zero restrictions on *all* structural equations (rather than just the first).

20-4 COMPARISON OF METHODS

As we have already pointed out, there is no reason why a simultaneous system must be estimated using a systems method; instead we can use a single equation method, estimating the system one equation at a time. These various approaches are briefly compared in Table 20-1. One point is worth

TABLE 20-1 Comparison of Various Estimation Methods for a System of Simultaneous Equations

↓ More complicated, conceptually and computationally

↓ More useful for large samples

↓ Asymptotically closer to target (more efficient)

Estimator	
OLS or GLS	If used in a simultaneous system, this yields a biased and inconsistent result. Really not a system method, it is being asked to do more than it was designed for. Nevertheless, it does have small variance.
2SLS LI	Like OLS, these methods concentrate on one equation at a time. But unlike OLS, they are consistent. All x's (included and excluded) are used to construct new instrumental variables.
3SLS FI	All equations are estimated simultaneously, to exploit the structure of all equations at once. But more computing time, and a larger sample size, are required. If there is specification error in an equation, then FI carries this defect throughout the whole system, whereas LI would isolate it to the one equation.

elaborating: a systems method requires a much larger sample size. For example, 2SLS can be applied with a small sample to estimate the few parameters in the first equation, then the few parameters in the second equation, and so on. But 3SLS requires a much larger sample, since the whole array of parameters in all equations is estimated in one pass.

In the interests of brevity, in these last two chapters we have derived only the point estimator for each method; we have not derived its variance or its distribution. Of course, without this information tests of significance and confidence intervals could not be developed. These obviously are such important issues for practical econometrics, that we shall sketch them briefly

With a few important exceptions, nobody has exactly derived the small sample distributions for the estimators of Chapters 19 and 20. Present theoretical knowledge is limited to their large sample (asymptotic) properties, and in particular the asymptotic variance.[8] Typically, when an equation is estimated with one of these methods, it is desirable to indicate the asymptotic standard error below each estimated coefficient [as, for example, in (3-15)]. Such an asymptotic standard error will most likely understate the true standard error in small samples; but at least it will give the reader some rough indication of magnitude just as standard errors based on the normal distribution gave statisticians some clues in the days before the t distribution was discovered.

Moreover, although few small sample properties have been theoretically derived, a great deal of work has been done in investigating these properties by "Monte Carlo," that is, by running experiments over and over again, and gathering statistics on how these estimators behave. These Monte Carlo studies assume a known set of structural equations along with the joint distribution of their errors (normal or otherwise), and then proceed as follows:

1. A set of X values is selected. Then the Monte Carlo wheel is spun, drawing a sample set of errors.
2. Because we know the true structure, we can solve for the Y values.
3. Repeat this procedure, say 20 times, to obtain a small sample of 20 Y and X observations.
4. From these Y and X values, estimate each coefficient θ in the structural equations—using in turn OLS, 2SLS, 3SLS, and any other method we wish to compare.
5. Repeat steps 1–4, say 100 times. In this way, we derive 100 $\hat{\theta}$'s, which provide a picture of how $\hat{\theta}$ is distributed around its target θ, for each of the methods. Thus, we have an empirical small sample distribution of the OLS estimator, 2SLS estimator, and so on.

These methods are then compared, using the various criteria of Appendix 2-2. We review three of these criteria, in the context of empirical distributions (instead of probability distributions):

[8] For example, the covariance matrix of the 2SLS estimator (19-20) is consistently (asymptotically) estimated by

$$\text{cov}\begin{bmatrix}\hat{\boldsymbol{\gamma}}_1\\ \hat{\boldsymbol{\beta}}_1\end{bmatrix} \approx s^2([\hat{\mathbf{Y}}_1, \mathbf{X}_1]'[\hat{\mathbf{Y}}_1, \mathbf{X}_1])^{-1} \qquad \text{like (13-32)}$$

where s^2 is the residual variance. (We make the usual assumptions of Chapter 19-2 in this formula, including that the sequence of errors e_t are serially uncorrelated.) For a proof, see for example, Goldberger, *op. cit.*, p. 332.

(a) *Bias* is a measure of how far, *on average*, $\hat{\theta}$ is off its target θ:

$$\text{bias} = \bar{\hat{\theta}} - \theta \tag{20-53}$$

where $\bar{\hat{\theta}} = \sum \hat{\theta}_i/100$ is the average of the estimates $\hat{\theta}_i$.

(b) *Variance* is a measure of how much $\hat{\theta}$ fluctuates:

$$\text{variance} = \frac{\sum (\hat{\theta}_i - \bar{\hat{\theta}})^2}{100} \tag{20-54}$$

(c) *Mean squared error*[9] (MSE), is a summary measure of how much $\hat{\theta}$ is off its target θ:

$$\text{MSE} = \frac{\sum (\hat{\theta}_i - \theta)^2}{100} \tag{20-55}$$

The results from Monte Carlo studies are difficult to summarize, because of their empirical nature. However, they tentatively suggest the following small-sample properties:

1. OLS generally exhibits greater bias. This was expected, since OLS is asymptotically biased, but the other methods are not.
2. OLS has relatively small variance; moreover, in very small samples its smaller variance may more than offset its greater bias, so that it has smallest mean squared error. Thus, OLS cannot be rejected out-of-hand in small samples merely because of its large sample deficiency of inconsistency.
3. However, 2SLS usually outperforms OLS. Moreover, some estimators are more sensitive than others to such problems as multicollinearity in the X variables and misspecification of the model; on both these counts, 2SLS performs relatively well.
4. It has often been difficult to justify the increased computional cost involved in LI. As suggested earlier, LI can be very unstable, especially in very small samples. Similarly, it has been difficult to justify the further increased cost in moving up to FI. Sometimes it yields better results, but not always. Hopefully, future econometric analysis will better indicate the appropriate situations for these more complicated estimation methods, especially as computation becomes cheaper.
5. The preferred estimator may depend on what is to be estimated (structure or reduced form?) and the eventual objective (explanation or prediction?)

---

[9] This third criterion depends on the other two. According to (2-82), mean squared error = bias^2 + variance.

These observations confirm that no estimator is preferred under all circumstances, and the selection of the estimator and evaluation of results is still based largely on judgment. Nevertheless, 2SLS is a very useful all-purpose technique even for systems estimation. And even if limited resources dictate OLS, the results in small samples may still compare well with more complicated techniques.

Appendix

LIST OF TABLES

TABLE I Squares and Square Roots

N	N^2	$\sqrt{N}$	$\sqrt{10N}$
1.00	1.0000	1.00000	3.16228
1.01	1.0201	1.00499	3.17805
1.02	1.0404	1.00995	3.19374
1.03	1.0609	1.01489	3.20936
1.04	1.0816	1.01980	3.22490
1.05	1.1025	1.02470	3.24037
1.06	1.1236	1.02956	3.25576
1.07	1.1449	1.03441	3.27109
1.08	1.1664	1.03923	3.28634
1.09	1.1881	1.04403	3.30151
1.10	1.2100	1.04881	3.31662
1.11	1.2321	1.05357	3.33167
1.12	1.2544	1.05830	3.34664
1.13	1.2769	1.06301	3.36155
1.14	1.2996	1.06771	3.37639
1.15	1.3225	1.07238	3.39116
1.16	1.3456	1.07703	3.40588
1.17	1.3689	1.08167	3.42053
1.18	1.3924	1.08628	3.43511
1.19	1.4161	1.09087	3.44964
1.20	1.4400	1.09545	3.46410
1.21	1.4641	1.10000	3.47851
1.22	1.4884	1.10454	3.49285
1.23	1.5129	1.10905	3.50714
1.24	1.5376	1.11355	3.52136
1.25	1.5625	1.11803	3.53553
1.26	1.5876	1.12250	3.54965
1.27	1.6129	1.12694	3.56371
1.28	1.6384	1.13137	3.57771
1.29	1.6641	1.13578	3.59166
1.30	1.6900	1.14018	3.60555
1.31	1.7161	1.14455	3.61939
1.32	1.7244	1.14891	3.63318
1.33	1.7689	1.15326	3.64692
1.34	1.7956	1.15758	3.66060
1.35	1.8225	1.16190	3.67423
1.36	1.8496	1.16619	3.68782
1.37	1.8769	1.17047	3.70135
1.38	1.9044	1.17473	3.71484
1.39	1.9321	1.17898	3.72827
1.40	1.9600	1.18322	3.74166
1.41	1.9881	1.18743	3.75500
1.42	2.0164	1.19164	3.76829
1.43	2.0449	1.19583	3.78153
1.44	2.0736	1.20000	3.79473
1.45	2.1025	1.20416	3.80789
1.46	2.1316	1.20830	3.82099
1.47	2.1609	1.21244	3.83406
1.48	2.1904	1.21655	3.84708
1.49	2.2201	1.22066	3.86005
1.50	2.2500	1.22474	3.87298
N	N^2	$\sqrt{N}$	$\sqrt{10N}$

N	N^2	$\sqrt{N}$	$\sqrt{10N}$
1.50	2.2500	1.22474	3.87298
1.51	2.2801	1.22882	3.88587
1.52	2.3104	1.23288	3.89872
1.53	2.3409	1.23693	3.91152
1.54	2.3716	1.24097	3.92428
1.55	2.4025	1.24499	3.93700
1.56	2.4336	1.24900	3.94968
1.57	2.4649	1.25300	3.96232
1.58	2.4964	1.25698	3.97492
1.59	2.5281	1.26095	3.98748
1.60	2.5600	1.26491	4.00000
1.61	2.5921	1.26886	4.01248
1.62	2.6244	1.27279	4.02492
1.63	2.6569	1.27671	4.03733
1.64	2.6896	1.28062	4.04969
1.65	2.7225	1.28452	4.06202
1.66	2.7556	1.28841	4.07431
1.67	2.7889	1.29228	4.08656
1.68	2.8224	1.29615	4.09878
1.69	2.8561	1.30000	4.11096
1.70	2.8900	1.30384	4.12311
1.71	2.9241	1.30767	4.13521
1.72	2.9584	1.31149	4.14729
1.73	2.9929	1.31529	4.19533
1.74	3.0276	1.31909	4.17133
1.75	3.0625	1.32288	4.18330
1.76	3.0976	1.32665	4.19524
1.77	3.1329	1.33041	4.20714
1.78	3.1684	1.33417	4.21900
1.79	3.2041	1.33791	4.23084
1.80	3.2400	1.34164	4.24264
1.81	3.2761	1.34536	4.25441
1.82	3.3124	1.34907	4.26615
1.83	3.3489	1.35277	4.27785
1.84	3.3856	1.35647	4.28952
1.85	3.4225	1.36015	4.30116
1.86	3.4596	1.36382	4.31277
1.87	3.4969	1.36748	4.32435
1.88	3.5344	1.37113	4.33590
1.89	3.5721	1.37477	4.34741
1.90	3.6100	1.37840	4.35890
1.91	3.6481	1.38203	4.37035
1.92	3.6864	1.38564	4.38178
1.93	3.7249	1.38924	4.39318
1.94	3.7636	1.39284	4.40454
1.95	3.8025	1.39642	4.41588
1.96	3.8416	1.40000	4.42719
1.97	3.8809	1.40357	4.43847
1.98	3.9204	1.40712	4.44972
1.99	3.9601	1.41067	4.46094
2.00	4.0000	1.41421	4.47214
N	N^2	$\sqrt{N}$	$\sqrt{10N}$

TABLE I (Continued)

N	N^2	$\sqrt{N}$	$\sqrt{10N}$
2.00	4.0000	1.41421	4.47214
2.01	4.0401	1.41774	4.48330
2.02	4.0804	1.42127	4.49444
2.03	4.1209	1.42478	4.50555
2.04	4.1616	1.42829	4.51664
2.05	4.2025	1.43178	4.52769
2.06	4.2436	1.43527	4.53872
2.07	4.2849	1.43875	4.54973
2.08	4.3264	1.44222	4.56070
2.09	4.3681	1.44568	4.57165
2.10	4.4100	1.44914	4.58258
2.11	4.4521	1.45258	4.59347
2.12	4.4944	1.45602	4.60435
2.13	4.5369	1.45945	4.61519
2.14	4.5796	1.46287	4.62601
2.15	4.6225	1.46629	4.63681
2.16	4.6656	1.46969	4.64758
2.17	4.7089	1.47309	4.65833
2.18	4.7524	1.47648	4.66905
2.19	4.7961	1.47986	4.67974
2.20	4.8400	1.48324	4.69042
2.21	4.8841	1.48661	4.70106
2.22	4.9284	1.48997	4.71169
2.23	4.9729	1.49332	4.72229
2.24	5.0176	1.49666	4.73286
2.25	5.0625	1.50000	4.74342
2.26	5.1076	1.50333	4.75395
2.27	5.1529	1.50665	4.76445
2.28	5.1984	1.50997	4.77493
2.29	5.2441	1.51327	4.78539
2.30	5.2900	1.51658	4.79583
2.31	5.3361	1.51987	4.80625
2.32	5.3824	1.52315	4.81664
2.33	5.4289	1.52643	4.82701
2.34	5.4756	1.52971	4.83735
2.35	5.5225	1.53297	4.84768
2.36	5.5696	1.53623	4.85798
2.37	5.6169	1.53948	4.86826
2.38	5.6644	1.54272	4.87852
2.39	5.7121	1.54596	4.88876
2.40	5.7600	1.54919	4.89898
2.41	5.8081	1.55242	4.90918
2.42	5.8564	1.55563	4.91935
2.43	5.9049	1.55885	4.92950
2.44	5.9536	1.56205	4.93964
2.45	6.0025	1.56525	4.94975
2.46	6.0516	1.56844	4.95984
2.47	6.1009	1.57162	4.96991
2.48	6.1504	1.57484	4.97996
2.49	6.2001	1.57797	4.98999
2.50	6.2500	1.58114	5.00000
N	N^2	$\sqrt{N}$	$\sqrt{10N}$

N	N^2	$\sqrt{N}$	$\sqrt{10N}$
2.50	6.2500	1.58114	5.00000
2.51	6.3001	1.58430	5.00999
2.52	6.3504	1.58745	5.01996
2.53	6.4009	1.59060	5.02991
2.54	6.4516	1.59374	5.03984
2.55	6.5025	1.59687	5.04975
2.56	6.5536	1.60000	5.05964
2.57	6.6049	1.60312	5.06952
1.58	6.6564	1.60624	5.07937
2.59	6.7081	1.60935	5.08920
2.60	6.7600	1.61245	5.09902
2.61	6.8121	1.61555	5.10882
2.62	6.8644	1.61864	5.11859
2.63	6.9169	1.62173	5.12835
2.64	6.9696	1.62481	5.13809
2.65	7.0225	1.62788	5.14782
2.66	7.0756	1.63095	5.15752
2.67	7.1289	1.63401	5.16720
2.68	7.1824	1.63707	5.17687
2.69	7.2361	1.64012	5.18652
2.70	7.2900	1.64317	5.19615
2.71	7.3441	1.64621	5.20577
2.72	7.3984	1.64924	5.21536
2.73	7.4529	1.65227	5.22494
2.74	7.5076	1.65529	5.23450
2.75	7.5625	1.65831	5.24404
2.76	7.6171	1.66132	5.25357
2.77	7.6729	1.66433	5.26308
2.78	7.7284	1.66733	5.27257
2.79	7.7841	1.67033	5.28205
2.80	7.8400	1.67332	5.29150
2.81	7.8961	1.67631	5.30094
2.82	7.9524	1.67929	5.31037
2.83	8.0089	1.68226	5.31977
2.84	8.0656	1.68523	5.32917
2.85	8.1225	1.68819	5.33854
2.86	8.1796	1.69115	5.34790
2.87	8.2369	1.69411	5.35724
2.88	8.2944	1.69706	5.36656
2.89	8.3521	1.70000	5.37587
2.90	8.4100	1.70294	5.38516
2.91	8.4681	1.70587	5.39444
2.92	8.5264	1.70880	5.40370
2.93	8.5849	1.71172	5.41295
2.94	8.6436	1.71464	5.42218
2.95	8.7025	1.71756	5.43139
2.96	8.7616	1.72047	5.44059
2.97	8.8209	1.72337	5.44977
2.98	8.8804	1.72627	5.45894
2.99	8.9401	1.72916	5.46809
3.00	9.0000	1.73205	5.47723
N	N^2	$\sqrt{N}$	$\sqrt{10N}$

TABLE I (Continued)

N	N²	√N	√10N
3.00	9.0000	1.73205	5.47723
3.01	9.0601	1.73494	5.48635
3.02	9.1204	1.73781	5.49545
3.03	9.1809	1.74069	5.50454
3.04	9.2416	1.74356	5.51362
3.05	9.3025	1.74642	5.52268
3.06	9.3636	1.74929	5.53173
3.07	9.4249	1.75214	5.54076
3.08	9.4864	1.75499	5.54977
3.09	9.5481	1.75784	5.55878
3.10	9.6100	1.76068	5.56776
3.11	9.6721	1.76352	5.57674
3.12	9.7344	1.76635	5.58570
3.13	9.7969	1.76918	5.59464
3.14	9.8596	1.77200	5.60357
3.15	9.9225	1.77482	5.61249
3.16	9.9856	1.77764	5.62139
3.17	10.0489	1.78045	5.63028
3.18	10.1124	1.78326	5.63915
3.19	10.1761	1.78606	5.64801
3.20	10.2400	1.78885	5.65685
3.21	10.3041	1.79165	5.66569
3.22	10.3684	1.79444	5.67450
3.23	10.4329	1.79722	5.68331
3.24	10.4976	1.80000	5.69210
3.25	10.5625	1.80278	5.70088
3.26	10.6276	1.80555	5.70964
3.27	10.6929	1.80831	5.71839
3.28	10.7584	1.81108	5.72713
3.29	10.8241	1.81384	5.73585
3.30	10.8900	1.81659	5.74456
3.31	10.9561	1.81934	5.75326
3.32	11.0224	1.82209	5.76194
3.33	11.0889	1.82483	5.77062
3.34	11.1556	1.82757	5.77927
3.35	11.2225	1.83030	5.78792
3.36	11.2896	1.83303	5.79655
3.37	11.3569	1.83576	5.80517
3.38	11.4244	1.83848	5.81378
3.39	11.4921	1.84120	5.82237
3.40	11.5600	1.84391	5.83095
3.41	11.6281	1.84662	5.83952
3.42	11.6964	1.84932	5.84808
3.43	11.7649	1.85203	5.85662
3.44	11.8336	1.85472	5.86515
3.45	11.9025	1.85742	5.87367
3.46	11.9716	1.86011	5.88218
3.47	12.0409	1.86279	5.89067
3.48	12.1104	1.86548	5.89915
3.49	12.1801	1.86815	5.90762
3.50	12.2500	1.87083	5.91608
N	N²	√N	√10N

N	N²	√N	√10N
3.50	12.2500	1.87083	5.91608
3.51	12.3201	1.87350	5.92453
3.52	12.3904	1.87617	5.93296
3.53	12.4609	1.87883	5.94138
3.54	12.5316	1.88149	5.94979
3.55	12.6025	1.88414	5.95819
3.56	12.6736	1.88680	5.96657
3.57	12.7449	1.88944	5.97495
3.58	12.8164	1.89209	5.98331
3.59	12.8881	1.89473	5.99166
3.60	12.9600	1.89737	6.00000
3.61	13.0321	1.90000	6.00833
3.62	13.1044	1.90263	6.01664
3.63	13.1769	1.90526	6.02495
3.64	13.2496	1.90788	6.03324
3.65	13.3225	1.91050	6.04152
3.66	13.3956	1.91311	6.04979
3.67	13.4689	1.91572	6.05805
3.68	13.5424	1.91833	6.06630
3.69	13.6161	1.92094	6.07454
3.70	13.6900	1.92354	6.08276
3.71	13.7641	1.92614	6.09098
3.72	13.8384	1.92873	6.09918
3.73	13.9129	1.93132	6.10737
3.74	13.9876	1.93391	6.11555
3.75	14.0625	1.93649	6.12372
3.76	14.1376	1.93907	6.13188
3.77	14.2129	1.94165	6.14003
3.78	14.2884	1.94422	6.14817
3.79	14.3641	1.94679	6.15630
3.80	14.4400	1.94936	6.16441
3.81	14.5161	1.95192	6.17252
3.82	14.5924	1.95448	6.18061
3.83	14.6689	1.95704	6.18870
3.84	14.7456	1.95959	6.19677
3.85	14.8225	1.96214	6.20484
3.86	14.8996	1.96469	6.21289
3.87	14.9769	1.96723	6.22093
3.88	15.0544	1.96977	6.22896
3.89	15.1321	1.97231	6.23699
3.90	15.2100	1.97484	6.24500
3.91	15.2881	1.97737	6.25300
3.92	15.3664	1.97990	6.26099
3.93	15.4449	1.98242	6.26897
3.94	15.5236	1.98494	6.27694
3.95	15.6025	1.98746	6.28490
3.96	15.6816	1.98997	6.29285
3.97	15.7609	1.99249	6.30079
3.98	15.8404	1.99499	6.30872
3.99	15.9201	1.99750	6.31664
4.00	16.0000	2.00000	6.32456
N	N²	√N	√10N

TABLE I (Continued)

N	N²	√N	√10N
4.00	16.0000	2.00000	6.32456
4.01	16.0801	2.00250	6.33246
4.02	16.1604	2.00499	6.34035
4.03	16.2409	2.00749	6.34823
4.04	16.3216	2.00998	6.35610
4.05	16.4025	2.01246	6.36396
4.06	16.4836	2.01494	6.37181
4.07	16.5649	2.01742	6.37966
4.08	16.6464	2.01990	6.38749
4.09	16.7281	2.02237	6.39531
4.10	16.8100	2.02485	6.40312
4.11	16.8921	2.02731	6.41093
4.12	16.9744	2.02978	6.41872
4.13	17.0569	2.03224	6.42651
4.14	17.1396	2.03470	6.43428
4.15	17.2225	2.03715	6.44205
4.16	17.3056	2.03961	6.44981
4.17	17.3889	2.04206	6.45755
4.18	17.4724	2.04450	6.46529
4.19	17.5561	2.04695	6.47302
4.20	17.6400	2.04939	6.48074
4.21	17.7241	2.05183	6.48845
4.22	17.8084	2.05426	6.49615
4.23	17.8929	2.05670	6.50384
4.24	17.9776	2.05913	6.51153
4.25	18.0625	2.06155	6.51920
4.26	18.1476	2.06398	6.52687
4.27	18.2329	2.06640	6.53452
4.28	18.3184	2.06882	6.54217
4.29	18.4041	2.07123	6.54981
4.30	18.4900	2.07364	6.55744
4.31	18.5761	2.07605	6.56506
4.32	18.6624	2.07846	6.57267
4.33	18.7489	2.08087	6.58027
4.34	18.8356	2.08327	6.58787
4.35	18.9225	2.08567	6.59545
4.36	19.0096	2.08806	6.60303
4.37	19.0969	2.09045	6.61060
4.38	19.1844	2.09284	6.61816
4.39	19.2721	2.09523	6.62571
4.40	19.3600	2.09762	6.63325
4.41	19.4481	2.10000	6.64078
4.42	19.5364	2.10238	6.64831
4.43	19.6248	2.10476	6.65582
4.44	19.7136	2.10713	6.66333
4.45	19.8025	2.10950	6.67083
4.46	19.8916	2.11187	6.67832
4.47	19.9809	2.11424	6.68581
4.48	20.0704	2.11660	6.69328
4.49	20.1601	2.11896	6.70075
4.50	20.2500	2.12132	6.70820
N	N²	√N	√10N

N	N²	√N	√10N
4.50	20.2500	2.12132	6.70802
4.51	20.3401	2.12368	6.71565
4.52	20.4304	2.12603	6.72309
4.53	20.5209	2.12838	6.73053
4.54	20.6116	2.13073	6.73795
4.55	20.7025	2.13307	6.74537
4.56	20.7936	2.13542	6.75278
4.57	20.8849	2.13776	6.76018
4.58	20.9764	2.14009	6.76757
4.59	21.0681	2.14243	6.77495
4.60	21.1600	2.14476	6.78233
4.61	21.2521	2.14709	6.78970
4.62	21.3444	2.14942	6.79706
4.63	21.4369	2.15174	6.80441
4.64	21.5296	2.15407	6.81175
4.65	21.6225	2.15639	6.81909
4.66	21.7156	2.15870	6.82642
4.67	21.8089	2.16102	6.83374
4.68	21.9024	2.16333	6.84105
4.69	21.9961	2.16564	6.84836
4.70	22.0900	2.16795	6.85565
4.71	22.1841	2.17025	6.86294
4.72	22.2784	2.17256	6.87023
4.73	22.3729	2.17486	6.87750
4.74	22.4676	2.17715	6.88477
4.75	22.5625	2.17945	6.89202
4.76	22.6576	2.18174	6.89928
4.77	22.7529	2.18403	6.90652
4.78	22.8484	2.18632	6.91375
4.79	22.9441	2.18861	6.92098
4.80	23.0400	2.19089	6.92820
4.81	23.1361	2.19317	6.93542
4.82	23.2324	2.19545	6.94262
4.83	23.3289	2.19773	6.94982
4.84	23.4256	2.20000	6.95701
4.85	23.5225	2.20227	6.96419
4.86	23.6196	2.20454	6.97137
4.87	23.7169	2.20681	6.97854
4.88	23.8144	2.20907	6.98570
4.89	23.9121	2.21133	6.99285
4.90	24.0100	2.21359	7.00000
4.91	24.1081	2.21585	7.00714
4.92	24.2064	2.21811	7.01427
4.93	24.3049	2.22036	7.02140
4.94	24.4036	2.22261	7.02851
4.95	24.5025	2.22486	7.03562
4.96	24.6016	2.22711	7.04273
4.97	24.7009	2.22935	7.04982
4.98	24.8004	2.23159	7.05691
4.99	24.9001	2.23383	7.06399
5.00	25.0000	2.23607	7.07107
N	N²	√N	√10N

TABLE I (Continued)

N	N^2	$\sqrt{N}$	$\sqrt{10N}$
5.00	25.0000	2.23607	7.07107
5.01	25.1001	2.23830	7.07814
5.02	25.2004	2.24054	7.08520
5.03	25.3009	2.24277	7.09225
5.04	25.4016	2.24499	7.09930
5.05	25.5025	2.24722	7.10634
5.06	25.6036	2.24944	7.11357
5.07	25.7049	2.25167	7.12039
5.08	25.8064	2.25389	7.12741
5.09	25.9081	2.25610	7.13442
5.10	26.0100	2.25832	7.14143
5.11	26.1121	2.26053	7.14843
5.12	26.2144	2.26274	7.15542
5.13	26.3169	2.26495	7.16240
5.14	26.4196	2.26716	7.16938
5.15	26.5225	2.26936	7.17635
5.16	26.6256	2.27156	7.18331
5.17	26.7289	2.27376	7.19027
5.18	26.8324	2.27596	7.19722
5.19	26.9361	2.27816	7.20417
5.20	27.0400	2.28035	7.21110
5.21	27.1441	2.28254	7.21803
5.22	27.2484	2.28473	7.22496
5.23	27.3529	2.28692	7.23187
5.24	27.4576	2.28910	7.23878
5.25	27.5625	2.29129	7.24569
5.26	27.6676	2.29347	7.25259
5.27	27.7729	2.29565	7.25948
5.28	27.8784	2.29783	7.26636
5.29	27.9841	2.30000	7.27324
5.30	28.0900	2.30217	7.28011
5.31	28.1961	2.30434	7.28697
5.32	28.3024	2.30651	7.29383
5.33	28.4089	2.30868	7.30068
5.34	28.5156	2.31084	7.30753
5.35	28.6225	2.31301	7.31437
5.36	28.7296	2.31517	7.32120
5.37	28.8369	2.31733	7.32803
5.38	28.9444	2.31948	7.33485
5.39	29.0521	2.32164	7.34166
5.40	29.1600	2.32379	7.34847
5.41	29.2681	2.32594	7.35527
5.42	29.3764	2.32809	7.56206
5.43	29.4849	2.33024	7.36885
5.44	29.5936	2.33238	7.37564
5.45	29.7025	2.33452	7.38241
5.46	29.8116	2.33666	7.38918
5.47	29.9209	2.33880	7.39594
5.48	30.0304	2.34094	7.40270
5.49	30.1401	2.34307	7.40945
5.50	30.2500	2.34521	7.41620
N	N^2	$\sqrt{N}$	$\sqrt{10N}$

N	N^2	$\sqrt{N}$	$\sqrt{10N}$
5.50	30.2500	2.34521	7.41620
5.51	30.3601	2.34734	7.42294
5.52	30.4704	2.34947	7.42967
5.53	30.5809	2.35160	7.43640
5.54	30.6916	2.35372	7.44312
5.55	30.8025	2.35584	7.44983
5.56	30.9136	2.35797	7.45654
5.57	31.0249	2.36008	7.46324
5.58	31.1364	2.36220	7.46994
5.59	31.2481	2.36432	7.47663
5.60	31.3600	2.36643	7.48331
5.61	31.4721	2.36854	7.48999
5.62	31.5844	2.37065	7.49667
5.63	31.6969	2.37276	7.50333
5.64	31.8096	2.37487	7.50999
5.65	31.9225	2.37697	7.51665
5.66	32.0356	2.37908	7.52330
5.67	32.1489	2.38118	7.52994
5.68	32.2624	2.38328	7.53658
5.69	32.3761	2.38537	7.54321
5.70	32.4900	2.38747	7.54983
5.71	32.6041	2.38956	7.55645
5.72	32.7184	2.39165	7.56307
5.73	32.8329	2.39374	7.56968
5.74	32.9476	2.39583	7.57628
5.75	33.0625	2.39792	7.58288
5.76	33.1776	2.40000	7.58947
5.77	33.2929	2.40208	7.59605
5.78	33.4084	2.40416	7.60263
5.79	33.5241	2.40624	7.60920
5.80	33.6400	2.40832	7.61577
5.81	33.7561	2.41039	7.62234
5.82	33.8724	2.41247	7.62889
5.83	33.9889	2.41454	7.63544
5.84	34.1056	2.41661	7.64199
5.85	34.2225	2.41868	7.64853
5.86	34.3396	2.42074	7.65506
5.87	34.4569	2.42281	7.66159
5.88	34.5744	2.42487	7.66812
5.89	34.6921	2.42693	7.67463
5.90	34.8100	2.42899	7.68115
5.91	34.9281	2.43105	7.68765
5.92	35.0464	2.43311	7.69615
5.93	35.1649	2.43516	7.70065
5.94	35.2836	2.43721	7.70714
5.95	35.4025	2.43926	7.71362
5.96	35.5216	2.44131	7.72010
5.97	35.6409	2.44336	7.72658
5.98	35.7604	2.44540	7.73305
5.99	35.8801	2.44745	7.73951
6.00	36.0000	2.44949	7.74597
N	N^2	$\sqrt{N}$	$\sqrt{10N}$

TABLE I (Continued)

N	N^2	$\sqrt{N}$	$\sqrt{10N}$
6.00	36.0000	2.44949	7.74597
6.01	36.1201	2.45153	7.75242
6.02	36.2404	2.45357	7.75887
6.03	36.3609	2.45561	7.76531
6.04	36.4816	2.45764	7.77174
6.05	36.6025	2.45967	7.77817
6.06	36.7236	2.46171	7.78460
6.07	36.8449	2.46374	7.79102
6.08	36.9664	2.46577	7.79744
6.09	37.0881	2.46779	7.80385
6.10	37.2100	2.46982	7.81025
6.11	37.3321	2.47184	7.81665
6.12	37.4544	2.47386	7.82304
6.13	37.5769	2.47588	7.82943
6.14	37.6996	2.47790	7.83582
6.15	37.8225	2.47992	7.84219
6.16	37.9456	2.48193	7.84857
6.17	38.0689	2.48395	7.85493
6.18	38.1924	2.48596	7.86130
6.19	38.3161	2.48797	7.86766
6.20	38.4400	2.48998	7.87401
6.21	38.5641	2.49199	7.88036
6.22	38.6884	2.49399	7.88670
6.23	38.8129	2.49600	7.89303
6.24	38.9376	2.49800	7.89937
6.25	39.0625	2.50000	7.90569
6.26	39.1876	2.50200	7.91202
6.27	39.3129	2.50400	7.91833
6.28	39.4384	2.50599	7.92465
6.29	39.5641	2.50799	7.93095
6.30	39.6900	2.50998	7.93725
6.31	39.8161	2.51197	7.94355
6.32	39.9424	2.51396	7.94984
6.33	40.0689	2.51595	7.95613
6.34	40.1956	2.51794	7.96241
6.35	40.3225	2.51992	7.96869
6.36	40.4496	2.52190	7.97496
6.37	40.5769	2.52389	7.98123
6.38	40.7044	2.52587	7.98749
6.39	40.8321	2.52784	7.99375
6.40	40.9600	2.52982	8.00000
9.41	41.0881	5.53180	8.00625
6.42	41.2164	2.53377	8.01249
6.43	41.3449	2.53574	8.01873
6.44	41.4736	2.53772	8.02496
6.45	41.6025	2.53969	8.03119
6.46	41.7316	2.54165	8.03741
6.47	41.8609	2.54362	8.04363
6.48	41.9904	2.54558	8.04984
6.49	42.1201	2.54755	8.05605
6.50	42.2500	2.54951	8.06226
N	N^2	$\sqrt{N}$	$\sqrt{10N}$

N	N^2	$\sqrt{N}$	$\sqrt{10N}$
6.50	42.2500	2.54951	8.06226
6.51	42.3801	2.55147	8.06846
6.52	42.5104	2.55343	8.07465
6.53	42.6409	2.55539	8.08084
6.54	42.7716	2.55734	8.08703
6.55	42.9025	2.55930	8.09321
6.56	43.0336	2.56125	8.09938
6.57	43.1649	2.56320	8.10555
6.58	43.2964	2.56515	8.11172
6.59	43.4281	2.56710	8.11788
6.60	43.5600	2.56905	8.12404
6.61	43.6921	2.57099	8.13019
6.62	43.8244	2.57294	8.13634
6.63	43.9569	2.57488	8.14248
6.64	44.0896	2.57682	8.14862
6.65	44.2225	2.57876	8.15475
6.66	44.3556	2.58070	8.16088
6.67	44.4889	2.58263	8.16701
6.68	44.6224	2.58457	8.17313
6.69	44.7561	2.58650	8.17924
6.70	44.8900	2.58844	8.18535
6.71	45.0241	2.59037	8.19146
6.72	45.1584	2.59230	8.19756
6.73	45.2929	2.59422	8.20366
6.74	45.4276	2.59615	8.20975
6.75	45.5625	2.59808	8.21584
6.76	45.6976	2.60000	8.22192
6.77	45.8329	2.60192	8.22800
6.78	45.9684	2.60384	8.23408
6.79	46.1041	2.60576	8.24015
6.80	46.2400	2.60768	8.24621
6.81	46.3761	2.60960	8.25227
6.82	46.5124	2.61151	8.25833
6.83	46.6489	2.61343	8.26438
6.84	46.7856	2.61534	8.27043
6.85	46.9225	2.61725	8.27647
6.86	47.0596	2.61916	8.28251
6.87	47.1969	2.62107	8.28855
6.88	47.3344	2.62298	8.29458
6.89	47.4721	2.62488	8.30060
6.90	47.6100	2.62679	8.30662
6.91	47.7481	2.62869	8.31264
6.92	47.8864	2.63059	8.31865
6.93	48.0249	2.63249	8.32466
6.94	48.1636	2.63439	8.33067
6.95	48.3025	2.63629	8.33667
6.96	48.4416	2.63818	8.34266
6.97	48.5809	2.64008	8.34865
6.98	48.7204	2.64197	8.35464
6.99	48.8601	2.64386	8.36062
7.00	49.0000	2.64575	8.36660
N	N^2	$\sqrt{N}$	$\sqrt{10N}$

TABLE I (Continued)

N	N^2	$\sqrt{N}$	$\sqrt{10N}$
7.00	49.0000	2.64575	8.36660
7.01	49.1401	2.64764	8.37257
7.02	49.2804	2.64953	8.37854
7.03	49.4209	2.65141	8.38451
7.04	49.5616	2.65330	8.39047
7.05	49.7025	2.65518	8.39643
7.06	49.8436	2.65707	8.40238
7.07	49.9849	2.65895	8.40833
7.08	50.1264	2.66083	8.41427
7.09	50.2681	2.66271	8.42021
7.10	50.4100	2.66458	8.42615
7.11	50.5521	2.66646	8.43208
7.12	50.6944	2.66833	8.43801
7.13	50.8369	2.67021	8.44393
7.14	50.9796	2.67208	8.44985
7.15	51.1225	2.67395	8.45577
7.16	51.2656	2.67582	8.46168
7.17	51.4089	2.67769	8.46759
7.18	51.5524	2.67955	8.47349
7.19	51.6961	2.68142	8.47939
7.20	51.8400	2.68328	8.48528
7.21	51.9841	2.68514	8.49117
7.22	52.1284	2.68701	8.49706
7.23	52.2729	2.68887	8.50294
7.24	52.4176	2.69072	8.50882
7.25	52.5625	2.69258	8.51469
7.26	52.7076	2.69444	8.52056
7.27	52.8529	2.69629	8.52643
7.28	52.9984	2.69815	8.53229
7.29	53.1441	2.70000	8.53815
7.30	53.2900	2.70185	8.54400
7.31	53.4361	2.70370	8.54985
7.32	53.5824	2.70555	8.55570
7.33	53.7289	2.70740	8.56154
7.34	53.8756	2.70924	8.56738
7.35	54.0225	2.71109	8.57321
7.36	54.1696	2.71293	8.57904
7.37	54.3169	2.71477	8.58487
7.38	54.4644	2.71662	8.59069
7.39	54.6121	2.71846	8.59651
7.40	54.7600	2.72029	8.60233
7.41	54.9081	2.72213	8.60814
7.42	55.0564	2.72397	8.61394
7.43	55.2049	2.72580	8.61974
7.44	55.3536	2.72764	8.62554
7.45	55.5025	2.72947	8.63134
7.46	55.6516	2.73130	8.63713
7.47	55.8009	2.73313	8.64292
7.48	55.9504	2.73496	8.64870
7.49	56.1001	2.73679	8.65448
7.50	56.2500	2.73861	8.66025
N	N^2	$\sqrt{N}$	$\sqrt{10N}$

N	N^2	$\sqrt{N}$	$\sqrt{10N}$
7.50	56.2500	2.73861	8.66025
7.51	56.4001	2.74044	8.66603
7.52	56.5504	2.74226	8.67179
7.53	56.7009	2.74408	8.67756
7.54	56.8516	2.74591	8.68332
7.55	57.0025	2.74773	8.68907
7.56	57.1536	2.74955	8.69483
7.57	57.3049	2.75136	8.70057
7.58	57.4564	2.75318	8.70632
7.59	57.6081	2.75500	8.71206
7.60	57.7600	2.75681	8.71780
7.61	57.9121	2.75862	8.72353
7.62	58.0644	2.76043	8.72926
7.63	58.2169	2.76225	8.73499
7.64	58.3696	2.76405	8.74071
7.65	58.5225	2.76586	8.74643
7.66	58.6756	2.76767	8.75214
7.67	58.8289	2.76948	8.75785
7.68	58.9824	2.77128	8.76356
7.69	59.1361	2.77308	8.76926
7.70	59.2900	2.77489	8.77496
7.71	59.4441	2.77669	8.78066
7.72	59.5984	2.77849	8.78635
7.73	59.7529	2.78029	8.79204
7.74	59.9076	2.78209	8.79773
7.75	60.0625	2.78388	8.80341
7.76	60.2176	2.78568	8.80909
7.77	60.3729	2.78747	8.81476
7.78	60.5284	2.78927	8.82043
7.79	60.6841	2.79106	8.82610
7.80	60.8400	2.79285	8.83176
7.81	60.9961	2.79464	8.83742
7.82	61.1524	2.79643	8.84308
7.83	61.3089	2.79821	8.84873
7.84	61.4656	2.80000	8.85438
7.85	61.6225	2.80179	8.86002
7.86	61.7796	2.80357	8.86566
7.87	61.9369	2.80535	8.87130
7.88	62.0944	2.80713	8.87694
7.89	62.2521	2.80891	3.88257
7.90	62.4100	2.81069	8.88819
7.91	62.5681	2.81247	8.89382
7.92	62.7264	2.81425	8.89944
7.93	62.8849	2.81603	8.90505
7.94	63.0436	2.81780	8.91067
7.95	63.2025	2.81957	8.91628
7.96	63.3616	2.82135	8.92188
7.97	63.5209	2.82312	8.92749
7.98	63.6804	2.82489	8.93308
7.99	63.8401	2.82666	8.93868
8.00	64.0000	2.82843	8.94427
N	N^2	$\sqrt{N}$	$\sqrt{10N}$

TABLE I (Continued)

N	N^2	$\sqrt{N}$	$\sqrt{N10}$
8.00	64.0000	2.82843	8.94427
8.01	64.1601	2.83019	8.94986
8.02	64.3204	2.83196	8.95545
8.03	64.4809	2.83373	8.96103
8.04	64.6416	2.83549	8.96660
8.05	64.8025	2.83725	8.97218
8.06	64.9636	2.83901	8.97775
8.07	65.1249	2.84077	8.98332
8.08	65.2864	2.84253	8.98888
8.09	65.4481	2.84429	8.99444
8.10	65.6100	2.84605	9.00000
8.11	65.7721	2.84781	9.00555
8.12	65.9344	2.84956	9.01110
8.13	66.0969	2.85132	9.01665
8.14	66.2596	2.85307	9.02219
8.15	66.4225	2.85482	9.02774
8.16	66.5856	2.85657	9.03327
8.17	66.7489	2.85832	9.03881
8.18	66.9124	2.86007	9.04434
8.19	67.0761	2.86182	9.04986
8.20	67.2400	2.86356	9.05539
8.21	67.4041	2.86531	9.06091
8.22	67.5684	2.86705	9.06642
8.23	67.7329	2.86880	9.07193
8.24	67.8976	2.87054	9.07744
8.25	68.0625	2.87228	9.08295
8.26	68.2276	2.87402	9.08845
8.27	68.3929	2.87576	9.09395
8.28	68.5584	2.87750	9.09945
8.29	68.7241	2.87924	9.10494
8.30	68.8900	2.88097	9.11043
8.31	69.0561	2.88271	9.11592
8.32	69.2224	2.88444	9.12140
8.33	69.3889	2.88617	9.12688
8.34	69.5556	2.88791	9.13236
8.35	69.7225	2.88964	9.13783
8.36	69.8896	2.89137	9.14330
8.37	70.0569	2.89310	9.14877
8.38	70.2244	2.89482	9.15423
8.39	70.3921	2.89655	9.15969
8.40	70.5600	2.89828	9.16515
8.41	70.7281	2.90000	9.17061
8.42	70.8964	2.90172	9.17606
8.43	71.0649	2.90345	9.18150
8.44	71.2336	2.90517	9.18695
8.45	71.4025	2.90689	9.19239
8.46	71.5716	2.90861	9.19783
8.47	71.7409	2.91033	9.20326
8.48	71.9104	2.91204	9.20869
8.49	72.0801	2.91376	9.21412
8.50	72.2500	2.91548	9.21954
N	N^2	$\sqrt{N}$	$\sqrt{N10}$

N	N^2	$\sqrt{N}$	$\sqrt{10N}$
8.50	72.2500	2.91548	9.21954
8.51	72.4201	2.91719	9.22497
8.52	72.5904	2.91890	9.23038
8.53	72.7609	2.92062	9.23580
8.54	72.9316	2.92233	9.24121
8.55	73.1025	2.92404	9.24662
8.56	73.2736	2.92575	9.25203
8.57	73.4449	2.92746	9.25743
8.58	73.6164	2.92916	9.26283
8.59	73.7881	2.93087	9.26823
8.60	73.9600	2.93258	9.27362
8.61	74.1321	2.93428	9.27901
8.62	74.3044	2.93598	9.28440
8.63	74.4769	2.93769	9.28978
8.64	74.6496	2.93939	9.29516
8.65	74.8225	2.94109	9.30054
8.66	74.9956	2.94279	9.30591
8.67	75.1689	2.94449	9.31128
8.68	75.3424	2.94618	9.31665
8.69	75.5161	2.94788	9.32202
8.70	75.6900	2.94958	9.32738
8.71	75.8641	2.95127	9.33274
8.72	76.0384	2.95296	9.33809
8.73	76.2129	2.95466	9.34345
8.74	76.3876	2.95635	9.34880
8.75	76.5625	2.95804	9.35414
8.76	76.7376	2.95973	9.35949
8.77	76.9129	2.96142	9.36483
8.87	77.0884	2.96311	9.37017
8.79	77.2641	2.96479	9.37550
8.80	77.4400	2.96648	9.38083
8.81	77.6161	2.96816	9.38616
8.82	77.7924	2.96985	9.39149
8.83	77.9689	2.97153	9.39681
8.84	78.1456	2.97321	9.40213
8.85	78.3225	2.97489	9.40744
8.86	78.4996	2.97658	9.41276
8.87	78.6769	2.97825	9.41807
8.88	78.8544	2.97993	9.42338
8.89	79.0321	2.98161	9.42868
8.90	79.2100	2.98329	9.43398
8.91	79.3881	2.98496	9.43928
8.92	79.5664	2.98664	9.44458
8.93	79.7449	2.98831	9.44987
8.94	79.9236	2.98998	9.45516
8.95	80.1025	2.99166	9.46044
8.96	80.2816	2.99333	9.46573
8.97	80.4609	2.99500	9.47101
8.98	80.6404	2.99666	9.47629
8.99	80.8201	2.99833	9.48156
9.00	81.0000	3.00000	9.48683
N	N^2	$\sqrt{N}$	$\sqrt{10N}$

TABLE I (Continued)

N	N^2	$\sqrt{N}$	$\sqrt{10N}$
9.00	81.0000	3.00000	9.48683
9.01	81.1801	3.00167	9.49210
9.02	81.3604	3.00333	9.49737
9.03	81.5409	3.00500	9.50263
9.04	81.7216	3.00666	9.50789
9.05	81.9025	3.00832	9.51315
9.06	82.0836	3.00998	9.51840
9.07	82.2649	3.01164	9.52365
9.08	82.4464	3.01330	9.52890
9.09	82.6281	3.01496	9.53415
9.10	82.8100	3.01662	9.53939
9.11	82.9921	3.01828	9.54463
9.12	83.1744	3.01993	9.54987
9.13	83.3569	3.02159	9.55510
9.14	83.5396	3.02324	9.56033
9.15	83.7225	3.02490	9.56556
9.16	83.9056	3.02655	9.57079
9.17	84.0889	3.02820	9.57601
9.18	84.2724	3.02985	9.58125
9.19	84.4561	3.03150	9.58645
9.20	84.6400	3.03315	9.59166
9.21	84.8241	3.03480	9.59687
9.22	85.0084	3.03645	9.60208
9.23	85.1929	3.03809	9.60729
9.24	85.3776	3.03974	9.61249
9.25	85.5625	3.04138	9.61769
9.26	85.7476	3.04302	9.62289
9.27	85.9329	3.04467	9.62808
9.28	86.1184	3.04631	9.63328
9.29	86.3041	3.04795	9.63846
9.30	86.4900	3.04959	9.64365
9.31	86.6761	3.05123	9.64883
9.32	86.8624	3.05287	9.65401
9.33	87.0489	3.05450	9.65919
9.34	87.2356	3.05614	9.66437
9.35	87.4225	3.05778	9.66954
9.36	87.6096	3.05941	9.67471
9.37	87.7969	3.06105	9.67988
9.38	87.9844	3.06268	9.68504
9.39	88.1721	3.06431	9.69020
9.40	88.3600	3.06594	9.69536
9.41	88.5481	3.06757	9.70052
9.42	88.7364	3.06920	9.70567
9.43	88.9249	3.07083	9.71082
9.44	89.1136	3.07246	9.71597
9.45	89.3025	3.07409	9.72111
9.46	89.4916	3.07571	9.72625
9.47	89.6809	3.07734	9.73139
9.48	89.8704	3.07896	9.73653
9.49	90.0601	3.08058	9.74166
9.50	90.2500	3.08221	9.74679
N	N^2	$\sqrt{N}$	$\sqrt{10N}$

N	N^2	$\sqrt{N}$	$\sqrt{10N}$
9.50	90.2500	3.08221	9.74679
9.51	90.4401	3.08383	9.75192
9.52	90.6304	3.08545	9.75705
9.53	90.8209	3.08707	9.76217
9.54	91.0116	3.08869	9.76729
9.55	91.2025	3.09031	9.77241
9.56	91.3956	3.09192	9.77753
9.57	91.5849	5.09354	9.78264
9.58	91.7764	3.09516	9.78775
9.59	91.9681	3.09677	9.79785
9.60	92.1600	3.09839	9.79796
9.61	92.3521	3.10000	9.80306
9.62	92.5444	3.10161	9.80816
9.63	92.7369	3.10322	9.81326
9.64	92.9296	3.10483	9.81835
9.65	93.1225	3.10644	9.82344
9.66	93.3156	3.10805	9.82853
9.67	93.5089	3.10966	9.83362
9.68	93.7024	3.11127	9.83870
9.69	93.8961	3.11288	9.84378
9.70	94.0900	3.11448	9.84886
9.71	94.2841	3.11609	9.85393
9.72	94.4784	3.11769	9.85901
9.73	94.6729	3.11929	9.86408
9.74	94.8676	3.12090	9.86914
9.75	95.0625	3.12250	9.87421
9.76	95.2576	3.12410	9.87927
9.77	95.4529	3.12570	9.88433
9.78	95.6484	3.12730	9.88939
9.79	95.8441	3.12890	9.89444
9.80	96.0400	3.13050	9.89949
9.81	96.2361	3.13209	9.90454
9.82	96.4324	3.13369	9.90959
9.83	96.6289	3.13528	9.91464
9.84	96.8256	3.13688	9.91968
9.85	97.0225	3.13847	9.92472
9.86	97.2196	3.14006	9.92975
9.87	97.4169	3.14166	9.93479
9.88	97.6144	3.14325	9.93982
9.89	97.8121	3.14484	9.94485
9.90	98.0100	3.14643	9.94987
9.91	98.2081	3.14802	9.95490
9.92	98.4064	3.14960	9.95992
9.93	98.6049	3.15119	9.96494
9.94	98.8036	3.15278	9.96995
9.95	99.0025	3.15436	9.97497
9.96	99.2016	3.15595	9.97998
9.97	99.4009	3.15753	9.98499
9.98	99.6004	3.15911	9.98999
9.99	99.8001	3.16070	9.99500
10.00	100.000	3.16228	10.0000
N	N^2	$\sqrt{N}$	$\sqrt{10N}$

Table IIa Random Digits

39 65 76 45 45	19 90 69 64 61	20 26 36 31 62	58 24 97 14 97	95 06 70 99 00
73 71 23 70 90	65 97 60 12 11	31 56 34 19 19	47 83 75 51 33	30 62 38 20 46
72 20 47 33 84	51 67 47 97 19	98 40 07 17 66	23 05 09 51 80	59 78 11 52 49
75 17 25 69 17	17 95 21 78 58	24 33 45 77 48	69 81 84 09 29	93 22 70 45 80
37 48 79 88 74	63 52 06 34 30	01 31 60 10 27	35 07 79 71 53	28 99 52 01 41
02 89 08 16 94	85 53 83 29 95	56 27 09 24 43	21 78 55 09 82	72 61 88 73 61
87 18 15 70 07	37 79 49 12 38	48 13 93 55 96	41 92 45 71 51	09 18 25 58 94
98 83 71 70 15	89 09 39 59 24	00 06 41 41 20	14 36 59 25 47	54 45 17 24 89
10 08 58 07 04	76 62 16 48 68	58 76 17 14 86	59 53 11 52 21	66 04 18 72 87
47 90 56 37 31	71 82 13 50 41	27 55 10 24 92	28 04 67 53 44	95 23 00 84 47
93 05 31 03 07	34 18 04 52 35	74 13 39 35 22	68 95 23 92 35	36 63 70 35 33
21 89 11 47 99	11 20 99 45 18	76 51 94 84 86	13 79 93 37 55	98 16 04 41 67
95 18 94 06 97	27 37 83 28 71	79 57 95 13 91	09 61 87 25 21	56 20 11 32 44
97 08 31 55 73	10 65 81 92 59	77 31 61 95 46	20 44 90 32 64	26 99 76 75 63
69 26 88 86 13	59 71 74 17 32	48 38 75 93 29	73 37 32 04 05	60 82 29 20 25
41 47 10 25 03	87 63 93 95 17	81 83 83 04 49	77 45 85 50 51	79 88 01 97 30
91 94 14 63 62	08 61 74 51 69	92 79 43 89 79	29 18 94 51 23	14 85 11 47 23
80 06 54 18 47	08 52 85 08 40	48 40 35 94 22	72 65 71 08 86	50 03 42 99 36
67 72 77 63 99	89 85 84 46 06	64 71 06 21 66	89 37 20 70 01	61 65 70 22 12
59 40 24 13 75	42 29 72 23 19	06 94 76 10 08	81 30 15 39 14	81 83 17 16 33
63 62 06 34 41	79 53 36 02 95	94 61 09 43 62	20 21 14 68 86	84 95 48 46 45
78 47 23 53 90	79 93 96 38 63	34 85 52 05 09	85 43 01 72 73	14 93 87 81 40
87 68 62 15 43	97 48 72 66 48	53 16 71 13 81	59 97 50 99 52	24 62 20 42 31
47 60 92 10 77	26 97 05 73 51	88 46 38 03 58	72 68 49 29 31	75 70 16 08 24
56 88 87 59 41	06 87 37 78 48	65 88 69 58 39	88 02 84 27 83	85 81 56 39 38
22 17 68 65 84	87 02 22 57 51	68 69 80 95 44	11 29 01 95 80	49 34 35 86 47
19 36 27 59 46	39 77 32 77 09	79 57 92 36 59	89 74 39 82 15	08 58 94 34 74
16 77 23 02 77	28 06 24 25 93	22 45 44 84 11	87 80 61 65 31	09 71 91 74 25
78 43 76 71 61	97 67 63 99 61	80 45 67 93 82	59 73 19 85 23	53 33 65 97 21
03 28 28 26 08	69 30 16 09 05	53 58 47 70 93	66 56 45 65 79	45 56 20 19 47
04 31 17 21 56	33 73 99 19 87	26 72 39 27 67	53 77 57 68 93	60 61 97 22 61
61 06 98 03 91	87 14 77 43 96	43 00 65 98 50	45 60 33 01 07	98 99 46 50 47
23 68 35 26 00	99 53 93 61 28	52 70 05 48 34	56 65 05 61 86	90 92 10 70 80
15 39 25 70 99	93 86 52 77 65	15 33 59 05 28	22 87 26 07 47	86 96 98 29 06
58 71 96 30 24	18 46 23 34 27	85 13 99 24 44	49 18 09 79 49	74 16 32 23 02
93 22 53 64 39	07 10 63 76 35	87 03 04 79 88	08 13 13 85 51	55 34 57 72 69
78 76 58 54 74	92 38 70 96 92	52 06 79 79 45	82 63 18 27 44	69 66 92 19 09
61 81 31 96 82	00 57 25 60 59	46 72 60 18 77	55 66 12 62 11	08 99 55 64 57
42 88 07 10 05	24 98 65 63 21	47 21 61 88 32	27 80 30 21 60	10 92 35 36 12
77 94 30 05 39	28 10 99 00 27	12 73 73 99 12	49 99 57 94 82	96 88 57 17 91

Eqn. 6-22 is $\rho e_{t-1} + V_t$

TABLE II*b* Random Normal Numbers, $\mu = 0$, $\sigma = 1$

.464	.137	2.455	−.323	−.068	.296	−.288	1.298	.241	−.957
.060	−2.526	−.531	−.194	.543	−1.558	.187	−1.190	.022	.525
1.486	−.354	−.634	.697	.926	1.375	.785	−.963	−.853	−1.865
1.022	−.472	1.279	3.521	.571	−1.851	.194	1.192	−.501	−.273
1.394	−.555	.046	.321	2.945	1.974	−.258	.412	.439	−.035
.906	−.513	−.525	.595	.881	−.934	1.579	.161	−1.885	.371
1.179	−1.055	.007	.769	.971	.712	1.090	−.631	−.255	−.702
−1.501	−.488	−.162	−.136	1.033	.203	.448	.748	−.423	−.432
−.690	.756	−1.618	−.345	−.511	−2.051	−.457	−.218	.857	−.465
1.372	.225	.378	.761	.181	−.736	.960	−1.530	−.260	.120
−.482	1.678	−.057	−1.229	−.486	.856	−.491	−1.983	−2.830	−.238
−1.376	−.150	1.356	−.561	−.256	−.212	.219	.779	.953	−.869
−1.010	.598	−.918	1.598	.065	.415	−.169	.313	−.973	−1.016
−.005	−.899	.012	−.725	1.147	−.121	1.096	.481	−1.691	.417
1.393	−1.163	−.911	1.231	−.199	−.246	1.239	−2.574	−.558	.056
−1.787	−.261	1.237	1.046	−.508	−1.630	−.146	−.392	−.627	.561
−.105	−.375	−1.384	.360	−.992	−.116	−1.698	−2.832	−1.108	−2.357
−1.339	1.827	−.959	.424	.969	−1.141	−1.041	.362	−1.726	1.956
1.041	.535	.731	1.377	.983	−1.330	1.620	−1.040	.524	−.281
.279	−2.056	.717	−.873	−1.096	−1.396	1.047	.089	−.573	.932
−1.805	−2.008	−1.633	.542	.250	−.166	.032	.079	.471	−1.029
−1.186	1.180	1.114	.882	1.265	−.202	.151	−.376	−.310	.479
.658	−1.141	1.151	−1.210	−.927	.425	.290	−.902	.610	1.709
−.439	.358	−1.939	.891	−.227	.602	.873	−.437	−.220	−.057
−1.399	−.230	.385	−.649	−.577	.237	−.289	.513	.738	−.300
.199	.208	−1.083	−.219	−.291	1.221	1.119	.004	−2.015	−.594
.159	.272	−.313	.084	−2.828	−.439	−.792	−1.275	−.623	−1.047
2.273	.606	.606	−.747	.247	1.291	.063	−1.793	−.699	−1.347
.041	−.307	.121	.790	−.584	.541	.484	−.986	.481	.996
−1.132	−2.098	.921	.145	.446	−1.661	1.045	−1.363	−.586	−1.023
.768	.079	−1.473	.034	−2.127	.665	.084	−.880	−.579	.551
.375	−1.658	−.851	.234	−.656	.340	−.086	−.158	−.120	.418
−.513	−.344	.210	−.736	1.041	.008	.427	−.831	.191	.074
.292	−.521	1.266	−1.206	−.899	.110	−.528	−.813	.071	.524
1.026	2.990	−.574	−.491	−1.114	1.297	−1.433	−1.345	−3.001	.479
−1.334	1.278	−.568	−.109	−.515	−.566	2.923	.500	.359	.326
−.287	−.144	−.254	.574	−.451	−1.181	−1.190	−.318	−.094	1.114
.161	−.886	−.921	−.509	1.410	−.518	.192	−.432	1.501	1.068
−1.346	.193	−1.202	.394	−1.045	.843	.942	1.045	.031	.772
−1.250	−.199	−.288	1.810	1.378	.584	1.216	.733	.402	.226
.630	−.537	.782	.060	.499	−.431	1.705	1.164	.884	−.298
.375	−1.941	.247	−.491	.665	−.135	−.145	−.498	.457	1.064
−1.420	.489	−1.711	−1.186	.754	−.732	−.066	1.006	−.798	.162
−.151	−.243	−.430	−.762	.298	1.049	1.810	2.885	−.768	−.129
−.309	.531	.416	−1.541	1.456	2.040	−.124	.196	.023	−1.204
.424	−.444	.593	.993	−.106	.116	.484	−1.272	1.066	1.097
.593	.658	−1.127	−1.407	−1.579	−1.616	1.458	1.262	.736	−.916
.862	−.885	−.142	−.504	.532	1.381	.022	−.281	−.342	1.222
.235	−.628	−.023	−.463	−.899	−.394	−.538	1.707	−.188	−1.153
−.853	.402	.777	.833	.410	−.349	−1.094	.580	1.395	1.298

TABLE IIIa Binomial Coefficients

n	$\binom{n}{0}$	$\binom{n}{1}$	$\binom{n}{2}$	$\binom{n}{3}$	$\binom{n}{4}$	$\binom{n}{5}$	$\binom{n}{6}$	$\binom{n}{7}$	$\binom{n}{8}$	$\binom{n}{9}$	$\binom{n}{10}$
0	1										
1	1	1									
2	1	2	1								
3	1	3	3	1							
4	1	4	6	4	1						
5	1	5	10	10	5	1					
6	1	6	15	20	15	6	1				
7	1	7	21	35	35	21	7	1			
8	1	8	28	56	70	56	28	8	1		
9	1	9	36	84	126	126	84	36	9	1	
10	1	10	45	120	210	252	210	120	45	10	1
11	1	11	55	165	330	462	462	330	165	55	11
12	1	12	66	220	495	792	924	792	495	220	66
13	1	13	78	286	715	1287	1716	1716	1287	715	286
14	1	14	91	364	1001	2002	3003	3432	3003	2002	1001
15	1	15	105	455	1365	3003	5005	6435	6435	5005	3003
16	1	16	120	560	1820	4368	8008	11440	12870	11440	8008
17	1	17	136	680	2380	6188	12376	19448	24310	24310	19448
18	1	18	153	816	3060	8568	18564	31824	43758	48620	43758
19	1	19	171	969	3876	11628	27132	50388	75582	92378	92378
20	1	20	190	1140	4845	15504	38760	77520	125970	167960	184756

Note. $\binom{n}{x} = \dfrac{n(n-1)(n-2)\cdots(n-x+1)}{x(x-1)(x-2)\cdots 3.2.1}$; $\binom{n}{0} = 1$; $\binom{n}{1} = n$. For coefficients missing from the above table, use the relation

$$\binom{n}{x} = \binom{n}{n-x}, \quad \text{e.g.,} \quad \binom{20}{11} = \binom{20}{9} = 167960.$$

TABLE III*b* Individual Binomial Probabilities $p(x)$

n	x	.05	.10	.15	.20	.25	.30	.35	.40	.45	.50
						π					
1	0	.9500	.9000	.8500	.8000	.7500	.7000	.6500	.6000	.5500	.5000
	1	.0500	.1000	.1500	.2000	.2500	.3000	.3500	.4000	.4500	.5000
2	0	.9025	.8100	.7225	.6400	.5625	.4900	.4225	.3600	.3025	.2500
	1	.0950	.1800	.2550	.3200	.3750	.4200	.4550	.4800	.4950	.5000
	2	.0025	.0100	.0225	.0400	.0625	.0900	.1225	.1600	.2025	.2500
3	0	.8574	.7290	.6141	.5120	.4219	.3430	.2746	.2160	.1664	.1250
	1	.1354	.2430	.3251	.3840	.4219	.4410	.4436	.4320	.4084	.3750
	2	.0071	.0270	.0574	.0960	.1406	.1890	.2389	.2880	.3341	.3750
	3	.0001	.0010	.0034	.0080	.0156	.0270	.0429	.0640	.0911	.1250
4	0	.8145	.6561	.5220	.4096	.3164	.2401	.1785	.1296	.0915	.0625
	1	.1715	.2916	.3685	.4096	.4219	.4116	.3845	.3456	.2995	.2500
	2	.0135	.0486	.0975	.1536	.2109	.2646	.3105	.3456	.3675	.3750
	3	.0005	.0036	.0115	.0256	.0469	.0756	.1115	.1536	.2005	.2500
	4	.0000	.0001	.0005	.0016	.0039	.0081	.0150	.0256	.0410	.0625
5	0	.7738	.5905	.4437	.3277	.2373	.1681	.1160	.0778	.0503	.0312
	1	.2036	.3280	.3915	.4096	.3955	.3602	.3124	.2592	.2059	.1562
	2	.0214	.0729	.1382	.2048	.2637	.3087	.3364	.3456	.3369	.3125
	3	.0011	.0081	.0244	.0512	.0879	.1323	.1811	.2304	.2757	.3125
	4	.0000	.0004	.0022	.0064	.0146	.0284	.0488	.0768	.1128	.1562
	5	.0000	.0000	.0001	.0003	.0010	.0024	.0053	.0102	.0185	.0312
6	0	.7351	.5314	.3771	.2621	.1780	.1176	.0754	.0467	.0277	.0156
	1	.2321	.3543	.3993	.3932	.3560	.3025	.2437	.1866	.1359	.0938
	2	.0305	.0984	.1762	.2458	.2966	.3241	.3280	.3110	.2780	.2344
	3	.0021	.0146	.0415	.0819	.1318	.1852	.2355	.2765	.3032	.3125
	4	.0001	.0012	.0055	.0154	.0330	.0595	.0951	.1382	.1861	.2344
	5	.0000	.0001	.0004	.0015	.0044	.0102	.0205	.0369	.0609	.0938
	6	.0000	.0000	.0000	.0001	.0002	.0007	.0018	.0041	.0083	.0156
7	0	.6983	.4783	.3206	.2097	.1335	.0824	.0490	.0280	.0152	.0078
	1	.2573	.3720	.3960	.3670	.3115	.2471	.1848	.1306	.0872	.0547
	2	.0406	.1240	.2097	.2753	.3115	.3177	.2985	.2613	.2140	.1641
	3	.0036	.0230	.0617	.1147	.1730	.2269	.2679	.2903	.2918	.2734
	4	.0002	.0026	.0109	.0287	.0577	.0972	.1442	.1935	.2388	.2734
	5	.0000	.0002	.0012	.0043	.0115	.0250	.0466	.0774	.1172	.1641
	6	.0000	.0000	.0001	.0004	.0013	.0036	.0084	.0172	.0320	.0547
	7	.0000	.0000	.0000	.0000	.0001	.0002	.0006	.0016	.0037	.0078

If $\pi > .50$, interchange π and $(1 - \pi)$.

TABLE III*b* (Continued)

		π									
n	x	.05	.10	.15	.20	.25	.30	.35	.40	.45	.50
8	0	.6634	.4305	.2725	.1678	.1001	.0576	.0319	.0168	.0084	.0039
	1	.2793	.3826	.3847	.3355	.2670	.1977	.1373	.0896	.0548	.0312
	2	.0515	.1488	.2376	.2936	.3115	.2965	.2587	.2090	.1569	.1094
	3	.0054	.0331	.0839	.1468	.2076	.2541	.2786	.2787	.2568	.2188
	4	.0004	.0046	.0185	.0459	.0865	.1361	.1875	.2322	.2627	.2734
	5	.0000	.0004	.0026	.0092	.0231	.0467	.0808	.1239	.1719	.2188
	6	.0000	.0000	.0002	.0011	.0038	.0100	.0217	.0413	.0703	.1094
	7	.0000	.0000	.0000	.0001	.0004	.0012	.0033	.0079	.0164	.0312
	8	.0000	.0000	.0000	.0000	.0000	.0001	.0002	.0007	.0017	.0039
9	0	.6302	.3874	.2316	.1342	.0751	.0404	.0207	.0101	.0046	.0020
	1	.2985	.3874	.3679	.3020	.2253	.1556	.1004	.0605	.0339	.0176
	2	.0629	.1722	.2597	.3020	.3003	.2668	.2162	.1612	.1110	.0703
	3	.0077	.0446	.1069	.1762	.2336	.2668	.2716	.2508	.2119	.1641
	4	.0006	.0074	.0283	.0661	.1168	.1715	.2194	.2508	.2600	.2461
	5	.0000	.0008	.0050	.0165	.0389	.0735	.1181	.1672	.2128	.2461
	6	.0000	.0001	.0006	.0028	.0087	.0210	.0424	.0743	.1160	.1641
	7	.0000	.0000	.0000	.0003	.0012	.0039	.0098	.0212	.0407	.0703
	8	.0000	.0000	.0000	.0000	.0001	.0004	.0013	.0035	.0083	.0176
	9	.0000	.0000	.0000	.0000	.0000	.0000	.0001	.0003	.0008	.0020
10	0	.5987	.3487	.1969	.1074	.0563	.0282	.0135	.0060	.0025	.0010
	1	.3151	.3874	.3474	.2684	.1877	.1211	.0725	.0403	.0207	.0098
	2	.0746	.1937	.2759	.3020	.2816	.2335	.1757	.1209	.0763	.0439
	3	.0105	.0574	.1298	.2013	.2503	.2668	.2522	.2150	.1665	.1172
	4	.0010	.0112	.0401	.0881	.1460	.2001	.2377	.2508	.2384	.2051
	5	.0001	.0015	.0085	.0264	.0584	.1029	.1536	.2007	.2340	.2461
	6	.0000	.0001	.0012	.0055	.0162	.0368	.0689	.1115	.1596	.2051
	7	.0000	.0000	.0001	.0008	.0031	.0090	.0212	.0425	.0746	.1172
	8	.0000	.0000	.0000	.0001	.0004	.0014	.0043	.0106	.0229	.0439
	9	.0000	.0000	.0000	.0000	.0000	.0001	.0005	.0016	.0042	.0098
	10	.0000	.0000	.0000	.0000	.0000	.0000	.0000	.0001	.0003	.0010

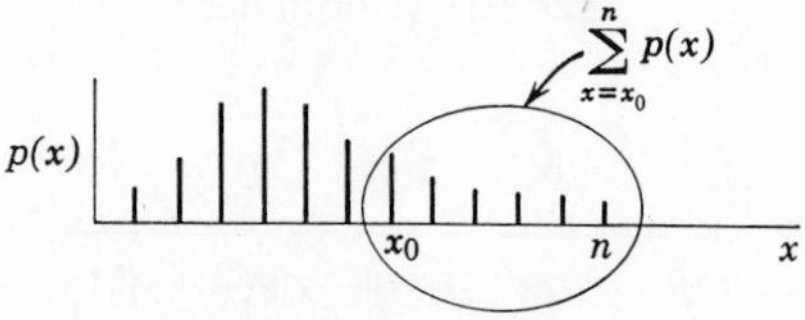

TABLE III*c* Cumulative Binomial Probabilities in Right-hand Tail

		π									
n	x_0	.05	.10	.15	.20	.25	.30	.35	.40	.45	.50
2	1	.0975	.1900	.2775	.3600	.4375	.5100	.5775	.6400	.6975	.7500
	2	.0025	.0100	.0225	.0400	.0625	.0900	.1225	.1600	.2025	.2500
3	1	.1426	.2710	.3859	.4880	.5781	.6570	.7254	.7840	.8336	.8750
	2	.0072	.0280	.0608	.1040	.1562	.2160	.2818	.3520	.4252	.5000
	3	.0001	.0010	.0034	.0080	.0156	.0270	.0429	.0640	.0911	.1250
4	1	.1855	.3439	.4780	.5904	.6836	.7599	.8215	.8704	.9085	.9375
	2	.0140	.0523	.1095	.1808	.2617	.3483	.4370	.5248	.6090	.6875
	3	.0005	.0037	.0120	.0272	.0508	.0837	.1265	.1792	.2415	.3125
	4	.0000	.0001	.0005	.0016	.0039	.0081	.0150	.0256	.0410	.0625
5	1	.2262	.4095	.5563	.6723	.7627	.8319	.8840	.9222	.9497	.9688
	2	.0226	.0815	.1648	.2627	.3672	.4718	.5716	.6630	.7438	.8125
	3	.0012	.0086	.0266	.0579	.1035	.1631	.2352	.3174	.4069	.5000
	4	.0000	.0005	.0022	.0067	.0156	.0308	.0540	.0870	.1312	.1875
	5	.0000	.0000	.0001	.0003	.0010	.0024	.0053	.0102	.0185	.0312
6	1	.2649	.4686	.6229	.7379	.8220	.8824	.9246	.9533	.9723	.9844
	2	.0328	.1143	.2235	.3447	.4661	.5798	.6809	.7667	.8364	.8906
	3	.0022	.0158	.0473	.0989	.1694	.2557	.3529	.4557	.5585	.6562
	4	.0001	.0013	.0059	.0170	.0376	.0705	.1174	.1792	.2553	.3438
	5	.0000	.0001	.0004	.0016	.0046	.0109	.0223	.0410	.0692	.1094
	6	.0000	.0000	.0000	.0001	.0002	.0007	.0018	.0041	.0083	.0156
7	1	.3017	.5217	.6794	.7903	.8665	.9176	.9510	.9720	.9848	.9922
	2	.0444	.1497	.2834	.4233	.5551	.6706	.7662	.8414	.8976	.9375
	3	.0038	.0257	.0738	.1480	.2436	.3529	.4677	.5801	.6836	.7734
	4	.0002	.0027	.0121	.0333	.0706	.1260	.1998	.2898	.3917	.5000
	5	.0000	.0002	.0012	.0047	.0129	.0288	.0556	.0963	.1529	.2266
	6	.0000	.0000	.0001	.0004	.0013	.0038	.0090	.0188	.0357	.0625
	7	.0000	.0000	.0000	.0000	.0001	.0002	.0006	.0016	.0037	.0078

TABLE III*c* (Continued)

n	x_0	.05	.10	.15	.20	.25	π .30	.35	.40	.45	50
8	1	.3366	.5695	.7275	.8322	.8999	.9424	.9681	.9832	.9916	.9961
	2	.0572	.1869	.3428	.4967	.6329	.7447	.8309	.8936	.9368	.9648
	3	.0058	.0381	.1052	.2031	.3215	.4482	.5722	.6846	.7799	.8555
	4	.0004	.0050	.0214	.0563	.1138	.1941	.2936	.4059	.5230	.6367
	5	.0000	.0004	.0029	.0104	.0273	.0580	.1061	.1737	.2604	.3633
	6	.0000	.0000	.0002	.0012	.0042	.0113	.0253	.0498	.0885	.1445
	7	.0000	.0000	.0000	.0001	.0004	.0013	.0036	.0085	.0181	.0352
	8	.0000	.0000	.0000	.0000	.0000	.0001	.0002	.0007	.0017	.0039
9	1	.3698	.6126	.7684	.8658	.9249	.9596	.9793	.9899	.9954	.9980
	2	.0712	.2252	.4005	.5638	.6997	.8040	.8789	.9295	.9615	.9805
	3	.0084	.0530	.1409	.2618	.3993	.5372	.6627	.7682	.8505	.9102
	4	.0006	.0083	.0339	.0856	.1657	.2703	.3911	.5174	.6386	.7461
	5	.0000	.0009	.0056	.0196	.0489	.0988	.1717	.2666	.3786	.5000
	6	.0000	.0001	.0006	.0031	.0100	.0253	.0536	.0994	.1658	.2539
	7	.0000	.0000	.0000	.0003	.0013	.0043	.0112	.0250	.0498	.0898
	8	.0000	.0000	.0000	.0000	.0001	.0004	.0014	.0038	.0091	.0195
	9	.0000	.0000	.0000	.0000	.0000	.0000	.0001	.0003	.0008	.0020
10	1	.4013	.6513	.8031	.8926	.9437	.9718	.9865	.9940	.9975	.9990
	2	.0861	.2639	.4557	.6242	.7560	.8507	.9140	.9536	.9767	.9893
	3	.0115	.0702	.1798	.3222	.4744	.6172	.7384	.8327	.9004	.9453
	4	.0010	.0128	.0500	.1209	.2241	.3504	.4862	.6177	.7340	.8281
	5	.0001	.0016	.0099	.0328	.0781	.1503	.2485	.3669	.4956	.6230
	6	.0000	.0001	.0014	.0064	.0197	.0473	.0949	.1662	.2616	.3770
	7	.0000	.0000	.0001	.0009	.0035	.0106	.0260	.0548	.1020	.1719
	8	.0000	.0000	.0000	.0001	.0004	.0016	.0048	.0123	.0274	.0547
	9	.0000	.0000	.0000	.0000	.0000	.0001	.0005	.0017	.0045	.0107
	10	.0000	.0000	.0000	.0000	.0000	.0000	.0000	.0001	.0003	.0010

Table IV Areas for a Standard Normal Distribution

An entry in the table is the area under the curve, between $z = 0$ and a positive value of z. Areas for negative values of z are obtained by symmetry.

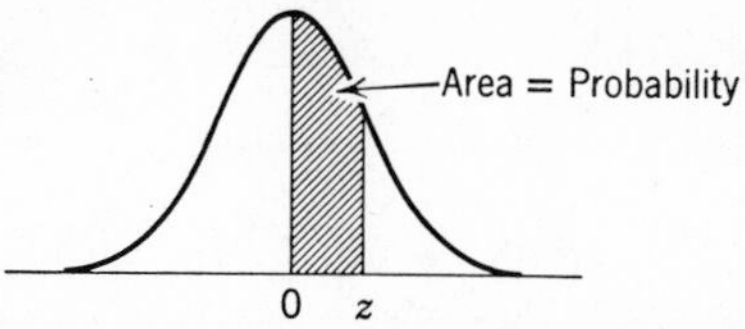

Second Decimal Place of z

→ ↓z	.00	.01	.02	.03	.04	.05	.06	.07	.08	.09
.0	.0000	.0040	.0080	.0120	.0160	.0199	.0239	.0279	.0319	.0359
.1	.0398	.0438	.0478	.0517	.0557	.0596	.0636	.0675	.0714	.0753
.2	.0793	.0832	.0871	.0910	.0948	.0987	.1026	.1064	.1103	.1141
.3	.1179	.1217	.1255	.1293	.1331	.1368	.1406	.1443	.1480	.1517
.4	.1554	.1591	.1628	.1664	.1700	.1736	.1772	.1808	.1844	.1879
.5	.1915	.1950	.1985	.2019	.2054	.2088	.2123	.2157	.2190	.2224
.6	.2257	.2291	.2324	.2357	.2389	.2422	.2454	.2486	.2517	.2549
.7	.2580	.2611	.2642	.2673	.2703	.2734	.2764	.2794	.2823	.2852
.8	.2881	.2910	.2939	.2967	.2995	.3023	.3051	.3078	.3106	.3133
.9	.3159	.3186	.3212	.3238	.3264	.3289	.3315	.3340	.3365	.3389
1.0	.3413	.3438	.3461	.3485	.3508	.3531	.3554	.3577	.3599	.3621
1.1	.3643	.3665	.3686	.3708	.3729	.3749	.3770	.3790	.3810	.3830
1.2	.3849	.3869	.3888	.3907	.3925	.3944	.3962	.3980	.3997	.4015
1.3	.4032	.4049	.4066	.4082	.4099	.4115	.4131	.4147	.4162	.4177
1.4	.4192	.4207	.4222	.4236	.4251	.4265	.4279	.4292	.4306	.4319
1.5	.4332	.4345	.4357	.4370	.4382	.4394	.4406	.4418	.4429	.4441
1.6	.4452	.4463	.4474	.4484	.4495	.4505	.4515	.4525	.4535	.4545
1.7	.4554	.4564	.4573	.4582	.4591	.4599	.4608	.4616	.4625	.4633
1.8	.4641	.4649	.4656	.4664	.4671	.4678	.4686	.4693	.4699	.4706
1.9	.4713	.4719	.4726	.4732	.4738	.4744	.4750	.4756	.4761	.4767
2.0	.4772	.4778	.4783	.4788	.4793	.4798	.4803	.4808	.4812	.4817
2.1	.4821	.4826	.4830	.4834	.4838	.4842	.4846	.4850	.4854	.4857
2.2	.4861	.4864	.4868	.4871	.4875	.4878	.4881	.4884	.4887	.4890
2.3	.4893	.4896	.4898	.4901	.4904	.4906	.4909	.4911	.4913	.4916
2.4	.4918	.4920	.4922	.4925	.4927	.4929	.4931	.4932	.4934	.4936
2.5	.4938	.4940	.4941	.4943	.4945	.4946	.4948	.4949	.4951	.4952
2.6	.4953	.4955	.4956	.4957	.4959	.4960	.4961	.4962	.4963	.4964
2.7	.4965	.4966	.4967	.4968	.4969	.4970	.4971	.4972	.4973	.4974
2.8	.4974	.4975	.4976	.4977	.4977	.4978	.4979	.4979	.4980	.4981
2.9	.4981	.4982	.4982	.4983	.4984	.4984	.4985	.4985	.4986	.4986
3.0	.4987	.4987	.4987	.4988	.4988	.4989	.4989	.4989	.4990	.4990

TABLE V Student's t Critical Points

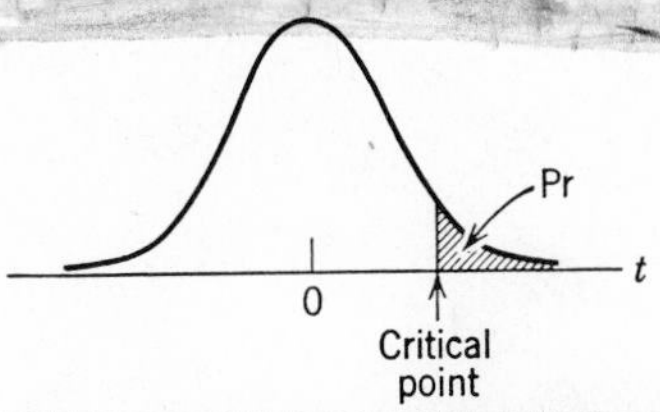

d.f. \ Pr	.10	.05	.025	.01	.005
1	3.078	6.314	12.706	31.821	63.657
2	1.886	2.920	4.303	6.965	9.925
3	1.638	2.353	3.182	4.541	5.841
4	1.533	2.132	2.776	3.747	4.604
5	1.476	2.015	2.571	3.365	4.032
6	1.440	1.943	2.447	3.143	3.707
7	1.415	1.895	2.365	2.998	3.499
8	1.397	1.860	2.306	2.896	3.355
9	1.383	1.833	2.262	2.821	3.250
10	1.372	1.812	2.228	2.764	3.169
11	1.363	1.796	2.201	2.718	3.106
12	1.356	1.782	2.179	2.681	3.055
13	1.350	1.771	2.160	2.650	3.012
14	1.345	1.761	2.145	2.624	2.977
15	1.341	1.753	2.131	2.602	2.947
16	1.337	1.746	2.120	2.583	2.921
17	1.333	1.740	2.110	2.567	2.898
18	1.330	1.734	2.101	2.552	2.878
19	1.328	1.729	2.093	2.539	2.861
20	1.325	1.725	2.086	2.528	2.845
21	1.323	1.721	2.080	2.518	2.831
22	1.321	1.717	2.074	2.508	2.819
23	1.319	1.714	2.069	2.500	2.807
24	1.318	1.711	2.064	2.492	2.797
25	1.316	1.708	2.060	2.485	2.787
26	1.315	1.706	2.056	2.479	2.779
27	1.314	1.703	2.052	2.473	2.771
28	1.313	1.701	2.048	2.467	2.763
29	1.311	1.699	2.045	2.462	2.756
30	1.310	1.697	2.042	2.457	2.750
40	1.303	1.684	2.021	2.423	2.704
60	1.296	1.671	2.000	2.390	2.660
120	1.289	1.658	1.980	2.358	2.617
∞	1.282	1.645	1.960	2.326	2.576

TABLE VI C^2 Critical Points* ($C^2 = \chi^2/\text{d.f.}$)

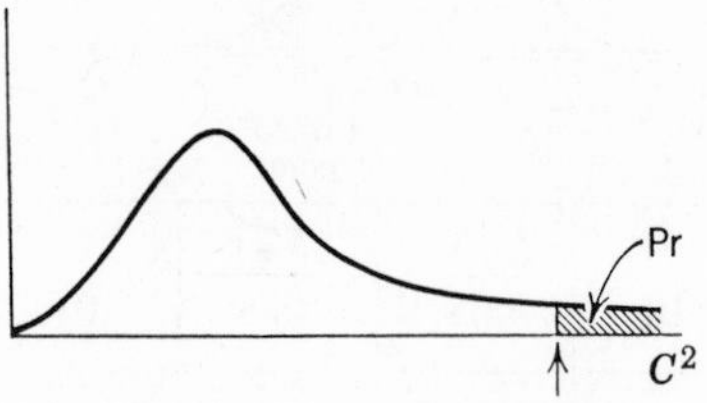

df \ Pr	.995	.99	.975	.95	.90	.10	.05	.025	.01	.005
1	.000039	.00016	.00098	.0039	.0158	2.71	3.84	5.02	6.63	7.88
2	.00501	.0101	.0253	.0513	.1054	2.30	3.00	3.69	4.61	5.30
3	.0239	.0383	.0719	.117	.195	2.08	2.60	3.12	3.78	4.28
4	.0517	.0743	.121	.178	.266	1.94	2.37	2.79	3.32	3.72
5	.0823	.111	.166	.229	.322	1.85	2.21	2.57	3.02	3.35
6	.113	.145	.206	.273	.367	1.77	2.10	2.41	2.80	3.09
7	.141	.177	.241	.310	.405	1.72	2.01	2.29	2.64	2.90
8	.168	.206	.272	.342	.436	1.67	1.94	2.19	2.51	2.74
9	.193	.232	.300	.369	.463	1.63	1.88	2.11	2.41	2.62
10	.216	.256	.325	.394	.487	1.60	1.83	2.05	2.32	2.52
11	.237	.278	.347	.416	.507	1.57	1.79	1.99	2.25	2.43
12	.256	.298	.367	.435	.525	1.55	1.75	1.94	2.18	2.36
13	.274	.316	.385	.453	.542	1.52	1.72	1.90	2.13	2.29
14	.291	.333	.402	.469	.556	1.50	1.69	1.87	2.08	2.24
15	.307	.349	.417	.484	.570	1.49	1.67	1.83	2.04	2.19
16	.321	.363	.432	.498	.582	1.47	1.64	1.80	2.00	2.14
18	.348	.390	.457	.522	.604	1.44	1.60	1.75	1.93	2.06
20	.372	.413	.480	.543	.622	1.42	1.57	1.71	1.88	2.00
24	.412	.452	.517	.577	.652	1.38	1.52	1.64	1.79	1.90
30	.460	.498	.560	.616	.687	1.34	1.46	1.57	1.70	1.79
40	.518	.554	.611	.663	.726	1.30	1.39	1.48	1.59	1.67
60	.592	.625	.675	.720	.774	1.24	1.32	1.39	1.47	1.53
120	.699	.724	.763	.798	.839	1.17	1.22	1.27	1.32	1.36
∞	1.000	1.000	1.000	1.000	1.000	1.00	1.00	1.00	1.00	1.00

Interpolation should be performed using reciprocals of the degrees of freedom.

* To obtain critical values of χ^2, multiply the critical value of C^2 by (d.f.)

TABLE VII *F* Distribution Critical Points 5% (Roman Type) and 1% (Boldface Type) Points

Degrees of freedom for denominator	Degrees of freedom for numerator																						
	1	3	3	4	5	6	7	8	9	10	11	12	14	16	20	24	30	40	50	75	100	200	500	∞
1	161 **4052**	200 **4999**	216 **5403**	225 **5625**	230 **5764**	234 **5859**	237 **5928**	239 **5981**	241 **6022**	242 **6056**	243 **6082**	244 **6106**	245 **6142**	246 **6169**	248 **6208**	249 **6234**	250 **6258**	251 **6286**	252 **6302**	253 **6323**	253 **6334**	254 **6352**	254 **6361**	254 **6366**
2	18.51 **98.49**	19.00 **99.01**	19.16 **99.17**	19.25 **99.25**	19.30 **99.30**	19.33 **99.33**	19.36 **99.34**	19.37 **99.36**	19.38 **99.38**	19.39 **99.40**	19.40 **99.41**	19.41 **99.42**	19.42 **99.43**	19.43 **99.44**	19.44 **99.45**	19.45 **99.46**	19.46 **99.47**	19.47 **99.48**	19.47 **99.48**	19.48 **99.49**	19.49 **99.49**	19.49 **99.49**	19.50 **99.50**	19.50 **99.50**
3	10.13 **34.12**	9.55 **30.81**	9.28 **29.46**	9.12 **28.71**	9.01 **28.24**	8.94 **27.91**	8.88 **27.67**	8.84 **27.49**	8.81 **27.34**	8.78 **27.23**	8.76 **27.13**	8.74 **27.05**	8.71 **26.92**	8.69 **26.83**	8.66 **26.69**	8.64 **26.60**	8.62 **26.50**	8.60 **26.41**	8.58 **26.30**	8.57 **26.27**	8.56 **26.23**	8.54 **26.18**	8.54 **26.14**	8.53 **26.12**
4	7.71 **21.20**	6.94 **18.00**	6.59 **16.69**	6.39 **15.98**	6.26 **15.52**	6.16 **15.21**	6.09 **14.98**	6.04 **14.80**	6.00 **14.66**	5.96 **14.54**	5.93 **14.45**	5.91 **14.37**	5.87 **14.24**	5.84 **14.15**	5.80 **14.02**	5.77 **13.93**	5.74 **13.83**	5.71 **13.74**	5.70 **13.69**	5.68 **13.61**	5.66 **13.57**	5.65 **13.52**	5.64 **13.48**	5.63 **13.46**
5	6.61 **16.26**	5.79 **13.27**	5.41 **12.06**	5.19 **11.39**	5.05 **10.97**	4.95 **10.67**	4.88 **10.45**	4.82 **10.27**	4.78 **10.15**	4.74 **10.05**	4.70 **9.96**	4.68 **9.89**	4.64 **9.77**	4.60 **9.68**	4.56 **9.55**	4.53 **9.47**	4.50 **9.38**	4.46 **9.29**	4.44 **9.24**	4.42 **9.17**	4.40 **9.13**	4.38 **9.07**	4.37 **9.04**	4.36 **9.02**
6	5.99 **13.74**	5.14 **10.92**	4.76 **9.78**	4.53 **9.15**	4.39 **8.75**	4.28 **8.47**	4.21 **8.26**	4.15 **8.10**	4.10 **7.98**	4.06 **7.87**	4.03 **7.79**	4.00 **7.72**	3.96 **7.60**	3.92 **7.52**	3.87 **7.39**	3.84 **7.31**	3.81 **7.23**	3.77 **7.14**	3.75 **7.09**	3.72 **7.02**	3.71 **6.99**	3.69 **6.94**	3.68 **6.90**	3.67 **6.88**
7	5.59 **12.25**	4.74 **9.55**	4.35 **8.45**	4.12 **7.85**	3.97 **7.46**	3.87 **7.19**	3.79 **7,00**	3.73 **6.84**	3.68 **6.71**	3.63 **6.62**	3.60 **6.54**	3.57 **6.47**	3.52 **6.35**	3.49 **6.27**	3.44 **6.15**	3.41 **6.07**	3.38 **5.98**	3.34 **5.90**	3.32 **5.85**	3.29 **5.78**	3.28 **5.75**	3.25 **5.70**	3.24 **5.67**	3.23 **5.65**
8	5.32 **11.26**	4.46 **8.65**	4.07 **7.59**	3.84 **7.01**	3.69 **6.63**	3.58 **6.37**	3.50 **6.19**	3.44 **6.03**	3.39 **5.91**	3.34 **5.82**	3.31 **5.74**	3.28 **5.67**	3.23 **5.56**	3.20 **5.48**	3.15 **5.36**	3.12 **5.28**	3.08 **5.20**	3.05 **5.11**	3.03 **5.06**	3.00 **5.00**	2.98 **4.96**	2.96 **4.91**	2.94 **4.88**	2.93 **4.86**
9	5.12 **10.56**	4.26 **8.02**	3.86 **6.99**	3.63 **6.42**	3.48 **6.06**	3.37 **5.80**	3.29 **5.62**	3.23 **5.47**	3.18 **5.35**	3.13 **5.26**	3.10 **5.18**	3.07 **5.11**	3.02 **5.00**	2.98 **4.92**	2.93 **4.80**	2.90 **4.73**	2.86 **4.64**	2.82 **4.56**	2.80 **4.51**	2.77 **4.45**	2.76 **4.41**	2.73 **4.36**	2.72 **4.33**	2.71 **4.31**
10	4.96 **10.04**	4.10 **7.56**	3.71 **6.55**	3.48 **5.99**	3.33 **5.64**	3.22 **5.39**	3.14 **5.21**	3.07 **5.06**	3.02 **4.95**	2.97 **4.85**	2.94 **4.78**	2.91 **4.71**	2.86 **4.60**	2.82 **4.52**	2.77 **4.41**	2.74 **4.33**	2.70 **4.25**	2.67 **4.17**	2.64 **4.12**	2.61 **4.05**	2.59 **4.01**	2.56 **3.96**	2.55 **3.93**	2.54 **3.91**
11	4.84 **9.65**	3.98 **7.20**	3.59 **6.22**	3.36 **5.67**	3.20 **5.32**	3.09 **5.07**	3.01 **4.88**	2.95 **4.74**	2.90 **4.63**	2.86 **4.54**	2.82 **4.46**	2.79 **4.40**	2.74 **4.29**	2.70 **4.21**	2.65 **4.10**	2.61 **4.02**	2.57 **3.94**	2.53 **3.86**	2.50 **3.80**	2.47 **3.74**	2.45 **3.70**	2.42 **3.66**	2.41 **3.62**	2.40 **3.60**

Table VII (Continued)

Degrees of freedom for denominator	Degrees of freedom for numerator: 1	2	3	4	5	6	7	8	9	10	11	12	14	16	20	24	30	40	50	75	100	200	500	∞
12	4.75 **9.33**	3.89 **6.93**	3.49 **5.95**	3.26 **5.41**	3.11 **5.06**	3.00 **4.82**	2.92 **4.65**	2.85 **4.50**	2.80 **4.39**	2.76 **4.30**	2.72 **4.22**	2.69 **4.16**	2.64 **4.05**	2.60 **3.98**	2.54 **3.86**	2.50 **3.78**	2.46 **3.70**	2.42 **3.61**	2.40 **3.56**	2.36 **3.49**	2.35 **3.46**	2.32 **3.41**	2.31 **3.38**	2.30 **3.36**
13	4.67 **9.07**	3.80 **6.70**	3.41 **5.74**	3.18 **5.20**	3.02 **4.86**	2.92 **4.62**	2.84 **4.44**	2.77 **4.30**	2.72 **4.19**	2.67 **4.10**	2.63 **4.02**	2.60 **3.96**	2.55 **3.85**	2.51 **3.78**	2.46 **3.67**	2.42 **3.59**	2.38 **3.51**	2.34 **3.42**	2.32 **3.37**	2.28 **3.30**	2.26 **3.27**	2.24 **3.21**	2.22 **3.18**	2.21 **3.16**
14	4.60 **8.86**	3.74 **6.51**	3.34 **5.56**	3.11 **5.03**	2.96 **4.69**	2.85 **4.46**	2.77 **4.28**	2.70 **4.14**	2.65 **4.03**	2.60 **3.94**	2.56 **3.86**	2.53 **3.80**	2.48 **3.70**	2.44 **3.62**	2.39 **3.51**	2.35 **3.43**	2.31 **3.34**	2.27 **3.26**	2.24 **3.21**	2.21 **3.14**	2.19 **3.11**	2.16 **3.06**	2.14 **3.02**	2.13 **3.00**
15	4.54 **8.68**	3.68 **6.36**	3.29 **5.42**	3.06 **4.89**	2.90 **4.56**	2.79 **4.32**	2.70 **4.14**	2.64 **4.00**	2.59 **3.89**	2.55 **3.80**	2.51 **3.73**	2.48 **3.67**	2.43 **3.56**	2.39 **3.48**	2.33 **3.36**	2.29 **3.29**	2.25 **3.20**	2.21 **3.12**	2.18 **3.07**	2.15 **3.00**	2.12 **2.97**	2.10 **2.92**	2.08 **2.89**	2.07 **2.87**
16	4.49 **8.53**	3.63 **6.23**	3.24 **5.29**	3.01 **4.77**	2.85 **4.44**	2.74 **4.20**	2.66 **4.03**	2.59 **3.89**	2.54 **3.78**	2.49 **3.69**	2.45 **3.61**	2.42 **3.55**	2.37 **3.45**	2.33 **3.37**	2.28 **3.25**	2.24 **3.18**	2.20 **3.10**	2.16 **3.01**	2.13 **2.96**	2.09 **2.89**	2.07 **2.86**	2.04 **2.80**	2.02 **2.77**	2.01 **2.75**
17	4.45 **8.40**	3.59 **6.11**	3.20 **5.18**	2.96 **4.67**	2.81 **4.34**	2.70 **4.10**	2.62 **3.93**	2.55 **3.79**	2.50 **3.68**	2.45 **3.59**	2.41 **3.52**	2.38 **3.45**	2.33 **3.35**	2.29 **3.27**	2.23 **3.16**	2.19 **3.08**	2.15 **3.00**	2.11 **2.92**	2.08 **2.86**	2.04 **2.79**	2.02 **2.76**	1.99 **2.70**	1.97 **2.67**	1.96 **2.65**
18	4.41 **8.28**	3.55 **6.01**	3.16 **5.09**	2.93 **4.58**	2.77 **4.25**	2.66 **4.01**	2.58 **3.85**	2.51 **3.71**	2.46 **3.60**	2.41 **3.51**	2.37 **3.44**	2.34 **3.37**	2.29 **3.27**	2.25 **3.19**	2.19 **3.07**	2.15 **3.00**	2.11 **2.91**	2.07 **2.83**	2.04 **2.78**	2.00 **2.71**	1.98 **2.68**	1.95 **2.62**	1.93 **2.59**	1.92 **2.57**
19	4.38 **8.18**	3.52 **5.93**	3.13 **5.01**	2.90 **4.50**	2.74 **4.17**	2.63 **3.94**	2.55 **3.77**	2.48 **3.63**	2.43 **3.52**	2.38 **3.43**	2.34 **3.36**	2.31 **3.30**	2.26 **3.19**	2.21 **3.12**	2.15 **3.00**	2.11 **2.92**	2.07 **2.84**	2.02 **2.76**	2.00 **2.70**	1.96 **2.63**	1.94 **2.60**	1.91 **2.54**	1.90 **2.51**	1.88 **2.49**
20	4.35 **8.10**	3.49 **5.85**	3.10 **4.94**	2.87 **4.43**	2.71 **4.10**	2.60 **3.87**	2.52 **3.71**	2.45 **3.56**	2.40 **3.45**	2.35 **3.37**	2.31 **3.30**	2.28 **3.23**	2.23 **3.13**	2.18 **3.05**	2.12 **2.94**	2.08 **2.86**	2.04 **2.77**	1.99 **2.69**	1.96 **2.63**	1.92 **2.56**	1.90 **2.53**	1.87 **2.47**	1.85 **2.44**	1.84 **2.42**
21	4.32 **8.02**	3.47 **5.78**	3.07 **4.87**	2.84 **4.37**	2.68 **4.04**	2.57 **3.81**	2.49 **3.65**	2.42 **3.51**	2.37 **3.40**	2.32 **3.31**	2.28 **3.24**	2.25 **3.17**	2.20 **3.07**	2.15 **2.99**	2.09 **2.88**	2.05 **2.80**	2.00 **2.72**	1.96 **2.63**	1.93 **2.58**	1.89 **2.51**	1.87 **2.47**	1.84 **2.42**	1.82 **2.38**	1.81 **2.36**
22	4.30 **7.94**	3.44 **5.72**	3.05 **4.82**	2.82 **4.41**	2.66 **3.99**	2.55 **3.76**	2.47 **3.59**	2.40 **3.45**	2.35 **3.35**	2.30 **3.26**	2.26 **3.18**	2.23 **3.12**	2.18 **3.02**	2.13 **2.94**	2.07 **2.83**	2.03 **2.75**	1.98 **2.67**	1.93 **2.58**	1.91 **2.53**	1.87 **2.46**	1.84 **2.42**	1.81 **2.37**	1.80 **2.33**	1.78 **2.31**
23	4.28 **7.88**	3.42 **5.66**	3.03 **4.76**	2.80 **4.26**	2.64 **3.94**	2.53 **3.71**	2.45 **3.54**	2.38 **3.41**	2.32 **3.30**	2.28 **3.21**	2.24 **3.14**	2.20 **3.07**	2.14 **2.97**	2.10 **2.89**	2.04 **2.78**	2.00 **2.70**	1.96 **2.62**	1.91 **2.53**	1.88 **2.48**	1.84 **2.41**	1.82 **2.37**	1.79 **2.32**	1.77 **2.28**	1.76 **2.26**
24	4.26 **7.82**	3.40 **5.61**	3.01 **4.72**	2.78 **4.22**	2.62 **3.90**	2.51 **3.67**	2.43 **3.50**	2.36 **3.36**	2.30 **3.25**	2.26 **3.17**	2.22 **3.09**	2.18 **3.03**	2.13 **2.93**	2.09 **2.85**	2.02 **2.74**	1.98 **2.66**	1.94 **2.58**	1.89 **2.49**	1.86 **2.44**	1.82 **2.36**	1.80 **2.33**	1.76 **2.27**	1.74 **2.23**	1.73 **2.21**

25	4.24 **7.77**	3.38 **5.57**	2.99 **4.68**	2.76 **4.18**	2.60 **3.86**	2.49 **3.63**	2.41 **3.46**	2.34 **3.32**	2.28 **3.21**	2.24 **3.13**	2.20 **3.05**	2.16 **2.99**	2.11 **2.89**	2.06 **2.81**	2.00 **2.70**	1.96 **2.62**	1.92 **2.54**	1.87 **2.45**	1.84 **2.40**	1.80 **2.32**	1.77 **2.29**	1.74 **2.23**	1.72 **2.19**	1.71 **2.17**
26	4.22 **7.72**	3.37 **5.53**	2.89 **4.64**	2.74 **4.14**	2.59 **3.82**	2.47 **3.59**	2.39 **3.42**	2.32 **3.29**	2.27 **3.17**	2.22 **3.09**	2.18 **3.02**	2.15 **2.96**	2.10 **2.86**	2.05 **2.77**	1.99 **2.66**	1.95 **2.58**	1.90 **2.50**	1.85 **2.41**	1.82 **2.36**	1.78 **2.28**	1.76 **2.25**	1.72 **2.19**	1.70 **2.15**	1.69 **2.13**
27	4.21 **7.68**	3.35 **5.49**	2.96 **4.60**	2.73 **4.11**	2.57 **3.79**	2.46 **3.56**	2.37 **3.39**	2.30 **3.26**	2.25 **3.14**	2.20 **3.06**	2.16 **2.98**	2.13 **2.93**	2.08 **2.83**	2.03 **2.74**	1.97 **2.63**	1.93 **2.55**	1.88 **2.47**	1.84 **2.38**	1.80 **2.33**	1.76 **2.25**	1.74 **2.21**	1.71 **2.16**	1.68 **2.12**	1.67 **2.10**
28	4.20 **7.64**	3.34 **5.45**	2.95 **4.57**	2.71 **4.07**	2.56 **3.76**	2.44 **3.53**	2.36 **3.35**	2.29 **3.23**	3.24 **3.11**	2.19 **3.03**	2.15 **2.95**	2.12 **2.90**	2.06 **2.80**	2.02 **2.71**	1.96 **2.60**	1.91 **2.52**	1.87 **2.44**	1.81 **2.35**	1.78 **2.30**	1.75 **2.22**	1.72 **2.18**	1.69 **2.13**	1.67 **2.09**	1.65 **2.06**
29	4.18 **7.60**	3.33 **5.52**	2.93 **4.54**	2.70 **4.04**	2.54 **3.73**	2.43 **3.50**	2.35 **3.33**	2.28 **3.20**	2.22 **3.08**	2.18 **3.00**	2.14 **2.92**	2.10 **2.87**	2.05 **2.77**	2.00 **2.68**	1.94 **2.57**	1.90 **2.49**	1.85 **2.41**	1.80 **2.32**	1.77 **2.27**	1.73 **2.19**	1.71 **2.15**	1.68 **2.10**	1.65 **2.06**	1.64 **2.03**
30	4.17 **7.56**	3.32 **5.39**	2.92 **4.51**	2.69 **4.02**	2.53 **3.70**	2.43 **3.47**	2.34 **3.30**	2.27 **3.17**	2.21 **3.06**	2.16 **2.98**	2.12 **2.90**	2.09 **2.84**	2.04 **2.74**	1.99 **2.66**	1.93 **2.55**	1.89 **2.47**	1.84 **2.38**	1.79 **2.29**	1.76 **2.24**	1.72 **2.16**	1.69 **2.13**	1.66 **2.07**	1.64 **2.03**	1.62 **2.01**
32	4.15 **7.50**	3.30 **5.34**	2.90 **4.46**	2.67 **3.97**	2.51 **3.66**	2.40 **3.42**	2.32 **3.25**	2.25 **3.12**	2.19 **3.01**	2.14 **2.94**	2.10 **2.86**	2.07 **2.80**	2.02 **2.70**	1.97 **2.62**	1.91 **2.51**	1.86 **2.42**	1.82 **2.34**	1.76 **2.25**	1.74 **2.20**	1.69 **2.12**	1.67 **2.08**	1.64 **2.02**	1.61 **1.98**	1.59 **1.96**
34	4.13 **7.44**	3.28 **5.29**	2.88 **4.42**	2.65 **3.93**	2.49 **3.61**	2.38 **3.38**	2.30 **3.21**	2.23 **3.08**	2.17 **2.97**	2.12 **2.89**	2.08 **2.82**	2.05 **2.76**	2.00 **2.66**	1.95 **2.58**	1.80 **2.47**	1.84 **2.38**	1.80 **2.30**	1.74 **2.21**	1.71 **2.15**	1.67 **2.08**	1.64 **2.04**	1.61 **1.98**	1.59 **1.94**	1.57 **1.91**
36	4.11 **7.39**	3.26 **5.25**	3.86 **4.38**	2.63 **3.89**	2.48 **3.58**	2.36 **3.35**	2.28 **3.18**	2.21 **3.04**	2.15 **2.94**	2.10 **2.86**	2.06 **2.78**	2.03 **2.72**	1.89 **2.62**	1.93 **2.54**	1.87 **2.43**	1.82 **2.35**	1.78 **2.26**	1.72 **2.17**	1.69 **2.12**	1.65 **2.04**	1.62 **2.00**	1.59 **1.94**	1.56 **1.90**	1.55 **1.87**
38	4.10 **7.35**	3.25 **5.21**	2.85 **4.34**	2.62 **3.86**	2.46 **3.54**	2.35 **3.32**	2.26 **3.15**	2.19 **3.02**	2.14 **2.91**	2.09 **2.82**	2.05 **2.75**	2.02 **2.69**	1.96 **2.59**	1.92 **2.51**	1.85 **2.40**	1.80 **2.32**	1.76 **2.22**	1.71 **2.14**	1.67 **2.08**	1.63 **2.00**	1.60 **1.97**	1.57 **1.90**	1.54 **1.86**	1.53 **1.84**
40	4.08 **7.31**	3.23 **5.18**	2.84 **4.31**	2.61 **3.83**	2.45 **3.51**	2.34 **3.29**	2.25 **3.12**	2.18 **2.99**	2.12 **2.88**	2.08 **2.80**	2.04 **2.73**	2.00 **2.66**	1.95 **2.56**	1.90 **2.49**	1.84 **2.37**	1.79 **2.29**	1.74 **2.20**	1.69 **2.11**	1.66 **2.05**	1.61 **1.97**	1.59 **1.94**	1.55 **1.88**	1.53 **1.84**	1.51 **1.81**
42	4.07 **7.27**	3.22 **5.15**	2.83 **4.29**	2.59 **3.80**	2.44 **3.49**	2.32 **3.26**	2.24 **3.10**	2.17 **2.96**	2.11 **2.86**	2.06 **2.77**	2.02 **2.70**	1.99 **2.64**	1.94 **2.54**	1.89 **2.46**	1.82 **2.35**	1.78 **2.26**	1.73 **2.17**	1.68 **2.08**	1.64 **2.02**	1.60 **1.94**	1.57 **1.91**	1.54 **1.85**	1.51 **1.80**	1.49 **1.78**
44	4.06 **7.24**	3.21 **5.12**	2.82 **4.26**	2.58 **3.78**	2.43 **3.46**	2.31 **3.24**	2.23 **3.07**	2.16 **2.94**	2.10 **2.84**	2.05 **2.75**	2.01 **2.68**	1.98 **2.62**	1.92 **2.52**	1.88 **2.44**	1.81 **2.32**	1.76 **2.24**	1.72 **2.15**	1.66 **2.06**	1.63 **2.00**	1.58 **1.92**	1.56 **1.88**	1.52 **1.82**	1.50 **1.78**	1.48 **1.75**
46	4.05 **7.21**	3.20 **5.10**	2.81 **4.24**	2.57 **3.76**	2.42 **3.44**	2.30 **3.22**	2.22 **3.05**	2.14 **2.92**	2.09 **2.82**	2.04 **2.73**	2.00 **2.66**	1.97 **2.60**	1.91 **2.50**	1.87 **2.42**	1.80 **2.30**	1.75 **2.22**	1.71 **2.13**	1.65 **2.04**	1.62 **1.98**	1.57 **1.90**	1.54 **1.86**	1.51 **1.80**	1.48 **2.76**	1.46 **2.72**

(*Contd*)

Table VII (Continued)

Degrees of freedom for denominator	Degrees of freedom for numerator																						
	1	2	3	4	5	6	7	8	9	10	11	12	14	16	20	24	30	40	50	75	100	200	500	∞
48	4.04 **7.19**	3.19 **5.08**	2.80 **4.22**	2.56 **3.74**	2.41 **3.42**	2.30 **3.20**	2.21 **3.04**	2.14 **2.90**	2.08 **2.80**	2.03 **2.71**	1.99 **2.64**	1.96 **2.58**	1.90 **2.43**	1.86 **2.40**	1.79 **2.28**	1.74 **2.20**	1.70 **2.11**	1.64 **2.02**	1.61 **1.96**	1.56 **1.83**	1.53 **1.84**	1.50 **1.78**	1.47 **1.73**	1.45 **1.70**
50	4.03 **7.17**	3.18 **5.06**	2.79 **4.20**	2.56 **3.72**	2.40 **3.41**	2.29 **3.18**	2.20 **3.02**	2.13 **2.88**	2.07 **2.78**	2.20 **2.70**	1.98 **2.62**	1.95 **2.56**	1.90 **2.46**	1.85 **2.39**	1.78 **2.26**	1.74 **2.18**	1.69 **2.10**	1.63 **2.00**	1.60 **1.94**	1.55 **1.86**	1.52 **1.82**	1.48 **1.76**	1.46 **1.71**	1.44 **1.68**
55	4.02 **7.12**	3.17 **5.01**	2.78 **4.16**	2.54 **3.68**	2.38 **3.37**	2.27 **3.15**	2.18 **2.98**	2.11 **2.85**	2.05 **2.75**	2.00 **2.66**	1.97 **2.59**	1.93 **2.53**	1.88 **2.43**	1.83 **2.35**	1.76 **2.23**	1.72 **2.15**	1.67 **2.06**	1.61 **1.96**	1.58 **1.90**	1.52 **1.82**	1.50 **1.78**	1.46 **1.71**	1.43 **1.66**	1.41 **1.64**
60	4.00 **7.08**	3.15 **4.98**	2.76 **4.13**	2.52 **3.65**	2.37 **3.34**	2.25 **3.12**	2.17 **2.95**	2.10 **2.82**	2.04 **2.72**	1.99 **2.63**	1.95 **2.56**	1.92 **2.50**	1.86 **2.40**	1.81 **2.32**	1.75 **2.20**	1.70 **2.12**	1.65 **2.03**	1.59 **1.93**	1.56 **1.87**	1.50 **1.79**	1.48 **1.74**	1.44 **1.68**	1.41 **1.63**	1.39 **1.60**
65	3.99 **7.04**	3.14 **4.95**	2.75 **4.10**	2.51 **3.62**	2.36 **3.31**	2.24 **3.09**	2.15 **2.93**	2.08 **2.79**	2.02 **2.70**	1.98 **2.61**	1.94 **2.54**	1.90 **2.47**	1.85 **2.37**	1.80 **2.30**	1.73 **2.18**	1.68 **2.09**	1.63 **2.00**	1.57 **1.90**	1.54 **1.84**	1.49 **1.76**	1.46 **1.71**	1.42 **1.64**	1.39 **1.60**	1.37 **1.56**
70	3.98 **7.01**	3.13 **4.92**	2.74 **4.08**	2.50 **3.60**	2.35 **3.29**	2.32 **3.07**	2.14 **2.91**	2.07 **2.77**	2.01 **2.67**	1.97 **2.59**	1.93 **2.51**	1.80 **2.45**	1.84 **2.35**	1.79 **2.28**	1.72 **2.15**	1.67 **2.07**	1.62 **1.98**	1.56 **1.88**	1.53 **1.82**	1.47 **1.74**	1.45 **1.69**	1.40 **1.63**	1.37 **1.56**	1.35 **1.53**
80	3.96 **6.95**	3.11 **4.88**	2.72 **4.04**	2.48 **3.56**	2.33 **3.25**	2.21 **3.04**	2.12 **2.87**	2.05 **2.74**	1.99 **2.64**	1.95 **2.55**	1.91 **2.48**	1.88 **2.41**	1.82 **2.32**	1.77 **2.24**	1.70 **2.11**	1.65 **2.03**	1.60 **1.94**	1.54 **1.84**	1.51 **1.78**	1.45 **1.70**	1.42 **1.65**	1.38 **1.57**	1.35 **1.52**	1.32 **1.49**
100	3.94 **6.90**	3.09 **4.82**	2.70 **3.98**	2.46 **3.51**	2.30 **3.20**	2.19 **2.99**	2.10 **2.82**	2.03 **2.69**	1.97 **2.59**	1.92 **2.51**	1.88 **2.43**	1.85 **2.36**	1.79 **2.26**	1.75 **2.19**	1.68 **2.06**	1.63 **1.98**	1.57 **1.89**	1.51 **1.79**	1.48 **1.73**	1.42 **1.64**	1.39 **1.59**	1.34 **1.51**	1.30 **1.46**	1.28 **1.43**
125	3.92 **6.84**	3.07 **4.78**	2.68 **3.94**	2.44 **3.47**	2.29 **3.17**	2.17 **2.95**	2.08 **2.79**	2.01 **2.65**	1.95 **2.56**	1.90 **2.47**	1.86 **2.40**	1.83 **2.33**	1.77 **2.23**	1.72 **2.15**	1.65 **2.03**	1.60 **1.94**	1.55 **1.85**	1.49 **1.75**	1.45 **1.68**	1.39 **1.59**	1.36 **1.54**	1.31 **1.46**	1.27 **1.40**	1.25 **1.37**
150	3.91 **6.81**	3.06 **4.75**	2.67 **3.91**	2.43 **3.44**	2.27 **3.13**	2.16 **2.92**	2.07 **2.76**	2.00 **2.62**	1.94 **2.53**	1.89 **2.44**	1.85 **2.37**	1.82 **2.30**	1.76 **2.20**	1.71 **2.12**	1.64 **2.00**	1.59 **1.91**	1.54 **1.83**	1.47 **1.72**	1.44 **1.66**	1.37 **1.56**	1.34 **1.51**	1.29 **1.43**	1.25 **1.37**	1.22 **1.33**
200	3.89 **6.76**	3.04 **4.71**	2.65 **3.88**	2.41 **3.41**	2.26 **3.11**	2.14 **2.90**	2.05 **2.73**	1.98 **2.60**	1.92 **2.50**	1.87 **2.41**	1.83 **2.34**	1.80 **2.28**	1.74 **1.17**	1.69 **2.09**	1.62 **1.97**	1.57 **1.88**	1.52 **1.79**	1.45 **1.69**	1.42 **1.62**	1.35 **1.53**	1.32 **1.48**	1.26 **1.39**	1.22 **1.33**	1.19 **1.28**
400	3.86 **6.70**	3.02 **4.66**	2.62 **3.83**	2.39 **3.36**	2.23 **3.06**	2.12 **2.85**	2.03 **2.69**	1.96 **2.55**	1.90 **2.46**	1.85 **2.37**	1.81 **2.29**	1.78 **2.23**	1.72 **2.12**	1.67 **2.04**	1.60 **1.92**	1.54 **1.84**	1.49 **1.74**	1.42 **1.64**	1.38 **1.57**	1.32 **1.47**	1.28 **1.42**	1.22 **1.32**	1.16 **1.24**	1.13 **1.19**
1000	3.85 **6.66**	3.00 **4.62**	2.61 **3.80**	2.38 **3.34**	2.22 **3.04**	2.10 **2.82**	2.02 **2.66**	1.95 **2.53**	1.89 **2.43**	1.84 **2.34**	1.80 **2.26**	1.76 **2.20**	1.70 **2.09**	1.65 **2.01**	1.58 **1.89**	1.53 **1.81**	1.47 **1.71**	1.41 **1.61**	1.36 **1.54**	1.30 **1.44**	1.26 **1.38**	1.19 **1.28**	1.13 **1.19**	1.08 **1.11**
∞	3.84 **6.64**	2.99 **4.60**	2.60 **3.78**	2.37 **3.32**	2.21 **3.02**	2.09 **2.80**	2.01 **2.64**	1.94 **2.51**	1.88 **2.41**	1.83 **2.32**	1.79 **2.24**	1.75 **2·18**	1.69 **2.07**	1.64 **1.99**	1.57 **1.87**	1.52 **1.79**	1.46 **1.69**	1.40 **1.59**	1.35 **1.52**	1.28 **1.41**	1.24 **1.36**	1.17 **1.25**	1.11 **1.15**	1.00 **1.00**

TABLE VIII Common Logarithms*

N	0	1	2	3	4	5	6	7	8	9
10	0000	0043	0086	0128	0170	0212	0253	0294	0334	0374
11	0414	0453	0492	0531	0569	0607	0645	0682	0719	0755
12	0792	0828	0864	0899	0934	0969	1004	1038	1072	1106
13	1139	1173	1206	1239	1271	1303	1335	1367	1399	1430
14	1461	1492	1523	1553	1584	1614	1644	1673	1703	1732
15	1761	1790	1818	1847	1875	1903	1931	1959	1987	2014
16	2041	2068	2095	2122	2148	2175	2201	2227	2253	2279
17	2304	2330	2355	2380	2405	2430	2455	2480	2504	2529
18	2553	2577	2601	2625	2648	2672	2695	2718	2742	2765
19	2788	2810	2833	2856	2878	2900	2923	2945	2967	2989
20	3010	3032	3054	3075	3096	3118	3139	3160	3181	3201
21	3222	3243	3263	3284	3304	3324	3345	3365	3385	3404
22	3424	3444	3464	3483	3502	3522	3541	3560	3579	3598
23	3617	3636	3655	3674	3692	3711	3729	3747	3766	3784
24	3802	3820	3838	3856	3874	3892	3909	3927	3945	3962
25	3979	3997	4014	4031	4048	4065	4082	4099	4116	4133
26	4150	4166	4183	4200	4216	4232	4249	4265	4281	4298
27	4314	4330	4346	4362	4378	4393	4409	4425	4440	4456
28	4472	4487	4502	4518	4533	4548	4564	4579	4594	4609
29	4624	4639	4654	4669	4683	4698	4713	4728	4742	4757
30	4771	4786	4800	4814	4829	4843	4857	4871	4886	4900
31	4914	4928	4942	4955	4969	4983	4997	5011	5024	5038
32	5051	5065	5079	5092	5105	5119	5132	5145	5159	5172
33	5185	5198	5211	5224	5237	5250	5263	5276	5289	5302
34	5315	5328	5340	5353	5366	5378	5391	5403	5416	5428
35	5441	5453	5465	5478	5490	5502	5514	5527	5539	5551
36	5563	5575	5587	5599	5611	5623	5635	5647	5658	5670
37	5682	5694	5705	5717	5729	5740	5752	5763	5775	5786
38	5798	5809	5821	5832	5843	5855	5866	5877	5888	5899
39	5911	5922	5933	5944	5955	5966	5977	5988	5999	6010
40	6021	6031	6042	6053	6064	6075	6085	6096	6107	6117
41	6128	6138	6149	6160	6170	6180	6191	6201	6212	6222
42	6232	6243	6253	6263	6274	6284	6294	6304	6314	6325
43	6335	6345	6355	6365	6375	6385	6395	6405	6415	6425
44	6435	6444	6454	6464	6474	6484	6493	6503	6513	6522
45	6532	6542	6551	6561	6571	6580	6590	6599	6609	6618
46	6628	6637	6646	6656	6665	6675	6684	6693	6702	6712
47	6721	6730	6739	6749	6758	6767	6776	6785	6794	6803
48	6812	6821	6830	6839	6848	6857	6866	6875	6884	6893
49	6902	6911	6920	6928	6937	6946	6955	6964	6972	6981
50	6990	6998	7007	7016	7024	7033	7042	7050	7059	7067
51	7076	7084	7093	7101	7110	7118	7126	7135	7143	7152
52	7160	7168	7177	7185	7193	7202	7210	7218	7226	7235
53	7243	7251	7259	7267	7275	7284	7292	7300	7308	7316
54	7324	7332	7340	7348	7356	7364	7372	7380	7388	7396

TABLE VIII (Continued)

N	0	1	2	3	4	5	6	7	8	9
55	7404	7412	7419	7427	7435	7443	7451	7459	7466	7474
56	7482	7490	7497	7505	7513	7520	7528	7536	7543	7551
57	7559	7566	7574	7582	7589	7597	7604	7612	7619	7627
58	7634	7642	7649	7657	7664	7672	7679	7686	7694	7701
59	7709	7716	7723	7731	7738	7745	7752	7760	7767	7774
60	7782	7789	7796	7803	7810	7818	7825	7832	7839	7846
61	7853	7860	7868	7875	7882	7889	7896	7903	7910	7917
62	7924	7931	7938	7945	7952	7959	7966	7973	7980	7987
63	7993	8000	8007	8014	8021	8028	8035	8041	8048	8055
64	8062	8069	8075	8082	8089	8096	8102	8109	8116	8122
65	8129	8136	8142	8149	8156	8162	8169	8176	8182	8189
66	8195	8202	8209	8215	8222	8228	8235	8241	8248	8254
67	8261	8267	8274	8280	8287	8293	8299	8306	8312	8319
68	8325	8331	8338	8344	8351	8357	8363	8370	8376	8382
69	8388	8395	8401	8407	8414	8420	8426	8432	8439	8445
70	8451	8457	8463	8470	8476	8482	8488	8494	8500	8506
71	8513	8519	8525	8531	8537	8543	8549	8555	8561	8567
72	8573	8579	8585	8591	8597	8603	8609	8615	8621	8627
73	8633	8639	8645	8651	8657	8663	8669	8675	8681	8686
74	8692	8698	8704	8710	8716	8722	8727	8733	8739	8745
75	8751	8756	8762	8768	8774	8779	8785	8791	8797	8802
76	8808	8814	8820	8825	8831	8837	8842	8848	8854	8859
77	8865	8871	8876	8882	8887	8893	8899	8904	8910	8915
78	8921	8927	8932	8938	8943	8949	8954	8960	8965	9971
79	8976	8982	8987	8993	8998	9004	9009	9015	9020	9025
80	9031	9036	9042	9047	9053	9058	9063	9069	9074	9079
81	9085	9090	9096	9101	9106	9112	9117	9122	9128	9133
82	9138	9143	9149	9154	9159	9165	9170	9175	9180	9186
83	9191	9196	9201	9206	9212	9217	9222	9227	9232	9238
84	9243	9248	9253	9258	9263	9269	9274	9279	9284	9289
85	9294	9299	9304	9309	9315	9320	9325	9330	9335	9340
86	9345	9350	9355	9360	9365	9370	9375	9380	9385	9390
87	9395	9400	9405	9410	9415	9420	9425	9430	9435	9440
88	9445	9450	9455	9460	9465	9469	9474	9479	9484	9489
89	9494	9499	9504	9509	9513	9518	9523	9528	9533	9538
90	9542	9547	9552	9557	9562	9566	9571	9576	9581	9586
91	9590	9595	9600	9605	9609	9614	9619	9624	9628	9633
92	9638	9643	9647	9652	9657	9661	9666	9671	9675	9680
93	9685	9689	9694	9699	9703	9708	9713	9717	9722	9727
94	9731	9736	9741	9745	9750	9754	9759	9763	9768	9773
95	9777	9782	9786	9791	9795	9800	9805	9809	9814	9818
96	9823	9827	9832	9836	9841	9845	9850	9854	9859	9863
97	9868	9872	9877	9881	9886	9890	9894	9899	9903	9908
98	9912	9917	9921	9926	9930	9934	9939	9943	9948	9952
99	9956	9961	9965	9969	9974	9978	9983	9987	9991	9996

* The log of *N* is "the power to which 10 must be raised to yield *N*." Thus log 100 = 2, because $10^2 = 100$. In this table, only the "mantissa" (the digits to the right of the decimal) is given for each log. The characteristic (the integer to the left of the decimal) is 1; for example log 19.1 = 1.281. Log $\frac{1}{10}$ *N* requires the characteristic 0, log 10 *N* the characteristic 2, log 100 *N* the characteristic 3, and so on. Thus log 537 = 2.73.

TABLE IX Critical Points of the Durbin-Watson Test for Autocorrelation [see equation (6–31)]

This table gives two limiting values of critical D (D_L and D_U), corresponding to the two most extreme configurations of the regressors; thus, for every possible configuration, the critical value of D will be somewhere between D_L and D_U:

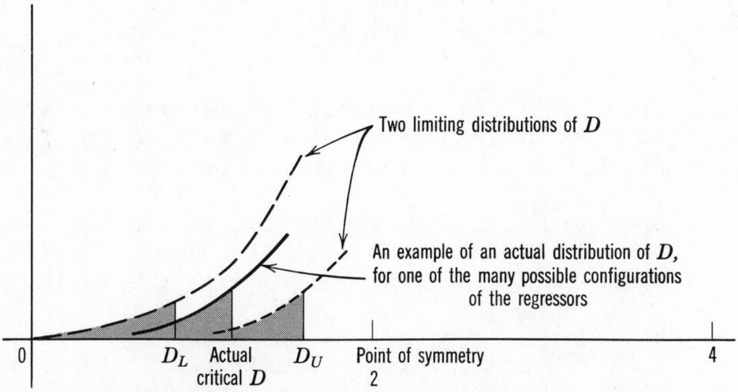

For example, suppose there are $n = 15$ observations and $k = 3$ regressors (as well as the constant), and we wished to test $\rho = 0$ versus $\rho > 0$ at the $\alpha = .05$ level of significance. Then if D fell below $D_L = .82$, we would reject H_0. If D were above $D_U = 1.75$, we could not reject H_0. If D were between D_L and D_U, this test is indecisive.

If your D falls below D_L, reject $\rho = 0$
If your D falls between D_L and D_U, test is inconclus
If your D falls above D_U, you cannot reject $\rho = 0$

THIS IS DESIGNED FOR A ONE-TAIL TEST.

Sample size = n	Pr = Probability in Lower Tail (Significance Level = α)	k = Number of Regressors (Excluding the Constant)									
		1		2		3		4		5	
		D_L	D_U	D_L	D_U	D_L	D_U	D_L	D_U	D_L	D_U
15	.01	.81	1.07	.70	1.25	.59	1.46	.49	1.70	.39	1.96
	.025	.95	1.23	.83	1.40	.71	1.61	.59	1.84	.48	2.09
	.05	1.08	1.36	.95	1.54	.82	1.75	.69	1.97	.56	2.21
20	.01	.95	1.15	.86	1.27	.77	1.41	.68	1.57	.60	1.74
	.025	1.08	1.28	.99	1.41	.89	1.55	.79	1.70	.70	1.87
	.05	1.20	1.41	1.10	1.54	1.00	1.68	.90	1.83	.79	1.99
25	.01	1.05	1.21	.98	1.30	.90	1.41	.83	1.52	.75	1.65
	.025	1.18	1.34	1.10	1.43	1.02	1.54	.94	1.65	.86	1.77
	.05	1.29	1.45	1.21	1.55	1.12	1.66	1.04	1.77	.95	1.89
30	.01	1.13	1.26	1.07	1.34	1.01	1.42	.94	1.51	.88	1.61
	.025	1.25	1.38	1.18	1.46	1.12	1.54	1.05	1.63	.98	1.73
	.05	1.35	1.49	1.28	1.57	1.21	1.65	1.14	1.74	1.07	1.83
40	.01	1.25	1.34	1.20	1.40	1.15	1.46	1.10	1.52	1.05	1.58
	.025	1.35	1.45	1.30	1.51	1.25	1.57	1.20	1.63	1.15	1.69
	.05	1.44	1.54	1.39	1.60	1.34	1.66	1.29	1.72	1.23	1.79
50	.01	1.32	1.40	1.28	1.45	1.24	1.49	1.20	1.54	1.16	1.59
	.025	1.42	1.50	1.38	1.54	1.34	1.59	1.30	1.64	1.26	1.69
	.05	1.50	1.59	1.46	1.63	1.42	1.67	1.38	1.72	1.34	1.77
60	.01	1.38	1.45	1.35	1.48	1.32	1.52	1.28	1.56	1.25	1.60
	.025	1.47	1.54	1.44	1.57	1.40	1.61	1.37	1.65	1.33	1.69
	.05	1.55	1.62	1.51	1.65	1.48	1.69	1.44	1.73	1.41	1.77
80	.01	1.47	1.52	1.44	1.54	1.42	1.57	1.39	1.60	1.36	1.62
	.025	1.54	1.59	1.52	1.62	1.49	1.65	1.47	1.67	1.44	1.70
	.05	1.61	1.66	1.59	1.69	1.56	1.72	1.53	1.74	1.51	1.77
100	.01	1.52	1.56	1.50	1.58	1.48	1.60	1.46	1.63	1.44	1.65
	.025	1.59	1.63	1.57	1.65	1.55	1.67	1.53	1.70	1.51	1.72
	.05	1.65	1.69	1.63	1.72	1.61	1.74	1.59	1.76	1.57	1.78

CITATIONS FOR TABLES

I. Reproduced, by permission, from the *Wiley Trigonometric Tables*, John Wiley and Sons, 1945.

II. (a) Reproduced, by permission, from R. C. Clelland et al, *Basic Statistics with Business Applications*, John Wiley and Sons, 1966.

(b) Reproduced, by permission, from the RAND Corporation.

III. Reproduced, by permission, from the *Chemical Rubber Company Standard Mathematical Tables*, 16th Student Edition.

IV. Reproduced, by permission, from P. Hoel, *Elementary Statistics*, 2nd Edition, John Wiley and Sons, 1966.

V. Reproduced, by permission, from R. Fisher and F. Yates, *Statistical Tables*, Oliver and Boyd, Edinburgh, 1938.

VI. Reproduced, by permission, from W. J. Dixon and F. J. Massey, *Introduction to Statistical Analysis*, 2nd Edition, McGraw-Hill, 1957.

VII. Reproduced, by permission, from *Statistical Methods*, 6th Edition, by George S. Snedecor and William G. Cochrane, 1967, by the Iowa State University Press, Ames, Iowa.

VIII. Reproduced from John E. Freund, *Moden Elementary Statistics*, 3rd Edition, © 1967, by permission of Prentice-Hall Inc., Englewood Cliffs, New Jersey.

IX. Reproduced, by permission, from Carl F. Christ, *Econometric Models and Methods*, John Wiley and Sons, 1966. Originally abridged from J. Durbin, and G. S. Watson, "Testing for Serial Correlation in Least Squares Regression. II." *Biometrika* **38** (June, 1951), pp. 159–178.

Answers to Odd-Numbered Problems

The student is *not* expected always to calculate the answer as precisely as the given answers below. These answers are given to a fairly high degree of precision merely for the benefit of those who want it; even so, the last digit may be slightly in error because of slide rule inaccuracy.

1-1 (a) $S = 760 + \frac{2.6}{18} y$

$= 760 + .144y$

or $= -396 + .144Y$

(b) $a = \$760$ = estimate of saving of the average person.
$a_o = -\$396$ = estimate of saving of a person with zero income. However, this is extrapolating recklessly.

1-3 (a) .068 bushel per pound (all units are "per acre").
(b) \$.136 per pound. Not economic.
(c) Less than \$.136 per pound.

1-5 (a) $S(a_o b) = \Sigma(Y_i - a_o - bX_i)^2$

(b) $\frac{\partial S}{\partial a_o} = -2\Sigma(Y_i - a_o - bX_i) = 0$

$\frac{\partial S}{\partial b} = -2\Sigma X_i(Y_i - a_o - bX_i) = 0$

(c) $a_o = -396$, $b = .144$, as before.
(d) The method in the text is easier than the method in this problem.

2-1 (a) $\beta = \frac{2.6}{18} \pm 3.18 \sqrt{\frac{.0388}{18}}$

$= .144 \pm .148$

(b) $\beta^* = \frac{15.4}{18} \pm 3.18 \sqrt{\frac{.0388}{18}}$

$= .856 \pm .148$

Note that $\beta^* = 1 - \beta$, and the error allowances for β^* and β are the same.

2-3 $t = \frac{2.6/18}{\sqrt{.0388/18}} = 3.11$ which falls

short of $t_{.01} = 4.54$. Therefore do not reject H_o.

2-5 (a) It is preferable to observe i in a period of wide fluctuation.
(b) The family with a \$10,000 income is more predictable, because it is closer to the center of the data.

2-7 (a)

$\bar{x}$	$p(\bar{x})$	$\bar{x}p(\bar{x})$
2	1/9	2/9
3	2/9	6/9
4	3/9	12/9
5	2/9	10/9
6	1/9	6/9
		36/9

$$E(\bar{X}) = 36/9 = \mu$$

Instead of using a table, this result could be proved theoretically and generally.
(b) Similarly,
$E(2\bar{X} + 1) = 81/9 = 2\mu + 1$
hence unbiased.
(c) Similarly,
$E(\bar{X}^2) = 156/9 \neq \mu^2$
$\text{Bias} = E(\bar{X}^2) - \mu^2$
$= 156/9 - 4^2$
$= 4/3$

2-9 $\bar{X}$ is a consistent estimate of μ, if the population has finite variance. Then $\bar{X}$ has zero bias, and its variance σ^2/n approaches zero, so that (2-83) applies.

3-1 (a) $S = 760 + .115y - .0294w$
(b) The coefficient of Y is now slightly less (dropped from .144 to .115). For most purposes, this new coefficient is better, since it shows the relation of S to Y, if W were fixed.
(c) 878
(d) \$230
(e) \$27
(f) 3930
(g) 2 d.f. are very few, in order to estimate σ^2 reliably. A larger sample would be much better.

3-3 (a) (1) $\hat{\alpha} = \bar{S}$

(2) $\Sigma Sy = \hat{\beta}\Sigma y^2 + \hat{\gamma}\Sigma wy + \hat{\Psi}\Sigma ny$

(3) $\Sigma Sw = \hat{\beta}\Sigma yw + \hat{\gamma}\Sigma w^2 + \hat{\Psi}\Sigma nw$

(4) $\Sigma Sn = \hat{\beta}\Sigma yn + \hat{\gamma}\Sigma wn + \hat{\Psi}\Sigma n^2$

(b) $\hat{\alpha} = 760$

$\hat{\beta} = .1054$

$\hat{\gamma} = -.0242$

$\hat{\Psi} = -38.1$

3-5 (a) 36.7
(b) 25.5, which is much better.

3-7 (a) $S = \dfrac{269}{8} - \dfrac{52.5}{42}(T - 7.5)$

$= 33.6 - 1.25(T - 7.5)$

(b) There is serious bias caused by the fact that we started at a seasonal high (Christmas), so that the time trend is downwards.

3-9 (a) Make B is better by .38 mpg.

4-1 (a) $C = 54.8 - 28.2Q + 5.43Q^2$

(b)

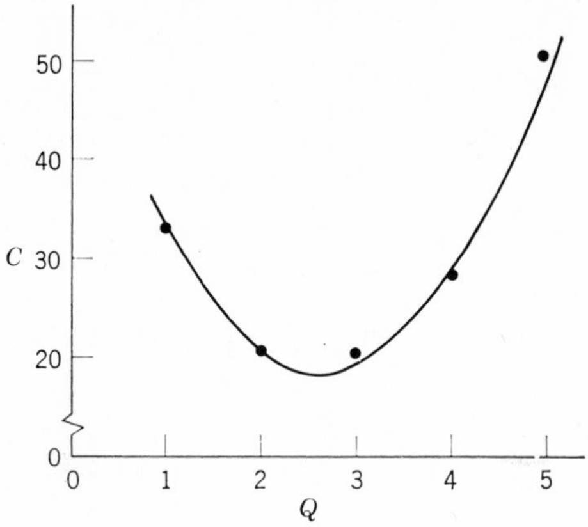

(c) $C = 18.3$

4-3 (a) Linear regression of Y on X^2.
(b) Intractable nonlinear model. Use a computer routine to minimize the sum of squares.
(c) Multiply linear regression of Y on t and sin $(2\pi t/12)$.
(d) Linear regression of log Y on t.
(e) Linear regression of log Y on t.
(f) Multiple linear regression of log Y on t and X.
(g) Intractable nonlinear model. Use a computer routine to minimize the sum of squares.

5-1 (a) $24/\sqrt{(44)(34)} = .62$
(b) $-.49 < \rho < .95$
(c) No.

5-3 (a) $35^2/(100)(20) = .62$
(b) .38
(c) $F = 4.7$ while $F_{.05} = 10.13$
$t = 2.2$ while $t_{.025} = 3.18$
$\beta = .35 \pm .51$

For any of these 3 reasons, do not reject H_o.

5-5 (e) Alone is false, and should be: "If $\hat{\beta} < 1$, no strict conclusion can be drawn about $\hat{\beta}_*$."

5-7 (a) .874
(b) .982
(c) .992
(d) .76, .984
(e) $R^2 \geq r^2$ necessarily
(f) $r_{SY \cdot W}$

5-9 (a) .22
(b) .016
(c) 1, 2
(d) 28
(e) For wealth, $t = -5.3$. Yes

6-1 (a) $\beta = .295 \pm 2.45$
(b) $\beta = 0 \pm 2.74$
(c) WLS is closer to the target than is OLS. Only WLS gives a valid 90% confidence interval.

6-3 (d) If the beginning value $Y_0 = 0$ is regarded as fixed, then the *OLS* line is also the *MLE* line.

7-1 (a)

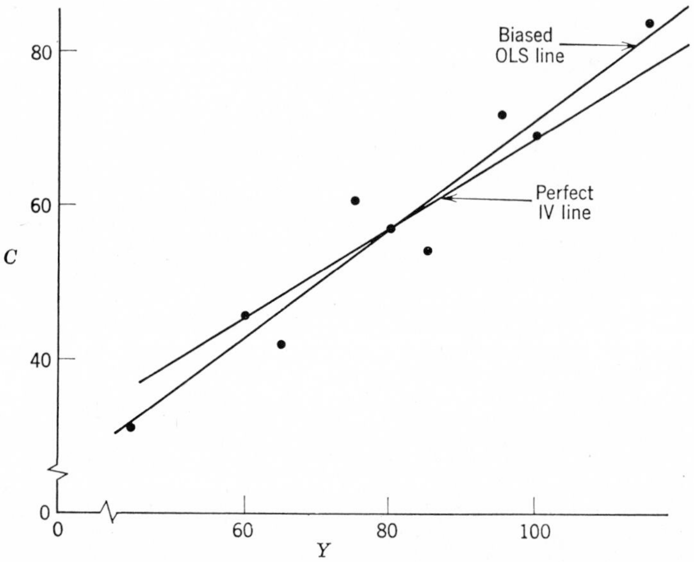

(*a*)

(b) $C = -1.5 + .744Y$
Inconsistent

(c) (i) $C = 10 + .60Y$,
Consistent

(ii) Exactly the same.

(d) The errors e_i exactly cancel, yielding a perfect estimate in part (c). Usually we would not be so lucky, and we would find $\hat{\beta}$ is slightly off target.

7-3 (a) .67, 3.0

(b) *OLS* yields the inconsistent estimate $\hat{\beta} = .77$

(c) (i) *OLS* estimator of β

(ii) *OLS* estimator of β of course, and *IV* estimator of β.

7-5 The weakness is in the vague phrase, "hence it has zero mean, etc." This model does not satisfy a crucial requirement for consistency: the error must be uncorrelated with the regressor.

8-1 Only equation 1 may be identified.

8-3 (a) The short equations

(b) (i) True, except for the last sentence, which should read:

"... if the number of variables on the right hand side (thus α_0 is not counted) is no more than the total number of exogenous variables in the system."

(ii) Corrected version: even though one equation in a system is identified, other equations may be unidentified as shown by Problem 8-1.

8-5 (a) The *D* and *S* bands have the same vertical spread. However, since demand has a greater slope, it has a much narrower band, and therefore has greater influence on the direction of the parallelogram.

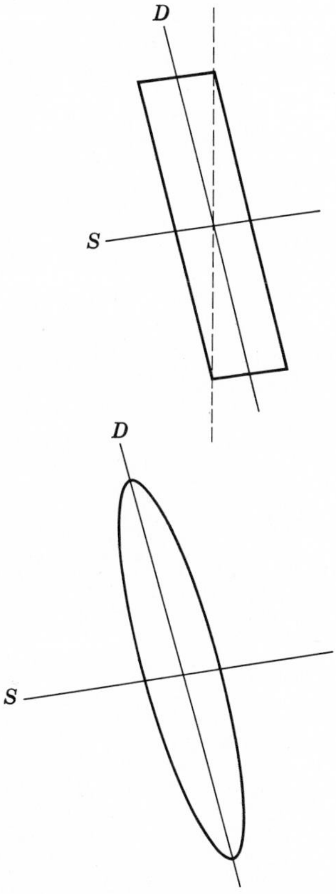

(b)

10-1 (a) .69, .31

(b) Wrong, since you may get a "rain" prediction when it shines. Correct conclusion: a "shine" prediction means that it is certain to shine.

(c) It is now more likely that the barometer will erroneously predict "rain" when it shines; hence a "rain" prediction is no longer as likely to guarantee rain.

10-3 (a) .1, .4, .5

(b) .28, .44, .28

10-5 (a) a_1

(b) a_1

(c) a_3

(d) False. It should be: Action a_1 is best when "rain" is predicted, and also when no prediction is possible. Action a_3 is best when "shine" is predicted. Action a_2 is never best.

10-7 (a) Midrange, median, mean, mode.
(b) Correct.

10-9 (a) Mode, 73 or 74
(b) Median, 73 to 74
(c) Mean, 73.5

10-11 Closer to 20, because the data are twice as reliable.

10-13 Estimate (a) is less believable, because it puts complete faith in a very small and unreliable sample.

10-15 (a) 103.54, $\alpha = .33$, $\beta = .020$
(b) 113.12, $\alpha = .05$, $\beta = .195$
Average loss increases by a factor of 3.16.
(c) $r_0/r_1 = 4/1$, which is unreasonable.

10-17 (a) You do not want to play, because the value of the game is 10/8 to me, which I could win by using the strategy mix: H played 5/8 of the time, T played 3/8.
(b) Each play H and T equally often, which results in a zero payoff. I would secretly choose my penny only if my opponent was secretly choosing also and seemed easy to outwit.

13-1 (a) (1) The region inside the ellipse
$$(\beta_2 - 1.15 \quad \beta_3 + .29) \begin{pmatrix} 18 & -18 \\ -18 & 144 \end{pmatrix} \begin{pmatrix} \beta_2 - 1.15 \\ \beta_3 + .29 \end{pmatrix} \leq 14.8$$
(2) $\beta_3 = -.29 \pm .24$
(3) $\beta_2 = 1.15 \pm .68$
(4) The region inside the ellipse
$$(\beta_1 - 7.6 \quad \beta_2 - 1.15) \begin{pmatrix} 5 & 0 \\ 0 & 15.8 \end{pmatrix} \begin{pmatrix} \beta_1 - 7.6 \\ \beta_2 - 1.15 \end{pmatrix} \leq 14.8$$

(b) $S = 7.6 + 1.15y - .29w$

s_i	.28	.157	.056
CI	± 1.2	$\pm .68$	$\pm .24$
t_i	27	7.2	-5.3

(c) Reject only the first 3.
(d) (1) \$487
(2) This family's income (or assets) is the average of the incomes (or assets) of D and E. Predicted savings will not exactly coincide with observed savings for either D or E, nor for the average of the two.
(3) $\$487 \pm 321$

14-1 (a) 3.84
(b) 6.64

14-3 (a) $7.1 < \sigma^2 < 69$
(b) $7.8 < \sigma^2 < 104$

15-3 $C = 2/7$.

15-5 (a) $\langle 2.33, .33 \rangle$
(b) $\langle -2.1, 3.6 \rangle$
(c) $\langle -.96, -.78 \rangle$, easiest.

15-7 (a) $y_1 \nwarrow \nearrow \langle 1, 0 \rangle$
$y_2 \swarrow \searrow \langle \frac{1}{2}, 1 \rangle$
$y_3 \longleftrightarrow \langle 1\frac{1}{2}, -1 \rangle$
(b) Although the three points y_i are close, their co-ordinates are very different because the basis vectors

point in nearly the same direction (are nearly collinear).

15-9 (a) $+\sqrt{\frac{.09}{.91}(45)} = 2.10$

(b) Since the prob-value $\approx .04$, reject H_o at the 5% level, but do not reject H_o at the 1% level.

(c) Since the prob-value $\approx .02$, reject H_o at the 5% level, but do not reject H_o at the 1% level.

(d) Since $\beta_2 < 0$ is the only alternative, accept $H_o: \beta_2 = 0$ because it is more plausible.

15-11 $F = \frac{.044}{.437}(23) = 2.32$, which does not exceed the critical $F_{.05} = 4.28$. Therefore do not reject $H_o: \beta_7 = 0$.

(b) $R = .77$

(c) .437

(d) .30

15-13 (a) All parts true.

15-15 (a) $\hat{\alpha}_2 \neq \hat{\beta}_2$ (unless $r_{xz} = 0$), as proved in part (b).

15-19 (a) Rarely; if $\mathbf{x} \perp \mathbf{z}$, or $c' = 0$ (i.e. $\hat{\mathbf{y}}$ in the multiple regression lies in the line generated by $\mathbf{x}$ alone).

(b) Always.

(c) Often; if $\mathbf{z}$ adds sufficiently to the explanation of $\mathbf{y}$ without driving $\mathbf{x}$ out of the picture.

(d) Sometimes; if $\mathbf{z}$ is so correlated with $\mathbf{x}$ that it reduces b' more than $\hat{\mathbf{e}}'$; or loss of 1 d.f. could conceivably do it.

16-3 (a) σ^2/n_i

(b) $480/68 = 7.06$

(c) $15/2 = 7.50$

(d) *GLS*, given in (b)

(e) *OLS* unduly weights the last $\bar{Y}$, which happens to be rather high.

16-7 (a) $e_t = .5, -.5, .5, -.5$
The serial correlation is -1 (perfectly negative).

(b) (i) .33
(ii) .92
(iii) *GLS* is much closer to β.

(c) (i) .415
(ii) .071
(iii) efficiency of *OLS* relative to *GLS* = 17%.

17-1 (a) The distribution of errors and hence of $\mathbf{y}$, is elliptical, rather than spherical.

(b) However, since the ellipse is still centered correctly, the *OLS* estimate is unbiased.

(c) Because of the greater variance of the *OLS* estimator, its *CI* should be wider. But instead it is narrower, because $\hat{\mathbf{e}}$ is an inappropriate $\perp$ projection, and hence understates.

18-1 Equation 1 is exactly identified.
2 is unidentified.
3 is overidentified.

19-1 *OLS* is biased (even asymptotically) because the regressors $\mathbf{Y}_1$ are correlated with $\mathbf{e}$. Hence *OLS* is inconsistent, and should not be used for large samples.

19-3 (a) Yes

(b) Yes

(c) Yes, but the expression of $\hat{Q}$ is different.

Glossary of Important Symbols

Symbol	*Meaning*	*Definition or Other Important Reference*
I SYMBOLS INTRODUCED IN PART I		
(a) ENGLISH SYMBOLS		
ANOVA	analysis of variance	p. 118
B	bias	(2-60)
BLUE	best linear unbiased estimator	p. 21
cov	covariance	(2-73)
d.f.	degrees of freedom	(2-105)
e	error term in regression model	(2-3)
$E(\ )$	expected value $= \mu$	(2-1)
$F_{r,n-k}$	F statistic on r and $(n - k)$ d.f. (variance ratio)	(5-21), (14-37), p. 278
H_0	null hypothesis	(2-33)
H_1	alternate hypothesis	(2-34)
iff	if and only if	(2-83)
ILS	indirect least squares	p. 161
IV	instrumental variable(s)	p. 153, p. 341
k	number of estimated regression parameters	(3-16)
$L(\ )$	likelihood function, or	(2-51)
	expected loss	(10-10)
MLE	maximum likelihood estimate(tion)	p. 36
n	sample size	(2-105)
$N(\ ,\ )$	normal distribution, with specified mean and variance	(6-51)

Symbol	*Meaning*	*Definition or Other Important Reference*
OLS	ordinary least squares	p. 132
$p(y)$	probability function of y	(10-5)
$p(y, z)$	joint probability function of y and z	(10-5)
$p(y/z)$	conditional probability function of y, given z	(10-5)
$\Pr(a \leq y \leq b)$	probability that y will fall between two specified values a and b	(2-27)
r	simple sample correlation, or regret	(5-4), (5-13) (10-61)
r^2	coefficient of determination	(5-29)
$r_{XY \cdot Z}$	partial correlation of X and Y, if Z were held constant	(5-39), (5-40)
R	multiple correlation coefficient	(5-43), (5-44)
s^2	sample residual variance about regression line, including	(2-24), (13-26)
	sample variance as a special case	(2-70)
s_{XY}	sample covariance of X and Y	p. 149
s_{XX}	sample variance of $X = s_X^2$	(7-9)
$S(\ )$	sum of squared residuals	(1-10)
2SLS	two-stage least squares	p. 190
t_{n-k}	Student's t variable on $(n - k)$ degrees of freedom $= \pm\sqrt{F_{1,n-k}}$	(2-26), (5-22), (14-30), p. 278
T	time	(3-24)
u	error (like e)	(8-9)
v	error (like e), or perturbation in serially correlated error	(8-2) (6-14)
var	variance	(2-8)
WLS	weighted least squares	(6-5), (16-26)
X	(also Y, Z, etc.) = variable in original form	(1-4)
x	(also y, z, etc.) = variable expressed as deviations from its mean	(1-5)
$\underline{x}$	variable in fully standardized form	(5-2)
Y_t	value of Y in time t	(6-13)

Symbol	*Meaning*	*Definition or Other Important Reference*
$\bar{Y}$	sample mean of Y	(2-61)
$\hat{Y}$	fitted value of Y	(2-25)
z	standard normal variable	Fig. 2-4

(b) GREEK SYMBOLS are generally reserved for population parameters, as follows:

α	population regression intercept	(2-3)
β	population regression slope	(2-3)
γ	population regression coefficient	(3-1)
θ	any population parameter	(2-59)
$\hat{\theta}$	sample estimator of θ	(2-59)
λ	Lagrange multiplier, or variance ratio of errors in two variables	(2-92) (7-50)
μ	population mean	Fig. 2-8
$\prod$	product of	(2-49)
ρ	population correlation, or serial correlation of time series error	(5-7) (6-22)
σ^2	population variance (about regression line, usually)	(2-4), (13-16)
σ_X	population standard deviation of X	(5-7b), (7-14)
σ_{XY}	population covariance of X and Y	(8-24)
$\sum$	sum of	(1-1)
τ	generalized differencing operator	(6-27), (16-57)

(c) OTHER MATHEMATICAL SYMBOLS

$\triangleq$	equals by definition	(2-60)
$\equiv$	equals identically	p. 155
$\approx, \simeq$	equals approximately	p. 79
$\hat{=}$	equals in the limit	(7-21), (7-37)
$\xrightarrow{p}$	has a probability limit of, i.e., is a consistent estimator of, (similar to $\hat{=}$ above)	(2-81b)
$\rightarrow$	has a limit of	(10-41)

II SYMBOLS INTRODUCED IN PART II

In Part II the symbolism of Part I is retained, but extended and modified as follows: A boldface capital letter such as **B** or **X** represents a matrix; a boldface small letter such as **β** or **x** represents a vector; to avoid too many transpose signs, a vector may be either row or column, depending on the context in which it is introduced. (Usually a set of observations on one variable is introduced as a column, while a set of variables is introduced as a row.) A single entry in a matrix or vector is an ordinary small letter. In Part II the variables x and y may refer either to their actual observed values or deviations from their mean; but as in Chapters 2 and 3 it is recommended that, unless otherwise specified, the y's be regarded as actual observed values and the x's as deviations from the mean.

The superscript hat (as in $\hat{\boldsymbol{\beta}}$) still means "estimated or fitted value (of $\boldsymbol{\beta}$)."

The "first" equation is the one being estimated (or identified).

We do not attempt to explain all the subscripted uses.

(a) MATRIX SYMBOLS EXTENDING USAGE OF PART I

$\boldsymbol{\beta}$	(with or without subscript) vector of coefficients of exogeneous variables in regression equation; hence	(13-13), (19-15)
$\mathbf{B}$	matrix of coefficients of all exogenous variables in all equations in the system	(18-1), (20-39)
$\mathbf{e}$	vector of error terms in regression model	(13-13)
$\mathbf{x}$	(with or without subscript) either a vector of observations on one exogenous variable, or	(19-13)
	vector of all exogenous variables in the model; hence	(13-12), (18-7)
$\mathbf{X}$	matrix of observations on all exogenous variables in the model, being comprised of	(13-13), (19-14)
$\mathbf{X}_1$	matrix of observation on all exogenous variables included in the first equation, and	(19-14)
$\mathbf{X}_1^*$	matrix of observations on all exogenous variables excluded from the first equation	(19-14)
$\mathbf{Y}$	matrix of observations on all endogenous variables of first equation, being comprised of	(19-54), (20-38)
$\mathbf{Y}_1$	matrix of observations on all endogenous variables on right side of first equation, and	(19-14)
$\mathbf{y}$	vector of observations on single endogenous variable on left side, determined by first equation, or	(13-13), (19-14)
	(in Chapter 18 only) vector of all endogenous variables in the system	(18-1)

(b) DIMENSIONS

k	number of regressors in first equation, or	(13-13)
	k-class estimator	(19-78)

M	number of exogenous variables in model (usually equal to number of instrumental variables), being the sum of	(18-7), (20-39)
m	number of exogenous variables in first equation, and	(18-7), (20-38)
m_0	number of exogenous variables excluded from first equation	(18-7), (20-38)
n	number of observations in sample	(13-13)
Q	number of endogenous variables in the system, being the sum of	(18-7), (20-39)
q	number of endogenous variables in first equation, and	(18-7), (20-38)
q_0	number of endogenous variables excluded from first equation	(18-7), (20-38)
r	number of regressors being simultaneously tested (note also its use as sample correlation coefficient as in Part I)	(13-35), (13-41)

(c) English Symbols

$\mathbf{C}$	linear transformation of $\boldsymbol{\beta}$	(13-35)
C_r^2	modified chi-square statistic on r d.f.	(14-24), p. 278
$\mathbf{D}$	transformation matrix; after use on GLS model, OLS becomes valid. *See* **M** *also.*	(16-27), (16-50)
FI/LGV FI/ML	full information	p. 392
GLS	generalized least squares	p. 318
LI/LGV LI/LVR LI/ML	limited information	p. 372
LWV	least weighted variance	(19-50)
$\mathbf{M}$	transformation matrix; e.g., after use on GLS model, OLS becomes valid. *See* **D** *also.*	(16-60)
$\bar{R}^2$	corrected R^2 (reduced for d.f.)	p. 311
$\mathbf{S}$	matrix of covariances of all instrumental variables with all variables on right side of first equation, or	(18-29)
	(Chapter 20 only) matrix of covariances of all instrumental variables with all right-hand variables in all equations in the system, in special block arrangement	(20-29)

$\mathbf{S}_1$	(Chapter 20 only) observations on all right-hand variables in first equation	(20-7), (20-27)
3SLS	three-stage least squares	p. 388
$\mathbf{U}$	covariance matrix of errors in GLS	(16-3)
$\mathbf{v}_i$	errors in ith reduced form equation; hence	(19-41)
$\mathbf{V}$	matrix of errors in reduced form, or	(19-17), (20-40)
	covariance matrix of $\hat{\boldsymbol{\beta}}$ (except for scalar σ^2)	(13-33)
$\mathbf{z}$	vector of observations on one instrumental variable; hence	(17-8)
$\mathbf{Z}$	matrix of observations on several instrumental variables	(17-18)

(d) Greek Symbols

$\boldsymbol{\alpha}_1$	vector of coefficients of all right-hand variables in first equation; hence	(20-7)
$\boldsymbol{\alpha}$	vector of coefficients of all right-hand variables in all equations	(20-28)
$\boldsymbol{\gamma}$	any linear combination, or	(13-35)
	vector of coefficients of all endogenous variables in first equation $= \begin{bmatrix} 1 \\ \boldsymbol{\gamma}_1 \end{bmatrix}$, where	(18-7), (19-54)
$\boldsymbol{\gamma}_1$	vector of coefficients of endogenous variables on right side of first equation	(19-15)
$\boldsymbol{\Gamma}$	matrix of coefficients of all endogenous variables in all equations in the system	(18-7), (20-39)
λ	Lagrange multiplier, which turns out to be the LVR	(19-75)
$\boldsymbol{\Pi}$	matrix of reduced form coefficients	(18-3)
χ_n^2	chi-square statistic on n d.f.	(14-1), p. 278
$\boldsymbol{\Omega}$	covariance matrix of $\mathbf{v}$, the errors in the reduced form	(19-52)

(e) Other Mathematical Symbols

$\lVert\mathbf{x}\rVert$	length (norm) of $\mathbf{x}$	(15-11)
$\mathbf{x} \cdot \mathbf{y}$	dot product of $\mathbf{x}$ and $\mathbf{y}$	(15-3)
$\perp$	perpendicular (orthogonal)	(15-13)
$\boldsymbol{\Pi}_0$ or $\boldsymbol{\Pi}_*$ (or $\mathbf{B}_0$, etc.)	selected submatrix of $\boldsymbol{\Pi}$ (or $\mathbf{B}$, etc.)	(18-9), (18-12)
*	(as a matrix element) any nonzero value	(18-22)
$._5371$	.00000371	p. 245

28_4	280000	p. 245
[ ]	a partitioned matrix	(18-12), (19-16)

III GREEK ALPHABET

Letters	*Names*	*English Equivalent*	*Letters*	*Names*	*English Equivalent*
$A\alpha$	Alpha	a	$N\nu$	Nu	n
$B\beta$	Beta	b	$\Xi\xi$	Xi	x
$\Gamma\gamma$	Gamma	g	Oo	Omicron	o
$\Delta\delta$	Delta	d	$\Pi\pi$	Pi	p
$E\epsilon$	Epsilon	e	$P\rho$	Rho	r
$Z\zeta$	Zeta	z	$\Sigma\sigma$	Sigma	s
$H\eta$	Eta	—	$T\tau$	Tau	t
$\Theta\theta$	Theta	—	$\Upsilon\upsilon$	Upsilon	u or y
$I\iota$	Iota	i	$\Phi\phi$	Phi	—
$K\kappa$	Kappa	k	$X\chi$	Chi	—
$\Lambda\lambda$	Lambda	l	$\Psi\psi$	Psi	—
$M\mu$	Mu	m	$\Omega\omega$	Omega	—

Index

as square root of *F*, 119, 130, 254, 277, 278

Applied Probability and Statistics (Continued)

YOUDEN · Statistical Methods for Chemists
ZELLNER · An Introduction to Bayesian Inference in Econometrics

Tracts on Probability and Statistics

BILLINGSLEY · Ergodic Theory and Information
BILLINGSLEY · Convergence of Probability Measures
CRAMÉR and LEADBETTER · Stationary and Related Stochastic Processes
JARDINE and SIBSON · Mathematical Taxonomy
RIORDAN · Combinatorial Identities
TAKÁCS · Combinatorial Methods in the Theory of Stochastic Processes